To Edward

Happy [...]

from the Phillips

Minerva Series

MINERVA SERIES OF STUDENTS' HANDBOOKS

No. 22

General Editor

BRIAN CHAPMAN

Professor of Government
University of Manchester

INTRODUCTION TO
ECONOMIC ANALYSIS

INTRODUCTION TO
ECONOMIC ANALYSIS

BY

MILES FLEMING

*Professor of Economics
University of Bristol*

LONDON
GEORGE ALLEN & UNWIN LTD
RUSKIN HOUSE MUSEUM STREET

FIRST PUBLISHED 1969
SECOND IMPRESSION 1970
THIRD IMPRESSION 1970
FOURTH IMPRESSION 1971

© George Allen & Unwin Ltd, 1969

ISBN 0 04 330140 1 *cased*

ISBN 0 04 330141 X *paper*

PRINTED IN GREAT BRITAIN
in 10 *point Times Roman type*
BY COMPTON PRINTING LTD
LONDON AND AYLESBURY

PREFACE

The form of this book is based on three considerations:

1. A new subject is best understood from an initial, broad picture of its whole field, into which more and more detail is painted as study progresses. Part I of the book describes different kinds of economic system in terms of the functions which they have to perform. The main questions about how they work—and the interconnections between these questions—are then spelt out to provide the framework for the detailed analysis of Parts II, III and IV.

2. The grasp of a subject is improved by an understanding of the similarities between the techniques of explanation used in its different branches. Parts II, III and IV cover different branches of economics, but the aim is to show that the methods of analysis are basically the same in all of them. Thus, it will be seen that the condition of aggregate supply, as well as the condition of aggregate demand, is used in Part III to show how the price level and national output are determined. This parallels the use of supply and demand concepts in Part II.

3. The objective of a scientific subject is to make predictions. In economics, the explanation of what the levels of quantities like prices, outputs, and incomes will be, in given circumstances, is a preliminary to predicting why they will go up or down. The emphasis in the book rests on the analysis of changes in economic quantities.

Suggestions for more advanced reading in economics are gathered together in appendices to Parts II, III and IV.

I have had valuable comments and suggestions from Mr F. S. Brooman and Professor P. Davidson at every stage in the composition of the book, and from Mr H. M. Clarke and Professor D. C. Rowan on parts of it. I am indebted to Professor S. Weintraub, and also to Professor P. Davidson, from whom I learned the essential role of an aggregate supply function in macroeconomic analysis. My grateful thanks to all of them and to my wife, who encouraged me to write the book, in no way implicates them in its shortcomings.

CONTENTS

PART III: MACROECONOMICS

PART I

THE NATURE OF ECONOMIC SYSTEMS

CHAPTER 1

THE FUNCTIONS OF AN ECONOMIC SYSTEM

Economics seeks to explain the working of economic systems. The beginner must therefore start by acquiring a general picture of what an economic system is. That picture consists of two things: a *description* of the system and an account of its *functions*. The description merely lists the activities which go on within the system; the functions show how these activities are systematically connected with one another.

Economic activity is an important part of daily experience. It is not difficult, therefore, to describe the main features of the kind of economic system which exists in the UK, Western Europe and North America. That is done in the following narrative, where all the descriptive terms are in common use.

People earn their incomes in a variety of ways, e.g. by working for wages and salaries, by renting out land, by receiving a share of the profits of business firms. They also spend their incomes in a variety of ways on tangible *goods* (e.g. bread, television sets) and intangible *services* (e.g. haircuts, holidays). But part of their incomes will usually go in the payment of taxes to the government, and yet another part may be withheld from spending, i.e. saved. The part of income which is spent on goods and services becomes the revenue of the business firms that produced and sold them.

To produce goods,[1] firms must use resources like raw materials (e.g. seeds, metals, chemicals), manpower, machines, buildings and land on which to put buildings or grow crops. They get these resources in two ways: by purchasing them (i) from people (e.g. manpower from workers, the use of land from landlords), and (ii) from other firms that produce them (e.g. raw materials, components). The payments a firm makes for the resources it uses are its costs of production. The costs it incurs therefore either go to people in the form of incomes (e.g. wages, rents) or to other firms in the form of revenue from goods sold.

[1] For brevity, the term goods will in future be used to cover both goods and services unless a contrary indication is given.

3

A distinction can be made between two kinds of goods produced by firms. There are those, like bread and haircuts, which are bought by people to give them personal satisfaction. Since these goods are used (or consumed) by people, they are called *consumer* goods. There are also those, like machines and buildings, which are bought by other firms in order to enlarge their capacity to produce goods. These are known as *capital* goods.

The government, as well as business firms, produces goods and especially services. It supplies the community, for example, with armed forces, police, law courts, roads and education. It purchases resources, like the manpower of soldiers, judges and teachers, in order to provide those public services, and thereby pays incomes to the people it employs. Usually the government does not sell its services to the community, but rather provides them collectively without charge.[1] It therefore gets little revenue from sales. On the other hand it does get revenue from taxation.

All the purchases of goods and resources described in the preceding paragraphs are paid for with money in the form of coins, notes and balances in bank accounts. The provision of a supply of money to carry out the buying and selling of things is one of the activities of banks. But money is not only used to buy goods and resources. It is also borrowed and lent. Sometimes the borrowing is by people to enable them to buy consumer goods (e.g. television sets). More importantly, the borrowing is by business firms to enable them to finance the purchase of capital goods (e.g. factories). A person or a firm which wants to borrow may do so directly from another person or firm. But some firms specialize in the business of borrowing and lending. These financial firms (like banks, hire purchase finance companies and building societies) provide the service of borrowing from some persons and firms and of lending to others. The interest received from lending provides the financial firm with revenue to pay interest on its borrowing and to cover the costs of purchasing resources (e.g. the manpower of clerks) to run the business. People who save out of their incomes can earn interest by lending their savings.

Goods and resources are not only bought and sold between persons and firms resident in the same country. They are also bought, or imported, from foreign countries, and sold, or exported, to those countries. Moreover, borrowing and lending takes place between persons and firms resident in different countries.

All the above activities of persons, firms and government—both within a country and between countries—are aspects of the working of

[1] There are very minor exceptions like fees to visit some museums.

one kind of economic system. A common feature of these activities is their concern with the use of money to buy resources, which are required to produce goods, which in their turn are sold for money. The buying and selling of resources and goods for money is the leading theme of the descriptive narrative. It is an obvious fact of existence that many of the goods we want for the enjoyment of life must be actively created (or produced) by human labour working on other resources. But what purposes are served by the buying and selling of the resources and the goods for money? The answer to that question provides an explanation of the functions of an economic system.

THE SCARCITY OF RESOURCES

The resources required to produce goods are not available, in any country, in unlimited amounts. The measurement of what resources are available must take account of two things: (i) the number of *units* of each resource, e.g. men (and women) able and willing to work, acres of land, quantities of minerals capable of being mined, machines and buildings; and (ii) the *effectiveness* of each unit in producing goods, i.e. the *physical* amount of any goods which each unit could produce. The productive capacity of a country depends on that effectiveness (or *productivity*) of its resources, as well as on their quantities. Countries differ a lot in both respects.

The proportion of the total population which is able and willing to work determines the quantity of manpower. Its productivity depends on the skills which have been acquired by education and training. Geography and geology account for the extent and the fertility of land, and for the quantity and quality of minerals. The amounts of capital goods (e.g. machines, buildings and other man-made instruments) are the outcome of a process of accumulation stretching back over many years. That accumulation requires that some of the resources available at any time be used for the production of those capital goods, i.e. that *not all* of the resources are devoted to producing consumer goods. The productivities of capital goods depend on the state of technical knowledge at the time they were built.

The size of the working population, the extent of land and the natural resources that go with it, the quantities of capital goods, together with their productivities, place a limit upon the amount of goods a country can produce. That limit is not fixed through time. Populations grow, hitherto unknown natural resources are discovered, more capital goods to use in production are accumulated, technical knowledge expands and human skills are improved by both education and training. But at any time there is a maximum amount of goods that can be produced given the quantities and productivities of the available resources. That maximum would be of little interest if it was *greater* than the amount of goods a country would like to have. But, of course, it is less than, not greater than, the desired amount. There may be a few people, like some millionaires, or alternatively those who think that human desires should be strictly curbed, who can get all the goods they want. But for nearly all mankind that state of bliss is not attainable. Even in the richest countries in the world, as well as in the many others in which malnutrition still abounds, an abundance of goods is not yet foreseeable.

Goods are scarce because there are not enough resources to produce all the goods we want. Consequently, the people of a country must have some *system* through which they can jointly decide the goods which are to be produced with the available resources. The word system has the same meaning here as it has in many other human contexts. Thus, we speak of the political system as comprising the political parties, Parliament, the Government, the Cabinet and so forth. These political institutions are the means through which the people of a country jointly decide the kind of society in which they want to live together, and the rules (or laws) which are to govern their social relations. A system, in its social sense, has two important features. It is a means of reaching decisions, and it is a set of institutions through which people can co-operate in that decision-making. The functions of an economic system, and of the institutions through which it works, centre upon co-operative decision-making about production.

The buying and selling of resources and goods for money described earlier is one way in which the people of a country can jointly decide the goods which are to be produced with their resources. That kind of economic system is known as a *price mechanism*, and it is widely used, in one form or another, throughout the world. Thus, while it is not the only kind of economic system, its present extensive use makes the study of it a major topic of economics. Most of this book is devoted to explaining how production decisions are determined through the price mechanism. There are, however, different—though related—aspects of those decisions which must be distinguished.

PRODUCTION DECISIONS

Because resources are limited, both in quantity and in productivity, a country has to decide upon the goods which it is going to produce.

That means also deciding upon the goods which it is not going to produce—at least until resources have increased. This choice between having and not having particular goods has both qualitative and quantitative sides. Modern technology makes possible the production of hundreds of thousands of different *kinds* of goods. In choosing between them a country might decide to produce one rather than another, e.g. hospitals rather than swimming pools. If it is poorly endowed with resources, there may indeed be a wide range of goods it will not consider producing at all. That is a qualitative decision. But within the range of goods it does decide to produce there remains the quantitative decision. How much of each good is to be produced? The limited resources must be allocated to produce particular quantities of each good. The more of one good that is produced, the less resources are available to produce others.

The production decisions made through the economic system are essentially quantitative in nature. The choices before the community are seldom, if ever, of an 'all or nothing' variety. They are of the form: some more of one thing at the cost of less of others. Even the qualitative decision—hospitals rather than swimming pools—involves quantities: some *number* of hospitals and *no* swimming pools. The first function of an economic system is to determine the precise quantities of different goods—both consumer and capital goods—to be produced.

PRODUCTION METHODS

What these quantities can be depends, of course, on the kinds and the amounts of the available resources. But it also depends on the ways in which the resources are used, i.e. on the *methods* of production. Most goods can be produced by a variety of methods. Thus motor cars can be turned out on a production line where a lot of machinery helps the workers assemble each car. Alternatively, a car can be 'hand-made' by a lot of labour aided by a relatively small amount of machinery. The difference between these two production methods is in the amount of machinery per worker employed, i.e. in the ratio of machinery to labour. Clearly, there is a wide spectrum of methods, involving more and less machinery (and also different kinds of machinery) per worker, between which firms can choose. This variability in the way resources can be combined is true for most goods. Each one can be made by more or less skilled labour, by different kinds of machines and out of different raw materials; and the kinds and amounts of labour, machinery and raw materials used can be varied in relation to one another.

Different methods of production are thus distinguished from one another by differences in the ratios between the quantities of the various kinds of resources used in them. A community has to decide, through its economic system, the particular method (or methods) to be used in producing each good. That is the second function of the system.

But that function and the first one are interrelated. The output of goods which a country is *able* to produce depends not only on the kinds and the amounts of its labour, natural resources and capital goods, but also on the ways (i.e. the ratios) in which those resources are combined. That is, the *productivities* of resources depend in part on the ways in which they are used together. Change the production methods, and the total output which can be achieved with the available resources will alter. Hence, an economic system cannot determine the quantities of different goods to be produced without *at the same time* determining their methods of production.

That is a point of great importance for the working of an economic system. Since a community cannot have all the goods it wants, it must try to produce as many as possible from its limited resources. It must, therefore, choose the production methods which are best in that respect. That is, it must use its resources in what are, in some sense, the most 'efficient' ratios. The phrase 'in some sense' has been used advisedly here, because the concept of *economic efficiency* is a complex one. It must not be confused with other meanings of the term, e.g. the one found in engineering. There are a number of considerations which enter into the idea of economic efficiency. An explanation of a few of them now will help in the understanding of the functions of an economic system.

The output of goods will be the larger, the harder men are willing to work. But the willingness to work depends in part on the 'rewards' from work. That is why the incentives to work offered by an economic system are relevant to its efficiency. But working hard is not the whole of economic efficiency. There is also the question of choosing the 'best' production methods within which to work hard. That is a matter of allocating workers (and other resources) to different jobs so that the most 'efficient' ratios between resources are achieved.

There are two considerations which are basic to the problem of allocating resources. First, each particular resource (like a man or a machine) will probably be able to do a variety of jobs, e.g. produce different goods. The man (or the machine) will have certain capabilities in each job. His degree of skill in doing one kind of work may rank high amongst those of other men, but in doing another kind of work his skill may only have a low ranking in relation to others. Clearly, that difference is relevant to the question of which job he should do. Hence, the economic system should provide a means of comparing the degrees of skill (or productivities) of himself and others in different kinds of work.

But, secondly, those productivities will not, on their own, be *sufficient* to indicate which job he should do. He may have a highly ranked skill in the production of some good of which the community only wants a small amount. That is, this kind of skill may not be especially scarce in relation to the community's need for it. On the other hand, the community may want a very large amount of a second good in the production of which his skill has only a low ranking. That is, the second kind of skill may be especially scarce in relation to the need for it. Consequently, it can be that, in order to give the community the quantities of different goods it wants, he should work at producing the second good rather than the first.

Thus the degree of scarcity attaching to each kind of resource must be allowed for in the choice of an efficient allocation of resources. That scarcity depends on the quantity available of the resource *relative* to the need for it in the production of the goods the community wants. The degrees of scarcity vary from one kind of resource to another. That is why an economic system should provide a means of assessing *both* the productivities, and the relative scarcities, of different kinds of resources.

It is not only, therefore, the overall scarcity of resources, but also the scarcities of particular resources in relation to one another, that is central to the functioning of an economic system. That point can be illustrated in yet another way. Compare the resources with which two countries are endowed. England, for example, is densely populated in comparison with Australia, i.e. the ratio of labour to land is much higher in the former. England must, therefore, be especially careful in husbanding its relatively scarce land, and Australia must do likewise in relation to labour. Hence, the economic system in England should so work as to encourage the adoption of production methods which use high ratios of labour to land (e.g. 'intensive' agriculture); while Australia's economic system should encourage methods using low labour-to-land ratios (e.g. 'extensive' agriculture). Exactly the same point applies to the relative scarcities of machinery in different countries. The economic system in England should encourage a more intensive use of machinery in relation to labour than would be appropriate in India, for example.

Those are some of the reasons for the complexity of the problem of getting an efficient allocation of resources; and why, in particular, the relative scarcities of resources, as well as their physical productivities, are relevant to economic efficiency. The functioning of an economic system is not only a matter of deciding the kinds and quantities of goods to produce with the available resources, it is also a matter of deciding the production methods which will give the community as much as possible of the kinds of goods it wants.

DISTRIBUTION DECISIONS

But there remains a third function which the system has to perform. The total output of goods has to be shared out (distributed) among the members of the community. There are two aspects of that sharing out which have to be distinguished. First, the economic system has to determine the relative sizes of the shares which are to go to each person (or household); and second, it has to determine the kinds and quantities of goods which are to make up each share. The distinction between the two is an important one whenever households are given some freedom of choice as to the kinds and quantities of goods in which they can take their shares. Broadly speaking, a household could get the *same* share of total output in a variety of forms, i.e. made up of different collections of goods. Hence, an economic system might determine the sizes of shares while still leaving the households free to choose the kinds and quantities of goods in which to take those shares.

Two things are required of the system if it is to work in that way. First, it must have some principle for determining the sizes of shares; and second, it must have some means of ensuring that the decisions about the production of goods are guided by the choices of goods by households. The goods produced must be those wanted by the households. Moreover, the total quantities of goods in which the households want to take their shares must equal what can be produced with the available resources.

The decisions about the production and the distribution of goods must therefore be consistent with each other. Hence, the third function of an economic system is necessarily interrelated with the first two. The system must *simultaneously* determine the kinds and quantities of goods to be produced, the production methods to be used, and the distribution of the resulting output between households.

Those are the basic functions which, because of the scarcity of resources, we need an economic system to perform. A price mechanism, of which some descriptive details were given at the beginning of this chapter, can perform the functions simultaneously. The next step in outlining the subject matter of economics must, therefore, provide an explanation in general terms of how production and distribution decisions are reached through the buying and selling of goods and resources for money. But the price mechanism is not the only possible kind of economic system; moreover, it can itself take a variety of forms. Hence an understanding of how the economic system performs its functions requires some knowledge of the different types of system.

CHAPTER 2

TYPES OF ECONOMIC SYSTEM:
A COMMAND ECONOMY

The economic systems of countries today differ from one another in various ways. But all of them, except the most primitive, can be regarded as a *mixture* of two basic types: a price mechanism and a 'command economy'. The latter can also be called an 'administratively planned' economy. A prefix has been deliberately given to the term 'planned', because that word has a number of meanings in relation to economic activity, others of which will be considered later. In one sense, all economic activity is planned since it is the result of decisions taken through the economic system. But the way in which a price mechanism plans the production and distribution of goods is often not clear to the layman. Therefore, in explaining the different types of economic system, it will be well to start with a kind of planning where the meaning is clear-cut.

Administration is the process of arriving at and executing decisions. An administration is that part of an institution (or organization) which has the tasks of making the decisions about the policies which the institution is to follow, and of seeing that those policies are carried out. Thus, there is the 'administrative grade' of the British Civil Service which helps the political Ministers with the formulation and execution of government policy. Indeed, as in the US, the government of a country may often be referred to as the Administration. Similarly, the policies of all business firms have to be administered in a way that depends on the size and complexity of their operations. In a large joint-stock company, the administration consists of the board of directors together with the senior office holders in the company who help and advise the board.

The process of administration can be broken down into three stages: (i) the collection and analysis of the *information* needed as a basis for the making of decisions, (ii) the *decision-making* itself, which depends on the objectives of the organization, and (iii) the issue of instructions for the *execution* of the decisions. Thus a business firm requires information about its costs of production and the state of the market to enable its directors to decide the quantities of goods it is to produce, and the prices at which it is to try to sell them. Once those decisions are reached, they have to be communicated to the men on the factory floor, and in the salesrooms, who are to carry them out. *Communication* is an essential and all-pervasive element in administration. Information must be communicated to the top decision-makers in the organization; they have to communicate among themselves in arguing out the policy to be adopted; and they have to communicate their instructions as to how the policy is to be followed.

The administration of an organization requires a chain of *command* within it. The top decision-makers must be able to command subordinates to gather the information needed for the taking of decisions; and they must also be able to command subordinates to carry out their decisions. The subordinates are the executives of an organization (e.g. the executive grade of the British Civil Service).

A command economy would operate through an administrative process of the nature just described; and it would do so without the use of money and the pricing of goods and resources in terms of money. To conceive of such an administration of the whole economy, it is therefore necessary to clear the mind of all preconceptions derived from everyday experience of the buying and selling of things for money. A command economy must be thought of as a department of government within which all decisions are taken on the production and distribution of goods. Let it be called the Ministry of Economic Planning. At its head will be the political Ministers upon whom lies the responsibility for the economic decisions taken. But they will have to be advised and helped in that task by senior officials, who in their turn will be served by the executive officers.

The Ministry has to perform the three functions of an economic system set out in Chapter 1. To do that, it needs certain information the nature of which must now be spelt out in detail, if the work of the Ministry is to be understood. The required information can be grouped under three heads.

THE COLLECTION OF INFORMATION

First, the kinds and quantities of all the resources available have to be discovered, in order to work out the kinds and quantities of goods that could be produced. The compilation of such an inventory is complicated by the fact that each resource (like a man or a machine) will probably have various capabilities (e.g. a mechanic might help to produce either cars or aeroplanes). Hence, the Ministry requires information on the various jobs each resource could do, in order to assess the country's potential capacity to produce different kinds of goods.

But a second type of information is also needed for a complete assessment of that capacity. The resources have to be used *together* to create goods: men must operate machines to work raw materials into finished goods. The productivities of the resources depend on the methods used, i.e. on the ratios in which they are combined. For each production method, there will be some relationship between the quantities of resources used and the amount of the good produced. If certain quantities of manpower, machine-power and raw materials are put in to the production of a good, a certain output of that good will result. These production relations between the 'inputs' of resources and the outputs of goods thus help to determine the productive capacity of a country. It is therefore not sufficient for the Ministry to know the kinds and quantities of the available resources. It must also have information on the quantities of goods that those resources could produce whenever they are used in the different possible production methods.

Moreover, the Ministry should try to discover the production relaons between inputs of resources and outputs for *all* possible methods of producing *all* goods. Otherwise, it may set the economy to produce a *smaller* total of goods than it is capable of doing. Suppose that the Ministry is ignorant of some method of producing a particular good which is feasible with existing technical knowledge. The introduction of this method would need the re-organization of the production, not only of the good in question, but also of other goods. This is so because if the quantities of resources used in producing one good are changed, that requires the quantities used in others to be changed also. If the good in question is to be produced with more machinery and less labour, then less machinery and more labour are available for other goods.

Now suppose that the method, of which the Ministry had been ignorant, is introduced and a re-organization of production throughout the economy takes place. How may this affect the total output of goods? The answer to that question is complicated by the fact that many different kinds of goods are being produced. If only one good was being produced, the effect of the re-organization of production on total output could easily be seen: the output of the single good either increases, decreases or is unchanged. But suppose that three goods—taken as representing what in fact will be many thousands—are being produced.

For brevity, let them be called A, B and C. Suppose that, before the re-organization, the following 'collection' of them is being produced:

$$6A + 8B + 4C \tag{i}$$

If the re-organization allows the collection

$$7A + 9B + 5C \tag{ii}$$

to be produced, then total output has clearly increased. For the outputs of *all* the goods have gone up. Even if the re-organization allows the collection

$$6A + 8B + 5C \tag{iii}$$

to be produced, it can still be said unequivocally that total output has increased. For, in comparison with collection (i), the output of one good (C) has gone up, without the outputs of the other two being reduced.

But suppose that the re-organization allows the collection

$$4A + 9B + 7C \tag{iv}$$

to be produced. It cannot now be said whether total output has increased or decreased. That collection contains more of B and C, but less of A, than collection (i). Insofar as A, B and C are different goods, the units of which cannot be added together, it is impossible to say which of the collections (i) and (iv) is the greater. For one collection to be *greater* than another, it must have more of some good (or goods), and not less of any others (as with collection (ii) in comparison with both (i) and (iii)).

The four collections of goods exemplify the kind of information that is required about production methods. Given it, the Ministry can see that the available resources should not be used to produce either (i) or (iii), since (ii) is greater than either of them. On the other hand, it is not possible to say which of (ii) and (iv) is the greater. How then could the Ministry choose between them?

That question leads to the third kind of information which is needed before the Ministry can decide the particular kinds and quantities of goods to have produced. It must discover what the community wants. The community cannot have all the goods it wants. It must therefore make a choice between the different collections of goods that could be produced by using the available resources in different ways. The wants of the community have to be expressed in terms of their tastes or *preferences* as between the different collections.

The concept of preferences is most easily illustrated by considering the case of an individual person. Suppose that Mr Smith is told that he can have *only* one of two collections of three goods A, B and C, e.g. either $7A$ plus $9B$ plus $5C$ or $4A$ plus $9B$ plus $7C$.[1] If he chooses the first collection rather than the second, he is then said to prefer the first to the second. More generally, we can conceive of an *order* of preferences between many collections of goods. Suppose that Mr Smith is now confronted with a large number of collections and asked to place them in his order of preference. What is required of him is that he say which would be his first choice, his second choice and so on. The way in which he chooses between the collections expresses the order of his preferences.

The third kind of information required by the Ministry is the order of the *community's* preferences between different collections of goods. The first two kinds of information, explained above, were necessary to discover the collections of goods that *could* be produced with the available resources. Given that knowledge, there remains the choice to be made between those feasible collections. Which of the many possible collections should actually be produced? The order of the community's preferences is needed for the making of that choice.

How then can the Ministry be informed of the community's order of references? What, indeed, *is* the 'community' in this respect? The answer to the latter question depends on the political organization of the country, and, in particular, on the extent to which different people are able to have a say in deciding the kinds and quantities of goods to be produced. In a democracy, it is presumed that at least all responsible adults should have some kind of say in the matter. In other societies, only the views of the ruler (or rulers) will count.

In the latter cases, the Ministry will only have to discover the 'government's' preferences between different collections of goods. If the government is a dictator, he must reveal his own tastes. If it is a group of people, they must get round a table and argue out any differences there may be in their tastes. That argument will involve both (i) the group's order of preferences between different collections of goods, and (ii) the rule (or rules) to be used in dividing the goods produced between the members of the community. It would not be sensible to judge the merits of different collections of goods without regard to the quantity of each good (e.g. toothbrushes) which is to go to each person.

The problem of discovering the community's preferences would be

[1] It should be noted that neither of these collections is greater than the other.

much more complicated in a democracy. The Ministry will have to be informed of *every* household's order of preferences between *all* the collections of goods that might be distributed to it. Some form of questionnaire to all households would be needed to collect that information. From the completed questionnaires, the Ministry would then have to construct, by aggregation, an order of preferences for the whole community. That order would, of course, depend on the way in which goods are to be divided between households.

THE DECISION-MAKING PROCESS

When the three kinds of information detailed above have been collected, the Ministry comes to the decision-making stage of its work. In principle, the decisions about the production and distribution of goods will have to be reached in the following manner. First, *all* the different ways of using the available resources have to be divided into two groups: the 'efficient' and the 'inefficient' ways. The latter are those which produce totals of goods which are unequivocally *smaller* than those which would result from other production methods. Thus, the methods which, for example, produce collections (i) and (iii) above are inefficient in that sense, and should be weeded out of the list of all the possible production methods.

But that will still leave a long list of efficient ways of using resources. These are the ways which produce collections of goods *none* of which is unequivocally greater than the others. Thus, the methods which produce collections (ii) and (iv) above are efficient in this sense: neither of these collections is greater than the other. But while it is impossible to say which collection is the *greater*, it is possible to ask which collection is *preferred*.

That is what the Ministry must now do in relation to all the collections of goods that could be produced by efficient production methods. It must confront those collections with the community's order of preferences, and attempt to discover which particular collection is highest in that order. That collection is the one that should be produced. Resources should be allocated to its production in the way indicated by the information collected by the Ministry. And the goods produced should be distributed to people according to the rules used in giving an order to the community's preferences. Those decisions bring the Ministry to the final stage of its work. It must now issue the commands for the decisions to be executed.

The magnitude of the task involved in the administrative planning of a *whole* economy can hardly be exaggerated.[1] In developed countries, there are large quantities of many different kinds of resources which are capable of producing hundreds of thousands of different kinds of goods. A command economy would require an enormous Ministry of Economic Planning to collect the information required for decision-making, and to execute the decisions. Moreover, that planning process would have to be an unceasing one, because of continual changes in resources, production methods and preferences.

It is, however, the actual decision-making which presents a problem of utter complexity. All the possible methods of using the available resources have to be scanned, in relation to the community's order of preferences, in order to discover that collection of goods which is most preferred among those that could be produced. There is no human brain, or committee of brains, or currently conceivable computer, that could digest all the relevant information, let alone hold it steadily 'before the mind' in order to pick out the most preferred collection of goods. That being so, it would be a mere accident if the Ministry got anywhere near the 'best' use of resources. To be precise, it would be prone to major errors in two respects: (i) in choosing production methods which yield a *smaller* output of goods than could be produced by other feasible methods, and (ii) in choosing to produce a collection of goods which is *less preferred* than other possible collections. The likelihood of those errors would, of course, be increased by any deficiencies in the information collected by the Ministry.

In view of those problems, it is maybe not surprising that the administrative planning of a *whole* economy has never been attempted. The *pure* command economy has yet to exist. However, important elements of administrative planning have been used, and are used (in conjunction with the price mechanism) in many countries. This was so in the belligerent countries during the Second World War; and it is currently so in, for example, the Soviet Union. The understanding of the nature— and the advantages and disadvantages—of these forms of administrative

---

[1] To ease the exposition at this stage, a number of important decisions which would have to be taken have been ignored. For example, capital goods as well as consumer goods can be produced. The former enlarge a country's capacity to produce the latter *in the future*, but at the cost of having fewer consumer goods in the present. Hence, the allocation of resources between the two types of goods depends in part on the community's preferences between consuming less now and more later.

Again, it may not be thought proper, at least in a democracy, simply to command people to work in particular ways. Some choice between jobs may be allowed. If so, a set of incentives and deterrents will have to be used to ensure that the allocation of workers between jobs fits in with the production decisions.

planning (sometimes called physical controls) is increased by conceiving what a complete command economy would be like.

But in addition, that conceptual exercise makes clear the problems with which any alternative economic system has to contend. In particular, it brings out clearly the three things which underlie the operation of any economic system; viz., (a) the kinds and quantities of resources available, (b) the alternative methods of production by which they can be used, and (c) the preferences of the community between different collections of goods. The stage has therefore been set for understanding the working of a price mechanism.

CHAPTER 3

TYPES OF ECONOMIC SYSTEM:
A PRICE MECHANISM

It is through the buying and selling of goods and resources for money that economic decisions are made under a price mechanism. This allows the whole community to participate directly in the decision-making process. That is in strong contrast to the operation of a command economy, in which the making of decisions is centralized in the Planning Ministry.

A price mechanism can, however, be used in conjunction with a variety of social and political institutions. The buying and selling of things for money did, in fact, first appear and then develop in capitalist (private enterprise) societies, in which most resources are privately owned rather than being the property of the state (i.e. publicly-owned). But a collectivist society, in which both natural and man-made resources are mainly owned by the state, can also have its economic decisions made through a price mechanism. In the present century, a number of collectivist societies (e.g. Yugoslavia) have set up 'socialist' price mechanisms.

A capitalist price mechanism can take a variety of forms. The best way to understand that variety is to consider its different aspects one at a time. To start with, therefore, let us ignore any economic activity that may be undertaken by government, and also any foreign trade with other countries; and assume that only consumer (and no capital) goods are being produced.

Let the term 'firm' be used to cover all organizations in which resources are used to produce goods. Under capitalism, the resources which belong to a firm are owned by private persons—either directly or through such legal instruments as stocks and shares. The firms sell their goods for money, the amount received being called their *revenue*. The resources they use (labour, natural and man-made resources) have to be paid for in money. These payments are their *costs*. A main objective of a privately-owned firm will be to make its revenue exceed its costs by as large an amount as possible. That is, it aims to maximize the excess of

20

revenue over costs. If that excess is called *profit*[1], then the firm's objective can be reworded as that of maximizing profit.

The resources used by firms are bought either directly from persons (e.g. labour), or from other firms (e.g. raw materials, components). However, since the firms are privately owned, all the payments for resources end up with persons. Most people live in family groups and make many of their economic decisions on a family basis. The term 'household' will be used for each family unit, whether it consists of one, two or more persons.

The finished consumer goods produced by firms are sold to these households. Thus, in its simplest form, the price mechanism involves firms which pay out money costs to buy resources from households, and also sell goods to those households for money revenue. Or put the other way round: the households receive income from selling resources to firms and spend that income in buying the goods produced with those resources. The price mechanism therefore works through a circular flow of money expenditure from households to firms and back to households again, and so on endlessly.

It is by means of this circular flow that decisions are made on the kinds and quantities of goods to be produced, on the production methods to be used and on the distribution of the goods between households. That is, the working of such an economic system depends on the ways in which households and firms behave in buying and selling goods and resources.

THE BEHAVIOUR OF HOUSEHOLDS

The labour, natural resources and capital goods in a capitalist society are owned by households. It is they who ultimately decide upon the uses to which these resources are put. Under a price mechanism, that means choosing the firms to which the resources are hired out. Those decisions depend on the prices for them offered by the firms: each household will want to get the most advantageous prices for its resources.

The income of each household depends on both the quantities of resources it owns and on the prices obtained for their use. Thus the size of an income from labour is got by multiplying the hours of work done during some period of time by the price of that work (the wage rate) per hour. In general, the quantities of different resources sold by a

[1] The terms revenue, cost and profit will be defined more rigorously later; see Chapters 9–11 below.

household, multiplied by their respective prices, give the total income of the household.

That income is now available for the purchase of consumer goods. From its size, and the prices that have to be paid for these goods, the household can work out the different collections of goods it *could* buy by spending its income in different ways. But which collection it *does* buy depends also on its preferences. Being free to spend its income as it wishes, it can pick out the most preferred collection of goods that its income can buy at the ruling prices.

The economic behaviour of a household thus has two sides. On the one hand, it hires out resources in return for income; and on the other, it uses that income to buy goods. Both aspects of its behaviour are conditioned by prices. The uses to which it puts its resources depend on the prices offered for them. The ways in which it spends its income depend on the prices of goods. These two aspects of household behaviour are, however, interconnected: the purpose of hiring out resources is to obtain the income required to purchase goods.

THE BEHAVIOUR OF FIRMS

The production decisions of firms are governed by their aim of maximizing the excess of revenue over cost (maximizing profit). The size of the revenue depends on the ways in which households spend their incomes. The costs are made up of payments for the resources used in production. To maximize profit, those costs must be made as low as possible, i.e. minimized. For the excess of revenue over cost for any output will only be at a maximum, if the cost is at a minimum. Profit maximization necessarily involves cost minimization.

Each firm has to decide upon the production method it is going to use, i.e. on the ratios in which different resources are to be employed. For example, it must choose between having a larger or a smaller amount of machinery per worker. The choice of the production method is governed by the need to minimize costs. The appropriate method of producing any output will be the one that gets costs as low as possible. But the amount of those costs depends on *both* the prices and the productivities of resources.

Consider a good that can be produced by using three resources: one kind of labour, one type of machine, and a particular raw material. Suppose that 4 men operating 1 machine and using 20 units of raw material can produce 50 units of the good in 8 hours. This relationship between the inputs of resources and the output of the good gives the productivity of the resources when they are used in that way; i.e. it tells how much output they can produce. But the *cost* of the good cannot be ascertained until the prices of the resources are known as well. Thus, if the wage rate (i.e. the price of labour) is £5 per man for 8 hours work, if the price for running the machine for 8 hours is £20, and if the raw material is £3 per unit, then the total cost of 50 units of the good will be £100. If the prices of resources were lower, the total cost, with productivity unchanged, would be lower (e.g. with a wage rate of £4 for 8 hours, total cost is £96). But also, if productivity were higher, the total cost, with resource prices unchanged, would be lower (e.g. with greater skill, 3 men could do the work of 4, and total cost would be £95).

Both the productivities of resources (which depend on the production methods used), and their prices, help to determine costs. In seeking out that production method which minimizes costs, a firm must therefore weigh the productivity of *each* resource against the price that has to be paid for it. The higher the productivity of any resource in relation to its price, the lower costs will be. Hence, it is by considering the productivity-to-price relationship for each and every resource that the firm can pick out the combination (i.e. ratios) of resources which minimizes cost.

The economic behaviour of a firm thus has two sides. On the one hand, it hires resources to produce goods, and thereby incurs costs; and on the other, it sells those goods to earn revenue. Both aspects of its behaviour are conditioned by prices. Its choice of resources depends on their prices. The quantities of goods that households will buy from it depend on their prices. These two aspects of the firm's behaviour are, however, interconnected: the purpose of incurring costs is to earn a revenue which will maximize profit.

The prices of goods and of resources are the connecting links between the behaviour of households and the behaviour of firms. They have, therefore, to reach agreement on what these prices are to be.

THE DETERMINATION OF PRICES

It is in seeking to minimize costs, in order to maximize profits, that firms decide what resources they want to use. The availability of those resources depends on the ability and willingness of households to provide them. The price of any resource will be bid up as long as firms are unable to get as much of it as they want. Hence, the price will depend on the amount which the firms want *in relation to* the households' ability and willingness to provide the resource.

Similarly, the price of a good will depend on the amount which the households want *in relation to* the firms' willingness to produce it. The price of any good will be bid up as long as the firms are unwilling to produce as much of it as the households want to buy.

Prices thus depend on the willingness of households to sell resources and buy goods, and of firms to buy resources and sell goods. The prices which are established must be such that *two* conditions are satisfied: (i) the quantities of goods produced must be the same as those which the households want to buy, and (ii) the quantities of resources used by firms must be the same as those which the households want to sell. If *either* of those conditions is not satisfied, then the prices of *both* goods and resources will change. Thus, if at ruling prices households want to buy more of a good than is being produced, its price will rise. The firms will now find it profitable to increase production, and therefore use more resources. That will raise the prices of the resources in question.

But similarly, if at ruling prices firms want to use more of a resource than households are willing to provide, its price will rise. That will increase the costs of the firms using the resource, and thereby reduce the quantities of goods they are willing to produce. As a result, the prices of those goods will rise.

The prices of goods and resources cannot be fixed independently of each other. They must be determined *simultaneously* in order that *both* the conditions given above are satisfied.

Those conditions show how the price mechanism performs the first two functions of an economic system. Prices will go on changing until the quantities of goods produced are the same as households want to buy. That is the way in which the price mechanism determines the kinds and quantities of goods produced.

Similarly, prices will go on changing until the quantities of the different resources used by firms are the same as households want to sell. That is the way in which the price mechanism determines the production methods used.

It is through the process of households and firms agreeing on prices that the available resources of a community come to be allocated to the production of different goods.

Moreover, in performing the first two functions, the price mechanism at the same time carries out the third function of an economic system. The prices of resources, together with the quantities provided by each household, determine the money incomes of the different households. These incomes, and the prices of goods, determine the quantities of goods which the different households can have. That is, it is through incomes and prices that the distribution of goods between households is brought about. In this process, each person is free to decide the kinds and quantities of goods in which to take his share of total output. Moreover, that freedom in no way prevents the sum of all households' shares being the same as the total output that can be produced with the available resources. For as has already been seen, the prices of goods and resources will be such that the quantities of goods which firms are able and willing to produce match those that households want to buy. That is the manner in which a price mechanism can simultaneously perform all three functions of an economic system.

The price mechanism works through households and firms making their economic decisions in relation to prices. The quantities of resources sold, and of goods bought, by households depend on their prices. Similarly, the quantities of goods produced, and of resources used, by firms depend on their prices. The prices change as long as the quantities (of both goods and resources) which households and firms decide to buy and sell do not match. The prices thus act to co-ordinate, or make consistent with one another, the various buying and selling decisions.

The quantities of resources available, the different possible methods of production, and the preferences of households, all enter into that decision-making process. The availability of resources is made known by the willingness of households to sell them. Firms have to choose between production methods in order to minimize their costs. Households express their preferences in the ways they spend their incomes.

The price mechanism therefore uses the same three kinds of information that, as noted at the end of the last chapter, are required by a command economy. But in the latter, the whole mass of information has to be centrally collected by the Ministry of Economic Planning; whereas, in the former, it is sufficient that each household and firm collect only the information which is relevant on its *own* decisions. This de-centralizing of the gathering of information makes it possible for human brains (and computers) to deal with the enormous amount of information needed to run an economic system. In addition to prices, each household has to know only the quantities of resources it possesses, and its own preferences between goods; and each firm has to know only the different production methods for the goods it is going to produce.

The economic decisions of separate households and firms can, therefore, be made on amounts of information which are relatively very small compared with what the Ministry would have to assemble. It was argued in the previous chapter that the Ministry's task of economic decision-making is quite impracticable. It would be simply incapable of digesting and scanning all the relevant information. But that task becomes much more practicable through the de-centralized working of a price mechanism. Separate decisions can be made by households and firms on the basis of relatively small amounts of information, which of course include the prices at which goods and resources can be bought and sold. It is then through adjustments in those prices that the separate decisions are co-ordinated, or made consistent with one another.

A command economy and a price mechanism are alternative ways of tackling the *same* problems, viz., those which arise from the scarcity of resources. In principle, they could both give the same 'efficient'[1] solution for the allocation of resources. But overall administrative planning is so impracticable, that the chance of getting an 'efficient' use of resources under it is exceedingly small.

A price mechanism is much more practicable. But that in itself does not guarantee that it will work 'efficiently'. Certain conditions need to be fulfilled for that to be so. For example, firms and households must in fact take account of all the available and relevant information. The mechanism must ensure that all the available resources are used (i.e. are 'fully employed'). The prices of goods and of resources must be related to one another in certain ways for the 'most preferred' collection of goods to be produced. These conditions are frequently not fulfilled in existing capitalist price mechanisms. Why that is so cannot be appreciated without a fuller understanding of how a price mechanism works. Hence, one of the motives for studying economics is to discover how economic systems could be made to work more 'efficiently'.

SOCIALIST PRICE MECHANISMS

In a collectivist society, the natural and man-made resources are owned by the state. But that does not debar the community from using a price mechanism as the means through which economic decisions are made. This could be done in the following way.

A variety of firms would be set up to hold and operate the publicly-owned natural resources and capital goods. Each firm would be administered by a manager (or managing committee) appointed or elected in some manner. He would be instructed to purchase with money (i.e. incur costs on) the resources needed for the firm's productive activities, and to sell the resulting output for money revenue. Thus, the firm would pay wages and salaries to its employees, would make payments to other firms for resources (e.g. raw materials, components) received from them, and would make payments to the government for the use of the natural resources and capital goods owned by it.

[1] In the same sense given to that term in the last chapter; see p. 18 above.

The wages and salaries are the incomes of households, out of which they can buy—in accordance with their preferences—the goods produced by the publicly-owned firms. The government can also use its income from natural resources and capital goods to buy goods and services for general use by the community.[1] The revenues of the firms are thus determined by the ways in which the households and the government wish to spend their incomes.

The manager of each firm would be instructed to run it so that its revenue just covers its costs. That is, the firm's objective would be to make the excess of revenue over cost equal to zero. Firms that are not meeting this objective would have to change their production policies, i.e. change their outputs of goods and/or inputs of resources. As a result, the prices of goods and resources would alter. Hence, as in a capitalist price mechanism, the prices of goods would go on changing until the quantities produced are the same as the community wants to buy; and the prices of resources would go on changing until the quantities required by firms are the same as those available.

Thus, there will clearly be some similarity between the ways resources are used, and goods are produced, by firms under capitalist and socialist price mechanisms. It might be thought, however, that the difference in the firm's objective as between the two systems will lead to different allocations of resources. But that is not necessarily so. The costs of a private enterprise firm (as of a socialist firm) must be taken to include appropriate payments for the resources it *owns*, as well as for the resources it buys from persons and other firms. If costs are thus defined (i.e. in the same way for both systems), then a capitalist price mechanism may operate—through competition between firms—so that costs are no more than covered by revenue. In that case, the working of a capitalist price mechanism would be similar to that of a socialist one.

The point at issue in the previous paragraph cannot, of course, be fully understood and debated without more knowledge of how a price mechanism works. But it is important to realize from the outset that the buying and selling of things for money is an economic system which can be used by collectivist as well as by capitalist societies. Although this book is couched in a form directly relevant to societies in which private enterprise predominates,[2] its analysis has a more general applicability than that.

---

[1] The ways in which a government can operate through a price mechanism (either capitalist or socialist in nature) are explained in the next chapter.

[2] Most societies of this kind do have some socialist firms, e.g. the nationalized industries in the UK, and many public utility companies elsewhere.

CHAPTER 4

GOVERNMENT AND MIXED ECONOMIC SYSTEMS

Any form of government must use some of a country's scarce resources. Even at a minimum, some manpower and buildings are needed for the formulation and execution of public policy. The provision of those resources for the 'public sector' of an economy has to be arranged through the economic system. More particularly, the system has to allocate the available resources between the public sector and the remaining 'private sector'. That does not raise any new problem for a command economy. In it, the Ministry of Economic Planning would take the government's preferences for goods into account, as well as those of anybody else who might be considered. But the existence of government in a country that uses a price mechanism does need further study.

It seems fairly obvious that all countries in the modern world do need to be governed to some extent. Clashes of interest between individuals would lead to fraud and violence without some form of external constraint. Therefore, communities have *at least* to provide themselves with police forces and law courts to maintain internal peace, and with armed forces to deter external aggression. These services have an important common characteristic from an economic viewpoint. If they are provided at all, they are, by their very nature, available collectively to everybody in the community. By living in a country, a person is, *ipso facto*, defended by its armed forces and is subject to its laws. He uses those public services in common with his fellow citizens, in contrast with his private use of, say, a loaf of bread. There are thus 'collective' goods and services to be distinguished from 'private' ones.

The collective goods are characterized by the *necessary* sharing of the benefits from them by all the members of the community. But there are many apparently private goods from which people other than their owners can derive pleasure (or displeasure). The architecture and state of repair of a person's house, his health and education (or lack of them) can be matters of interest to his neighbours. These and other goods he can buy may—intentionally or unintentionally—confer benefits on other members of the community (e.g. the improvement in social relations that education can bring); or can involve them in costs (e.g. medical bills as a result of infectious illnesses). Such 'external effects' of some private goods give them a character akin to that which distinguishes collective goods. That is one—but only one—reason why many modern governments provide a range of public services which extends beyond those that are unequivocally collective in nature. But what that range should be is a matter of controversy, in part because people differ in their judgements on the external effects of private goods.[1]

Under a price mechanism, people are free to buy, or not to buy, different private goods. Conceivably, the same arrangement could be made as regards collective goods. For example, each person could inform the government of the amount of external defence he wished to purchase per annum. The sum of these individual purchases would then determine the government's total expenditure on defence. But there are obvious shortcomings to this method. Since the armed forces of a country must act as an integrated unit, an individual could not tell how much defence he was in fact buying without knowing the amounts of other people's purchases of it. Moreover, he could decide not to spend anything in the expectation that his more apprehensive fellow citizens will provide him, as well as themselves, with the defence he does want. Thus, with collective goods, there is no clear and certain relation between an individual's expenditure and the benefits he gets from it. In that respect, they differ from private goods, where the individual can assess what he gets for the price he pays.

There are thus good reasons why a government should not sell collective goods to the community. But there are no special difficulties in it buying the resources (e.g. the labour of civil servants and soldiers) which are needed to provide the services. For that to be achieved, however, *not all* the resources of the country must be drawn into the production of goods for the private sector. Some must be freed for use in the public sector. Hence the expenditures of households on private goods must be curtailed. This would of course happen automatically if the households had to spend some of their incomes directly on collective goods. But when that is not the case, the government must find an alternative way of reducing household expenditure. The alternative is taxation, which is a compulsory payment to the government.

The various types of taxes may be broadly classified under three

[1] Cf. many discussions of the merits and de-merits of the public provision of education and health services.

heads. First, there are the *outlay* (or expenditure) taxes,[1] which are levied on the purchase and sale of goods. These take the form either of a specific amount per unit of a good, or of a percentage of the price of a good (e.g. either 1s per unit, or 10 per cent of the price). Since these amounts have to be paid over to the government when goods are bought and sold, a likely consequence is that the prices of the taxed goods will be higher than they would otherwise be.[2] Secondly, *income* taxes[3] are levied on the earnings of households,[4] and the amount payable may be (as is often the case) a larger percentage of income, the higher that income is. Thirdly, *capital* taxes may be levied on the accumulated wealth of households. Thus, from time to time each household may have to pay over some percentage of its wealth to the government.

All three forms of taxation are likely to reduce the *quantities* of goods bought by households. Outlay taxes raise prices, and as a result money incomes cannot buy as many goods. Income taxes reduce the amounts of money income at the free disposal of households. Capital taxes may induce people to cut expenditure so as to meet at least a part of those taxes out of income, rather than let them fall entirely on their wealth. By reducing the quantities of goods bought, taxation ensures that not all the resources of a country are used by the private sector. The total amount of taxation should, therefore, be sufficient to free the resources that are to be bought by the public sector. That is the manner in which, through the combination of government expenditure and taxes, the price mechanism allocates resources between the two sectors.

But taxation can also be used for other purposes. The rates of outlay taxes often vary as between different goods. As a result, the prices of some goods are raised relatively more than those of others. That alters the ways in which households spend their incomes. Thus, as a matter of social policy, a government may tax some goods more heavily (e.g. alcohol) than others (e.g. food), in order to discourage the purchase of the former to a greater extent. Indeed, that kind of policy can be carried farther by the granting of outlay subsidies to some goods, which is likely to reduce their prices and encourage the purchase of them.

Again, income taxes can be levied at proportionately higher rates on large as compared with small incomes. That will reduce, to a greater extent, the quantities of goods that richer people can buy, than it will

[1] Sometimes called indirect taxes.
[2] By how much is analysed later; see Chapter 15 below.
[3] Sometimes called direct taxes.
[4] And maybe, additionally, on the profits of firms.

for poorer people. Taxation may thus be used to alter the relative sizes of the shares of total output going to different households. That kind of policy can be carried farther by the granting of income subsidies to some groups in the community, e.g. social security benefits to the sick and the unemployed.

Since a country cannot produce all the goods it wants, it is sensible for it to have as few unemployed resources as possible. Price mechanisms, however, have not always in the past brought about the 'full employment' of available resources. In the Great Depression of the 1930s, over 20 per cent of the workers in, e.g. the US, the UK and Germany, were unemployed. But a government can, through the relation between its own expenditure and taxation, prevent that from happening. It was shown above that taxation, by reducing private expenditure, frees resources for use by the government. The level of taxation should, therefore, be such that frees *no more* than the amount of resources that is going to be bought by public spending. If taxation is higher than that level, some of the freed resources will be left unemployed. Therefore, having decided the size of public expenditure, a government can choose the rates of taxation which will allow sufficient private expenditure to ensure 'full employment'. Changes in taxation can thus be used to make a country's *total* expenditure (both private and public) on goods enough to cause all its resources to be used in production.

It has now been shown how a government operating (i.e. spending and taxing) through a price mechanism can do a number of things. It can change the kinds and quantities of goods produced. It does this partly by public spending, which expresses *collective* preferences as contrasted with the private preferences of households, and partly by taxes (and subsidies), which by altering prices and incomes change the kinds and quantities of goods bought by households. By taxes on (or subsidies to) the use of different kinds of resources, it can give firms an incentive to alter production methods. Through taxation and spending on social security benefits, it can change the way in which total output is shared between households. And by changing the relation between total public spending and total taxation, it can influence the overall level of employment of resources.

The term 'planning' is often used to indicate some form of governmental control over economic activity. Administrative planning, explained in Chapter 2, clearly fits that usage. But so do the activities described in the previous paragraph. They are, however, so different in character from administrative planning that it is well to have a separate term for them. A properly descriptive one would seem to be 'Planning through the Price Mechanism'. But even the distinction between those two kinds of 'planning' does not avoid all the pitfalls of that highly ambiguous (and emotive) word. It suggests that only government can 'plan' economic activity. Yet, as was explained in Chapter 3, a price mechanism can be used to decide (i.e. to plan) the production of goods in accordance with the preferences of households. The understanding of that point can clear the ambiguities from the term 'planning'. To plan anything is to do it according to somebody's preferences. And so it is with the production of goods. They can be in accord with private preferences, or collective preferences, or with some combination of both. But it is only by specifying *whose* preferences are to be considered, that one can give sense to the word 'planning'.

MIXED ECONOMIC SYSTEMS

It is customary to draw a sharp distinction between capitalist and collectivist economies, and to speak of a mixed economy as one in which there is both private and public ownership of resources. But that is not the only, or indeed the most significant, set of distinctions for understanding the working of different economic systems.

A more significant set is based on two considerations: (i) whose preferences it is that govern the production of goods, and (ii) what kind of system is used to relate production to those preferences. A command economy and a price mechanism are the two basic or pure types of economic system. But elements from both can be used together in a variety of mixtures. Under both types of system, both private and collective preferences for goods can be allowed to influence production decisions. But it has been seen above that it is much more practicable to take private preferences into account under a price mechanism than it would be in a command economy. That mechanism, however, can be used by both capitalist and collectivist economies.

Existing economic systems differ a lot from one another in respect of (*a*) the combination of private and public ownership of resources in them, (*b*) the relative importance of private and collective preferences for the production of goods, and (*c*) the mixture of price mechanism and administrative planning used by them.

In the countries of the world where private enterprise predominates, economic activity is today mainly determined through a price mechanism. There usually are no more than a few elements of administrative planning (e.g. control over the uses to which land may be put). But most of these countries have public sectors which provide 15 per cent or more of the total outputs of goods and services in them. That is, collective preferences play a significant role in production decisions. Moreover, with public sectors as large as that, government taxing and spending inevitably affect incomes and prices, and thereby change the purchasing decisions of households. Indeed, taxation policy is now widely used to influence both the details and the overall level of private expenditure. Some degree of 'Planning through the Price Mechanism' is thus standard practice in capitalist economies.

With 15 per cent or more of total output determined by collective preferences, the remaining 85 per cent or less depends on private preferences. But while that output is mainly provided by privately-owned firms, a portion of it usually comes from publicly-owned (i.e. nationalized) firms. The latter are not part of the public sector in the sense of that term used above. Their production decisions are based upon what they can sell, and therefore their behaviour is more akin to that of privately-owned firms than that of government departments. Unfortunately, the existence of socialized firms imparts ambiguity to the term 'private sector'. It can mean either (i) the sector in which private goods are produced for sale at a price (some of them maybe by publicly-owned firms), or (ii) the sector containing privately-owned firms. The term will be used only in the first sense in this book.

Those countries in which the public ownership of resources predominates could use a price mechanism, with a division between 'public' and 'private' sectors as in a capitalist economy. Some collectivist societies (e.g. Yugoslavia) openly aspire to that kind of system. But it is broadly true today of collectivist societies that they make extensive use of administrative planning. Some goods and resources are, however, bought and sold for money in these countries. They do have some *elements* of the price mechanism explained in Chapter 3. The conjunction of administrative planning and those elements increases the influence of collective (i.e. government) preferences, as compared with private preferences. That indeed is usually the intention.

Administrative planning can alter the working of a price mechanism in a variety of ways. For example, production decisions might be made by the government on the basis of the kinds and quantities of goods *it* thinks the community should have. These goods could then be sold at prices which just induce the households to buy them. There would, therefore, be freedom of choice for *each* household—known as 'consumers' choice'—as between the *available* goods. But the households' purchases would have no influence on production decisions as in the price mechanism of Chapter 3. Where that influence does exist, it gives the consumers a wider range of choice, because production will be adjusted to the ways in which they spend their incomes. Hence, that situation is known as one of 'consumers' sovereignty'—which involves more than consumers' choice.

Again, although workers may be paid incomes in money to allow them to exercise consumers' choice, these payments (or prices) for labour may not be taken into account in deciding production methods. That is, the concept of money costs may not be used in choosing the ratios in which to combine different resources.

Those are two examples of the ways in which collectivist societies (e.g. the Soviet Union) have combined some elements of the price mechanism with administrative planning. But in recent years, their dissatisfaction with the results has become clear. As the range of goods a country can produce increases, it becomes more difficult for a government to decide (*a*) the kinds and quantities of goods the community should have, and (*b*) what are the efficient ways of producing those goods. It is then that countries turn for guidance on those matters—as the Soviet Union seems to have been doing—to a greater use of the price mechanism.

The widespread existence of capitalist price mechanisms, and the development of socialist ones, determine the central topic of economics. The general way in which that mechanism performs the three functions of an economic system has already been explained. It is therefore time to specify precisely the questions which have to be answered to give a fuller understanding of its working.

CHAPTER 5

THE PROBLEMS FOR
ECONOMIC ANALYSIS

This chapter, and the next one, aim to provide the framework within which the connections between the chapters of Parts II, III and IV of the book can be understood. What they will do is to give a more precise picture than hitherto of a price mechanism, and indicate the questions that have to be asked about its working.

Continual reference will be made to households, firms and the goods they produce, and resources. It will help if a simple way of referring to these things is established now and is kept unchanged throughout the book. The use of alphabetic symbols rather than proper names (e.g. the Smith household, motor-cars, particular kinds of labour) will save space and reading time. The letters at the beginning of the Roman alphabet will be used as names for the different goods (A, B, C, . . .). Each good will be said to be produced by an *industry*, which will contain one or more separate firms (each of course producing the same good[1]). An industry will be given the same name as the good it produces (e.g. industry A). To make the distinction more easily remembered, resources will be given names from the beginning of the Greek alphabet (α, β, γ, . . .). These resources are classified in a general way into labour, natural resources (or land[2]) and capital (man-made resources). But for many purposes it is important to make finer distinctions between the different *kinds* of labour, of land and of capital. The term *factor of production* will be used for a particular kind of resource (e.g. all the workers with a specific skill, or all the machines of a certain type); and the names α, β, γ, . . . will refer to factors in that sense. Letters from the middle of the Roman alphabet will be used as names for households (J, K, L, . . .).

A precise picture of a price mechanism cannot be drawn to include all the millions of households, hundreds of thousands of goods, and simi-

[1] For simplicity, each firm will be supposed to produce only one good. In fact, there are many firms which produce a whole range of goods.

[2] This is the traditional name, but it must be remembered that it covers the things (e.g. minerals) contained in the land—and the sea and air.

larly large number of factors of production, which exist in a country like the UK. But it will be sufficient to take a few of each as representative of the large numbers in question. In Fig. 5.1, three households (*J*, *K* and *L*) are shown buying three goods (*A*, *B* and *C*) from firms grouped in industries with the same names. The firms are buying three resources (*α*, *β* and *γ*), which may be thought of as particular kinds of labour,

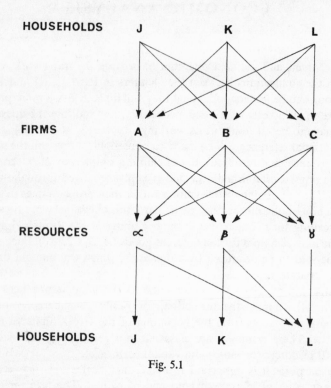

Fig. 5.1

land and capital respectively. These factors are owned by households, who hire them out to firms for money payments. But in order to bring out the way in which households thus derive incomes from the sale of factors, the latter have been separated from the former. The diagram pictures the *circular* flow of expenditures in a price mechanism from households to firms and back to households again. But since the page is flat, the line representing households has had to be repeated at the bottom in order to show the return flow of expenditures to the same households who are at the top.

The arrows represent the separate flows of expenditure which occur as goods and resources are bought and sold; the arrow heads indicate who is receiving payment. Thus, all three households buy the three goods, and the top set of nine arrows stand for their expenditures on those goods, which are at the same time the revenues of the firms. (In a more sophisticated version of the diagram, the relative sizes of the separate expenditures could be indicated by the thicknesses of the arrow shafts.)

All three industries use the three kinds of resources in the production of their goods, and the second set of nine arrows stand for their expenditures in hiring the factors. The totals of these expenditures for each firm are their costs of production plus any profits which are paid out to the owners of the firms. The costs and profits are, at the same time, the incomes of the households who own the factors and the firms. How much income a particular household will earn depends on the kinds and quantities of resources it provides. Thus, in the diagram, J only receives income from α (e.g. labour), K only from β (e.g. land), while L is apparently more affluent in having income from γ (e.g. capital), as well as from the first two kinds of resource.

These incomes of the households allow them to carry out the expenditures on goods with which the diagram begins. And similarly, the resulting revenues of firms enable them to incur costs and earn profits, and thereby create the incomes. All the flows of expenditures, and the corresponding receipts, have to be measured in relation to some period of time, say a week or a month. In the diagram, the households are shown as spending all of their incomes, and therefore doing no saving. The firms are shown as producing consumer goods for sale to households, but no capital goods to enlarge their productive capacities. There is neither government nor foreign trade. These aspects of a price mechanism will be introduced later in the chapter.

The diagram also excludes another feature of the real world. Few, if any, goods are produced in their entirety by a single firm. It is usual for most goods to be worked up to their finished form by the efforts of a series of firms. Thus, wheat is grown by one firm, milled by another into flour, which is baked by a third into a loaf of bread, that is finally retailed by yet another. Moreover, those four firms will all have been provided with other constituents of the load, as well as with transport and other services by a host of different firms. A good passes through a variety of such *intermediate* stages, in which its components are bought and sold between firms. These 'intermediate' transactions have been ignored in the diagram, because they are not essential to present purposes. Only the 'final' transactions in which finished goods are sold have been shown.

The diagram can now be used to specify the questions which have to be asked about the working of a price mechanism. The first set of questions comes under the head of microeconomics, the significance of which term will become clear presently.

MICROECONOMICS

Each flow of expenditure in the diagram can be broken down into a price times a quantity of the good or resource in question. A price is the amount of money paid per unit of a thing. A quantity is the number of physical units of the thing. Thus, if household J buys 5 units of A per month at a price of £1, the expenditure flow from J to A will be £5 per month. Again, if industry A employs 10α (say men) for a month at a price of £100 each (i.e. a monthly salary of that amount), the expenditure flow from A to α will be £1,000 per month. The letter p will throughout this book signify a price (of either a good or a factor); and the letter q a quantity. Hence, an expenditure flow equals $p \cdot q$.

The expenditure flows in the diagram therefore involve, on the one hand, both the quantities of goods bought and their prices; and on the other hand, both the quantities of factors bought and their prices. These quantities show how the resources α, β and γ are being allocated between the production of the goods A, B and C. But what the quantities are depends in part (as was shown in Chapter 3) on the prices. Hence, to understand how economic activity is decided through a price mechanism, it is necessary to explain how the prices and the quantities of goods and factors bought and sold are determined.

Whenever anything is traded between two people, the buyer and the seller must be in agreement on *both* the price at which the thing is traded and the quantity which is traded at that price. If they disagree on *either* the price or the quantity, an exchange (i.e. purchase and sale) of money for the thing cannot take place. Thus, a firm might offer to make chairs for a person at £5 each, if he will buy a dozen of them. He may be willing to buy only ten at that price, but would be ready to take the dozen if the price is reduced to £4. Since they disagree on the quantity (viz., 12 as against 10 units) to be exchanged at a price of £5, and also disagree on the price (viz., £5 as against £4) to be paid for 12 units, they are unable to trade.

The point of the last paragraph also applies to a market, in which many buyers and many sellers come together to trade the same thing. For continuing trade to be possible, they must reach agreement on both the price of the thing and the quantity to be traded at that price. It is through the process by which the two sides of the market reach agreement, that the price and the quantity are determined. To show how a price mechanism works, it is necessary to explain how buyers and sellers behave in trying to agree on the prices at which certain quantities of goods and resources will be exchanged.

That explanation can be broken down into three parts. First, it is necessary to discover the influences which determine the willingness of buyers to buy. Second, the influences which determine the willingness of sellers to sell must be discovered. Third, an account must be given of how prices are adjusted in markets so as to make the quantities that buyers wish to buy equal to the corresponding quantities that sellers wish to sell.

Consider these points in relation to the buying and selling of goods. The quantities (say per month) of A, B and C that households J, K and L are willing to buy, depend on a number of influences. Clearly, the sizes of their incomes (per month) play an important part in determining their willingness to buy. But so also will their tastes for (or preferences between) different goods. People with the same incomes, but different preferences, will not spend their incomes in the same way. The prices of A, B and C also play a part in determining the quantities of them that the households are willing to buy. For the higher the price of, say, A, compared with those of B and C, the more will purchases be shifted from the dearer A to the relatively cheaper B and C.

The willingness to buy a good is called the *condition of demand* for that good. This condition indicates how the quantity that households are willing to buy of the good depends on such influences as incomes, preferences and prices. Thus, it may well show that the *quantity demanded* will be greater, the larger are people's incomes, the stronger is their liking for the good, and the lower is its price. The condition of demand and the quantity demanded must not be confused. The latter is the amount of a good that households are willing to buy. The condition of demand shows the way the quantity demanded depends on incomes, preferences and prices. It is that condition which tells how households will behave in trying to reach agreement with firms on the prices and quantities of A, B and C.

The quantities per month that industries A, B and C are willing to produce for sale depend on a number of influences. Each firm is trying to maximize profit, i.e. the excess of its revenue over its costs. The revenue equals the price times the quantity of the good in question. The costs depend, as has already been explained,[1] on both the prices and the

[1] See pp. 22–23 above.

productivities of the factors of production. The problem facing each firm is to discover the particular size of output at which the excess of revenue over costs will be greatest. That is, out of the various possible levels of output, it has to find the most profitable one. But the revenue from each output will depend on the price at which it can be sold. And the costs of producing each output will depend on the prices and productivities of the factors. Hence, the willingness of any firm to produce for sale is dependent on the price it can get for its goods, and on the prices and productivities of the factors.

The willingness of an industry to produce a good for sale is called the *condition of supply* for that good. The *quantity supplied* must not be confused with the condition of supply. The quantity supplied is the amount of a good that firms are willing to produce as a result of their search for maximum profits. The condition of supply shows the way the quantity supplied depends on the price of the good, and on the prices and productivities of factors. It is that condition which tells how firms will behave in trying to reach agreement with households on the prices and quantities of *A*, *B* and *C*.

The reaching of agreement in a market involves the adjustment of the price of the good to the level at which quantity demanded equals quantity supplied. What that level will be depends on the *conditions* of both demand and supply. But it is also necessary to explain the nature of the adjustment process through which the market *finds* the price in question. That is why the explanation of how the price and quantity of a good are determined can be divided into three parts, viz. (i) the nature of the demand condition, (ii) the nature of the supply condition, and (iii) the way in which the price will change as long as quantity demanded does not equal quantity supplied.

Precisely the same technique can be used to explain the prices and quantities of the factors of production. For them, demand comes from the firms and supply from the households. The condition of demand for a factor shows the influences which determine the quantity demanded of it by firms. The condition of supply shows the influences which determine the quantity supplied of it by households. But, in addition, it is necessary to explain how the price of the factor will move to the level at which quantity demanded equals quantity supplied.

The last few paragraphs give meaning to the saying 'prices depend on demand and supply'. That statement in itself throws no light on how prices are determined, and learning to parrot it does not make one into an economist. It is no more than the trite observation that prices depend on the behaviour of buyers and sellers. Content is only given to the statement when explanations of that behaviour are offered in the form of the conditions of demand and supply, and the price adjustment process. The concepts of demand and supply are a *technique* for distinguishing, and relating to one another, the various influences which help to determine prices and quantities.

That technique can also be used to explain *changes* in prices and quantities. Such changes will occur whenever there are alterations in the *conditions* of demand and supply. Thus, if incomes or preferences alter, the households will wish to buy different quantities of goods at existing prices. Consequently, the quantities demanded and the corresponding quantities supplied will no longer be equal, and prices will be adjusted to new levels. Similarly, if the productivities of factors, and therefore the costs of production, alter, the firms will wish to produce different quantities of goods for sale at existing prices. Once again, quantities demanded and quantities supplied will no longer be equal, and prices will adjust to new levels.

In Fig. 5.1, the price mechanism is shown as consisting of two sets of markets: the markets in which goods are bought and sold, and those in which factors are bought and sold. Demand and supply analysis attempts to disentangle the influences which determine the prices and quantities in those markets. This is a complex task, because the prices and quantities of different goods and of different factors are interrelated in a number of ways. Thus, the quantity of A that J, K and L will want to buy depends on the prices of B and C, as well as on that of A itself. The lower the prices of B and C, the more the households will shift their purchases away from the relatively dearer A. Similarly, the quantity of α that industries A, B and C will want to employ depends on the prices of β and γ, as well as on that of α itself. For, given the productivities of the factors, the lower the prices of β and γ, the more the costs of the firms can be reduced by using more of β and γ and less of α.

Moreover, the prices and quantities of goods and of factors respectively are interrelated. For example, suppose that a change in preferences makes J, K and L want to buy more A and less B. The price and quantity of A will rise, and those of B will fall. For this to happen, industry A must use more α, β and γ, and industry B use less of those factors. But suppose that the ratio of α to β (say of labour to land) used in the production of A is higher than the ratio used in the production of B. Hence, the extra quantity demanded of α by A may be greater than the decrease in quantity demanded of α by B. And vice versa in the case of β. As a consequence, the price of α (labour) will rise, and that of β (land) will fall.

Those examples illustrate the necessity of a clear-cut technique for the analysis of the working of a price mechanism. The number of influences which affect prices and quantities is large. The interrelations between different prices and quantities are complex. Without a clearly-defined set of concepts, the student of economics will quickly lose his way in the maze of connections between the various parts of the mechanism. Demand and supply analysis is a technique for mapping one's way through that maze.

That technique is basic to microeconomics—the economics 'of the small'. The small refers to the separate decision-making units (viz., households and firms) which are, so to speak, the atomic elements of the price mechanism. Microeconomics studies the behaviour of households and firms in relation to the buying and selling of goods and resources, in order to explain the determination of their prices and quantities. Its central concern is with the *allocation* of resources, i.e. with the way in which the price mechanism sets resources to produce different kinds and quantities of goods.

But the microeconomic view is not the only possible one. A second set of questions about the working of a price mechanism comes under the head of macroeconomics, which will now be explained.

MACROECONOMICS

In Fig. 5.1, the separate flows of expenditure by households on different goods, and by firms on different resources, are shown. These flows can be added together to present an overall picture of the working of the price mechanism. The sum (or aggregate) of all the households' expenditures on consumer goods is called consumption expenditure or simply *consumption*. The aggregate of all the firms' expenditures on resources is the total of the incomes flowing to the factors. For a whole country, that aggregate of the factors' incomes is called the *national income*. It is therefore equal to the aggregate of costs incurred by firms plus the profits earned by their owners.

But since profits equal revenues minus costs, the revenues equal costs plus profits. The aggregate of the firms' revenues is the money value of the goods they produce, i.e. is the sum of the quantities of goods multiplied by their respective prices. The money value of all the goods produced by a country is called its *national product* (or output). It follows from these definitions that the national product is equal to the national income. The national product equals the aggregate revenues of firms from finished goods—which equal costs plus profits—which equal national income. The identity between the value of national product and national income is another way of saying that it is the spending on goods that creates the incomes of the factors which produce the goods.

The separate expenditure flows of Fig. 5.1 are shown added together in Fig. 5.2a. The aggregate consumption expenditure (say per month) of the three households becomes the three firms' aggregate revenue—and out of this is paid the costs plus profits which constitute the national income per month flowing to the three resources. All that national income is then shown as flowing on to become the aggregate *personal*

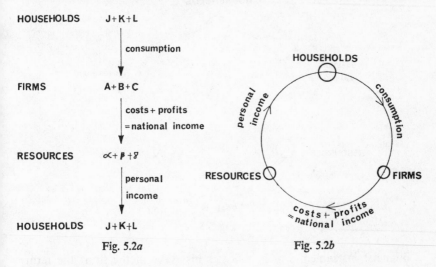

Fig. 5.2a   Fig. 5.2b

income of the households. This picture can now be generalized to refer to all households, firms and resources, and can also be presented—in Fig. 5.2b—in a more convenient form, which brings out directly the circular nature of the aggregate flow of expenditure from households to firms and back to households again.

Fig. 5.2b shows the households spending the whole of personal income on consumer goods, which are the only ones produced by firms. But, in fact, households often save some of their incomes; and there are firms which produce capital goods. These two aspects of a price mechanism can now be introduced.

Saving is that part of income which is not spent on consumption. Hence, in Fig. 5.3 (which elaborates on the previous diagram), the whole of the households' personal income is not shown as being spent on consumption. The arrow shaft leading from 'households' indicates that a certain amount of personal saving (say per month) is being undertaken.

Saving is one way[1] of adding to personal wealth. That wealth can be held in three forms: (i) money, (ii) on loan to other people, firms or governments, and (iii) durable goods. When wealth is loaned out, some financial instrument (e.g. an IOU) is normally acquired by the lender; the term 'bond' will be used for the piece of paper which acknowledges a loan. Durable goods (e.g. a house or a factory) may either be directly owned by a person, or may belong to a firm of which the person is the sole or part owner. When the latter is the case, the person will have a

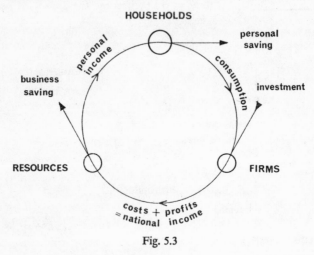

Fig. 5.3

financial instrument which indicates his stake in the firm; the term 'share' will be used for the piece of paper which acknowledges his part-ownership of the firm. The term 'securities' is a more general word that covers both bonds and shares.

Personal wealth can thus be held in the forms of money, bonds, shares and durable goods. When a person saves, he has to decide how to distribute the addition to his wealth between those forms. To the extent that he decides to hold his saving in money, no further action is needed. His income was paid in money, and therefore in the first instance, his saving will be in the form of money. But if he decides to hold some of his saving in bonds, shares or durable goods, he must now purchase these things.[2] From whom he buys them is a question that will be considered in a moment.

[1] The receipt of gifts and bequests are others.

[2] It should be noted that saving was defined as the part of income not spent on *consumption*. The use of savings to buy (i.e. spend on) bonds, shares and durable goods is not inconsistent with that definition.

By analogy, business firms may also be said to save. The profit of a firm can be called its income (which must not be confused with its revenue). Many firms do not distribute—in the form of 'dividends'— the whole of this income to the people who own shares in them. The undistributed profits—i.e. the unspent income—are called business saving. The firms may, indeed, be thought of as saving on behalf of their owners. Since this saving is done out of profits, it is shown in Fig. 5.3 by an arrow shaft from the part marked 'resources'. As with households, the firms have to decide how to distribute their saving between money, bonds, shares and durable goods.

It can be seen from the diagram that the existence of business saving means that not all of the national income is passed on to households. That is why the flow of incomes to households is called aggregate *personal income*; and is so marked in the diagram to distinguish it from national income.

Currently-produced capital goods either replace those that have worn out (by use in production), or are an addition to the stock of capital. The process of accumulating capital is called *investment*. It is therefore necessary to distinguish replacement investment—the replacement of worn-out capital goods—from net investment, which is the *net* addition to the capital stock after the required replacement has been done. The sum of the two kinds of investment is called gross investment.

Firms will thus invest in new capital goods either to prevent their productive capacity from falling, as existing capital wears out, or to enlarge that capacity. Other firms (e.g. in the building and engineering industries) will have to use resources to produce the capital goods. The expenditure on capital goods, by the investing firms, becomes the revenue of the capital goods industries, out of which they meet their costs and earn profits. Investment thus provides a flow of revenue to firms, in addition to that from households to the consumer goods industries. That is indicated in Fig. 5.3 by the separate arrow shaft going into 'firms'. The national product (and income) is now the outcome of the sum of consumption and investment expenditures.[1]

The spending on investment has to be financed, i.e. the firms undertaking it require money to pay for the capital goods. The financing can be done in a number of ways. The firms may have accumulated money, bonds and shares by not distributing all their profits in the past. Those bonds and shares can be sold, and in addition new ones can be issued, to raise the necessary funds.

---

[1] To simplify the diagram, investment by households has been ignored. It does of course take place (e.g. in houses), but is very much smaller than that of firms.

But who will have the money with which to buy the bonds and shares sold by investors? Clearly, both the households and firms who are currently saving are in a position to do that. The markets in which securities are bought and sold thus act as a means of channelling saving into the financing of investment. But those markets work in a much more complex way than that suggests. In the first instance, a large number of firms have come to specialize in the business of borrowing and lending money. They borrow from one set of people (e.g. savers) in order to lend to another set (e.g. investors). Hence they are called 'financial intermediaries', and include banks, insurance companies, pension funds, building societies and hire-purchase finance companies. Because of their specialized knowledge in different kinds of borrowing and lending operations, these financial firms provide a lot of the funds needed by investors.

Secondly, banks as well as being financial intermediaries are also the providers of money to a community. Their ability to create money[1] is a further source of finance for investment.

Thirdly, there already exists a very large stock of bonds and shares as a result of financing operations in the past. These 'old' securities are frequently bought and sold, as people decide to change the ways in which they hold their wealth. The trading in old securities, and the issue and purchase of 'new' securities, go on at the same time, and thus complicate the working of the markets (e.g. stock exchanges) in which they are bought and sold.

The latter—known as the capital[2] or financial markets—are a third set of markets in the price mechanism, in addition to those for goods and for factors. There are interconnections between all three sets of markets. The quantities demanded of factors depend on the quantities demanded of goods. The willingness of firms to buy capital goods depends on the availability of finance and on the interest rates that have to be paid for that finance. The level of interest rates is determined through the working of the financial markets, and it depends on the *condition* of demand for finance in relation to the *condition* of supply.

---

[1] Exactly how they do this will be explained in Chapter 29 below.

[2] There is a potential source of confusion here, which comes from the variety of everyday meanings attaching to the word "capital". Unless otherwise indicated, economists use the word to mean a stock of *goods* (e.g. buildings, machines); and similarly, the term "investment" to mean an addition to that stock. The money required to purchase capital goods is, therefore, best called "finance" or "funds" or maybe "money capital". The so-called capital markets are markets in money capital, and not in capital goods. Similarly, the everyday use of "investment" to mean the buying of bonds and shares must not be confused with the economists' use of that word.

Investment is one source of demand for that finance, and saving is one source of supply of it. An investor may, of course, provide out of his own saving some or all of the finance to cover his expenditure on investment (e.g. when a firm buys capital goods with its own current business saving, and when a household uses its current saving to purchase a house). But more usually, investors get a lot of their finance through the financial markets, and savers lend a lot of their savings to financial intermediaries or buy bonds and shares with them.

The overall working of, and interconnections between, the markets in goods, in factors, and in finance, is the subject matter of macroeconomics —the economics 'of the large'. The large refers to the *aggregate* flows of expenditure between households and firms, and through the financial markets. Whereas microeconomics is concerned to explain the separate flows of expenditure, the task of macroeconomics is to explain the sizes of the aggregate flows on consumption and investment. Hence, while the former centres on the *allocation* of resources between the production of different goods, the latter deals with the overall *level* of production of goods (i.e. the national product).

The money value of the national product (and income) is got by multiplying the quantities of goods produced by their respective prices. Hence, in explaining what determines the size of the national product, macroeconomics must show what determines the general level of the prices of those goods, as well as their quantities. It is on the latter, that the level of employment of resources depends. Therefore, the possibility that the price mechanism may so work as to leave some resources unemployed is a problem within the field of macroeconomics. Moreover, as has been seen, the working of the financial markets plays a part in determining aggregate expenditure. One kind of financial intermediary, the banks, provides money to the economy. Hence, the role of money in the working of a price mechanism comes within the field of macroeconomics.

GOVERNMENT AND FOREIGN TRADE

Fig. 5.3 can now be elaborated to show the places of government economic activity, and of trade with the rest of the world, in the overall working of a price mechanism.

The different ways in which a government can operate through that mechanism were described in Chapter 4. It can provide goods and services collectively to the community, either by employing resources itself (e.g. civil servants, teachers), or by buying the goods from firms (e.g. armaments, medical supplies). It can give benefits to certain groups of people (e.g. the unemployed). Those benefits are personal incomes from the point of view of their recipients. But since these incomes do not come from the sale of resources (i.e. are not *factor incomes*), they are called *transfer incomes*—viz., because they are transferred from the community as a whole to the groups in question.[1] The government can obtain revenue by taxes on the personal incomes of households, on the profits of firms (e.g. in the form of a 'corporation tax'), and on expenditures on goods.[2] The different aggregate expenditure flows from the government, and to it, as a result of the above activities, are labelled 1 to 6 in Fig. 5.4 (where the government is represented by the letter *G* in a box).

Expenditure flow number 1 represents the purchase of resources directly from households, which creates factor incomes and therefore some national income. Flow number 2 is the purchase of goods from firms, which leads them to employ resources and thereby create factor incomes. Flow number 3 is made up of the transfer incomes, which are part of the personal income of households, but do not enter into national income because they are not earned from the sale of resources. Flow number 4 is the revenue from the taxes on personal income. That income, less the taxes on it, is called personal *disposable* income. Hence, personal saving must now be re-defined as the part of personal disposable incomes not spent on consumption. Flow number 5 is the revenue from the taxes on profits. Since those profits are part of the national income, the taxes on them are (like business saving) elements of national income which do not become personal income of households. Flow number 6 is the revenue from the taxes on expenditures, which are included in the prices of goods when they are sold. Those taxes are usually collected by firms and passed on to the government.

Through flows 1, 2, and 3, the government *increases* aggregate expenditure in the economy. Through flows 4, 5, and 6, it *reduces* the ability of the private sector to buy goods. The *net* effect of the two sets of flows on the *level* of economic activity is one more problem for macroeconomics. Moreover, should government expenditure exceed its revenue, it will require additional finance; while, should the reverse be the case, it will be in a position to lend or to repay debt. In either case, the government will have an effect on the working of the financial markets.

---

[1] Just as a parent may allow his children to have some of his income.
[2] Taxes on wealth cannot be shown, since the diagram only deals with current expenditures and incomes.

The existence of government presents problems for microeconomics as well as for macroeconomics. The effects of its activities on different prices, and on the allocation of resources, as well as on the level of economic activity, have to be explained.

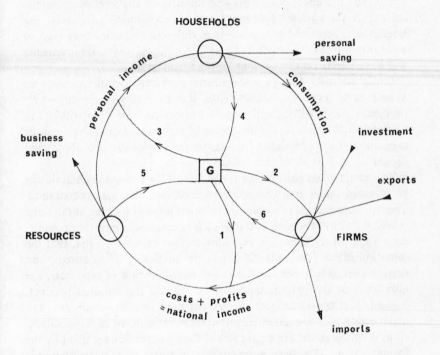

KEY: 1.   resources bought from households.
      2.   goods bought from firms.
      3.   transfer incomes.
      4.   personal income taxes.
      5.   taxes on profits.
      6.   taxes on expenditures.

Fig. 5.4

A country may sell (export) goods to the rest of the world. These exports provide revenue to the firms producing them (as indicated by the arrow in Fig. 5.4), and thereby create some national income. When the country buys (imports) goods from the rest of the world, there is a flow of expenditure abroad from that country's firms[1] (as indicated by the arrow in Fig. 5.4). Such expenditure is a *reduction* in the aggregate flow within the country; it leads to the production of goods, and a consequent creation of factor incomes, abroad rather than at home. The net effect of exports and imports on the *level* of economic activity is yet another problem for macroeconomics. Moreover, the households, firms and governments of different countries may lend to and borrow from one another. These international financial movements will have effects on the working of the financial markets.

But in addition, foreign trade present problems for microeconomics as well as for macroeconomics. Thus, it is necessary to explain which particular goods will be exported and imported, and what will be the consequential effects on the allocation of resources. For convenience of exposition, the problems of international economics are all treated separately in Part IV of this book.

This chapter has shown how the problems for economic analysis can be grouped under two heads: microeconomics and macroeconomics. The two approaches, however, are different ways of looking at the same thing; and one of the aims of this book is to emphasize how they complement each other. There are two sides to that emphasis. First, that the same influences (viz., quantities and productivities of resources, and preferences), which help to determine the allocation of resources, are also basic to the determination of the size of the national product. Second, that the techniques of analysis used in microeconomics and macroeconomics are essentially the same. The flows of expenditure, studied by the latter, are aggregates of the separate flows studied by the former. It is therefore appropriate to start with microeconomic analysis, in Part II, before going on to the macroeconomic analysis of Part III. But before doing either, there must be some consideration of the way in which economic analysis proceeds in seeking an explanation of the working of a price mechanism.

[1] To simplify the diagram, only firms are shown as exporting and importing. Only a small amount of both is usually done by households.

CHAPTER 6

THE NATURE OF
ECONOMIC ANALYSIS

The last chapter indicated the questions that have to be asked about the working of a price mechanism. The present one will consider the methods to be used in discovering the answers.

By their nature, the economic decisions made by people are about *quantities*, e.g. the quantities of different resources to be used, and the quantities of different goods to be produced, consumed, and invested. Economics tries to explain the behaviour of people in making those decisions. That is why much of economic analysis runs in terms of quantities. But it must always be borne in mind that the quantities are the outcome of human behaviour within the institutions of the economic system.

A thing (or an event) is 'explained' by the discovery of the influences on which it 'depends'. For example, the quantity demanded of a good is said to *depend* on prices, and on the incomes and preferences of households. This statement means that, if any of the latter influences change, the quantity demanded will change. Thus, if incomes rise, more of the good may be bought. Prices, incomes, and preferences are the 'causes', of which the quantity demanded is the 'effect'. The explanation of the quantity is expressed in terms of its (causal) dependence on the influences in question.

That dependence is a complex matter. To begin with, the relation between cause and effect is expressed by means of the related *changes* in them. Quantity demanded depends on incomes because a *change* in the latter brings about a *change* in the former. The causal relation is shown by the *different* quantities which will be demanded at *different* levels of income. If that is known, it can be seen how a change in income will bring about a change in quantity demanded.

But secondly, there is usually a variety of influences (causes) all working on any one quantity. The effects of those different influences have to be distinguished from one another. Thus, it is necessary to discover whether an increase in the quantity demanded of a good is due

51

3

to, say, a fall in its price or a rise in incomes (or some combination of both). That can only be done by discovering (i) the way in which the quantity will change when price *alone* changes, and (ii) the way in which the quantity will change when incomes *alone* change. The effects of the price and income changes have to be considered *separately* in order to distinguish their respective influences on quantity demanded. Only then is it possible to tell if a particular quantity change was due to a price change or an income change (or some combination of both).

In order to explain economic quantities, it is therefore necessary to find out the ways in which they will change as a result of changes in other things. That is the basic procedure which will be followed in the rest of this book. It will be helpful to establish, once and for all, a precise manner of expressing the related changes between a quantity and the influences on which it depends. There are a number of possibilities. We could say that the quantity varies or performs or functions in certain ways whenever the influences on it change. The term 'function' is now generally used in that respect in mathematics[1] and science, and there is merit in standardizing, as far as possible, the vocabulary of different branches of knowledge.

It will therefore be said that, for example, the quantity demanded of a good is a *function* of prices, incomes, and preferences. 'Is a function of' means that changes in the latter influences will bring about changes in the quantity; i.e. it is another way of saying that the quantity *depends on* the influences in question. Since that dependence is indicated by the related changes (variations) in the quantity and its influences, these things are all called 'variables'. The quantity demanded is the 'dependent' variable, and the influences determining it are the 'independent' variables, since the former depends on the latter.

For brevity, the statement of a functional relation can be written in the form:

$$\text{quantity demanded} = f(\text{prices, incomes, preferences})$$

where the symbol f means that the variable on the left is a function of the variables listed within the brackets.[2] That form can be further abbreviated by using symbols (e.g. letters) for the different variables.

---

[1] Mathematicians, however, use the term in a more general sense than the one to be used here.

[2] It will be noticed that the functional relation in the text is what was earlier called the condition of demand (cf. p. 39 above). It should now be quite clear why the quantity demanded and the condition of demand must not be confused. Indeed, clarity is one of the benefits of writing functional relations in the above form.

CONCEPTS AND THEORIES

The form of a functional relation indicates how two problems are involved in the explanation of any quantity. First, it is necessary to specify the variables on which it is thought to depend. Second, the nature of that dependence has to be discovered.

The specification of the variables is a matter of defining them, i.e. of deciding to what feature (or features) of experience they will refer. Thus, it is necessary to decide to what aspects of economic behaviour the concepts of 'price', 'income' and 'preferences' will refer. That appears to be fairly obvious in the case of 'price': it is the amount of money that has to be paid for one unit of something. But the meanings to be given to 'income' and 'preferences' are far from obvious. Economics was quite a developed subject before the concept of preferences given earlier[1] was hit upon. That household purchases depend in some way on their 'tastes' as between goods may not be difficult to perceive. But that those tastes involve an order of preferences between different collections of goods is a difficult notion to arrive at. Similarly, despite the glib way in which we use the word every day, 'income' is a complex idea. That becomes all too clear the farther one goes in economics; but the reader can test the matter now by asking himself what precisely is the distinction between his 'income' and his 'wealth'.

The point of the previous paragraph is not only that the student of economics has to go through a lengthy and difficult process of learning the meanings of economic concepts. It is also—and more importantly— that the construction of those concepts is continually going on. The task of explaining economic events is not just one of discovering (functional) relations between variables whose meanings come to us ready formed in some miraculous way. We have literally to 'think up' the concepts (variables) as a means of referring to our experience of the world. The history of economics—as of any science—shows that the 'thinking up' of new concepts goes hand in hand with the discovery of relationships between concepts.

Those relationships are found not by simply *looking at* the facts, but rather by *asking questions* of the facts. Suppose an attempt is made to find out how the quantity demanded of some good depends on prices and incomes. Numerous facts about those variables can be collected and listed—the lists giving the quantities bought of the good (e.g. apples) at different times, the various prices paid for it at those times, the prices of other goods (e.g. oranges) with which it is competitive, and the

[1] On p. 16 above.

incomes of the purchasers. Merely looking at those lists—for however long—will not disclose how the quantity purchased was dependent on prices and incomes. For, as was explained above, what is being sought is the effects which *changes* in prices and incomes have had on the quantity. One must therefore *ask* what the effects were. Asking means supposing (or postulating) some set of effects, and then seeing (or testing) whether the supposition accords with the facts.

There are many different effects which the changes in prices and incomes may have had on the quantity purchased. The problem is to discover which particular effects they did in fact have. There is only one known way of doing that, viz., postulating different sets of effects in the hope of finding a set which fits the facts. That is why the method of explanation used in all science starts off by postulating theories (or hypotheses). The theories can be regarded as questions asked of the facts. Did the quantity purchased of apples increase because, for example, their price fell, or the price of oranges rose, or people's incomes increased, or because of some combination of all these changes? Questions like that have to be asked in order to discover the relationships in the facts.

That part of scientific procedure is now well established. But, unfortunately, we have no infallible recipe for constructing concepts, and using them to frame theories which will fit the facts. The progress of knowledge still depends on good fortune in hitting upon new concepts (and modifying old ones); and upon the lengthy process of trying out different theories in order to find those, out of the many possible ones, which will explain the facts. It is often said that the great scientist is the one with vision and imagination. But, while those words properly compliment his work, they do nothing to explain how he arrived at his concepts and theories.

The nature of scientific method does however provide one guideline for the construction of concepts and theories. Since the aim of theories is to explain the facts, they must be capable of being tested against the facts. Hence, it must be known how the concepts, used in the theories, can be given factual content. For example, the concept of 'income' will only be useful in theorizing if we know the operations by means of which incomes can be measured. Similarly, we must know the operations by which people's preferences can be discovered. It is therefore often said that scientific concepts should be defined in an 'operational' manner.[1] The point is worth stressing, if only because people often do

---

[1] This expression is not a fortunate one, for it invites confusion between the definition and the operations. The definition of a concept is what it refers to, e.g. national income is the sum of factor incomes. The operations are the means by which factual content is given to the concept, e.g. the gathering of statistics to measure national income.

use concepts without knowing the operations by means of which they can be given content. It is, indeed, easy to find examples in the writings of economists.

PREDICTIONS

Now consider the problem of testing an economic theory which has been expressed in the form of a *single* functional relation, e.g. as in the case of quantity demanded of a good. The theory can be said to *predict* what the dependent variable will be when the independent variables are of certain sizes (i.e. have certain 'values'), e.g. it predicts what the quantity demanded will be at various prices and various levels of income. It is those predictions of the theory that are tested. That is, in the first instance, the procedure in testing a theory is to ask: what are its predictions? These are then compared with the facts: are they or are they not in accord with the facts? For example, is the quantity, which the theory predicts will be demanded at certain prices and incomes, the same as the quantity which is actually purchased at those prices and incomes?

Where a theory takes the form of a *single* functional relation, it is usually easy to see what its predictions are. Thus, an inspection of the condition of demand for a good will quickly reveal the various quantities which it is predicted will be demanded at various prices and incomes. But economic theories are seldom as 'simple' as that. To be precise, they usually contain more than one functional relation. That is necessary because of the complexity of an economic system.

Consider, for example, the problem of explaining how the prices and quantities of goods and resources are determined. It was shown in Chapter 5[1] that there are three elements in that explanation, viz., (i) the condition of demand, (ii) the condition of supply, and (iii) the way in which a market adjusts the price so as to make quantity demanded equal quantity supplied. Suppose we have a theory which comprises explanations of all three elements. To test the theory it is necessary to discover its predictions. But these will not be obvious from a mere inspection of the explanations of its three elements. It is through the *interaction* of the conditions of demand and supply, and the price adjustment process, that prices and quantities are determined. It is therefore necessary to work out what the nature of that interaction will be. That is, one must ask: given the explanations of the three elements, what prices and quantities are predicted by their interaction?

[1] See pp. 39–40 above.

The complexity of such an interaction, and the difficulty of perceiving its predictions, can be precisely illustrated by a piece of analysis carried out in Chapter 5[1]. The problem there was the effects (i.e. the predictions) of a change in households' preferences, away from one good, and towards another. It was shown that the consequent disruption of the equalities between the quantities demanded and supplied of the two goods would change their prices; that, as a result of the price changes, the firms would alter their outputs; that, therefore, the quantities demanded of factors would change; and that consequently their prices would alter. Even this bare summary of an analysis, that earlier took quite some space to spell out, gives an idea of the magnitude of the task of setting out the predictions of a theory. The elements of the theory in question are the demand and supply conditions of the goods and the factors, and the price adjustment processes. But before the theory can be tested, it is necessary to understand how the elements taken *together* explain prices and quantities.

That is why the construction of theories, in all sciences, involves long chains of *analysis*, through which the predictions of the theories are set forth. This analysis is a matter of logical deduction—of discovering the implications of combining the various elements that make up the theory. Those implications are the predictions which have to be tested against the facts.

THE TESTING OF THEORIES

There are two considerations which are relevant to the manner in which economic theories can be tested. The first concerns the content of the theories; the second concerns the way in which factual information can be obtained for the testing.

An economic theory may be either *qualitative* or *quantitative* in content. Suppose it is postulated that quantity demanded of a good will increase if its price falls, or if incomes rise. That theory is limited in its scope by only making statements about the *direction of change* of the variables. It goes no further than saying that the quantity will go up or down, according as the other variables go up or down. It says nothing of the *magnitude* (or quantity) of the up and down movements. Theories which are restricted to predictions about the directions of change in variables are termed qualitative.

On the other hand, theories which predict the magnitudes, as well as

[1] See p. 41 above. It is strongly recommended that the reader refresh his memory of that analysis before proceeding.

the directions, of change in variables are called quantitative. Insofar as they are successful, they obviously provide more knowledge than do qualitative theories about the working of economic systems. It is through the introduction of quantities into the functional relations in a theory that it becomes quantitative. Thus, suppose it is postulated that quantity demanded will be of certain magnitudes, if prices and incomes are at particular levels. That theory predicts the precise amounts which will be purchased at specified levels of prices and incomes. It gives the sizes, as well as the directions of change, in the variables. It therefore says *more* about household behaviour than does a qualitative theory. But the latter, of course, still says *something*.

There are two different ways in which the factual information required for the testing of theories can be collected. First, the information may be simply a *record* of what has happened in the past. In this case, the collector is essentially a passive observer of the facts. He notes them down as they occur. This is the way in which governments, and other bodies, collect statistics of prices, outputs, incomes, and so on.

But secondly, it is possible, in some cases, to control the nature of the information collected. That is done by *experiment*, in which the collector actively arranges the kind of information he wants to have. He does that by deliberately setting up situations (or experiments) from which the required information will emerge. For example, suppose that an economist is given powers to manipulate prices and incomes. He could then experiment to discover how quantity demanded actually behaves when those two variables change. By keeping incomes constant, and varying prices, he can record the effects of the latter on quantity demanded. And similarly, he can discover the effects of varying incomes, by keeping prices constant.

The object of experimenting is to distinguish the *actual* effects which the different independent variables have had on the dependent variable. A theory tries to predict those different effects. It is tested by a comparison of the effects it *predicts* with the *actual* effects. The testing of it will, therefore, be helped if the factual information comes in a form in which the actual effects of the different variables are separated.

But economists, like astronomers, are unable to experiment—at least at present. They must, therefore, make do with passively recorded factual information. This presents a considerable problem in the testing of economic theories. Economists have to separate out, in that information, the *actual* effects which the different variables have had. This separation is necessary in order to confront the predicted effects with the actual effects. For example, take the predictions of the theory of demand which have been used throughout this chapter. The information available to test that theory will be in the form of a list of quantities bought of a good (at various times in the past), at various levels of prices and incomes. That list will show how the quantity demanded changed as *both* prices and incomes changed. It will not show, as would the experiment discussed above, how the quantity changed as prices changed, with incomes constant, or how the quantity changed as incomes changed, with prices constant. That is, the information is not in a form which separates the actual effects of prices and incomes on quantity demanded. This shortcoming of passively recorded information requires the use of certain techniques for the testing of economic theories. The techniques are those of statistical theory.

The separation of the effects of different variables has to be done *quantitatively*. Thus, to separate the effects of price and income on quantity demanded is a matter of determining how much of the change in the quantity was due to a price-change, and how much to an income-change. As a result of this, quantitative theories have an inherent advantage over qualitative ones. Suppose that two variables (e.g. price and income) influence a third one (e.g. quantity demanded) in *opposite* directions. Without knowing the *magnitudes* of the opposing effects of the first two, one cannot predict even the direction of change of the third. Thus, if the price of a good rises at the same time as incomes increase, a qualitative theory cannot predict what will happen to quantity demanded. That would, however, be possible in a quantitative theory, in which the magnitudes of the effects of price and income changes are specified.

This limitation of qualitative theories very much restricts the possibility of testing them whenever they reach some degree of complexity. For as has been seen, that testing requires the separation of the effects of different variables whenever their influence works in opposite directions; and it can only be done quantitatively.

If the predictions of a theory are not found to accord with the facts, it may be difficult to discover what is wrong. There may be a flaw in the method used to test it. Thus, the operations used to give factual content to the concepts of the theory may be at fault, e.g. the measurements of prices and incomes may be incorrect. Repeated testing may therefore be necessary before it is judged that the theory has been falsified. In that case, it will be difficult to tell, for a complex theory, which of its elements —i.e. the different functional relations in it—is (or are) wrongly specified. The predictions are the implications of the elements as a *whole*. One wrong element, with the remainder correct, is still sufficient to bring about the falsification of the theory. But even when that wrong element (or elements) is thought to have been detected, a further problem remains. The error may lie in the specification of the concepts (variables) used in the element; or it may be in the nature of the relationship which is supposed to hold between the variables.[1]

The discovery of what is wrong with a falsified theory can be important, since it may act as a guide either to the modification of that theory, or to the construction of a new one. Much of the development of established sciences in fact takes the form of modifying and extending existing theories, rather than of abandoning them completely. That extension occurs even where the existing theories appear to be in accord with the facts. The verification of a theory cannot be certain. Although it may have been confirmed so far by all the tests to which it has been subjected, it may always be falsified by further testing.

But there is a further point to be made in relation to the development of human knowledge. The functional relations in all theories only refer to limited domains of experience. Yet those domains are interconnected; and the interconnections require explanation. More general theories— i.e. those covering wider domains—have therefore to be constructed on the basis of the successful, but more limited, theories.

Thus, one might have what appears to be a verified theory of the price and output of a single good. That theory, however, must be based on assumptions about the situations in other markets; as has been seen, there are close interconnections between markets. A more general theory of the whole economy is therefore required. But an economic system works in the context of the technical knowledge of the community, the private and collective preferences of its members, and its social and political institutions. Changes in technical knowledge, preferences, and institutions will alter the decisions made through an economic system. Hence, predictions of economic events cannot be made except on assumptions about those non-economic influences. A more general theory of human society is therefore required.

The verification of a theory is a challenge to construct a more general theory.

ECONOMIC ANALYSIS

While the method of enquiry used in economics is essentially a unified one, it may be thought of as having three parts:

  (i) The construction of concepts and theories.

---

[1] It should be noted, for completeness, that a theory may not accord with the facts because there are logical errors in the deduction of its predictions.

    (ii) The deduction of the predictions of the theories.

    (iii) The testing of the theories.

The predictions of a theory can refer either to past events, or to future events. An explanation of the economic happenings of the year 1844 makes predictions for that year in the same sense as a theory which attempts to predict the economic events of 1975. And the theories of both past and future events must be similarly tested by reference to what has actually happened. Explanations of past economic events is called economic history, while the future is usually left to economics.

    Quantitative economic theories are grouped under the name of econometrics. But the method of enquiry used by that branch of economics is the same as that explained in this chapter. The content of econometrics is distinguished by the functional relations of its theories being expressed in a quantitative rather than a qualitative form. This calls for the use of various mathematical techniques to deduce the predictions of econometric theories. Since only passively recorded factual information is available, the testing of those theories employs the techniques of statistical theory.

    Much of economic theory is still qualitative in nature. That is so simply because the subject has not yet developed further. Since its subject-matter is largely made up of quantities, the aim should be (and in fact is) to make its functional relations quantitative in nature. Progress in that respect will depend on the accumulation of factual information (about prices, output, incomes, and so on), and on the development of mathematical and statistical techniques for expressing and testing econometric theories. But those developments will not obviate the need for people to think up new concepts and theories.

    This book is confined to qualitative economic theory. It was shown that, when qualitative theories become at all complex, it is not possible to test them rigorously. The joint effect of different variables, whose influence runs in opposite directions, can only be determined quantitatively. Hence, the testing of qualitative theories is restricted to an 'impressionistic' judging of the validity of the *separate* elements (functional relations) in them. Any attempt to dress up the process of testing, by comparing the *whole* theories with factual information, misconceives the nature of the problem.

    The content of this book will, therefore, be restricted to the first two parts of the method of enquiry in economics, viz., the construction of concepts and theories, and the deduction of their predictions. That coverage of the subject (which is typical of most introductory books, and of many more advanced works) is referred to as economic theory or economic analysis.[1] The latter term is the better description, because it draws attention to the analysis or deduction of the predictions of theories, which is the central part of economic analysis. It was shown earlier that analysis in that sense becomes a lengthy and difficult task as the complexity of theories increases. A training in economics (as in any science) must, therefore, be grounded in an acquisition of the techniques of analysis.

Those techniques are best learned by progressing from the analysis of simple theories (with few functional relations) to that of complex ones (with many functional relations). The pattern of this book is based on that progression. All the functional relations will be (to repeat) qualitative in nature, and the arguments used to support them will not be susceptible to rigorous testing. But an attempt will be made to keep two basic considerations in mind: What are the operations by means of which factual content could be given to the concepts? And, are the predictions of the theories capable of being tested?

---

[1] Mathematical economics, as contrasted with econometrics, is economic analysis which uses the more powerful forms of mathematical technique.

PART II

MICROECONOMICS

CHAPTER 7

THE CONSUMER

Microeconomics tries to explain the determination of prices and quantities in both the goods and the factor markets. This part of the book is organized on the following pattern. The analysis of the markets for consumer goods is undertaken first (Chapters 7–17), and is followed by the analysis of the markets for factors (Chapters 18–21). An analysis of the interrelations between the two sets of markets completes the part (Chapter 22).

The explanations of the prices and quantities of both goods and factors are broken down into the *three* stages already discussed in Chapter 5,[1] viz., (i) the behaviour of buyers, (ii) the behaviour of sellers, and (iii) the working of markets. Thus the analysis of the consumer goods markets progresses from the explanation of the behaviour of households as consumers (in this chapter and the next one), to the explanation of the behaviour of firms as suppliers of goods (in Chapters 9–12), to the explanation of how prices and quantities are determined by markets (in Chapters 13–17). The analysis of the factor markets progresses in a similar fashion (as explained in Chapter 18).

PRICES AND INCOMES

The nature of consumer behaviour was outlined in general terms in Part I above. What has to be explained are the ways in which consumers allocate their expenditures in buying various quantities, per period of time, of different goods. It is fairly obvious from personal experience that the *quantity demanded* of any good depends on a number of influences, viz., the price of the good, the prices of other goods, the incomes of consumers, their wealth, and their tastes (or preferences) as between goods. It is now necessary to enquire how that quantity will change whenever those influences change. Consider them one at a time.

Suppose that the money price of a good falls. Such a change is significant in two ways for a consumer of it. First, his *money* income is now capable of buying a larger total of *all* goods. Suppose that he has been

[1] See pp. 39–40 above.

buying 10 units of good A per month at 5s each, making a total expenditure on it of £2 10s 0d per month. If the price falls to 4s—while the prices
of all other goods stay the same—he can now buy the same quantity of
A and have 10s left over. That 10s enables him to enlarge the total of all
goods he can buy. His *real* income—as measured by the quantity of all
goods that his money income could buy—has been increased by the
price fall. Therefore, it is not possible to tell how the quantity demanded
of a good will react to a price change, without knowing the effect of a
real income change on that quantity.

Second, when the price of a good falls, it becomes *relatively* cheaper
than other goods. In deciding whether or not to purchase various goods,
a consumer will compare their prices. It would not be sensible to spend
on one thing without considering the others that could alternatively be
acquired with that expenditure. It is not possible, therefore, to tell how
the quantity demanded of a good will react to a change in its price
except in the context of other prices and of real income.

A rise in money income, with prices unchanged, increases real income.
A larger total of goods can now be bought. But it does not follow
that the consumer will buy more of *all* the goods he was previously
purchasing. The quantities of some may be unaffected by the rise in real
income. The amounts purchased of some may actually fall. These are
called *inferior* goods; they are replaced in consumption by other goods
as people become better off. Thus, potatoes and margarine are often
replaced by other foodstuffs, and motor cycles by motor cars. The
remaining goods, for which quantity demanded increases as real income
rises, are called *superior* goods. In a broad sense, the majority of things
belong to this category. But there is the complication of differences in
the qualities of goods. As people become better off, they often change
from goods of poor quality to similar ones of better quality. However
we may allow for the factor of quality differences, there is no general
principle covering the dependence of quantity demanded on real income.
The former may either increase or decrease as the latter rises.

Goods may be either *substitutes* or *complements* of one another.
Substitute goods are alternative means of satisfying our wants, e.g.
apples and oranges are alternative foodstuffs. The substitutability between goods is best understood by starting from the extreme case. Two
apples are *perfect* substitutes for each other to a consumer if he would
get exactly the same satisfaction from either. An apple and an orange
are unlikely to be perfect substitutes in that way. Nevertheless, in that
they will both satisfy hunger, they are *imperfect* substitutes for each
other. How imperfect depends on the tastes of the consumer. It is

necessary, therefore, to conceive of a range of substitutability between particular things. That, indeed, is the basis of the economic distinction between different goods. A single good comprises all those things which are perfect substitutes for one another, e.g. all the apples which would give a consumer the same satisfaction. Oranges are a different good— as far as the analysis of economic behaviour is concerned—simply because they are not perfect substitutes for apples. But clearly the degree of substitutability between pairs of goods varies a great deal. Oranges are probably, for most people, less imperfect substitutes for apples than are fish. Goods can thus be ranged in relation to one another by the degree of imperfection in their substitutability. Some will be fairly 'close' substitutes (apples and oranges); some will be fairly 'distant' substitutes (apples and fish).

The degree of substitutability between goods helps to determine how the quantities demanded will react to changes in prices. Suppose the price of apples falls; they are now relatively cheaper than oranges and fish. Since these goods are alternative ways of satisfying hunger, people will consider shifting to some extent from consuming oranges and fish to consuming more apples. The amount of substitution in favour of apples will be relatively greater against oranges, than against fish, be- cause the former is the closer substitute. The quantity demanded of a good thus depends on its own price in relation to the prices of substitutes.

Some goods, however, are complements rather than substitutes of one another. That is, the satisfaction to be got from the one complements (or increases) the satisfaction to be got from the other. Thus, for some people, steak is not palatable without onions. But the relation of complementarity in the consumption of goods depends not only on tastes. There may also be technical reasons for it, e.g. motor cars and petrol.

The two effects of a fall in the price of a good—the prices of all other goods staying the same—can now be considered together. The fall increases *real* income; it has an *income* effect. It also makes the good *relatively* cheaper than its substitutes; it has a *substitution* effect. The latter will increase the quantity demanded of the good to the extent that it is substituted for the others. The income effect will do likewise in the case of superior goods. Since both effects work in the same direction, the quantity demanded of a superior good will increase as its price falls.

But for inferior goods, the income and substitution effects work in opposite directions, since the former effect reduces quantity demanded as price falls (and real income increases). A qualitative analysis cannot say which effect will be stronger, and therefore cannot establish the relation between quantity demanded and the price for an inferior good. There is, however, a strong presumption, for all goods, that the income effect of a price change will be small in size. People only spend a small fraction of their incomes on any one good. A change in its price will therefore make little difference to their real incomes. If income effects are thus negligibly small, the substitution effect will lead to the same relation between quantity demanded and price for an inferior, as for a superior, good.

But that relation may not always hold because of another consideration. People do sometimes judge the merits of goods partly on the basis of their prices. High-priced goods may be thought to be 'better' than low-priced ones. This may be due to snobbery. But it may also occur when people are unable to be sure of the characteristics of goods, e.g. the durability and reliability of today's durable consumer goods like washing machines. In that case, they may presume, for lack of other evidence, that a lower price indicates a poorer performance. Whether this consideration does ever outweigh the substitution effect could only be discovered by a quantitative enquiry.

The nature of the dependence of the quantity demanded of a good on the prices of *other* goods depends on whether they are substitutes or complements. But the existence of income effects makes it impossible to reach general conclusions on qualitative grounds only. Suppose that two superior goods A and B are substitutes. The substitution effect from a fall in the price of B will reduce the quantity demanded of A, but the income effect will increase it. Suppose that two superior goods A and C are complements. The 'complementarity' effect from a fall in the price of C will increase the quantity demanded of A, and the income effect will do likewise. But if A is an inferior good, the income effect will work in the opposite direction. Only if it is assumed that income effects are negligibly small, can the following principles be stated: the quantity demanded of a good will increase if the price of a substitute rises, or if the price of a complement falls.

The consumption of different goods thus depends on their money prices *relative* to one another, and on *real* incomes. If we neglect the influence of wealth (to be considered next), an important point can be brought out. Suppose that all money prices and all money incomes are doubled. Then, both *relative* prices and *real* incomes are unchanged. Twice the amount of money will now buy the same quantity as before of each and every good, and the same total of all goods. Consequently, if households had been satisfied with the quantities of goods they were previously consuming, there is no good reason for them to change those quantities simply because all money values have doubled.

To generalize: if all money values change in the *same* proportion, and households are aware of this, the *quantities* demanded of goods will not be affected.[1] This is another way of saying that it is changes in *relative* prices, and in *real* incomes, that cause quantities demanded to change.

WEALTH AND TASTES

A person's wealth at any moment of time is equal to his assets minus his liabilities. The assets comprise all things of value owned by him, viz., goods, securities, and money. The liabilities are his debts. Since those debts have to be subtracted from the assets to discover what the person is worth at any time, wealth is also called *net worth*. Apart from gifts and bequests, net worth can be increased by saving, i.e. by spending less than the whole of income on consumption. On the other hand, an excess of consumption expenditure over income (i.e. dissaving) reduces net worth, since that excess has to be financed either by a reduction of assets, or by an increase in debts.

Wealth can be used to finance consumption in the present, or in the future. Since human life has a limited span, the more wealth one has, the larger is the task of spending it before death. Hence, unless one has a strong desire to leave monuments to oneself or bequests to others, consumption expenditure will be larger, the greater is one's wealth.[2] That is, the quantities demanded of goods will depend on real net worth as well as on real income. It seems likely that the goods which are superior or inferior with respect to income will be similarly so in relation to wealth, i.e. the greater is wealth, the larger (smaller) will be the quantities demanded of superior (inferior) goods.

Tastes are the remaining influence on quantity demanded to be considered. It was shown earlier[3] that they have to be expressed, for any person, in the form of an order of preferences between different collection of goods. That can be done by means of the technique of 'indifference curves'. It is, however, possible to carry out a lot of economic analysis without the aid of that technique; and it is here judged that time and space in an introductory book are better spent on other matters. It is sufficient for present purposes to note that changes in tastes will alter the quantities demanded of goods. Those changes occur for a

---

[1] Behaviour contrary to this is said to indicate a "money illusion" on the part of households.

[2] The complex question of the various influences which determine the proportion of income spent of consumption is analysed in Chapter 24 below.

[3] On p. 16 above.

variety of reasons, both personal and social, amongst which is the advertising of goods by firms.

THE DEMAND FUNCTION

The quantity demanded of a good has now been seen to depend on (i.e. to be a function of) prices, incomes, net worths, and tastes. This statement can be expressed in the form which was explained in the previous chapter,[1] viz.,

quantity demanded $= f$(prices, incomes, net worths, tastes)

A further abbreviation, through the use of alphabetic symbols, allows it to be written (and read) more quickly. Let D stand for quantity demanded, with a subscript indicating the good in question, e.g. D_A. With p standing for a price, subscripts can again indicate the goods, e.g. p_A. The money incomes, out of which households spend on consumption, are personal incomes less income taxes, viz., personal disposable incomes. Since the symbol Y is used for national income,[2] a superscript d is added to distinguish the aggregate of personal disposable incomes, viz., Y^d. Let NW stand for net worths, and T for tastes (preferences). The condition of demand for good A can then be written:[3]

$$D_A = f(p_A, p_B, p_C, \ldots, Y^d, NW, T)$$

This statement is called a demand function, since it indicates that D_A will change in some way when any of the independent variables in the brackets change. In a qualitative analysis, the *direction* of change in D_A has to be specified. That can be done in the following words. If the dependent variable in a function increases, as a result of an increase in an independent variable, the former is said to be an *increasing* function of the latter. Thus, since for superior goods quantity demanded will increase when incomes increase, D_A is an increasing function of Y^d. If the dependent variable decreases, as a result of an increase in an independent variable, the former is said to be a *decreasing* function of the latter.

The qualitative[4] theory of consumer demand can now be stated in terms of the above functional relation. If the income effects of price changes are negligibly small, D_A is a decreasing function of p_A; it is an increasing function of p_B, where B is a substitute of A, and is a decreasing

---

[1] P. 52 above.
[2] The letter I being used for investment.
[3] The dots after p_C indicate that the prices of still other goods will influence D_A.
[4] In the sense explained on p. 56 above.

function of p_C, where C is a complement of A; it may be either an increasing, or a decreasing, function of Y^d, i.e. A may be either a superior or an inferior good—and similarly with respect to NW; finally, it is an increasing function of T, i.e. of people's preference for it.

It is those predictions about consumer behaviour that have later to be related to the predictions about the behaviour of firms, in order to explain the determination of prices and quantities. The way in which the former predictions can be expressed, for that purpose, must now be considered.

CHAPTER 8

DEMAND CURVES

The previous chapter showed the theory of consumer demand to be fairly complex: not only do many variables influence quantity demanded, but they do so in different directions. It is important, therefore, to have an easy and quick means of separating out, in any piece of analysis, the effects of the different variables. That will be appreciated whenever the conditions of both demand and supply are brought together to explain the determination of price and quantity. Plane geometry is one helpful device in this respect; and it is widely used as a means of exposition in economics. In applying it now to the theory of demand, it should be noted that nothing new will be added to what has already been said in the last chapter. The aim of the diagrams is to clarify the analysis, and to put it in a form which will be simpler to use later on.

In Fig. 8.1 the price of good A is measured on the vertical axis and its quantity per period of time on the horizontal axis. Any point on the diagram refers to both a price and a quantity of A, e.g. point P refers to[1] price OF and quantity OG. If the quantity is taken to mean quantity demanded, then the point P can be interpreted as saying 'if the price of A is OF, then the quantity demanded of A by consumers will be OG'. And similarly for any other point.

The statement that quantity demanded will rise as price falls can now be expressed in the diagram by means of a curve which is downward sloping to the right,[2] e.g. D_1. This curve is made up of a series of points, all of which are to be interpreted in the same manner as was the point P above. It is the downward slope of the curve which indicates that quantity demanded rises as price falls. For example, at point R, the price (OE) is lower, and the quantity (OH) is larger, than at point P. In general, a movement down the curve shows that quantity demanded rises as price falls. Once the 'language' of the diagram is understood, the shape of the curve is seen to be merely another way of saying that the quantity demanded of a good is a decreasing function of its price.

[1] I.e. has co-ordinates with respect to the origin O.
[2] I.e. of negative slope.

D_1 is called a demand curve, because it is a graphical representation of *one part* of the demand function. It separates the effect of the price of a good on the quantity demanded from the effects of the other variables. For that purpose, the latter have to be held constant, otherwise the shape of the demand curve would not indicate the effect of the price change *alone*. It is therefore necessary to have some other way (i.e. other than

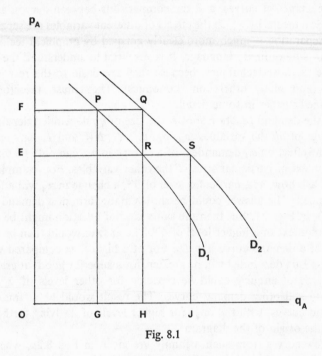

Fig. 8.1

the *shape* of the curve) of indicating the effects of the other variables on quantity demanded. That is done by means of *'shifts'* in the curve.

Compare the two demand curves, D_1 and D_2, in Fig. 8.1. At a p_A of OF, the quantity demanded is OG on D_1, and is OH on D_2; and at a p_A of OE, the quantity demanded is OH on D_1, and is OJ on D_2. In general, the quantity demanded is greater at every p_A on D_2, than it is on D_1. A comparison between demand curves D_1 and D_2 can be used to show the effect on the quantity demanded of a change in some variable *other than* p_A. For example, suppose that A is a superior good; an increase in incomes (Y^d) will increase the quantity demanded. It is essential to be clear on what that means, viz., that, at *any* given p_A, the effect of the increase in Y_D will be to increase the quantity demanded.

That is what the curve D_2 shows in comparison with D_1. For, whatever is p_A (e.g. OE or OF or any other price), the quantity demanded is greater on D_2 than it is on D_1. Hence, D_2 can represent the relation between p_A and the quantity demanded at a *higher* Y^d, and D_1 represent that relation at a *lower* Y^d; a comparison between D_2 and D_1 will then indicate the effects of an increase in Y^d on the quantity demanded.

The shapes of curves, and the comparisons between curves, are the graphical means by which the effects of different variables are separated. This separation is much more clearly grasped by graphical techniques than it is by ordinary language. It is essential to understand the exact nature of those techniques, because they are basic to the rest of this book (and many others on economics). They must, therefore, be explained further in some detail.

As the demand function shows, the size of q_A demanded depends on the sizes of *all* the variables, p_A, p_B, p_C, Y^d, NW and T. Any enquiry into the effect on q_A demanded, of a change in p_A, can only be made in the context of particular sizes of the other variables. For example, one might ask how, at a particular level of Y^d, a change in p_A will affect q_A demanded. The answer could be shown in the form of a demand curve like D_1 in Fig. 8.1. But then the same kind of question might be asked in the context of a higher level of Y^d. The answer would then be in the form of a demand curve like D_2. For at a higher, as compared with a lower Y^d, q_A demanded will be greater (for a superior good) at *every* p_A. This type of enquiry could be repeated for other levels of Y^d, thus yielding still other demand curves. The result would be a 'family' of demand curves, with the ones for higher levels of Y^d lying farther out from the origin of the diagram.

A few curves from such a family are given in Fig. 8.2a, where D_4 shows how changes in p_A affect q_A demanded at one level of Y^d (say Y_4^d), D_3 shows the effects of p_A on q_A demanded at a lower Y^d (Y_3^d), and so on. If a particular price, like OF, is now taken, the diagram also indicates how the q_A demanded *at that price* increases as Y^d increases. Thus, as Y^d increases from Y_1^d to Y_4^d, the demand curves D_1 to D_4 show how the q_A demanded at price OF increases from OG, at point P on D_1, to OK, at point S on D_4.

The same information can also be presented on the diagram in Fig. 8.2b. Y^d is there measured on the vertical axis and q_A per period of time on the horizontal axis. The points P' to S' show the quantities demanded at *different* levels of Y^d—but at the *same* p_A, viz., OF as in Fig. 8.2a. Thus, the quantity demanded is OG at Y_1^d (point P' in Fig. 8.2b)—and this is derived from point P on D_1 (in Fig. 8.2a), which is the demand curve for income level Y_1^d. Similarly, points Q', R' and S', in Fig. 8.2b, are derived from points Q, R and S respectively in Fig. 8.2a. The curve E_1, through points P' to S', shows how changes in Y^d affect q_A demanded at *one* level of p_A (viz., OF).

The effects on q_A demanded of changes in Y^d, at *other* levels of p_A, can be similarly extracted from Fig. 8.2a and graphed on Fig. 8.2b. The result will be a family of curves, like E_1 to E_4, which give the relations

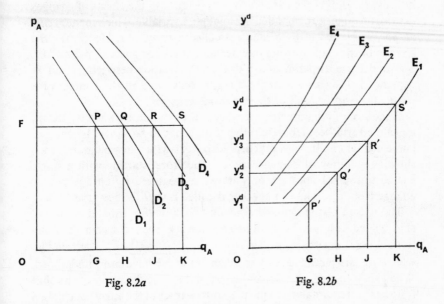

Fig. 8.2a   Fig. 8.2b

between Y^d and q_A demanded at *different* levels of p_A (E_4 being for the highest, and E_1 for the lowest, level of p_A).

The two families of curves, in Figs. 8.2a and 8.2b, are thus different graphical representations of the *same* demand function. The curves in Fig. 8.2b might, therefore, be called demand curves, since they are derived from the demand function.[1] But the term is conventionally used only for the curves in Fig. 8.2a, because that diagram is the more convenient way of representing the demand function for microeconomic analysis. This is so because microeconomics is concerned to explain the determination of prices and quantities. It is therefore convenient to have price and quantity (rather than income and quantity) shown explicitly in the diagrams used.

---

[1] They are in fact called Engel curves after the German statistician who first used them; hence the label E.

THE PARAMETERS OF THE DEMAND CURVE

When the relation between price and quantity demanded is shown by means of a demand curve, the effects of the variables *other than* price, on quantity demanded, have to be indicated by means of families[1] of demand curves. In drawing any *one* demand curve in a family, the other variables have to be treated *as if* they were 'constants', i.e. unchanging in magnitude. Only if they are taken as constant can the effects of changes in price on quantity demanded be isolated. A variable, which for a *specific purpose* is treated as a constant, is called a *parameter*. Hence, for the specific purpose of drawing one demand curve for good A, p_B, p_C, Y^d, NW and T are its parameters.[2] That is, the relation between p_A and q_A demanded, shown by a single curve, is only valid in the context of a particular size for each of those parameters.

If the size of a parameter is changed, the relation between p_A and q_A demanded will be altered, and therefore it has to be shown by another curve in a family. It is not practicable to work with many diagrams, each showing a family of demand curves. Therefore, starting with a single curve, additional ones are only drawn as required by an analysis. A change from one curve to another is called a *shift* in the curve.

The nature of the demand *function* tells how the demand *curve* will shift whenever any of its parameters changes. Thus, consider the function for good A, viz., $D_A = f(p_A, \underline{p_B}, \underline{p_C} \ldots, \underline{Y^d}, \underline{NW}, \underline{T})$. The variables which are the parameters of the demand curve have been underlined. When they change, the demand curve shifts. The direction of the shift follows from the analysis in the previous chapter of the effects of changes in p_B, p_C, Y, NW and T on q_A demanded. Consider them one at a time, and assume that the income effects of price changes are negligibly small.

Since q_A demanded will increase as p_B rises (where B is a substitute of A), a rise in p_B will shift the demand curve for A upwards to the right, e.g. from D_1 to D_2 in Fig. 8.2a. Thus, if p_A was OF before the rise in p_B, q_A demanded will increase from OG to OH as a consequence of the consumers transferring some purchases away from the now relatively dearer substitute B. And vice versa for a fall in p_B.

---

[1] With one family for *each* of the other variables p_B, p_C, Y^d, NW and T, as in the case of Y^d in Fig. 8.2a.

[2] That the treatment of variables as parameters is entirely relative to the purpose in hand, can be seen in this way. To isolate the effects of changes in p_A on q_A demanded, Y^d must be taken as a parameter—as it is of the curves in Fig. 8.2a. On the other hand, to isolate the effects of Y^d on q_A demanded, p_A must be taken as a parameter—as it is of the curves in Fig. 8.2b.

Since q_A demanded will decrease as p_C rises (where C is a complement of A), a rise in p_C will shift the demand curve for A downwards to the left, e.g. from D_2 to D_1 in Fig. 8.2a. Thus, if p_A was OF before the rise in p_C, q_A demanded will decrease from OH to OG as a consequence of less A being required to complement the smaller consumption of C, which occurs when its price rises. And vice versa for a rise in p_C.

Increases in Y^d, and in NW, will shift the demand curve upwards to the right in the case of superior goods; but in the reverse direction for inferior goods. A change in tastes in favour of A will shift the demand curve upwards to the right. And vice versa in all these cases.

The shapes of demand curves, and shifts in them, are thus a precise technique for expressing the effects of changes in different variables on quantity demanded. But despite that, beginners are still prone to confuse a *movement* along a curve with a *shift* in it, i.e. to confuse the effects of changes in p_A on q_A demanded with the effects of changes in p_B, p_C, Y^d, NW and T on q_A demanded. The richness of the English language in synonyms allows a verbal distinction which may help in the avoidance of that confusion. In future, a movement along a curve will be referred to as an *expansion* or *contraction* of quantity demanded; while a shift in a curve will be called an *increase* or a *decrease* in demand. Thus a fall in p_A will be said to expand q_A demanded, and a rise to contract it (which are movements along a single curve); while a change in a parameter which shifts the demand curve upwards to the right will be said to increase demand, and one that shifts it downwards to the left will be said to decrease demand.

THE TOTAL EXPENDITURE CURVE

The total expenditure of consumers on a good is got by multiplying the quantity purchased (q) by the price (p), i.e. it equals $p \cdot q$. Expenditure may either rise or fall when more of the good is bought as its price falls. Thus, suppose that $q_A = 10$, when $p_A = 5s$; total expenditure ($p_A \cdot q_A$) equals £2 10s 0d. If p_A falls to 4s, and q_A expands to 13, $p_A \cdot q_A$ rises to £2 12s 0d; but if q_A only expands to 12, $p_A \cdot q_A$ falls to £2 8s 0d.

The relation between total expenditure and quantity demanded can be shown graphically, as in Fig. 8.3a. Total expenditure on good A ($p_A \cdot q_A$) is measured on the vertical axis and—as with a demand curve—q_A on the horizontal axis. The total expenditure (TE) curve shows $p_A \cdot q_A$ rising at first, and then falling as q_A expands; whether or not that will be generally so will be considered later in this chapter.

The point to be made at the moment is that a total expenditure curve and a demand curve are two ways of conveying the *same* information. Consider the connections between Fig. 8.3a and the corresponding demand curve in Fig. 8.3b. In the latter, $q_A = OG$ when $p_A = OF$; $p_A \cdot q_A$ is therefore measured by the rectangle $OGPF$ ($= OG \times OF$) subtended by the point P. Similarly, the rectangle $OHQE$ measures $p_A \cdot q_A$ when $q_A = OH$ at $p_A = OE$. Hence the rectangles subtended by

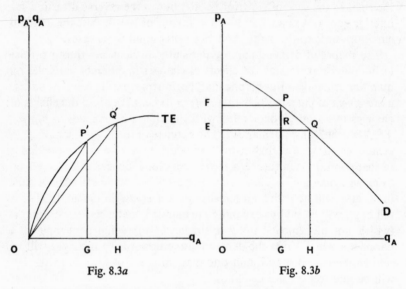

Fig. 8.3a   Fig. 8.3b

the various points on a demand curve give the information required to draw the corresponding total expenditure curve.

Thus in Fig. 8.3a a vertical distance measures what is measured by an area in Fig. 8.3b. At $q_A = OG$, $p_A \cdot q_A$ in the latter diagram is represented by the rectangle $OGPF$, while in the former it is given by the height GP'. And similarly for the other corresponding points on the two curves. Starting with a demand curve, one can therefore plot the corresponding total expenditure curve.

Obviously, one can also do the reverse operation. In Fig. 8.3a, $p_A \cdot q_A = GP'$ at $q_A = OG$. Since price is total expenditure divided by quantity bought $\left(\text{i.e. } p = \dfrac{p \cdot q}{q}\right)$, p_A equals $\dfrac{GP'}{OG}$ at point P'. That ratio is mathematically expressed as tan angle $P'OG$, and it measures the slope of the line OP'. Hence, the slope of a straight line (like OP'), drawn from the origin to a point on the total expenditure curve, measures the price at which the quantity in question is demanded. The prices obtained in this way, together with the corresponding quantities demanded, allow the demand curve to be plotted.

The total expenditure curve shows explicitly how q changes as $p \cdot q$ changes. The demand curve shows explicitly how q changes as p changes. It will be helpful in later analysis to have both ways of looking at the same matter.

DEMAND ELASTICITIES

The quantities of different goods are measured in a variety of ways—by weight, by length, by area, by volume. In each case there is a choice between different units of measurement, e.g. as between ounces and tons in the case of weight. There is, similarly, a choice between different units in which to measure the price of a good, e.g. shillings or pounds, or again, pounds or dollars.

A change from one unit to another will not alter the *direction* of the slope of a demand curve. Thus, in Fig. 8.2a, if we change from measuring q_A in tons to measuring it in ounces, the curves will still be downward sloping to the right; and in Fig. 8.2b, they will still be upward sloping. But the *degrees* of slope will alter. The change from tons to ounces increases the scale on the horizontal axis, and therefore makes the curves in both diagrams less steep, i.e. reduces their slopes at each level of p_A.

As far as the *qualitative* relations between variables (e.g. p_A and q_A) are concerned, it does not matter what units of measurement are chosen. If q_A demanded is a decreasing function of p_A, that will be so whatever the units in which p_A and q_A are measured. But problems arise when an attempt is made to assess the *quantitative* relations between variables. Suppose it is asked by how much q_A demanded will expand when p_A falls. If A is measured by weight, the answer could be given in ounces or tons; and it will depend on whether the fall in p_A is measured in, say, shillings or pounds. Moreover, if another good B is measured by length, there is the additional problem of *comparing* the extent to which q_B demanded expands, when p_B falls, with that extent in the case of A.

These problems arising from the choice of the units of measurement can be simply avoided by measuring changes in variables in *proportional* rather than in *absolute* terms. Thus an expansion of q_B demanded can be expressed as, say, $\frac{1}{10}$ (or 10 per cent) of the original level of q_B, rather than so many feet or yards. The proportional statement of a change will be the *same* whatever the units of measurement used, e.g. an expansion in q_B, from 300 feet to 330 feet, is still an expansion of one-tenth when it is measured in yards rather than in feet. Similarly, the proportional measurement of a change in price will be the same whatever the unit of measurement, e.g. shillings or pounds.

The Greek letter Δ, prefixed to a variable, is used to indicate a change (an increment or a decrement) in that variable. For example, Δq stands for a rise of some magnitude in the variable q, and $-\Delta q$ for a fall of some magnitude; and similarly with Δp and $-\Delta p$. The proportional change in a variable is the amount of the change in it divided by its original value. For q, the proportional change is therefore $\dfrac{\Delta q}{q}$, and for p it is $\dfrac{\Delta p}{p}$. Suppose that, when p_B falls from £10 to £9, q_B demanded expands from 300 feet to 330 feet. Then,

$$\frac{\Delta q_B}{q_B} = \frac{30}{300} = \frac{1}{10} \quad \text{and} \quad \frac{\Delta p_B}{p_B} = \frac{-1}{10} = -\frac{1}{10}$$

The demand function for a good (say A) indicates how the dependent variable (q_A demanded) will change whenever the independent variables ($p_A, p_B, p_C \ldots, Y, NW$ and T) change. The quantitative assessment of those relations is a matter of discovering to what extent q_A demanded will change, whenever p_A changes by some amount, and similarly for changes in p_B, etc. As it has been shown, all those changes have to be measured in proportional terms. Hence a quantitative study of the condition of demand asks questions of the form: what will be the size of $\dfrac{\Delta q_A}{q_A}$ (the proportional expansion in quantity demanded) following from some $\dfrac{-\Delta p_A}{p_A}$ (some proportional fall[1] in A's price); what will be the size of $\dfrac{-\Delta q_A}{q_A}$ (the proportional decrease in quantity demanded) following from some $\dfrac{-\Delta p_B}{p_B}$ (some proportional fall[1] in substitute B's price); what will be the size of $\dfrac{\Delta q_A}{q_A}$ (the proportional increase in quantity

---

[1] A change in the reverse direction (viz., a rise) could be taken instead. The significance of taking a change in one direction, rather than the other, will be considered later in this chapter.

demanded, when A is a superior good) following from some $\dfrac{\Delta Y^d}{Y^d}$ (some

proportional increase[1] in personal disposable incomes)?

The answers to those questions can all be expressed in a uniform way, viz., the proportional change in quantity demanded *divided* by the proportional change in the variable which caused quantity demanded to change. Thus, the extent of the response of q_A demanded, to a fall in p_A,

is $\dfrac{\Delta q_A}{q_A} \bigg/ \dfrac{-\Delta p_A}{p_A}$; the extent of the response of q_A demanded, to a fall in

p_B, is $\dfrac{-\Delta q_A}{q_A} \bigg/ \dfrac{-\Delta p_B}{p_B}$; and the extent of the response of q_A demanded,

to a rise in Y^d, is $\dfrac{\Delta q_A}{q_A} \bigg/ \dfrac{\Delta Y^d}{Y^d}$. The uniformity in those three quotients lies

in the fact that the proportional change in the *dependent* variable is always the numerator, and that in the *independent* variable is always the denominator.

The magnitudes of the quotients measure the reaction of the dependent variable to a change in an independent variable. Thus, if q_A demanded expands from 400 to 500, when p_A falls from 10 to 9, the

extent of the expansion $\dfrac{\Delta q_A}{q_A} \bigg/ \dfrac{-\Delta p_A}{p_A}$ is $\dfrac{100}{400} \bigg/ \dfrac{-1}{10} = -2 \cdot 5$; and if q_A

demanded expands from 500 to 600, when p_A falls from 9 to 8, the

extent of the expansion is $\dfrac{100}{500} \bigg/ \dfrac{-1}{9} = -1 \cdot 8$. The reaction of q_A de-

manded, to a change in p_A, is thus smaller at the lower level of p_A. The extent of a change in a dependent variable (e.g. q_A), as a result of a change in an independent variable (e.g. p_A), is called the former's *elasticity* with respect to the latter.

Elasticity is thus a *quantitative* measure of the relation between two variables, which is independent of the units in terms of which the variables are measured. The three quotients given above are the elasticities of q_A demanded with respect to p_A, p_B, and Y^d. Elasticity is a completely general concept; it can be applied to the relation between any two variables. In the further applications of it later in this book, the concept will always take the same form, viz., a proportional change in a dependent variable divided by a proportional change in an independent variable. In referring to an elasticity, it is therefore necessary to specify *both* the variables whose relationship it measures.

[1] Once again, a change in the reverse direction (viz., a decrease) could be taken instead.

$- \dfrac{\Delta q_A}{q_A} \Big/ \dfrac{\Delta p_A}{p_A}$ is called *a price elasticity of demand*, because it measures the response of the quantity demanded of the good to a change in its *own* price. It has a negative sign, since, with q_A demanded a decreasing function of p_A, Δq_A is positive when Δp_A is negative, and vice versa. The size of this elasticity depends on the number and closeness of the substitutes for good A. The larger the number of close substitutes, the more will purchases shift between them and A—and the more, therefore, will q_A demanded change—whenever p_A changes; and hence the larger (e.g. -4 as against -2)[1] the price elasticity of demand for A will be.

$\dfrac{\Delta q_A}{q_A} \Big/ \dfrac{\Delta p_B}{p_B}$ is called a *cross price elasticity of demand*. It measures the response of the quantity demanded of a good to a change in the price of *another* good. When that good (B) is a substitute, this elasticity has a positive sign, since, with q_A demanded an increasing function of p_B, Δq_A is positive or negative according as Δp_B is positive or negative.[2] When that good is a complement, this elasticity has a negative sign, since, with q_A demanded now a decreasing function of p_B, Δq_A is positive when Δp_B is negative, and vice versa.[2] This elasticity will be the larger, the more closely the other good is related to A as a substitute or a complement.

$\dfrac{\Delta q_A}{q_A} \Big/ \dfrac{\Delta Y^d}{Y^d}$ is the *income elasticity of demand*; and $\dfrac{\Delta q_A}{q_A} \Big/ \dfrac{\Delta NW}{NW}$ the *wealth elasticity of demand*. They both have positive signs for superior goods, since q_A demanded and Y^d (or NW) change in the same direction; and negative signs for inferior goods, since q_A demanded and Y^d (or NW) then change in opposite directions. Since T has not been specified here in a quantitative manner, an elasticity in respect of it cannot be given.

Any elasticity has to be measured at particular levels of *all* the variables, p_A, p_B, p_C, Y^d, NW and T. Thus the price elasticity of demand for good A is based on the Δq_A, which results from Δp_A, at a particular level of p_A—*and* at particular levels of the other variables. There are no grounds for presuming that the price elasticity of demand will be the same at *different* levels of p_A, with p_B, p_C, Y^d, NW and T unchanged. Nor that it will remain unchanged at *one* level of p_A, whenever any of p_B, p_C, Y^d, NW or T change.

---

[1] It should be noted that in relation to elasticities, economists normally speak of a bigger negative number as being *larger* than a smaller negative number, which of course is the reverse of what a mathematician would say.

[2] Assuming that the income effects of price changes are negligibly small.

THE MEASUREMENT OF PRICE ELASTICITY

In Fig. 8.4, two points P and Q are marked on a demand curve for good A. The straight line joining P and Q is extended to cut the axes in J and K. A *fall* is p_A, from OF to OE (so that $-\Delta p_A = EF = RP$), expands

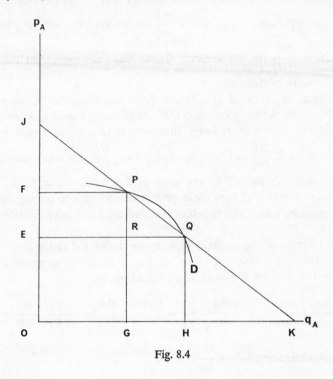

Fig. 8.4

q_A demanded from OG to OH (so that $\Delta q_A = GH = RQ$). The price elasticity of demand is symbolized by ε_D.

Hence:

$$\varepsilon_D = \frac{\Delta q_A}{q_A} \bigg/ \frac{-\Delta p_A}{p_A} = -\frac{GH}{OG} \bigg/ \frac{EF}{OF} = \frac{GH}{EF} \cdot \frac{OF}{OG}$$

But that elasticity can also be measured for a *rise* in p_A, from OE to OF, which contracts q_A demanded from OH to OG. Hence:

$$\varepsilon_D = \frac{-\Delta q_A}{q_A} \bigg/ \frac{\Delta p_A}{p_A} = -\frac{GH}{OH} \bigg/ \frac{EF}{OE} = -\frac{GH}{EF} \cdot \frac{OE}{OH}$$

4

That is, the price elasticity of demand can be measured either for a movement down the arc PQ of the curve (i.e. from P to Q), or for a movement up the arc (from Q to P). In general, the two measures will not be of the same size, because the ratio of the original values of p_A and q_A (at P and Q respectively) will not be the same in two cases. Thus, in the two expressions of ε_D above, $\dfrac{OF}{OG}$ (in the first) will not, in general, be equal to $\dfrac{OE}{OH}$ (in the second). These measures are called the *arc* price elasticity of demand.

However, as the point Q is taken closer and closer to the point P, the differences between OE and OF, on the one hand, and between OH and OG on the other hand, diminish. If Q is taken a very small distance from P, $\dfrac{OF}{OG}$ can be taken as equal to $\dfrac{OE}{OH}$, and the measure of ε_D for a fall in price will be the same as that for a rise in price. The procedure of taking Q very close to P is tantamount to measuring ε_D *at* the point P; hence, this measure is called the *point* price elasticity of demand.

That concept of the ε_D leads to a simple device for seeing what it is at any point on a demand curve. In Fig. 8.4, the ε_D at point P, as measured in relation to a very small fall in p_A, is:

$$\frac{\Delta q_A}{q_A}\bigg/\frac{-\Delta p_A}{p_A} = -\frac{\Delta q_A}{\Delta p_A}\cdot\frac{p_A}{q_A} = -\frac{GH}{EF}\cdot\frac{OF}{OG} = -\frac{RQ}{RP}\cdot\frac{GP}{OG}$$

By similar triangles, $\dfrac{RQ}{RP} = \dfrac{GK}{GP}$; hence:

$$-\frac{RQ}{RP}\cdot\frac{GP}{OG} = -\frac{GK}{GP}\cdot\frac{GP}{OG} = -\frac{GK}{OG} = -\frac{PK}{PJ}$$

Since P and Q are very close together, the line JK is a tangent to the demand curve at the point P, as shown in Fig. 8.5a. The distance from P, along that tangent to the horizontal axis (i.e. PK), divided by the distance from P, along the tangent to the vertical axis (i.e. PJ), then measures ε_D at the point P $\left(\text{i.e. } \dfrac{PK}{PJ}\right)$. Thus, by drawing a tangent to any point P on a demand curve, one can see from the lengths of PK and PJ what is the magnitude of the point ε_D.

This procedure also has the advantage—because of a potential confusion in this respect—of showing that the elasticity, and the slope, at a point on the curve are *not* the same thing. The slope of the curve, and the slope of its tangent, are the same. In Fig. 8.5a, the slope of the curve at P is therefore $-\dfrac{OJ}{OK}$; but its elasticity is $-\dfrac{PK}{PJ}$[1].

The difference between elasticity and slope is most obvious in the case

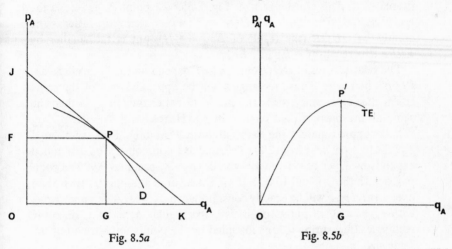

Fig. 8.5a   Fig. 8.5b

of a straight line demand curve. Suppose that the line JK, in Fig. 8.5a, is a demand curve. Its slope is the same at all points on it. But the ε_D ranges from infinity at J, down to unity at its mid-point, and then down to zero at K. When point P is at J, $PJ = 0$, and therefore $\dfrac{PK}{PJ} = \infty$; when point P is at the mid-point, $PJ = PK$, and $\dfrac{PK}{PJ} = 1$ (as illustrated in the diagram); and when point P is at K, $PK = 0$, and $\dfrac{PK}{PJ} = 0$.

The point measure of ε_D is convenient for graphical analysis. But any actual measurements will give arc elasticities. It has then to be remembered that the ε_D, measured in one direction over an arc of a demand

[1] In the language of calculus, the slope at a point on the demand curve is $\dfrac{dp}{dq}$. Since the limiting value of $\dfrac{\Delta p}{\Delta q} = \dfrac{dp}{dq}$, the point ε_D is measured by $\dfrac{dq}{dp} \cdot \dfrac{p}{q}$, which is not the same thing as the slope $\dfrac{dp}{dq}$.

curve, will not in general be the same as that measured in the reverse direction.

The shape of the total expenditure curve can now be specified by means of price elasticities. When q demanded expands as a result of a fall in p, there are two contrary influences working on total expenditure $(p \cdot q)$. The expansion in q (Δq) increases $p \cdot q$; but the fall in p $(-\Delta p)$ decreases it. This can be seen in Fig. 8.3b.[1] At point P, $p_A \cdot q_A$ is the rectangle $OGPF$; at Q, it is $OHQE$. As between them, the latter is the greater by $GHQR$ (the result of $\Delta q_A = GH$), but is the smaller by $ERPF$ (the result of $-\Delta p_A = EF$).

The relative sizes of $GHQR$ and $ERPF$ depend on the ε_D over the arc PQ of the curve. Those rectangles will be approximately of the same size if that ε_D is unity, since the proportional change in q_A is then the same as the proportional change in p_A. Hence, with $\varepsilon_D = 1$, $p_A \cdot q_A$ will be approximately the same at both P and Q. For example, if p_A falls by 1 per cent from 100 to 99, and as a consequence q_A demanded expands by 1 per cent from 100 to 101, $p_A \cdot q_A$ becomes 9,999 as compared with the original 10,000. If ε_D is measured at a point, rather than over an arc, $p \cdot q$ will be exactly constant when $\varepsilon_D = 1$. A demand curve, with $\varepsilon_D = 1$ at *all* points on it, is a rectangular hyperbola, since the rectangles (measuring $p \cdot q$) subtended by the points on it are all of the same size.

If $\varepsilon_D > 1$, the proportional change in q_A is greater than the proportional change in p_A; hence, $p_A \cdot q_A$ increases as p_A falls—and decreases as p_A rises. If $\varepsilon_D < 1$, the proportional change in q_A is smaller than the proportional change in p_A; hence, $p_A \cdot q_A$ decreases as p_A falls—and increases as p_A rises.

The total expenditure curve, in Fig. 8.5b, has price elasticities >1 in the range from 0 to P', over which $p \cdot q$ is increasing; it has $\varepsilon_D = 1$ at P', where $p \cdot q$ is constant (which therefore corresponds to the mid-point P of the straight line demand curve JK in Fig. 8.5a); and it has price elasticities <1 in the range beyond P', over which $p \cdot q$ is decreasing.

The ε_D of a *single* consumer, for most goods, is probably smaller at lower than at higher prices. The lower the price, the closer he comes to being satiated with a good. His total expenditure curve for a good will then look like that in Fig. 8.5b. But the total expenditure curve for *all* consumers, in aggregate, will probably have a variety of ranges as price falls, with low price elasticities followed by high price elasticities which are followed by more low price elasticities—with maybe that pattern repeating itself again at still lower prices. As the price of a good falls, it

[1] On p. 78 above.

comes successively within the reach of lower and lower income groups. As each new group begins to consume it, the ε_D increases. But at some low price, the ε_D will probably become and remain small. That is why the demand curves in this book are drawn concave on the side facing the origin—such curves have small price elasticities at low prices.

CHAPTER 9

THE FIRM: REVENUE AND COST CONDITIONS

The behaviour of consumers having been investigated, the second stage of demand and supply analysis is now reached. The behaviour of firms has to be analysed to discover the condition of supply for a good. The quantity of it produced for sale is the sum of the outputs of the firms in an industry. To explain the supply which will be forthcoming, it is therefore necessary to explain *both* the output of the individual firm and the number of firms there will be in the industry. The former task will be undertaken in this chapter and the next two; the latter will then be analysed in Chapter 12.

However, the behaviour of the individual firm depends on the nature of the industry within which it operates; and in particular on the ways in which it competes with other firms in offering its good to consumers. The conditions under which firms compete with one another are called the 'market situation'. That situation can take different forms, and it is necessary to distinguish (or classify) them, because the output of a firm depends on the kind of market which it is supplying.

In the first instance, the behaviour of the firm will be studied in the market situation of 'perfect competition'.[1] That will be done, not because perfect competition is a situation commonly found—it is in fact comparatively rare—but because it comprises, in a number of respects, the easiest set of conditions in which to understand how the output of an industry is determined.[2] A lot of economic analysis starts with the assumption of perfect competition as a limiting case from which progress can be made to an understanding of what will happen in more complex market situations. In that way, it is an analogue of the simpler experiments carried out in the natural sciences. A physicist finds it helpful to consider how a perfect sphere would roll down a smooth inclined plane, before attempting to predict the behaviour of a football

---

[1] Other market situations will be analysed in Chapters 16 and 17.

[2] In addition, it has considerable importance for the concept of the "efficient" working of a price mechanism as studied in "welfare economics".

on an uneven pitch. Economists—and especially apprentice ones—can, similarly, benefit by progressing from the simple to the complex.

A market situation comprises the conditions on *both* sides of the market, i.e. in the markets for goods, the conditions under which firms supply goods, and those under which consumers demand them. On the supply side, a perfectly competitive industry has these characteristics:

(i) There is a large number of independent firms, so that the output of any single firm is a negligibly small part of the total output of the industry.

(ii) The product[1] of each firm is a perfect substitute for the products of all the other firms in the industry. The good produced by the industry is therefore homogeneous, in that the consumers do not differentiate between the products of the different firms.

(iii) There are no obstacles to the entry of new firms into the industry, or to the exit of existing firms from it.

On the demand side, perfect competition requires (*a*) that there is a large number of independent buyers of the good, in the sense that the purchases of each one are a negligibly small part of total purchases in the market; and (*b*) that each buyer knows the prices at which all the firms are offering their products.

Some of the implications of perfect competition are immediately obvious. The products of the different firms are identical to the consumers, and they know the prices of all of them. No consumer will therefore pay more for the product of one firm than for that of another. Hence a *uniform* price will rule in the market for the products of all the firms.

Again, the output of each firm and the purchases of each consumer are negligibly small in relation to the totals for the industry. Hence, neither the *individual* firm, nor the *individual* consumer, can have any influence over the market price of the good. If the firm produces more or less, or the consumer buys more or less, those changes will not have a significant effect on the relation between the quantity supplied of the good and the quantity demanded of it; and that being so, the changes will not disturb its price. As a consequence, the individual firm and consumer have to take the price ruling in the market as given to them, and decide on the basis of it what quantity of the good they wish, respectively, to sell and to buy. For the specific purpose of deciding their sales and purchases, the market price is a *parameter* to be reacted to, rather than

---

[1] The term 'product' is usually employed for what is produced by a firm, while the term 'good' is used for the thing produced by the whole industry.

a variable to be determined.[1] As compared with some other market situations, in which the individual buyer or seller *can* influence price, this feature of perfect competition is one which makes the analysis easier.

In aiming to maximize profit, a firm has to discover that level of output at which its total revenue from sales exceeds its total costs by the greatest amount. That is, it has to pick out the most profitable output from the whole range of possible outputs. To do this, it must know what total revenue and total costs would be at *different* levels of output. How total revenue will change, as the quantity sold changes, is called the revenue condition (or revenue function) of the firm; and how total costs will change, as the quantity produced changes, is its cost condition (or cost function).

THE REVENUE CONDITION

The revenue of firms from the sale of consumer goods is the same thing as the expenditure of households on them. For an *industry* as a whole, the total expenditure curve (like that in Fig. 8.3a[2]), of all the consumers of its good, shows how the total revenue will change as quantity sold changes. It may, therefore, also be called the *total revenue* curve of the industry. The corresponding demand curve (as in Fig. 8.3b), of the consumers for the industry's good, may also be called the *average revenue* curve of the industry. The price of a good is the same thing as the average amount of revenue received per unit of it, i.e. total revenue divided by quantity sold. The geometrical connections between a total revenue curve, and the corresponding average revenue curve, are of course the same as those already explained[3] for a total expenditure curve and the corresponding demand curve.

The revenue curves for the individual firm are *not* the same as those for the industry. The firm only sells a part of the industry's output. Moreover, under perfect competition, they are not even of the same *shape*. Since the output of the firm is very small compared with that of the industry, it will sell its product at a price which is the same as those of the other firms. It could sell nothing at a higher price, because its product is identical to theirs; on the other hand, if it charged a lower price than the rest, it would attract the whole demand for the good to

---

[1] Cf. the earlier discussion of the distinction between parameters and variables on p. 76 above.

[2] On p. 78 above.

[3] On pp. 78–79 above.

itself. But being very small in size, it could not meet that demand. Hence, in charging a lower price, it would merely be getting a smaller total revenue (and therefore smaller profit) than it could get by selling at the same price as the other firms.

Since the firm cannot charge a higher price than the others do, and finds it unnecessary to charge a lower one, its average revenue (AR) curve is a horizontal straight line, like AR_1 in Fig. 9.1a. This line indicates that—as long as the firm is very small—it can sell as much as it

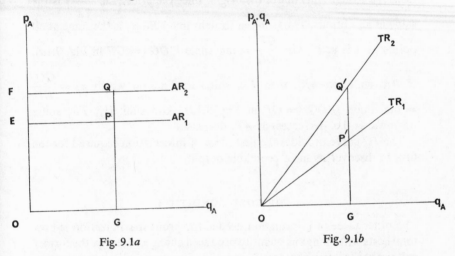

Fig. 9.1a   Fig. 9.1b

wishes at the ruling market price OE of good A. AR_1 is a demand curve for the *individual* firm under perfect competition. Its price elasticity is the same, viz., infinity, at all points on it: at each point, a small fall in price would lead to an infinitely large expansion in quantity demanded.

What the market price facing the individual firm will be at any time depends on the conditions of demand and supply for the industry as a whole. The determination of the market price will be analysed in due course[1]. But *whatever* is its level, the average revenue (or demand) curve of the individual firm under perfect competition will be infinitely price-elastic at that level. Thus, if for some reason the market price rises from OE to OF (in Fig. 9.1a), the average revenue curve will *shift* upwards (i.e. increase) from AR_1 to AR_2. A fall in price will shift the curve downwards (i.e. decrease it). In general, since the price is given, i.e. is a parameter, to the firm, a change in that parameter shifts its demand curve.

[1] In Chapters 13–15 below.

The total revenue (TR) curve of the firm can now be derived from its average revenue curve. At point P on AR_1 (Fig. 9.1a), the total revenue, i.e. $p_A \cdot q_A$, is measured by the rectangle $OGPE$. In Fig. 9.2b, total revenue is measured on the vertical axis; and for the quantity OG, it is given by GP', at the point P'. TR is measured by an *area* in Fig. 9.1a, and by a *length* in Fig. 9.1b. The other points on the TR_1 curve are similarly obtained from AR_1. The TR curve, for a perfectly competitive firm, is a straight line out of the origin, since the price $\left(\text{i.e. } \dfrac{TR_A}{q_A} \right)$ is the same at all outputs. Thus, on the straight line TR_1, p_A is the same at all points as it is at P', viz., $\dfrac{GP'}{OG} = \tan$ angle $P'OG$ ($= OE$ in Fig. 9.1a).

If AR_1 shifts to AR_2, then TR_1 shifts to TR_2, on which $p_A = \dfrac{GQ'}{OG}$ $= \tan$ angle $Q'OG$ ($= OF$ in Fig. 9.1a). And similarly, TR_1 shifts downwards (i.e. decreases) as AR_1 decreases.

The TR curve provides the first piece of information required for the firm to discover its most profitable output.

THE COST CONDITION

The other piece of information needed for profit maximization is how total costs will change as quantity produced changes. Clearly, the former will rise as the latter increases. No sensible firm would plan its production in such a manner that a smaller output would cost more in total to produce than a larger one. The question to be analysed is therefore the precise way in which total costs will rise as output increases.

It has already been explained, by means of an arithmetic example,[1] how the costs of production depend on *both* the prices, and the physical productivities, of the factors. The physical productivities determine how much output of a good will result from the inputs of particular quantities of the factors. The sum of those quantities multiplied by the respective factor prices is then the total cost of the output in question. How total cost will rise, as output increases, therefore depends on what the physical productivities, and the prices, of factors will be at larger as compared with smaller outputs.

To specify the cost condition of a firm, it is therefore necessary to enquire into two matters, viz., what will be (i) the *prices*, and (ii) the

---

[1] On pp. 22–23 above. It is recommended that the reader refresh his memory of the details.

physical productivities of the factors used by the firm. Consider the prices first.

Just as a perfectly competitive firm produces only a very small part of the output of the industry, so it will use relatively only very small quantities of the factors employed within the industry. Hence, the *individual* firm will be no more able to influence the prices of those factors, than it is able to influence the price of its product. However much, or little, of the factors the firm uses, it will have no significant effect on the relations between the quantities demanded and supplied of them. It can, therefore, expand or contract its employment of factors on the assumption that their prices will not change on *that* account. They will of course change for any *other* reasons[1] that significantly disturb the equalities between the quantities demanded and supplied of them. That is, factor prices are parameters for the perfectly competitive firm, in the same sense as the price of its product is a parameter.

THE PRODUCTION FUNCTION

Now consider the physical productivities of the factors used by the firm.

The production of a good requires a number of different factors to be combined with one another, e.g. various kinds of labour, land and capital. Those factors have to be used together for any of the good to be produced; a single factor on its own will not be sufficient. The output of the good therefore depends on the *combination* of quantities of the factors used. Suppose that the production by a firm of good A requires three factors, α (say a kind of labour), β (a kind of natural resource), and γ (a type of machine). The firm's output of A will depend on the quantities it uses of α, β and γ. Change any of those quantities and the output will change. That is to say, the output of A (q_A) is a function of the inputs of α, β and γ (viz., q_α, q_β and q_γ). This can be expressed more briefly in the usual functional form:

$$q_A = f(q_\alpha, q_\beta, q_\gamma)$$

q_A represents the number of (physical) units produced per period of time. q_α, q_β and q_γ have, similarly, to be measured in terms of the time periods for which the factors are used (e.g. man-hours of labour, machine-hours of capital). The functional relation then shows what the size of q_A will be for different combinations of quantities of α, β and γ (e.g. $10\gamma + 7\beta + 8\gamma$ produce $100A$, while $12\gamma + 9\beta + 15\gamma$ produce

[1] Which will be analysed in Chapters 18–22 below.

150A, and so on). This relationship is called a *production function*. It is purely 'technical', in the sense that money prices in no way appear in it. It shows, given the technical knowledge available to a firm, the *physical* relationship between the inputs of factors and the output of its product.

It is by means of the production function of a firm that the physical productivities of the factors have to be expressed. Their output (i.e. their physical productivity) is the result of their *joint* use. Hence, the physical productivity of any one factor (say labour) can only be measured in the context of the particular quantities of the other factors (land and capital) with which it is used. Here again is an example of the problem, discussed in Chapters 6 and 8, of separating out the effects of different variables. The variables q_α, q_β and q_γ all help to determine q_A. To separate the effect of, say, q_α on q_A, it is necessary to hold q_β and q_γ constant (i.e. treat them as parameters) and then see how q_A changes as q_α changes. Only in that way can the physical productivity of one factor be separated from that of the others with which it is used.

The nature of the production function of a firm has to be carefully specified. The factors of production are defined in a precise sense. All the units grouped in a particular factor are *perfect technical substitutes* for one another. Thus if α is a kind of labour, all the men classified under it are identical in their abilities (i.e. are perfect technical substitutes). It will make no difference to the output of a firm whether it uses one unit (viz., man), rather than another, of the particular factor. And similarly for the units classified respectively under β and γ.

The characteristics of the factors of production, and the ways in which a firm will combine them, depend on the state of technical knowledge at any time. The skills of men are the outcome of their education and training; the productivities of machines depend on the technology embodied in them; and the ways in which men, machines, and natural resources are used together depend on the technical knowledge of the people who make the production decisions within firms. All these features of the productive process are subsumed under the term 'the state of technical knowledge' (or technology). That state is taken as given (i.e. as a parameter) for the purpose of specifying a production function. The factors α, β and γ are supposed to have given technical characteristics; and the decision-makers in the firms are supposed to have given knowledge of the ways in which the factors can be combined. The production function indicates the outputs which would result, in the state of technical knowledge in question, from different combinations of the factors.

This way of putting the matter has the purpose of separating the effects on costs of *changes* in technical knowledge from the effects of changes in other variables. If the production function (and hence the cost condition based on it) is first of all specified for a given state of technology, it can then be shown how a change in technology will alter the cost condition. That change means a *shift* to another production function. For example, if technology improves, any output of a good can then be produced by *smaller* quantities of at least some of the factors. The new form of the function, for a firm producing good A, would then show that any q_A would, in the improved state of technology, be produced by a smaller q_α and/or a smaller q_β and/or a smaller q_γ. The reductions in those inputs will depend on the nature of the technological improvement, which can take a variety of forms, e.g. improved labour skills, new kinds of raw materials, technically better machines, improved knowledge of the ways in which to combine the different factors.

The state of technology is, then, a *parameter* of the production function. A change in that state, which shifts the function, will be called an *improvement* or a *deterioration*. In the former case, any output can be produced by smaller quantities of at least some of the factors; or what amounts to the same thing, any combination of quantities of the factors can produce a larger output; and vice versa in the latter case. An improvement (deterioration) in technology of course means an increase (decrease) in the physical productivities of at least some of the factors.

Now consider, in respect of any one production function, the ways in which the quantities of the factors can be changed in order to alter output. The quantity of a factor has to be measured in terms of the length of time for which it is used, e.g. in man-hours, machine-hours and so on. While a firm cannot employ less than a *whole* man or machine, it can employ them for longer or shorter periods of time, and in that way can vary the *quantities* of these factors used. But there are obvious difficulties in reducing, beyond some point, the amount of time for which a unit of a factor is available to a firm. Most people want to work for something like the standard number of hours per week. They could divide their time by working for a number of different firms, but that would be inconvenient and time-wasting. Except for part-time workers, and for short-time and over-time working, there is a *minimum* size of unit in terms of which labour has to be employed, viz. a whole man for the standard work period (usually a week for wage-earners, and a month for salary-earners).

The existence of such a minimum is more significant in the case of capital. It would be highly inconvenient, in many cases, for firms to vary the quantities of capital they employ by sharing the use of capital goods like machines and buildings.[1] Moreover, each physical unit of those goods has often a minimum size for technical reasons, e.g. it is not technically feasible to reduce the size of a blast-furnace, or a motor-car assembly plant, beyond a certain point. Hence, partly because of the costs of sharing the use, and partly for reasons of technology, there is a minimum size of unit in terms of which a firm has to acquire many kinds of capital. That minimum is frequently quite large, as measured by the output it can help to produce (e.g. as with a blast-furnace).

When the quantity used of a factor cannot be reduced below some amount, it is said to be only available in *indivisible* units. If, however, it can be obtained in any amount, however small—e.g. man-hours or man-minutes rather than man-weeks—it is said to be *perfectly divisible*.

Output is changed by varying the quantities used of the factors. The quantities of all of them may be varied at the same time, or only those of some of them. Clearly, the effect on output will depend on which is the case. If the quantity of a factor is kept unchanged for some reason, when the quantities of the others are varied, it is called a *fixed* factor; the others are called the *variable* factors.

Both the variability or fixity of factors, and their perfect divisibility or indivisibility, have to be taken into account in specifying the production function of a firm. These features help to determine the nature of a production function, and hence what the physical productivities of the factors will be at different levels of output.

The prices of factors, and their physical productivities as given by the production function, jointly determine the cost condition of a firm. How this comes about is analysed in the next chapter.

---

[1] Though the renting, for limited periods of time, of some movable capital equipment (e.g. cranes) has increased in importance in recent years.

CHAPTER 10

COST CURVES

It will be sufficient for present purposes to consider three different production functions and their associated cost conditions. They are those in which (i) all the factors are both variable and perfectly divisible; (ii) only one factor is both variable and perfectly divisible, the rest being both fixed and indivisible; and (iii) one factor is both variable and perfectly divisible, a second factor is variable but only in indivisible units, and the rest are both fixed and indivisible.

THE VARIABLE FACTORS CASE

Take the production function for a firm producing good A, viz. $q_A = f(q_\alpha, q_\beta, q_\gamma)$, where α, β and γ are all variable and perfectly divisible. Suppose that 10 units of A can be produced per hour by 1 unit of α working with 1 unit of β and 1 unit of γ (e.g. one man working for an hour on a raw material with the help of a tool). All units of α are identical (i.e. perfect technical substitutes); and similarly in the cases of β and γ. Hence, 20 units of A can be produced by 2α plus 2β plus 2γ: a second set of 1α plus 1β plus 1γ will produce $10A$, just as the first set did. Similarly, $30A$ will be produced by 3α plus 3β plus 3γ; and so on. In general, if *all* the factors are increased by some scale, the output will increase by the same scale. The production function is then said to exhibit *constant returns to scale*.[1]

The term 'returns' refers to the return of output from the inputs of the factors; it is thus a way of referring to the physical productivity of the factors. An increase in the scale of use of *all* the factors means that their quantities are increased in the *same* proportion; and that, therefore, the proportions *between* the quantities are unchanged. *Constant returns to scale* only holds when the proportions between the factors remain unchanged. In the example above, the ratios between α, β and γ remain at $1:1:1$; that is why a doubling, a trebling and so on of their quantities does likewise to output.

[1] In the language of mathematics, the function is homogeneous of degree one.

97

The cost condition for this kind of production function can now be derived. To maximize profit, a firm must minimize total cost. In order to pick out the most profitable output, the firm must know the total cost of each and every level of output between which it has to choose. It must, therefore, find the *lowest* total cost at which each and every output could be produced.

To minimize the total cost of any output is a matter of finding that *combination* of quantities of the factors which, given their prices, is the *least cost combination* for that output. The firm does have a choice in this respect; any output can be produced in a variety of ways, i.e. by different combinations of factor quantities. Total cost is the sum of the factor quantities multiplied by their respective prices, viz., $p_\alpha \cdot q_\alpha$ plus $p_\beta \cdot q_\beta$ plus $p_\gamma \cdot q_\gamma$. Minimizing the total cost of any output means minimizing $(p_\alpha \cdot q_\alpha + p_\beta \cdot q_\beta + p_\gamma \cdot q_\gamma)$ for it. Given $p_\alpha, p_\beta,$ and $p_\gamma,$ that is a matter of choosing the appropriate $q_\alpha, q_\beta,$ and $q_\gamma.$ The range of choice in that respect is given by the production function: it shows the different combinations of q_α, q_β and q_γ which could all produce the output in question.

The prices of the factors are given by the market (i.e. are parameters) to the perfectly competitive firm, and do not change as a result of it buying more or less of them. Suppose that at particular prices of $\alpha,$ β and $\gamma,$ it finds that the *least cost combination* of factors which will produce $10A$ is 1α plus 1β plus $1\gamma.$[1] Then, at the same prices, the least cost combination for $20A$ is 2α plus 2β plus 2γ; and so on. Output can be doubled by duplicating the original set of factor quantities; and if the original set was a least cost combination, so also must be its duplicate. At given factor prices, the least total cost for $20A$ will be twice that for $10A.$ In general, total cost will rise in proportion to output.

This is shown in Fig. 10.1*a*, where the least total cost (TC) to a firm of producing different outputs is measured on the vertical axis. A total cost curve (like TC_1)[2] indicates, for each output (e.g. OG), what will be the minimum total cost (e.g. GP') at which it can be produced, given its production function and the prices of the factors. It is essential to note that each point on TC_1 implies the use of a method of production which gives the *minimum* total cost for the corresponding output. There are other ways known to the firm (i.e. other combinations of factors) of producing each output that would incur higher total costs. The latter are not indicated in the diagram, since it is assumed that the firm is aiming to maximize profit.

[1] The condition necessary for this to be so will be analysed in Chapter 19 below.
[2] Ignore TC_2 for the moment.

As has been seen, with constant returns to scale and given factor prices, total cost rises in proportion to output; TC is doubled when q_A is doubled. TC_1 is therefore a straight line out of the origin. The average cost (AC) of any output is its total cost divided by that output. AC at point P' (Fig. 10.1a) is $\dfrac{GP'}{OG}$ = tan angle $P'OG$. Since TC_1 is a straight line out of the origin, the AC is the same at all points on it. The curve AC_1 (in Fig. 10.1b, where AC is measured on the vertical axis) can

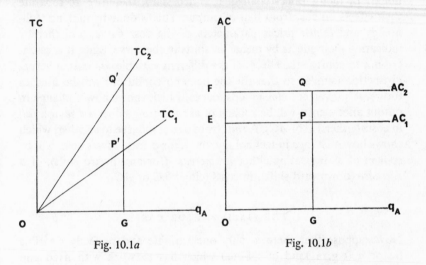

Fig. 10.1a Fig. 10.1b

thus be derived from TC_1 in precisely the same manner as the AR curve was earlier derived from the corresponding TR curve.[1] AC_1 is a horizontal straight line, since AC is constant at all outputs.

TC_1 (and AC_1) have been constructed on the basis of a particular production function, and a particular set of factor prices. The function, and those prices, are therefore parameters of the curves. If any of them change, the curves will shift. Suppose there is a deterioration in the state of technology, i.e. a decrease in factor productivities; each output now requires larger quantities of at least some factors for its production. At given factor prices, the TC of each and every output will be increased. The TC curve will be shifted upwards, e.g. from TC_1 to TC_2, with the latter showing how TC varies with output in the new state of technology (the AC curve also shifts upwards from AC_1 to AC_2). An improvement

---

[1] The reverse derivation is, of course, also possible. Thus, at point P (Fig. 10.1b), $TC_A = AC_A \cdot q_A$ = rectangle $OGPE$, which gives GP' in Fig. 10.1a.

in technology shifts the curves downwards, since smaller quantities of at least some factors are now required to produce each output.

If the prices of factors rise, the quantities of them used to produce any output will cost more. The *TC* (and *AC*) curve will shift upwards— and vice versa for a fall in factor prices.

A cost curve shows, by means of its shape, how *TC* (or *AC*) changes as output changes, i.e. it shows cost as a function of output, and is called the cost condition of the firm. But costs also change when technology or factor prices change. It is necessary, therefore, to separate their effects on cost from that of output. This is done by making technology and factor prices parameters of the cost curve, and thereby indicating their effects by means of shifts in the curve. Since it is essential not to confuse the effects of the different variables on cost, a verbal distinction (similar to that for the demand condition) will be used in future. A movement *along* a cost curve, which shows how a change in output affects cost, will be spoken of as indicating either a *rise* or a *fall* in costs (either *TC* or *AC*). A *shift* from one cost curve to another, which shows how a change in technology, or factor prices, affects cost, will be spoken of as indicating either an *increase* (for an upward shift), or a *decrease* (downward shift), in costs (either *TC* or *AC*).

THE FIXED FACTOR CASE

Now suppose that there is only one variable and perfectly divisible factor α (e.g. a kind of labour) which has to work with fixed and indivisible factors β and γ (e.g. some raw material and a machine). The level of output per period of time (e.g. per hour) can now be varied only by changing the input of α. Only by putting more and more men to work the machine, can output per hour be increased.

In this case, an increase in α means an increase in the *ratio* of α to $\beta + \gamma$ (or a decrease in the ratio of $\beta + \gamma$ to α, as it will sometimes be useful to regard it). As contrasted with the case where all the factors are variable, a production function with fixed and indivisible factors does not permit a scale increase in all the factors, with the proportions between them unchanged. A new question therefore arises: how will output per period of time change as more and more α is used in conjunction with the fixed β and γ?

To illustrate the analysis of this question, suppose that a number of operations (say six) are required to work the machine. Put one man on the machine, and he has to spend time in walking round it to perform the six operations in turn. Add a second man, and they can share the work; and so on for additional men. When a second man is added, it might appear that the output per period from the machine will be doubled, for each man now only does three operations. But, in fact, it will be *more* than doubled, because less time per man will be required to walk between the fewer operations, and less effort per man will be needed to adjust to the task of performing each operation in turn. Thus output per period will increase in *greater* proportion than the number of men. The addition of the third up to the sixth man will, similarly, by saving more time and effort per man between operations, continue to

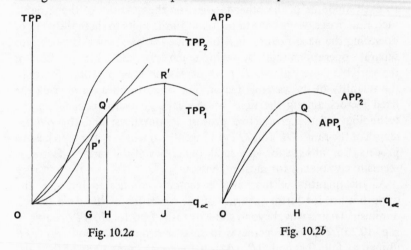

Fig. 10.2*a*　　　　　　　　　Fig. 10.2*b*

increase output in greater proportion than the increase in the number of men. If seven or more men are now used, *each* operation has to be shared by more than one man. How this can be done depends on the technology of the machine. The possibility of breaking down each operation into smaller ones may be limited. In that case, while the increase in men beyond six may still increase output, it will do so in *smaller* proportion than itself. Moreover, if more and more men are added, there will come a point at which there are so many of them around the machine that they begin to impede one another. If more are added beyond that point, the output per period from the machine will fall.

Three ranges can thus be distinguished in the response of the output of A to increases in the input of α in the above illustration. First, q_A increases in greater proportion than q_α does; then q_A continues to increase as q_α does, but in smaller proportion; and finally, q_A decreases as q_α increases still more. All this is shown in Fig. 10.2*a*, where q_A per period of time is measured on the vertical axis and q_α on the horizontal.

Since q_A here changes as a result of changes in q_α, q_A is called the *total physical product* (*TPP*) of that factor. The TPP_1 curve[1] then shows how α's *TPP* changes, as more of it is set to produce A. From O to P' on the curve, q_A increases in greater proportion than q_α (the curve is concave on its upper side); from P' to R', q_A increases as q_α increases, but in smaller proportion (the curve is now convex on its upper side[2]); and beyond R', q_A decreases as q_α increases.

Those three ranges in the response of *TPP* are what can, in general, be expected to occur when an increasing quantity of one factor is applied to fixed amounts of the other factors. As the quantity of the variable factor increases, ways have to be found for its units to share the work of operating the fixed factors. It is the scope for breaking this work into separate operations that, by saving some time and effort per unit of the variable factor, allows *TPP* to increase in greater proportion than the quantity of the variable factor. The opportunities for sharing the fixed factors among the units of the variable factor depend on the technology of the productive process in question; and the *relative* length of the range OP' (on TPP_1 in Fig. 10.2a) will vary from process to process. But, at least for very small quantities of the variable factor, it seems likely to exist for most processes.

As the quantity of the variable factor continues to increase, the opportunities for further sharing of the operating of the fixed factors diminish. That is why, beyond some quantity (OG for the TPP_1 curve in Fig. 10.2a), *TPP* only increases in smaller proportion; and why *TPP* ultimately falls (behond OJ), when there are so many units of the variable factor that they impede one another in sharing the fixed factors. That point brings out the symmetry between the first range (O to P'), and the third (beyond R'), on the TPP_1 curve. In the latter, there is a high ratio of α to $\beta + \gamma$; in the former, there is a low ratio of α to $\beta + \gamma$, i.e. a high ratio of $\beta + \gamma$ to α. With that high ratio, it is the fixed factors that are impeding themselves in sharing the variable factor. As the latter increases (towards OG), the degree of impediment diminishes —which is another way of saying that the variable factor can save time and effort per unit in sharing the fixed factors.[3]

It is thus the sharing of each other by the variable and the fixed factors that determines the shape of the *TPP* curve. That sharing is a

---

[1] Ignore TPP_2 for the moment.

[2] P' is therefore a 'point of inflexion' in the curve.

[3] No sensible firm would employ more than OJ of α (on TPP_1 in Fig. 10.2a), for that would reduce output. It can also be shown that, for any amount of α less than OH (note: not OG), there is too much of $\beta + \gamma$, in the sense that a *reduction* in them (if it were possible), with α unchanged, would *increase* output.

matter of the *ratio* between them. As the variable factor changes, the ratio changes, and the variable and fixed factors share different amounts of each other. That is why *TPP* does not change in the same proportion as the variable factor. This is in marked contrast with the case of *constant returns to scale*, where *all* the factors change in the same proportion. There, the quantity of output changes in the same proportion as the factors, because a unit of each factor continues to share the same amounts of the other factors.

The change in the product of the variable factor, as more of it is used, can be expressed in average as well as in total terms. The *average physical product* (*APP*) is total physical product divided by the number of units of the variable factor which is used to produce it, i.e. q_A/q_α. The *APP* curve is derived from the *TPP* curve in the same way as *AR* and *AC* curves were obtained from the corresponding *TR* and *TC* curves.

In Fig. 10.2a, the *APP* at point Q' on the TPP_1 curve is $\dfrac{q_A}{q\alpha} = \dfrac{HQ'}{OH}$ = tan angle $Q'OH$, where OQ' is a straight line joining Q' and the origin. The *APP* at any other point on the TPP_1 curve is, similarly, given by the tan of the angle which a straight line from the origin to the point makes with the horizontal axis. Given the shape of the TPP_1 curve, as explained above, that angle increases for the points from O up to Q', where OQ' is a tangent to the curve, and then decreases for successive points beyond Q'. That is, *APP* increases to a maximum at Q', and then diminishes.[1] This is shown by the APP_1 curve in Fig. 10.2b, where *APP* is at a maximum at point Q, which corresponds to Q' in Fig. 10.2a.

The shape of the APP_1 curve shows, in a different form, what has already been argued will happen when the *ratio* of the variable to the fixed factors increases. *APP* rises from O up to Q because, as more units of a α share the operations on $\beta + \gamma$, *each* unit saves some time and effort. Hence, the output per unit (i.e. the *APP*) increases. But beyond Q, the opportunities for further sharing of the operations have so diminished, that output per unit decreases. The APP_1 curve is said to exhibit *increasing average returns* to the variable factor up to the point Q, and *diminishing average returns* to it beyond Q. This behaviour of the average returns to a factor occurs because the quantity of it is increased, while the quantities of all the other factors are held constant. That is, increasing and diminishing average returns *to a factor* are the outcome of *variable proportions* between factors. In contrast, if all the

---

[1] The significance of the fact that Q' lies to the right of the point of inflexion P' will be considered later; see pp. 203–204 below.

factors are increased in the same proportions, the average return to each factor remains constant. With *constant returns to scale*, output increases in the same proportion as the input of each and every factor.

The TPP_1 curve (and the corresponding APP_1 curve) for a factor is a graphical representation of the production function when there is only one variable factor. It shows output as a function of the input of that factor. As was explained in the previous chapter, that function is based on a given technology. If the latter improves, the TPP_1 and the APP_1 curves shift upwards (e.g. to TPP_2 and APP_2 in Figs. 10.2a and 10.2b),

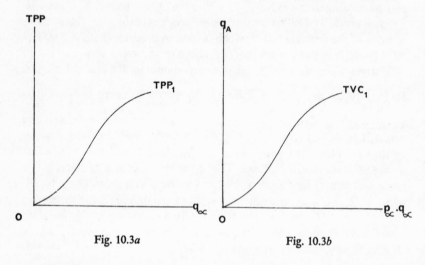

Fig. 10.3a   Fig. 10.3b

thus indicating that a larger output can now be produced by any quantity of the variable factor. A deterioration in technology shifts the curves downwards.

With a knowledge of the prices of the factors, which are given by the market to the perfectly competitive firm, its cost condition can now be derived from the production function in the present case. In Fig. 10.3a, the range of decreasing TPP has not been drawn, since a sensible firm would not operate in it. The TPP_1 curve shows how output (q_A) increases as the quantity of the variable factor (q_α) increases. The total expenditure on employing that factor is got by multiplying its quantity by its price, i.e. it equals $p_\alpha \cdot q_\alpha$. If each q_α on the horizontal axis of Fig. 10.3a is multiplied by p_α, that gives the total expenditures on the variable factor which would have to be incurred in the production of the corresponding q_As. Those expenditures are called the *total variable costs* (*TVC*) of the outputs.

The multiplication of the q_α axis in Fig. 10.3a by p_α thus changes the TPP_1 curve into the TVC_1 curve which is shown in Fig. 10.3b. Apart from the change of scale on the horizontal axis (which measures $p_\alpha \cdot q_\alpha$ $= TVC$), the latter diagram has the same properties as the former.

It is usual, however, in a diagram giving a cost curve, to put cost on the vertical axis and output on the horizontal, as was done in Fig. 10.1 above. If the axes in Fig. 10.3b are interchanged, the TVC curve is rotated about the line which bisects the axes. The TVC_1 curve[1] now appears as in Fig. 10.4a. This shows how TVC at first rises in *smaller*

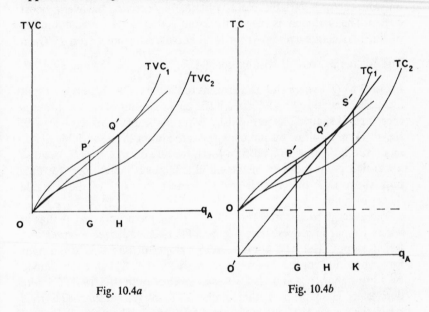

Fig. 10.4a   Fig. 10.4b

proportion than output (where the curve is convex on its upper side, from O to the point of inflexion P'), and then rises in *greater* proportion than output (beyond P', where the curve is concave on its upper side). The smaller than proportional rise in TVC over the range OP' simply reflects the fact that, over this range, output (TPP) increases in greater proportion than the input of the variable factor; and similarly for the range beyond P', the greater than proportional rise in TVC reflects the fact that output now increases in smaller proportion than input.[2]

The expenditures on the fixed factors (β and γ) have also to be taken into account. With given factor prices, these total $p_\beta \cdot q_\beta + p_\gamma \cdot q_\gamma$, and

[1] Ignore TVC_2 for the moment.
[2] I.e., point P' in Fig. 10.4a corresponds exactly to point P' in Fig. 10.2a.

that sum is called the *total fixed costs* (*TFC*) of the firm. The addition of *TFC* and the *TVC* of any output gives the *total cost* (*TC*), i.e. the total of payments to all factors, for the output. That addition is shown graphically, in Fig. 10.4*b*, by the device of lowering the horizontal axis, as compared with Fig. 10.4*a*, by an amount OO' which equals the *TFC*. The curve, which with respect to origin O gives TVC_1, now gives TC_1 with respect to origin O', because a *TFC* of OO' has been added to the *TVC* at every level of output.

Further understanding of the properties of the cost condition, when only one factor is variable, can be obtained by deriving the average cost curves. The procedure is exactly the same as that already used a number of times to derive average from total curves. At point Q' on TVC_1 in Fig. 10.4*a*, the average variable cost $(AVC) = \dfrac{HQ'}{OH} = $ tan angle $Q'OH$.

From O to Q' (where OQ' is a tangent to the curve), *AVC* falls as output increases; beyond Q', *AVC* rises.[1] The curve relating *AVC* to output is therefore 'U shaped', as in Fig. 10.5. That shape again reflects—as with the *TVC* curve—how output changes as the input of the variable factor increases. *AVC* falls to its lowest level, for any output, at OH, because up to that point the *APP* of the variable factor is increasing;[2] for outputs above OH, the *AVC* is rising, because the *APP* of the variable factor is falling.

The average fixed cost (*AFC*) falls in the same proportion as that in which output increases, because the *TFC* is spread over a larger and larger output. The *AFC* curve therefore slopes downwards to the right throughout its length.[3] The average total[4] cost (*ATC*) curve is obtained by adding the *AVC* and *AFC* at each level of output. The *ATC* curve derives its U shape from that of the *AVC* curve, because *ATC* rises when the rising *AVC* outweighs the falling *AFC*. The point S, beyond which this occurs (in Fig. 10.5), is to the right of the point Q because, between the outputs OH and OK, the fall in *AFC* is greater than the rise in *AVC*. The same thing can be seen in Fig. 10.4*b*. The *ATC* at any point on the TC_1 curve is given by the slope of a straight line joining the point to the origin O'. *ATC* is at its lowest at S' on TC_1, where $O'S'$ is a tangent to the curve, whereas *AVC* is at its lowest at point Q'.

The total and average cost curves have been constructed on the basis

[1] The significance of the fact that Q' lies to the right of the point of inflexion P' will be considered later; see pp. 121–122 below.

[2] I.e., point Q in Fig. 10.5 corresponds exactly to point Q in Fig. 10.2*b*.

[3] It is a rectangular hyperbola, since the rectangles subtended by all points on it measure the *TFC* and are therefore equal.

[4] Total here means the total of the *average* variable and the *average* fixed costs.

of a particular production function, and a particular set of factor prices, which are therefore parameters of the curves. It has been seen how the *TVC* curve is derived directly from the *TPP* curve. An improvement in technology shifts the latter curve *upwards* (e.g. from TPP_1 to TPP_2 in Fig. 10.2a), and therefore shifts the former curve *downwards* (e.g. from

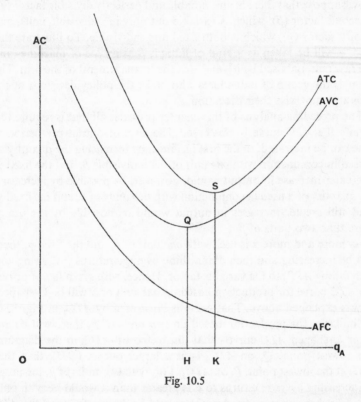

Fig. 10.5

TVC_1 to TVC_2 in Fig. 10.4a, with a consequential downward shift in TC_1 to TC_2 in Fig. 10.4b).[1] That is, an increase in the productivities of the factors *decreases* costs, because any output can now be produced by a smaller quantity of the variable factor in conjunction with the fixed factors. And vice versa for a deterioration in technology.

A rise in the price of the variable factor shifts the *TVC* and *AVC* curves (and therefore the *TC* and *ATC* curves) upwards. A rise in the prices of the fixed factors shifts the *TFC* and *AFC* curves (and therefore

[1] There will, of course, be associated downward shifts in the *AVC* and *ATC* curves in Fig. 10.5.

the *TC* and *ATC* curves) upwards. And vice versa for reductions in factor prices.

THE INDIVISIBLE FACTOR CASE

Now suppose that there is one variable and perfectly divisible factor (α), a second factor (β), which is variable but only in indivisible units, and a third factor (γ), which is both fixed and indivisible. To illustrate this case, α will be taken as a kind of labour, β as a type of machine (and the raw material used by it), and γ as the 'management' of the firm. The latter is the group of individuals who make the policy decisions of the firm and supervise their execution.

The preceding analysis of this chapter provides all that is required to specify the *ATC* curve in this case.[1] The level of output per period of time can be increased, in the first instance, by increasing the quantity of α used in conjunction with *one* unit of the indivisible β, and the fixed γ. A greater increase in output would, however, be possible by increasing the quantity of α used in conjunction with *two* units of β, and the fixed γ. And still greater increases in output would be possible by the use of more than two units of β.

As more and more α is used with *one* unit of β, and the fixed γ, there will be increasing and then diminishing average returns (i.e. rising and then falling *APP*) to the variable factor. Hence, with given factor prices, the *ATC* curve for production based on *one* unit of β will be U-shaped, as was explained above. That curve is illustrated by ATC_1 in Fig. 10.6.

Similarly, for production based on *two* units of β, there will be another U-shaped *ATC* curve—that illustrated by ATC_2 in the diagram. The lowest point, Q, on ATC_2 is at a larger output (OH), than that (OG) at the lowest point, P, on ATC_1. For, with two units of β, the range of increasing average returns to α is greater than it would be with only one β. If there were no fixed γ, OH would be double OG, and the *ATC* at Q and P would be the *same*. This follows because the production methods with two units of β would simply duplicate those with one unit. But with a fixed γ there is, to begin with, increasing average returns to α *plus* β as more of both of them is used in conjunction with the fixed factor. This means that, as is shown in the diagram, the *AVC* at the lowest point (Q) of ATC_2 is below that at the lowest point (P) of ATC_1. The increasing returns to α plus β means that their *APP* is higher at output OH than at OG.

---

[1] The *TC* curve will not be drawn, but can easily be deduced in the manner already explained for the derivation of total from average curves.

The curves ATC_3, ATC_4 and ATC_5 represent the cost conditions for production with three, four and five units of β respectively. It has been assumed in their construction that the fixed quantity of γ gives increasing returns to α plus β up to three units of β, and diminishing returns beyond that. Hence, the ATC at the lowest point (R) of ATC_3 is below that at Q, and also below those at the lowest points (S and T) and ATC_4 and ATC_5.

Given these five cost conditions, the firm can see which one of them

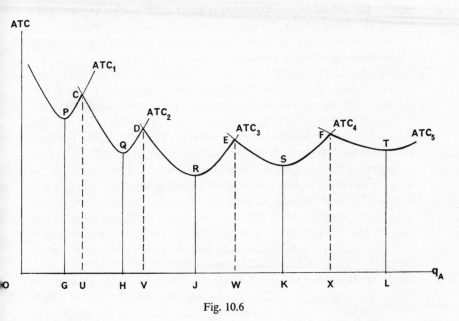

Fig. 10.6

(and therefore which quantity of β) will give the minimum ATC for the production of any output. For outputs up to OU (at which ATC_1 intersects ATC_2), the ATC is lower with the use of one unit of β than with two units. If output is expanded beyond OU, a second unit of β has to be employed to keep ATC for any output at a minimum; beyond OV, a third unit must be used, and so on. The complete cost curve for the firm, which gives the minimum ATC at which each output could be produced, is therefore made up from certain ranges on the five curves in the diagram, viz., the range up to point C on ATC_1, that from C to D on ATC_2, and so on. It is the curve marked out by the points $PCQDRESFT$.

The firm's cost curve thus has the appearance of a 'scalloped' U. It is U-shaped because of the fixed factor γ. The smaller the size (as measured in relation to output) of each indivisible unit of β, the smaller is the length of each scallop on the curve, and the more the latter approaches the shape of a smooth U. Thus, in the limiting case where a unit of β is so small that it can be treated as perfectly divisible, we are back with the kind of cost curve analysed in the fixed factor case above.

Moreover, suppose that there is no fixed γ. The lowest points of the five curves in Fig. 10.6 would then be at the same level. In that case, the smaller the size of β—i.e. the closer it approaches perfect divisibility— the smaller is the length of each scallop on the curve, and the more the latter approaches to a horizontal straight line. We are then back with the variable factors case analysed earlier.

Instead of increasing the *number* of units of one indivisible factor (like β), a firm might substitute a *larger* indivisible factor for it, as the means of expanding productive capacity. Thus it frequently happens that the type of machinery used at higher outputs is different from that used at lower ones. For that to be so, two conditions have to be fulfilled. First, the cost curve of the larger indivisible factor (like ATC_2 in Fig. 10.6) must lie *above* that of the smaller indivisible factor (like ATC_1) at lower levels of output. This condition ensures that the smaller one is used at the lower outputs. Second, the cost curve for the larger indivisible factor must lie *below* that for production with *two* units of the smaller one. This condition ensures that the larger one is substituted for the smaller one at higher levels of output. A change from smaller to larger indivisible units of machinery appears, in fact, to be a frequent reason for the achievement of lower ATC at high as compared with low levels of output.

As with the earlier cost curves in this chapter, both the production function, and factor prices, are parameters of the present one. The curve shifts upwards or downwards as the parameters change, and for the same reasons as have already been explained.

THE DIFFERENCES BETWEEN COST CONDITIONS

The purpose of the present chapter has been to distinguish the influences which together determine costs, and to present the analysis in a form (viz., of cost curves) which enables the effects of those influences to be separated. Costs are dependent on the physical productivities, and the prices, of factors. The productivities, as given by a production function, can vary from one level of output to another. That is why it is necessary to show, by the *shape* of a cost curve, how a change in output will affect costs—and to distinguish, by means of a *shift* in the cost curve, how a change in productivities, for reasons *other* than a change in output, will affect costs.

What the productivities will be at different levels of output depends on the extent to which factors are divisible and variable. The three cases analysed above specify various possibilities in these respects, and show the significance of them for the shape of a cost curve.

Some factors are divisible into fairly small units, e.g. many kinds of labour and raw materials. Some factors come in indivisible units of quite large size, e.g. certain types of machinery. There is one factor which has a form of indivisibility which is peculiar to itself. This is the management of a firm—the group of people who make the policy decisions. That group can become larger and larger—it is variable in quantity. As it increases in size, the people within it specialize more and more on the different aspects of management, e.g. production, personnel, sales, market research, accounting. But since management means decision-making, there must be some way, i.e. some administrative process, in which the decisions of the different departments of the management are integrated and made consistent with one another. The need for that integration is the form of indivisibility which is peculiar to management.

The variability of different factors depends on a number of circumstances. These will be taken into account at appropriate points in later chapters. The analysis of the present chapter, together with the revenue condition specified in the previous chapter, now provides the basis for seeing how a perfectly competitive firm will find that level of output which maximizes profit.

CHAPTER 11

THE FIRM: PROFIT MAXIMIZATION

Profit is the excess of *TR* over *TC*. The last two chapters have explained how *TR* and *TC* may vary from one level of output to another. To maximize profit, a firm has to discover the *particular* level of output—in the whole range of possible outputs—at which the excess of *TR* over *TC* is greatest. The nature and implications of the firm's behaviour in this respect will now be analysed.

A *complete* and *certain* knowledge of its cost and revenue conditions is required for a firm to deduce the level of output at which it would maximize profit. The knowledge must be *complete* in the sense that it can predict the total cost it would incur, and the total revenue it would receive, at each and every possible level of output. Otherwise, the firm could not know which level will yield a maximum profit. The knowledge must be *certain* in the sense that it can predict correctly. If it makes mistakes in prediction, its aim of maximizing profit will not be realized.

The probability is that the revenue and cost conditions of any firm will change as time passes. The *TR* curve will shift as a result of changes in incomes, preferences, and the prices of other goods. The *TC* curve will shift as a result of changes in factor prices and physical productivities (i.e. shifts in the production function). Most firms will expect these changes to occur, and will not expect that the output, which maximizes profit in the present revenue and cost conditions, will continue to do so in the future. If a firm aims to maximize profit *continuously*, it must therefore allow for changing levels of output through time. Any plans for future outputs depend on the firm's predictions about its future revenue and cost conditions. For more and more distant periods of time, these predictions become more and more uncertain. The difficulties in predicting correctly for the more remote future force firms to work within a time *horizon*. That is, they limit their forward planning of output levels to a period of time for which they think they can make predictions, which stand some chance of being approximately realized.

The probability of future changes in revenue and cost conditions is, however, not a *sufficient* reason for forward planning by a firm. If it could instantaneously adapt its production to new conditions, there

112

would be no need to plan for them. The firm would simply make the necessary adjustments to them as they occur. That is, it would immediately alter the quantities of the factors it uses, so as to produce what is the most profitable output in the new circumstances. But it takes time to bring about a change in the rate of output. If an increase is required, a larger flow of raw materials and components must be arranged, additional labour will have to be hired, and it may be necessary to acquire more capital goods in the form of factory space and machinery. Moreover, when a change occurs in the cost condition, the management of the firm will have to go through the process—which may well be a lengthy one—of working out afresh what are the least cost combinations of the factors for different outputs in the new situation.

It is especially in the planning of an increased rate of output, and in the acquisition of additional capital goods to make it possible, that time is taken up. Buildings and machinery can take months, or even years, to construct. Consequently, a firm, which thinks it will be profitable to expand output in the future, must make advance plans for that expansion.

But not only do buildings and machinery take time to construct; they are durable and take time to wear out in the process of producing goods. The physical lives of many capital goods can run not only into years but into decades. Consequently, a firm which experiences an unforeseen decrease in demand (i.e. downward shift in its *TR* curve) will be left with an excess amount of capital. It can allow this to wear out in time and not be replaced, or it may sell the surplus quantity. However, a lot of capital goods are limited (or specific) to the production of a narrow range of products. In the circumstances of decreased demand for its product, a firm will seldom be able to sell its excess capital for other than scrap prices.

For each firm, there will consequently be some period of time during which it can do little to vary the quantity of capital at its disposal. The length of that period depends, on the one hand, on the time required to construct and instal new capital and, on the other hand, on the rate at which existing capital is worn out by use over time. The period within which the quantity of capital is fixed will differ from firm to firm, and from industry to industry, especially since it depends on the technology of the capital. Capital is a *fixed factor* for that period of time. It is only over a longer period that it becomes a variable factor. Herein lies an important reason for distinguishing, as in the previous chapter, between a cost condition, where all the factors are variable, and one where some factors are fixed.

For these reasons, the concept of profit maximization is a complex one. If a firm is to succeed in its *aim* of maximizing profit in current conditions, it must know what its *TR* and *TC* would be at all possible levels of output. However, if it is uncertain about its predictions in these respects, the question arsies as to what should be its behaviour in the face of that uncertainty. Should it, for example, take what it regards as the most probable levels of *TR* and *TC* for each output, and choose what it expects to be the most profitable one on that basis? Or should it play safe, in some way, by allowing for the chance that its predictions will be wrong?

Moreover, since a firm cannot immediately adapt itself to changes in its revenue and cost conditions, profit maximization must involve an attempt to predict those changes and to plan future outputs accordingly. But when a firm is faced with *unforeseen* changes, its immediate scope for changing its policy is restricted by its capital being a fixed factor for some time ahead. Profit maximization, under that restriction, will have a different outcome from that in which the firm is able to vary the quantities of all the factors it uses.

These different aspects of profit maximization cannot all be dealt with at once. To start with, it will be assumed that the firm has complete and certain knowledge of its revenue and cost conditions, and that it expects them to remain unchanged in the foreseeable future. Within that period of time, the quantities of *all* the factors used by the firm will be supposed to be variable. Profit maximization will, therefore, be analysed initially on the basis of a cost condition derived from a production function in which all the factors are variable. An understanding of that case will lead into the analysis of profit maximization by firms which have to operate for a time with fixed quantities of capital, as a result of unforeseen changes.[1] The problems arising from incomplete, and uncertain, knowledge of revenue and cost conditions will be taken up still later.[2]

The present assumptions fit the market situation of perfect competition much better than they do other situations. The perfectly elastic *AR* curve of the firm is given completely, and with certainty, by the market price of the good. Since the prices of factors are also given by the market, a knowledge of the firm's production function allows its cost condition to be derived. The market prices of goods and factors depend on industry demand and supply conditions. The individual firm is unlikely to be able to predict these, and it will consequently take its revenue and cost conditions as given until such times as they change.

[1] This will be dealt with in Chapter 14 below.
[2] In Chapters 16 and 17.

THE ELEMENTS IN TOTAL COST

It was explained in the previous chapter how the cost condition of a firm depends on the prices and physical productivities of factors. It is now necessary to specify carefully the various elements which make up the total cost of production.

Cost of production comprises all the payments which have to be made by a firm in order to acquire the factors it wants to use. Factors are the *productive services* provided by persons, pieces of land, and capital goods. The owners of a firm will hire or rent some productive services from other people, e.g. their labour, maybe some land for the firm to operate on, and maybe some capital goods, which may include machinery, but of which buildings are the more usual example. The payments of wages and salaries to employed labour, and of rents for hired land, machinery, and buildings, are all elements in the firm's cost of production because these payments are necessary to acquire the factors in question.

A firm, however, usually itself owns most of the capital goods (and maybe the land) whose productive services it requires. The purchase of those goods has to be financed. That is, *money* capital is needed to buy the capital goods. As indicated earlier, to prevent ambiguity the term *finance* will be used for money capital, the word capital being used only for capital goods. The *cost of finance* for the acquisition of capital goods is part of a firm's costs of production.

Finance can be raised in two distinct ways. The owners of the firm may borrow some of it (usually not all) from other people (or firms).[1] And they may provide some (or maybe all) from their own wealth.[2]

The *interest* which a firm has to pay on its borrowed finance is an element in its cost of production, since the payment of interest is necessary to induce the creditors to continue their financing. The owners of a firm are not, of course, themselves creditors of it, and therefore cannot be said to earn interest on the finance they provide. Nevertheless, they will expect and require some rate of return to induce them to continue providing it. They could, alternatively, lend out their own finance to someone else at the market rate of interest. The rate of return necessary to induce the owners to continue the financing of their firm is, therefore, an element in its cost of production.

There is a final element of cost to be taken into account. The capital

---

[1] E.g., on the basis of financial instruments like debentures, loan stock, mortgages, and overdrafts from banks.

[2] Their titles of ownership in the firm being in the form of, e.g. stocks and shares.

goods used by the firm will wear out in time—or become obsolete, in the sense that it becomes profitable to replace them by technically more advanced capital. The wearing out of capital necessarily happens during production; consequently, an expense must be allowed in respect of it. That expense, viz., 'depreciation', should be such, per period of time, that the total of allowances for depreciation will be sufficient to replace the capital at the end of its life. Since that life cannot be foreseen with certainty, the element allowed in cost for depreciation can only be estimated.

The excess of total revenue over total cost was designated earlier as profit. The specification of the elements entering into total cost, in the present circumstances, brings to light some of the problems involved in using the highly ambiguous term 'profit'. In everyday speech, profit is what is left out of revenue when the owners of a firm have made all the payments to *other people* for productive services hired from them. That use of the term is quite arbitrary from the viewpoint of economic analysis. It leaves the distinction between cost and profit dependent on the dividing line, which varies from firm to firm, between those productive services which are provided by other people, and those which are provided by the owners themselves. A consistent use of the term 'cost' requires that *all* the payments, which have to be made for productive services, are treated, irrespective of their ownership, as elements in the cost of production.

The *cost of finance* for the capital goods owned by a firm must, therefore, be included in cost, as well as the payments of wages, salaries, and rents to other people. That is why the rate of return, expected and required by the firm's owners on their financing, is here treated as an element of cost. For brevity, economists usually refer to it as 'normal profit'. With normal profit included in total cost, any excess of total revenue over that cost has to be distinguished as a 'supernormal' profit. It is the latter which the firm aims to maximize. Since most references in future will be to supernormal profit, it will be convenient to drop the adjective. That is, unless otherwise indicated, profit means supernormal profit.[1]

THE OUTPUT OF THE PERFECTLY COMPETITIVE FIRM

Under perfect competition, the individual firm is unable to influence the price of its product. There must, therefore, be some constraint that

---

[1] The nature of profit will be further considered later; see pp. 238–239 below.

prevents its most profitable output from being more than a very small part of the industry's output.

The firm can obtain the factors it requires at given market prices. Suppose, initially, that all the factors are *both* variable and perfectly divisible. With the production function therefore showing constant returns to scale, TC will rise in the same proportion as output. The TC curve will be a straight line out of the origin (as in Fig. 10.1a^1), and ATC will be constant.

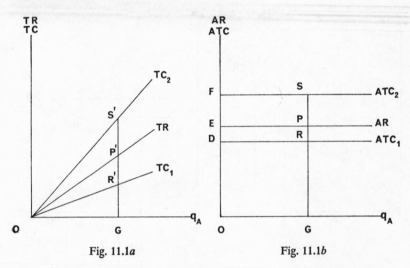

Fig. 11.1a Fig. 11.1b

In Fig. 11.1a, the TR curve, of a perfectly competitive firm producing good A, is a straight line out of the origin, since the firm can sell any output at the given market price. If its cost condition is the straight line TC_2, TR is less than TC at every level of output. At output OG, the firm would make a loss (i.e. an excess of TC over TR) of $P'S'$. That loss would be larger at higher outputs, since the straight line TC and TR curves diverge from each other. Any firm with these cost and revenue conditions would cease production.

If the cost condition is TC_1, TR exceeds TC at every level of output. The profit at output OG would be $R'P'$; and that profit would increase steadily as output rises. Any firm with these cost and revenue conditions would expand indefinitely. That means its output would become more than a very small part of the industry's output. Perfect competition would then cease to exist. The same outcome would result if the firm's TC

¹ On p. 99 above.

curve coincided with its *TR* curve. For although it could, in those circumstances, no more than cover its *TC* at any output, it would have the incentive to grow to a size at which it could influence the market price of the good, and therefore the level of its profit.

The same argument can be put in terms of average curves. In Fig. 11.1*b*, the perfectly elastic *AR* curve corresponds to the *TR* curve in Fig. 11.1*a*, and ATC_1 and ATC_2 correspond to TC_1 and TC_2. At output *OG*, profit *per unit* of output (i.e. *AR* minus *ATC*) is *RP*, with the cost

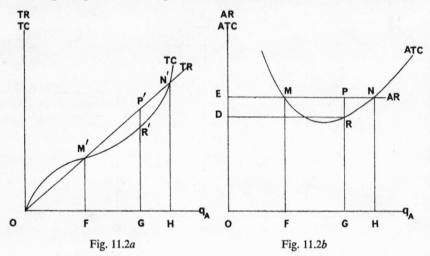

Fig. 11.2*a*   Fig. 11.2*b*

condition ATC_1. Profit on the *whole* output (i.e. profit per unit multiplied by output) is measured by the rectangle *DRPE*—which corresponds to *R'P'* in Fig. 11.1*a*. With the cost condition ATC_2, the loss *per unit* of output is *PS*; and the loss on the *whole* output is *EPSF*. Since ATC_2 lies above *AR* at all outputs, the firm would cease production. With ATC_1 (and also with an *ATC* curve which coincides with the *AR* curve), the firm would expand indefinitely, and its output would cease to be a very small part of that of the industry.

A cost condition based on factors, which are *both* variable and perfectly divisible, is thus incompatible with perfect competition. With *ATC*, as well as *AR*, constant at all outputs, there is no constraint to prevent a firm, which can cover its costs, from being so large as to destroy perfect competition. As long as *AR* is constant—as required by perfect competition—*ATC* must *rise* as output increases, in order to prevent the indefinite expansion of the firm. This means that, with factor prices given to the firm, its *ATC* curve must be U-shaped (as in

Fig. 10.5[1]). Moreover, that U shape must be such in relation to the *AR* curve, that the most profitable output of the firm is very small in relation to that of the industry.

On the *TC* curve in Fig. 11.2*a*, *TC* at first rises in smaller proportion, and then in greater proportion, than output. The corresponding *ATC* curve, in Fig. 11.2*b*, is therefore U-shaped. The straight line *TR* curve corresponds to the perfectly elastic *AR* curve. For all outputs from *O* to *F*, and for those beyond *H*, *TC* exceeds *TR*. In the range of outputs between *OF* and *OH*, *TR* exceeds *TC*. And similarly for the relations between *ATC* and *AR*.

The most profitable output for the firm is *OG*, where, in Fig. 11.2*a*, the *TR* curve at *P'* is a maximum vertical distance above the *TC* curve at *R'*. Given its revenue and cost conditions, *R'P'* is the maximum profit the firm can earn, and it will do so by producing and selling the output *OG*. In Fig. 11.2*b*, the maximum profit is measured by the rectangle *DRPE*, which is the profit per unit of output (*RP*) multiplied by the level of output (*OG*). Thus, in terms of the average curves, the most profitable output is where the largest rectangle can be inscribed between the corresponding points (viz., *P* and *R*), on the *AR* and *ATC* curves, and the vertical axis. It should be noted that the profit *per unit* of output (*RP*) will *not*, in general, be at a maximum when the profit on the *whole* output (*DRPE*) is at a maximum.

It can be seen by inspection that, at the maximum vertical distance (*R'P'*) of the *TR* curve above the *TC* curve, the two curves are parallel. Where they are not parallel, they are either moving farther apart (e.g. for outputs from *OF* up to *OG*), or moving closer together (e.g. for outputs from *OG* up to *OH*). Hence, where the curves are diverging in the range between *OF* and *OG*, profit can be increased by raising output; and where they are converging in the range between *OG* and *OH*, it can be increased by lowering output.

Two curves are parallel when their slopes are the same. Hence, a necessary condition, for an output to be the most profitable one, is that the slopes of the *TR* and *TC* curves be the same at that output. The economic meanings of these slopes must, therefore, be enquired into.

MARGINAL COST AND MARGINAL REVENUE

The *TC* curve shows how *TC* varies with output. At each level of output, it can be seen from the curve by how much *TC* will change if output changes by a small amount. Thus, in Fig. 11.3*a*, if output increases from

[1] On p. 107 above.

OG to OH, TC rises from GP' to HQ'. An increment of TC (ΔTC) equal to $R'Q'$ results from an increment of output (Δq_A) equal to GH ($= P'R'$). Hence, the rate at which TC rises, between the outputs OG and OH, is measured by $\dfrac{\Delta TC}{\Delta q_A} = \dfrac{R'Q'}{P'R'}$. The rate at which TC is rising can, similarly, be measured from the other points on the curve. It can then be seen whether TC is rising more rapidly over one range of output as compared with another.

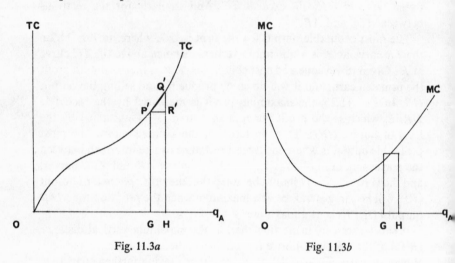

Fig. 11.3a   Fig. 11.3b

Join the points P' and Q' by a straight line. Then the rate at which TC rises between P' and Q', viz., $\dfrac{R'Q'}{P'R'}$, is equal to tan angle $Q'P'R'$. If the points P' and Q' are taken closer and closer together, the slope of the straight line $P'Q'$ (i.e. tan angle $Q'P'R'$) approaches more and more to the slope of the tangent at P'. Hence, for a very small increase in output from P', the rate at which TC rises can be measured by the slope of the tangent, and therefore of the curve, at P'.

The rate at which TC rises as output increases can thus be thought of in either of two ways. On the one hand, it is the rise in cost (ΔTC) for some *particular* increase in output (Δq_A), e.g. an increase of one unit in the output of A. If GH in Fig. 11.3a is one unit, then the ratio $\dfrac{R'Q'}{P'R'}$ shows the rate at which TC rises for a unit increase in output. This rise in TC is called the *marginal cost* (MC) of the unit in question. It is the *additional* cost of producing the unit, i.e. additional to the *TC* of output *OG*. It is shown in Fig. 11.3*b* by the height of the rectangle erected on the points *G* and *H* (*MC* being measured on the vertical axis). The *MC* for a unit increase in output, from any other level of output, can be similarly derived from the *TC* curve; and the corresponding rectangle can be drawn in Fig. 11.3*b*.

On the other hand, the rate at which *TC* rises can be taken for a very small increase in output. If *GH* is very small, the ratio $\frac{R'Q'}{P'R'}$ can be measured by the slope of the *TC* curve at *P'*. The rate at which *TC* is rising, i.e. *MC*, is now being measured at a *point* on the *TC* curve. This gives the *MC* of an output (e.g. *OG*), rather than, as above, the *MC* over a *range* of output (e.g. *GH*).[1] The *MC* of each output—as given by the slope of the *TC* curve at each output—can now be plotted in Fig. 11.3*b* to give the *MC* curve of the firm. It is more convenient to show *MC* by means of a continuous curve than by a series of rectangles, like the one drawn in Fig. 11.3*b*.[2]

Since the *MC* curve is derived from the *TC* curve, it gives the same information, but in a different form—as does the *ATC* curve. The connections between the three ways of showing the costs of a firm can now be shown.

The *ATC* and *MC* curves in Fig. 11.4*b* correspond to the *TC* curve in Fig. 11.4*a*. The *ATC* is falling up to output *OG*, where the straight line *OP'* is a tangent to the *TC* curve, and is rising at larger outputs. The *MC*, at any point on the *MC* curve, is equal to the slope at the corresponding point of the *TC* curve[3] (e.g. *FN* = slope at *N'*). *TC* is rising in smaller proportion than q_A up to the point of inflexion *N'*, i.e. the slope of *TC* diminishes up to *N'*. Hence *MC* is falling for outputs up to *OF*. Beyond that, *TC* is rising in greater proportion than q_A, i.e. the slope of *TC* is increasing. Hence *MC* is rising for outputs above *OF*.

The *ATC* is at its lowest at output *OG*, where *OP'* is a tangent to the *TC* curve. That tangent has the same slope as the curve at *P'*. Therefore *MC* is necessarily the same as *ATC* where the latter is at its lowest; the *MC* curve necessarily goes through the lowest point (*P*) of the *ATC* curve. When *MC* is *below ATC*, the latter is falling; if the cost of an additional unit of output is less than the average cost of the previous

[1] This distinction is, therefore, analogous to that between arc and point elasticity; cf. p. 84 above.
[2] But while *MC* will be interpreted here as the *MC of* a particular output, any actual measurements of it have to be over a range of output.
[3] In the language of calculus, *MC* is the first derivative (or rate of change) of *TC* with respect to *q* (viz., d*TC*/d*q*).

units, that average will be pulled down by an expansion of output.[1] Similarly, *ATC* will be rising if *MC* is *above* it. The lowest point of the *MC* curve is thus reached at a smaller output (*OF*) than that at the lowest point of the *ATC* curve (*OG*); the point of inflexion *N'* on the *TC* curve comes before *P'*, where *OP'* is a tangent to the curve.

It has already been seen how the *TC* curve can be constructed from the *ATC* curve; e.g. at point *P* on the latter (in Fig. 11.4*b*), *TC* is measured by the rectangle *OGPD*, which gives *GP'* in Fig. 11.4*a*. The *TC* curve can

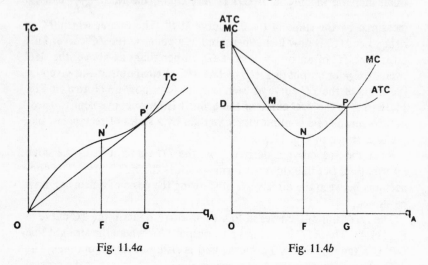

Fig. 11.4*a*   Fig. 11.4*b*

also be derived from the *MC* curve. Suppose—for the purpose of exposition—that *MC* is measured in relation to unit increases in output. The successive points on the *MC* curve then give the cost of producing the first unit of output, the *additional* cost of producing a second unit, the *additional* cost of producing a third unit, and so on. The *TC* of three units is therefore the *sum* of the *MC*s of those three units; and similarly for any size of output. Thus, in Fig. 11.4*b*, the *TC* of output *OF* is the sum of the *MC*s given by points *E* to *N* on the *MC* curve. That sum is measured by the area underneath the *MC* curve up to the output *OF*, viz. by the area *OFNME*, which is bounded on the top by the range *EMN* of the *MC* curve.[2] Similarly, the *TC* of output *OG* is given by the area *OGPNME* underneath the *MC* curve, which is equal in size to the

---

[1] Note that *MC* may be *rising* even though it is *below ATC*, as in the output range *FG*.

[2] In the language of calculus, the *TC* of any output is the integral of *MC* up to that output, since *MC* is the first derivative of *TC* with respect to output.

rectangle $OGPD$, since the latter is the same TC derived from the ATC curve.[1] The TCs, thus derived from the MC curve, allow the whole TC curve to be drawn.

The concept of *marginal revenue* (MR) bears precisely the same relation to TR as MC does to TC. MR measures the rate at which TR rises, when the quantity sold of a good increases. Like MC, the MR can be measured for some particular increase (e.g. of one unit) in sales, or for such a very small increase that it is given by the slope at a point on the TR curve. With the latter procedure, the MR curve can be derived from the TR curve by plotting the slopes on the latter against the corresponding outputs. In Fig. 11.2a[2], the perfectly competitive firm's TR curve is a straight line out of the origin. Its constant slope gives a horizontal straight line MR curve, which coincides with the AR curve in Fig. 11.2b. Since the firm can sell any number of units at the same price, the additional revenue from one more unit is equal to the average revenue from the previous units.

The relationship between *any* two economic quantities can be expressed in a *total*, an *average* or a *marginal*[3] form. The connections between the three forms are always the same as those explained above for TC, ATC and MC. If complete information is given in any one of the forms, it can always be translated into the other two. Now that the mathematical relations between total, average and marginal quantities have been established, it will be possible in later analyses to choose the form which is most enlightening for the problem in hand.

ALTERNATIVE EXPOSITIONS OF PROFIT MAXIMIZATION

The determination of the perfectly competitive firm's most profitable output has already been explained by means of both the TR and TC curves and the AR and ATC curves. The TR and TC curves have the same slopes at that output. The slopes of those curves have been seen to measure MR and MC respectively. The exposition of profit maximization under perfect competition can now be completed by showing it in the alternative total, average and marginal forms.

In Fig. 11.5a, the maximum profit $R'P'$ is earned at output OJ. The MR and MC curves in Fig. 11.5b therefore intersect at that output. Total profit can also be discovered from the marginal curves. It is the

---

[1] Hence, the area EDM under the MC curve is equal to the area MNP above the MC curve, which is bounded on the top by the straight line MP.

[2] On p. 118 above.

[3] It should therefore be helpful for students with a knowledge of calculus to note that the word 'marginal' is simply the economist's term for a first derivative.

area $OJPE$ under the MR curve, which equals the TR of output OJ, *less* the area $OJPQNG$ under the MC curve, which equals the TC of output OJ. It has already been seen that the rectangle $DRPE$, inscribed between the AR and ATC curves, also measures profit.

The MR and MC curves are shown as intersecting at output OH, as well as OJ. It is evident from the total curves that, in the initial range of output over which TC exceeds TR, OH is the one at which a maximum *loss* $N'M'$ ($=$ rectangle $ENMF$ in Fig. 11.5b) will be incurred. The TC

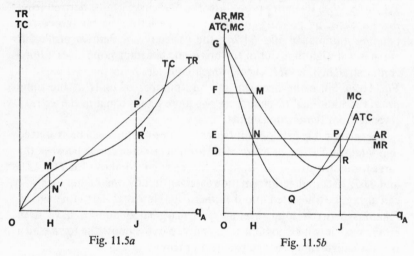

Fig. 11.5a Fig. 11.5b

and TR curves are, of course, parallel at M' and N'. $MR = MC$ thus indicates either a profit *maximum* or a profit *minimum* (which is the same thing as a maximum loss). In general, the TC and TR curves of a firm may be parallel at two or more levels of output. $MR = MC$ is therefore a *necessary* but not a *sufficient* basis for distinguishing the output which gives the maximum profit. For a profit maximum, the MC curve must intersect the MR curve from *below* on the left to *above* on the right, as at point P in Fig. 11.5b. The reverse occurs at point N, which is therefore a profit minimum.[1]

With a perfectly elastic AR curve, it is *rising ATC* which prevents the perfectly competitive firm from expanding indefinitely. It is therefore

[1] In the language of calculus, second and maybe higher order conditions are required to distinguish a maximum from a minimum. Let π stand for profit ($= TR - TC$). $MR = MC$ means $\dfrac{\mathrm{d}TR}{\mathrm{d}q} - \dfrac{\mathrm{d}TC}{\mathrm{d}q} = 0$, i.e. $\dfrac{\mathrm{d}\pi}{\mathrm{d}q} = 0$. For π to be a maximum, it is necessary that $\dfrac{\mathrm{d}^2\pi}{\mathrm{d}q^2} < 0$.

necessary to ask if there is some circumstance, compatible with perfect competition, which will give a U-shaped *ATC* curve.

Being very small, the perfectly competitive firm can purchase as much as it requires of any factor at its ruling market price. The quantities of all factors are therefore variable to it. Some of the factors may, of course, come in indivisible units (e.g. machines). The *ATC* curve for *each* indivisible unit will be U-shaped. The complete *ATC* curve is made up from the series of curves for more and more units of the indivisible factor.[1] If there is *no* fixed factor, the lowest points of all those curves will be on the same level, and the complete *ATC* curve will not rise when the number of units of the indivisible factor can be increased.[2]

There is, however, as was seen in the previous chapter, one factor which has a special form of indivisibility, viz. management. The quantity of management—i.e. the number of people participating in it —can be varied, but the unity of decision-making has to be maintained. The need to integrate the decisions, made by the different parts of the management of a firm, accounts for its special form of indivisibility. Increased specialization, as between the persons in management, can lower *ATC* as output increases. But it will become more difficult to reach consistent decisions as the size of the management increases. Because of this, *ATC* will begin to rise at some level of output. What that level will be depends on the managerial capabilities of the people available to the firm.

With given factor prices, and with the quantities of all factors variable, there is thus only one circumstance which can explain the U-shaped *ATC* curve required under perfect competition, viz. the special form of indivisibility inherent in management. This will cause the *ATC* for *any* firm to rise at *some* level of output. What is required for perfect competition, however, is that *ATC* rises sufficiently at a very *low* level of output, so that the individual firm is prevented from expanding to a size at which it can influence the price of its product. That will occur only if managerial capabilities are very restricted.

It will become clear at a later stage that there are a number of reasons why few industries even approximate to the conditions of perfect competition. The above analysis, however, shows that it will not exist where people have the ability to take advantage of specialization in management, without encountering significant difficulties in the co-ordination of decisions.

[1] See pp. 108–110 above.
[2] I.e. the complete *ATC* curve approximates to a horizontal straight line; see p. 110 above.

CHANGES IN OUTPUT

Qualitative[1] predictions can now be made as to how the output of a firm will change when its revenue and cost curves shift. The analysis of changes in output will be made with only the average and marginal curves, but it can easily be extended to the total curves.

Suppose that initially, in Fig. 11.6a, the market price of good A is OD. The AR_1 (and the coincident MR_1) curve of the firm in question is perfectly elastic at that price. Given the ATC and MC curves, the most

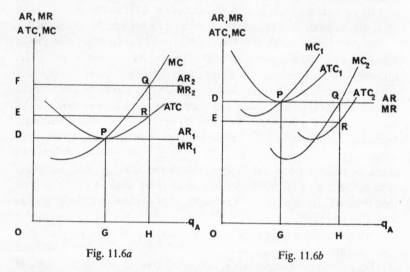

Fig. 11.6a   Fig. 11.6b

profitable output, with $MC = MR$, is OG, where the firm is shown as earning a zero profit, since $ATC = AR_1$ at point P.

If p_A rises to OF, the revenue curves shift (i.e. *increase*) to AR_2 and the coincident MR_2. The MC curve is intersected by MR_2 at a higher output (OH), than it was by MR_1. The firm therefore expands its output to the new most profitable level, where it will earn a profit $ERQF$ (profit per unit RQ multiplied by output).

In general, as p_A rises above OD, the horizontal line, representing AR and MR, shifts further and further upwards. The most profitable output at each p_A is given by the point on the MC curve where it is cut by the MR curve for that p_A. Since $MR = AR$ (price) under perfect competition, those points indicate the outputs which the firm will produce at different prices (e.g. at Q the output OH is produced at the price OF). A curve which shows how output varies with price is called a *supply*

[1] In the sense explained on p. 56 above.

curve; it shows what quantity supplied will be at different prices. The points on the perfectly competitive firm's MC curve, from its intersection with the ATC curve upwards, form its supply curve (the firm will not produce at a price less than ATC, since it would make a loss). In Fig. 11.6a, the firm's supply curve is coincident with the MC curve from the point P upwards. It shows that the firm will expand output if the price of its product rises.

Now consider the effect on output of a shift in the firm's *cost* curves. These curves have two parameters, the prices of the factors and the production function. If factor prices fall, or technology improves, the curves shift downwards (i.e. costs *decrease*); and vice versa. Suppose that initially, in Fig. 11.6b, the cost curves are ATC_1 and MC_1. With p_A at OD, the most profitable output is OG (giving a zero profit, since $ATC = AR$ at point P). If either factor prices fall, or technology improves, costs decrease at all levels of output, and the curves shift downwards to, say, ATC_2 and MC_2. The MR curve is intersected by MC_2 at a higher output (OH), than it was by MC_1. The firm now expands its output to the new most profitable level where it will earn a profit $ERQD$. A rise in factor prices, or a deterioration in technology, will *increase* costs, i.e. shift the cost curves upwards, and cause the firm to contract output.

The theory of the perfectly competitive firm, as developed above, can now be used to explain the number of firms which there will be in an industry.

CHAPTER 12

THE INDUSTRY SUPPLY CURVE

The *revenue* conditions of the firms in a perfectly competitive industry are all the same. With a uniform price ruling for their products, the AR curve of each firm is perfectly elastic at that price.

Whether the *cost* conditions of perfectly competitive firms are the same or not depends on their managements. The latter may differ in two respects: in knowledge and skill, and in the salaries required to draw them into the industry in question.

Management needs knowledge of the technical capabilities of the different factors of production, and of the various ways in which they can be combined. It also needs administrative skill to run the firm, i.e. to arrange that the factors are combined in the chosen way. When managements differ in knowledge and skill the production functions of their firms will be different, i.e. given quantities of factors will produce a larger output in one firm as compared with another. That is the *technical* sense in which it can be said that one firm is more efficient than another. Differences between firms in technical efficiency are shown by differences in their production functions.

The persons in the management of a firm will have to be paid salaries at least as large as they could earn in other firms.[1] Otherwise, they will transfer themselves to other firms. Any firm will therefore have to pay each member of its management his *transfer price*, i.e. the highest price (viz. salary rate) he could obtain from some other firm.[2] A manager can consider moving between industries as well as moving between firms in the same industry. For example, he may have the technical ability to help in organizing the production of good B as well as of good A. In that case, he will work in industry A only for a salary at least as great as he could earn in industry B. Some firm producing A will have to pay him at least his transfer price in relation to industry B.

The managers capable of working in industry A may not have the same transfer prices in relation to other industries. Thus, while Mr J and Mr K might be equally capable of organizing the production of

[1] Assuming that they have no other grounds for preferring one firm to another.
[2] This point of course applies to all factors.

good A, they may have quite different abilities in relation to the technology of good B. If J is technically superior in the latter field, he could then earn a higher salary than K could in a firm producing B. In that case, J's transfer price to industry A will be higher than K's.

The cost condition of a firm depends on its production function and the prices of the factors. The firms in a perfectly competitive industry can thus have different cost conditions *either* because their managements differ in knowledge and skill *or* because the managers have different transfer prices in relation to other industries. Of two firms producing good A, one will be said to be the *higher cost* firm (and the other the lower cost one) if its ATC curve lives above that of the other. The higher average total cost for all outputs of the one will be due either to the inferior knowledge and skill of its management in respect of the technology of good A, or to the higher transfer prices of its managers in relation to other industries.[1] It follows that a higher cost firm is not necessarily less efficient *technically* than a lower cost one. Its higher costs may be due to the higher salaries it has to pay to its managers in order to attract them away from other industries.

It will be supposed, initially, that the firms in a perfectly competitive industry do have different cost conditions. For the purpose of illustrating the analysis of what determines the number of firms in the industry (producing good A), three firms—A_1, A_2 and A_3—will be taken as representing the large number involved. The ATC and MC curves of the firms are given in the three sections of Fig. 12.1, where A_1 is the lowest cost, and A_3 the highest cost, firm. The output of A_1 is measured from origin O', of A_2 from origin O'', and of A_3 from origin O''', with ATC and MC measured on the respective vertical axes from these origins. AR and MR are also measured on those vertical axes. Since there is a uniform price for the products of all the firms, a continuous horizontal straight line across the diagram gives the AR (and MR) curve for each firm.

Which firms will find it profitable to exist, and what outputs they will produce, can be read from Fig. 12.1. If the market price of A is below $O'D$, it is less than the lowest ATC of each firm, and all of them would make losses at any output level. At the price $O'D$, at which AR_1 is a tangent to the ATC curve of A_1, that firm can just cover its costs at its most profitable output $O'J'$, where $MR = MC$. The other two firms would still make losses at this price. As the price of A rises from $O'D$ to $O'E$, A_1 will expand its output (along its MC curve) from $O'J'$ to $O'K'$. At the latter price, it will be profitable for A_2 to come into existence and produce $O''K'''$, where its $MR = MC$. As price rises from

[1] Or, of course, to some combination of both features of management.

$O'E$ to $O'F$, A_1 further expands its output from $O'K'$ to $O'L'$, and A_2 expands its output from $O''K''$ to $O''L''$. At the latter price, A_3 comes into existence with an output $O'''L'''$.

The output of an industry is the sum of the outputs of the firms in it. There are thus two reasons why the industry output will expand as the price of its good rises. On the one hand, it will be profitable for existing firms to produce larger outputs at higher prices. On the other hand, new firms, which could not have covered their costs at lower prices, will

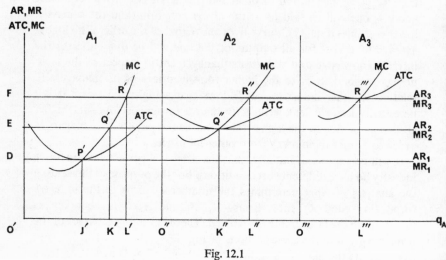

Fig. 12.1

enter the industry as price rises. The way in which the industry output changes, as price changes, can be expressed by means of a *supply curve*.

In Fig. 12.2, the price of the good (p_A) is measured on the vertical axis, and the quantity supplied (q_A) by the industry per period of time is measured on the horizontal axis. Any point on the diagram refers to both a price and a quantity of A, e.g. point P refers to (or has co-ordinates) price OD and quantity OJ. If the quantity is taken to mean quantity supplied, then the point P can be interpreted as saying 'if the price of A is OD, then the quantity supplied of A by the industry will be OJ'. And similarly for any other point.

The quantities that will be supplied by the industry at different prices follow from Fig. 12.1 and the explanation already given of it. At a price below OD, no firm finds it profitable to exist, and the industry output up to that price will be zero. At price OD, firm A_1 comes into existence and produces output $O'J'$. This is recorded in Fig. 12.2 at point P, where the industry output OJ equals $O'J'$ of Fig. 12.1. At price OE, firm A_1 has expanded its output to $O'K'$, and A_2 has come into existence with output $O''K''$. The industry output is now $O'K' + O''K''$; and this is recorded at point Q in Fig. 12.2, where the industry output OK equals the sum of $O'K'$ and $O''K''$. Similarly, point R is given by the sum of the outputs

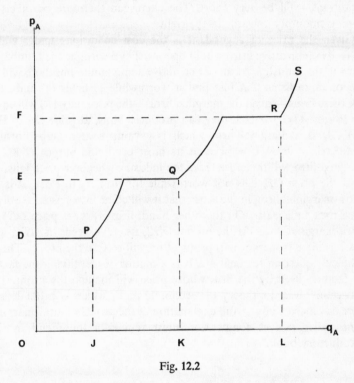

Fig. 12.2

of A_1, A_2 and A_3 at price OF; thus, the industry output OL equals $O'L' + O''L'' + O'''L'''$.

The other industry supply points between P, Q and R can be similarly derived from Fig. 12.1. When all the points are joined, they give the industry supply curve (labelled S). Its horizontal range from D to P shows that output below price OD is zero, and that at this price firm A_1 produces an initial output of OJ ($= O'J'$ in Fig. 12.1). The upward sloping range of the S curve beyond point P indicates the expansion in the output of A_1 as price rises from OD to OE. The horizontal range on the curve before point Q indicates the initial output of firm A_2 at price

OE. Similarly, the upward sloping range beyond Q indicates the combined expansions in the outputs of A_1 and A_2 as price rises from OE to OF; and the horizontal range before R indicates the initial output of firm A_3 at price OF. Since the outputs of the firms are very small in relation to that of the industry, the horizontal ranges of the industry S curve—indicating the successive entry of new firms with different cost conditions—will be very short. The curve can therefore be taken as sloping smoothly upwards to the right.[1]

Given the price of a good, it is the cost conditions under which perfectly competitive firms would operate that determine the number of firms in the industry. At any price above some minimum, there will be one or more firms that just find it worthwhile to enter the industry. For these firms—called the marginal firms—the price (i.e. AR) will equal the lowest ATC at which they can produce. Thus, at price OE in Fig. 12.1, A_2 is a marginal firm which is earning a zero (supernormal) profit[2], since its ATC = price at its most profitable output $O''K''$. A marginal firm will therefore leave the industry whenever price falls.

At the price OE, it is not worthwhile for firm A_3 to exist; it is an 'extra-marginal' firm, in the sense that it will come into existence only if price rises sufficiently. On the other hand, firm A_1 is (at price OE) an 'intra-marginal' firm. At the output $O'K'$, its AR exceeds its ATC, and it is earning a (supernormal) profit. Who will receive the profit? This is a difficult question for analysis. It is a matter of identifying the factor (or factors) used by the firm whose price will include the profit. The answer involves the theory of 'economic rent', which is better left to more advanced study. A full explanation of the profits of intra-marginal firms under perfect competition must remain a loose end in this introductory book.[3]

THE PARAMETERS OF THE SUPPLY CURVE

From the foregoing analysis, it can be seen that the quantity supplied by the industry depends on the price of its good in relation to the cost conditions of the firms. The latter conditions depend on the prices of the factors and the firms' production functions. Hence the output of the

---

[1] I.e. the slope is positive.

[2] It is, of course, earning the normal profit (the cost of its finance) which is included in its costs.

[3] A clue to the explanation can, however, be provided. Under present assumptions, as the industry expands, the prices (salaries) of the managers in the intra-marginal firms will be bid up by competition between the firms in the industry for them. The managers will appropriate the profits.

industry will change not only when the price of its good changes, but also when factor prices and production functions change. This can be expressed in the form of the *supply function* for the industry:

$$S_A = g(p_A, p_\alpha, p_\beta, p_\gamma \ldots, PF)$$

where S_A stands for quantity supplied, p_A for the price of the good. $p_\alpha, p_\beta, p_\gamma \ldots$ for the prices of the factors used by the industry, and PF for *all* the production functions of the firms.[1]

Since the industry supply curve shows how S_A changes as p_A changes, the other independent variables within the brackets are held constant for the purpose of drawing the curve. The factor prices ($p_\alpha, p_\beta, p_\gamma \ldots$), and the production functions, are the parameters of the supply curve. When they change, the curve shifts to a new position. That is, the *condition* of supply (i.e. the supply function) has to be expressed by means of a whole family of supply curves, with each curve showing how S_A varies with p_A at a particular set of factor prices and production functions. This way of expressing the condition of supply is, of course, the same as that already used for the condition of demand.

It was shown in the previous chapter how the output of the individual firm will change whenever its cost curves shift. That analysis can now be used to show how the industry supply curve will *shift* whenever the factor prices and the production functions (which determine the firms' cost curves) change.

Suppose that the S_1 curve in Fig. 12.3 is derived from the cost curves of firms A_1, A_2 and A_3 in Fig. 12.1. Thus, at price OE, the quantity supplied by the industry is OK, which equals $O'K'$ from A_1 plus $O''K''$ from A_2. Now suppose that either factor prices fall, or technology improves, so that the cost curves of all the firms in Fig. 12.1 shift downwards. With this *decrease* in costs, the outputs of A_1 and A_2 will expand, at price OE, to their new most profitable levels at which MR against equals MC.[2] If the cost curves of A_3 are shifted down sufficiently by the parameter change—i.e. so that it could now cover its costs at some output—it will come into existence and contribute to the industry output. The latter will, therefore, increase above OK at price OE in Fig. 12.3, partly because of the expansions in the outputs of existing firms, and partly because of the entry of new firms. If the industry output thereby increases to OM at price OE, then T is a point on the new supply curve (S_2). The outputs which the industry would produce, at all

---

[1] The letter 'g' is used to indicate the functional relation, since 'f' has already been used in the demand function.

[2] See p. 127 above.

other prices of its good, are similarly increased by the decrease in costs. Hence, the points that make up S_2 all lie to the right of the corresponding ones on S_1.

The shift in the supply curve from S_1 to S_2 means that the industry is now willing, because of the fall in factor prices, or the improvement in technology, to supply a larger output at every price of its good. That

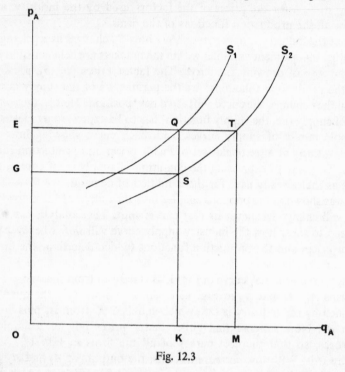

Fig. 12.3

can be put another way: the industry is now willing to supply any output at a lower price than before. Thus, on the original supply curve S_1, the output OK would be forthcoming if the price were OE. The latter is called the *supply price* of that output. When the supply curve has shifted to position S_2, the same output OK will be forthcoming at the supply price OG—which is lower than OE.

A rise in factor prices, or a deterioration in technology, will increase the costs of firms, i.e. shift their cost curves upwards. The industry supply curve will then *shift* to the left (e.g. from S_2 to S_1). The industry will now be willing only to supply a smaller output at each price; or what is the same thing, the supply price of each output will be higher.

The terminology already used to distinguish between movements *along* a demand curve, and shifts *in* it, will also be used in relation to the supply curve. A rise (fall) in price will be said to *expand* (*contract*) the quantity supplied—this is a movement along the supply curve. A change in factor prices, or technology, which shifts the curve, will be said to *increase* or *decrease* supply. That terminology will help to prevent confusion between the effects which changes in the different variables—viz. the price of the good, factor prices, and technology—have on quantity supplied.

THE PRICE ELASTICITY OF SUPPLY

A quantitative measure of the relation between the quantity supplied and price of a good must—as in the case of demand—be independent of the units in terms of which the variables are measured. It is therefore necessary to ask what will be the *proportional* change in quantity supplied as a result of some *proportional* change in price. The proportional change in quantity is $\dfrac{\Delta q}{q}$, and that in price is $\dfrac{\Delta p}{p}$. With an industry supply curve sloping upwards to the right, q supplied expands as p rises; hence Δq is positive (negative) when Δp is positive (negative).

The quantitative relation between q supplied and p is expressed in the usual form of an elasticity, i.e. the proportional change in the dependent variable (q) divided by the proportional change in the independent variable (p). The *price elasticity of supply* (ε_S) is therefore $\dfrac{\Delta q}{q} \bigg/ \dfrac{\Delta p}{p}$ where q means quantity supplied. ε_S can be measured either over an *arc* of the supply curve, or at a *point* on it. In the latter case, the same device, as that already derived for the point price elasticity of demand,[1] can be used to see what the ε_S is at any point on the supply curve. In Fig. 12.4, tangents are drawn to the S curve at points P, Q, and R, and are extended to intersect both axes. The distance along a tangent to the horizontal axis divided by the distance along it to the vertical axis measures the point ε_S. At P it is $\dfrac{PK}{PJ}$, which is greater than unity; at R it is $\dfrac{RK'}{RJ'}$, which is less than unity. Since the tangent at Q goes through the origin, the ε_S at Q is unity $\left(= \dfrac{QO}{QO} \right)$. As in the case of demand, the ε_S is *not* the same thing as the slope of the S curve.

[1] On pp. 84–85 above.

As price rises, the quantities supplied by existing firms in an industry expand, and new firms enter the industry. The size of ε_S therefore depends on the magnitudes of both those forms of expansion of the industry output. The more rapidly rising is the MC of a firm, the less it will increase its output as the price of its product rises. Hence, the ε_S will be the smaller, the more rapidly rising are the MCs of existing firms. New firms enter an industry because a rise in the price of its good

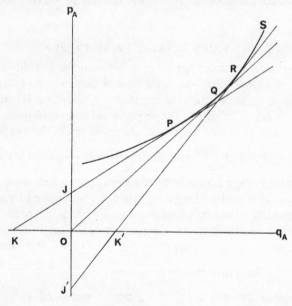

Fig. 12.4

allows them to cover their costs. The bigger the differences between the costs of extra-marginal and existing firms—as indicated by the lowest points on their ATC curves—the fewer firms will come into existence as a result of any rise in price. Thus, in Fig. 12.1, the greater the vertical distance between Q'' on the ATC curve of A_2, and R''' on the ATC curve of A_3, the larger the rise in price above OE needed to bring A_3 into the industry. Hence, the ε_S will be the smaller, the greater is the cost differences between firms.

If the cost conditions of all the actual and potential firms in a perfectly competitive industry are identical, the ε_S is infinite, and the S curve is a horizontal straight line. Thus if the ATC curves of the three firms in Fig. 12.1 are all identical to that of A_1, the industry supply

price (with given factor prices and productivities) will stay constant at
OD. Below that price, no firms would exist and the industry output
would be zero; above that price, an indefinitely large number of firms
would be drawn into the industry. The output of the industry will vary,
at the constant supply price OD, as a result of changes in the *number* of
firms in the industry. The output of *each* firm will remain unchanged at
the lowest point of its ATC curve (viz., P' on the ATC curve of A_1).

With given factor prices and production functions, the S curve of a
perfectly competitive industry is either a horizontal straight line, or is
upward sloping to the right. It cannot be downward sloping to the
right, since each firm must be producing at *rising MC* in order to keep
it very small in relation to the industry. Cost conditions are likely to
differ between firms, because of differences in the knowledge and skill,
and/or transfer prices, of their managements. Hence, a supply curve,
sloping upwards to the right, will now be used, in conjunction with the
already constructed demand curve, to explain the determination of the
industry price and output under perfect competition.

CHAPTER 13

PRICE AND OUTPUT
DETERMINATION: I

It was shown in Chapter 5[1] that there are three elements in the explanation of how the price and output of a good are determined, viz. (i) the condition of demand, (ii) the condition of supply, and (iii) the way in which the price is adjusted in the market so as to make the quantity demanded equal to the quantity supplied.

The condition of demand shows what quantities will be demanded at different prices and different values of the other variables which influence consumer behaviour. The earlier analysis yielded the demand function (for good A):

$$D_A = f(p_A, p_B, p_C, \ldots, Y^d, NW, T)$$

The condition of supply shows what quantities will be supplied at different prices and different values of the other variables which influence the behaviour of firms. The analysis of a perfectly competitive industry has given the supply function (for good A):

$$S_A = g(p_A, p_\alpha, p_\beta, p_\gamma, \ldots, PF)$$

Continuing trade between the consumers and the firms requires that they reach agreement on *both* terms of the trade, i.e. the price of A and the quantity of it to be traded at that price. When the consumers have given incomes, net worths, and preferences, and are confronted by a given set of prices of other goods ($B, C \ldots$), they are willing to buy a larger quantity of A, the lower is its price. When the firms operate at given factor prices and with given production functions (i.e. under given cost conditions) they are willing to produce and sell a larger quantity of A, the higher is its price. It is in the context of those quantities, which consumers and firms are willing to buy and sell respectively at different prices, that the market has to *find* a price which equates quantity demanded and quantity supplied. A theory of price and output therefore has to explain how the market tries to find that price.

[1] On pp. 38–40 above.

The nature of this problem is clarified by putting the demand and supply curves for a good, produced under perfect competition, on the same diagram. In Fig. 13.1, the D curve shows the various q_As per period of time which the consumers are willing to buy at different p_As— given their incomes, net worths, and preferences, and the prices of other goods. The S curve shows the various q_As the firms are willing, over the

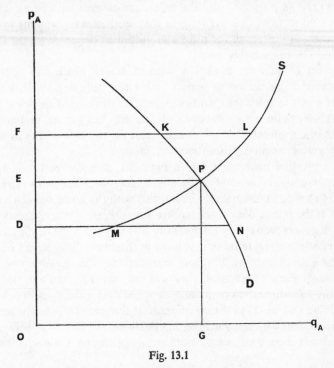

Fig. 13.1

same period, to produce and sell at different p_As—given the prices of factors, and the production functions. With the D curve sloping downwards to the right throughout its length, and with the S curve sloping upwards, they intersect once at point P.

Since that point is on both the curves, it indicates that, at price OE, the quantity demanded ($OG = EP$) equals the quantity supplied. There is no other price at which this would be so. At prices higher than OE (e.g. OF), the quantity which would be supplied (FL) exceeds that which would be demanded (FK). At prices lower than OE (e.g. OD), the quantity demanded (DN) exceeds the quantity supplied (DM).

If the price ruling in the market were OE, the consumers and firms would be in agreement on *both* the price and the quantity to be traded at that price. The market would then be said to be in *equilibrium*; *OE* being called the equilibrium price, and *OG* the equilibrium output. The concept of equilibrium means that both sides of a market are simultaneously satisfied with the terms on which they are trading. The buyers are content with the quantity being purchased in each period of time at the price in question; and the sellers are content with this quantity being sold at the price. As long as they both remain content in that way, there is no reason for price and output to depart from the levels *OE* and *OG* respectively.

Market equilibrium is thus a state of affairs which will continue unchanged from period to period until either side decides that it no longer wants to trade the quantity in question at the existing price. That would happen on the consumer side if incomes, net worths, preferences, or the prices of other goods change; and on the side of the firms, if factor prices, or production functions, change.

At any other price than *OE* in Fig. 13.1, the market would be in *disequilibrium*. The concept of disequilibrium means that both sides of a market cannot simultaneously be satisfied with the terms on which they trade. *If* the price ruling in the market were *OF*, the *D* curve shows that the consumers would buy the quantity *FK*. But the *S* curve shows that the firms in aggregate think it is most profitable to produce an output *FL* for sale at that price. Their expectations will, however, be disappointed. For at that price, they will only sell *FK*, and will find the quantity *KL*—the excess of quantity supplied over quantity demanded—remaining unsold. Thus if they do trade at the price *OF*, the consumers will be content with the outcome, but the firms will not. In this way, the market will show its disequilibrium at any price above the equilibrium one.

If the price ruling in the market were *OD*, the *S* curve shows that the firms in aggregate think it is most profitable to produce an output *DM* for sale. But the *D* curve shows that the consumers will want to buy the quantity *DN*. If the firms hold sufficient *stocks* of the good, they could meet the excess (*MN*) of quantity demanded over quantity supplied by allowing their stocks to run down.[1] But if they do not hold any (or sufficient) stocks, they will have to disappoint some consumers by not selling them as much as they want to buy at price *OD*. Thus, if they do trade at that price, the consumers will or will not be content with the

---

[1] What determines the quantity of stocks a firm will want to hold cannot be investigated at this point. It comes under the theory of investment in capital, which is dealt with in Chapter 21 below.

outcome, according as the firms can or cannot draw sufficiently upon stocks; but the firms will not be content, since their output is less than they could sell. Disequilibrium in the market at any price below the equilibrium one can thus show itself in a number of ways.

Market disequilibrium is a state of affairs which will not continue unchanged from period to period. At a disequilibrium price, the firms will not be selling the quantities they expected to, and upon which they based their production decisions. Since that state is general to the industry, the firms will all want to adjust the price of the good upwards, or downwards, to try and make the quantity they can sell equal to the quantity produced. The present problem for analysis is to explain how that price adjustment process will take place.

The placing of a demand and a supply curve on the same diagram can indicate that there is an equilibrium price and output for an industry. But in themselves the curves do not show how the market may find that equilibrium.

THE SEARCH FOR EQUILIBRIUM

The search for an equilibrium price must start from *knowledge* of the kind of disequilibrium which would exist at other prices. The firms need to know whether the aggregate quantity they would produce at a particular price exceeds, or falls short of, what can be sold at that price. Only with knowledge of the excess, or the deficiency, can they tell whether to raise, or to lower, the price. The way that knowledge comes to them depends on the organization of the market.

Some goods are traded by means of an *auction*. In this, the organization of the market centres on the auctioneer, whose function it is to guide the buyers and sellers to an agreed price. Agreement requires that the sellers are willing to sell at the price, and that there are no buyers who are willing to pay a *higher* price. Only then would both sides of the market be content with the outcome. The auctioneer calls out different prices[1] on a *provisional* basis, so that no trading takes place at any price until agreement in the above sense has been reached. Thus an auction provides knowledge of the disequilibrium prices without any trading occurring at those prices. Trade only takes place when the equilibrium price has been discovered.

Auctions, however, are mostly confined to goods that have already been produced, e.g. houses, works of art, raw materials, and foodstuffs. That is, they are mainly used as a means of fixing the prices at which

[1] In either an ascending or descending order.

existing stocks of goods are to be traded, rather than as a means of agreeing prices in anticipation of production. An auction thus discovers the price at which the quantity demanded equals the *existing* supply of a good. It is not widely used to find the price at which quantity demanded equals the quantity which firms are willing to set about *producing*.

The main exception in this respect is where a prospective buyer invites *tenders* from the firms who could produce the good he wants. Tendering is a form of auction—but an auction which takes place before, rather than after, goods have been produced. The prices tendered by the potential suppliers allow the buyer to reach agreement with one of them on both the price and the quantity to be produced. In that way, production only occurs at equilibrium prices. As a form of market organization, tendering is important where the buyers differ in regard to the characteristics they require in a particular type of good. That is why tenders are much used in the building and construction industry. Some people have individual requirements as regards the kind of house they want to have built; and many firms require features, special to themselves, in new factories.

But for the vast majority of goods there are many buyers who, in respect of each one, are satisfied to take a standardized product. Whether it is a brand of margarine, or television set, or motor car, most firms can count on being able to sell some number of identical units of each good. That being so, it is a more convenient and less costly form of market organization for the firms to take the initiative in producing for the market. Instead of waiting for orders from buyers, they produce in *anticipation* of sales to come—and do so on the expectation of being able to sell the quantity produced at a particular price.

With this form of market organization, the firms in an industry cannot tell, before they produce and put their products up for sale, whether the market price is an equilibrium or a disequilibrium one. It is the comparison between the rate at which they are *selling* per period of time and the rate at which they are *producing* in the same period which gives them that information.

The explanation already given of Fig. 13.1 was directed to precisely that point. The diagram is intended to show how price and output will be determined in the most prevalent form of market organization, viz. where production takes place in anticipation of demand. Thus the supply curve indicates that if the market price is *OF*, the firms in aggregate *expect* that *FL* is the most profitable output to produce per period of time—and that they proceed to produce it. For as was shown in the previous chapter, each firm decides on its own production level by means of its cost condition and the market price. But the quantity which the firms will actually sell per period at price *OF* is shown by the demand curve to be *FK*. Hence, it is in the process of marketing the output *FL* that the firms acquire the knowledge that *OF* is a disequilibrium price.

In contrast to what happens in an auction, trading can actually take place at disequilibrium prices whenever production is in anticipation of demand. This means that at least one side of the market is dissatisfied with the outcome of the trading, and will therefore seek new terms on which to continue it into the future. The search for new terms will go on as long as the quantity demanded and the quantity supplied are not equated by the ruling market price. The problem with respect to the price adjustment process can therefore be re-stated in this way: Will the knowledge of disequilibrium, as derived from actual trading, make the market converge to the equilibrium position?

THE CONDITIONS FOR CONVERGENCE TO EQUILIBRIUM

Consider this further with the aid of Fig. 13.1. Suppose that the market price happens to be *OD*. The firms therefore expect it to be profitable to supply in aggregate an output *DM* per period of time. However, as they market that output, they find that they are selling it at the rate of *DN* per period. Consequently, they must either allow their stocks to decline, or they must turn customers away when they have sold all their production.[1] As soon as this situation becomes clear to the firms, it will be possible for *all* of them to raise the price at which they are selling. Since quantity demanded exceeds quantity supplied at the existing price, the firms will be able to sell all they are currently producing at some higher price—and thereby get a larger revenue and profit.

As price rises in this way *both* the quantity demanded and the quantity supplied change. At a higher price, the consumers are only willing to buy a smaller quantity of the good; quantity demanded *contracts* along the *D* curve in Fig. 13.1 from point *N* towards point *P*. The higher price, however, makes it profitable—as was shown in the previous chapter[2]— for existing firms to expand output, and for new firms to enter the industry. The quantity supplied by the industry *expands* along the *S* curve from point *M* towards point *P*.

The rise in price therefore reduces the excess of quantity demanded over quantity supplied, i.e. the *D* and *S* curves are converging towards each other at prices above *OD*. But as long as the price remains below

[1] Or some combination of both.
[2] On pp. 130–132 above.

OE, the firms will find when they market their products that they can sell more than they are producing. The price will therefore converge to the equilibrium level *OE*, at which both the buyers and the sellers are content with the terms on which they are trading; and it will remain there as long as the *D* and *S* curves do not shift their positions.

A similar analysis shows how the price of a good will converge towards the equilibrium level from an initial position which is above it. Thus, at price *OF*, the quantity supplied (*FL*) exceeds the quantity demanded (*FK*). On marketing their products, the firms will find that they are selling less than they are producing. As soon as this situation becomes clear to the firms, they will *all* want to reduce the price at which they are selling, in order to prevent unsold stocks of their products from accumulating. As price falls, quantity demanded *expands* along the *D* curve in Fig. 13.1 from point *K* towards point *P*; and quantity supplied *contracts* along the *S* curve from point *L* towards point *P*, as some firms leave the industry, and the remaining ones reduce their outputs. Price will continue to fall as long as quantity supplied exceeds quantity demanded. It will therefore converge to the equilibrium level *OE*.

Given the nature and shapes of the *D* and *S* curves for a perfectly competitive industry, the above analysis shows how the market would *find* its way to the equilibrium price and output. Firms discover that there is disequilibrium at a particular market price by means of the discrepancy between quantity produced and quantity sold. The discrepancy leads them to change the price. That the price will then converge to the equilibrium level is an exceedingly important conclusion for a lot of economic analysis; and it merits a precise statement.

For brevity, an excess of quantity demanded over quantity supplied at any price is called the *excess demand* at that price. In Fig. 13.1, there is an excess demand of *MN* at price *OD*. Similarly, an excess of quantity supplied over quantity demanded is called the *excess supply* at that price. In the same diagram, there is an excess supply of *KL* at price *OD*. At an equilibrium price, the excess demand (and excess supply) is, of course, zero.

The behaviour of the market price in a perfectly competitive industry, as analysed above, can now be summarized in the statement: price will rise if there is excess demand; it will fall if there is excess supply; and it will remain unchanged if excess demand is zero.

If, as has been shown for a perfectly competitive industry, the *D* curve is downward sloping to the right, and the *S* curve is upward sloping, that behaviour of price will cause it to converge to the equilibrium level. For, as Fig. 13.1 shows, a rise in price reduces excess demand (i.e. the curves converge at prices above *OD*), and a fall in price reduces excess supply (i.e. the curves converge at prices below *OF*).

Two conditions are therefore necessary to ensure that a perfectly competitive market will find the equilibrium price. It is not sufficient that *excess demand* should *raise price* (and excess supply lower it); it

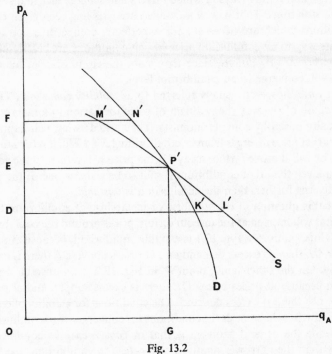

Fig. 13.2

is also necessary that a *rise in price* should *reduce excess demand* (and a fall reduce excess supply).

The need for both those conditions is illustrated by Fig. 13.2. In it, the *S* curve is shown—solely for the exposition of the present point—as downward sloping to the right, but less steeply so than the *D* curve. The curves intersect at *P*; there is an equilibrium price *OE*. But the market would only find the equilibrium by accident. At higher prices (e.g. *OF*), there is excess demand (*M'N'*); price will rise and therefore diverge from the equilibrium level. At lower prices (e.g. *OD*), there is excess supply (*K'L'*); price will fall and again diverge from the equilibrium level. That is, the trading at disequilibrium prices, which causes the firms to change the price, will lead them away from, rather than towards, the equilibrium. That happens, in the present hypothetical case, because a rise in price *increases* excess demand (and a fall increases excess supply).

Understanding of the price mechanism will be vitiated by any glib assumption[1] that prices are always either at, or moving towards, equilibrium levels. Whether or not this is so depends on the organization of markets, and on the ways in which buyers and sellers react to disequilibrium situations. That is why a detailed analysis has been given of the conditions which are necessary for a perfectly competitive market to find its way to an equilibrium price.[2] Such conditions are best described as *convergence conditions*, since they state the circumstances in which price will converge to an equilibrium level.

They are, however, usually referred to as *stability conditions*. This is so because of the way the problem of price formation in a market was originally posed by some economists. They asked: what will happen if the market price diverges from its equilibrium level? Will it return to that level, or will it move farther away? If the price will return to the equilibrium level, then that equilibrium is said to be a *stable* one. If the price will diverge further, then the equilibrium is *unstable*.

But this question of the stability, or instability, of equilibrium turns on what will happen at the disequilibrium prices around the equilibrium one. Thus, point P in Fig. 13.1 is a stable equilibrium, because at prices below OE there is excess demand and at prices above OE there is excess supply. On the other hand, point P' in Fig. 13.2 is an unstable equilibrium because at prices below OE there is excess supply, and at prices above OE there is excess demand. The conditions for stability of equilibrium are thus the same as the conditions for convergence to equilibrium. But while the general problem is that of *convergence* to equilibrium, rather than the narrower question of a *return* to equilibrium, the term stability conditions has continued to be used for what are more properly called convergence conditions.

The circumstances in which, as analysed above, a perfectly competitive market will find its way to an equilibrium price are known as *Walrasian*[3] stability conditions. But these conditions only deal with a part of the process of convergence to equilibrium. That process usually takes *time*, and it is necessary to examine in detail what happens within an industry during that time.

---

[1] Which is, in fact, frequently made by advocates of a freely working price mechanism.

[2] Moreover, as will be seen in Chapter 15, it is these conditions which explain how price and output will change whenever the D or S curve shifts.

[3] After the French economist Léon Walras (1834–1910), who first used them extensively in economic analysis.

CHAPTER 14

PRICE AND OUTPUT DETERMINATION: II

CONVERGENCE TO EQUILIBRIUM OVER TIME

Consider again the account given in the previous chapter of how the price, in a perfectly competitive market, will converge to equilibrium.

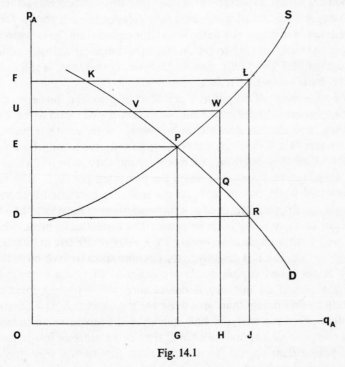

Fig. 14.1

Suppose that the price is initially OF in Fig. 14.1. When the industry markets the output FL (= OJ) at this price, the excess supply KL means that sales fall short of production by that amount. All the firms therefore reduce price by some amount—say to OU.

It was implicit in the earlier analysis that, *each* time the firms reduce the price, the quantity supplied is adjusted to the new price as indicated by the *S* curve. Hence, when the price is reduced to *OU*, the industry output contracts to *UW*. It will now be discovered in due course that there is an excess supply *VW* at the new price. That knowledge leads to a further reduction in price, and a further contraction in the industry output. If there is still some excess supply at this lower price, the process of reducing price, and contracting output, is repeated until the equilibrium price *OE* is found. The industry thus 'gropes' its way to equilibrium, by discovering the excess supply at each price at which it sells.

The term *path* will be used for the *series* of values taken by price and output, as they converge to a new equilibrium. Thus the particular path followed in the above analysis is along the *S* curve from point *L* down to point *P*. This explanation of the convergence process assumes, however, that the industry output is *fully adjusted* to each price *before* a move is made to a new one in the search for equilibrium. Thus when the price is reduced from *OF* to *OU*, it is assumed that the industry adjusts its output to *UW*, and only *then*, on discovering that there is still excess supply, makes a further reduction in price.

The adjustment of output to a new level of price can, however, be a lengthy matter. When price is reduced, some firms will want to leave the industry, and the remaining ones will want to reduce their outputs. The owners of a firm which leaves the industry have to stop hiring the factors which they get from other people, and they have to dispose of the capital (and maybe land) which the firm itself possesses. The contracts under which labour and raw materials are purchased will probably not run for very long; and in a few weeks—or at most months—the purchase of these factors can be ended. The capital equipment, which may well from a physical viewpoint have years of life left in it, can be put up for sale. But it is unlikely in the circumstances to fetch more than scrap prices. Most capital goods are designed to produce particular products. When an industry is contracting, the departing firms are unlikely to find others that have a use for the capital. A new question therefore arises for analysis: how quickly will firms leave an industry when the price of its good falls? Will they do so more or less immediately, selling their capital for what they can get; or will they think it better to continue producing as long as the capital is physically capable of being operated? Should the latter be the case, the process of contraction in the industry could be very lengthy.

A firm which decides to remain in the industry, when price falls, has to contract output. It therefore has to reduce its purchases of the factors which it gets from other people. This can be done as soon as the contracts of purchase run out. But the firm will be left with a quantity of capital which is appropriate to a larger output than it is now going to produce. If the capital is divisible into separate units, only that number of units appropriate to the new output need be used. But if the capital is indivisible, the firm will only be able to adjust the quantity of it to the lower level of output when the time comes for replacement. In the meantime, that capital is a *fixed* factor.

The convergence of price to the equilibrium level must now be reconsidered with the above features of the contraction process in mind. Start once again, in Fig. 14.1, with the price at OF. The excess supply KL causes the firms to reduce price—say initially to OU. But suppose that, because of existing contracts with factors, the rate of production cannot be reduced quickly, i.e. it remains at OJ. The continuing excess supply may now force further reductions in price *within* the period of time during which output remains at OJ. Indeed, the speed with which the price is adjusted downwards may be great enough to eliminate any excess of quantity produced over quantity demanded *before* the industry has time to reduce output below OJ.[1] In that case, the price will fall to OD, where at the point R on the D curve, the quantity demanded is the same as the current rate of production OJ. The price has fallen to OD because the firms have adjusted price *more quickly* than they have been able to adjust output.

This statement indicates a difference between the present account of the convergence process and that given in the previous chapter. Both have the same starting point, viz. that price will fall when there is excess supply, as at price OF in Fig. 14.1. But the account in the last chapter then assumes that output adjusts to the lower price *before* another reduction in price occurs (e.g. when price falls to OU, output adjusts to UW). The present account, on the other hand, assumes that output cannot be quickly adjusted as price falls, and that in the meantime the price will fall to the extent necessary to eliminate any excess of quantity produced over quantity demanded (viz. to OD). It is now necessary to analyse how *output* will adjust in this situation.

OUTPUT ADJUSTMENTS

How output will change, as a result of price being adjusted down to OD in Fig. 14.1, is best explained by going back to the behaviour of the individual firms, from which the industry S curve is derived. The revenue

---

[1] This would, in fact, happen if the output was sold by auction.

and cost conditions of a single firm are shown in Fig. 14.2. To keep the diagram as uncluttered as possible only those parts of the cost curves which are relevant to the analysis have been drawn.

The capital equipment (or 'plant') used by the firm is supposed to be available only in indivisible units of larger and larger size. An ATC

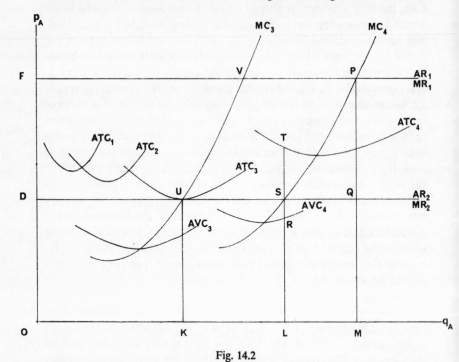

Fig. 14.2

curve can be drawn for production with each size of plant. The complete ATC curve is made up from ranges of the curves for the different sizes of plant. This has already been explained by means of Fig. 10.6.[1]

The ATC curves for four sizes of plant are shown in Fig. 14.2. The lowest point on ATC_3 is below those on ATC_1, ATC_2, and ATC_4. This is because of the special form of indivisibility inherent in management, which gives increasing returns to all the other factors up to plant size number 3, and diminishing returns in relation to larger plants. The AVC[2] and MC curves have been drawn only for plant sizes 3 and 4.

---

[1] On p. 109 above.
[2] As already explained by means of Fig. 10.5 on p. 107 above.

The AR_1 (and the coincident MR_1) curve gives the revenue condition of the firm when p_A is OF. At that price, the firm will produce with plant size number 4, because it can earn the largest profit at output OM, where MR_1 cuts MC_4 at point P. (It would, e.g. earn a smaller profit by producing with plant size number 3, at point V where MR_1 cuts MC_3.) The output OM is this firm's contribution to the output OJ, in Fig. 14.1, which the industry will supply at price OF.

When, as a result of the excess supply shown in Fig. 14.1, the market adjusts p_A down to OD, the revenue condition of the firm becomes that given by the AR_2 (and MR_2) curve in Fig. 14.2. Hence at output OM—which the firm cannot change immediately—MC (at point P on MC_4) exceeds MR (at point Q on MR_2). The firm will therefore want to reduce output as soon as possible. But as long as it operates with plant size number 4, it can do that only by reducing the inputs of factors other than capital. That is, until such time as it might be worthwhile to replace the existing plant with another one, it must—if it stays in business—operate with the cost condition of plant size number 4.

MC_4 and MR_2 intersect at point S. Hence, OL is now the firm's most profitable output. It will contract to that output as soon as it can reduce the inputs of the variable factors. At output OL, price is LS, the AVC per unit of output is LR, and the ATC_4 curve indicates that the AFC ($= ATC - AVC$) is RT per unit of output.

The fixed factor in question is the firm's capital equipment. The fixed cost of the firm is the *cost of finance* for this capital. But the capital has already been acquired, and the financing of it is a matter of past history. As was explained in Chapter 11,[1] the cost of finance is the *expected* rate of return from the capital purchased with the finance, which is just sufficient to induce people to provide it. Investment in capital depends on what people *expect* to earn on it. What they do *in fact* earn is another matter. The AFC of RT in Fig. 14.2 measures the *expected* return per unit of output on plant size number 4, which was a sufficient inducement *at the time* to bring about the investment in it. The excess of price over AVC per unit of output, i.e. RS, measures the *actual* return per unit of output which will be earned on the plant in the existing revenue and variable cost conditions.

It is those conditions which determine what the *already existing* capital will earn. In that situation, the only relevance of the AFC is to indicate whether or not the expectations of investors are being realized. At the price OD in Fig. 14.2, those expectations are being disappointed. The *actual* return on plant number 4 (as given by RS) is below the

[1] On pp. 115–116 above.

expected return (as given by RT). But the present rate of return is the best that can be got, since given MR_2 and MC_4, OL is the most profitable output.

With its plant already in existence, the problem facing the firm is whether to continue operating it or to dispose of it. The sum of money for which it can be sold will itself bring a rate of return (e.g. by being lent out at a rate of interest) to the people who financed the capital.[1] If that return is greater than the one now expected, given the current situation, to be got from continuing to operate the plant, the firm will sell up and go out of business. But since in the circumstances the plant is unlikely to fetch more than its scrap value, the return on the sum realized by its sale will be relatively small. Hence the firm will most likely continue to operate the existing plant as long as it can expect *some* return from it.

It can now be deduced from Fig. 14.2 what the different firms in the industry will do when the market price is reduced from OF to OD. The firm, whose cost condition is shown in the diagram, will stay in business, and as soon as it can reduce the inputs of the variable factors, will contract output from OM to OL. At the latter output it can earn some return (as given by RS) on its existing plant. But any firm whose AVC curve (for its existing plant) lies wholly *above* AR_2 will go out of business. There is no output at which it can even cover its variable costs, let alone earn some return on its capital.

For the firms which stay in business there is still the question of what they will do when their existing plants need to be replaced. That decision will depend upon the return which a new plant is *expected* to earn. For investment in it to take place, the expected return must be sufficient to induce people to put up the finance. In this situation the firms are free to decide whether or not to invest, i.e. the quantity of capital is now variable. Hence the ATC curve, which includes the cost of finance, and not the AVC curve, is the one which has to be compared with the AR curve to see if there is an output which it would be profitable to produce with a new plant.

The firm depicted in Fig. 14.2 would not, at price OD, replace plant size number 4 with an identical one. At the most profitable output (OL) with this plant, the ATC at point T exceeds the AR at S. The expected return on the plant would, therefore, be insufficient to call forth the finance for it. But plant size number 3 would just be worthwhile. At the most profitable output (OK) with this plant, the AR equals the ATC at

[1] It is this rate of return which is the *current* cost of the capital, since it is all that its owners forego in using it.

point *U*. The expected return would therefore be just sufficient to call forth the required finance.

The substitution of a smaller for a larger plant means that the firm reduces its output (from *OL* to *OK*) when replacement takes place. There will, however, be some firms (viz. at least those which were marginal ones at the price *OF*) which will go out of business rather than replace their plants. These are the ones for which the *ATC* curves, for *all* plant sizes, lie wholly above the *AR* curve.

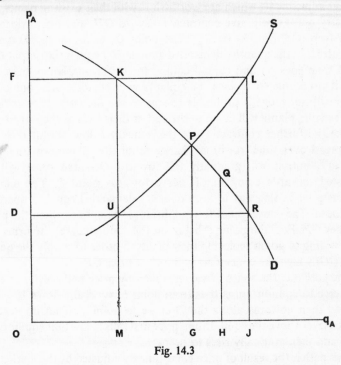

Fig. 14.3

SHORT AND LONG PERIOD ANALYSIS

The convergence over time to equilibrium by a perfectly competitive industry, as analysed above in terms of the behaviour of the individual firms, can now be summed up with the help of Fig. 14.3.[1] The excess supply *KL*, at price *OF*, causes that price to fall. For a period of time the output *OJ* cannot be reduced. Within that period, the price is adjusted down to *OD* at which there is no excess of quantity produced over quantity demanded (at point *R*). As soon as firms can reduce their

[1] Which repeats the essential features of Fig. 14.1.

inputs of variable factors, some of them go out of business (viz. those for which the AVC with the existing plant exceeds price OD at *every* level of output). The remaining firms contract output to the new most profitable levels (at which AVC either equals, or exceeds, price OD). In these two ways the industry output contracts below OJ. As it does so, the price is adjusted upwards by the market to keep quantity demanded equal to quantity produced. The rise in price of course requires further adjustments in the outputs of the firms. When they have made all the output adjustments which are worthwhile with their existing plants, the industry output will have contracted, say, to OH, and price will have risen from OD ($= JR$) to HQ. The point Q, being on the D curve, indicates that the quantity demanded at price HQ equals the output OH.

As time goes on and capital equipment wears out, some firms will find it profitable to replace their plants with smaller ones, but other firms will not judge it profitable to stay in the industry. It is unlikely that existing plants will come to the end of their lives at the same time. Hence the further contraction of the industry below output OH will be spread over time. As firms change to smaller plants, or leave the industry, output will gradually fall towards OG, and price will be adjusted upwards along the D curve towards point P. The market adjusts price in this way to keep quantity demanded equal to quantity produced. The convergence to equilibrium is completed when the price reaches GP. For, the point P being on the supply curve, the firms are now willing to go on replacing their plants in order to supply the quantity (OG) which the consumers will buy at price GP.

The *path* (i.e. the series of values) taken by price and output as they converge to equilibrium is thus from point L, vertically down to point R, and then upwards along the D curve to point P. That is, starting from a level above the equilibrium, price first falls below that equilibrium level and then gradually rises to it.

This path is the result of price being quickly adjusted by the market, to keep quantity demanded equal to quantity produced, while the latter is only slowly adjusted to the price. It is in contrast with the path (analysed at the beginning of this chapter) which price will follow down the S curve from point L to point P, if, after *each* fall in it, the quantity supplied is *fully adjusted* before another change in price occurs. The full adjustment in quantity supplied requires that the capital equipment of the industry is variable, as well as the quantities of the other factors. That is the basis on which the S curve in Fig. 14.3 was originally constructed.[1]

[1] I.e. in the analysis of Chapter 12.

There are three stages in the explanation of the path from L down to R, and up to P, in Fig. 14.3. In the first, the rate of output is fixed (at OJ) for some period of time: that during which none of the inputs of factors can be varied. This length of time is called the *market period*. The analysis assumes that, within this period, the market will adjust the price to equate quantity demanded and quantity produced (viz. from point L down to R).

In the second stage, the capital equipment of the industry is fixed in quantity,[1] but output can be altered by varying the inputs of other factors. This length of time is called the *short period*. It will vary in length from firm to firm and from industry to industry depending (when an industry is contracting) on the age and durability of existing capital. During the short period, the plants of firms are in the process of being adjusted to what is appropriate at the ruling market price. The length of time required for the adjustment to be completed is called the *long period*. In it, the quantities of *all* factors are variable. Since the S curve in Fig. 14.3 is constructed on that basis, it is known as a long period supply curve.

The equilibrium price to which a market may converge is given by the point of intersection between the D curve and the long period S curve (at point P). The market period price (at R) and the short period prices (e.g. at Q) are only *temporary* equilibria. They are the *demand prices* for the outputs in question and are less—when the industry is contracting —than the corresponding (long period) *supply prices* (e.g. for output OJ, the demand price JR is less than the supply price JL). That is why the industry proceeds to reduce output.

The above analysis is easily adapted to explain how price converges to equilibrium from a level below it. Suppose that, in Fig. 14.3, the price is initially OD. The firm in Fig. 14.2 will then have a most profitable output at OK, with plant size number 3. There will be excess demand (in Fig. 14.3) of UR. With output fixed in the market period at OM, price will be adjusted up to OF, in order to eliminate (at point K) the excess of quantity demanded over quantity produced. It is now profitable for existing firms to expand output and for new firms to enter the industry. But in the short period all that can happen is that the existing firms expand by employing more of the variable factors with their fixed capital equipment. Thus, at price OF, the firm in Fig. 14.2 will expand to point V, where MR_1 cuts MC_3. As industry output increases in the short period, price will fall (along the D curve) below OF in Fig. 14.3. It will converge to point P in the long period when existing firms have had

---

[1] Except in respect of those firms which go out of business.

time to enlarge their plants and new firms have been able to enter the industry.

The path which price and output follow is thus from point U, up to K, and then down to D curve to the long period equilibrium at P. The market period price (at K), and the short period prices below it, are all demand prices, and are greater than the corresponding (long period) supply prices (e.g. for output OM, the demand price MK exceeds the supply price MU). That is why the industry proceeds to expand output.

The way in which *output* will converge, during the short period, towards the long period equilibrium is thus explained by these conditions: *output* will *expand* from any level at which the *demand price exceeds the supply price* (e.g. as $MK > MU$ at output OM in Fig. 14.3); and it will *contract* from any level at which the *supply price exceeds the demand price* (e.g. as $JL > JR$ at output OJ). These principles are known as *Marshallian*[1] stability (i.e. convergence) conditions.

Both the Walrasian, and the Marshallian, stability conditions are involved in the explanation of how price and output converge to the long period equilibrium. The former deals with how the market adjusts *price*, at each stage of the convergence process, to equate quantity demanded and quantity produced; the latter deals with how the industry adjusts *output* to equate demand price and supply price. That is, the Walrasian conditions relate to *trading*, while the Marshallian conditions relate to *production*. Thus in Fig. 14.3, with excess supply KL at price OF, the price falls in the market period to OD (the Walrasian stability condition). The industry now proceeds to contract output because supply price exceeds the demand price (the Marshallian stability condition).

THE COBWEB THEOREM

It has been the intention of this chapter, and the previous one, to emphasize that the theory of price and output determination involves much more than discovering that there is a possible equilibrium. It is also necessary to explain how the equilibrium may be reached. Two paths, along which the price and output of a perfectly competitive industry might converge to equilibrium, have now been analysed. But these are not the only possible paths. The importance (and complexity) of this matter makes it worthwhile to consider one more possibility.

The analysis so far is particularly applicable to goods that take a relatively short time to produce, and are coming on to the market

---

[1] After the English economist Alfred Marshall (1842–1924), who developed the time period analysis of output adjustment which underlies these conditions.

continually. In this case, the firms can keep a more or less continual watch on the relation between quantity produced and quantity sold, and can, if necessary, adjust price and output frequently. But where goods take a relatively long time to produce (as with agricultural crops) the firms have to decide their outputs on the basis of what they *expect* the price will be some time ahead. In default of indications to the contrary they may well expect that the current market price will continue unchanged into the period in which their output will be marketed.

To illustrate this situation, suppose that good A takes six months to produce. The size of the output decided upon at the beginning of a six-month period—i.e. the quantity to be supplied at the end of the period—is based on the price expected to be got at the end of the period. The expected price, however, is assumed to be the same as the current price, i.e. as the price ruling in the market at the beginning of the period. Hence quantity supplied at any time depends on what the price was six months *previously*; or what is the same thing, the current price determines the quantity which will be supplied six months *later*.

The S curve in Fig. 14.4 is to be interpreted in that way.[1] The price on the vertical axis is the *current* p_A, but the corresponding quantity supplied on the S curve is that which will be forthcoming six months later. The D curve, however, is of the same nature as before: it shows the current quantity demanded as depending on the current price.

Suppose that, as a result of price OF ruling six months previously, the industry produces the output OU (= FJ, at point J on the S curve). The quantity demanded, at price OF, is FH. This is a disequilibrium situation, since there is excess supply HJ. The problem is to determine the paths which price and output will follow, given the nature of the S curve in this case.

When the output OU is marketed, the price will be adjusted down to UK, where (at point K on the D curve) the quantity demanded equals the quantity produced. That price now becomes the *expected* one, on which the next period's production will be based. The S curve shows that, at price UK (= VL), the industry will produce an output OV during the coming six months. When that output is marketed, however, it will fetch a price, VM, as given by the D curve (at M). The price VM (= WN) will now lead to an output OW in the succeeding period, which will sell at price WP (at P on the D curve). Price and output will continue to fluctuate from period to period in this manner, but, as the diagram shows, they gradually converge to the equilibrium at T.

---

[1] In contrast to the S curves used above, where the current quantity supplied depends on the *current* price.

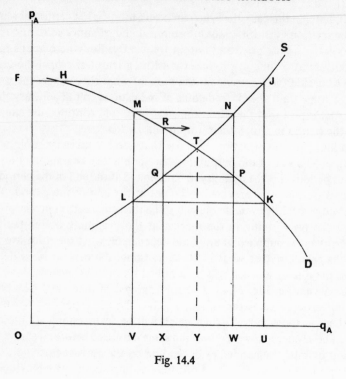

Fig. 14.4

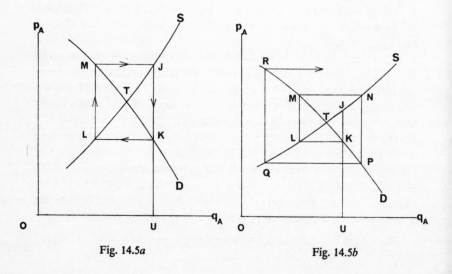

Fig. 14.5a

Fig. 14.5b

Output alternately falls and rises from OU to OV to OW to OX, and so on; but its fluctuations diminish in size as it approaches the equilibrium output OY. Price also alternately rises and falls from UK to VM to WP to XR, and so on; and its fluctuations diminish in size as it approaches the equilibrium price YT. The paths followed by price and output are both a series of *convergent* fluctuations. That will be so whatever the disequilibrium output from which the adjustment process begins. It is obvious from the shape of the diagram why the analysis is referred to as the Cobweb Theorem.

It can be shown that the paths followed by price and output depend on the slopes of the D and S curves. Moreover, these paths may not be convergent ones. The S curves in Figs. 14.5a and 14.5b are constructed on the same basis as that in Fig. 14.4. The slopes of the D and S curves in Fig. 14.5a are such that, starting from the output OU, price and output will alternately fluctuate up and down, between the same two values respectively, without approaching the equilibrium at T (price fluctuates between points K and M on the D curve, and output between J and L on the S curve). The fluctuations are *constant* ones. In Fig. 14.5b, the fluctuations are *divergent* ones. Starting from output OU, the price follows the path given by the points K, M, P, R, etc., on the D curve, and output that given by the points J, L, N, Q, etc., on the S curve. Both price and output move farther away from the equilibrium at T.

This book is mainly concerned with situations in which prices and outputs converge to equilibrium. The analysis of divergent (or unstable) price and output paths requires techniques which go beyond the introductory level. It must however be stressed once again that, as has now been shown, the existence of an equilibrium does not ensure that the market will find it; and that, in any case, the process of convergence (if there is one) is an essential element in the explanation of price and output determination.

That process of convergence usually takes time. The 'long period' required for it may be so long that the D and S curves shift their positions before it is completed. In that case, there will then be a new equilibrium towards which the industry will start to converge. What the new equilibrium will be is the next problem to be analysed.

CHAPTER 15

PRICE AND OUTPUT CHANGES

It is the conditions for convergence to equilibrium (the stability conditions) that enable predictions to be made as to how price and output will change whenever the demand and supply curves shift. The last two chapters have shown how those conditions explain the behaviour of price and output in *disequilibrium* situations. Starting from an equilibrium, a shift in the demand or the supply curve brings about a disequilibrium. The resulting changes in price and output will then depend on the stability conditions which apply to the industry in question.

The present chapter will be confined to what happens *within* a perfectly competitive industry whenever its equilibrium is disturbed. The effects of this on other industries will be analysed in Chapter 22 below.

DEMAND CURVE SHIFTS

Suppose that, in Fig. 15.1, industry A is initially in equilibrium at price OE and output OJ, where the (long period) S curve and the D_1 curve intersect. An *increase* in demand now takes place, e.g. the demand curve shifts up from D_1 to D_2. This could happen for a number of reasons, since the D curve has a number of parameters. A rise in personal disposable incomes, or net worths, will, if A is a superior good, increase the demand for it; so will a rise in the prices of substitute goods and a fall in the prices of complements; and so will a change in consumer preferences in favour of A. For any of these reasons, the consumers will wish to buy a larger q_A at any p_A, as is shown by D_2 in comparison with D_1.

Hence, at the initial equilibrium price OE, q_A demanded increases from EP (on D_1) to ER (on D_2). Since q_A supplied at that price is EP (on the S curve), the market is now in disequilibrium, with an excess demand PR. As soon as the firms become aware that their sales are exceeding production by that amount per period, they will all raise p_A by some amount (as indicated by the Walrasian stability condition). The path now followed by price and output depends on two things: (i) the speed with which the market adjusts p_A upwards by an amount sufficient to eliminate the excess demand, and (ii) the speed with which the firms expand output in response to the higher p_A.

The last two chapters explored a number of possibilities in these respects. Thus the firms may be relatively slow in detecting the excess demand and in raising p_A; but they may be relatively quick in achieving the 'long period' adjustment[1] of output to each new price. In that case,

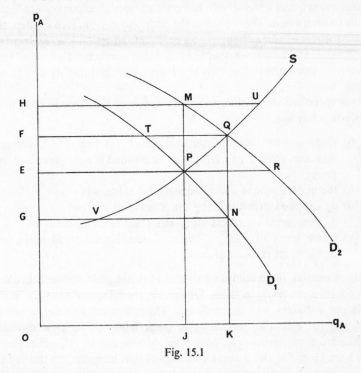

Fig. 15.1

as the firms raise p_A step by step above OE, they are able to adjust output fully at each step. Output therefore expands along the long period S curve from P towards Q. But as p_A rises, the q_A demanded contracts along D_2 from R towards Q. Hence, at each step in the process of raising p_A, the firms find that excess demand has diminished (as indicated by a smaller excess of sales over production per period of time). Finally, at price OF, excess demand is eliminated, and p_A and q_A are once again in equilibrium (at Q).

Thus, under the conditions of perfect competition, an *increase* in demand for a good—for any of the reasons given above—*raises* both its

[1] I.e. by changing the inputs of *all* factors appropriately.

price and its output. Those are the qualitative predictions which follow from the theories of consumer and business firm behaviour developed in earlier chapters.

It is, however, much more important to understand the reasoning by which those conclusions are reached, than it is merely to remember them. When the techniques of economic analysis are used to explain actual events, it is necessary to understand which techniques are applicable to each event. That requires the ability to reason, step by step, the consequences of some change in an economic situation (e.g. an increase in demand) and to test whether the reasoning is in accord with the facts. Merely to know the predictions of theories does not qualify one to use them.

It is therefore worthwhile to repeat concisely the steps in the above analysis. They are:

(i) starting from equilibrium at point P (in Fig. 15.1), demand increases from D_1 to D_2, i.e. q_A demanded is now greater at *any* price;

(ii) the consequential excess demand PR raises p_A;

(iii) q_A supplied expands along the S curve as p_A rises;

(iv) q_A demanded contracts along the D curve as p_A rises;

(v) hence, from (iii) and (iv), excess demand is eliminated, and a new equilibrium reached at point Q.

It is essential, in an analysis like this, to distinguish movements *along* the curves from *shifts* in them. Otherwise, the effects of changes in the different variables will be confused. Thus demand initially *increases* because, for example, incomes rise (shift from D_1 to D_2); quantity demanded then *contracts* as price rises (movement up D_2). No reason has been given for the S curve to shift; all that happens, on the supply side, is that quantity supplied *expands* as price rises (movement up the S curve).

That analysis, however, assumes a particular set of responses by the firms to a disequilibrium situation, viz. that price is adjusted relatively slowly, and output relatively quickly. But other responses are possible. Indeed, the reverse set is much more likely, under perfect competition, in the case of industries which use significant amounts of capital. The long period adjustment of output to a new price will then take some time, and it will be the price changes which occur relatively more quickly. The path from the old to the new equilibrium, in this case, is explained by the Marshallian time period analysis.

When demand increases from D_1 to D_2 (in Fig. 15.1), and excess demand *PR* appears, the market will—as in the above analysis—raise p_A above *OE* (as indicated by the Walrasian stability condition). In the market period,[1] when output is fixed at *OJ*, there may be sufficient time for p_A to be adjusted right up to the level *OH*, at which the excess of quantity demanded over output is eliminated (at point *M*). This elimination of excess demand in the market period is due entirely to the contraction in quantity demanded as p_A rises (viz. the movement from *R* to *M* on D_2).

The 'market period' price *OH* is above the long period supply price *OE* of the output *OJ* (at point *P* on the *S* curve). Hence the industry will find it profitable to expand output (as indicated by the Marshallian stability condition). At the price *OH*, existing firms are producing outputs for which $MR > MC$, and they will therefore expand production; moreover, some extramarginal firms could now produce profitability.[2]

During the short period, output is first expanded above *OJ* (but not up to *OK*), by the use of more of the variable factors in conjunction with the existing capital equipment. This expansion leads to excess supply at price *OH*. Hence—by Walrasian stability condition—the market adjusts price downwards (but not as far as *OF*) to keep quantity demanded equal to output. Output then rises further in the short period, as firm after firm installs new plant, and as new firms enter the industry. As this happens, price follows a path down D_2. When the industry has completed the adjustment of its capital stock, the price will have reached the new long period equilibrium level *OF*.

The new equilibrium is the same as in the initial analysis of this problem, but the path to it followed by the price is different. Instead of rising gradually along the *S* curve (from *P* to *Q*), the price first of all rises to *OH* (at point *M*), and then falls along D_2 to the equilibrium at *Q*.

If, however, good *A* takes a lengthy period of time to produce, the disturbance of equilibrium by an increase in demand may lead to fluctuations in price and output (in accordance with the Cobweb Theorem). Thus, when demand increases from D_1 to D_2 in Fig. 15.1, the output *OJ*—whose size was determined some time previously—will fetch a price *OH* (at point *M* on D_2). That price will lead the industry to *start* production at a new level, as given by point *U* on the *S* curve. But this output will not come on to the market until some time in the future. When it does, it will sell for the price given by the point on D_2

[1] In which *none* of the inputs of factors can be varied.
[2] As was explained on pp. 155–156 above.

vertically below U. This is the start of a series of fluctuations in price and output like those already analysed.[1] Whether or not the path of these fluctuations will be one of convergence to the new equilibrium (at Q) depends on the slopes of the D_2 and S curves.

It is thus the *time* required for price and output changes to take place that especially complicates the analysis of those changes. This is why an explanation cast *entirely* in terms of a comparison of long period equilibria[2]—without reference to the stability conditions—may not only be misleading, but also wrong. It is misleading to say that (in Fig. 15.1) an increase in demand from D_1 to D_2 raises price from OE to OF, and output from OJ to OK. It may do so eventually—in the long period. But the long period may be exceedingly long. In the short period, the price will lie above OF; and that period may not be particularly 'short' in terms of actual time.

An analysis in terms of a comparison of long period equilibria may be wrong in two respects. First, when equilibrium is disturbed, price and output may fluctuate without converging to a new equilibrium (e.g. as shown by the Cobweb Theorem). Second, although the conditions for convergence exist, the new equilibrium may never be reached, because *further* shifts in the D and/or S curves occur while the industry is moving towards it. In that case, the actual paths followed by price and output through time will be made up of a series of short period (or *temporary*) equilibria. It might, of course, be argued that an industry is always 'tending' towards the (current) long period equilibrium. But without a knowledge of the stability conditions, the statement that there is such a tendency amounts to no more than saying that there *is* an equilibrium. Whether or not the industry is moving towards it—and if so along what path—depends on the nature of the stability conditions. As Alfred Marshall put it: 'The fact that the general conditions of life are not stationary is the source of many of the difficulties that are met with in applying economic doctrines to practical problems.'[3]

The corresponding analyses for a decrease in demand can now be briefly given. Suppose that in Fig. 15.1 the initial equilibrium is at point Q, where the D_2 and S curves intersect. A decrease in demand to D_1 will cause price and output to change along one of a variety of paths. There is now excess supply TQ at price OF. If price reacts relatively slowly, and output relatively quickly to this disequilibrium, the industry will converge to the new equilibrium along the path from Q to P on

[1] On pp. 156–159 above.
[2] I.e. the points of intersection between D and (long period) S curves.
[3] *Principles of Economics*, 8th ed., 1920, p. 347.

the S curve. As price falls, output contracts down the S curve, and quantity demanded expands down the D_1 curve (from T to P). The excess supply is thereby eliminated.

But if price reacts more quickly to the disequilibrium than does output, the price will fall in the market period to OG (at point N). This new price is below the long period supply price OF of the output OK. Hence (in accordance with the Marshallian stability condition) the industry will set about contracting. As it does so, the price will gradually rise over the short period along D_1 towards OE (at P). But if the capital equipment of the industry is very durable, it will take a long time for it (and the level of output) to be adjusted to the long period equilibrium. During that time, the industry will be a 'depressed' one, in the sense that the *actual* earnings on capital will be less than normal profits.[1]

A decrease in demand can lead to fluctuations in price and output when the good in question takes some time to produce. In accordance with the Cobweb Theorem, the decrease in demand from D_1 to D_2 (in Fig. 15.1) will lower the price of the output OK to OG (at point N). This price will cause the industry to start production at a new level, as given by point V on the S curve. But that output, when it comes on the market, will sell for the price given by the point on D_1 vertically above V. This is the start of a set of fluctuations in price and output whose path depends on the slopes of the D_1 and S curves.

SUPPLY CURVE SHIFTS

The supply curve of a perfectly competitive industry will shift whenever factor prices, or physical productivities (i.e. production functions), change. The principles involved in analysing the consequences of such shifts are the same as those for demand curve shifts. The analysis will therefore concentrate on the differences in detail.

Starting from an initial equilibrium at the intersection of the D and S_1 curves in Fig. 15.2, suppose that there is an increase in supply to S_2, due to a fall in factor prices. The path now followed by price and output depends on the relative speeds with which they are adjusted in this disequilibrium situation. The fall in factor prices has shifted the cost curves of all firms downwards. Each firm now expects it to be profitable to supply a larger output at any price; this is what—in aggregate for the industry—S_2 shows in comparison with S_1. If existing firms (and the new ones that now find it profitable to enter the industry) can adjust

[1] As was explained on pp. 151–152 above.

outputs quickly, in response to the decrease in costs, the industry output
at price OE will increase from OJ (at P on S_1) to OL (at R on S_2).

However, when the output OL is marketed, the firms will discover that
there is now excess supply (PR) at price OE. As price is adjusted downwards (in accordance with the Walrasian stability condition), quantity
supplied *contracts* along S_2 (from R towards Q), and quantity demanded

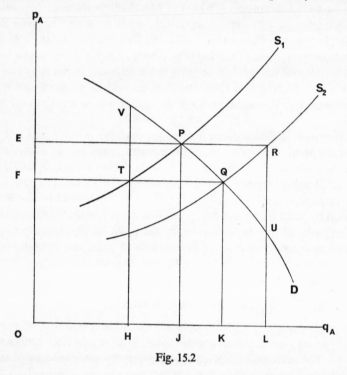

Fig. 15.2

expands along the D curve (from P towards Q). The excess supply is
eliminated when price falls to OF. The path followed by the industry to
the new equilibrium is thus from point P to R, and then down S_2 to Q.
That is, while the price falls gradually (from OE to OF), the output first
increases beyond the new equilibrium (viz. to OL), and then contracts
back to it.

New capital equipment—which takes time to produce—will be required by both existing and new firms. It is more likely, therefore, that
the initial response to a fall in factor prices will be increased use of the
variable factors in conjunction with existing plants. Output will not
therefore increase all the way to OL (as indicated by point R on the long

period supply curve), but by some smaller amount. If the market now adjusts price relatively quickly, so as to keep the quantity demanded equal to the increased output, the price will fall along the D curve. As more and more new plant is installed in the short period, output will expand, and price will fall still further along the D curve towards the long period equilibrium at Q. Thus, the industry follows a different path between equilibria whenever price is adjusted relatively more quickly than output.

If the conditions underlying the Cobweb Theorem are present, the increase in supply will cause fluctuations in price and output. The decrease in costs will increase output from OJ (at P) to OL (at R). When the new output is marketed, it will sell at a price LU (at U on the D curve); and so on, along a path determined by the slopes of the D and S_2 curves.

The corresponding analyses for a decrease in supply (from S_2 to S_1), due to a rise in factor prices, involve no new points. The resulting paths which may be followed by price and output need only be summarized. If output adjusts relatively more quickly than price, it will fall initially to OH (at T on S_1). The excess demand TQ then raises price. Hence the quantity supplied expands from T towards P on S_1 and the quantity demanded contracts from Q towards P on the D curve. The path followed by price and output is from point Q to T, and then up S_1 to P. But if price adjusts relatively more quickly than output, the path will be from Q to P along the D curve. Output will be contracted only gradually during the short period (as capital wears out) from OK to OJ. If the Cobweb Theorem is applicable, the fluctuations in price and output will follow the path from point Q to T to V, and so on.

An improvement in technology shifts the cost curves of all firms downwards. The resulting *increase* in the industry supply curve will have the same effects on price and output as a fall in factor prices. However, the speed with which those effects operate depends upon the form that the improvement takes. Sometimes an increase in technical knowledge allows the productivity of *existing* resources to be raised. This will happen through labour and machines being used in new ways, or in new combinations. It is often the outcome of past experience in using the resources, i.e. it is an example of 'learning by doing'. Since the decrease in costs brought about by this kind of technical improvement can be quickly achieved, there will be correspondingly rapid effects on output and price.

On the other hand, many advances in technology require the installation of new types of machinery, and may also require new forms of labour skill. The technical improvement has to be 'embodied' in new resources. A considerable time may be needed to produce the new resources and also for it to be worthwhile for firms to replace their existing resources with them. In that case, the effects on output and price will be spread over a lengthy period of time.

THE RELEVANCE OF ELASTICITIES

A shift in the demand or the supply curve usually, but not always, affects *both* price and output. Given the size of the shift, the magnitudes of the effects depend on the price elasticities of demand and supply.

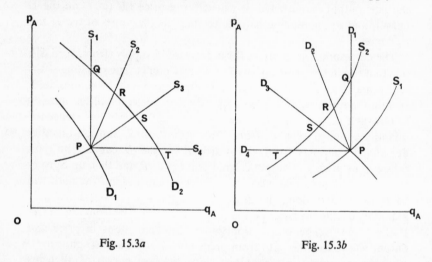

Fig. 15.3a   Fig. 15.3b

Starting from an equilibrium at point P in Fig. 15.3a, suppose that demand increases from D_1 to D_2. Four alternative supply curves have been drawn, all radiating from the point P. The price elasticity of supply (ε_S)—as measured for a rise in price from that point—is in increasing order of magnitude from that on S_1 up to that on S_4.[1] It is zero on the vertical straight line S_1, and infinity on the horizontal straight line S_4. A comparison between the alternative new equilibrium points Q, R, S, and T shows that an increase in demand has a greater effect on output, and a smaller effect on price, the larger is ε_S. This is because ε_S

---

[1] The $\varepsilon_S = \dfrac{\Delta q_A}{q_A} \Big/ \dfrac{\Delta p_A}{p_A} = \dfrac{\Delta q_A}{\Delta p_A} \cdot \dfrac{p_A}{q_A}$. The term $\dfrac{p_A}{q_A}$ is the same on all four curves at point P; $\dfrac{\Delta q_A}{\Delta p_A}$ is largest ($= \infty$) on S_4, and smallest ($= 0$) on S_1.

measures the extent of the proportional expansion in quantity supplied due to a given proportional rise in price. When $\varepsilon_S = 0$ (as in the market period), the increase in demand raises price without affecting output. When $\varepsilon_S = \infty$, output expands without any change in price. In the short period, as compared with long period, price rises more and output less because ε_S is smaller during the former (e.g. on S_2 as compared with S_3). A similar diagram can be used to show that for a decrease in demand, output contracts more, and price falls less, the greater is ε_S.

The corresponding construction in Fig. 15.3b shows that a decrease in supply (from S_1 to S_2) contracts output more, and raises price less, the greater is the price elasticity of demand (ε_D). This is smallest ($= 0$) on D_1, and largest ($= \infty$) on D_4. In the former case, the decrease in supply raises price without affecting output, and in the latter case, it contracts output without changing price. A similar diagram can be used to show that, for an increase in supply, output expands more, and price falls less, the greater is ε_D.

OUTLAY TAXES AND SUBSIDIES

The techniques of demand and supply analysis can now be used to explain the effects on prices and outputs of the levying of outlay taxes, and the granting of outlay subsidies.

Outlay taxes are those levied on the purchase and sale of goods. They take one or other of two forms: (i) a specific amount per unit of a good (e.g. 1s per unit)—called a *specific* tax; or (ii) a given percentage of the price of a good—called an *ad valorem* tax. An outlay tax can be collected either from the seller, or from the buyer, of the good. The former is the more usual, since, there being normally fewer sellers than buyers, it is the less costly method of collection.

In that case, the price at which an industry will offer any output to the market will include the amount of tax levied on each unit of that output. It is therefore necessary to distinguish two supply prices for each output: that *excluding* the tax, and that *including* it. In Fig. 15.4, the (long period) supply curve S_1 shows the supply prices, *exclusive* of any tax, at which a perfectly competitive industry is willing to produce the corresponding outputs. The curve S_2 gives the supply prices *inclusive* of any tax. The vertical distances (e.g. QT) between the two curves therefore measure the amount of tax per unit of output at each level of output. The diagram illustrates the imposition of a *specific* tax, since S_1 and S_2 are parallel, i.e. the vertical distances between them are the same, because the amount of tax per unit of output is the same at a higher price as at a lower one. In the case of an *ad valorem* tax, the two curves will diverge from each other as they rise to the right, i.e. the vertical distances between them increase, because the amount of tax per unit of output is greater at a higher price than at a lower one.[1]

Suppose that, initially, there is no tax on the good. Equilibrium is then

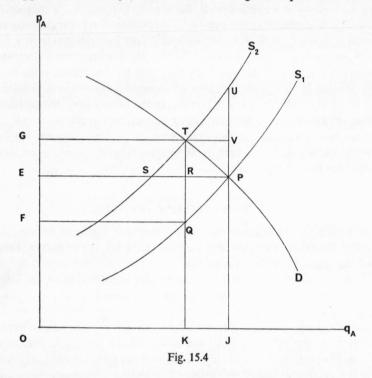

Fig. 15.4

at the intersection (P) of the D and S_1 curves. The imposition of a tax means a *decrease* in supply, because S_2 rather than S_1 now shows the terms on which the good is supplied to the market. The industry requires a higher supply price, inclusive of tax, for *any* output (e.g. OG as against OF for output OK). There is now excess demand SP at price OE, and this disequilibrium causes price and output to change along one of the paths already analysed in this chapter. It is unnecessary, for the

---

[1] If the tax is collected from the buyers of a good, it is necessary to distinguish two demand prices for each output; that excluding the tax, and that including it. The D curve in Fig. 15.4 would then show demand prices *inclusive* of the tax; and a new curve, lying below it to the left, would be required to show demand prices *exclusive* of the tax. The vertical distances between them would measure the amount of tax per unit of output at each level of output.

present purpose, to repeat that analysis, and it will be assumed that there is convergence to the new (long period) equilibrium at T.

The imposition of the tax, therefore, has these long period effects: (a) output is reduced from OJ to OK; (b) the price *inclusive* of the tax is raised from OE to OG; and (c) the price *exclusive* of the tax is lowered from OE to OF (at point Q on S_1). The difference between OG and OF (viz. $FG = QT$) is the amount of the tax per unit of output; and the total tax revenue is the rectangle $FQTG$.

The price *paid* by the consumers (i.e. the one inclusive of the tax) rises by $EG (= RT)$. The price *received* by the firms (i.e. the one exclusive of the tax) falls by $FE (= QR)$. The sum of those two changes is the tax per unit (QT). Thus (in Fig. 15.4), the consumers and the firms share what is called the *incidence* of the tax. That is, the tax in part raises the price paid by the consumer, and in part lowers the price received by the firms.

The proportion in which the incidence is shared depends on the price elasticities of *both* demand and supply. The relevance of the demand elasticity can be seen from Fig. 15.3b. The smaller is the ε_D, the greater is the rise in the price paid by the consumers as a result of a decrease in supply, and therefore the more the incidence of a tax falls on them. If $\varepsilon_D = 0$ (as on D_1), the price rises by the full amount of the tax, and the consumers bear the whole incidence. If $\varepsilon_D = \infty$ (as on D_4), the price to the consumer does not change; and the price received by the firms therefore falls by the full amount of the tax, and they bear the whole incidence.

It is rather more complicated to show in general the relevance of the supply elasticity. Two extreme cases should, however, indicate the principle involved. In Fig. 15.5a, $\varepsilon_S = \infty$. When S_1 shifts to S_2, as a result of the specific tax (QT), the price paid by the consumers rises by the full amount of the tax.

In Fig. 15.5b, $\varepsilon_S = 0$. The S curve being vertical, the imposition of the tax cannot be shown by a shift in it. However, the equivalent device of a decrease in the D curve can be used.[1] When D_1 shifts to D_2, as a result of the specific tax (of QP), the price *paid* (i.e. inclusive of tax) by the consumers (OE) is unchanged; and the price *received* (i.e. exclusive of tax) by the firms (OF) is lower by the full amount of the tax. In general, the smaller is the ε_S, the greater is the reduction in the price received by firms, and the more the incidence of the tax falls on them.

When an outlay subsidy[2] is granted to an industry, it is again necessary

---

[1] As explained in the footnote on p. 170 above.
[2] Either specific, or *ad valoerm*, in the same sense as with a tax.

to distinguish two supply prices for each output: that *excluding* any allowance for the subsidy, and that *including* an allowance for it. Fig. 15.4 can be used again for the analysis in this respect.[1] The S_2 curve shows the supply prices, *before* any allowance is made for the subsidy, at which the corresponding outputs will be produced. S_1 gives the supply prices *after* the subsidy has been allowed for. The vertical distance

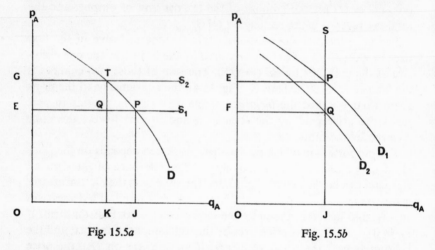

Fig. 15.5a   Fig. 15.5b

(e.g. *PU*), between the two curves, measures the amount of the specific subsidy per unit of output.

The granting of the subsidy alters the equilibrium from *T* to *P*, and therefore has these long period effects: (*a*) output expands from *OK* to *OJ*; (*b*) the price *paid* by the consumers falls from *JV* to *JP*; this indicates their benefit from the subsidy; and (*c*) the price *received* (including the subsidy) by the firms rises from *JV* to *JU*; this indicates their benefit from the subsidy. The proportion in which the benefit from the subsidy is shared depends on the price elasticities of both demand and supply. By the same reasoning as that used above in respect of a tax, the smaller the ε_D, and the greater the ε_S, the larger the share of the benefit which goes to the consumers, i.e. the more the price paid by them will fall. And vice versa in relation to the firms.

PRICE SUPPORT POLICIES

Governments sometimes support the prices, received by firms for their goods, at levels above the market equilibria. The intention is usually

[1] Thus indicating that a subsidy can be treated analytically as a *negative tax*.

that of enabling firms to earn larger revenues than they would otherwise do, thereby allowing their owners to enjoy larger incomes. There are three different ways of pursuing this policy.

(1) In the first, the government guarantees a price to the producers of a good, by committing itself to buy any of the output which is not bought at that price by the consumers. Thus, suppose that in terms of Fig. 15.6 a government decides to support the price received by the

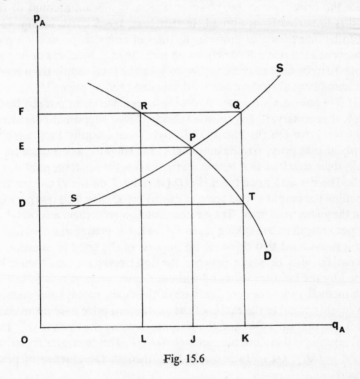

Fig. 15.6

firms in industry A at the level OF, i.e. it guarantees the firms a price OF for whatever quantity they produce. Without state intervention, the market price (in equilibrium) would be OE, and the output OJ. When the firms are assured of getting the price OF, they will produce OK ($= FQ$, at point Q on the S curve). If they now sell to consumers at the guaranteed price, their sales will only amount to FR (at point R on the D curve). There is excess supply (of RQ), since the price OF is above the equilibrium level. But by itself purchasing the excess supply the government prevents the price from falling below OF. The government may now find some use for the output it buys, e.g. as a form of aid to particular groups of people (at home or abroad) or as a stockpile—if the good is durable—for use in the future.

(2) If the government does not wish to purchase the excess supply it can still support the price by taking administrative measures to curtail the quantity supplied. Thus it may by law prevent the firms within the country from producing more than FR at the price OF. This quantitative control on output eliminates the excess supply that would otherwise lower the price. It may be, however, that a significant amount of the good is imported from abroad. In that case, the S curve in Fig. 15.6 has to be interpreted as showing the total of domestic production plus imports at each price. Restrictions on imports (e.g. by tariffs or import quotas) can be used in this situation to keep the total supply from home and abroad equal to the quantity demanded (FR) at price OF.

(3) The government can guarantee the firms a particular price by being ready, if necessary, to pay them a subsidy. Thus, suppose it guarantees them the price OF (in Fig. 15.6) for whatever quantity they want to supply at that price, viz. the output OK. But suppose, at the same time, it tells them to sell *all* that output on the market for whatever price it will fetch. The demand price for it is OD (at point T on the D curve). But by selling the output at this price, the firms get $DF (= TQ)$ *less* per unit than the guaranteed price. The government now pays them a subsidy[1] of TQ per unit, thereby making up the price it has guaranteed them.

If it is assumed that there are no imports of the good in question, a comparison can be made between the total revenues that would be earned by the industry with and without a price support policy. Under both method 1 (government purchase of the excess supply) and method 3 (a subsidy equal to the excess of the guaranteed price over the market price), the output is OK, and the price received by the firms is OF. The total revenue is therefore the rectangle $OKQF$. This is greater than that ($OJPE = OJ \times OE$) which would be earned in the absence of price support.

Under method 2 (quantitative restriction of output) the output is OL (at point R). Whether the total revenue ($OLRF$) from this output is greater or less than that ($OJPE$), which would be earned in the absence of price support, depends on the price elasticity of demand (ε_D) over the range RP of the D curve.[2] If that $\varepsilon_D > 1$, then $OJPE > OLRF$; but if $\varepsilon_D < 1$, $OJPE < OLRF$. Thus, a quantitative restriction on the output of an industry, over a range in which $\varepsilon_D < 1$, will *increase* its total revenue.

---

[1] Known, in the UK, as a deficiency payment.
[2] As was explained on p. 86 above.

There are many governments which today have price support policies for agricultural products. They have been adopted for a variety of reasons; and their merits and de-merits can be argued on a variety of grounds. The above analysis provides the basis for understanding their nature. Thus, speaking broadly for the present time (1968): the US government supports the market prices of agricultural products by a commitment to purchase any excess supplies at those prices, but supplements this policy by some quantitative controls on outputs; the European Economic Community (the 'Common Market') supports the market prices by restricting imports (by means of variable import duties) to levels which, together with domestic outputs, will equal the corresponding quantities demanded at the support prices; and the UK government pays subsidies (deficiency payments) to farmers which give them higher prices than those at which their products sell on the market. That is why the market prices of food are now lower in the UK than in the other countries mentioned.

In some circumstances (especially wartime) governments attempt—by legally imposed price controls—to hold market prices below their equilibrium levels. This means that there are excess demands at the controlled prices (just as in Fig. 15.6 there is excess demand of ST at price OD). Consumers are unable to buy as much as they wish to at the prices in question. A variety of consequences may follow. The price controls may be evaded and the goods sold at higher ('black market') prices. The goods may be supplied on a 'first come, first served' basis, which leads to queueing by the customers. The firms may operate an informal rationing scheme of their own. Or the government may institute an official rationing system to work in conjunction with the price control.

CHAPTER 16

IMPERFECT COMPETITION: I

The conditions under which firms compete with one another are called the *market situation*. The analysis of the preceding chapters was restricted to perfect competition because that market situation is the easiest framework in which to study the determination of prices and outputs. The basis has thus been provided for the study of more complex market situations, and of the ways in which they affect prices and outputs.

Firms compete with one another for customers by means of the prices they charge for their products. The effectiveness of that competition depends on the willingness of consumers to substitute one product for another as a result of price changes.

Most goods are substitutes for one another to a greater or lesser extent. Some may be *perfect* substitutes: the consumers regard them as being identical in all respects. Others may be *close* substitutes: while they are not identical, they have sufficient similarities for consumers to think of them as alternative ways of satisfying some want. Different brands of toothpaste are close substitutes in this sense. They perform the same function, but people differentiate between them on a variety of grounds, e.g. on their supposed teeth-cleaning powers, their tastes, their names, their forms of packaging, and the ways in which they are advertised.

But goods may be substitutes even though they do not perform the same function. Because of the scarcity of resources, consumers cannot satisfy all their wants. They have therefore to consider whether it would be worthwhile to have more of one kind of good (e.g. foodstuffs) and less of another (e.g. clothing). It is in this respect that most goods are at least *distant* substitutes for one another.

An indication of the degree of substitutability between any two goods can be obtained from a 'cross price elasticity of demand'. This is the ratio of the proportional change in the quantity demanded of *one* good to a given proportional change in the price of the *other*.[1] If the price of a good falls, the quantity demanded of a substitute for it will decrease.[2]

[1] See p. 82 above.
[2] Assuming that the income effects of price changes are negligibly small.

The extent of the decrease, as given by the cross price elasticity, indicates how close or distant the goods are as substitutes. This elasticity is infinity for perfect substitutes: a small fall in the price of one will reduce the quantities demanded of the others to zero.

The cross price elasticity is less than infinity for close substitutes: a small fall in the price of one will reduce the quantities demanded of the others to some extent, but *not* to zero. Thus, if the price of one brand of toothpaste falls, this will take some customers away from the other brands. But those people who are strongly attracted by the distinctive features of the latter will not switch their purchases because of the small change in relative prices. In general, the more sharply consumers differentiate between the various brands, the less switching of purchases between them there will be as a result of price changes, i.e. the smaller will be the cross price elasticities of demand.

The distinction between *close* and *distant* substitutes is a matter of degree. Motoring and gardening are substitute ways of getting satisfaction. But the cross price elasticity between motor cars and garden implements is very small as compared with that between rival makes of cars. That is why cars and gardens are regarded as distant substitutes, and rival makes of cars as close substitutes. This distinction, however, involves the problem—which will be considered presently—of drawing the line between what are 'small' and what are 'large' cross price elasticities. What one finds, in fact, is a whole spectrum of degrees of substitutability between goods—ranging from the infinite cross price elasticities of perfect substitutes to those of very distant substitutes, which are little more than zero.

It can now be appreciated that the effectiveness of competition between firms depends on the sizes of the cross price elasticities of demand between their products. The larger these are, the more the sales of one product will expand when its price falls relatively to those of other products.

But the nature of competition also depends on how each firm *reacts* whenever other firms change their prices. If one firm lowers its price, the sales of firms producing substitutes will be reduced. They may then react—in order to maximize profits in the new situtation—by lowering their own prices. Whether or not this happens will depend on the magnitudes of their losses of sales.

The size of the sales loss for each firm will vary with the total number of the competing firms. If there are only a few of them, each will lose a significant amount of sales to the price-cutting firm. In this case, the latter will realize that it is likely to call forth reactions from its competitors. But if there is a large number of competing firms, the sales loss will be spread so thinly over them that each one is not affected significantly. In that case a firm will be able to assume that a price change by it will not call forth reactions from its competitors. The number of competing firms must, therefore, be taken into account in characterizing a market situation. That number will depend on the ease or difficulty with which new firms can enter the market.

Hence, in order to specify the nature and effectiveness of competition, a market situation has to be defined, on the supply side,[1] in terms of *three* conditions: (i) the degrees of substitutability between the products of the firms in it, (ii) the number of those firms, and (iii) the condition (i.e. ease or difficulty) of entry to it. It will be recalled that perfect competition was defined[2] as the situation in which there is a large number of firms, all producing perfect substitutes, and in which there are no obstacles to the entry of new firms to the market.

When one or more of the conditions of perfect competition is not fulfilled, there is a state of imperfect competition. It will be sufficient, at an introductory level, to distinguish three forms of imperfect competition, viz. monopolistic competition, monopoly, and oligopoly.

Monopolistic competition exists when there is a large number of firms all producing close (but not perfect) substitute products, and when there are no obstacles to the production of further close substitutes by new firms.

A firm has a *monopoly* when no close substitutes for its product are being produced and there are obstacles which prevent this from happening.

Oligopoly exists when there are only a few firms producing either perfect, or close, substitute products, and there are obstacles which prevent their number from becoming large.[3]

The definitions of these three situations all depend on the meaning given to the term *close* substitute. Monopolistic competition exists when there are many close substitutes, oligopoly when there are only a few, and monopoly when there is none. To distinguish the situations, it is therefore necessary to demarcate close from distant substitutes. The problem is that these shade gradually into one another. Consequently, the concept of an 'industry' loses definiteness under imperfect competition.

---

[1] The conditions on the demand side have also to be specified. It will continue to be assumed here that there is a large number of independent buyers, each of whom has knowledge of the prices at which all firms are offering their products.

[2] See p. 89 above.

[3] Perfect and imperfect oligopoly are distinguished according as the products are perfect or only close substitutes respectively.

The division of an economy into separate industries is a device for breaking down the study of prices into stages. In the first stage, the effects on prices of competition *within* each industry are analysed, on the assumption of a given state of affairs in the rest of the economy. This means that the effects on other industries of changes within the industry in question are ignored. In the second stage, the effects on prices of competition *between* industries are analysed. This, of course, is necessary—whatever the state of competition within the various industries—since all prices are mutually interdependent.

The analysis of perfect competition in earlier chapters did not progress beyond the first stage: the effects outside an industry of changes within it were ignored. The nature of this procedure is quite precise in that the boundary of an industry is clear-cut under perfect competition, viz. it is the line between the identical products within it and the different products outside it.

The same kind of procedure will be adopted in the following analyses of industries under monopolistic competition, monopoly, and oligopoly. But, insofar as there is no clear-cut line of division between close and distant substitutes, economists must make a judgment as to where the line should be drawn. That is, they have to decide in each particular case which competitive effects between products are to be ignored in the first stage of explaining prices.

Thus the drawing of boundary lines around industries is not meant to deny the obvious fact that they compete with one another for shares in the expenditures of consumers. Rather, it is a means of distinguishing the effects on prices of the stronger competition between close substitutes from those of the weaker competition between distant substitutes. The former effects will now be analysed; the latter will be considered in Chapter 22 below.

MONOPOLY AND MONOPOLISTIC COMPETITION

The market situation specifies the nature of competition between firms within an industry. It therefore indicates how the sales of each firm depend on the price of its product relative to the prices charged by the other firms. That is, the form of the *demand curve* for each firm is dependent on the kind of market situation in which it operates.

Under monopolistic competition, the individual firm can, by reducing its price, attract to itself some—but not all—of the consumers of close substitute products. By raising its price, it will lose some—but not all—of its own customers to rival firms. However, these gains from, or losses to, other firms are spread over a large number of them. The effect on each will therefore be negligibly small. The firm which is changing its price can assume in this situation that the other firms will not react by altering their prices. It can thus try to predict the effect of a change in its own price on the quantity demanded of its product, on the assumption of unchanged prices for close substitutes. This means it can try to

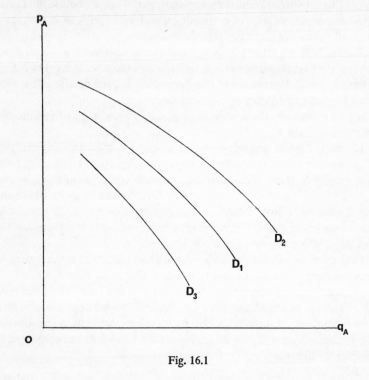

Fig. 16.1

discover the details of the particular demand curve confronting it at any time.

This curve will be downward sloping to the right, like D_1 for product A in Fig. 16.1. The price elasticity at each point on it is, in contrast to the position for the firm under perfect competition, less than infinite. As p_A rises, the q_A demanded contracts, but not to zero, because some people so prefer the distinctive qualities of A that they will continue to buy it even at a higher price. Similarly, as p_A falls, the q_A demanded only expands to a limited extent, since some people will prefer to continue buying close substitutes even when they become relatively dearer. The greater the substitutability between the various products, the larger will be the price elasticity at any point on D_1. But it is always less than infinite because the products are not perfect substitutes.

The *position* of D_1 depends on the prices of all the other products of the industry; these prices are parameters of D_1. If they rise, D_1 will shift upwards to the right, e.g. to D_2. That is, the demand for A will *increase*, since it is a substitute for the others. If the prices of the latter fall, D_1 will *decrease* to, e.g. D_3.

The implications of the fact that, under monopolistic competition, the individual firm can change its price without calling forth reactions from other firms, can now be expressed more precisely. With the prices of close substitutes given at any time, each firm will be confronted with a demand curve like D_1 in Fig. 16.1. It can therefore vary p_A and affect the q_A demanded *in the way shown* by the curve. This is possible because the other firms do not react by changing their prices. If they did, then D_1 would shift its position. As a consequence, the firm in question would have to know the nature of the shift (e.g. to D_2 or D_3) before it could say how a change in p_A would affect the q_A demanded. As it is, the large number of firms under monopolistic competition ensures that each firm is confronted by a single determinate demand curve at any time.

Now consider the demand curve for the firm under monopoly. There are distant, but no close substitutes, for the product of a monopoly.[1] It is a one-firm industry. It has been explained that in the first stage of price analysis the interactions between different industries are ignored. This means it is assumed that a monopolist is confronted by a single determinate demand curve at any time. He can vary his price and try to predict how the quantity demanded of his product will be affected, without having to consider reactions from distant competitors. That is, he can try to discover the position and shape of the demand curve, like D_1 in Fig. 16.1, which confronts him at any time.

The prices of other goods are, of course, parameters of this curve. If they change, the curve will shift. But if they are taken as given, the curve has a determinate shape and position. It is downward sloping to the right because, as a monopoly reduces its price, it only attracts a limited amount of custom away from other goods (i.e. from distant substitutes).

Under perfect competition, the individual firm must charge the same price as its competitors. It must *take* the price given by the market. It has therefore only to discover the level of output which it is most

---

[1] Monopoly does not, therefore, imply the complete absence of competition, but only of that from *close* substitutes.

profitable to produce at that price. Under both monopoly and monopolistic competition, on the other hand, the individual firm has a choice as to which price to charge for its product. It can raise its price and sell less, or lower the price and sell more. It has therefore to discover the particular price at which its sales will be at the most profitable level. The firm under imperfect competition is a *price maker*, in contrast to the perfectly competitive firm which is a *price taker.*

What is the most profitable level of output for a firm depends, of course, on its cost condition as well as on its revenue (or demand) condition. The cost curve of a firm (in either its total, average, or marginal form) has a variety of possible shapes. The reasons for this were explained at length in Chapters 9 and 10. Only one point need be added here.

The firm under perfect competition will only remain small in size if its ATC is rising at a low level of output.[1] With a perfectly elastic AR curve, the firm could expand indefinitely and thus destroy perfect competition, if that condition is not fulfilled. It is not necessary to make any particular assumption about the shape of the cost curve under imperfect competition. But, because of the form of indivisibility which is peculiar to management,[2] it is likely that the ATC of *any* firm will begin to rise at *some* level of output. Before this level is reached, however, it is quite possible for ATC to be falling or constant over a wide range of output.[3] In that case, the shape of the ATC curve will resemble a saucer rather than a 'U'.

PROFIT MAXIMIZATION

It was explained in Chapter 11[4] how the search by a firm for maximum profits depends on knowledge of its revenue and cost conditions, and of how they may change over time. The behaviour of the firm, under monopoly and monopolistic competition, will now be analysed under two assumptions, viz. (i) that it has *complete* and *certain* knowledge of its revenue and cost conditions, and (ii) that they remain unchanged for a sufficiently long period of time to allow the firm to acquire that size of plant (i.e. capital equipment) which is the most profitable. The latter assumption means that the analysis applies to the 'long period' in the Marshallian sense.[5]

Two alternative sets of average and marginal revenue and cost curves,

[1] See pp. 118–119 above.   [2] See p. 111 above.
[3] For the reasons given on pp. 108–110 above.
[4] See pp. 112–114 above.   [5] Cf. p. 155 above.

for a firm producing product A, are drawn in Figs. 16.2a and 16.2b[1] (all
the lettering is identical as between the two diagrams). Since the AR
curve is downward sloping to the right for a firm under both monopoly
and monopolistic competition, the MR curve lies everywhere below it.
MR is the addition to TR obtained by selling one more unit of the
product.[2] When price has to be reduced in order to sell that extra unit,
the TR is affected in two ways. On the one hand, it gains from the price
(i.e. the AR) at which the extra unit is sold. On the other hand, it loses

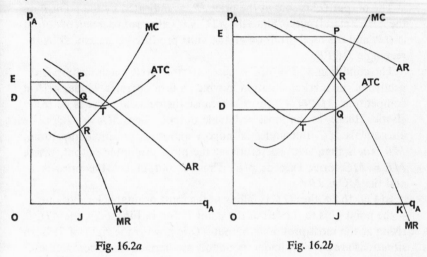

Fig. 16.2a Fig. 16.2b

from the reduction in the price (AR) at which the other units were being
sold. The MR therefore falls short of the corresponding AR by the sum
of the reductions in price on all the other units.

MR is shown as being zero at output OK, and negative at greater
outputs. The TR is consequently at a maximum at that output; and the
price elasticity of demand is unity at the corresponding point on the AR
curve.[3] Moreover, the elasticity is greater than unity at outputs below
OK (where MR is positive and TR is rising); and less than unity at
outputs above OK (where MR is negative and TR is falling).

The ATC curve, rather than the AVC curve, is the relevant one for a
long period analysis.[4] It is drawn, for the reasons already discussed, as

[1] The analysis could alternatively, of course, be conducted in terms of TR and
TC curves.
[2] See p. 123 above.
[3] As was explained by means of Figs. 8.5a and 8.5b on p. 85 above.
[4] This has already been explained by means of Fig. 14.2 on p. 150 above.

first falling, and then rising, to the right. The *MC* curve intersects it at its minimum point T.[1]

The *MR* curve intersects the *MC* curve at point *R*—and does so from *above* on the left of *R* to *below* on the right of it. Hence *OJ* is the most profitable level of output for the firm. Units of output beyond *OJ* add more to *TC* than to *TR* (i.e. *MC* exceeds *MR* for them), and therefore reduce the amount of profit. And on the other hand, profit is rising with output up to the level *OJ*, since *MR* exceeds *MC* over this range.[2]

The output *OJ* is sold at the price *JP*, as indicated by the point *P* on the *AR* (demand) curve. Since the *ATC* is *JQ*, the profit *per unit* of output is *QP*, and the total profit on all the units produced is measured by the rectangle *DQPE*.

The condition $MR = MC$ is necessary for profit maximization irrespective of the market situation in which a firm operates. Under perfect competition, $MR = AR$ (price), because the demand curve is perfectly elastic. Hence, at the most profitable output where $MR = MC$, price also equals *MC*. But under monopoly and monopolistic competition, *MR* is less than *AR*. Therefore, at the most profitable output, where $MR = MC$, price exceeds *MC*. Thus, at output *OJ*, the price is *JP* and the *MC* is *JR*.[3]

In Fig. 16.2*a*, the *ATC* is falling at the most profitable level of output —the point *Q* is to the left of the point *T*. But in Fig. 16.2*b*, the *ATC* is rising at the most profitable output—*Q* is now to the right of *T*. Both situations are possible under monopoly and monopolistic competition.[4] Which of them obtains will depend on the *positions* and *shapes* of the revenue curves relative to those of the cost curves.

The position of the demand curve for a firm depends on competition from other firms. The more competition there is, the smaller will be the demand for the firm's product. That is, the larger the number of

[1] See pp. 121–122 above.
[2] It should be noted that, if *MC* is always greater than zero, *MR* must be greater than zero at point *R*. Hence the price elasticity of demand at the most profitable output (i.e. at point *P*) must be greater than unity.
[3] The relation between *MR* and the corresponding *AR* depends on the price elasticity of demand. It is shown in more advanced texts that $AR = \dfrac{\varepsilon}{\varepsilon + 1} \cdot MR$, where ε is that elasticity (which is negative). At the most profitable output, therefore, price $= \dfrac{\varepsilon}{\varepsilon + 1} \cdot MC$. The larger negative number ε is, the smaller $\dfrac{\varepsilon}{\varepsilon + 1}$ is, and hence the lesser is the extent to which price exceeds *MC*. When ε is infinity (under perfect competition), $\dfrac{\varepsilon}{\varepsilon + 1} = 1$ and price $= MC$.
[4] It will be remembered that, under perfect competition, *ATC* cannot be falling at the most profitable level of output; see pp. 129–130 above.

competing firms, the closer to the origin of the diagram will the demand curve lie. This is the significant respect in which monopolistic competition differs from monopoly.

In both Figs. 16.2*a* and 16.2*b*, the firm is shown as earning a sizeable (supernormal) profit *DQPE*. This represents a return to it over and above the cost of financing the capital it uses. As was explained earlier,[1] both the interest paid on borrowed finance, and the rate of return expected and required by the firm's owners on their financing, are elements of cost. They are included in the *ATC* curve. The supernormal profit *DQPE* therefore means that the firm is earning more than a normal profit on its capital. This is an inducement for new firms to enter the industry.

That is not possible under monopoly—for reasons which will be discussed in a moment. Hence the 'monopoly' profit *DQPE* is secure from competition.

But under monopolistic competition, new firms producing close substitutes *can* enter the industry. As they do, they take some customers away from existing firms. The *AR* (and *MR*) curves of the latter therefore *shift* downwards to the left. Their *MR* curves now intersect their *MC* curves at lower levels of output. This is illustrated by Fig. 16.3 in comparison with Figs. 16.2*a* and 16.2*b*.

In Fig. 16.3, the *AR* curve lies everywhere below the *ATC* curve, except where they touch at point *P*. The firm can only cover its costs at the output *OJ*; and that output is the most profitable one (with *MR* = *MC* at point *R*). Thus in comparison with Figs. 16.2*a* and 16.2*b*, the *AR* curve has been shifted—by the competition from new firms— downwards to the left. Moreover, it has been shifted to the greatest extent consistent with the firm in question remaining in the industry. If the *AR* curve lay further to the left, the firm could not cover its costs at any level of output.

When new firms enter the industry, the effects on the *AR* curves of existing firms depend on the degrees of substitutability between their products. It is possible that the new firms may attract so many customers away from existing firms, that the latter are able to earn only normal profits. That is the situation portrayed in Fig. 16.3. But this outcome is not inevitable. The products of some firms, under monopolistic competition, may be sufficiently distinctive to prevent the complete elimination of their supernormal profits by competition from other firms. In given conditions, some (large) number of firms will find it profitable to operate in an industry under monopolistic competition.

[1] See pp. 115–116 above.

Some of them will earn only normal profits—as in Fig. 16.3. But others may well be able to earn supernormal profits—as in Fig. 16.2*a* or 16.2*b*.

Monopolistic competition is a blend of monopoly and competition—hence the term. Because the products of the firms are differentiated in one or more respects, each firm has—in the strict sense—a monopoly

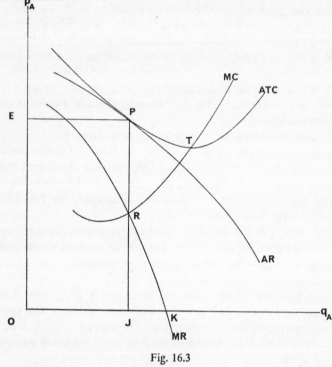

Fig. 16.3

of its own product. But, at the same time, it is subject to a considerable degree of competition from other firms producing close substitutes.

That element of competition is absent under *monopoly*. This can be so for a variety of reasons. A monopoly can be created by law. Or it can depend on sole access to the technical knowledge required to produce the product in question—as a result of secrecy, or protection by patent. Or it can depend on sole control of some natural resource, or type of labour skill. Or again, it can exist because, with given cost conditions, it is thought that the condition of demand would not make it profitable for more than one firm to produce for the market.

Those are the circumstances which make a monopoly *possible*. But they do not in themselves ensure that it will be either a particularly profitable, or a 'big', firm. Its size and profitability depend on its revenue and cost conditions, as has been shown above. The conjunction of a large demand, and ATC falling over a wide range of output, can lead to 'bigness' and high profitability. But some monopolies—e.g. a single newspaper serving a town—can be quite modest in both size and profitability. What the analysis above shows is that conclusions in these respects cannot be reached without a knowledge of the facts in any particular case.

Moreover, monopolies can be quite impermanent. Especially when technical progress is rapid, new close substitutes for the monopolized product will appear. Unless this is offset by demand increasing over time, the new competition will—by shifting the monopoly's AR curve down to the left—reduce its size and profitability.

The above analysis has spelt out the implications of profit maximization for the equilibrium of the firm under monopoly and monopolistic competition. It has therefore used precisely the same *technique* as has already been employed[1] in studying the behaviour of the firm under perfect competition. What is different, as between the analyses, is the nature of the *condition of demand* facing the individual firm in the three market situations. However, there may be a further difference. It has yet to be considered[2] whether the assumption that the firm has *complete* and *certain* knowledge of its revenue and cost conditions is appropriate to the circumstances of imperfect competition.

PRICE AND OUTPUT CHANGES

The equilibrium of a firm at its most profitable level of output will be disturbed by changes in its revenue and cost conditions. The AR and MR curves will shift as a result of changes in consumers' incomes, or preferences, or in the prices of close substitute products. The AC and MC curves will shift as a result of changes in factor prices, or in technology (i.e. in the production function).

Given a complete and certain knowledge of the new revenue and/or cost conditions, the firm can identify the new most profitable level of output. This knowledge therefore ensures that price and output will converge to their new equilibrium values. The process of convergence will, of course, take a period of time, whose length depends on the

[1] In Chapter 11 above.
[2] In the next chapter.

magnitudes of the changes required in factor inputs (especially of capital equipment).[1]

Qualitative[2] analysis can predict the direction (but not the magnitude) of the effects on *output* of increases, or decreases, both in demand and in costs under monopoly and monopolistic competition. With an increase in demand, which shifts both the AR and MR curves upwards to the right, output will rise, since the MR and MC curves now intersect at a higher output. And vice versa for a decrease in demand, which shifts both the AR and MR curves downwards to the left. With a decrease in costs, which shifts both the AC and MC curves downwards, output will rise, since the MR and MC curves will now intersect at a higher output. And vice versa for an increase in costs.

But qualitative analysis cannot predict the direction (let alone the magnitude) of the effects on *price* of increases, or decreases, in *demand*. Output rises when there is an increase in demand. The MC curve may be either falling, or rising, over the range of output in question. If it is falling, this *may* bring about a reduction in price; while, if it is rising, it *may* bring about a rise in price. It is necessary to say '*may*', because the behaviour of price also depends on what happens to the shape (i.e. the elasticities) of the demand curve whenever it shifts.[3] A little experimentation with diagrams like Figs. 16.2*a* and 16.2*b* will show that upward shifts in the AR and MR curves can either raise or lower price; and similarly for downward shifts in the curves. Thus, in contrast to what can happen under perfect competition, an *increase* in demand under monopoly and monopolistic competition may *lower* price, and a *decrease* in demand may *raise* price.

Qualitative analysis can, however, predict the direction (but not the magnitude) of the effects on *price* of increases or decreases in *costs*. Output rises when there is a decrease in costs. Price must therefore fall, since, with the AR curve unchanged, the larger output can only be sold at a lower price. And similarly, price must rise when costs increase.

---

[1] A Marshallian period analysis, similar to that conducted in Chapter 14, can be used to explain the paths of price and output during convergence.

[2] In the sense explained on p. 56 above.

[3] This can be seen directly from the formula, price $= \dfrac{\varepsilon}{\varepsilon + 1}$. MC at the most profitable level of output (see fn. 3 on p. 184 above). When that output alters, the change in price depends on what happens to both ε and MC.

CHAPTER 17

IMPERFECT COMPETITION: II

There is only a small number of firms in competition with one another under oligopoly. A change in the price charged by one of them will therefore have significant effects on the sales of the others. When one firm lowers its price, the sales and the revenues of the others will decrease. As a result of their altered revenue conditions, the latter will have to change their prices in order to maximize profits in the new situation. Those price changes will now have an effect on the sales of the firm which initially reduced price.

The individual firm, therefore, cannot predict the effect on sales of a change in its own price without knowing the reactions of the other oligopolists. This means that it is not faced at any time with a single determinate demand curve for its product. The prices charged by competing firms are parameters of such a curve. If they change, the curve shifts its position. But if the firm in question changes its price, the other firms will probably react by changing theirs. That is, if the individual firm tries (by means of a price change) to *move along* a particular demand curve, the result will be a *shift* in the curve because of the price changes by competing firms.

The search for the most profitable output is therefore much more complex under oligopoly than in other market situations. In order to know its revenue condition, the firm has to predict not only the reactions of consumers to a change in its price, but also those of competing firms. It may well make wrong forecasts in both respects. But it is likely to be particularly concerned about its competitors' reactions. This is so, because a mistaken prediction about other firms' behaviour may lead to a series of price changes, the consequences of which it will be exceedingly difficult to foresee. Suppose, for example, that an oligopolist thinks he can predict the reactions to a change in his own price; and that, given his predictions, a reduction in price will alter his sales to the most profitable level (given his cost condition). If his predictions are wrong he will not get the desired volume of sales, and will therefore have to consider whether a further price change should be made. But this will involve predicting afresh how the other firms will then react. Thus, in considering the initial price change, an oligopolist must take into account the *uncertainty* of the consequences of that change.

The existence of uncertainty under oligopoly can lead to collusion between firms in the fixing of prices. They may prefer to assure themselves of smaller profits by means of restrictive agreements than to take the uncertain chance of higher profits by competition. The collusion may be quite open. Or it may be secret, because it is illegal. Or again, it may be achieved by unspoken agreement that prices will only be changed in certain circumstances, e.g. when factor prices common to the whole industry alter,[1] or when some firm, which is accepted as a 'price leader', makes a change.

Ideally, from the viewpoint of the industry as a whole, prices should be fixed so as to maximize the *sum* of the (supernormal) profits of all firms taken together. The industry would then be behaving in the same way as a monopolist.[2] There are, however, difficulties in achieving this outcome by means of collusion. In the first place, the resulting distribution of profits, as between the different firms, may not commend itself to some of them. They, taken separately, might do better with a different set of prices in the industry. And secondly, when collusive agreements are made, it is then profitable for individual firms to take customers away from their competitors by whatever *secret* price-cutting they can get away with.

The literature of economics abounds with different explanations of the determination of prices under oligopoly. It is possible to think of a great variety of predictions which firms might make about their reactions to one another's policies. And it is possible to argue in a variety of ways as to how the behaviour of firms will be affected by the uncertainty attaching to their revenue conditions. Different hypotheses about the predictions, and about the effects of uncertainty, yield different theories of price. In these circumstances it may be helpful to enquire into the procedures through which firms actually arrive at their prices.

AVERAGE COST PRICING[3]

Many firms, in both the UK and the US where oligopoly is prevalent, set their prices by adding a percentage to 'average direct costs'. The

---

[1] E.g. changes in nationally-agreed wage rates.

[2] Hence, the desire for monopoly profits, as well as for escape from uncertainty, may be a motive for collusion between firms.

[3] Sometimes also called Full Cost pricing.

meaning of the latter term is not entirely uniform as between firms. However, since there are a large number of firms which each produce more than one product, the term usually refers to those costs (e.g. on raw materials and workshop labour) which are directly attributable to each product. Average direct costs (ADC) is, therefore, a concept analogous to that of AVC, as used above. A percentage is added to ADC in computing price in order to cover the other costs, including the cost of financing capital. It may, however, be sufficient to give a return on capital which is greater than normal profit.

This account of the price fixing procedure of many firms hardly merits being called a theory of price—for two reasons. First, ADC will probably vary with output, for the same reasons as AVC does. It is therefore not possible to identify the *particular* value of ADC, to which a percentage is to be added, until the relevant output is known. But the output the firm can sell depends on the price it charges. Hence, since (i) the price cannot be decided until output is known, and (ii) output cannot be determined until the price is fixed, the above account is, to say the least, an incomplete explanation of price. And secondly, it is also inadequate as a theory, in that it gives no explanation of the size of the percentage added to ADC to compute the price.

An attempt to provide a *theory* to explain average cost pricing can be made along the following lines. It appears that, for many manufacturing firms, the ADC curve is saucer-shaped, as in Fig. 17.1. The ADC falls at low levels of output, and rises at high ones, but it is roughly constant over a wide range of intermediate outputs. The reasons for this are probably as follows. The ADC curve depicted here is derived from a set of ADC curves for *different* sizes of plant.[1] If there are indivisibilities in capital equipment, the individual ADC curves will be U-shaped. But unless the indivisibilities are very significant, an increase in plant size will yield a fairly flat, complete ADC curve. Only a small range of *each* of the U-shaped ADC curves for different plants will be encompassed in the complete curve.[2]

The falling and rising sections of the latter can be explained by the special form of indivisibility inherent in management.[3] The ADC falls at low levels of output as management combines more effectively with the other factors of production. It rises at high outputs because of the difficulties in reaching decisions in a large organization. But over the intermediate range of output, increases in the size of (and specialization

[1] In the way explained on pp. 108–110 above.
[2] See p. 110 above.
[3] See p. 111 above.

within) management can keep pace with the increased use of other factors; and can do so without much change in productivity, and therefore in ADC.

With ADC constant over a wide range of output, MC will coincide with it over that range. But, as shown in Fig. 17.1, MC lies below ADC where the latter is falling; and lies above ADC where the latter is rising.

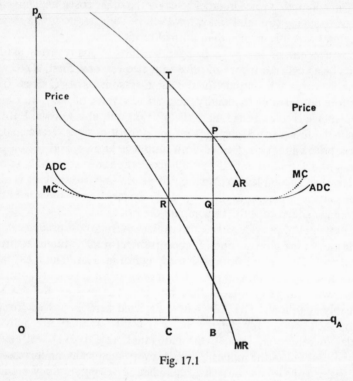

Fig. 17.1

Now suppose that a firm adds a given percentage to ADC in order to fix the price of its product. What that price should then be, at different levels of output, is shown in the diagram by the line marked 'Price'. The prices on this line exceed the corresponding ADCs by a constant percentage of the latter. It can be seen that, as observed earlier, the price cannot be computed until the level of output—and its ADC—is specified. However, if the firm expects to operate only within the range of output over which ADC is constant, a price can be fixed *before* the level of sales (and therefore output) is known. For with a given percentage mark-up on ADC, the price will be the same at all levels of output within that range.

If the firm acts on the assumption that *ADC* will not vary with output, the determination of its output can now be shown. The *AR* curve, in Fig. 17.1, plots the various quantities of its product the firm will *actually* sell at different prices. This curve must be interpreted in a slightly different way from the demand curves used earlier. The latter were drawn on the assumption of *given* prices for competing products. The present *AR* curve, on the other hand, assumes that in relation to *each* price on it, the prices of competing products have been adjusted to the levels that their firms think appropriate. In other words, the curve allows for the reactions of competing firms to a change in the price charged by the firm in question. This is necessary in order for the *AR* curve to show the *actual* sales of the firm at different prices for its product.

The output of the firm will be at the point *P*, where the *AR* curve intersects the price line. Its product has been marketed at a price (*BP*), decided by adding a given percentage (*QP*) to the *ADC* (*BQ*) in the range over which it is constant. The *AR* curve indicates that at the price *BP* an output *OB* will be sold.

No explanation has yet been given of how the size of the percentage mark-up (*QP*) is determined. One possibility is that it is varied from time to time in trial-and-error attempts to find the most profitable level of output. The nature of such a process can be seen from Fig. 17.1, in which the *MR* curve, corresponding to the already explained *AR* curve, has been drawn. The most profitable output is *OC*, as indicated by the intersection of the *MR* and *MC* curves at point *R*; and the price at which it can be sold is *CT*, as given by the *AR* curve. The amount of the percentage mark-up on *ADC* is *RT*.

The firm is therefore making less than maximum profit at output *OB*. If it now lowers its price, by reducing the percentage mark-up on *ADC*, it will sell more, but it will make a smaller profit (since *MC* exceeds *MR* for outputs beyond *OB*). But if it raises its price, by increasing the mark-up, it will find that it is earning a larger profit despite the fall in sales. By a progressive raising of the mark-up, it will converge to the most profitable output *OC*. Any further rise in the mark-up will be checked by the discovery that profit is now falling (since *MR* exceeds *MC* at lower outputs). Similarly, if the firm starts with a price at which the volume of sales is less than *OC*, it will converge to that output by discovering that a progressive lowering of the mark-up increases profit.

This is one possible explanation of how the size of the percentage mark-up on *ADC* is determined. However, if it is correct, then the average cost pricing theory of the *equilibrium* of the firm (as interpreted above) is the same as the theory developed in previous chapters.[1] Under both theories, the equilibrium price and output of the firm is where it is maximizing profit in relation to its revenue and cost conditions.

But another interpretation of average cost pricing is possible. The firm under oligopoly has to take into account the reactions of competing firms to a change in its price. These reactions have been allowed for in drawing the AR (and MR) curve in Fig. 17.1. The curves are so drawn[2] that the firm can easily and assuredly converge to the most profitable output. If it is producing beyond the output OC, a little experimentation will show that increases in the mark-up will lead it to the most profitable output; and vice versa if it is producing below OC. But the firm cannot, in fact, know what is the shape of this AR curve, since it cannot predict the reactions of its competitors with certainty. The curve could have a great variety of shapes. It need not even be downward sloping to the right.[3] This would be the case if, when the firm reduces its price, its competitors reduce theirs to an even greater extent. Its sales would then contract, rather than expand, as a result of the price reduction.

With this uncertainty as to the shape of the AR curve, the firm may be reluctant to embark on experimental price changes. These *may* lead it to a more profitable level of output.[4] But, on the other hand, they *may not*. At each and every step in its experiments with price, it has to reckon with the reactions of its competitors. It is always *possible* that, whatever the series of price changes it makes, it will move to a less profitable level of sales—because of its competitors' reactions. That, indeed, is what can happen during a 'price war' between oligopolists. All of them become less profitable as a result of price cutting.

Because of uncertainty, oligopolists may avoid experimental price changes, and thus never obtain the knowledge of their revenue conditions which is necessary to maximize profits. That is, they may prefer the profits they are actually earning to the uncertain chance of higher profits as a result of price changes. Their prices, in this case, will be arrived at by adding a 'conventional' percentage mark-up to ADC, rather than by adjusting the mark-up so as to maximize profits. Their adherence to

[1] This theory is sometimes rejected on the ground that businessmen do not use the terms MR and MC. That fact is irrelevant, since, as was explained earlier, MR and MC are alternative ways of presenting the same information as that given by TR and TC. The latter terms are, of course, widely understood.

[2] Viz. falling to the right with continuously increasing slopes.

[3] In contrast to the demand curves used earlier, for which the prices of competing products are taken as given.

[4] But not necessarily to the *most* profitable level: the AR curve may be so shaped that the MR curve intersects the MC curve a number of times.

some convention in this respect arises from their conviction that to do otherwise would be too risky.

If the mark-up is only a conventional one, then this interpretation of average cost pricing is a *different* theory of price from the 'profit maximization' theory of earlier chapters. With the mark-up fixed at a conventional level, profits will be maximized only by accident. In terms of Fig. 17.1, the firm will have a fixed mark-up of QP, and will produce the output OB. Because of uncertainty, it will not make the experimental price-changes through which it could converge to the most profitable output OC.

The two theories—viz. that of profit maximization, and that of average cost pricing with a mark-up which does not maximize profits—are, in principle, capable of being tested. Some progress has been made in this respect. But it is limited by economists' inability to experiment with prices, and therefore to discover the revenue conditions of firms.

The mark-ups actually used are certainly not rigid. Firms do vary them, from time to time, and from one class of customer to another. This suggests at least some attempt to take the position and shape of the AR curve into account in fixing prices. But there is a degree of rigidity in many mark-ups which does not seem to be consistent with profit maximization in changing conditions. This, and the above analysis of uncertainty, suggest that the attempt to maximize profits is not a complete explanation of the behaviour of the firm—and of the determination of prices—at least under oligopoly.

PRICE AND OUTPUT CHANGES

Suppose that a firm practises average cost pricing, with the mark-up adjusted so as to maximize profits. The effects on price and output of parameter changes, which shift the demand or cost curves, will then be the same as those already analysed for a profit-maximizing firm at the end of the last chapter.[1]

But the effects on price may be different if the firm maintains a *fixed* percentage mark-up. Price is now 'cost-determined', in the sense that it depends on the ADC of the output produced by the firm. This output, however, depends on the position of the AR curve (as shown in Fig. 17.1). An increase (decrease) in demand will raise (lower) output. What then happens to price depends on the shape of the ADC curve over the

[1] See pp. 187–188 above.

range of output in question. Changes in the *shape* of the demand curve, as it shifts, do not in themselves affect the price.[1]

Suppose that the firm operates only along the horizontal range of the *complete ADC* curve. Increases and decreases in demand will then not change price in the long period, i.e. when the firm is using the desired size of plant. However, it might be thought that in the short period price would vary with output, since the *ADC* of a given size of plant will itself vary with output. But price may not be changed in the short period if the firm is uncertain of its competitors' reactions.[2] That is, its pricing policy may be based on the estimated *long period ADC*.

The *ADC* curve itself will shift as a result of changes either in the prices of labour and raw materials or in technology. A rise in factor prices, or a deterioration in productivity, will increase *ADC*, and therefore raise price. Lower factor prices or improved technology will reduce price.

Firms that are reluctant to compete by means of price changes—because of uncertainty as to their competitors' reactions—may go in for various forms of 'non-price' competition. They can try to draw customers away from their rivals by means of advertising, or by varying the nature of their products so as to make them more attractive to consumers. The aim, of course, is to shift the *AR* curve upwards to the right. But both advertising and product variations will increase costs. The firm is therefore faced, in these respects, with further problems of comparison between costs and revenues. These, however, must be left for more advanced study.

----

[1] I.e. the formula, price $= \dfrac{\varepsilon}{\varepsilon + 1}$. *MC* (see fn. 3 on p. 184 above) does not apply.

[2] This implies that the mark-up on short period *ADC* is variable.

CHAPTER 18

THE MARKETS FOR FACTORS

All the analysis of the prices of goods in the previous chapters has proceeded on the assumption of given prices for the factors of production. It is now necessary to enquire into their determination, and to explain how the prices of goods and of factors are interconnected.

Factors of production are the *productive services* rendered by human beings, natural resources, and (man-made) capital goods. It is essential to distinguish between a productive *service* and the *thing* that renders it. Both the service and the thing may have prices; and although these prices will be interconnected, they are not the same prices. Thus an acre of land may be rented out for so much per year: this is the price (per year) of the productive service obtained from the natural resource. But the acre itself may be sold outright for a sum of money: this is the price of the acre as distinct from the price of its productive service per period of time. Since the acre will presumably be purchased because of the productive services it can give, there will be a connection between the prices, that would be paid for those services, and the price of the acre itself. This is one of the problems which will have to be analysed presently.

In order to avoid confusion in this respect, a strict terminology will be used henceforward. The term *factor* will be used only to denote a *productive service* per period of time. The term *resource* will be used only to refer to the *thing* which renders a productive service. The resources of an economy are its men and women, its land and mines, and its capital goods. The factors of production are the man-hours, the acre-hours, and the machine-hours of productive services which the resources provide.

A clear distinction can now be drawn between two different sets of prices, viz. the prices of factors and the prices of resources. Unfortunately, everyday usage in these respects can be confusing. It is therefore necessary to be precise about the meanings which will be given to certain terms. The price per period of time of the productive services of men and women is a wage rate or a salary rate[1]; that of the services of

---

[1] The usual distinction between the two is that wages are paid weekly and salaries monthly.

land and mines is a rent.[1] The owners of capital goods (e.g. buildings, machines) may either hire them out to others or may themselves use the goods for productive purposes. To avoid confusion with the rents of land, the price paid for the renting of a capital good will be called a *capital rental*. This is the price paid per period of time for the productive services of the capital good. When capital goods are used by their owners, the earnings from their productive services are called profits. The relationship between capital rentals and profits will be analysed in due course.

The prices paid for *resources* may be referred to simply as the prices of capital goods, of land and mines, and (in a slave-owning society) of men and women. But—and it is here that more confusion can arise—these prices are often called the *capital values* of the resources. The reason for that will become clear later.[2] For the moment, it is enough that the prices (or capital values) of resources be clearly distinguished from the wage rates, salary rates, rents, capital rentals, and profits that are paid for their productive services per period of time. The importance of this distinction can be further emphasized in the following way. Productive services (factors) are *flows*, which have to be measured over some *period* of time, e.g. man-hours, machine-hours. The prices of factors, therefore, always have a time-dimension, e.g. a wage rate per week, a machine-rental per hour. On the other hand, resources are *stocks*, which are measured at a *point* in time, e.g. some number of machines which are in existence at a particular moment. The prices of resources therefore do not have a time-dimension, e.g. the price of a machine is quoted as of a particular moment in time.

The analysis of the coming chapters will involve another price, viz. the rate of interest. Interest is the amount of money paid for a loan for some period of time, e.g. £5 for the loan of £100 for one year. What this means is that, in return for £100 today, £105 has to be repaid in one year's time. Interest is usually expressed in the form of a rate per cent, in relation to the amount of the loan, per annum. Thus, interest of £5 on a loan of £100 for a year is at the rate of 5 per cent p.a. The rate of interest is the price per period of time of a loan of money, i.e. of *finance*. It is *not* the price of a factor, in the sense of the productive services of labour, land, or capital goods. While the rate of interest will enter into the analysis of the coming chapters, the explanation of

---

[1] This must not be confused with 'economic rent', which has a specialized meaning for economists, and does not refer to the earnings of any particular class of factor. The theory of 'economic rent' (which was referred to on p. 132 above) is not dealt with in this book.

[2] In Chapter 21; see pp. 240–241 below.

THE MARKETS FOR FACTORS

how it is determined must await the study of macroeconomics in Part III.[1]

THE PROBLEMS FOR ANALYSIS

At any time, a community will have a given and fixed stock of resources, viz. of human beings, natural resources, and capital goods. But at the same time, the quantity of productive services available will be variable to some extent. Labour, land, and capital can all be worked for a smaller, or a larger, number of hours during any period of time; they can also be worked less or more intensively during those hours.

Moreover, many resources are capable of providing a variety of alternative productive services. Most men can turn their hands to a variety of jobs. Many pieces of land can be used to produce different crops, or to have different kinds of buildings put on them. Some machines at least are capable of performing different tasks.

The price mechanism determines the uses to which resources are put. That is, it determines the kinds and quantities of productive services, from those resources, that are used in the production of goods. There are *three* interrelated problems in this respect, and it is essential to distinguish between them.

(i) The kinds and quantities of factors (i.e. productive services) bought by firms, and sold by households, per period of time will depend on their prices. An explanation has to be given of what those prices will be, and why they may change. A theory of wage rates,[2] rents, capital rentals, and profits has to be provided. This will be done in the next two chapters.

(ii) Although the stock of resources is fixed at any one time, it can increase or decrease over time. Population can grow or decline. Land can be reclaimed for productive use, or can be abandoned to nature. Capital goods can be accumulated, or the existing stock can be allowed to wear out without replacement.

What happens to the stock of resources will depend to some extent on the current, and the expected future, prices for the productive services of those resources. Thus the size of a country's population, and therefore of its labour force, depends in some way on the level of real wage rates.[3] The rates at which land is reclaimed and improved, and at which natural

---

[1] See Chapter 30 below.

[2] From now on, the term wage rates will be taken to include salary rates.

[3] As measured by the quantities of goods which money wage rates can buy at ruling prices.

resources are exhausted by extraction, also depend on the prices, both current and expected, of the productive services rendered by natural resources. The economic aspects of population changes, and of the conservation of natural resources, are too complex to be studied here.

The accumulation (or decumulation) of capital goods over time will clearly depend on the revenues which are *expected* to be carried from their productive services as they are used. It will only be worthwhile acquiring a capital good if its cost is expected to be at least covered by the revenue which will be earned from it during its lifetime. That revenue will be the capital rentals paid for its use, or the profits received from its use. The *expected* capital rentals (or profits) thus play a central role in determining the changes over time in the stock of capital goods— which in turn alter the quantities of productive services available from the stock at any one time. Changes in the stock of capital are called *investment* (disinvestment if the change is negative). This aspect of the theory of factor prices will be analysed in Chapter 21 below. It is in this context that the determination of the prices (capital values) of resources —as distinct from factors—will be considered.

(iii) The distribution of income in a community depends on the prices paid for factors. It can be analysed from at least two viewpoints. The income of a person is determined by the kinds and quantities of resources he owns, and the prices paid for their productive services. An explanation of the distribution of incomes between *persons* thus requires a knowledge of the distribution of the ownership of resources in the community. Traditionally, resources have been classified into three categories, viz. labour, land, and capital. Economists have for long debated whether there are any principles which explain the *functional* distribution of income as between these categories, i.e. which explain the division of the national income into wages, rents, and profits (including capital rentals). This is a highly complex matter on which little agreement has been reached. Neither it, nor the personal distribution of income, will be analysed systematically in this book.[1]

A start can now be made on the first problem in respect of factor prices, viz. how they are determined. This will initially (in the next chapter) be undertaken in general terms. The aim there will be to emphasize that the same form of analysis can be applied to *all* factor prices, irrespective of whether the productive services come from labour, land, or capital goods. Differences of detail between the various factors will then be taken into account in Chapter 20.

---

[1] Though the functional distribution of income will enter, to some extent, into the macroeconomic analysis of Part III below.

The analysis of the determination of the price, and quantity employed, of a factor will be broken down into precisely the same steps as were followed for the determination of the price and output of a good. First, the condition of demand (viz. the demand function) for the factor is explained. Second, the supply function for the factor is specified. Third, given the demand and supply functions, an explanation is provided of how the market finds (if it does) the equilibrium price and quantity, i.e. a convergence (stability) analysis is given. And fourth, predictions as to the effects, on price and quantity, of shifts in the demand and supply curves are derived.

The precise results will depend on the kind of *market situation* in which the factor is bought and sold. For simplicity at the general level, *perfect competition* will be assumed in the next chapter: i.e. that there is a large number of firms demanding the factor in question, all the units of which are identical in the sense of being perfect technical substitutes for one another; and that there is a large number of households supplying the factor, all of them having complete knowledge of the prices offered for it by the different firms. In these circumstances, the price of the factor will be uniform throughout the market.

CHAPTER 19

THE PRICES OF FACTORS

THE CONDITION OF DEMAND

A profit maximizing firm will try to discover the *least cost combination* of factors with which to produce its output. Once the combination is known, the quantities demanded of the different factors to produce the output in question are determined. It has already been explained[1] how costs depend on the prices and the physical productivities of the factors. The minimizing of cost for any output has to be undertaken in relation to these factor prices and productivities. Hence the quantity demanded of any factor depends (i) on the output levels of the firms using it, (ii) on the price and physical productivity of the factor in question, and (iii) on the prices and physical productivities of the other factors used with it. The nature of this demand function for a factor has now to be explained in terms of the *conditions* under which a combination of factors will be a *least cost* one for a particular output.

The contributions of the different factors to the output of a firm have to be separated from one another in order to measure their physical productivities. All the factors have to be used together for any output at all to be produced; a single factor on its own will not suffice. Output is the result of *combining* the factors. The separation of the factors' contributions to output (i.e. their physical productivities) can only be done by varying the quantity of *one* factor at a time, while keeping the quantities of the other factors constant. In this way, it is possible to measure the *additional* output which will result from using more units of a particular factor.

The amount of the additional output can be explained with the help of a diagram used earlier.[2] If the quantities, used by a firm, of all factors *except one* are held constant, then changes in the level of employment of that one (α) will affect the output of the firm in the way shown by the curve in Fig. 19.1a. This is a *total physical product* curve, which shows how output (i.e. *TPP*, as measured on the vertical axis) first rises in

[1] In Chapters 9 and 10 above.
[2] Viz. Fig. 10.2a on p. 101 above.

greater proportion than the input of α, then rises in smaller proportion, and finally decreases as the ratio of α to the other factors continues to increase. The reasons for this were explained earlier.[1]

The concept of the *marginal physical product* (*MPP*) of a factor can now be derived from the *TPP* curve. If the quantity employed of α increases by *BC* from *OB* to *OC* (the quantities of all other factors remaining constant), *TPP* rises by *RQ* from *BP* to *CQ*. An increment of

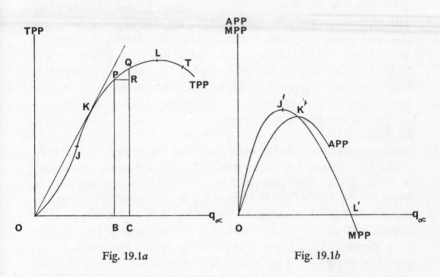

Fig. 19.1a   Fig. 19.1b

TPP, equal to *RQ*, results from an increment of input equal to *BC* (= *PR*). Hence the rate at which *TPP* rises is measured by $\dfrac{\Delta TPP}{\Delta q_\alpha} = \dfrac{RQ}{PR}$.

This ratio is the *MPP* of factor α over the range in question. Like all marginal concepts,[2] *MPP* can be thought of in either of two ways. On the one hand, it can be regarded as the additional output resulting from a particular increase (e.g. of one unit) in the quantity of the factor. On the other hand, it can be thought of as the rate at which *TPP* rises in response to a very small increase in the input. If *PR* in Fig. 19.1a is very small, the ratio $\dfrac{RQ}{PR}$ can be measured by the slope of the *TPP* curve at the point *P*. Thus, the *MPP* can be measured either at a *point* (e.g. *P*) on the *TPP* curve, or over a *range* (e.g. *PQ*) of it. As with the

[1] See pp. 100–103 above.
[2] Cf. the explanation of *MC* on pp. 119–121 above.

other marginal concepts, it will usually be more convenient to work with the 'point' concept.[1]

The slope of the *TPP* curve (i.e. the *MPP*) increases from *O* up to the point of inflexion *J*, and then decreases to zero at *L*. Beyond *L*, the slope is negative. There are increasing *marginal* returns to the factor α between *O* and *J*, diminishing marginal returns between *J* and *L*, and negative marginal returns beyond *L*.[2] The marginal returns to a factor (its *MPP*s) must be distinguished from its average returns (its *APP*s[3]). As with all average and marginal concepts, the *APP* is rising as long as the *MPP* exceeds it; and is falling when the *MPP* is less than it. *MPP* = *APP* when the latter is at its maximum. This is shown in Fig. 19.1*b*. Point *J* of Fig. 19.1*a* corresponds to *J'* in Fig. 19.1*b*, where *MPP* is at a maximum; point *K* to *K'*, where *APP* is at a maximum[4]; and point *L* to *L'*, where *MPP* is zero, and beyond which it is negative. It can thus be seen that increasing and diminishing returns to a factor can be stated in terms of either its *MPP* or its *APP*; and that the two statements are not identical, since *J'* and *K'* in Fig. 19.1*b* do not coincide.

The *MPP* measures the contribution to output from a given increase in the input of a single factor, with the inputs of other factors remaining constant. The *MPP* of factor α is negative for quantities of it beyond the point *L* in Fig. 19.1*a*. A profit maximizing firm will never use those quantities of α in conjunction with the given amounts of other factors, since it can obtain a *larger* output from a *smaller* input of α (e.g. at point *L* as compared with *T*). That is, in general, it will never use *ratios* of α to the other factors which are so *high* as to make the *MPP* of α negative.

Moreover, just as a high ratio of α to the other factors will make *its* *MPP* negative, so a high ratio of the other factors to α will make *their* *MPP*s negative. The *MPP*s of the *other* factors are, in fact, negative in the range of the *TPP* curve from *O* to *K* (at which the *APP* of α is at a maximum).[5] If the quantities of the other factors are variable, a profit maximizing firm will therefore never use those quantities of α (viz. between *O* and *K*) in conjunction with the given amounts of the other factors. Since the latters' *MPP*s are negative, a *decrease* in the quantities

---

[1] Once again, readers with a knowledge of calculus should note that the term 'marginal' means a first derivative. The *MPP* of α is the first derivative of *TPP* with respect to q_α.

[2] Where there are so many units of α that they impede one another in working with the constant quantities of the other factors; see pp. 101–102 above.

[3] Which have already been explained by means of Fig. 10.2*b* on p. 101 above.

[4] *OK* is a tangent to the *TPP* curve in Fig. 19.1*a*.

[5] A rigorous proof of this is given in more advanced texts.

of them used relative to α will *increase* output. That is, in general, the firm will never use *ratios* of α to the other factors (if they are variable) which are so *low* as to make the *MPP*s of the other factors negative. This is merely another way of saying that it will not use those ratios of the other factors to α which are so *high* as to have that outcome.[1]

Thus, when the quantities of all its factors are variable, a profit maximizing firm will only operate in the range of outputs between K and L in Fig. 19.1a. The *MPP* of α is both *positive* and *diminishing* for increases in q_α within this range. By the same argument, the firm will employ the other factors only in such quantities that their *MPP*s are also positive and diminishing.

The conditions for a combination of factors to be a *least cost* one for a particular output can now be specified. Consider a good that is produced by two factors α and β, whose prices p_α and p_β are given and constant. The *MPP*s of the factors will be written as MPP_α and MPP_β.

The ratio $\dfrac{p_\alpha}{MPP_\alpha}$ shows the additional expenditure *per unit of output* incurred by employing more of α. Thus, if $p_\alpha = £2$, and $MPP_\alpha = 10$ units, $\dfrac{p_\alpha}{MPP_\alpha} = \dfrac{£2}{10}$, which shows that an additional cost of 4s per unit of output will be incurred when output is increased by using more α. Similarly, if $p_\beta = £6$, and $MPP_\beta = 20$ units, $\dfrac{p_\beta}{MPP_\beta} = \dfrac{£6}{20}$, which shows that an additional cost of 6s per unit of output will be incurred when output is increased by using more β.

Now suppose that a particular combination of α and β is being used, and that their prices and *MPP*s are those just given. Then, the combination is *not* the least cost one for the output in question. The *same* output could be produced by using *more* of α and *less* of β, i.e. by substituting some of α for some of β. This substitution of α for β would, in the circumstances, decrease cost. The additional output from using more α costs 4s per unit, and the reduction in output, from using less β, saves a cost of 6s. per unit. Hence each substitution of α for β—in such way as to leave output *unchanged*—gives a *net* reduction in total cost.

However, as α is substituted for β, the ratio of q_α to q_β, used by the firm, increases. Hence MPP_α falls and MPP_β rises because there are diminishing marginal returns to the factors. With p_α and p_β unchanged,

[1] The nature of the symmetry (already referred to on p. 102 above) between the range O to K on the *TPP* curve, and the range beyond L, has now been made clearer. It lies in the negative *MPP*s of the other factors, and of α, respectively.

$\dfrac{p_\alpha}{MPP_\alpha}$ rises, and $\dfrac{p_\beta}{MPP_\beta}$ falls, i.e. the additional cost per unit of the out-put, got from using more α, rises, and the saving in cost per unit of the output, lost by using less β, falls. When, through continued substitution of α for β, the ratio $\dfrac{p_\alpha}{MPP_\alpha}$ has risen to equality with $\dfrac{p_\beta}{MPP_\beta}$, further substitution will no longer decrease cost for the output in question. It will, of course, now increase cost. The condition $\dfrac{p_\alpha}{MPP_\alpha} = \dfrac{p_\beta}{MPP_\beta}$ is therefore necessary for the combination of factors to be the *least cost* way of producing a particular output.[1] Thus suppose that in the above example MPP_α falls to 8 units, and MPP_β rises to 24 units, as α is substituted for β. Then the additional cost per unit of output is the same (viz. 5s) in respect of increases (or decreases) in the use of either factor. In that situation, there can be on balance no saving in cost for the output in question by using more of one factor and less of the other.

It follows that the *MC* of *additional* output will be the same irrespective of whether it is produced by using more of one factor, or of another, or of both of them. The additional cost per unit of the output, obtained by using more of a factor, is merely another name for the *MC* of that output. This additional cost is the same for *all* the factors in a least cost combination. Hence, the ratio $\dfrac{p}{MPP}$ for each factor equals *MC* (which is therefore 5s in the above example). The above analysis can be extended to cover any number of factors, so that the condition for a combination of factors to be a *least cost* one for a particular output can be written:

$$\frac{p_\alpha}{MPP_\alpha} = \frac{p_\beta}{MPP_\beta} = \frac{p_\gamma}{MPP_\gamma} = \cdots = MC$$

The demand function for a factor of production can now be explained by means of this condition. Suppose that the firms using α, β, and γ are initially in equilibrium, and are therefore demanding given quantities of these factors. Consider how the quantity demanded of α will alter in response to a change in its price. If p_α falls, $\dfrac{p_\alpha}{MPP_\alpha}$ is reduced, and the

---

[1] The condition can be written in the alternative forms $\dfrac{MPP_\alpha}{p_\alpha} = \dfrac{MPP_\beta}{p_\beta}$ and $\dfrac{p_\alpha}{p_\beta} = \dfrac{MPP_\alpha}{MPP_\beta}$.

least cost condition is no longer satisfied. Factor α will now be substituted for β and γ until MPP_α has so fallen, and MPP_β and MPP_γ so risen (because of diminishing returns), that the condition is one again satisfied. There is a *substitution effect* which causes the quantity demanded of α to expand when its price falls. But in addition, the reduction in p_α *decreases* the costs[1] of the firms using α. They will now—with given demand conditions for their products—expand their outputs, and therefore the quantities demanded of *all* the factors. This *expansion effect* works in the same direction as the substitution effect as far as α is concerned, and so ensures that the quantity demanded of α will expand when its price falls.

If p_β falls, $\dfrac{p_\beta}{MPP_\beta}$ is reduced, and the substitution effect expands the quantity demanded of β, but contracts the quantity demanded of α (and γ). The expansion effect, as before, expands the quantities demanded of all the factors. The substitution and expansion effects work in *opposite* directions for α, and without quantitative information, it is not possible to say whether a fall in p_β will increase, or decrease, the quantity demanded of α.

An improvement in technology (i.e. a change in the production functions) will increase the productivities of some, or all, of the factors. This will have a *factor saving effect* on the quantities demanded of those whose productivity has increased. Smaller amounts of them will now be required to produce *given* quantities of goods. But since the MPPs of at least some of the factors have increased, costs will have decreased. There will, therefore, also be an expansion effect on the quantities demanded of all the factors. Moreover, there may also be a substitution effect as between the factors. The technical change may be of a nature which increases the productivities of the factors to *different* extents. For example, MPP_α may increase more than MPP_β, which itself increases more than MPP_γ. Hence, $\dfrac{p_\alpha}{MPP_\alpha}$ will now be smaller than $\dfrac{p_\beta}{MPP_\beta}$, which in turn is smaller than $\dfrac{p_\gamma}{MPP_\gamma}$. Factor α will therefore be substituted for β, and both α and β will be substituted for γ. Technical change thus affects the quantity demanded of a factor in a complex fashion. The factor saving effect of an improvement in technology decreases the quantity demanded, the expansion effect increases it, and the substitution (if it exists[2]) may work in either direction. Without quantitative

[1] I.e., shifts the cost curves downwards.
[2] It will not exist if the MPPs of all factors increase in the *same* proportion.

information it is not possible to say what will be the net outcome of these effects.

Lastly, *increases* in demand[1] for the goods, which α, β, and γ help to produce, will increase the outputs of the goods, and therefore increase the quantities demanded of all the factors. The firm's cost curve is drawn on the assumption that the firm chooses the least cost combination of factors for each possible level of output. An increase in demand moves the firm along its cost curve to a higher output. The least cost condition is satisfied there for larger quantities of all the factors.

The quantity demanded of a factor thus depends on its own price, on the prices of the other factors used with it, on the productivities of all the factors, and on the conditions of demand for the goods which use the factors. This condition of demand for a factor will presently be expressed in the form of demand curves.

THE CONDITION OF SUPPLY

The owner of a resource has to decide upon the use to which to put it. A man who is capable of doing various different kinds of work must choose which of them he will actually do. That is, he has to decide upon the kind of productive service (factor) to be supplied by his labour resource.

The decision will depend in part upon the prices of the different productive services he could supply. With a training in chemistry, he could, for example, teach or do research work or go into a business firm. His choice will depend in part on the wage rates, relative to one another, offered by these jobs. But he will not necessarily choose the job which offers the highest wage rate. Irrespective of the wage rates, he is likely to have *preferences*[2] as between the different kinds of work he would like to do, and the conditions under which he will have to do them. His decision will be the outcome of a comparison of the alternative wage rates in relation to his preferences between the jobs in question. In principle, the same considerations apply to decisions about the uses to which land, and capital goods, are put. The owners of land and capital are, however, much less likely than workers to have preferences as between different uses of their resources. The latter will, therefore, usually be directed to supplying the most highly priced productive services of which they are capable.

---

[1] I.e. upward shifts in demand curves.
[2] The preferences of resource-owners must, of course, be distinguished from the preferences (between goods) of the same people in their capacity as consumers.

Thus, given the relative prices of factors, and the preferences of resource-owners, particular quantities of the various factors will be supplied. If the price of one of them now rises (the prices of the others remaining constant) the quantity supplied of it is likely to expand. At least some resource-owners will switch to supplying this factor rather than the others. If the wage rates paid by industry for chemists rise, some of them may decide to leave teaching and go into business. By the same reasoning, a rise in the prices of other factors is likely to decrease the quantity supplied of the factor in question.

There is, however, a further consideration in these respects—at least in the case of labour. The quantity of a factor has a time dimension, e.g. so many man-hours of work *per week*. The quantity supplied depends not only on the number of men willing to do the work in question, but also on the number of hours per week for which each man is willing to work. It is therefore necessary to enquire how a change in a wage rate will affect the hours of work per week supplied by each man.

This question involves a choice between *work* and *leisure*. If a wage rate rises, an hour's work will now purchase a larger quantity of goods. The value of another hour's work has thus increased in relation to the value placed on another hour's leisure. This provides a motive for doing more work and taking less leisure per week. The wage rate rise produces a *substitution effect* in favour of work and against leisure.

Leisure, however, probably has the same characteristics as a superior good, namely that more of it is demanded as income increases. The better off we are, the more time we want in order to enjoy the larger quantity of goods available to us. A rise in a wage rate increases the income to be got from a *given* amount of work. It therefore produces an *income effect*, which operates to reduce the amount of work supplied.

The substitution and income effects of a wage rate change thus operate in opposite directions; and without quantitative information it is not possible to say whether a man will work longer or shorter hours as a result of a rise in his wage rate. This conclusion qualifies (in the case of labour, at any rate) the earlier presumption that a rise in the price of a factor will expand the quantity supplied of it. While the *number* of units of resources (e.g. men) supplying the factor will probably expand, *each* unit may supply a smaller amount of the factor. Once again, it is not possible to say, without quantitative information, whether the former or the latter effect will be the greater, i.e. whether the quantity supplied of the factor will expand or contract as its price rises.

A shift in resources from one use to another will probably give rise to *transfer costs* for their owners. When a man changes the kind of work he does, he may have to undergo a period of re-training, and may also have to move house. When the job done by a machine is changed, it may take time to re-set it; and similarly in the preparation of land for some new use. Hence, when the price of a factor rises, the amount of additional resources, which are now switched to supplying it, will depend on the costs of transferring them from other uses. The rise in the factor price will have to be more than sufficient to compensate for the transfer costs incurred.

The quantity supplied of a factor thus depends on its own price, on the prices of other factors, on the preferences of resource-owners, on transfer costs, and on the total existing stock of resources from which factors can be made available. This condition of supply for a factor, and the condition of demand which has already been explained, will now be expressed by means of supply and demand curves.

PRICE AND EMPLOYMENT LEVEL DETERMINATION

The quantity demanded of a factor will expand as its price falls; this is shown by the demand curve for factor α in Fig. 19.2. All the other influences on q_α demanded are the parameters of the demand curve for the factor, viz. the prices of the other factors used with it, the physical productivities of the factors, and the conditions of demand for the goods which use the factors. A change in one or other of these parameters will shift the demand curve.

The quantity supplied of a factor may expand as its price rises; this is shown by the supply curve in Fig. 19.2.[1] All the other influences on q_α supplied are the parameters of the supply curve, viz. the prices of other factors, the preferences of resource-owners, transfer costs, and the existing stock of resources. A change in one or other of these parameters will shift the supply curve.

The D and S curves intersect at point P, giving an equilibrium price OA, and level of employment OH, for the factor. It has already been explained at length, in relation to the markets for goods,[2] that the *existence* of an equilibrium does not in itself ensure that the market will find its way there. Whether it does so or not depends on the convergence (stability) conditions, which specify the behaviour of the market when

---

[1] It is possible, as has been seen particularly in the case of labour, that the quantity supplied may contract as the factor price rises. In this event, the supply curve will slope upwards from *right* to *left* over at least part of its length. It is then said to be *backwards bending* over this range.

[2] See Chapters 13 and 14 above.

it is in disequilibrium. It is that behaviour which determines whether or not the price and quantity will converge to the equilibrium.

A complete analysis of the conditions for convergence to equilibrium in a factor market cannot be made without taking into account what is happening in the markets for the goods which use the factor. If the market for a factor is in disequilibrium—e.g. if p_α is above or below OA

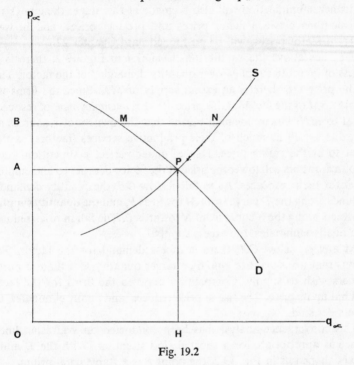

Fig. 19.2

in Fig. 19.2—then its price will change. The combinations of factors which are producing the goods which use factor α will no longer be *least cost* ones.[1] The prices and outputs of the goods will therefore start adjusting to new levels. How that adjustment takes place depends on the convergence conditions in the goods' markets. Hence, since factors are demanded in order to produce goods, the process of convergence in a factor market is necessarily dependent on the convergence process which is occurring simultaneously in the markets for the goods made by the factor.[2]

[1] I.e. the cost curves of the firms will have shifted.
[2] The converse is also true, since factor prices help to determine *incomes*, which in turn help to determine the demands for goods.

8

It is not possible to tackle the whole of this complex matter at once. In particular, a Marshallian long period analysis, in which the *stock* of capital is variable, cannot be undertaken until Investment has been studied in Chapter 21 below. For the present, a *short period* analysis must suffice. This restricts the discussion[1] to the determination of the prices of the factors which can be supplied by a *fixed* stock of resources. A further simplification will also be made at this stage: the analysis of the relations between factor prices and product prices, and between different factor prices, will be postponed until Chapter 22.

If p_α lies above the equilibrium level OA in Fig. 19.2, there is an excess of quantity supplied over quantity demanded of the factor. Thus at the price OB there is an excess supply of MN. Since the firms will employ BM of the factor at this price, there is *unemployment* of resources equal to MN. Unemployment means that the owners of resources are not able to sell as much of their productive services (factors) as they want to at the ruling price. Hence, under perfect competition, those resource-owners will lower the price of the factor in order to find employment for their resources. As p_α falls below OB, the quantity demanded expands along the D curve from M towards P, and the quantity supplied contracts along the S curve from N towards P. The fall in price reduces, and finally eliminates, the excess supply.

At any p_α below OA, there is excess demand for the factor. This means that firms want to employ a larger quantity of it than resource-owners wish to supply. Competition between the firms for the factor will bid up its price. The rise in price reduces, and finally eliminates, the excess demand.

This convergence analysis has been conducted on Walrasian lines,[2] as seems appropriate for a short period situation. With the D and S curves shaped as in Fig. 19.2, the point P is a stable equilibrium.

PRICE AND EMPLOYMENT LEVEL CHANGES

It is the convergence conditions that enable predictions to be made as to the effects on the price and the employment level of a factor brought about by shifts in its D and S curves.[3] In Fig. 19.3, the curves D_1 and S intersect so as to give equilibrium at point P. If an increase in demand shifts the D curve to D_2, there is now an excess demand of PR at the

---

[1] As already explained in the previous chapter; see pp. 199–200 above.

[2] In the same sense as already used in relation to the market for goods; see p. 146 above.

[3] This role of the convergence conditions has already been explained in relation to the goods' markets; see p. 160 above.

ruling price OA. Competition between firms for factor α will therefore raise its price. As p_α rises, the q_α supplied will expand along the S curve from P towards Q, and the q_α demanded will contract along D_2 from R towards Q. The rise in p_α thus gradually eliminates the excess demand and the market converges to the new equilibrium at Q. Since

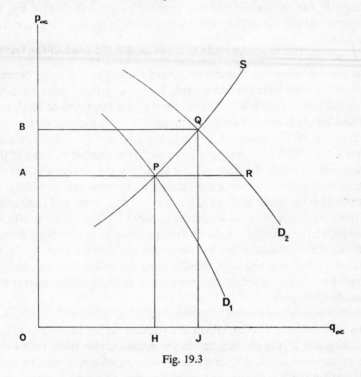

Fig. 19.3

the S curve is upward sloping to the right, the increase in demand raises both the price and the employment level of the factor.

As the earlier analysis of the demand function showed, an increase in demand for a factor can have a variety of causes. It will occur if there is an increase in the demands for the goods which the factor helps to produce. It *may* occur if the prices of the other factors used with it *either* rise or fall. If the latter *fall*, and the substitution effect against the factor in question is outweighed by the expansion effect, the demand for it will increase. If the prices of the other factors *rise*, and the substitution effect in favour of the factor in question is *not* outweighed by the contraction effect, the demand for it will increase.

An improvement in technology *may* increase the demand for a factor.

Whether or not this happens depends on the net outcome of the factor saving, the expansion, and the substitution effects already analysed.[1]

The magnitudes of the effects of an increase in demand on the price and employment level of a factor depend on its price elasticity of supply. Like all other elasticities, this one is measured by the proportional change in the dependent variable (quantity supplied) divided by the proportional change in the independent variable (price). It is therefore $\dfrac{\Delta q}{q} \Big/ \dfrac{\Delta p}{p}$, where q is the quantity supplied, and p the price of the factor. It is positive when the S curve is upward sloping to the right, because Δq and Δp then have the same signs. The greater is the price elasticity of supply, the larger will be the increase in the employment level, and the smaller the rise in the price, which result from an increase in demand.

The size of the elasticity depends on two sets of considerations, namely the effects of a change in price on (i) the number of units of the resource (e.g. men) which are willing to supply the factor, and (ii) the amount of productive service which each resource-unit is willing to supply. It is the preferences of the owners of resources, and their costs of transfer, which are relevant under heading (i). The elasticity will be the smaller, the stronger are the owners' preferences as between different uses for their resources, and the larger are the costs of transfer. With marked preferences and high transfer costs not many resources will be induced to shift by a small change in price. In those circumstances the *mobility* of resources will be low.

It is the substitution and income effects, in relation to the choice between work and leisure, which are relevant under heading (ii). The elasticity will be the smaller, the larger is the income effect relative to the substitution effect. A strong desire for more leisure, as income rises, will weaken the inducement to resource-owners to supply more productive services as price rises; and may even, as has been seen, bring a reduction in supply.

A reversal of all the changes in the above analysis makes it applicable to a decrease in demand for a factor.

Now consider the effects of an increase in the supply of a factor. If the S curve in Fig. 19.4 shifts from S_1 to S_2, an excess supply of PR now appears at the original equilibrium price OA. The consequent unemployment will cause a fall in the price of the factor. As p_α falls, q_α demanded will expand along the D curve from P towards Q, and the q_α supplied will contract along S_2 from R towards Q. The fall in p_α thus

[1] On pp. 207–208 above.

gradually eliminates the excess supply, and the market converges to the
new equilibrium at *Q*. The increase in supply lowers the price and raises
the employment level of the factor.

As the earlier analysis of the supply function showed, an increase in
the supply of a factor can have a variety of causes. It will occur if the

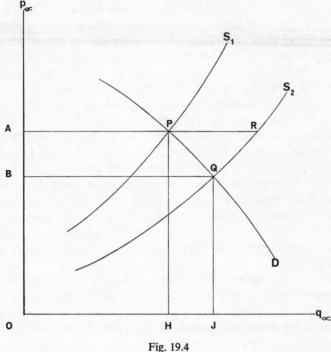

Fig. 19.4

stock of resources which provide the factor increases (e.g. if population
or the stock of capital increases). It will also occur if there is a fall in the
prices of the other factors which the resources could alternatively
provide, or if the resource-owners change their preferences in favour of
supplying more of the factor in question. An increase in supply *may*
occur if transfer costs are reduced. Such a reduction may, at given
factor prices, now make it worthwhile for some owners to shift their
resources to different uses. But the net outcome of these shifts may either
increase or decrease the supply of any particular factor.

The magnitudes of the effects of an increase in supply on the price
and employment level of a factor depend on its price elasticity of

demand. This is measured by $\dfrac{\Delta q}{q} \Big/ \dfrac{\Delta p}{p}$, where q is the quantity demanded, and p the price of the factor. It is negative because Δq and Δp have opposite signs. The greater is the price elasticity of demand, the larger will be the increase in the employment level, and the smaller the fall in the price, as a result of an increase in supply.

When the price of a factor falls, the quantity demanded expands as a result of both the substitution and expansion effects. It is therefore the magnitudes of these two effects which determine the size of the price elasticity of demand. The substitution effect depends on the technical possibilities of using one factor instead of another, e.g. machines rather than men. The easier it is—in this technical sense—to use one factor rather than another, the greater will be the substitution of the one for the other as the result of a price change.

The expansion effect follows from the decrease in costs brought about by the fall in the factor price. The decrease in costs lowers the prices of the goods made by the factor, and expands the quantities demanded of them. The extent of those expansions—and therefore the extent of the expansion in the quantity demanded of the factor—depends on the price elasticities of demand for the goods. Moreover, the greater are the proportions of the costs of the goods which are attributable to the factor whose price has fallen, the more the prices of the goods will fall.

Hence, taking the substitution and expansion effects together: the price elasticity of demand for a factor will be the greater, the more easily it can be substituted for other factors, the larger it bulks as an element in costs, and the greater are the price elasticities of demand for the goods it helps to produce.

A reversal of all the changes in the above analysis makes it applicable to a decrease in the supply of a factor.

CHAPTER 20

WAGES, RENTS AND CAPITAL RENTALS

The previous chapter distinguished the influences which affect the price and employment level of a factor. It was deliberately cast in a general form so as to make clear how the techniques of demand and supply analysis can be applied to *any* factor, irrespective of whether it comes from a labour, land, or capital resource. The analysis will now be used to discuss the *relative* sizes of different wage rates, rents, and capital rentals.[1]

WAGES

There is perennial interest in the question of why there are differences, sometimes very great, between the wage rates earned by different people. The only simple answer is that the demand and supply conditions differ as between the various labour factors. But that in itself is not very illuminating. What is required is an explanation of why the demand and supply curves, for the various labour markets, intersect at different heights, i.e. at different prices.

The positions of the demand curves for two kinds of labour may be quite different, since they depend on the variety of technologies and demand conditions for the goods which can be made by the factors. As between Figs. 20.1a and 20.1b (for labour factors α and β respectively), the demand for α is clearly the 'greater', i.e. the D curve for α is much further out to the right than that for β. The relation between p_α and p_β now depends on the positions of their S curves. Given the S curve for α in Fig. 20.1a, $p_\alpha = p_\beta$ with the latter's S curve at S_2, $p_\alpha > p_\beta$ with S_1, and $p_\alpha < p_\beta$ with S_3.[2]

The positions of the S curves for the two kinds of labour depend on their parameters. As has been seen, these are the wage rates for other jobs, the preferences of workers as between different kinds of job, the

---

[1] The determination of the *absolute* levels of factor prices has to be analysed in macroeconomic terms; for an explanation of this see pp. 264–265 below.

[2] I.e. since price depends on both the D and S conditions, the factor with the 'greater' demand does not necessarily have the higher price.

costs of transferring between jobs, and the size and nature of the stock of labour resources. Suppose that there are some workers who are capable of doing *both* the jobs represented by α and β. The position of the S curve for β in Fig. 20.1b then depends on p_α. At higher and higher wage rates for α, more workers will want to supply α rather than β. The S curve for β will therefore shift upwards to the left (e.g. from S_1 to S_2). The S curve for α, of course, depends on p_β in the same way.

Differences in wage rates can now be explained as follows. Suppose that $p_\alpha = OA$. Why then will the S curve for β not take up the position

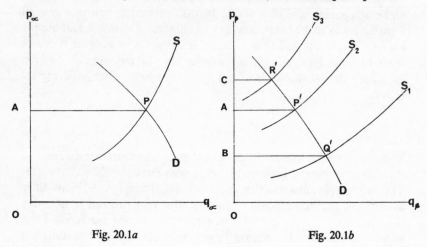

Fig. 20.1a Fig. 20.1b

S_2, which also makes $p_\beta = OA$? That is, why will workers not distribute themselves between α and β so as to make the wage rates the same in both jobs? The other parameters of the S curves give a number of possible reasons, all of which may operate at the same time.

The position of the S curve for β depends not only on p_α (given at OA), but also on the workers' preferences between job α and job β. Insofar as *all* workers do not like (or dislike) the two jobs to the same extent, it would be quite accidental for the supply curve to be S_2. Each worker, who prefers job α to job β, would be willing to do the former for a somewhat lower wage rate than he could earn at the latter; and similarly for those who prefer β to α. Given $p_\alpha = OA$, the preferences between the jobs of all the workers will determine the position of the S curve for β. There will be a different S curve for β (with $p_\alpha = OA$) for *every set* of preferences which all the workers might have. The larger is the number of workers who prefer β to α, the further downwards to the right will lie the S curve for β (e.g. S_1 rather than S_2). There is no reason why the workers should have the particular set of preferences which produces the S_2 curve, and thus makes $p_\alpha = p_\beta = OA$. Their preferences may lead to either S_1, which makes $p_\alpha > p_\beta$, or S_3, which makes $p_\alpha < p_\beta$.[1]

The willingness of those men, who are initially doing job α at any time, to move to job β depends on the costs of transfer. If they have no preference as between the two jobs, they will not move unless p_β exceeds p_α by an amount sufficient to compensate them for the transfer costs. The S curve for β can therefore keep a position (like S_3 in Fig. 20.1b) which makes $p_\beta > p_\alpha$. Precisely the same point applies to those men who are initially doing job β. The costs of transfer from β to α may be such that the S curve for β keeps a position (like S_1 in Fig. 20.1b) which makes $p_\alpha > p_\beta$. The transfer costs (e.g. of re-training and of moving house) need not be the same in each direction, or for each man.

The kinds and quantities of the different labour skills that *could* be made available at any time depend on the nature and size of the population. The innate qualities and the past education of the people who make up the population determine the range of jobs each person is *capable* of doing. The capacities of people therefore place a constraint on the shapes, and positions, which the S curves for different labour factors can take. Thus, however high one wage rate rises in relation to others, there will be a limit at any time to the quantity of the factor in question that could be supplied. The limit is given by the number of people who are capable of providing this productive service.

Consider this point in relation to factors α (e.g. operatic singing) and β (e.g. teaching). Suppose (it seems a realistic assumption) that of those people who could be teachers only a few would be acceptable as operatic singers. The higher is p_α relative to p_β, the more teachers will want to become singers. That is, as p_α rises, the S curve for β in Fig. 20.1b shifts upwards to the left—the supply of teaching decreases. The shifting of the S curve for β is, however, constrained by the limited capacity of teachers to be singers. Hence, with $p_\alpha = OA$, the supply curve for β may stay at S_1. Consequently, p_β remains less than p_α, because no more teachers are able to sing.

In general, the positions—*relative* to one another—which the S curves of all kinds of labour can take, will be constrained in this way. Each person has a limited range of abilities, and that range varies from person to person. Given the demand conditions for the different kinds of

---

[1] It is not of course necessarily correct to say that, if a majority of people prefer α as compared with β, then $p_\alpha < p_\beta$. The prices depend on the conditions of demand as well as those of supply.

ability, people may not have the capabilities which are necessary for them to distribute themselves among jobs in such a way as to equalize wage rates. This is one way in which an element of monopoly can exist in a labour market. A person with some unique ability is a class of factor with only one member. The quantity supplied of the factor can only be varied by the person working longer or shorter hours. A large demand for his services will allow him to earn a wage rate much in excess of those of most people, since the productive services of the latter are supplied in competition with those of many others.[1]

COLLECTIVE BARGAINING

There is another way in which monopoly can exist in a labour market. All the workers who supply a particular kind of labour skill may combine themselves into a trade union. Instead of each worker negotiating his wage rate (and conditions of work) separately with employers, the union bargains on behalf of all the workers. They therefore do not compete with one another. The union—when *all* the workers in question belong to it[2]—is a monopoly, because it acts as the sole seller of the productive service.

In developed industrial countries, where trade unions are widespread, it is usual for firms employing similar kinds of labour to combine themselves into employers' associations for the purpose of negotiating with unions. Instead of each firm reaching agreement separately with the unions on wage rates, the association to which they belong bargains on their joint behalf. This is called *collective bargaining*, which is an example of the market situation known as 'bilateral monopoly'.[3]

The process by which the market reaches agreement on the wage rate is quite different under bilateral monopoly from that under perfect competition. In the latter situation, as has been seen in the previous chapter, the wage rate will change as long as there is excess demand or supply for labour. It will settle at the level which equates the quantities demanded and supplied. When a trade union and an employers' association confront each other over the bargaining table, the presence

[1] There will be an oligopoly situation in a labour market when there are only a few people capable of supplying the same or closely similar productive services.

[2] E.g. when there is a 'closed shop'.

[3] There is a philological objection to this term. Monopolist means a 'single seller'. The union is a single seller, but the association of firms is a single *buyer*. The term 'monopsonist' has been coined for a single buyer (the market situation then being a monopsony). Most economists, however, prefer to say bilateral monopoly rather than monopoly-monopsony.

(or absence) of excess demand or supply at the ruling wage rate will undoubtedly influence their negotiations. But it will not be the only consideration. It is therefore necessary to consider how collective bargaining can affect wage rates relative to one another.

The prime function of a union is to get better wage rates (and working conditions) for its members. It tries to do this in the first instance by negotiation, but it will usually be ready to support that action at a later stage by calling a 'strike' in one form or another.[1] The extent to which a union will press for higher wage rates at any time depends on a variety of considerations. If the condition of demand for its members' work remains unchanged,[2] an increase in the wage rate may reduce their level of employment. This will happen if there is no excess demand for the labour at the time of the bargaining. If it is likely to happen, the union must balance the gain from the higher wage rate for its members who will remain in employment, against the loss to those who will become unemployed.

The willingness to back negotiations by strike action will depend on an assessment of the various prospective gains and losses. The disbursement of strike pay will deplete the financial resources of the union, and weaken its negotiating power in the future. During the strike, the earnings of its members will be reduced. Their willingness to endure this will influence the union's strategy. The longer the strike goes on, the more the current loss of wages will offset the prospective increase in wage rates. The union must therefore try to predict the length of time for which the firms will resist the wage claim.

An employers' association will put up at least some resistance to a claim for higher wage rates. If the conditions of demand for the goods produced by its firms remain unchanged,[2] an increase in the wage rate will, by increasing costs, reduce profits. But strike action by the union will also reduce profits, and may cause losses, for a time. The willingness of the separate firms to endure this will influence the association's strategy. It must therefore try to predict whether or not the union will strike; and if so, for what length of time it would persist with a strike.

Expectations with regard to their rival strategies thus play a central role in the wage bargaining between unions and employers' associations. This is the major respect in which the collective bargaining process, by which the market reaches agreement on the wage rate, differs from perfect competition. But this does *not* mean that the conditions of

---

[1] E.g. of all its members, or only against selected firms.
[2] Whether or not this can be expected to happen can only be analysed at the macroeconomic level; see Chapter 27 below.

demand and supply for labour are irrelevant to the outcome under
bilateral monopoly. The quantity demanded of labour by the firms will
still depend on the wage rate. With given conditions of demand for
their goods, that quantity will be smaller, the higher is the wage rate.
The quantity supplied of labour will still depend on the wage rate in
question relative to other wage rates.

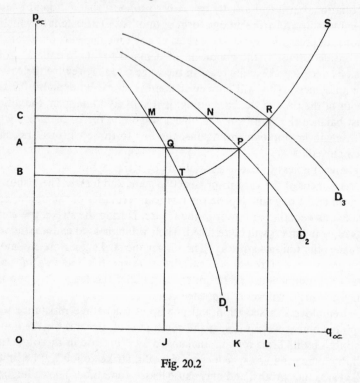

Fig. 20.2

However, the shape of the supply curve for a particular kind of
unionized labour will not be the same as it would be under perfect
competition. Trade unions will not agree to reductions in wage rates
except when there is considerable unemployment among their members.[1]
Moreover, their members, except under the pressure of high unemployment, will respect this policy by not accepting work at wage rates below
the agreed levels. As a consequence, the supply curve for a particular
labour factor will have the shape shown in Fig. 20.2.

Suppose that the ruling wage rate for α, as agreed between the union

[1] As, for example, happened during the Great Depression of the 1930s.

and the employers' association, is OA. Given the wage rates in alternative jobs, there will be some number of workers who want to supply α at the wage rate OA, and want to do some number of hours of work per period of time. Suppose that the quantity supplied of α is, in these circumstances, OK at the price OA (viz., at point P). Because the workers, in line with union policy, will not accept a lower wage rate, the S curve is perfectly elastic to the left of point P. The horizontal straight line section of the curve (AP) depicts the unwillingness of the workers to do the job for a lower wage rate. But to the right of P the curve will probably be upward sloping. A wage rate higher than OA will be required to attract workers from other jobs (and/or increase the hours of work offered), and so expand the quantity supplied beyond OK.

If the demand condition for the factor is given by the curve D_2, then its level of employment, at the ruling wage rate OA, will be OK (at point P). Since all the workers who are willing to supply α at that wage rate will find employment, a situation of 'full employment' may be said to exist for them. But if the demand condition is D_1, the level of employment will be only OJ (at point Q). There will be unemployment among the workers to the extent JK ($= OK - OJ$).[1] That is, there will be an excess supply (QP) of labour at the ruling wage rate. If—as yet a third possibility—the demand condition is D_3, the equilibrium level of employment is OL (at point R). This can be achieved only if the firms are willing to pay a wage rate in excess of the agreed level (viz. OC rather than OA). They may do so, and thereby attract workers from other jobs, and/or increase the hours of work. However, if they are unwilling to do so for some reason, an excess demand for labour will exist at the wage rate OA.

The position of the D curve depends on the demand conditions for the goods made by the factor. The quantities demanded of the goods depend on the incomes of households. These in turn depend on the prices paid for the factors supplied by the households. Wage rates are prices of factors. Hence, from the viewpoint of *all* labour markets, the *positions* of their D curves depend on the wage rates ruling in them. This set of interrelationships has to be analysed at the *macroeconomic* level. For that reason, the analysis of wage determination under collective bargaining will have to be taken further at a later stage in this book.[2]

For the present, however, it is now possible to see the significance of

---

[1] Which can take the form of workers being wholly unemployed, of workers being underemployed (i.e. on 'short time') or some combination of both.

[2] In Chapter 27 below.

the demand and supply conditions for the wage rate which emerges from a process of collective bargaining. Unions usually make wage claims periodically. Thus, after the rate OA in Fig. 20.2 has obtained for some time, a claim for a higher rate may be put to the employers' association. The amount of the claim, and the vigour with which it is pressed, will depend on the various considerations discussed above. One of these is the amount of excess demand or supply at the existing wage rate. If there is a significant amount of unemployment (excess supply) among the workers in question, this is likely to inhibit the union in its campaign for a higher wage rate. It will be more difficult to maintain solidarity among its members when there is a division of interests between them, i.e. when those in employment want a higher wage rate, but those out of work want a job. Moreover, on the other side of the market, the existence of unemployment may well mean that there are depressed conditions of demand and low profits for the goods made by the labour. In these circumstances, the employers are likely to be especially reluctant to agree to an increase in the wage rate. Hence unions are likely to be more militant in their claims, and employers more compliant in their responses, the lower is the level of unemployment.

The outcome of the bargain will still depend on additional considerations. But the above argument suggests that the agreed wage rate increase will be the greater, the lower is the existing level of unemployment. There is, in fact, some evidence that this is so. This conclusion will be of considerable importance in the macroeconomic analysis of Chapter 27 below.

The precise nature of the conclusion can be seen in terms of Fig. 20.2. Start with the wage rate at OA, and the S curve marked by the letters APS. The level of employment then depends on the position of the D curve. The further to the right it lies (e.g. D_2 as against D_1), the lower is the level of unemployment. That level plays a part in determining the increase in the wage rate, e.g. from OA to OC, which results from the current bargaining process. At the new rate, the S curve is that marked CRS.[1] The amount of the upward shift in the curve will be greater, the smaller is the existing unemployment (e.g. at point P, as compared with Q). It can be seen from the diagram that, if the D curve does not shift, the employment level will fall (e.g. to M on D_1, or to N on D_2).[2]

---

[1] The upward sloping range RS is unchanged, since other wage rates are assumed constant.

[2] It does not change with D_3, because the new *agreed* wage rate OC simply ratifies the rate which had already been competed above the previous agreed level OA.

At higher levels of unemployment, the employers are likely to take the initiative and press for a wage rate reduction. If they succeed in getting it down to, OB for example, the new S curve will be BTS. If the D curve does not shift, any unemployment which exists will be reduced (e.g. from Q to T on D_1). But that conclusion cannot necessarily be drawn for reductions in *all* wage rates, since the D curves for labour may then shift downwards to the left as incomes fall. This, again, is a question for the macroeconomic analysis of Chapter 27 below.

The process by which the market reaches agreement on the wage rate under collective bargaining can now be contrasted with that under perfect competition. There are two major differences. First, under perfect competition, the rate changes only if there is excess demand, or supply, for labour; while under collective bargaining, the rate is the outcome of the strategies of unions and employers' associations—and these depend on a variety of considerations, of which the existence of excess demand or supply is only one. Second, under competition, the wage rate will rise only if there is excess demand; while under collective bargaining it is possible for it to rise even when there is some excess supply (unemployment).

Three reasons for *differences* between wage rates were analysed earlier in the chapter, namely workers' preferences, transfer costs, and the ranges of abilities of the available workers. To these must now be added the effects of collective bargaining. The strength and militancy of trade unions vary from one to another. This is likely to have some effect on the pattern of relative wage rates. Moreover, some unions place restrictions on the entry of new members. This puts a constraint on the position of the supply curve of the workers in question, and operates to raise their wage rate relative to others. These various reasons for wage differences may of course work in the same or in opposite directions. The difference as between any two jobs will be the net outcome of all their effects.

Even if the total labour force is constant, the supply curves for different kinds of job will shift relative to one another over time, as workers retire or die, and young people enter the labour force. Since the young will be attracted by highly-paid work, and repelled by low-paid work, it might be thought that wage rate differences will decline as time goes on. But population changes are slow, and the conditions of demand for labour are changing at the same time. There can therefore be no presumption of a movement towards less inequality. Empirical studies do, however, suggest some movement in this direction as the standard of living in a country rises. This may be because parents (or the government) are better able to meet the large costs of entry (viz. for education and professional training) which exist for many highly-paid jobs.

RENTS

Now consider why rents may differ from one kind of land to another. There are a number of differences between pieces of land which are relevant to the determination of the prices for their productive services. They differ in their agricultural fertilities, in the minerals they bear, in the geological features which are important for the support of buildings, in their scenic attractions (or lack of them) and in their locations in space. These differences parallel those between the capabilities of human beings. They help to explain why the demand and supply curves for the various markets in land intersect at different heights, i.e. at different rents.

The positions of the demand curves for two kinds of land may be quite different, since they depend on the variety of technologies and demand conditions for the goods which can be made by the factors. Thus the demand for land which bears oil will be different from that for land which has no oil.

Location in space is a very important determinant of the differences in the demand conditions for various kinds of land. People are not uniformly distributed, either for work or by domicile, over the earth's surface. The complex subject of *location theory* deals with the economic, geographic, historic and social reasons for this. The congregation of people in cities and towns brings a much greater demand for land within them, and in their environs, than in the countryside. The time and effort (i.e. the transport costs) involved in moving goods and people from place to place is an essential element in that difference.

Given the demand curves for the productive services of different kinds of land, their rents depend on the *positions* of their supply curves. The explanation of differences in rents can be conducted in the same way as that used (with the aid of Figs. 20.1a and 20.1b above) for wage rates. The positions of the supply curves depend on the preferences of land owners as between different uses for it, on the costs of transferring land from one use to another and on the size and nature of the stock of land.

Preferences do not seem to be important for the majority of landowners. There may be a few who will choose to take a smaller rent for one use (e.g. as a private park or a golf course) than a larger rent for another (e.g. as a housing or industrial estate). But by and large, land will be attracted to the uses which pay the highest rents.[1]

But that will not equalize rents if there are costs of transfer between different uses. These may not be very significant in some cases, e.g. in changing from one agricultural crop to another. But they can be important, e.g. where a change of use involves the demolition of existing structures.

The main reason why the S curves, for the productive services of land, do not take up positions in *relation* to their D curves which equalize rents is, of course, the nature and location of the stock of land. Agricultural land cannot become oil-bearing land just because the rent of the latter exceeds that of the former. A portion of Dartmoor is not put to the same uses at the Strand in London because of the location of people and the costs of transport.

As the national income of a country increases over time, the D curves for the productive services of land will shift upwards to the right. In a settled country, the S curves, for the services of natural resources, can be increased only by reclamation, or by the discovery of hitherto unknown features of the land (e.g. natural gas deposits). Hence, the rents of land are likely to increase over time *relatively* to the prices of many goods. But what will happen to rents, *relatively* to the prices of labour and capital factors, is a more complex matter. It is part of the problems tackled by the theory of the functional distribution of income.

CAPITAL RENTALS

In view of the long analysis of wage rates and rents above, there would be little to add on capital rentals but for one consideration. Some capital goods (especially buildings) are rented through the market; but many of them (especially machinery) are not.

The capital rentals paid for the productive services of the former are determined by the conditions of demand and supply for them. These conditions depend on all the considerations analysed in the previous chapter. Differences between the rentals of the various capital goods may exist because of the preferences of their owners between uses,[2] the costs of transfer between uses, and the size and nature of the existing stock of capital goods. In all these respects, there exist only differences

---

[1] This, of course, has to be qualified if there is governmental control over the use of land.

[2] Which are not likely to be of much importance in relation to capital goods.

of detail between the analysis of capital rentals, on the one hand, and that of wage rates and rents on the other.

One cannot speak of market demand and supply curves for the productive services of capital goods which are not in fact rented through the market. Nevertheless, the earnings (i.e. what are usually called the profits) which their owners get directly from them are determined by the *same* influences as are capital rentals.

The owner of a capital good, who does not rent it out, has to decide upon the use to which to put it.[1] Given the nature of the good, he will seek out its most profitable use, subject to the costs of transfer between uses. Each capital good—like a human being or a piece of land—has only a limited range of capabilities, i.e. it can help in the production only of certain goods. The earnings of the capital good, in its alternative uses, will be determined by the revenue conditions for the goods it produces relative to their cost conditions. The latter depend on technology, and on the prices of the factors used with the capital good. The considerations just listed are, of course, precisely those which appear in the market demand condition for a *rented* capital good.

Suppose that there are no costs of transfer. Then, the owners of the existing units of the capital good will distribute these units between different uses in such a way as to equalize their rates of earnings. That is, they will set the units to produce those quantities of different goods which equalize the rates of profit on the capital good in the various production lines. The profit rate on one line may, however, remain above that on another, because transfer costs inhibit the shifting of the capital good between different uses. The considerations just noted are, of course, precisely those which appear in the market supply condition for a *rented* capital good.

The rates of profit on *existing* capital goods are thus determined by the same influences as are capital rentals. The theory of capital rentals embraces the theory of *short period* profits.[2] This can also be seen from a re-reading of the analysis of the 'short period' in Chapter 14.[3] It was shown there that the rate of profit, on the existing plant of a particular firm, depends on its revenue condition, and on its variable cost condition;[4] and that, if this rate is greater than or equal to zero, *and* greater than the rates on alternative uses of the plant, the firm will continue to

[1] He may *delegate* that decision to someone else as, e.g. the shareholders in a company do to the board of directors.
[2] Which Alfred Marshall, for this very reason, called *quasi-rents*.
[3] Especially pp. 149–153 above.
[4] Which depends on the firm's technology, and on the prices of the factors other than capital.

operate it. If that analysis is now extended to allow for transfer costs, it is merely another way of presenting the above argument, that *short period* profits are determined by the same influences as capital rentals.

The stock of capital can, however, be increased or decreased. This takes time, and any desired change in it can be achieved only in the *long period*. The analysis of capital rentals and profit rates in the long period therefore requires an investigation into the determinants of investment.

CHAPTER 21

INVESTMENT

A capital good may have a life which spans many months, years, or even decades. A decision to acquire it will therefore depend on the capital rentals (or profits) which are *expected* to be earned on it over its life. Neither the length of time for which it will be used, nor the capital rentals[1] which will *actually* be earned, can be known with certainty. A firm (or a person) embarking on an investment project must predict, to the best of its ability, both the expected life and the capital rentals.

A firm can invest either by acquiring a newly produced capital good or by purchasing an existing one from someone else. In the latter event, the other party disinvests to the same extent. A country[2] as a whole can therefore invest only through the production of new capital goods. The investment may either be in *replacement* of capital goods, that are currently wearing out (depreciating), or be a *net* addition to the capital stock. The following analysis will be specifically directed to net investments by firms, and will be couched in terms of the acquisition of newly-produced capital goods.[3]

The investor in a capital good has to pay the ruling *supply price* for it. This is the cost he must incur in order to get the revenue in the form of the expected capital rentals. Suppose that the supply price is paid entirely at a particular moment of time, e.g. at the beginning of some year when the capital good is delivered. Also suppose that the firm makes up its accounts on an annual basis, so that its capital rentals will be computed in *per year* terms.

Consider a firm which is thinking of investing in a capital good which has an expected life of *n* years. An expected capital rental has then to be predicted for each of these years. They will either be the rentals (e.g. for a building) which the owner expects to get from others for the use of

---

[1] Since capital rentals and short period profits are determined by the same influences, for brevity the former term will now be used to include the latter.

[2] Which has no foreign trade. The question of foreign investment will be dealt with in Part IV below.

[3] But the same principles apply to replacement investment and to investment in already existing capital goods.

the good; or they will be short period profits (e.g. on a machine) which he expects to earn by using the good himself for productive purposes. These profits will be determined by the revenue and variable cost conditions, in each of the years in question, for the goods produced by the capital good. The owner will therefore have to predict those conditions.

Suppose that he expects to earn a capital rental of a_1 in the first year, a_2 in the second year, and so on to a_n in the last year of the capital good's life.[1] The expected revenue from the good will then be the stream of capital rentals

$$a_1 + a_2 + \ldots + a_n$$

Let the supply price of the good be S. In the first instance, the investor will have to compare S and the stream of expected rentals, in order to compute the return he expects to get on an outlay of S.

That return cannot be computed by simply adding a_1 to a_n together and comparing their sum with S. The first year's rental, a_1, becomes available (assuming annual accounting) for use by the investor at the end of the first year. Similarly, a_2 becomes available at the end of the second year. The amounts, a_1 and a_2, are not directly comparable, because they are sums of money which become available *at different dates*. Thus, if a_1 is lent out at some rate of interest for a year, it will accumulate to a larger total by the end of the second year. It is that larger total which is directly comparable with a_2, since they have the *same* dates. The same point applies to all the rentals. A simple addition of a_1 to a_n therefore lacks economic significance.

Since the rate of interest has now entered the analysis, it may be well to pause and make clear the nature of accumulation at *compound* interest.

COMPOUND INTEREST

Suppose that a person lends out a sum of money for n years at a particular rate of interest, and that the interest is computed annually. Moreover, suppose he arranges that the annual amounts of interest are not in fact paid over to him as they fall due, but are retained by the borrower and are added to the original debt for repayment with it at the end of n years. In that case, the lender will earn interest, not only on the original sum, but also on the accumulating interest which is retained by the debtor. The sum repayable at the end of n years is then the original

[1] a_n will include the estimated price for which the good can be sold to another user or for scrap.

loan plus the interest *compounded* annually on it. What is now required is the formula for the accumulated sum repayable at the end of *n* years.

If £100 is borrowed for one year at 5 per cent per annum, the sum to be repaid at the end of the year is the original £100 plus 5 per cent of £100, i.e. £100(1 + 5 per cent), or £105. If the £105 is not repaid, but is now borrowed for an additional year on the same terms, the amount repayable at the end of two years is £105(1 + 5 per cent), or £110·25. Since the £105 is equal to £100(1 + 5 per cent), the amount to be repaid at the end of the second year can be expressed as £100(1 + 5 per cent) (1 + 5 per cent), or £100(1 + 5 per cent)^2; this can also be written as £100(1·05)^2, since 5 per cent (i.e. $\frac{5}{100}$) is 0·05. At the end of a third year of *compound* interest, the amount to be repaid will be £100(1·05)^3. This can be generalized with the aid of symbols as

$$A = P(1 + i)^n$$

where *P* is the amount of the loan, *n* is the number of years for which it is made, *i* is the percentage interest rate per annum (expressed in a decimal form), and *A* is the amount to which the loan will eventually accumulate at *compound* interest. Thus *A* is the *terminal value* to which *P* will *accumulate* at the end of *n* years.

The formula for compound interest can be looked at from another angle. It can be asked, what is the size of the sum which *would* accumulate to *A*, by the end of *n* years, at compound interest of *i* per cent p.a.? That is, instead of starting with *P* and asking what *A* will be, one can start with *A* and ask what *P* would have to be. A re-arrangement of the formula gives the answer

$$P = \frac{A}{(1 + i)^n}$$

That is, *P* is the amount which, if lent out at compound interest of *i* per cent p.a., would accumulate to a terminal value of *A* after *n* years.

P is called the *present value* of *A*. The method of obtaining *P*—as given by the formula—is known as that of *discounting* the sum *A*. The processes of accumulating and discounting at interest are thus two aspects of one and the same thing, namely the relation between a present value *P* and a terminal value *A* given by a compound interest rate. *P* accumulates at interest to *A*; or *A* is discounted at interest to *P*.

THE RETURN ON INVESTMENT

The process of discounting is required to calculate the expected return on an investment. It has been seen above that this return involves a comparison between the supply price S of the capital good and the expected stream of rentals $a_1 + a_2 + \ldots + a_n$.

Suppose that the ruling market rate of interest is i per cent p.a. It can now be asked, what sum of money would accumulate, at that rate, to a terminal value of a_1 by the end of *one* year? The answer, from the formula for discounting, is $\dfrac{a_1}{(1 + i)}$: this is the 'present value' of a_1. The present value of a_2 is similarly obtained as $\dfrac{a_2}{(1 + i)^2}$. Hence, given the interest rate, the present value of the *whole* stream of expected capital rentals can be computed by adding the present values of all its elements, giving

$$P' = \frac{a_1}{(1 + i)} + \frac{a_2}{(1 + i)^2} + \ldots + \frac{a_n}{(1 + i)^n}.$$

This formula is only a more complex version of the first one above. Instead of giving the relation between *one* present value P and *one* terminal value A, it gives the relation between the sum P' of a *number* of present values and the corresponding terminal values[1] a_1, a_2 to a_n. It indicates that at the given compound interest rate the sum P' can accumulate to the *series* of terminal values a_1, a_2 to a_n. This can be thought of as follows. Suppose that a person lends out P' at a compound interest rate of i. He could then arrange with the borrower to repay, not in a single amount at one date, but in a series of amounts at different dates. The formula shows that one possible series of repayments—of both the original loan and the accumulated interest on it— is a_1 at the end of one year, a_2 at the end of two years, and so on. That series will exactly repay the loan and accumulated interest on it by the end of n years.[2]

A comparison can now be made between S, the required outlay on the capital good, and P' the present value of its expected rentals. P', as has just been seen, can be thought of as the amount of a loan which would generate, at the ruling market interest rate, a series of repayments which are the same as the expected rentals.

---

[1] All of which are discounted at the same interest rate.

[2] It can be helpful to see that all this can also be presented in terms of accumulating, rather than of discounting. Multiply the present formula through by $(1 + i)^n$. Then

$$P'(1 + i)^n = a_1(1 + i)^{n-1} + a_2(1 + i)^{n-2} + \ldots + a_n.$$

That is, the terminal value of P', given on the left-hand side, is equal to the *sum* of the terminal values of a_1, a_2 to a_n, given on the right-hand side. This corresponds to $P(1 + i)^n = A$ for a single present value and a single terminal value.

Suppose that $S > P'$. The outlay of S on the capital good is expected to yield the stream of rentals a_1, a_2 to a_n. A loan of P', at a compound interest rate of i, can yield the same stream, a_1, a_2 to a_n, of repayments (including interest). In these circumstances, it is not expected to be profitable to invest in the capital good in question. The loan of the *smaller* sum (P') will bring the *same* series of returns as that expected from the *larger* outlay (S) on the investment. A profit maximizing firm, which has the finance for the investment, would therefore prefer to lend it out at interest, rather than to buy the capital good.

But if $S < P'$, the *smaller* outlay on investment is expected to bring the *same* series of returns as that which the loan of a *larger* sum could bring. If the uncertainty attaching to the expected capital rentals is ignored, a profit maximizing firm will therefore prefer to use finance to buy the capital good rather than to make a loan.

It is thus the relation between (i) the supply price of a capital good, and (ii) the present value, at the ruling interest rate, of its expected rentals, which shows whether or not investment in it is expected to be profitable.[1] This is known as the *present value* method[2] of evaluating an investment. It involves the explicit use of the rate of return on lending, i.e. the rate of interest. But it does not make explicit the expected *rate* of return on the investment. The same procedure can, however, easily be used to do that.

Suppose, once again, that a capital good, with supply price S, has expected rentals, a_1, a_2 to a_n. It can now be asked: what is the rate of discount (r) which would make the present value (P'') of those rentals equal to S? This is given by:

$$S = P'' = \frac{a_1}{(1 + r)} + \frac{a_2}{(1 + r)^2} + \ldots + \frac{a_n}{(1 + r)^n}.$$

The formula is the same as before, but it is used in a different way. Instead of using the rate of interest to find the present value of the rentals, the present value is taken as given (viz. $= S$), and the r which will discount the stream of rentals to it is calculated That is, the formula is used to solve for r (with P given), rather than for P (with i given).

The rate of discount, r, is called the *internal rate of return* which is expected to be earned on the capital good, i.e. it is the expected rate of

---

[1] It should be noticed that this assessment of profitability allows for the recovery of the outlay on the capital good. Just as the payments, a_1, a_2 to a_n, cover repayment of the loan P' as well as interest on it, so the capital rentals, a_1, a_2 to a_n, cover the depreciation charges on the capital good as well as its earnings in excess of its supply price.

[2] Or the *discounted cash flow* (D.C.F.) method.

return which is 'internal' to the investment project in question. It measures the expected earnings of the capital good in *excess* of its supply price;[1] and it does so in the form of their ratio to the supply price. Thus, with annual accounting, r will be a rate per cent p.a. (e.g. 10 per cent p.a.). The expected internal rate of return on a capital good, over its life, can therefore be compared directly with the ruling interest rate (i), as given 'externally' in the financial markets.

If $i > r$ for a particular investment, it is not expected to be profitable. It would be better to lend out available finance at i, rather than to buy a capital good which is only expected to earn r. Or, if the finance for the investment would have to be borrowed, it would not be profitable, since the *cost of finance* (at i per cent) exceeds the expected return from using the finance.

If $i < r$, and if the uncertainty attaching to the expected capital rentals is ignored, it is then expected to be profitable to carry out the investment. Available finance will earn less by lending, or borrowed finance will cost less, than the rate of return expected on the investment.

If $i > r$ for a particular investment, then (from the last two formulae in the text above) it necessarily follows that $S > P'$ for it. If $i > r$, then $P' < P''$, since P' is obtained by discounting the expected rentals at a *higher* rate (viz. i) than the rate r by which P'' is obtained. But $P'' = S$; hence, $S > P'$. By both tests—viz. $i > r$, and $S > P'$—the investment is unprofitable. Similarly, if $i < r$, then $S < P'$; and if $i = r$, then $S = P'$. Thus the *present value* and the *internal rate of return* methods of evaluating the profitability of a particular investment project necessarily give the same answer.[2]

It is more convenient, for present purposes, to work with an explicit comparison between the expected internal rate of return, r, on an investment and the rate of interest, i, on the borrowing of finance. But this comparison, as a test for profitability, has to be qualified to allow for the uncertainty attaching to the expected capital rentals. These are either, as has been seen, the rentals (e.g. for a building) which the owner of a capital good expects to get for its use by someone else; or they are the short period profits (e.g. on a machine) he himself expects to earn by using the good for productive purposes. In both cases, the *actual* capital rentals in the future will be determined by the revenue and variable cost conditions then ruling for the goods make by the capital good.

[1] As has just been explained (p. 234, fn. 1), the discounting formula allows for the recovery of the outlay on the good.
[2] But this is not necessarily so in respect of a *comparison* of the profitabilities of *alternative* investment projects. That, however, is a more complex question, which cannot be investigated here.

These conditions cannot be predicted with certainty. They will depend on the prices at which goods can be sold, on the prices at which factors can be bought, and on the state of technology in the future. All of these things may be exceedingly difficult to predict, especially for capital goods which may have long lives in front of them. That is why it is essential to emphasize that the internal rate of return on a capital good is an *expected* rate. Some investors—especially large firms with market research departments—may attempt a careful prediction of the rentals and the implied rate of return. Others may use the *current* rentals being earned on similar types of capital as a guide to expected rates of return.

The necessity of allowing for uncertainty can be formalized in the following manner. Suppose that $i = 7$ per cent p.a., and that the most *probable* value expected for the r of an investment project is put at 12 per cent p.a. On a straight comparison of i and r, the firm would make the investment. But the actual r may turn out to be less than 12 per cent. The investor must therefore ask himself: is the difference between a *certain* i of 7 per cent and an *uncertain* r of 12 per cent, i.e. 5 per cent, sufficient to cover the risk of disappointment?[1] The degree of uncertainty depends on the objective difficulties of predicting r. But the willingness to bear the risk of disappointment is subjective to the investor. Not all (if any) investors may regard a 5 per cent difference between i and the most probable r on the project as a sufficient inducement to bear the risk.

The investor's assessment of that risk can be expressed in the form of a percentage rate p.a., to be deducted from the most probable r. Suppose this *risk premium* is put at 3 per cent by the investor. The r, adjusted for uncertainty, is then 12 per cent $-$ 3 per cent, i.e. 9 per cent, and this is still sufficient to justify the investment when $i = 7$ per cent. But with greater difficulties in predicting r, and/or with a more cautious investor, the risk premium might be put at 6 per cent. The investment would not then be undertaken.

Denote the risk premium by p. Then an investment project will be expected to be profitable only if

$$r - p > i$$

i.e. if

$$r > i + p$$

---

[1] This assumes that interest on the borrowed finance will be paid at a rate of 7 per cent over the *whole* life of the capital good. If re-financing will be possible during that life, at a different interest rate, then i as well as r is uncertain.

INVESTMENT AND PROFITS

The interconnections between short-period profits, long-period profits, and the profitability of investment, can now be analysed. This is most easily done in relation to the analysis of Chapter 14.[1]

A firm is able to vary, in the long period, the quantities of *any* of the factors which it wants to use. It will, in equilibrium, be using the least cost combination of *all* factors to produce the most profitable output, given its revenue condition. It does not, therefore, need any net addition to its capital resources in order to provide more capital factors. That is, with its existing stock of capital equal to the most profitable stock with which it could operate, *net* investment by it will be zero.[2] This means that for a firm which is in long-period equilibrium, $r < i + p$ for any conceivable net investment project.

On the other hand, a firm which is in short-period, but not in long-period, equilibrium, has *not* got its most profitable stock of capital goods. Given its revenue and cost conditions, it wishes either to enlarge or to reduce the size of its plant. Its revenue and *variable* cost curves determine the highest *short-period* profit it can earn with the given and fixed size of plant. Thus, with plant size 4, and the AR_2 curve, in Fig. 14.2 on p. 150 above, the most profitable output is OL. In the long period, however, the firm can vary the size of its plant. Hence in order to discover the highest *long-period* profit it could earn, it is necessary to add the *cost of finance* for the plant—which is given by $i + p$, when uncertainty is taken into account—to the costs of the other factors. That is, in the terminology of Chapter 14, a cost curve which includes both *fixed* and *variable* costs has to be set against the revenue curve. The fixed cost, as was explained at the time, is the cost of finance for each particular size of plant.

The fixed cost for each plant size, plus the associated variable costs, give the long-period cost condition for the firm. This is shown by the complete cost curve derived from the ATC_1, ATC_2, ATC_3, and ATC_4 curves in Fig. 14.2. The relation between it and the revenue curve determines the most profitable output and therefore the most profitable size of plant in the long period. These are output OK, and plant size 3, in relation to the AR_2 curve in Fig. 14.2. The firm will want to change from its existing plant size to a new plant size if *both* of two conditions are fulfilled, namely that (i) a higher profit can be earned with the new

[1] See especially pp. 149–153 above.
[2] But positive *replacement* investment will be required to maintain the desired capital stock intact.

than with the existing plant, and (ii) the profit on the new plant will at least cover the cost of finance for it. The latter condition means, in terms of the present chapter's analysis, that the r for the *whole* of the new plant must at least equal $i + p$.

The new plant may be bigger or smaller than the existing one. It will be bigger if $r > i + p$ for *additions* to the existing plant. Net investment by the firm will then be positive. But the new plant will be smaller than the existing one if $r < i + p$ for the *replacement* of the existing plant size. Thus, plant size 4, in Fig. 14.2, is not replaced because AR_2, at point S, is less than ATC_4, at point T. Instead, plant size 3 is invested in, both because it is more profitable and because $AR_2 = ATC_3$ at point U, i.e. $r = i + p$ for the whole of this plant.

The relation between r and $i + p$ thus indicates the profitability of a *change* in the size of the capital stock. Such a change is profitable only for a firm which is not in long-period equilibrium. Net investment (either positive or negative) is the means by which it adjusts during the short period towards the long-period equilibrium.

The rate of interest is a *price* which, like all prices, is determined by the whole working of the economic system. The profitability of investment projects depends on the level of the interest rate. Hence a full explanation of investment cannot be given until the determination of the interest rate is analysed in Chapter 30 below. Moreover, that explanation involves a further problem. Investment is a *rate* per period of time. The condition, $r > i + p$, shows that an investment is expected to be profitable. But it does not in itself explain the rate (e.g. per year) at which a community will carry out all its investment projects. The whole question of the determinants of the *rate* of investment will be analysed at the macroeconomic level in Chapter 31 below.

It has been stressed before that the everyday use of the term profit is highly ambiguous. This is in part because of differences between the accounting conventions of firms. But it is also because the determination of profits is, as has been seen, a complex matter. It may be helpful, therefore, to give a summary of the relations between, and the determinants of, the different forms of profit which have been analysed in this book.

In all cases here the term 'profit' refers to the earnings of the productive services of capital goods. Profits are distinguished from capital rentals in that the latter are obtained from the renting out of capital goods, while the former are earned when their owners (or their delegates) themselves control the uses to which they are put.

Short-period profits are the earnings from the use of the productive services of a given and fixed stock of capital goods. They are determined by the revenue and variable cost conditions of the firms using them.

Long-period profits are those earned by firms which are in long-period equilibrium. They will be greater than, or equal to, the cost of the finance required to purchase the firms' capital goods. The cost of finance is $i + p$, when uncertainty is taken into account.[1]

Normal profits are those which equal the cost of finance.

Supernormal profits are those earned by a firm in excess of normal profit. They can exist in long-period equilibrium because of monopoly elements in the system. Without monopoly, competition in the use of capital goods would bring the earnings of their productive services down to equality with the cost of finance.

Profit must not be confused with the rate of interest, which is the price charged for a loan of money. But there are important relationships between profits and the interest rate.

Long-period profits are greater than or equal to $i + p$. They will be greater if there are monopoly elements in the system. They can therefore exceed the interest rate for two reasons, viz uncertainty and monopoly. This excess is sometimes called *pure* profit. But short-period profits need not bear any systematic relation to the interest rate. They may be above or below it, and can be negative (viz. losses).

It should now be clear that the *recorded* profits of firms need to be interpreted very carefully. *Actual* profits are short-period profits. The firms earning them may, or may not, be in long-period equilibrium at the time. If they are, it may be possible to draw deductions about uncertainty, and/or the presence of monopoly elements, from a comparison between their profit rates and the interest rate. But if they are not in long-period equilibrium, net investment (or disinvestment) by them will occur. The consequential expansion (or contraction) of the firms will affect their profit rates. The effects will have to be predicted before a comparison with the interest rate can yield any deductions about uncertainty and/or monopoly. Thus, actual profit rates which are high relative to the interest rate might be due to monopoly; but they might also be due to the fact that firms have not yet had time to complete the investments required by some change in demand and/or supply conditions.

[1] The *average* rate of profit (as given by AVC and AR) can exceed $i + p$ even when the *marginal* rate of profit (as given by MC and MR) equals $i + p$. If the latter condition obtains, net investment will be zero, because *additional* units of capital would not be profitable. Hence, the average rate of profit can exceed $i + p$ in long-period equilibrium.

THE PRICES OF RESOURCES

The price of an existing resource (e.g. a piece of land or a machine) depends on the prices which are expected to be paid for its productive services over the rest of its life. This is true at any point in the life. A resource is acquired because of the services it may yield. It is the values of those services which give value to the resource.

In the absence of uncertainty, the price of a resource will equal its present value, as obtained by discounting the expected prices of its services over its life by the ruling interest rate. The sum of money paid for the resource could alternatively be lent out at compound interest. The purchaser of a resource will therefore not pay more for it than the amount of a loan that could generate a series of repayments which is the *same* as the series of expected prices for the services of the resource. The principle here is, of course, exactly the same as that involved in computing the present value of a resource yet to be created. Once it is in existence, its market price will equal that present value.

The prices which will be paid for the services of a resource are, however, uncertain. On the other hand, the ruling interest rate is known and certain.[1] Therefore, the price of a resource will be obtained by discounting the expected prices of its services at a rate *greater* than the ruling interest rate, viz. at $i + p$, where p is the risk premium to cover the chances that the prices of the resource's services will be lower than expected. If a_1, a_2 to a_n are the expected prices of the services (e.g. the expected rents of a piece of land, or the expected rentals of a capital good) and P is the price of the resource, then

$$P = \frac{a_1}{(1 + i + p)} + \frac{a_2}{(1 + i + p)^2} + \cdots + \frac{a_n}{(1 + i + p)^n}$$

Thus, if $i = 7$ per cent, and $p = 5$ per cent, P will be lower when the expected prices of its services are discounted at 12 per cent, than it would be if they were discounted at 7 per cent. The price of a resource reflects the uncertainty of the returns which may be got from using it. It will be lower the more uncertain they are.

The process of discounting the expected prices of a resource's services is also called *capitalizing* them. The prices of resources are therefore also known as their *capital values*.[2]

---

[1] Except to the extent that the borrower may default on repayments. This is one reason why interest rates differ as between various classes of borrowers.

[2] However long the expected life of a resource, its capital value converges to a finite limit, since the present values of more and more distant prices for its services converge to zero; i.e. $\frac{a_n}{(1 + i + p)^n}$ converges to zero, as n increases, since $(1 + i + p) > 1$.

The capital values of existing buildings, machines, and pieces of land are continually being computed in order to fix their market prices. Thus, when one company is bidding to purchase ('take over') another one, there will be a lot of argument about the capital values of the existing buildings, machinery, and land owned by the latter.

Largely because of the absence of slavery, the capital values of human beings are seldom computed.[1] Estimates of the *national capital* of countries have been made by aggregating the capital values of their buildings, machines, land, etc. These estimates do not include *human capital*. This can be misleading because of the great importance to a country of its labour resources. Investment in human beings, through education and training, can bring returns in the form of higher incomes (both personal and national). The relation between that investment and those returns can be analysed by the principles developed in this chapter.[2] A comparison can then be made between the expected rates of return on investment in human capital and in capital goods. The comparison is obviously important for the determination of the best use of the resources available for investment.

[1] Except, e.g. to decide the compensation which should be paid for disablement.
[2] This is central to the economics of education.

CHAPTER 22

THE RELATIONS BETWEEN THE PRICES OF GOODS AND FACTORS

The determination of the prices of goods, and of changes in them, has so far been analysed on the assumption of given prices for factors. Similarly, the determination of the prices of factors, and of changes in them, has been analysed on the assumption of given prices for goods. Since prices are interrelated, an understanding of the working of a price mechanism requires the ability to trace the effects of a change in one price on other prices. The microeconomic analysis of this book will be rounded off by some demonstrations of how that can be done.

The prices of goods are interrelated because they are substitutes or complements of one another. The prices of factors are interrelated because they are used jointly in the production of goods. The prices of goods and of factors are interrelated both because factors are demanded in order to make goods, and because the incomes derived from the sale of factors help to determine the demands for goods. It is all these interrelations, together with the analyses of the preceding chapters, which enable the effects of a change in one price on other prices to be traced in a systematic manner.

For brevity and simplicity, most of the ensuing analyses will assume perfect competition, and will refer to the short period in which the stock of resources is given and fixed.

CHANGES IN THE DEMANDS FOR GOODS

Consider first the effects of an increase in demand for a particular good (A) upon the prices of the factors (α, etc.) which are used to produce it. The increased demand for A increases the demand for α, a larger quantity of which is now required to produce a greater output of A. The D curve for α shifts upwards to the right (since the demand condition of A is a parameter of it), e.g. from D_1 to D_2 in Fig. 22.1.

With an S curve for α which is upward sloping to the right, an increased demand for it raises its price, e.g. from point P to Q. The extent of the rise depends on the price elasticity of supply over the range of the S curve in question. Thus the more willing are the owners of resources, who can provide α, to shift them between uses in response to a small change in price, the smaller will be the rise in p_α. Given the supply elasticity, the rise in p_α will be the larger, the greater is the increase in demand for A and therefore for α.

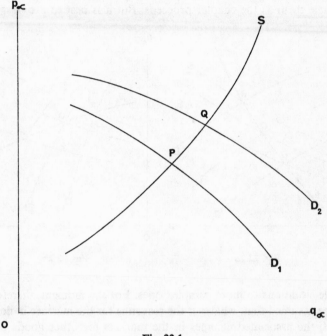

Fig. 22.1

In order to continue the analysis of this situation, it is essential to specify the reason for the increase in demand for A. That is, it is necessary to identify the parameter change which shifted the D curve for A. This could be a change in consumer preferences in favour of A, and against some other goods. If the latter also employ α, the analysis would have to take into account the effects, on the demand for it, of the decreases in demand for these other goods. Again, the demand for A could increase if incomes rise (and A is a 'superior' good). In this case, the demand for some other goods will also increase (or decrease for 'inferior' goods). If the latter employ α, the analysis would have to take into account the effects on the demand for it of the shifts in demand for these other goods. And yet again, the demand for A could increase if the prices of substitutes for it rise, or those of complements fall. It would then be necessary to enquire into the reasons for those other price changes to see if they have any connections with the D and/or S conditions of α.

These are some of the problems which have to be faced in the analysis of any economic situation. An attempt will be made to disentangle them as the chapter proceeds. But it is best to progress from

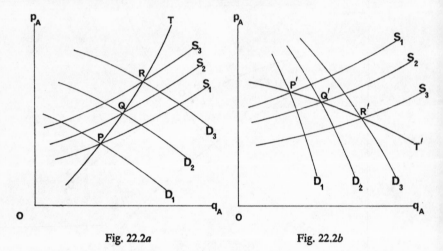

Fig. 22.2a   Fig. 22.2b

simple situations to more complex ones. For the moment, therefore, it will be assumed that, whatever the reason is for the increase in demand for A, the associated changes in the markets for other goods do not affect the D and/or S conditions for α.

Suppose, then, that the demand for α increases solely because of the increased demand for A. With a given S curve for α, its price will rise. p_α is a parameter of the S curve for A. As p_α, and the prices of the other factors used by A, rise, the costs of the firms producing A increase.[1] Hence the S surve for A shifts upwards to the left.

This is shown in Fig. 22.2a. The price of A is in equilibrium at point P, given by the D_1 and S_1 curves. Suppose there is an increase in demand to D_2. The consequential increases in the demands for factors raise their prices. The S curve for A shifts to S_2. The new equilibrium p_A is therefore given at the intersection (Q) of D_2 and S_2. If demand now increases to D_3, and the consequential rises in factor prices decrease

---

[1] I.e. their cost curves shift upwards.

supply to S_3, p_A will move to the equilibrium where D_3 and S_3 intersect at R.

The intermediate equilibria between P, Q, and R can be found in the same way. The curve T, which joins all these equilibria, then shows the path which p_A will follow as demand for A increases (or decreases). The price of A rises, partly because the individual S surves slope upwards to the right, and partly because factor prices rise as the output of A expands. The expansion in output will be smaller than it would have been if factor prices had not risen. This can be seen by comparing an upward movement along T with an upward movement along, e.g. S_1, on which factor prices are given and constant.[1]

There is, however, another possibility. The firms producing A may use *intermediate* products (like raw materials and components) as well as factors provided by labour, land, and capital resources. These intermediate products are the outputs of other industries. If they are operating under imperfect competition, an increase in the demands for their products may lower their prices.[2] In that case, as industry A expands, it may be able to purchase intermediate products at lower prices, because of economies which are *internal* to the other industries. This is one species of economy which is *external* to industry A. Of course, the prices of intermediate products may rise as industry A demands more of them; and this will necessarily happen[3] if the other industries are operating under perfect competition. In that case there will be external diseconomies for industry A.

Suppose that the prices of intermediate products do fall as industry A expands. Its S surve will, on that account, shift downwards to the right.[4] This could (but will not necessarily) lead to the outcome shown in Fig. 22.2b. The D_1 and S_1 curves give an equilibrium at P'. When the demand curve shifts to D_2, the expansion in output increases the demands for intermediate products and lowers their prices. The supply curve then shifts to S_2, giving an equilibrium in relation to D_2 at Q'. And similarly for D_3 and S_3 at R'. The path followed by p_A is given by the curve T', which is downward sloping to the right. The price of A

---

[1] But output *will* expand along T as long as the industry can get more factors, since factor prices rise only because output expands. That is, T will be upward sloping to the right.

[2] See pp. 187–188 above.

[3] On present assumptions. The subject of external economies (and diseconomies) is a complex one, because the production functions of different goods may be interconnected (e.g. when river water, which is used in the productive process of a firm downstream, is polluted by the productive process of another firm upstream). This cannot be taken further here.

[4] There will, of course, be some offset to this shift from higher factor prices.

falls as output expands because the *decreases* in the costs of the firms (as shown by the shifts in the S curve) more than offset their condition of *rising* costs (as shown by the upward slope of each S curve). The expansion of output will therefore be greater than it would have been if the prices of intermediate products had not fallen (or had risen).

CHANGES IN THE SUPPLIES OF FACTORS

It has now been shown how an increase in demand for a good affects factor prices; and how the resultant changes in the latter react back on the price of the good.[1] The next stage, in analysing the interconnections between prices, is to enquire how an increase in the supply of a factor will affect the prices of both factors and goods.

A shift in the S curve of a factor downwards to the right will reduce its price, since the D curve for it is downward sloping to the right. The costs of the firms using the factor will decrease.[2] The S curves of the goods made by the factor will increase, viz. shift downwards to the right. The prices of the goods will therefore fall and their outputs will expand.

In order to continue this analysis, it is necessary to specify the reason for the shift in the S curve of the factor (e.g. a particular kind of labour α). This could be a fall, for some other reason, in the wage rates of *other* kinds of labour, which cause some workers to switch to supplying α. Those reductions in wage rates will decrease the costs of the goods made by the other kinds of labour. If some of these goods also employ α, two sets of effects on their prices will have to be disentangled, namely that of the initial wage rate changes, and that of the consequential fall in p_α. Again, the supply of α could increase if workers come to prefer this kind of work to a greater extent, or if the costs of transferring to it from other jobs are reduced. In this case, the S curves of some other labour factors will decrease. The resulting rise in their prices may affect the costs and prices of some of the goods which use α. Again, the supply of α could increase if population increases. Since the supplies of other labour factors would also increase, there would be a host of effects on the prices of goods to be analysed. Yet again, the supply of α could increase if the workers doing the job come to prefer it more as against leisure. That change need not involve shifts in the S curves of other labour factors,

---

[1] Except that the effects on the demands for goods of the changes in incomes, which result from the changes in factor prices, have not been allowed for. These effects will be brought into the analysis later in the chapter.

[2] I.e. their cost curves shift downwards.

since other workers need not change their preferences between work and leisure.

It is thus seen, once more, how essential it is to specify the reason for a shift in a particular D or S curve. The same shift can lead to quite different consequences, according to the different reasons why the shift took place. The scope of the present piece of analysis will be restricted by taking the case of a change in preferences between work α and leisure. An increase in the supply of α, because of a reduced preference for

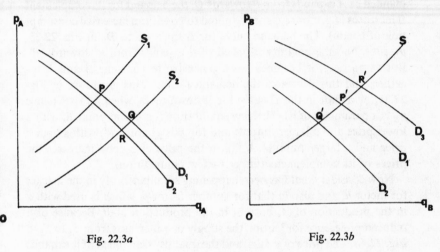

Fig. 22.3a   Fig. 22.3b

leisure, can be assumed not to be accompanied by shifts in the S curves of other factors.

Suppose that A and B are *substitute* goods; and that α is used in the production of A, but not in that of B. Before the increase in the supply of α, p_A is in equilibrium at point P in Fig. 22.3a, given the D_1 and S_1 curves; and p_B is in equilibrium at P' in Fig. 22.3b, given the D_1 and S curves for it.

The increase in the supply of α reduces p_α, and shifts the S surve of A down to S_2. p_A falls, and the quantity demanded of it expands from P towards Q. Since A is now relatively cheaper, it is substituted for B. The demand for B therefore decreases; its D curve shifts down to D_2 (since p_A is a parameter of it).[1] p_B falls, and the quantity supplied of it contracts from P' towards Q'. But as p_B falls, this offsets to some extent the

[1] Assuming that the 'income effects' of price changes are negligibly small; see p. 68 above.

fall in p_A, and reduces the amount of substitution of A for B.[1] This is shown in Fig. 22.3a by a shift in the D curve for A down to D_2 when p_B falls (since p_B is a parameter of it). The new equilibrium for A is at point R, with a lower price and a larger output; and for B is at point Q', with a lower price and a smaller output.[2] A fall in the price of a good reduces the prices of its substitutes (under perfect competition).

Suppose now that B is a *complement* of A. As before, the fall in p_α increases the supply of A to S_2, and reduces p_A. As the quantity demanded of A expands from P towards Q, the demand for its complement B increases (e.g. more eggs are required to go with an increased consumption of bacon). The demand curve for B shifts up to D_3 in Fig. 22.3b. p_B rises, and the quantity supplied of it expands from P' towards R'. But as p_B rises, it becomes more expensive to consume A and B together, and this decreases the demand for A.[3] This is shown, in Fig. 22.3a, by a shift in the D curve for A down to D_2 when p_B rises (since p_B is a parameter of it). The new equilibrium for A is at point R, with a lower price and a larger output; and for B is at point R', with a higher price and a larger output.[4] A fall in the price of a good increases the prices of its complements (under perfect competition).

Now consider what has been happening simultaneously in the market for factor α, and also in that for another factor β, which is used with α in the production of A, but not in the production of B. Because of a reduced preference for leisure, the supply of α increases from S_1 to S_2 in Fig. 22.4a. The price of α falls, and the quantity demanded of it expands from the original equilibrium at point J towards K. This results from both the *expansion* and the *substitution* effects.[5] An expansion in the quantity demanded of α is caused by the expansion in the quantity demanded of A as p_A falls. Thus the movement from J towards K in Fig. 22.4a is in part the result of the movement from P towards Q in Fig. 22.3a. The latter movement is caused by the downward shift in A's supply curve from S_1 to S_2; and this, in its turn, was caused by the

---

[1] But *some* substitution will occur, since p_B falls only in so far as A is substituted for B.

[2] It must be remembered that p_A is a parameter of B's demand curve, and p_B is a parameter of A's demand curve. Hence, in the final equilibrium, the position of the D_2 curve for B is dependent on the p_A at point R, and the position of the D_2 curve for A is dependent on the p_B at point Q'.

[3] But the quantity consumed of A (and B) still increases, since p_B rises only in so far as p_A falls.

[4] Once again, in the final equilibrium, the position of the D_3 curve for B is dependent on the p_A at point R, and the position of the D_2 curve for A is dependent on the p_B at point R'.

[5] See pp. 206–207 above.

fall in p_α resulting from the increase in the supply curve of α from S_1 to S_2 in Fig. 22.4a.

But when p_α falls, there is also a substitution effect in favour of α, and against β. The least cost condition,[1] $\dfrac{p_\alpha}{MPP_\alpha} = \dfrac{p_\beta}{MPP_\beta}$, was satisfied at the original equilibrium for good A (viz. at P in Fig. 22.3a). The fall in p_α makes $\dfrac{p_\alpha}{MPP_\alpha} < \dfrac{p_\beta}{MPP_\beta}$, and thus leads to a substitution of α for β. The

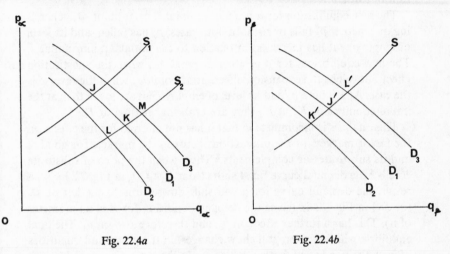

Fig. 22.4a   Fig. 22.4b

expansion in the quantity demanded of α, as its price falls (viz. from J towards K in Fig. 22.4a) is due to this substitution effect as well as to the expansion effect.

Although the substitution effect decreases the demand for β, the expansion effect increases it. Either effect can be the larger. If the substitution effect is the larger, the demand curve for β shifts from D_1 to D_2 in Fig. 22.4b (since p_α is a parameter of it). p_β falls, and the quantity supplied of it contracts from J' towards K'. If the expansion effect is the larger, the demand curve for β shifts from D_1 to D_3. p_β rises, and the quantity supplied of it expands from J' towards L'.

The change in p_β will react back on the market for α. If p_β falls, this offsets to some extent the fall in p_α, and reduces the amount of substitution of α for β.[2] This is shown in Fig. 22.4a by a shift in the D curve

---

[1] See pp. 205–206 above.
[2] But *some* substitution will occur, since p_β falls only in so far as α is substituted for β.

for α down to D_2 when p_β falls (since p_β is a parameter of it). Hence p_α moves from J towards L (the intersection of D_2 and S_2) rather than towards K. p_α thus falls to a greater extent, because the fall in p_β does not allow so much substitution of α for β.

On the other hand, if p_β rises, the substitution in favour of α is reinforced. The demand curve for α shifts up to D_3, and p_α moves from J towards M (the intersection of D_3 and S_2) rather than towards K. p_α thus falls to a lesser extent, because the rise in p_β allows more substitution of α for β.[1]

The new equilibrium for α is either at point L or at point M, depending on whether p_β falls or rises. In both cases, p_α has fallen, and its level of employment has increased in relation to the initial equilibrium at J. The new equilibrium for β is either at point K', when the substitution effect outweighs the expansion effect, or at point L', when the reverse is the case. At K', both p_β and its level of employment are lower than at the initial equilibrium J'; at L', they are both higher than at J'.[2]

This analysis is incomplete in that it has not allowed for the effects on the factor markets of the interactions between the markets for good A and its substitutes or complements.[3] Thus, when the price of substitute B falls,[4] the demand curve for A shifts from D_1 to D_2 in Fig. 22.3a. As a result, the demand curve for α will shift downwards to the left of D_2 (or D_3) in Fig. 22.4a (since the demand condition for A is a parameter of it). This has a further effect on p_α, and therefore also on p_β. The final equilibria will, however, still show changes, in the prices and quantities of both the goods and factors, which are in the same directions (though of different sizes) as those deduced above.[5]

CHANGES IN PRODUCTIVITY

A change in the physical productivity of a factor[6] shifts *both* the S curves of the goods made by it, and the D curve for the factor.

[1] p_α will still fall, since the whole sequence of events depends on it falling.

[2] It must be remembered that p_α is a parameter of β's demand curve, and p_β is a parameter of α's demand curve. Hence, in the final equilibrium, the position of the D_2 (D_3) curve for β is dependent on the p_α at point L (M), and the position of the D_2 (D_3) curve for α is dependent on the p_β at point K' (L').

[3] This is a simplification, in the present case, merely to prevent the diagrams becoming too cluttered with curves.

[4] Or rises, when it is a complement.

[5] The effects on the demands for goods of the changes in incomes, which result from changes in factor prices, have once again been left for analysis later in the chapter.

[6] I.e., a change in the production functions of goods.

Consider good A which is made by two factors α and β. Suppose that, as a result of some technical improvement, the physical productivity of α increases, but the physical productivity of β remains unchanged. This means that in relation to each and every combination of α and β, MPP_α increases and MPP_β remains unchanged.[1]

The increase in MPP_α decreases the costs of the firms producing A. The S curve of A shifts downwards to the right. The price of A falls and

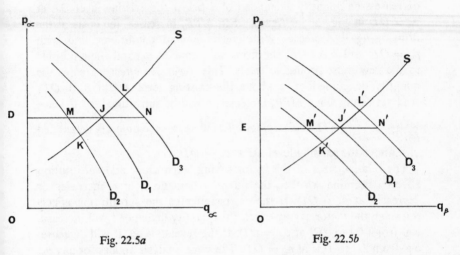

Fig. 22.5a   Fig. 22.5b

its output expands. The prices of substitutes of A will fall, and those of complements rise, in the way already analysed above.[2]

The effect of the increase in MPP_α on the D curves for α and β is more complex.[3] Suppose that, before the increase, p_α is in equilibrium at OD in Fig. 22.5a, viz. at the intersection J of the D_1 and S curves; and that p_β is also in equilibrium at OE in Fig. 22.5b, viz. at the intersection J' of its D_1 and S curves. The firms producing A will be using those quantities of α and β that satisfy the least cost condition, $\dfrac{p_\alpha}{MPP_\alpha} = \dfrac{p_\beta}{MPP_\beta}$, with $p_\alpha = OD$ and $p_\beta = OE$.

How the D curve for α will shift can be analysed by asking what will happen to the quantity demanded of α at $p_\alpha = OD$, when MPP_α increases. This question must be asked in relation to a particular p_β,

---

[1] It will be remembered that the MPPs of the factors are the only means by which their contributions to the output of a good can be separated from one another; see pp. 202–204 above.

[2] This assumes that the substitutes and complements do not use α and/or β.

[3] As has already been seen on pp. 207–208 above.

because the quantity demanded of α depends on p_β, as well as on its own price (i.e. p_β is a parameter of the D curve for α). At the original equilibrium, $p_\beta = OE$; this price is assumed in asking what happens to the quantity demanded of α at $p_\alpha = OD$, when MPP_α increases. There are three effects which have to be distinguished.[1]

When MPP_α increases, *any* output of A can be produced by a *smaller* quantity of α than was previously required. This *factor saving effect* decreases the quantity demanded of α below the existing level DJ, at $p_\alpha = OD$ in Fig. 22.5a. Again, when MPP_α increases, the costs of the firms using it decrease. With given demand conditions, and with $p_\alpha = OD$ and $p_\beta = OE$, the firms will want to expand their outputs to the new most profitable levels. This *expansion effect* increases the quantity demanded of α above the existing level DJ at $p_\alpha = OD$. And yet again, when MPP_α increases, α will be substituted for β, since $\dfrac{p_\alpha}{MPP_\alpha} < \dfrac{p_\beta}{MPP_\beta}$. This *substitution effect* increases the quantity demanded of α above the existing level DJ at $p_\alpha = OD$.

The relative sizes of the factor saving, expansion, and substitution effects determine whether the quantity demanded of α increases or decreases at $p_\alpha = OD$. If the expansion plus the substitution effects outweigh the factor saving effect, the quantity demanded will increase, e.g. from DJ to DN at $p_\alpha = OD$. If the reverse is so, it will decrease, e.g. from DJ to DM at $p_\alpha = OD$. The same analysis applies for any p_α. Hence, when MPP_α increases, the demand for α can either increase or decrease, i.e. the D_1 curve can either shift to D_3 or D_2.

The effect of the increase in MPP_α on the D curve for β has to be investigated with a given p_α, namely that of OD in Fig. 22.5b (since p_α is a parameter of the D curve for β). There is no factor saving effect on the quantity demanded of β at $p_\beta = OE$, since MPP_β is unchanged. The expansion effect increases the quantity demanded at $p_\beta = OE$, and the substitution effect decreases it. Hence, depending on the relative sizes of the latter two effects, the quantity demanded of β can either increase, e.g. from EJ' to EN' at $p_\beta = OE$, or decrease, e.g. from EJ' to EM'. The same analysis applies for any p_β. Hence, when MPP_α increases, the demand curve for β can either increase from D_1 to D_3, or decrease from D_1 to D_2.

The demand curve for α can shift to either D_2 or D_3 as a result of a technical improvement which increases MPP_α, but leaves MPP_β unchanged. p_α and its level of employment will therefore either both fall,

[1] Called respectively the factor saving, the expansion, and the substitution effects on p. 207 above.

from point J towards K, or both rise, from point J towards L. At the same time the demand curve for β can shift to either D_2 or D_3. Hence, p_β and its level of employment will either both fall, from point J' towards K', or both rise, from point J' towards L'.

However, as p_α and p_β change *relatively* to each other, in any of the above ways, substitution between them will be affected. Factor α is being substituted for β because MPP_α has increased. But if, as determined by the shifts in the D curves for α and β, p_β rises *relatively* to p_α,[1] further substitution of α and β will take place. And if p_β falls *relatively* to p_α, there will be some offset to the substitution which is occurring because MPP_α has increased. The effects of all this can be analysed by *further* shifts in the D curves for α and β (since p_β and p_α are parameters of them respectively). That has already been explained in relation to Figs. 22.4a and 22.4b above.

Moreover, the interactions between the market for A and those for its substitutes and complements, as p_A falls, shift the D curve for A.[2] That shift in turn produces shifts in the D curves for α and β (since the demand condition for A is a parameter of them). It has already been explained how these further complications can also be taken into account in determining the new equilibria to which the markets for α and β will move.

RELATED CHANGES IN DEMAND AND SUPPLY

One element has been ignored so far in all the analyses of this chapter, namely changes in incomes. A change in the prices of factors will alter the distribution of incomes between the resource-owners who provide the factors. Incomes help to determine the demands for goods (i.e. they are parameters of the D curves for goods). Changes in incomes will therefore shift these D curves.

Moreover, changes in the physical productivities of factors will also alter incomes. Some workers are paid a wage rate per unit of work done, i.e. a 'piece-rate'.[3] If their physical productivity increases, their wage earnings per period of time will rise.[4] The productivity increase will also change short-period profits: the costs of some firms will have decreased, and they will move to the new most profitable levels of output.

---

[1] Which will happen either if p_β rises more, or falls less than p_α, or if p_β rises and p_α falls.

[2] This was explained in relation to Figs. 22.3a and 22.3b above.

[3] Those paid a wage rate per period of time are on a 'time-rate'.

[4] Unless their hours of work per period of time fall in greater proportion than the increase in productivity.

An increase in the physical productivities of factors will lower the money prices of goods if the money prices of factors are unchanged. It is therefore necessary to distinguish between what happens to *money* incomes, and to *real* incomes, in this situation. Real incomes are measured by the quantities of goods that money incomes can buy at given money prices of those goods. With money incomes unchanged, a fall in the money prices of goods increases real incomes. Hence, even if a person's money income does not rise, he will benefit from a physical productivity increase because of the consequential fall in the money prices of goods.

Of course, as has been seen, an increase in physical productivity will change the prices of factors as well as those of goods. The money prices of particular factors may rise or fall. The money incomes of the various resource-owners may therefore either rise or fall. What happens to the real income of each one will then depend on the change in his money income *relative* to the changes in the money prices of the goods he buys.

If resources remain fully employed, someone must benefit from an increase in physical productivity. It will enlarge the quantity of goods produced, and thus raise the *real* income of the community as a whole. Some people at least must therefore have higher real incomes; though others may have unchanged or lower real incomes. How this works out depends on the changes in the prices of the different factors *relative* to those in the prices of goods.

The effects of changes in incomes, resulting from changes in factor prices and in profits, can be incorporated in the above analyses by means of appropriate shifts in the demand curves for goods. This was not done at the time because the effects of income changes will be quantitatively unimportant in those contexts. Only a few goods (A and its close substitutes and complements) and two factors (α and β) appeared in the analyses. The only incomes directly involved were those of the resource-owners providing α and β. These people are unlikely to spend more than a small fraction of their incomes on A and its substitutes and complements. Hence, when changes in p_α and p_β alter those incomes, the consequential changes in the demands for A, and for the goods closely related to it, are unlikely to be significant. That is, the D curves for the goods in question are unlikely to shift by much.

But once the analysis is broadened to encompass changes in the prices of *many* goods and factors, the effects of changes in incomes cannot be ignored. The consequential shifts in the demand curves for goods will be significant, since many incomes have been affected. This point, of course, is of vital importance when the working of the *whole* price mechanism is under scrutiny. The demands for *all* goods depend on the total income of the community. That income is derived from the prices paid for the factors, so that a change in factor prices alters incomes. This will shift the demand curves for goods and therefore affect their prices. Any analysis of the whole price system which ignores the effects of income changes on the demands for goods would be completely inadequate.

The role of income changes in the determination of price changes will now be demonstrated by analysing what happens in these respects as the total output of an economy grows in physical terms. The growth in output will be supposed to result from technical improvements which increase the physical productivities of factors. The supply curves of goods will shift on that account. The demand curves for goods will also shift because of the changes in incomes which are occurring. The shifts in the demand and the supply curves are thus related to each other. They are both caused by the increases in physical productivity. The analysis will be carried out in terms of a particular good (A), with the intention of showing how its price may change *relatively* to the prices of other goods. But since real incomes are increased by the increase in physical productivity, it is necessary to be explicit about the changes in money incomes and in the money prices of goods. This investigation will be of use in relation to some of the problems of Macroeconomics to be tackled later; and indeed it provides a bridge to macroeconomic analysis.[1]

To make the analysis applicable to present-day industrial economies, money wage rates will be supposed to be determined by collective bargaining. But for simplicity perfect competition will be assumed in the markets for goods.

Consider, with the help of Fig. 22.6, what may happen to the money price and output of A over a period of time, say a year. At the beginning of the year, the market for A is in equilibrium at point P, where the D_1 and S_1 curves intersect. During the year, physical productivity increases; this, if it were the only influence at work, would shift S_1 downwards to the right. But also, sometime during the year, the trade unions may well be successful in getting an increase in money wage rates. On that account alone, S_1 would shift upwards to the left. How S_1 will in fact shift depends on the relation between the money wage rate and the physical productivity increases per annum in respect of good A. If, on

---

[1] It will be assumed in the present analysis that resources remain fully employed as productivity increases, though they will of course have to switch to some extent between different uses. The problem of unemployment is dealt with in the next part of the book on macroeconomics.

average for all the workers involved, the percentage increase in money wage rates is *greater* than the percentage increase in physical productivity, the money cost of producing A will increase. Its S curve will decrease, e.g. to S_2. In the reverse case, the S curve will increase, e.g. to S_3.

The total money income of the economy will increase over the year as a result of the higher money wage rates. It will, moreover, rise relatively to the money prices of goods, since *real* income is raised by

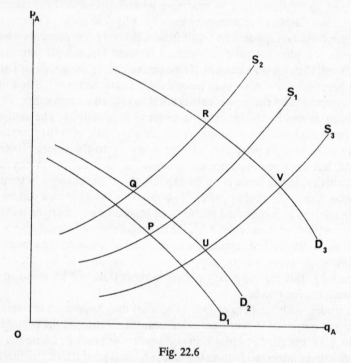

Fig. 22.6

the increase in physical productivity. The demand curves for superior goods will therefore shift upwards to the right. The amount of the shift in the D curve for A depends on how responsive the quantity demanded of A is to a change in *real* income, i.e. on its income elasticity of demand.[1] The greater that elasticity, the more the D curve shifts up, e.g. to D_3 as compared with D_2, as real incomes rise.

Various possible changes in the money price and output of A can now be read from Fig. 22.6. If the money cost of A *increases*, because the

[1] See p. 82 above.

increase in money wage rates outweights that in physical productivity, the *price* of A will rise. This is shown by the intersections of S_2 with D_2 and D_3 at Q and R respectively. But the *output* of A may either contract or expand. With smaller income elasticities of demand for A, it will contract, e.g. at Q with curve D_2; but with larger income elasticities, it will expand, e.g. at R with curve D_3.

If the money cost of A *decreases*, because the increase in physical productivity outweighs that in money wage rates, the *output* of A will expand. This is shown by the intersections of S_3 with D_2 and D_3, at U and V respectively. But the *price* of A may either fall or rise. With smaller income elasticities, it will fall, e.g. at U with curve D_2; but with larger income elasticities, it will rise, e.g. at V with curve D_3.

Both the income elasticities of demand, and the rates of physical productivity increase which are possible, vary a great deal between goods. Hence, even with a uniform increase in all money wage rates, the money prices of different goods will change to different extents, either upwards or downwards. That is, the prices of goods will change *relatively* to one another as total output expands. Fig. 22.6 is a means of understanding the continual changes in *relative* prices which take place on that account.[1] Thus there is a high income elasticity of demand for many services (e.g. recreation, education, and medical care). But the scope for physical productivity increases in the provision of them is not great. Their prices are bound to rise through time *relatively* to those of most manufactured goods, for which technical change is a fecund source of productivity increases.

The purpose of this chapter has been to demonstrate how the techniques of demand and supply analysis can be used to trace the related *changes* in prices which result from some disturbance of an economy. The analysis has progressed from less to more complex situations. It will have been noticed that, as this occurred, the increasing number of effects to be taken into account often operated in *opposite* directions on prices. It was therefore not possible, without quantitative information, to predict the directions of change in the prices and quantities of goods and factors. This is the limitation of *qualitative* theories which was explained in Chapter 6.[2] But qualitative theories at least identify the questions to which quantitative theories have to provide the answers.

---

[1] The diagram does not take into account the shifts in demand between goods as their prices change relatively to one another. This can be allowed for in the way explained in terms of Figs. 22.3a and 22.3b above.

[2] See p. 58 above.

FURTHER READING

MICROECONOMICS

More advanced analysis of the problems of microeconomics is given in G. J. Stigler, *The Theory of Price* (third edition, 1966), and in W. J. L. Ryan, *Price Theory* (1958). Similar ground is covered by K. J. Cohen and R. M. Cyert, *Theory of the Firm* (1965), which also investigates at length whether there are other objectives, as well as profit maximization, which govern the behaviour of the firm. A particular theory in this respect is developed in W. J. Baumol, *Business Behaviour, Value and Growth* (revised edition, 1967).

A mathematical approach to microeconomics can be found in J. M. Henderson and R. E. Quandt, *Microeconomic Theory* (1958). The 'general equilibrium'[1] of the whole price mechanism is analysed in R. E. Kuenne, *Microeconomic Theory of the Market Mechanism* (1968).

WELFARE ECONOMICS

Welfare economics enquires into the criteria which may be used to judge the efficiency with which an economic system allocates resources between different uses. T. Scitovsky, *Welfare and Competition* (1952), discusses these criteria in the context of a full treatment of micro-economic theory. F. Bator, 'The Simple Analytics of Welfare Economics', *American Economic Review*, March 1957, provides a short introduction to the subject. Its problems are analysed intensively in W. J. Baumol, *Welfare Economics and the Theory of the State* (second edition, 1965), and in J. de V. Graaff, *Theoretical Welfare Economics* (1957).

[1] Which is explained in Chapter 23 below.

PART III

MACROECONOMICS

GENERAL EQUILIBRIUM

The microeconomic analysis of the preceding part has shown that there are two distinct questions which have to be asked about the working of any particular market. Firstly, is there an *equilibrium* price which would equate the quantity demanded of the good (or factor) and the quantity supplied; and secondly, if there is such an equilibrium price, will the market in fact *converge* to it? These two questions are concerned respectively with the *existence* and the *stability* of equilibrium.

No reason has so far been given why any market might have no equilibrium price at all. But it has been shown that there is at least one set of circumstances in which, even though an equilibrium price exists, a market for a good might not converge to it. The Cobweb Theorem[1] demonstrates how it is possible for the price of a good to fluctuate endlessly without settling at an equilibrium level.

It was, moreover, shown in the previous chapter how the price of any good or factor depends on the prices ruling in other markets. The demand for, and therefore the price of, a good depends on the prices of its substitutes and complements. The demand for, and therefore the price of, a factor depends on the prices of the other factors which can be used with it. The prices of goods and of factors depend on one another, both because factor prices help to determine the costs of producing goods, and because they also help to determine the incomes which are spent on goods. All of this means that the price of one good or factor cannot be in equilibrium unless all other prices are *simultaneously* in equilibrium. Thus, the price of apples cannot be in equilibrium unless the price of oranges is also in equilibrium. If the latter condition does not prevail, the price of oranges will change. This will shift the demand curve for apples and change their price. Similarly, if the wage rate for one kind of labour is in disequilibrium, the resultant change in it will lead to substitution between it and other factors which will alter their prices. These changes in factor prices will, by their effects on costs and incomes, lead to changes in the prices of goods.

[1] See pp. 156–159 above.

The dependence of any one price on other prices implies the idea of a *general* equilibrium of the whole system of prices.[1] A single price is in equilibrium if the quantity demanded of the good (or factor) in question is equal to the quantity supplied of it. But that price can be in equilibrium only if all other prices are simultaneously in equilibrium. This will be so if the prices of all other goods and factors are such that the quantity demanded equals the quantity supplied in *every* market. The *set* of prices, which simultaneously equates *all* quantities demanded of goods and factors with the corresponding quantities supplied, is the condition for the general equilibrium of the price system.

It is of great practical importance *both* whether there is such a set of prices, and if so, whether the price mechanism would so work as to converge to it. Prices are a means of allocating resources between the production of different goods. Since resources are scarce, it is to the benefit of society to employ them as fully as possible. Only thus can it make its standard of living as high as possible. Suppose *either* that there is no set of prices which would bring about general equilibrium, *or* that if there is, the price mechanism does not work so as to converge to it. In either case, the result may be that some resources are left *unemployed* against the wishes of their owners.

In general equilibrium, the quantities demanded of goods equal the quantities supplied of them, and the quantities demanded of factors equal the quantities supplied of them. The latter condition means that resources are *fully employed*. At the equilibrium price for each factor, the quantity of it which resource-owners want to put on the market is precisely the quantity which firms want to buy. Hence no resources which are seeking employment at that price are unable to find it.[2]

If there is *no* set of equilibrium prices for all factors, then quantity demanded will not equal quantity supplied for at least some of them. And in particular there could be excess supply for some of them. This means there is some amount of unemployment. But even if there is an equilibrium set of prices for all factors, there is still the question of whether the price mechanism will converge to it. If it does not, there could be excess supply of some factors, i.e. some amount of unemployment.

---

[1] The concept of the general equilibrium of the whole price mechanism was first rigorously developed by Léon Walras, whose stability conditions have been used in earlier analyses.

[2] It is irrelevant, to an understanding of how a price mechanism works, that owners of resources *could* work them for longer hours per day than the full employment level. All that is relevant is the amount of productive services the owners *want* to supply at particular factor prices.

Many arguments for freely working price mechanisms tacitly imply a belief in the existence and the stability of a general equilibrium for such an economic system. Probably, most people feel intuitively that there must be a set of prices which will simultaneously equate the quantities demanded and supplied of all goods and factors.[1] But it has never, in fact, been proved at the *microeconomic* level, except under very restrictive assumptions, that such a set of prices will necessarily exist; nor that, if it does exist, the price mechanism will necessarily converge to it.

The lack of proof is not surprising. There are some millions of prices in a modern developed economy. They are all either directly interrelated, or indirectly interrelated through other prices. To demonstrate the existence of a general equilibrium set of prices for all markets, it is necessary to take into account all those interrelationships. This is an enormous (and necessarily mathematical) problem.

Large scale unemployment has in fact occurred, at least from time to time, under many price mechanisms.[2] This is one indication of the need to enquire into the existence and stability of general equilibrium. Because of the formidable difficulties of analysing these questions in microeconomic terms, economists have developed macroeconomic analysis.

MACROECONOMICS

Macroeconomics simplifies the task of analysing the overall working of a price mechanism.[3] Microeconomics attempts to explain the *particular* flows of expenditure on different consumer goods that go from households to firms; those on different capital goods that go from firms (and households) to other firms; and those on different factors that go from firms to households. Macroeconomics *aggregates* the particular flows of expenditure. It concentrates attention on the total of the particular expenditures on *consumption*; and on the total of the particular expenditures on *investment*; and on the total of the particular expenditures on factors which constitutes the *national income*.[4]

The sum of consumption and investment is the *national expenditure*.

---

[1] Though intuition usually fails them in relation to the question of stability.

[2] 20 per cent or more of the working populations of the UK, the US, and Germany were unemployed at the height of the Great Depression in the 1930s.

[3] This was shown in Chapter 5, in which (on pp. 42–50 above) the main concepts of macroeconomics, and the definitional relations between them, were explained. It is strongly recommended that the reader refresh his memory of the definitions, and especially of their interconnections, before proceeding.

[4] This ignores government and foreign trade for the present.

This expenditure makes it worthwhile for firms to produce goods and employ factors, i.e. it calls forth the national output, and thereby creates the national income. National expenditure is the *aggregate* demand for goods, and national output (income) is the *aggregate* supply.

It is essential to be clear on the nature of the aggregation process by which one goes from the microeconomic to the macroeconomic level. The flow of expenditure, per period of time, by all houesholds on a particular consumer good (A) is equal to its price times the quantity bought, viz. $p_A \cdot q_A$. Aggregate consumption expenditure, per period of time, is the *sum* of the $p \cdot q$s for all consumer goods, viz. $p_A \cdot q_A + p_B \cdot q_B + \ldots$. Similarly, aggregate investment expenditure, per period of time, is the *sum* of the $p \cdot q$s for all capital goods, viz., $p_F \cdot q_F + p_G \cdot q_G + \ldots$. National expenditure, per period of time, is the *sum* of the $p \cdot q$s for all consumer and capital goods, viz., $p_A \cdot q_A + p_B \cdot q_B + \ldots + p_F \cdot q_F + p_G \cdot q_G + \ldots$.

It is convenient to represent national output as the product of a single price (P) and a single quantity (X), viz. $P.X$. P is the money price of a unit of national output, and X is its physical volume. P is an *average* of the money prices (the ps) of all the consumer and capital goods bought by households and firms. It is called the *General Level of Prices* (of consumer and capital goods). It will, however, be necessary at times to distinguish the general level of the prices of consumer goods (P_C) from that of capital goods (P_K).

In principle, the computation of the average or general level of prices is a straightforward matter. But there is a basic problem in measuring X. It stands for the *physical volume* of the national output, i.e. for the *sum* of the quantities (the qs) of consumer and investment goods produced. These qs are measured in a great variety of units, e.g. pounds of butter, square yards of cloth. As such they cannot be added together. The only way of adding them is to value them in the common unit of money. This means multiplying the physical quantities (the qs) by their respective money prices (the ps). But that seems merely to take the problem back to its starting-point: in valuing all goods in terms of money in order to add them together, one ends up with $p_A \cdot q_A + p_B \cdot q_B + \ldots + p_F \cdot q_F + p_G \cdot q_G + \ldots$. Apparently, a measure of X which is *independent* of money prices is not possible.

ABSOLUTE AND RELATIVE PRICES

There is, however, a way out of the apparent dilemma. It lies in the different natures of the general price level P, and the ps of the various individual goods. Both P, and the ps, are measured in terms of money. But the significance of P is that it indicates the *absolute* level of prices in terms of money, while the significance of the ps is that they indicate the prices of goods *relative* to one another. Absolute prices can change without altering relative prices. For example, suppose that $p_A = £1$, $p_B = £2$, and $p_C = £3$. The average of these prices (P) is £2. Now suppose that $p_A = £2$, $p_B = £4$, and $p_C = £6$. P is now equal to £4. The *absolute* level of money prices has doubled. But *relative* prices are unchanged, viz. p_C is still twice p_B, and three times p_A. While the absolute money prices of the goods have changed, the *ratios* between them are unaltered. It is thus possible to discuss changes in absolute prices without necessarily getting involved in the problems of changes in relative prices.

The concept of the absolute price level was not used in the analysis of Part II of this book. Of course, prices there were stated in terms of money. It is convenient to measure all of them in the same unit; and to do so in terms of money rather than in terms of some good (e.g. cigarettes).[1] But the behaviour of consumers and firms was explained in Part II in terms of *relative* prices. Thus the quantities of goods demanded by consumers were shown to depend on their prices *relative* to one another, and the quantities of factors demanded by firms were shown to depend on their prices *relative* to one another.

It is necessary, however, to explain how the *absolute* prices of goods in terms of money, as well as their relative prices, are determined. This involves an enquiry into the significance of the absolute price level of goods for the behaviour of consumers and firms. That is why it is convenient to work with the concept of P. But it is also necessary to explain how the absolute prices of factors, as well as of goods, are determined. In particular, the absolute level of money wage rates has to be explained. This *General Level of Money Wage Rates* is an average of all money wage rates. The symbol W will be used for it.[2]

The difference between the relative prices and the absolute prices of goods provides a way of measuring X which is independent of *absolute*

---

[1] But it is not necessary. The price of A (or any good) can be expressed in the form of a quantity of B (or any other good) for which it will exchange, e.g. $2B$ for $1A$. This is a *barter* price. It is implicit in all money prices, e.g. the barter price of $1A$ is $2B$, if $p_A = £2$ and $p_B = £1$.

[2] It should be noted that, while P and W taken separately are absolute prices, their use together gives a relative price, viz. the average price of labour services in terms of goods. Wages, however, are spent on consumer goods. Hence $\dfrac{W}{P_C}$ is the average *real* wage rate, i.e. the amount of consumer goods which the average money wage rate will buy.

money prices. The national output has to be computed by putting prices on the physical quantities of goods in order to add them together. *Relative* prices—i.e. the ratios between money prices—can be used for this purpose. Thus, suppose that $p_A = £1$, and $p_B = £2$. q_A and q_B can be multiplied respectively by those prices in order to add them, and the similarly valued outputs of other goods, to get X. But since it is the *ratios* of the prices which are being used for the purpose of aggregation, the £ signs on them can be dropped. The operation of measuring X in this example then means: count every unit of q_A *once* and every unit of q_B *twice*, in adding them to get X. The measure of X—for given q_A and q_B—will then be independent of the absolute sizes of p_A and p_B as long as their ratio is unchanged. It does not matter if $p_A = £1$ and $p_B = £2$, or $p_A = £2$ and $p_B = £4$, and so on. It is only the ratio of 1 to 2 between them which is being used in the computation of X. Irrespective of the absolute sizes of p_A and p_B, X is obtained by counting every unit of A once, and every unit of B twice.

Now suppose that the absolute prices of goods in terms of money change between different time periods (e.g. years), but that relative prices remain unchanged. That is, suppose that P goes up or down, but that the ratios between the ps of all goods do not change. The national output X in *each* year can then be computed by using the *same* set of relative prices. Thus suppose that the ratio of p_A to p_B remains unchanged at 1 to 2 from year to year. X is computed for the first year by counting every unit of q_A once, and every unit of q_B twice. Similarly, the X of the second year is computed by also counting each unit of the q_A of *this* year once, and each unit of the q_B of *this* year twice. The q_As and the q_Bs will probably be different in the various years, e.g. the quantities produced of most goods will be increasing from year to year in an expanding economy. The Xs of the various years will therefore be different. But that difference is *not* the result of any change there may have been in the absolute level of money prices.

A given set of *relative* prices can thus be used to compute the Xs of different years, quite independently of what is happening to absolute money prices. In this way the behaviour of P can be distinguished from the behaviour of X. This is the basis on which the concepts of P and X are used in macroeconomics. P is the absolute price level of goods in terms of money. X is the volume of national output, computed by using a particular set of price-ratios to value[1] the quantities produced of different goods, in order to aggregate them. The national output X, in this sense, is also known as the national output (or product) 'at *constant*

[1] The technical term is to *weight* the quantities produced of different goods.

prices'—since only one set of prices is used to compute X in different time periods; or as the *real* national product—since it is the volume of goods produced, rather than their money value, which is the concern of the measure. On the other hand, P . X is known as the national output (product) 'at *current* prices'—since X is now valued at the ruling absolute price level; or as the money value—in contrast to the real value—of the national product.

MACROECONOMICS AND MICROECONOMICS

The method of computing X for macroeconomic analysis makes clear one limitation of that form of analysis. Suppose that *relative* prices change as the national output changes—as in fact usually happens to some extent.[1] The problem then arises as to *which* set of relative prices is to be used in computing the Xs of the different time periods. Unfortunately there is no unequivocally correct answer to this question.[2] In such circumstances, a microeconomic analysis of the effects of the changes in relative prices is required as well as the macroeconomic analysis. It is the intention of this part of the book to demonstrate in some detail how microeconomics and macroeconomics are two inter-related ways of looking at the working of a price mechanism. They are necessarily complements of each other.

This, indeed, should already be clear from the manner in which the problems of macroeconomics were introduced earlier in this chapter. The existence and stability of a *general* equilibrium for a price system has to be investigated. It is of great practical importance to discover how a price system might ensure the full employment of resources. This problem is too complex to tackle in (general) microeconomic terms.[3] Reformulated in macroeconomic terms, it centres on the determination of the real national output X and the price level P. The level of employment of all resources depends on the level of X. The higher X is, the more fully those resources will be employed. The level of X—and also of P—depends on the *aggregate* demand for it, for the purposes of consumption and investment, in relation to the willingness of firms in *aggregate* to supply it.

The magnitudes of the aggregate money expenditures on both consumption and investment have to be explained. The explanation of them

---

[1] For the reasons analysed in the last section of the previous chapter; see pp. 255–257 above.

[2] This problem is central to the theory of *index numbers*.

[3] Viz. in terms of a Walrasian system of general equilibrium.

is given by the *aggregate demand function*. The willingness of firms in aggregate to supply particular amounts of national output has to be explained. The explanation is given by the *aggregate supply function*. Given these functions, it has to be explained how their interaction determines X and P, and also how shifts in them will change X and P. It will be noticed that this programme for macroeconomics progresses through the same four stages of analysis as those encountered in microeconomics.[1]

[1] This form of macroeconomic analysis is called 'Keynesian', because it is in the main based on the work of John Maynard Keynes (Lord Keynes, 1883–1946); and in particular derives from his book *The General Theory of Employment, Interest and Money* (1936).

CHAPTER 24

AGGREGATE SUPPLY AND DEMAND

The explanation of how P and X are determined is a large task, and it will be undertaken one step at a time. Monetary influences will not be introduced until Chapters 28–30. Until then, the effects of money on economic activity will be kept out of the picture by the assumption that the monetary authorities hold the rate of interest at a given level. Their ability to do so, by means of variations in the quantity of money, will be considered later. The effects of government expenditure and taxation will not be allowed for until Chapter 32. Foreign trade will not be brought into the analysis until Chapter 36.

Macroeconomic analysis starts with the construction of the aggregate supply and aggregate demand functions.

AGGREGATE SUPPLY

The aggregate supply function shows what influences determine the willingness of firms to supply particular amounts of national output, which is the aggregate of the outputs of the individual firms. How those outputs are determined has already been explained in Part II above. Microeconomic analysis can therefore be drawn on to explain the determinants of aggregate supply.

It will be assumed here that all firms produce under conditions of perfect competition. The analysis will start with a Marshallian *short period* situation, in which the total stock of capital (K) is a given and fixed quantity (call it K_0, and include the fixed stock of land with it).[1] It follows that, in the short period, the level of national output (X) can be varied only by means of changes in the general level of employment of labour (N). The state of technology, together with the given quantities of capital and land, determine how the size of X will vary with the

---

[1] Since the accumulation of capital through net investment will enter into the analysis, it will have to be assumed for the present that the investment rate per period of time is not large enough to change K_0 significantly. In fact, net investment per annum in the UK is small compared with the total capital stock. The problems arising from changes in the stock of capital will be analysed in Chapter 31 below.

level of N. That relationship can be expressed by a single production function for the whole economy, $X = F(N,K_0)$. This will be assumed to have the same properties as the production functions used in microeconomics.

In accordance with the principle of diminishing returns, as more and more labour is employed to use the given amount of capital and land, national output will increase but at a decreasing rate, i.e. the marginal physical product of labour (MPP_L) will fall. With a given general level of money wage rates (W), the marginal cost of national output will therefore rise as output increases. Labour is the only variable factor. The employment of additional units of it adds less and less to national output. But each unit of labour is paid at the same rate, W. Hence each additional unit of output costs more and more to produce, i.e. the marginal cost of X $\left(\text{which, it will be recalled,[1] is equal to } \dfrac{W}{MPP_L}\right)$ is rising.

Under perfect competition, the supply price of a good equals its marginal cost. Hence at the macroeconomic level, the *aggregate supply price* of X will equal the MC of X.[2] The aggregate supply price of a particular national output is the price level (P) at which the firms in aggregate are willing to supply the output in question, i.e. it is the *supply-P* of the output in question. With W given, a rise in the price level is therefore necessary, in the short period, to induce firms to supply a larger national output, since the MC of output is rising.

The quantity supplied of X thus depends on P. Under perfect competition, the P at which a particular quantity of X will be supplied equals the MC of that X. That MC is determined by W and the MPP_L. The MPP_L at each X is given by the production function $X = F(N,K_0)$. These are the relationships which make up the aggregate supply function, i.e. which explain the willingness of firms to produce the national output.

The aggregate supply function is depicted by the curve labelled Y in Fig. 24.1. Aggregate *money* expenditure ($\equiv P . X$) is measured on the vertical axis and the *volume* of national output (X) on the horizontal. The Y curve is upward sloping to the right, and its slope increases as national output rises.

The points on the curve show the different amounts of aggregate money expenditure which will just be sufficient to induce firms to supply

---

[1] See the microeconomic analysis on pp. 205–206 above.
[2] Since relative prices are taken as given and constant in measuring X, this implies that the *relative MCs* of goods do not change as X changes.

the corresponding national outputs. That is, they show the total revenues which the firms must *expect* to get, in order to make it worthwhile for them to produce the corresponding national outputs. Thus, at point Q, an expected expenditure of OJ ($= DQ$) will call forth the output OD, The slope of the straight line OQ, joining Q to the origin, is equal o .

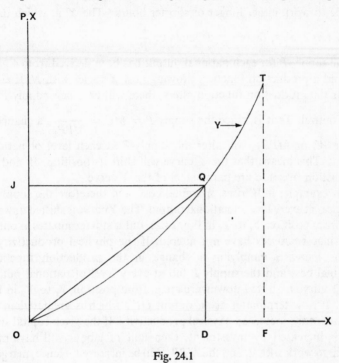

Fig. 24.1

the aggregate supply price of OD. The ratio $\dfrac{DQ}{OD}$ measures the slope.

DQ is the value of $P \cdot X$, where P here stands for the aggregate supply price (i.e. the supply-P); and OD is the amount of national output.

Therefore, $\dfrac{DQ}{OD} = \dfrac{P \cdot X}{X} = P$. The Y curve has increasing slope as the

point Q moves up it. This means that the supply-P rises as national output increases (because the MC of output is rising).[1]

The Y curve terminates at the output OF (point T): this is the 'full

[1] The aggregate supply curve is thus drawn in a 'total' rather in an 'average' form, i.e. X is shown as dependent on $P \cdot X$, rather than on P. This is to allow aggregate money expenditure on C and I to be set against $P \cdot X$.

employment'[1] level of national output. But the level of full employment depends on the *real* wage rate $\left(\dfrac{W}{P_C}\right)$, and on workers' preferences between work and leisure. For example, if $\dfrac{W}{P_C}$ rises, workers may decide to work either longer or shorter hours.[2] The X, at which the Y curve terminates, therefore depends on $\dfrac{W}{P_C}$.

The supply-P for each national output has been derived from a given W, and a production function showing how X varies with N. If either W, or the production function alters, there will be a new supply-P for *each* output. That is, since the supply-$P = MC = \dfrac{W}{MPP_L}$, a change in either W, or MPP_L, will alter the supply-P at each level of national output. This means that the Y curve will shift its position. W and the production function are parameters of the Y curve.

For example, if W rises, marginal cost, and therefore the supply-P, increases at every level of national output. The Y curve is shifted upwards (e.g. from position Y_1 to Y_2 in Fig. 24.2). But it still terminates at output OF, since resources have not altered. If the physical productivity of labour increases (implying a change in the production function), marginal cost and the supply-P fall at every level of national output. The Y curve is shifted downwards (e.g. from position Y_1 to Y_3 in Fig. 24.2). It now terminates at an output OF', which is greater than OF because of the increased physical productivity. If the given capital stock (K_0) is increased by investment, each unit of labour will have more capital to work with it, and the MPP_L will be increased. Hence, marginal cost and the supply-P fall at every level of national output. The Y curve is shifted downwards (e.g. from position Y_1 to Y_3 in Fig. 24.2). The full employment level of output is raised from OF to OF' by the increase in the stock of capital.[3]

The shape of the Y curve, and shifts in it, show how the production function, the available labour and capital resources, and the money wage rate, all help to determine the levels of national output which

---

[1] This does not mean 100 per cent employment of all resources, since some labour will be changing jobs, and some capital will be out of commission for maintenance work, at any time.

[2] See p. 209 above.

[3] The effect of any change in the real wage rate, $\dfrac{W}{P_C}$, would also have to be taken into account in these shifts in the Y curve.

firms are willing to supply at different expected amounts of aggregate money expenditure. An understanding of all this is necessary for the

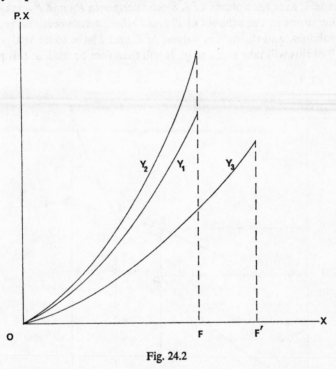

Fig. 24.2

analysis of how national output, employment, and the price level are determined. Moreover, the shifts in the Y curve, caused by the accumulation of capital, and by technical change, enter into the analysis of economic growth.

AGGREGATE DEMAND

The aggregate demand function has now to be constructed. In the absence of government and foreign trade, aggregate demand (Z) is the sum of the aggregate expenditures on consumption and on investment, i.e. $Z \equiv C + I$.[1] The explanations of both C and I are complex. To begin with, it is necessary to distinguish between the physical *volumes*, and the *money values*, of both C and I. The money value of C equals its

[1] It should be noted that the '$\equiv$' sign is used for an identity which is true by definition, while the '$=$' sign is used for a functional relation.

volume multiplied by P_C; and the money value of I equals its volume multiplied by P_K. The volume of C is determined by a variety of influences, as is the volume of I. Since changes in P_C and P_K may lead to alterations in the *volumes* of C and I, the interconnections between the volumes, and the money values, of C and I have to be analysed.

All of this will take some time. It will therefore be well, at this point,

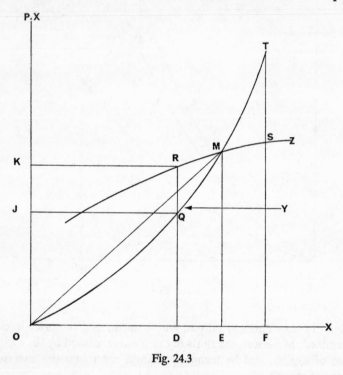

Fig. 24.3

to outline the general way in which the conditions of aggregate supply and aggregate demand determine the levels of X and P. The reader will then have in his mind the form which the aggregate demand function takes, and the purpose for which it is required, to guide him through its derivation.

Aggregate *money* demand is the sum of the money values of consumption and investment. Its amount, at each level of national output, is shown by means of an aggregate demand curve drawn in the same diagram as that used for the aggregate supply curve. The aggregate demand curve (labelled Z) will probably have a shape like the one in Fig. 24.3, where aggregate *money* expenditure ($\equiv P \cdot X$) is measured on the vertical axis and the *volume* of national output (X) on the horizontal. Each point on the Z curve shows the aggregate money demand which will be forthcoming at the corresponding level of national output, e.g. the point R shows that consumers plus investors will want to spend an amount OK (= DR) when output is at the level OD. The spending of consumers will depend in part on the sizes of their money incomes. One of the things which has to be explained, therefore, is the total of the money incomes which will be earned at each level of national output.

The Z and Y curves[1] can be used in the following way to explain how the levels of X and P are determined. Their point of intersection (M) shows that if the national output OE is produced, the aggregate money expenditure EM on it (as given by the Z curve) will be equal to the total revenue which firms expect to get from it (as shown by the Y curve). The national output will therefore be in *equilibrium* at the level OE, since firms in aggregate will be receiving the total revenue from it, which is just sufficient to induce them to produce it.[2] The national output OE is being supplied at the price level (i.e. the supply-P) given by the slope of OM, which is the straight line joining the origin to the point M on the Y curve. This will be the equilibrium price level.

The national output will be in *disequilibrium* at any level other than OE. For example, the firms will produce the national output OD if they expect to get a total revenue of DQ for it (as shown by point Q on the Y curve). But if OQ is produced, consumers plus investors will spend an amount DR on it (as shown by point R on the Z curve). There will consequently be an *excess* aggregate money *demand* of QR (= $DR - DQ$) for the national output OD. Similarly, there will be an *excess* aggregate money *supply* of ST (= $FT - FS$) if the national output OF is produced. With either excess aggregate demand or supply, the firms will want to change the quantities of goods which they are producing. An analysis is therefore needed of whether or not, in these circumstances, the national output will converge to the equilibrium level OE.

The determination of X and P can thus be explained along lines analogous to the demand and supply analyses at the microeconomic level. But as has been indicated, the explanation of the nature and shape of the Z curve is a complex matter, because the determination of both the volumes and the money values of consumption and investment has to be investigated. It will therefore be best to proceed in two stages. The determinants of the *volumes* of consumption and investment will

---

[1] Given the level of money wage rates (W).
[2] As explained on pp. 270–271 above.

be analysed in the rest of this chapter. For this purpose, the absolute money prices of consumer and capital goods (i.e. P_C and P_K) will have to be taken as given and constant. This assumption will be relaxed in Chapter 26 below, in order to analyse the determinants of the *money values* of consumption and investment. It will then be possible to show how the Z curve is derived.

THE VOLUME OF CONSUMPTION

The expenditures of households on different consumer goods have already been analysed in Chapters 7 and 8 above. They were shown to depend on *real* income, *real* personal wealth, preferences, and *relative* prices. But that analysis was limited to explaining the allocation of a household's total consumption expenditure as between different goods. It did not explain what determines the *total* expenditure on consumption.

An explanation is now required, not only of the determinants of that total for each household, but also of the aggregate of such totals for all households. It must be remembered that the present macroeconomic analysis is being carried out on the assumption of given and constant *relative* prices. The magnitude of aggregate consumption will be explained on that basis. Moreover, for the moment, absolute money prices are being assumed constant. Hence the coming analysis is directed to explaining the *volume* of C, i.e. 'real' C; and all the references to income and wealth mean *real* income and *real* wealth.[1] The analysis will start at the individual household level and then proceed to aggregate consumption for all households.

The total consumption expenditure of a household, per period of time, can be financed in one, or a combination, of three ways: out of the income of the period in question, by the sale of assets (e.g. securities), and by borrowing, i.e. by adding to liabilities. A person's wealth (or net worth) is equal to his total assets minus his total liabilities. Therefore any financing of consumption by selling assets or adding to liabilities implies a decrease in personal wealth. If a household spends more than its current income on consumption (i.e. dis-saves), it must draw on its wealth. If it spends less than its current income (i.e. saves), it automatically adds to its wealth (by acquiring assets, or by paying off debts).

Suppose a household always wants to spend the whole of its current income on consumption, and does not use any wealth it may have received as a gift or a legacy. Then the amount of its consumption

[1] I.e. the quantities of goods that the money values of income and wealth could buy at the given absolute money prices.

expenditure depends simply on the size of its current income. But if it spends either less or more than its income, there are other influences, in addition to income, that are helping to determine its total spending. In deciding to spend less or more than 100 per cent of its current income, it is deciding to add to or subtract from its wealth. There must be reasons why it wishes to alter the size of its wealth. That is, the *proportion* of income spent on consumption depends on the motives for accumulating or decumulating personal wealth.

A person may spend less than the total of his income over his *whole* lifetime because he wishes to make bequests. But even if he does not wish to enrich his heirs and successors, he may spend less than his income in some periods of time, and more in others. The assets acquired by the saving of the earlier periods enable him to finance an excess of spending over income later on. In this way, he can allow the flow of consumption over his lifetime to have a *different* pattern from that of the flow of income. There are many reasons why a person will not wish the consumption expenditures of every time period to be exactly equated to the respective incomes of those periods. People save in the winter towards a summer holiday; they save early in married life to finance their children's upbringing; they save during their working years[1] in order to support themselves in retirement.

The *proportion* of income spent on consumption by a person during any period of time can therefore be explained in many ways. But it is possible to distinguish a number of influences which are generally at work in this respect. Saving in the present provides the means for financing future expenditure. The larger a person's wealth, and the better his expectations for rising income over the future, the less urgent it will be to hold down the proportion of income spent in order to provide for planned future expenditures. The nature of these plans will depend on his age, his preferences, and his family situation (e.g. the ages of his children). The future, however, is uncertain, and some saving can be regarded as an insurance against unforeseen contingencies, such as a loss of income due to ill-health. But the amount of saving will vary with the degree of foresight exercised by the person. In that regard, a person may be sensitive to the level of the interest rate, since savings lent out at interest will grow in amount over time.

Hence, two households, which have exactly the same income in the same period of time, may consume quite different proportions of that income for a variety of reasons; namely differences in wealth, income

[1] E.g., by contributions to pension funds, and by the purchase of life assurance policies.

expectations, ages, preferences, number of children, degree of foresight exercised about the uncertain future, sensitivity to the rate of interest, and the desire to make bequests. All these personal attributes of house-holds, together with the sizes of current incomes, determine the total consumption expenditures per period of time by the different households.

The determinants of aggregate consumption expenditures (C) for the whole community can now be considered. The proportion of the national income which is consumed (i.e. the ratio C/Y) in any period of time is obtained by aggregating the consumption expenditures (to get C) and the incomes of all households (to get Y).[1] The C/Y ratio thus depends on the consumption-to-income ratios of all the individual households. These, in turn, depend on the various personal attributes listed in the last paragraph. The higher the households' consumption-to-income ratios are, the higher is the aggregate ratio C/Y. The personal attributes of the households therefore all play a part in determining the national ratio C/Y.

But since the attributes differ from one household to another, the *distribution* of income also helps to determine the aggregate C/Y ratio. If some national income is redistributed away from households with high consumption-to-income ratios to households whose ratios are low, C/Y will be reduced.

Moreover, the rate at which real income per head of the population has grown over some decades up to the present time will influence C/Y. The consumption expenditures of people who are now in retirement are financed out of assets which they accumulated in earlier years. They are dis-saving by drawing on assets accumulated in past years, when real income per head was *lower*. On the other hand, the saving of people in work at the present time is being made out of the *higher* current real income per head. Unless the other influences affecting the proportions of incomes saved have changed significantly, larger saving will result from higher real income. It is probable, therefore, that the saving of the workers will outweigh the dis-saving of the retired.[2] That is, the growth of real income per head will probably make the aggregate personal saving (S) of a country a positive amount. This means that $S/Y > 0$, and therefore that $C/Y < 1$.[3] Moreover, the more rapidly real income

[1] Saving by business firms (i.e. undistributed profits) are ignored here, because it is more convenient not to bring them into the analysis until Chapter 32 is reached.

[2] Whether this happens also depends on the present age composition of the population.

[3] Since $\dfrac{S}{Y} \equiv 1 - \dfrac{C}{Y}$; e.g. if $\dfrac{1}{10}$ of Y is saved, $\dfrac{9}{10}$ is consumed.

per head has increased in the past, the greater will be the current excess of the workers' saving over the retired people's dis-saving. Hence, the smaller will be C/Y.

The determinants of the level of real C can now be summarized. They are: the level of real Y, all the personal attributes of households listed earlier, the amounts of their real personal wealth, the distribution of Y between households, and the rates of growth of real income per head over time.

THE CONSUMPTION FUNCTION

Thus far, the magnitude of C has been explained in terms of the size of Y, and the various influences which determine the proportion of Y (i.e. C/Y) spent on C. But it is also necessary to know what the C/Y ratio would be at *different* levels of Y. The discussion of this matter will be helped by putting the C to Y relationship in a diagram. In Fig. 24.4, *real C* is measured on the vertical axis, and *real Y* on the horizontal. A curve drawn on the diagram indicates how real C varies with real Y; it is called a *consumption function*, for it shows C as a function of Y.[1] It is usually symbolized as $C = C(Y)$.

The broken line in Fig. 24.4 bisects the angle between the two axes, and therefore makes an angle of 45° with each of them. All points on this line are equidistant from the two axes, e.g. $FR = HR$ by construction. Hence at any point on the 45° line, the real C, as measured on the vertical axis, is necessarily equal to the corresponding real Y. Now consider, with the help of this '45° line' diagram, a number of different shapes which the consumption function might take.

If the consumption function happened to coincide with the 45° line, all points on it would be equidistant from the two axes, and C would equal Y at all levels of Y. An alternative is the straight line consumption function C_1, which starts at the origin and lies below the 45° line. At all points along C_1, C is less than Y (e.g. $FK < FR$), and $C/Y < 1$. The ratio C/Y is called the *average propensity to consume* (symbolized by APC). It has the same value at all points on C_1 (since at points J, K and L respectively, $\dfrac{C}{Y} = \dfrac{EJ}{OE} = \dfrac{FK}{OF} = \dfrac{GL}{OG}$, by similar triangles). In general, any straight line consumption function, which goes through the origin, has constant APCs at all levels of Y.

A third possibility is shown by the straight line consumption function

[1] Keynes called it a *propensity to consume*.

C_2, which does not have constant APCs. For example, at point J on C_2, the $APC = \dfrac{EJ}{OE}$, which is the slope of the straight line OJ that joins J to the origin. At point M, the slope of $OM\left(= \dfrac{FM}{OM}\right)$, which measures

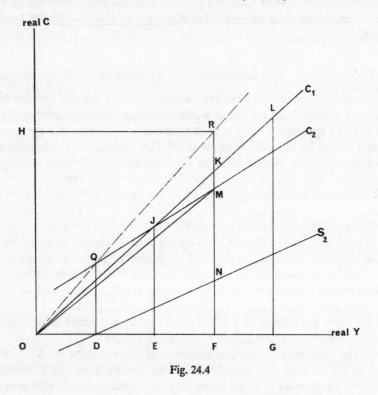

Fig. 24.4

the APC there, is less than the slope of OJ. Thus the APC on C_2 is smaller at higher levels of Y. Moreover, given that property, C_2 must intersect the 45° line (at Q). This means both that there is a level of Y at which $C = Y$ and that, below this level of Y, $C > Y$.

It is important to measure another characteristic of the consumption function, namely what expansion in C (ΔC) would result from a small change in Y (ΔY). The ratio $\dfrac{\Delta C}{\Delta Y}$ is called the *marginal propensity to consume* (symbolized by MPC). Since it indicates the rate at which C

changes in relation to Y, it is measured by the slope of the consumption function at each level of Y.[1]

The MPC and the APC must not be confused. For example, at point J, the slope of the function C_2 (which is its MPC) is smaller than the slope of OJ (which is its APC at J). The slopes of the two consumption functions in Fig. 24.4 are constant, i.e. straight line functions have constant MPCs.[2] But only C_1 has constant APCs. That is, only straight line functions which go through the origin have $MPC = APC$ at *all* levels of Y.

The consumption function shows how real C varies in relation to real Y. But it has been seen above that there are other determinants of C, viz. the personal attributes which determine the consumption-to-income ratios of households, real personal wealth, the distribution of income, and the past rates of growth of real income per head. These other determinants are the parameters of the consumption function. If they change, the function will shift upwards (viz. increase) or downwards (viz. decrease). A shift in the function means that C becomes larger or smaller at each level of Y. Therefore, the APC (C/Y) becomes larger or smaller at each Y. But the MPC $\left(\dfrac{\Delta C}{\Delta Y}\right)$ at each Y may not alter. This will be the case where the function shifts parallel to itself, and so retains the same slope at each level of Y.

Saving, by definition, equals income minus consumption. The relation between real S and real Y therefore follows by arithmetic, once the relation between C and Y is known. If S is now measured on the vertical axis of Fig. 24.4, the *saving function* (which shows how S varies with Y) corresponding to any consumption function can be plotted. For example, at the Y level OF ($= FR$) on the C_2 curve in Fig. 24.4, $C = FM$, and the rest of that income, MR, is saved. Mark the point N, so that $FN = MR$. N is one point on the saving function. The points for the other Y levels can be derived in the same way. The resulting curve, S_2, gives the same information about the division of income between consumption and saving as the curve C_2 does, but it gives it from a different viewpoint (e.g. at income OD, S is zero because $C = Y$ at point Q; and below that income S is negative because C exceeds Y).

[1] The MPC is an analogous concept to MC, and all the other marginal concepts used in Part II. It was shown, on pp. 119–121 above, how MC is measured by the slope at each point on the TC curve. Precisely the same form of reasoning shows MPC to be measured by the slopes at the points on the curve giving total consumption.

[2] For simplicity, only straight line functions will be considered here. On a curved function, MPC (and APC) will vary from point to point.

The remainder of the necessary interconnections between the C and S functions now follow. Since $C + S \equiv Y$, $\dfrac{C}{Y} + \dfrac{S}{Y} \equiv 1$. $\dfrac{S}{Y}$ is called the *average propensity to save* (APS). The $APS \equiv 1 - APC$ (if $\tfrac{9}{10}$ of income is consumed, $\tfrac{1}{10}$ is necessarily saved). The *marginal propensity to save*

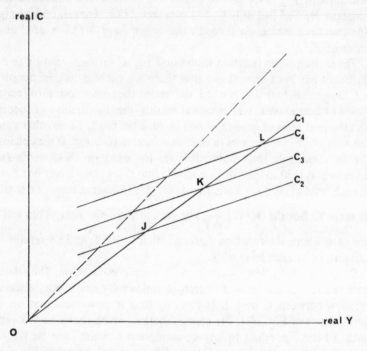

Fig. 24.5

(MPS) is $\dfrac{\Delta S}{\Delta Y}$, and is measured by the slope of the saving function at each level of Y. The $MPS \equiv 1 - MPC$ (e.g. if $\tfrac{9}{10}$ of an increment of income is consumed, $\tfrac{1}{10}$ of the increment is necessarily saved). If the consumption function shifts, because of a parameter change, the saving function necessarily shifts in the *opposite* direction: an increase in C, at any level of Y, *means* the same thing as a decrease in S at any level of Y.

Fig. 24.5 can be used to analyse the remaining question about the determination of real C, namely what will the C/Y ratio be at different levels of Y? It can now be seen that this is a question of the shape of the consumption function. Despite two decades of intensive research, economists have not reached an agreed answer. The reason for this is not difficult to understand.

The earlier analysis has shown that the volume of consumption is determined by a large number of variables. To specify the shape of the consumption function, one has to separate out the dependence of C on Y from its dependence on the other variables. There are great difficulties in making such a separation.[1] The *actual* amounts of C which have occurred in the past, at different levels of Y, do not in themselves give the C to Y relation. For example, suppose that C and Y have had, in three different years in the past, the values given by the points J, K, and L in Fig. 24.5. J, K, and L are all on the C_1 curve. It might then be argued that the behaviour of C, as between the three years, can be explained by means of a function with the shape C_1. But this would imply that the changes in Y were the *sole* reason for the changes in C, i.e. that the other variables determining C (such as the distribution of income and the other parameters of C_1) had not altered over the years in question.

But J is also on the C_2 curve, K on C_3, and L on C_4. Hence the first argument could be countered with the view that the behaviour of C is to be explained by a function with the shape C_2 shifting up, as a result of parameter changes, to the C_3 and C_4 positions. This view implies that changes in other determining variables, as well as in Y, had helped to alter C. Therefore the influence of those other variables on C has to be discovered, before one can decide that the consumption function has a shape like C_1 or C_2 (or some other shape). That is the problem on which work is still in progress.

But some shape for the consumption function has to be adopted to allow this book to continue. A function like C_2 in Fig. 24.5 seems fairly plausible for the short-period analysis being undertaken at the moment. Many industrial countries have experienced cycles of rising, followed by falling, economic activity, each cycle lasting 4–5 years. The C/Y ratio has usually been the smaller, the higher the level of Y during each cycle. The C_2 type of function is at least consistent with those facts. It may not, of course, be a complete explanation of them, since changes in other variables, like the distribution of income, may have shifted the function during the cycle. However, the working assumption of the following analysis will be that the APC is smaller at higher than at lower levels of Y, as is shown by the C_2 function.

[1] As was explained in general terms in Chapter 6; see especially pp. 57–58 above.

THE VOLUME OF INVESTMENT

Investment has already been analysed at the microeconomic level in Chapter 21. It was there shown that an individual investment project is expected to be profitable if the expected internal rate of return on it exceeds the interest rate after an allowance for uncertainty, i.e. if $r > i + p$. It was, however, pointed out that microeconomic analysis cannot explain the *rate* per period of time at which the volume of aggregate investment (I) will proceed.[1]

The interest rate[2] has to be determined before the number of investment projects, which are expected to be profitable, can be known. That number is likely to be so large that all the projects will not be carried out at once. It is therefore necessary to explain how the rate of I period by period (e.g. year by year) is determined. Moreover, the volume of investment per period is likely to depend on the *expected* future level of aggregate demand for the national output. Capital goods are needed to produce the national output. The higher the national output is expected to be in the future, the more capital goods will be required to produce it, and therefore the more investment will have to be undertaken. All these macroeconomic aspects of investment cannot be analysed until this part of the book has progressed farther.[3]

For the present, therefore, the volume of investment[4] per period of time will be taken to depend on the interest rate and on expected internal rates of return after an allowance for uncertainty. In particular, it will be assumed that the volume of investment per period will be larger, the lower is the interest rate. This is consistent with the microeconomic analysis; and it will be justified by later analysis. The investment function therefore takes the form $I = I(i)$, and it can be depicted by a horizontal straight line on the '45° line' diagram, at a level equal to the given rate of investment per period. All this will be demonstrated in the next chapter.

[1] See p. 238 above.
[2] Which is analysed in Chapter 30 below.
[3] They will be taken up in Chapter 31.
[4] Unless otherwise indicated, I is to be interpreted in the *gross* sense, i.e. as covering both replacement and net I. This is necessary since in explaining the determination of X and N, the production of *all* capital goods has to be taken into account.

CHAPTER 25

NATIONAL OUTPUT DETERMINATION

The previous chapter's analysis of the determinants of the *volumes* of consumption and investment has prepared the ground for the explanation of their *money values*. However, before this is undertaken, it will be helpful to have an understanding of how the volume of national output is determined, on the assumption of given and *constant* levels of money wage rates and prices.

The aggregate demand for goods is the sum of consumption and investment expenditures, i.e. $Z \equiv C + I$. The aggregate supply of goods (Y) is equal to $P \cdot X$. With P assumed to be constant, Y measures the volume of national output. For an economy to be in equilibrium, the volume of goods supplied by firms in aggregate must equal the quantity demanded of them, i.e. Y must equal the sum of C and I. The '45° line' diagram is widely used by economists to explain how the volume of national output is determined. By the very nature of the diagram, this means that P and W are assumed to be constant. Consequently, the aggregate supply function cannot be depicted on the diagram, because the function shows how national output depends on W and P. The 45° line diagram is therefore of limited use, since *both* the aggregate demand and supply functions are needed to explain how X and P are determined.[1] However, as long as its limitations are clearly recognized, it is a helpful introductory device for macroeconomic analysis. It will be so used here, as a preparation for the analysis (in the next chapter) of how *both* X and P are determined.

Since real[2] C expands as real Y rises, real Z expands as real Y rises. This is shown in the 45° line diagram in Fig. 25.1, where real Z (and its constituents real C and real I) is measured on the vertical axis and real Y on the horizontal. The C curve is given the shape discussed in the previous chapter: it is a straight line, and therefore the MPC $\left(\dfrac{\Delta C}{\Delta Y}\right)$ is the same at all points on it. The fact that it is sloping upwards to the right

---

[1] As explained on pp. 274–275 above.
[2] It will be recalled that 'real' means the same thing as 'volume of'.

shows that C expands as Y rises. It cuts the $45°$ line (at H), and has a smaller slope than it; hence as Y rises, C expands by a *smaller amount*, i.e. the $APC \left(\dfrac{C}{Y} \right)$ is less than one, and is falling as Y rises. The constant MPC is therefore also less than one. The *position* of the C curve depends on all the other influences, apart from Y, which determine consumption.

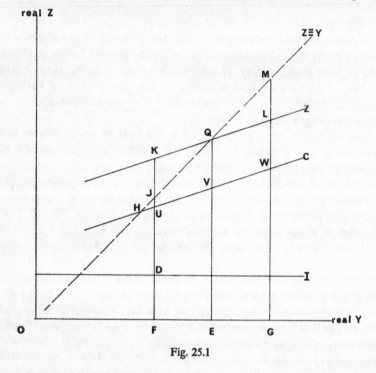

Fig. 25.1

If these parameters of the curve change, it shifts either upwards (increases) or downwards (decreases).

The I curve is, in accordance with the discussion in the previous chapter, a horizontal straight line. It shows the volume of investment which will be undertaken, given the expected internal rates of return on investment projects, the interest rate, and attitudes towards uncertainty. These determinants of investment are the parameters of the I curve. If they change, the curve shifts either upwards (increases) or downwards (decreases), but remains a horizontal straight line. In particular, the I curve will increase if the interest rate falls, and vice versa.

How aggregate demand will expand as Y rises can be seen by adding consumption and investment at *each* level of Y. For example, at the OF level of national output, C is FU, and I is FD; hence, $Z = FU + FD = FK$, at the output level OF. The size of Z is similarly obtained at the other output levels; and this enables the aggregate demand curve Z to be drawn. Since investment is constant at all output levels, the Z curve is parallel to the C curve. The vertical distances between the two curves (e.g. UK) equal the constant amount of investment. Z expands as Y rises, because C expands as Y rises. With investment constant, Z and C expand at the same rate as Y rises, i.e. the Z and C curves have the same slope. In other words, the slope of the Z curve equals the MPC.

Since the 45° line bisects the angle between the two axes, it is equidistant from both of them. At any point on it, the value of Z (measured on the vertical axis) is necessarily equal to the corresponding value of Y (on the horizontal axis). That is why the line is labelled $Z \equiv Y$.

Consider the economic significance of the point of intersection (Q) between the Z curve and the 45° line. Since Q is on the Z curve, EQ is the aggregate expenditure which the economy wants to make, on consumption plus investment, when the output level is OE. Since Q is also on the 45° line, the Z level EQ necessarily equals the Y level OE. Aggregate demand equals aggregate supply at Q. The economy is there producing the same amount of goods as consumers plus investors want to buy. Firms in aggregate are able to sell all that they are producing—neither more nor less.

The national output is therefore in *equilibrium* at Q. When the firms in aggregate produce the output OE, they create that amount of real income for households by their payments for factors. At that level of income, the consumers will spend EV, as shown by the C curve. This consumption, plus the constant amount of investment VQ, give an aggregate expenditure of EQ. Since the firms are therefore selling exactly the amount which they produce, there is no reason for them either to increase or to decrease that output. This is the sense in which the national output is in equilibrium at Q.

Now consider the relation between aggregate demand and supply at other levels of Y. If the firms in aggregate produce the national output OG, they create that amount of real income for households. Consumption will therefore be GW, as shown by the C curve at the national output OG. This consumption, plus the constant amount of investment WL, gives an aggregate demand of GL. But the aggregate supply of goods is OG (= GM, where M is on the 45° line). Thus, when the firms produce OG, they will find that there is an excess of aggregate supply over aggregate demand (viz. an *excess aggregate supply*) equal to

$GM - GL = LM$. The quantity of goods LM, which was produced in the expectation of being sold, in fact remains unsold. They are *involuntarily* added to the stocks of the firms. That is, they are an *unintended* investment; and must therefore be distinguished from the *intended* investment level shown by the I curve.

At the given general level of prices, excess aggregate supply results in some part of the national output remaining unsold. This situation is the macroeconomic counterpart of that discussed for the individual industry in Chapter 13.[1] It was there seen that excess supply, at a particular price for a good, would result in an unintended accumulation of stocks by the industry. It was then argued that the price would fall, *relative* to other prices, and would converge to an equilibrium level as the quantity supplied of the good contracts and the quantity demanded expands.

It is, however, a much more complex matter to analyse what will happen to excess *aggregate* supply if the *absolute* price level, P, falls. If P falls, the money value of $Y (\equiv P . X)$ falls, and this means a reduction in the money incomes of households, since these are created by Y. Hence the size of their money expenditure on consumption will fall. The effects of *all* these changes in *money* values have to be taken into account before a conclusion can be reached on the effect that a fall in the price level will have on excess aggregate supply. These complications are the reason why the analysis of the price level has been postponed (to the next chapter) until a separate analysis of national output has been completed. In any case, the price level is in fact fairly inflexible in a downward direction in many industrial economies, because trade unions resist reductions in W.[2] The present explanation of the determination of national output does, therefore, have some applicability to such economies.

Continue, then, to assume that the price level is given and constant. In that case, the excess aggregate supply of LM at the national output level OG, in Fig. 25.1, will lead to a reduction in national output. As long as national output is maintained at OG, there will be an unintended accumulation of stocks at the rate of LM per period of time. To prevent this from happening, firms will reduce their outputs. National output will fall, and will converge to the level OE, at which excess aggregate supply has been eliminated. The convergence to equilibrium occurs because, as Y falls, Z contracts to a *lesser* extent; since the MPC is less than 1, the contraction in C is less than the fall in Y.

[1] By means of Fig. 13.1 on p. 139 above.
[2] As has already been considered in the analysis of pp. 222–225 above.

If the firms produce a national output less than OE, the consequent *excess aggregate demand* will cause output to converge to OE. Thus, at the output OF ($= FJ$, where J is on the 45° line), consumption is FU, and with the constant amount of investment UK, aggregate demand is FK. There is an excess aggregate demand of JK. This means that firms in aggregate, having produced an output OF, find that they can sell an amount of goods larger than OF. If they hold sufficient stocks, they can meet the excess demand by running down stocks. This disinvestment, however, is *unintended*. If stocks are insufficient, the firms must either engage in *ad hoc* rationing of goods, and/or lengthen their order books. In any of these cases, there is an incentive for firms to increase their outputs. National output will rise, and will converge to OE, because, as Y rises, Z expands to a *lesser* extent; since the MPC is less than 1, the expansion in C is less than the rise in Y.

EMPLOYMENT AND UNEMPLOYMENT

Point Q is thus not only an equilibrium for the national output, it is also a *stable* equilibrium. The convergence analyses above have shown that, given the C and I curves, the economy will operate at the output level OE. The general level of employment of labour (N) now follows from the production function for the whole economy, viz. $X = F(N, K_0)$. K_0 (capital plus land) is given and constant in the short period. National output can therefore be varied only by changing the amount of labour services used in conjunction with the given K_0. There will be a different N at every level of X—N being higher, the greater is X. The size of N is therefore determined, once the level of real Y (i.e. X) is determined. There is no necessity, *under present assumptions*, for the N in question to be the full employment level of labour.

The equilibrium level of Y, and therefore of N, is given by the intersection of the Z curve and the 45° line. The higher the Z curve lies in the diagram, the larger will be the equilibrium Y, since the Z curve now intersects the 45° line at a larger Y. That is, the greater is the aggregate demand at *every* level of Y, the larger will be the equilibrium Y. The position and shape of the Z curve depends on the positions and shapes of the C and I curves—since the former is obtained by adding the latter two. The position and shape of the C curve depends on all the influences analysed in the previous chapter, viz. the personal attributes of households, their real personal wealth, and the distribution of income. The position of the horizontal straight line I curve depends on the expected internal rates of return, the interest rate, and attitudes towards uncertainty.

The C curve can thus lie higher, or lower, in the diagram for a variety of reasons; and so can the I curve. With P, W, and the interest rate given and constant, there is consequently no assurance that the Z curve will cut the 45° line at the full employment level of Y.

Thus suppose that, with the given K_0, and a given willingness of workers to supply labour services at the ruling real wage rate $\left(\dfrac{W}{P_C}\right)$, the national output OG in Fig. 25.1 could be produced by using all the available labour. OG is then the *full employment* level of output. But it is not, as has been seen, the *equilibrium* level of output. Given the Z curve in the diagram, the equilibrium level is OE. This is the level at which the economy will operate. Hence, a quantity of goods EG (= $OG - OE$), which *could* be produced by the available factors, is not in fact produced. The economy works below its productive capacity, and fails to employ all of its available labour services. The amount of unemployment is indicated by the quantity of goods EG which could be, but is not, produced. The larger EG is, relative to the full employment national output OG, the greater will be the percentage level of unemployment.

Full employment will not be achieved unless the Z curve lies higher up in the diagram. This would be so if the C and/or the I curves lie higher up. Thus, if investors come to expect larger internal rates of return on their projects, a greater investment per period will be undertaken. The higher I curve means a higher Z curve. If the latter now intersects the 45° line at point M, full employment will be assured. The equilibrium level of national output (at OG) now coincides with the full employment level. As it is, with the Z curve in the diagram, full employment cannot be maintained even if it happens to exist initially. The *deficiency* of aggregate demand at the full employment—i.e. the excess aggregate supply LM—will cause firms to reduce output and employment until they can sell all they produce (viz. the national output OE).

The relation between this process of adjustment in national output, and those going on concurrently in individual labour markets, can be shown by means of an analysis made in Chapter 20. Fig. 20.2[1] was based on the assumption that trade unions will resist reductions in money wage rates. The horizontal range of the S curve for the labour market in the diagram corresponds to the macroeconomic assumption

[1] On p. 222 above.

of a given and constant W. It was then shown how the level of employment of the labour factor will depend on the *position* of its demand curve. The greater the demand for the factor, the higher will be its level of employment. But the demand for the factor depends on the demands for the goods it helps to make. The *position* of the demand curve for the factor therefore depends on the aggregate demand for goods. Hence, the higher up the Z curve lies in Fig. 25.1, the more to the right the D curve in Fig. 20.2 will lie. The Z curve has to intersect the 45° line at point M (where OG is the full employment level of national output), if the D_2 curve is to intersect the S curve (viz. APS) at the full employment level OK for the factor.[1]

It is essential to remember the main assumptions on which the above analysis has proceeded, namely that the absolute price level (P), the absolute money wage rate level (W), and the interest rate (i), are all given and constant. The consequences of relaxing these assumptions will be investigated in due course, and it will then be seen whether the conclusion just reached—that national output can be in equilibrium *below* the full employment level—needs to be changed, and if so, in what way.

NATIONAL OUTPUT CHANGES

The C and I curves will shift if any of their parameters change. Thus, if the distribution of income changes, the amount spent on consumption at any level of national output is likely to change. If the distribution becomes less unequal, consumption will probably increase at every level of Y, i.e. the C curve will shift upwards. People with smaller incomes usually spend a higher proportion of any increase in income on consumption than do people with larger incomes. A redistribution of income towards the former will therefore increase their consumption expenditure by more than it reduces the consumption of the latter. Aggregate consumption therefore increases. An increase in C at every level of Y means an increase in the APC $\left(\dfrac{C}{Y}\right)$ at every level of Y. But the MPC $\left(\dfrac{\Delta C}{\Delta Y}\right)$, at each level of Y, will not necessarily change. It does not change if the C curve makes a parallel upward shift.

The I curve will shift upwards if, for example, the interest rate falls,

---

[1] It will be noticed that nothing has yet been said about the possibility of the Z curve intersecting the 45° line to the *right* of point M (when OG is the full employment level of Y). This will be considered in the next two chapters because it involves changes in P and W.

or investing firms come to expect higher internal rates of return on their projects. The new I curve will lie above, and be parallel to, its original horizontal position.

If either consumption or investment increases, the Z curve shifts up to a new position. Aggregate demand is now greater at *every* level of Y, as is shown in Fig. 25.2. The initial Z_1 curve intersects the 45° line at Q,

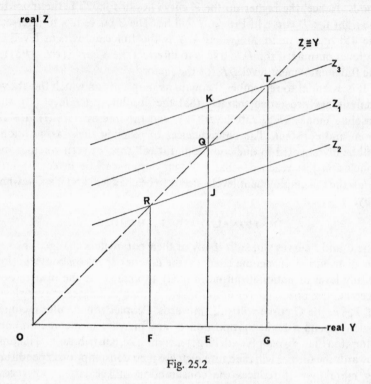

Fig. 25.2

giving an equilibrium national output OE. An increase in aggregate demand, arising from an increase in either consumption or investment, is shown by Z_3. For simplicity, Z_3 is drawn parallel to Z_1; since both are straight lines, the *MPC* is the same at all points on both of them.

With the increase in aggregate demand, the national output level OE is now a *disequilibrium* one. Aggregate demand on Z_3 is EK at output level OE ($= EQ$), the latter being the amount of aggregate supply. Consequently, there is an excess aggregate demand of QK ($= EK - EQ$) at the output level OE. As in microeconomics, it is the convergence (stability) conditions which determine what will happen in a disequilibrium situation. The macroeconomic convergence conditions for the present analysis have already been studied above.

Excess aggregate demand means that firms in aggregate find they can sell more goods than they have produced. With the price level constant, stocks are therefore run down, or order books are lengthened, or *ad hoc* rationing occurs. In any of these cases the firms will proceed to increase output. National output will therefore rise[1] and converge to OG, where $Z = Y$ on the Z_3 curve at point T. The convergence occurs because, as Y rises, Z expands to a lesser extent; since the MPC is less than 1, the expansion in C is less than the rise in Y. Hence the excess aggregate demand is gradually eliminated as output rises. The increase in aggregate demand raises Y, and therefore N as well.

A decrease in aggregate demand, arising from a decrease in either consumption or investment, will reduce both Y and N. Thus, if Z_1 in Fig. 25.2 shifts down to Z_2, there will be an excess aggregate supply of JQ at the original equilibrium national output OE. Firms in aggregate sell less than they are producing, and *unintended* investment in stocks occurs. The firms therefore reduce output, Y falls and converges to OF, where $Z = Y$ on the Z_2 curve at point R. The convergence occurs because the excess aggregate supply is gradually eliminated as Y falls, and Z contracts to a lesser extent; since the MPC is less than 1, the contraction in C is less than the fall in Y.

THE MULTIPLIER

The *magnitude* of the rise in national output, when aggregate demand increases, will now be investigated. Fig. 25.3 shows in detail what happens when aggregate demand increases. Aggregate demand at each level of Y is initially given by the Z_1 curve, which is obtained by adding consumption on the C curve to investment on the I_1 curve at each level of Y.

Suppose that investment per period of time increases from the I_1 to the I_2 curve, so that Z_1 shifts up to Z_2. The Z_2 curve is obtained by adding consumption on the (unchanged) C curve to investment on the I_2 curve, at each level of Y. The vertical distances between Z_1 and Z_2 are all equal to the *increase* in investment, i.e. to the vertical distance between I_1 and I_2. For example, at the OF level of national output, $NR (= Z_2 - Z_1)$ is by construction equal to $HJ (= I_2 - I_1)$.[2]

---

[1] This assumes that there are sufficient unemployed factors to allow the rise to take place. The consequences, when this is not so, will be analysed in the next two chapters.

[2] It should be noted that a parallel upward shift in the C curve leads to a parallel upward shift in the Z curve, in the same way as the present shift in the I curve does.

Z_1 intersects the 45° line at point Q, giving an equilibrium national output OE; and Z_2 intersects the 45° line at R, giving an equilibrium output OF. Thus, as a result of the increase in aggregate demand, national output rises from OE (= EQ) to OF (= FR). The rise in output is therefore measured either by EF (= $OF - OE$), or by MR (= $FR - EQ$). The length MR is the sum of MN and NR. It has already

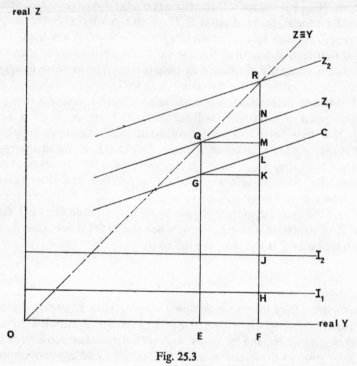

Fig. 25.3

been seen that NR (= HJ) is the increase in investment, which is the initial cause of the rise in output. But MR, the rise in output, is *greater* than NR, the increase in investment. That is, although the increase in investment (ΔI) initiates the rise in output (ΔY), the latter turns out to be greater than the former; in other words, ΔY is a *multiple* of ΔI. The relationship between ΔY and ΔI is therefore called the *Multiplier*.

This important relationship will now be explained in a number of different ways. First of all, consider further the geometrical expression of the multiplier in Fig. 25.3. The rise in output (MR) exceeds the increase in investment (NR) by the amount MN. What is the explanation of that amount?

MN is the *expansion* in consumption caused by the rise in national output from *OE* to *OF*. At the *OE* level of national output, consumption is *EG*, as given by point *G* on the *C* curve. At the output level *OF*, consumption is *FL*. The expansion in consumption along the *C* curve from *G* to *L*, as national output rises, is *KL*. And *KL* is equal, by construction, to *MN* (since the *C* and Z_1 curves are parallel).

The explanation of the magnitude of the rise in output can now be seen. The national output level *OE* is called forth by consumption expenditure of *EG* plus I_1 expenditure of *GQ*. The output level *OF* is called forth by consumption expenditure of *FL* plus I_2 expenditure of *LR* (= *FJ*). The rise in output of *MR* is partly the result of the *increase* in investment of *NR* (= *HJ*, i.e. the upward shift in the *I* curve), and partly of the *expansion* in consumption of *MN* (= *KL*, i.e. the movement along the *C* curve as *Y* rises). It is the *expansion* in consumption expenditure which occurs as *Y* rises that explains why *Y* rises by *more* than the increase in investment. The multiplier results from the consumption function.

The process of expansion in national output through the multiplier occurs in the following way. Start with *Y* in equilibrium, equal to the sum of consumption and investment expenditures. Suppose that investors decide—because, for example, of a fall in the interest rate—to invest at a greater rate, viz. to demand a greater quantity of capital goods in each period of time. The output of the capital goods industries will rise, and they will employ greater quantities of factors.[1] National output will therefore rise, initially by the amount of the increased output of capital goods; and the real incomes of the household which own the newly-employed resources will go up by the same amount.

Those households will spend some, but probably not all, of the increase in their incomes on consumer goods. This means an *increase* in the demands for consumer goods. The output of the consumer goods industries will rise, and they will employ greater quantities of factors. National output will therefore rise by a *further* amount, equal to the increased output of consumer goods. But this secondary rise will be less than the initial one caused by the increased output of capital goods: not all of the increase in incomes resulting from the initial rise in national output is spent on consumption; some is saved. The real incomes of the households, which own the resources that are now newly-employed in the consumer goods industries, will go up by the amount of the secondary rise in national output.

[1] As before in this chapter, it is assumed that there are sufficient unemployed resources to allow output to rise.

That will cause a *further* increase in the demands for consumer goods. But this further increase will be less than the first one (for consumer goods), because not all of the secondary rise in incomes will be spent on consumption; some will be saved. The output of consumer goods therefore rises again. National output rises yet again; incomes rise yet again; demands for consumer goods increase yet again, and so on. At each successive stage in this process of expansion, the *rise* in national output gets smaller and smaller. Each successive increase in incomes is not completely spent on consumption; some is saved. As the *expansion* in consumption gradually comes to an end, national output converges to its new, higher equilibrium level.

In terms of Fig. 25.3, the successive expansions in consumption, as Y rises to the new equilibrium, all add up to KL ($= MN$). And MN, plus the increase in demand for capital goods HJ ($= NR$), explains the rise in national output by MR.

The multiplier is thus seen as a process by which successive increases in national output give rise to further increases, because consumption expands as Y rises. This is another aspect of the circular flow of expenditure through which a price mechanism works. Expenditure calls forth output, which creates incomes, out of which expenditure takes place, and so on endlessly. The process of expansion involved in the multiplier can be expressed precisely in terms of the *MPC*.

Suppose that the community will spend four-fifths of *any* rise in its income on consumption, i.e. $\Delta C = \tfrac{4}{5}\Delta Y$. Hence the *MPC* $\left(\dfrac{\Delta C}{\Delta Y}\right) = \dfrac{4}{5}$, and is the same at all levels of Y. Suppose that investment increases by 10. Output therefore rises, initially, by 10. Consumption now expands by $\tfrac{4}{5} . 10$; this is the secondary rise in output. But this leads to a further expansion in consumption of $\tfrac{4}{5} . \tfrac{4}{5} . 10 = (\tfrac{4}{5})^2 . 10$. This, in turn, causes a tertiary rise in output of the same amount, giving rise to additional consumption of $(\tfrac{4}{5})^3 . 10$. Thus, the eventual rise in national output through the multiplier is the sum of the series

$$10 + \tfrac{4}{5} . 10 + (\tfrac{4}{5})^2 . 10 + (\tfrac{4}{5})^3 . 10 + \ldots$$

In general, if the increase in investment $(\Delta I) = a$, and the *MPC* $= c$, the rise in national output (ΔY) is the sum of the series

$$a + c . a + c^2 . a + c^3 . a + \ldots$$

This is a convergent series if $c < 1$, and its sum tends to a limit given by the formula,[1] $\dfrac{a}{1 - c}$. Hence,

$$\Delta Y = a \cdot \left(\frac{1}{1 - c} \right), \quad \text{i.e. } \Delta Y = \Delta I \cdot \left(\frac{1}{1 - MPC} \right).[2]$$

The term $\left(\dfrac{1}{1 - MPC} \right)$ is the multiplier, which shows by how much ΔI has to be multiplied in order to get ΔY. Its size depends on the size of the MPC, because the multiplier results from the *expansion* in consumption as Y rises. The MPC $\left(\dfrac{\Delta C}{\Delta Y} \right)$ measures that expansion. The more consumption expands as Y rises, the greater is the increase in demand for consumer goods, and therefore the larger is the resultant rise in Y. The larger is the MPC, the larger is the multiplier.[3] Thus, if MPC is $\tfrac{9}{10}$, $\left(\dfrac{1}{1 - MPC} \right)$ equals 10; but if MPC is $\tfrac{4}{5}$, the multiplier equals only 5.

In terms of Fig. 25.3, suppose that $\Delta I = NR = 10$, and $MPC = \tfrac{4}{5}$. Then, $\Delta Y = MR = 50$; and $\Delta C = MN = \tfrac{4}{5} . 50 = 40$. That is, when $\Delta Y = 50$, $\Delta C = 40$, and this together with $\Delta I = 10$, gives $\Delta Z = 50$; hence the rise in aggregate supply matches the rise in aggregate demand. In geometrical terms, MPC is the slope of the C curve, and the slopes of the Z curves are the same as it. It is the slope of Z_1 which determines the size of MN, for a given rise in Y. The greater is the slope (viz. MPC), the larger is MN (viz. ΔC); and the larger is MN, the larger is the rise in Y as a result of a given increase in I.

The multiplier operates during falls, as well as rises, in Y, because consumption contracts as Y falls, just as it expands when Y rises. The above analysis can be applied in reverse for a *decrease* in investment. Thus, in Fig. 25.3, a decrease in investment, from I_2 to I_1, will reduce Y

---

[1] As explained in textbooks on algebra.

[2] This can be derived in another way. $\Delta Y = \Delta C + \Delta I$, and $\Delta C = c . \Delta Y$. Hence $\Delta Y = c . \Delta Y + \Delta I$. From which $\Delta Y = \Delta I . \left(\dfrac{1}{1 - c} \right)$.

[3] The multiplier can also be expressed in terms of the MPS $\left(\dfrac{\Delta S}{\Delta Y} \right)$. $MPS = 1 - MPC$ (see p. 282 above). The multiplier is therefore $\left(\dfrac{1}{MPS} \right)$. It is the larger, the smaller is MPS; because, of course, MPS is smaller, the larger is MPC.

by a multiple of the decrease, and the magnitude of the reduction in Y will depend on the MPC.

The multiplier also operates as a result of *increases* (or decreases) in consumption. Thus, suppose that the C curve, rather than the I curve in Fig. 25.3, *shifts* upwards in a parallel fashion by the amount HJ, because of a redistribution of income. Z_1 then shifts to Z_2, and the resultant rise in Y is a multiple of the *increase* in consumption. That *increase* raises Y, and the consequential *expansion* in consumption raises Y still further. The only difference from the case where investment increases, is that the *initial* rise in Y is due to increased demand for consumer goods, rather than for capital goods.[1]

The above analysis has been simplified by assuming that the MPC is the same at all levels of Y, i.e. that the C curve is a straight line. This may not be so. Thus, the C curve, in Fig. 25.3, may be 'curved' between points G and L. The MPC (i.e. slope) will vary over this range of it. Hence the expansion in consumption between points G and L will be measured by the *average* of the MPCs in question. The size of the multiplier will then depend on that average of the MPCs.[2]

The multiplier helps to explain how prosperity and depression can spread throughout an economy—or the whole world. An increase (decrease) in spending in one part of an economy (or the world) will, by raising (reducing) incomes there, lead to an increase (decrease) in spending on goods produced elsewhere. Only the simplest form of the multiplier has so far been explained. It will be discovered—especially when government economic activity and foreign trade are allowed for—that the multiplier is in fact more complex in form.

---

[1] I.e. in the formula $\Delta Y = a \cdot \left(\dfrac{1}{1 - MPC} \right)$, a now stands for the *increase* in consumption, rather than in investment.

[2] It has been assumed, quite plausibly, that $MPC < 1$. If $MPC > 1$, the C curve, and therefore the Z curve, intersect the 45° line from *below* on the left to *above* on the right. The equilibrium Y is therefore unstable. If $MPC > 1$, the multiplier has a negative value. This is because a higher, as compared with a lower, Z curve intersects the 45° line at a *smaller* level of Y. But, since the equilibrium Y is unstable, Y would not converge to a lower level as a result of an increase in Z. The reader can easily verify this by drawing the diagram.

CHAPTER 26

NATIONAL OUTPUT AND THE PRICE LEVEL

The assumptions of a constant price level (P) and a constant money wage rate level (W), in the previous chapter, allowed the analysis to concentrate on the determination of the volume of national output (X). This has prepared the ground for the study of both X and P—which are determined in relation to each other. The analysis becomes more complex when P and W are variable: not only must the levels of P and W themselves be explained, but the effects of changes in them on X must also be explained.

A change in P alters the money value of Y ($\equiv P \cdot X$). The change in Y, on this account, means a change in the amount of *money* income which flows to households. A change in money income will probably alter the level of *money* expenditure on consumption. But it will not necessarily alter the *volume* of consumer goods which is demanded, since the absolute prices of goods, as well as money incomes, have changed. It has been emphasized in earlier analyses that the quantities demanded of consumer goods depend on *real* incomes. These are given by the relation between money incomes and money prices. Hence, when the price level and money incomes change together, it is what happens to the *real* incomes of different people that determines the change (if any) in the volume of consumption.

When W changes, this alters the amount of money income which flows to households at any level of employment. But it also alters the cost conditions of firms, and therefore leads to a change in P. Hence, when W, P, and money incomes change together, it is essential to distinguish between changes in the volume, and changes in the money value, of consumption.

The 45° line diagram is of no direct help in analysing these problems. By its very nature, it assumes P and W constant. It is necessary, therefore, to use a diagram[1] which shows the relations between X, P, and W, by means of the aggregate supply and the aggregate demand curves.

[1] Like Fig. 24.3 on p. 274 above.

The nature and shape of the aggregate supply (Y) curve has already been explained in detail.[1] But the properties of the aggregate demand (Z) curve have only been outlined, with the purpose of giving a preliminary indication of how it, together with the Y curve, can be used to explain the determination of both X and P.[2] The Z curve shows what the sum of the money expenditures on consumption and investment will be at each level of national output. Those expenditures have now to be analysed in order to derive the Z curve.

AGGREGATE MONEY EXPENDITURE ON CONSUMPTION

The *volume* of consumption depends on the sizes of people's *real* incomes. The latter are given by the sizes of their money incomes in relation to the average money prices of consumer goods (P_C). Therefore, to discover the *money value* of consumption, at any level of national output, it is necessary to know what (i) the total of money incomes, and (ii) the P_C, will be at that level of output. The aggregate supply function is needed to provide this information. It may be well, therefore, to recapitulate briefly, with the help of Fig. 26.1, the main properties of the Y curve.

Aggregate money expenditure ($\equiv P \cdot X$) is measured on the vertical axis of Fig. 26.1 and the national output (X) on the horizontal. The Y curve shows, at each point on it, the aggregate money expenditure which would be just sufficient to induce firms to produce the corresponding national output. Thus, the point Q indicates that an expected total revenue from sales of OJ ($= DQ$) would make it worthwhile for the firms to produce the national output OD. The supply price (the supply-P) of that output is $\dfrac{DQ}{OD} \left(= \dfrac{P \cdot X}{X} = P \right)$; this ratio is the slope of the straight line OQ, joining the origin and point Q. Under perfect competition, the supply-P equals the MC of national output. The MC $\left(= \dfrac{W}{MPP_L} \right)$, and therefore the supply-P, rises as national output increases, because of diminishing returns to labour. The curve terminates at the full employment level of national output OF. W is a parameter of the Y curve: a rise in W will shift the curve upwards, since $\dfrac{W}{MPP_L}$ is now higher at every level of national output.

---

[1] On pp. 269–273 above.
[2] See pp. 273–276 above; it is recommended that the reader refresh his memory of the guide to the coming analysis which is given in those pages.

Suppose that national output is at the level OD in Fig. 26.1. What will be the total of money incomes which flows to households at that volume of national output? For simplicity in the present analysis, natural resources are being grouped along with capital goods. Only two classes of income need therefore be distinguished, namely wages and profits

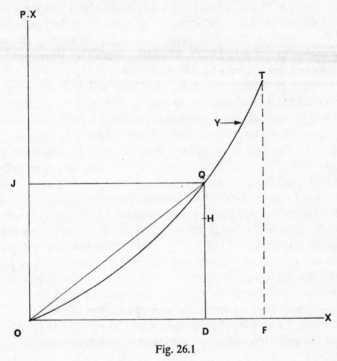

Fig. 26.1

(which include rents).[1] What then will be the amounts of money wages and profits at the output level OD?

The amount of labour services needed to produce the national output OD is given by the aggregate production function, $X = F(N, K_0)$.[2] It is the level of N, working on the given K_0, which determines the size of X. Hence the production function shows the number of man-hours of labour required to produce a particular national output. W is the average money wage rate per hour. Therefore, if W is multiplied by the number of man-hours needed to produce the national output OD, the total of money wages paid to produce that output is obtained. In

[1] If the firms use borrowed finance, the interest payable on it comes out of the profits, as that term is being used here.
[2] See pp. 269–270 above.

general, the total of money wages, at any level of national output, is $W \cdot N$—where N is the quantity of labour services required to produce the output in question. Suppose that, at the output level OD in Fig. 26.1, DH is the aggregate money expenditure of firms on the purchase of labour services. Then, $DH (= W \cdot N)$ is the amount of money wage income which is created when a national output OD is produced.

The Y curve shows that the firms in aggregate are willing to produce OD if they expect to get a total revenue of DQ from its sale. The wage cost of that output is DH. Hence, when the output OD is produced, the firms are *expecting* to earn a total of profits equal to $HQ (= DQ - DH)$. They cannot, of course, be certain that they will in fact earn those profits, since most production is in anticipation of demand. Expected profits will be realized only if demand is predicted correctly. *If* the firms in aggregate decide to produce the national output OD, they are predicting that the aggregate money expenditure of consumers plus investors on it will be DQ. That is, they are predicting that incomes from profits will total HQ.

The money wage income which is *actually* earned at output level OD is DH. This income will play a part in determining the money expenditure on consumption of wage earners. The money profit income which is *expected* at output level OD is HQ. This expected income will play a part in determining the money expenditure on consumption of profit earners.[1] But the quantities demanded of consumer goods depend on *real* incomes. It is therefore necessary to know the price level of the consumer goods (P_C) on which the money incomes of the community will be spent. To simplify the diagram, it will be assumed that P_C is the same as the price level of all goods (capital as well as consumer), i.e. that $P_C = P$.

The national output OD will be offered for sale at its *supply-P*, which is given by the slope of $OQ \left(= \dfrac{DQ}{OD} \right)$. This is the price level which, in conjunction with the above money incomes, gives the real incomes of people when output is OD. Those real incomes, together with the personal attributes of households, their real personal wealth, and the distribution of income between them, determine the *volume* of consumption.[2] That volume, multiplied by the P_C in question, is the aggregate *money* expenditure on consumption which will occur when national output is OD.

---

[1] It was explained in Chapter 24 (on p. 277 above) that *both* current, and expected, real incomes help to determine real consumption.
[2] As explained on pp. 276–279 above.

The total of money incomes, and the supply-P_C, can be similarly derived from the Y curve for the other levels of national output. This gives the real incomes at the other output levels; and these, together with the other influences on consumption, determine what the volumes of consumption will be at the different levels of national output. If these volumes are now multiplied by the corresponding supply-P_Cs, the amounts of money expenditure of consumption, which will occur at the

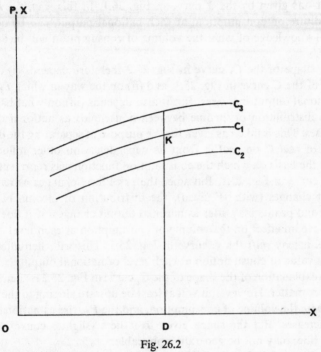

Fig. 26.2

different levels of output, are discovered. This information can now be expressed by means of a curve in the same diagram as that used for the Y curve.

Aggregate money expenditure ($\equiv P \cdot X$) is measured on the vertical axis of Fig. 26.2, and the national output (X) on the horizontal. The C_1 curve shows what the aggregate *money* expenditure on consumption will be at different levels of national output, e.g. it will be DK when output is OD. The derivation of this curve can, in line with the analysis above, be thought of in the following way. Suppose that the *consumption function* is known, and that it is shown by the C curve in Fig. 25.1.[1]

---

[1] On p. 286 above.

The consumption function, it will be recalled, shows the relation between real C and real Y (i.e. X), on the assumption of a *given* distribution of income between households. Suppose, for the moment, that the income distribution does not change as national output increases. Then the C_1 curve in Fig. 26.2 can be obtained by multiplying the volumes of consumption at the different levels of real Y—as given by the C curve in Fig. 25.1—by the corresponding P_Cs at the different levels of national output—as given by the Y curve in Fig. 26.1. In this way, the *money* expenditure on consumption, at each national output, can be derived from a knowledge of what the volume of consumption will be at each real Y.

The shape of the C_1 curve in Fig. 26.2 therefore depends (i) on the shape of the C curve in Fig. 25.1, and (ii) on the way in which P_C rises as national output increases. But it also depends (iii) on what happens to the distribution of income between households as national output increases. This is taken as given for the purpose of separating the dependence of *real C* on *real Y* from its dependence on other influences: that is the basis on which the consumption function was represented by the C curve in Fig. 25.1. But since the price level changes as national output changes (with W given), the distribution of income between wages and profits may alter as national output changes. If it does, this may have an effect on the volume of consumption at each level of real Y,[1] i.e. it may *shift* the C curve in Fig. 25.1. This will then affect the money value of consumption at each level of national output.

The explanation of the shape of the C_1 curve in Fig. 26.2 is therefore a complex matter. However, it will at least be upward sloping to the right, since *both* the volume of consumption, and the P_C, rise as national output increases. But the shape given to it here (slightly convex on its upper side) may not be generally applicable.

The C_1 curve in Fig. 26.2 has the same parameters as the C curve in Fig. 25.1. Changes in the personal attributes of households, their real wealth, and the distribution of income between them, alter the real C at each level of real Y. They therefore alter the money expenditure on consumption at each level of national output. The C_1 curve will then shift, either upwards (*increase*) to C_3, or shift downwards (*decrease*) to C_2.

But in addition, the position of the C_1 curve depends on what the supply-P_C is at each level of national output, which, in turn, depends on the level of W. The derivation above of the C_1 curve assumed a given W, since it was based on a given aggregate supply curve (of which W is a

[1] See p. 278 above.

parameter). If W increases, *both* the total of money incomes, and the supply-P, will be higher at *every* level of national output. Aggregate *money* expenditure on consumption will, therefore, be increased at every level of output. This follows because the increase in W leaves the sizes, and the distribution, of *real* incomes unchanged, and therefore does not affect the volume of consumption. W and P go up in the same proportion, since $P = MC = \dfrac{W}{MPP_L}$. Real incomes, and their distribution between wages and profits, do not change. Therefore, with the volume of consumption unchanged at each level of national output, the money expenditure on consumption at each level of output increases in the same proportion as W and P.

W is thus a parameter of the C_1 curve in Fig. 26.2. If W rises, C_1 will shift upwards to C_3; if it falls, C_1 will shift downwards to C_2. This is an essential point for a correct understanding of how the price level and the national output are determined.

AGGREGATE MONEY EXPENDITURE ON INVESTMENT

Now consider what the aggregate money expenditure on investment will be at each level of national output. The *volume* of investment depends on the expected internal rates of return in relation to the rate of interest, after an allowance has been made for uncertainty.[1] The *money* expenditure on investment is its volume multiplied by the price level of capital goods (P_K). The supply-P_K rises as national output increases. Hence, to discover what the money expenditure on investment will be at each level of output, it is necessary to know the effect (if any) of a change in P_K on the volume of investment.

The present analysis assumes constant *relative* prices. Hence, the absolute money prices of capital goods and consumer goods change in the same proportion. P_K and P_C always go up (or down) in the same proportion. This assumption is significant in the present context because capital goods are bought in order to produce consumer goods.[2] The revenue from producing consumer goods depends on P_C. The cost of investing in capital goods depends on P_K. Hence, the profitability of investing in capital goods depends on the relation between P_C and P_K. The higher P_K is relatively to P_C, the less profitable it will be to invest in capital goods. This point will not be pursued here, but it will be an

---

[1] See p. 284 above.
[2] And also, of course, to produce other capital goods.

important element in the analysis of what determines the rate of investment per period of time, to be given in Chapter 31 below.

Continue, then, to assume that P_K and P_C always change in the same
proportion. Suppose that P_K rises. In itself, this reduces the expected
internal rates of return on investment projects. For each project,[1]

$$S = P = \frac{a_1}{(1 + r)} + \frac{a_2}{(1 + r)^2} + \cdots + \frac{a_n}{(1 + r)^n}$$

where S is the supply price of the capital good, a_1, a_2 . . . a_n, are the
rentals expected from it, and r is the internal rate which gives a present
value (P), of the rentals, equal to the supply price S. A rise in P_K means
a higher supply price (S) for any capital good. Hence the r, which now
gives a present value (P) of the expected rentals, equal to the higher S, is
lower than it was before. The rise in P_K in itself reduces r.

This, however, assumes that the expected rentals remain unchanged
when P_K rises—which is unlikely to be so. P_K and P_C rise together.
Firms are therefore likely to revise their expectations of the *future* P_K
and P_C in an upward direction. When the money prices of all goods
increase, it is improbable that there will be grounds for expecting that
they will fall back to their original level. Rather, people will expect
prices in future to be higher than they had previously expected. The
capital rentals are predicted on the basis of *expected* prices. When
expected prices are revised upwards, the expected capital rentals are
also revised upwards.

The effect on r of a rise in P_K therefore depends on the extent to
which expected prices are revised upwards. Suppose that when P_K
(and P_C) rises by 10 per cent, people expect all prices in the future to be
10 per cent higher than they had previously expected. All the expected
capital rentals will then be revised upwards by 10 per cent. With S, and
a_1, a_2 . . . a_n, all increased by 10 per cent, r is unchanged. In these
circumstances, a rise in the *absolute* money prices of capital goods does
not affect the expected internal rates of return on them. Hence, at a
given interest rate, the *volume* of investment will be unchanged. And
the *money value* of investment will increase in the same proportion as
P_K, i.e. by 10 per cent in the above example.

It is, of course, possible that when current money prices rise, people
will revise expected prices upwards to a smaller or to a greater extent.
In the former case, the expected rentals will rise by less than the supply
prices of capital goods. Expected internal rates of return will therefore

[1] See pp. 234–235 above.

fall, and the *volume* of investment will decrease. But the money expenditure on investment will still increase if the proportional fall in the volume of investment is less than the proportional rise in P_K.

The case in which expected prices are revised upwards by *more* than the current increase in prices is of particular interest. This will happen if people think that the current increase is going to be followed by a *further* increase in the future. Thus, suppose that P_K and P_C rise by 10 per cent, and that this leads people to expect a further increase of say 5 per cent. This means that they are expecting money prices to be 15 per cent higher in the future than they had previously expected. Consequently, expected capital rentals go up by 15 per cent, compared with the 10 per cent rise in the current prices of capital goods. Expected internal rates of return increase. Hence, at a given interest rate, the *volume* of investment increases. The money expenditure on investment will then increase in greater proportion than P_K, i.e. by more than 10 per cent in the present example.[1]

This, however, assumes that the interest rate does not change as a result of the increase in money prices. But the interest rate may rise in these circumstances. This will be explained, and allowed for in the analysis, at a later stage.[2]

The amount of money expenditure on investment, at each level of national output, can now be shown by a curve in the same kind of diagram as that already used in respect of money expenditure on consumption. The I curves, in Fig. 26.3, all show the money expenditure on investment rising as national output increases. This will be so, as has been seen, as long as the volume of investment does not fall in greater proportion than the rise in P_K, which occurs as output increases. But how the volume of investment will behave, as P_K rises, depends on the way in which the expected future P_C is revised, as P_K rises. Since there is no general principle in this respect, the shapes of the I curves in Fig. 26.3 cannot be specified in general terms.

The internal rates of return on investment projects, the rate of interest, and the attitudes towards uncertainty, which determine the volume of investment, are parameters of the curves in Fig. 26.3. If they change, the curves will shift their positions, e.g. I_1 will *increase* to I_3, or *decrease* to I_2.

But, in addition, the position of the I_1 curve depends on what the

---

[1] The same point applies to the volume of durable consumer goods. If P_C is expected to rise, people will anticipate future consumption by purchasing more durable consumer goods in the present.

[2] In Chapter 30 below.

supply-P_K is at each level of national output, which, in turn, depends on the level of W. If W increases, the supply-P_K increases at each and every level of output. The effect of this on the volume of investment, and therefore on the money expenditure on investment, depends—as the analysis above has shown—on how expected future prices are revised

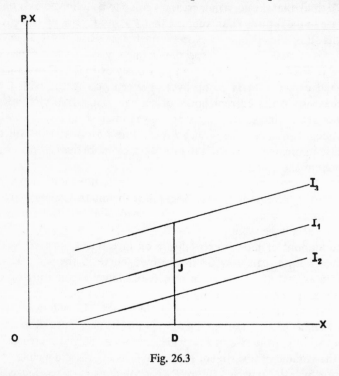

Fig. 26.3

when current prices change. As long as the volume of investment does not fall in greater proportion than the increase in P_K, money expenditure on investment will increase. That is, the I curve will shift upwards (e.g. from I_1 to I_3) as a result of the increase of W. Thus W is a parameter of the I curves, just as it was seen to be a parameter of the C curves in Fig. 26.2 above.

THE AGGREGATE DEMAND CURVE

Aggregate money demand, at each level of national output, is obtained by adding together the money expenditures on consumption and investment at each level of output. The C and I curves in Fig. 26.4 have been given the shapes already discussed in terms, respectively, of Figs. 26.2 and 26.3 above. The summation, vertically, of these two curves gives the aggregate money demand (Z) curve. For example, when output is at the level OD, money expenditure on consumption will be DK, and money expenditure on investment will be DJ; hence, $Z = DJ + DK = DL$, at the output level OD. The amount of aggregate demand is

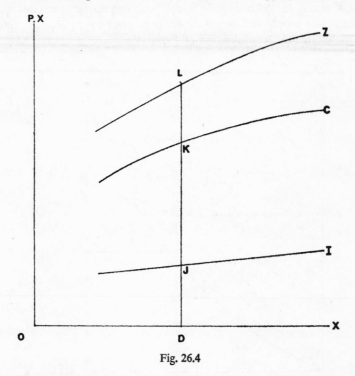

Fig. 26.4

similarly obtained at the other levels of output, and this allows the Z curve to be drawn.

The Z curve will shift upwards or downwards if either the C or the I curve shifts upwards or downwards. This means that the parameters of *both* the C and I curves are parameters of the Z curve. In particular, it must be emphasized again, W is a parameter of the Z curve—*as well as* of the Y curve. Thus, if money wage rates increase, this will raise the total of money incomes and the supply-P at *each* level of national output. Money expenditure on consumption will be higher at each level of output; and so will the money expenditure on investment, unless the rise in P_K causes a more than proportionate fall in the *volume* of investment. This will not happen if expected prices are revised upwards in line with the increase in current prices. The Z curve will therefore shift upwards as a result of an increase in W.

NATIONAL OUTPUT AND PRICE LEVEL DETERMINATION

The Y and Z curves in Fig. 26.5, depicting respectively the conditions of aggregate supply and aggregate demand, can now be used to explain the simultaneous determination of P and X.

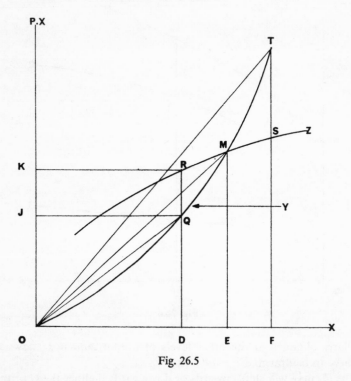

Fig. 26.5

The curves intersect (point M) at the output level OE. Firms in aggregate will produce this output if they expect to receive a total revenue of EM from it—as shown by point M on the Y curve. They will offer it for sale at the supply-P which is given by the slope of OM. If the output OE is produced, consumers plus investors will spend an amount EM on it—as shown by point M on the Z curve. Hence, at the output level OE, aggregate money expenditure on consumption plus invest-ment equals the total revenue which firms require to make it worthwhile, at the given W, to produce that national output. OE is the equilibrium level of national output, and the slope of OM is the equilibrium price level.

If the national output OE is produced, firms in aggregate will get the total revenue which they expected, and will therefore have no incentive to alter their outputs as long as the Y and Z curves remain unchanged. But it has still to be shown whether, and how, the economy will in fact converge to the equilibrium P and X. Suppose that output is at the level OD. The supply-P, at which it will be offered for sale, is given by the slope of OQ, where point Q is on the Y curve. Given that supply-P, given the money incomes created by OD at the given W, and given the other determinants of consumption and investment, then aggregate money expenditure is DR, where R is on the Z curve. There is excess aggregate demand $QR (= DR - DQ)$ at the output level OD.

The firms can respond to this excess demand in a variety of ways. They can raise the supply-P *above* the level given by the slope of OQ. They can keep the supply-P unchanged, and meet the excess demand by running down stocks, by *ad hoc* rationing, or by a lengthening of order books. Or they can take some combination of these measures. But whatever is the response, there will be an incentive to expand national output towards the equilibrium level OE.

The supply-P of the output OD is given by the slope of OQ. But the price level at which OD is sold can be *higher* than its supply-P, since consumers plus investors are willing to spend DR (which is greater than DQ) at this supply-P. That is, they want to buy a larger *quantity* of goods than OD, when it is offered for sale at the price level given by the slope OQ. If firms do raise the price level at which they sell the output OD, it will now exceed the MC (marginal cost) of that output, since the supply-P equals MC. With $P > MC$, it is profitable (under perfect competition) for firms to expand their outputs. And they will continue to do so until national output reaches the level OE, since there is excess aggregate demand at any lower level.

If the firms do not raise price level above the supply-P given by the slope of OQ, they must run down stocks, or ration goods, or lengthen their order books. In all these cases, there is an incentive to expand outputs and raise national output, as long as there is any excess aggregate demand, i.e. up to the equilibrium level OE.

The whole of the above convergence analysis can be applied in reverse to levels of national output at which there is excess aggregate supply. Thus, at the full employment level of output, which is OF in Fig. 26.5, there is an excess aggregate supply of $ST (= FT - FS)$. Firms will produce the output OF if they expect to get a total revenue of FT from it—as shown by point T on the Y curve. They will offer it for sale at the supply-P which is given by the slope of OT. But if they do produce OF, consumers plus investors will spend only an amount FS on it, as shown by point S on the Z curve.

In this situation, the firms can either reduce the price level at which they sell OF, below its supply-P, or they can allow stocks to accumulate at an unchanged supply-P. If they lower the price level, the MC of the output OF now exceeds that price level. With $P < MC$, firms will contract their outputs. Either the reduction of the price level, or the accumulation of unwanted stocks at an unchanged supply-P, will lead them to reduce national output, as long as there is any excess aggregate supply, i.e. down to the equilibrium level OE.

Fig. 26.5 shows an equilibrium X and P at less than full employment. Some resources are left unemployed because there is a *deficiency* of aggregate money demand $(= ST)$ at the full employment level of output. Firms in aggregate would not find it profitable to produce OF at the given level of W, which has been assumed in drawing both the Y and Z curves. It is essential to note that this conclusion has been reached on the assumption of a given W. The significance of that assumption will be analysed in the next chapter.

The analysis of this chapter has taken an important step beyond that of the previous one. It is now possible to see how the price level, as well as national output, is determined. The reasons for changes in the price level can therefore be investigated.

CHAPTER 27

PRICE LEVEL CHANGES

The price level for goods depends on the level of money wage rates. It is not possible, therefore, to explain changes in P without at the same time explaining how W is determined. The working of the labour markets must enter explicitly into the analysis of this chapter.

The basis for this has already been provided at the microeconomic level.[1] The determination of individual wage rates was there analysed for two different market situations, viz. perfect competition and bilateral monopoly (collective bargaining).

In a perfectly competitive labour market, the wage rate will rise relatively to other wage rates if there is excess demand for the labour service in question, and it will fall if there is excess supply. Suppose that all labour markets are perfectly competitive. The total amount of labour services (N) that will be supplied depends on the number of people willing to work, and on the hours for which they are willing to work, at the ruling level of the *real* wage rate $\left(\dfrac{W}{P_C}\right)$. The quantity demanded of labour services depends, as has been seen,[2] on the level of the national output. If there is an excess aggregate supply of labour, this means that there is unemployment. Under perfect competition, the unemployed will bid down *money* wage rates in an attempt to get jobs. Excess aggregate supply of labour (unemployment) will cause a fall in W.

On the other hand, the aggregate demand for national output may be so high that firms in aggregate demand a quantity of labour services in excess of the full employment level. That is, the firms offer a level of N which is greater than the N which people are ready to supply at the ruling *real* wage rate. Under perfect competition, the firms will bid up *money* wage rates in an attempt to get the labour they want. Excess aggregate demand for labour (at full employment) will cause a rise in W.

It therefore follows from the definition of full employment, that W can be in *equilibrium*, in perfectly competitive labour markets, *only*

---

[1] In Chapters 19, 20, and 22 above.
[2] See pp. 289–291 above.

when the aggregate demand for N equals the full employment level of N. Full employment is the aggregate quantity of N which people want to supply at the ruling real wage rate. If it is greater than the aggregate demand for N, W will fall; if it is smaller, W will rise; and if it is the same, W will remain unchanged, i.e. be in equilibrium.

The situation will be different if collective bargaining is the rule in all labour markets. It has been seen[1] that trade unions will resist reductions in *money* wage rates except in the face of significant unemployment among their members. Hence, at the macroeconomic level, excess aggregate supply of N will not necessarily cause a fall in W under collective bargaining—in contrast to what would happen under perfect competition. The excess supply (unemployment) has to reach some level before the unions will agree to a reduction in W.

On the other hand, trade unions will press periodically for increases in *money* wage rates. Each time they succeed, W rises. Their degree of success, however, depends on the current situation in labour markets.[2] If there is a significant amount of unemployment, they are unlikely either to demand, or to succeed in getting, much of an increase in W. Indeed, when unemployment goes above some critical level, employers will probably demand, and succeed in getting, a reduction in W. But the lower the level of unemployment, the greater will be the increase in W that the unions are likely to achieve. This is a further contrast with perfect competition. Under the latter, W will rise only if the aggregate demand for N exceeds the full employment level. But under collective bargaining, W can rise even when there is some unemployment, i.e. when the aggregate demand for N falls short of the full employment level.

The preceding argument can be expressed by means of Fig. 27.1. The rate of increase in W, i.e. $\dfrac{\Delta W}{W}$, which occurs during each period of time (e.g. some percentage amount per year), is measured on the vertical axis; the horizontal axis measures the rate of unemployment (U), i.e. the percentage of the supply of N which is not being employed. Any curve on the diagram will show a relationship between $\dfrac{\Delta W}{W}$ per period of time and the rate of unemployment: the particular one which has been drawn indicates that W will rise at a *greater* rate in each period, the *lower* is the unemployment rate. Thus, if the unemployment rate is OK, $\dfrac{\Delta W}{W}$ per

[1] On pp. 222–223 above.   [2] See pp. 223–225 above.

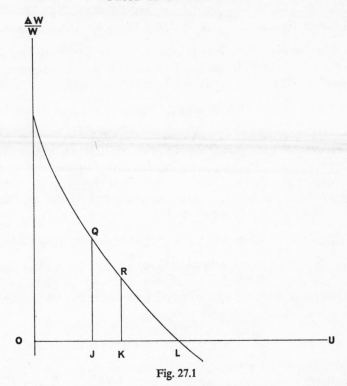

Fig. 27.1

period is KR; but if it is lower at OJ, $\dfrac{\Delta W}{W}$ per period is higher at JQ.

The curve also shows that at a particular unemployment rate, in this case OL, W will neither rise nor fall; and that at higher rates, W will fall in each period of time.[1] The curve thus expresses the analysis given above of the determination of W under collective bargaining. It is known as a *Phillips Curve*.[2]

---

[1] Post-war unemployment rates have been so low in the UK (seldom above 2½ per cent), that it is difficult to say what OL is for this country. It has been estimated to lie between 5 per cent and 10 per cent for the US.

[2] After Professor A. W. Phillips, who pioneered the work on the relationship between $\dfrac{\Delta W}{W}$ and the unemployment rate. It should be noted, however, that Phillips' study was an 'econometric' one (in the sense explained on p. 60 above). The statistical relation he found between $\dfrac{\Delta W}{W}$ and the unemployment rate does not, in itself, imply any particular explanation of that relation, e.g. the explanation in terms of the strategies of trade unions and employers' associations given on pp. 220–221 above. The term Phillips Curve, as used here, is to be interpreted with that in mind.

However, the size of $\dfrac{\Delta W}{W}$ per period depends on other influences, as
well as on the unemployment rate. Recent changes in the price level for
goods is a factor in the bargaining between trade unions and employers'
associations. The prime objective of the unions is to improve the *real*
wage rate $\left(\dfrac{W}{P_C}\right)$ of their members. Hence, $\dfrac{\Delta W}{W}$ per period will be
larger, the more rapidly P_C has been rising. Moreover, the 'degree of
unionization' (i.e. the proportion of workers belonging to trade unions)
probably influences the bargaining strategies of the unions, and thereby
the outcome of collective bargains. The rate of change in P_C, and the
degree of unionization are therefore parameters of the Phillips Curve.
For example, if either of them increase, the curve will shift upwards to
the right, i.e. $\dfrac{\Delta W}{W}$ will be larger at each level of the unemployment rate.

Price level changes will now be analysed on both sets of assumptions
about the determination of money wage rates, i.e. (i) under perfect
competition in labour markets, and (ii) under collective bargaining.

PRICE LEVEL AND NATIONAL OUTPUT CHANGES

Suppose that P and X are initially in equilibrium, with national output
below the full employment level. Thus, in Fig. 27.2, the Z_1 and Y curves
intersect at point Q, and give an equilibrium national output OD, and
equilibrium price level equal to the slope of OQ. The full employment
national output is OF. A given W is assumed in drawing the Z_1 and Y
curves.

Since there are unemployed resources with national output at OD,
W would fall if the labour markets were perfectly competitive. Suppose,
however, that collective bargaining is the rule, and that W will not fall
at the unemployment rate which exists when national output is OD.
The situation in this respect, when labour markets are perfectly competitive, will be analysed in the last section of this chapter. Consider
now the effects on P and X of an *increase* in aggregate demand.

Aggregate money demand can increase at each level of national output
—i.e. Z_1 can shift up to Z_2—for a variety of reasons. Either aggregate
money expenditure on consumption, or on investment, can increase.
The volume of consumption, and therefore the aggregate money expenditure on consumption, will increase if people decide to devote larger
proportions of their current real incomes to consumption, because of

some change in the personal attributes[1] which determine those proportions; or if real income is redistributed from those with high incomes to those with low ones. The volume of investment, and therefore the aggregate money expenditure on investment, will increase if investors come to expect higher capital rentals in the future, i.e. if expected internal rates of return increase; or if the interest rate falls. It will be

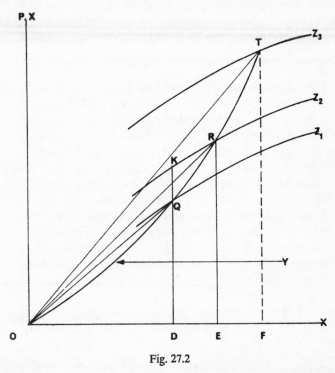

Fig. 27.2

seen later[2] that the interest rate will fall if the monetary authorities increase the quantity of money in the economy. An increase in the quantity of money is thus one reason—but not the only one—for a possible increase in aggregate money demand.

Z_1 will also shift upwards if W rises[3]; but in that case, so will the Y curve. On that account, the effects of a rise in W will be left for separate analysis later in the chapter.

Suppose that Z_1 increases to Z_2, for any of the above reasons (except a rise in W). The position of the Y curve is unchanged, i.e. none of its

[1] See pp. 277–278 above.   [2] In Chapter 30 below.
[3] See pp. 309–310 above.

parameters has altered. There is now excess aggregate demand, at the initial equilibrium national output OD, equal to QK ($= DK - DQ$), where point K is on Z_2. It has already been shown[1] that excess aggregate demand will lead to a rise in national output. Hence, X and P will converge to the new equilibrium at the intersection (point R) of Z_2 and Y. National output has risen from OD to OE; and the price level has also risen, from the level given by the slope of OQ to that given by the slope of OR.

The price level rises as national output expands because the marginal cost $\left(\dfrac{W}{MPP_L}\right)$ of national output is rising; and this is happening, because it has been assumed that MPP_L will diminish as more labour is used to work the given stock of capital. That assumption must now be reconsidered. When it was made earlier,[2] it was implicitly assumed that the given stocks of capital (viz. plants) of the firms are *indivisible*. This means that each firm must always use the *whole* of its existing plant, irrespective of its level of output. It is for this reason that MPP_L will fall as more labour is employed to work the existing plant.

But the plants of many firms do not form indivisible units. Thus, an engineering firm, which has a number of machine tools (lathes, etc.), does not need to keep all of them in use. When output falls, some of the tools will be left idle. That is, the reduction in output causes *un*employment[3] of capital goods, as well as of labour. If the employment of *both* capital and labour fall in the same proportion, the MPP_L will not change.

Similarly, when plants are not indivisible, an expansion of output may come from the employment of previously idle machines, as well as previously unemployed workers. If the ratio of capital to labour then remains unchanged, the MPP_L will not diminish. Hence, the MC of national output, and therefore the price level, will not rise as national output expands.[4]

This point seems to be of some importance in relation to industrial economies which are recovering from a high level of unemployment. At least in the early stages of recovery, the price level changes little as national output rises. This could result from idle capital, as well as unemployed workers, being drawn back into employment as national

[1] On p. 311 above.
[2] See pp. 269–270 above.
[3] As contrasted with *under*employment.
[4] MC, and therefore the price level, could even fall as national output expands, because some parts of the firms, e.g. their managements, are used more effectively as outputs rise.

output expands. MPP_L, the MC of national output, and the price level would then be little affected until the existing plants, in their entirety, are back in operation. But from there on, any further expansion in national output, brought about by a further rise in N, will lower MPP_L and raise the MC of national output and therefore the price level.

This means, in terms of Fig. 27.2, that the Y curve will not have increasing slope over its whole length. It may have a range, e.g. between points Q and R, where it is a straight line which, if extended, would go through the origin. In that case, the *supply-P* will be constant over the range QR. The increase in Z_1, to Z_2, would then expand national output without any change in the price level.

But the nearer the economy approaches the full employment level of national output, the more likely it is that the slope of the Y curve will increase. The existing plants in the economy will now be operating in their entirety. For example, from point R on the Y curve up to the full employment point T, the supply-P is very likely to be rising. A further increase in aggregate demand—from Z_2 to Z_3—will therefore raise the price level as well as national output.

An increase in aggregate demand causes a multiplier process to operate. It was seen in Chapter 25[1] that, with P constant, an *increase* in the *volume* of consumption or investment will raise national output by a greater amount. The initial increase in aggregate demand raises real Y. The volume of consumption then *expands*, according to the size of the MPC. This raises national output and real Y again. The volume of consumption expands again, and so on.

The same kind of multiplier process also operates when the price level is variable. But a rise in the price level, as national output increases, can affect the process in two ways. Suppose that initially there is an increase in the volume of investment. Both output and the price level now rise. But, as has been seen,[2] a rise in P_K may affect the volume of investment. This will not happen if the *expected P*, on which expected capital rentals are predicted, is revised upwards in the same proportion as the rise in the current P_K. But if the upward revision is less, the *volume* of investment will *decrease*. Hence, the expansion in national output will be smaller than if the price level had not risen.

Secondly, the *distribution* of real income may change as a result of the price level rising along with national output. If it does, this will probably affect the sizes of the $MPCs$[3] over the range of national output

---

[1] On pp. 293–298 above.   [2] On pp. 305–307 above.
[3] As measured in *real* terms, i.e. by the ratio of the increment in the real C (ΔC) to the increment in real Y (ΔY).

in question. The size of the multiplier $\left(\text{viz. } \dfrac{1}{1-c}\right)$ is determined by the *average* of those MPCs.[1] The behaviour of the price level, therefore, helps to determine by how much national output will rise as a result of an increase in aggregate demand.

National output cannot increase beyond the full employment level, namely beyond OF in Fig. 27.2. It is now necessary to analyse what will happen if the Z curve shifts above Z_3.

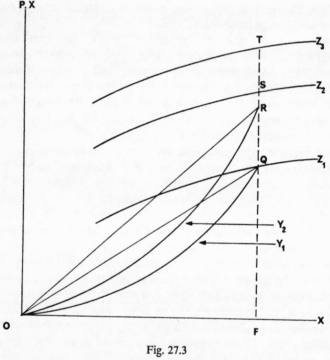

Fig. 27.3

DEMAND INFLATION

Suppose that X and P are, initially, in equilibrium at the full employment level of national output. This is shown by the Z_1 and Y_1 curves which intersect at point Q in Fig. 27.3. The equilibrium national output is at the full employment level OF where the Y_1 curve terminates. The equilibrium price level is given by the slope of OQ.

[1] See p. 298 above.

Now suppose that Z_1 increases to Z_2, for any of the reasons detailed in the last section of this chapter[1] (except a rise in W). This means that, at the current price level (slope of OQ), either consumers or investors now want to buy a larger *volume* of goods than previously. At point S on Z_2, the aggregate *money* demand is FS, at the current price level (slope of OQ). At point Q on Z_1, it was FQ, at the current price level (slope of OQ). Hence QS—the increase in aggregate money demand—divided by the current price level measures the increase in the *volume* of goods demanded.

There is now excess aggregate demand at the full employment level of national output. It is important to think of this in both money and real terms. The excess aggregate *money* demand is QS. The excess aggregate *real* demand is QS divided by the current price level (slope of OQ).

Since national output cannot expand in the short period beyond the full employment level, the impact of the excess demand for goods will be entirely on the price level. But it will also raise W. When the firms find that they can sell larger quantities of goods than they are producing, they will increase their demands for labour. That is, the upward shifts in the demand curves for goods lead to upward shifts in the demand curves for labour services. Excess demand for goods, at the ruling price level, leads to excess demand for labour at the ruling W.

If the labour markets are perfectly competitive, the excess demand for labour will then raise W. The competition between firms for more labour services, to produce more goods, will bid up money wage rates. Hence the $MC\left(=\dfrac{W}{MPP_L}\right)$ and the supply-P of the national output OF (and every other possible level of national output) will increase. That is, the Y_1 curve will shift upwards, e.g. to Y_2. The supply-P of the full employment output, at the higher W, is now given by the slope of OR (where R is on Y_2, at the national output OF). The increase in W has raised the supply-P of the output OF, from the slope of OQ to that of OR.

But as has already been seen,[2] the increase in W will also shift the Z_2 curve upwards, e.g. to Z_3. Hence, at the new higher W, it is the Y_2 and Z_3 curves which show the relation between the conditions of aggregate supply and aggregate demand. With these curves, there is now an excess aggregate *money* demand of RT at the full employment national output. That is, the excess money demand of QS, with the original Z_2 and Y_1 curves, has, by raising W, shifted both curves upwards to the new positions Z_3 and Y_2. Hence there is now an excess money demand

[1] On pp. 316–317 above.
[2] See pp. 309–310 above.

for goods of *RT*. There will consequently still be an excess demand for labour, and *W* will increase again. The Z_3 and Y_2 curves will now *both* shift upwards to new positions, at which there will still be an excess money demand for goods. *W* will therefore increase yet again.

This obviously raises the question: will this *inflationary* process continue indefinitely? Will *W* and *P* both rise endlessly? Or will something occur during the process to make them converge to equilibrium at some higher levels?

W and *P* can only reach a new equilibrium if the *Z* and *Y* curves, in shifting upwards, come to intersect once again at the full employment national output. Only then will there be *no* excess aggregate money demand to drive *W*, and *P*, still higher. This will happen if the upward shifts in the *Z* curve, each time *W* increases, are *smaller* than the corresponding upward shifts in the *Y* curve. With aggregate demand, at the full employment national output, increasing by *less* than aggregate supply, each time *W* rises, excess money demand will gradually be reduced. It will be finally eliminated when the *Y* curve catches up with the *Z* curve, and intersects it once again at the national output *OF*. *W* and *P* will then not rise any further. They have converged to new higher equilibrium levels. The inflationary process has come to an end.

Whether or not this will in fact happen can best be analysed by first considering the circumstances in which it will *not* happen. The excess aggregate money demand of *QS*, with the Z_2 and Y_1 curves in Fig. 27.3, leads to an increase in *W*. The supply-$P \left(= \dfrac{W}{MPP_L} \right)$ at each level of national output, rises in the *same* proportion as *W*. The upward shift in Y_1 to Y_2 is therefore in the same proportion as the increase in *W*.

The total of *money* wage incomes earned, at the full employment national output, increases in the same proportion as *W*. What happens to the total of money profit incomes depends on the behaviour of the price level. Suppose that the price level, at which the national output *OF* is offered for sale, is raised, as a result of the excess demand, from the original supply-*P* (slope of *OQ*) to the new supply-*P* (slope of *OR*). This means that *P* has increased in the *same* proportion as *W*. Hence the total of expected *money* profit incomes has increased in the same proportion as *P* (and *W*). Thus, with *W* and *P* increased in the same proportion, all *real* incomes are unchanged. Therefore the *volume* of consumption is unchanged: the aggregate money expenditure on consumption increases in the same proportion as the rise in the price level.

It has been seen earlier[1] that the *volume* of investment will not change

[1] See pp. 305–306 above.

as prices rise, if the *expected* prices rise in the same proportion, and if the interest rate does not alter. Suppose that those conditions obtain. Then with an unchanged volume of investment, the aggregate money expenditure on investment increases in the same proportion as the rise in the price level.

On the above assumptions, the *volume* of aggregate demand (for consumption plus investment) does not change as W and P rise. The excess aggregate *real* demand, which is driving W and P upwards, does not diminish as they rise. Hence they will not converge to a new equilibrium. The inflationary process is an *unstable* one.

This means, in terms of Fig. 27.3, that the Z curve always increases, with each rise in W, in the *same* proportion as the Y curve increases. With aggregate *real* demand unchanged, aggregate money demand increases in the same proportion as W and P. Hence excess aggregate money demand increases in the same proportion as P, and will therefore continue to drive W and P upwards.

The above analysis shows what is necessary for an inflationary process to come to an end. Aggregate *real* demand must *decrease* as the price level rises. The *volumes* of consumption and/or investment must be reduced as the price level rises. If this happens, the aggregate money expenditures on consumption and/or investment will not increase as rapidly as the price level. Therefore the Z curve will not shift upwards to the same extent as the Y curve, each time W increases. Excess aggregate demand (in both real and money terms) will be gradually eliminated.

Three ways in which this may happen can be seen from earlier analyses. (i) If the *expected P* is revised upwards in smaller proportion than the rise in the current P, the volume of investment (and consumption) will decrease.[1] (ii) If the interest rate rises as P rises,[2] the volume of investment (and maybe consumption) will decrease.[3] (iii) If W rises less than P, real income will be redistributed from wages to profits, and the volume of consumption may decrease.[4] Under collective bargaining, where money wage rates are only increased periodically, the rise in W may not keep pace with the rise in P.

W and P will converge to new (higher) equilibrium levels for any of the above three reasons. The inflationary process is then a *stable* one.

---

[1] See pp. 306–307 above. Of course, if the expected P is revised upwards in *greater* proportion, the volume of investment (and consumption) will *increase*, and this will make the excess aggregate real demand greater.

[2] It will be seen, in Chapter 30 below, that this will happen if the monetary authorities do not let the quantity of money increase as rapidly as P.

[3] See p. 284 above.

[4] See p. 304 above.

Thus, price expectations, the interest rate, or a redistribution of real income, can act as *stabilizers*[1] on an inflation, and prevent W and P from rising endlessly.

The inflationary process which has just been analysed is the result of *excess aggregate demand* at the full employment level of national output. It is therefore given the name *demand inflation*. Whether a demand inflation is stable or unstable depends on the operation, or lack of it, of the stabilizers considered above. It is not, however, the only kind of inflation which may exist.

COST INFLATION

Once again, suppose that X and P are initially in equilibrium at the full employment level of national output. This is shown by the intersection of the Z_1 and Y_1 curves at point Q in Fig. 27.4. Consider what will happen when there is collective bargaining in the labour markets.

It has already been argued[2] that money wage rates will increase periodically under collective bargaining, even when there is some unemployment; and that the rate of increase in W per period of time will be greater, the lower is the rate of unemployment. This is expressed by means of a Phillips Curve.

The W assumed in drawing the Z_1 and Y_1 curves of Fig. 27.4 is that agreed in the last round of collective bargains. Since national output is at the full employment level, W will increase in the next round of bargaining. The rate of increase is shown by the Phillips Curve. This increase in W will shift *both* the Y_1 and Z_1 curves upwards, and cause a rise in the price level. If W again increases in future bargaining rounds, the price level will rise further. This inflationary process is different in a number of respects from that of the demand inflation analysed above. It therefore needs a separate analysis.

The Z_1 and Y_1 curves intersect at the full employment national output. There is *no* excess aggregate demand to drive W and P upwards. In the present analysis, the increase in W, and the consequential rise in P, result from the bilateral monopoly situation in the labour markets. It is the latter, and *not* any excess demand for labour, which brings about the increase in W. That it is the first respect in which the present inflationary process differs from demand inflation.

This can be seen from a comparison of Figs. 27.3 and 27.4. In the

---

[1] Further stabilizers will be found when government and foreign trade are introduced into the analysis.

[2] See pp. 314–315 above.

former,[1] the Z_1 and Y_1 curves give an equilibrium at the full employment national output. Z_1 increases to Z_2, and causes excess aggregate demand for goods, and for labour. P and W therefore rise; and Y_1 shifts up to Y_2. In Fig. 27.4, the Z_1 and Y_1 curves also give an equilibrium at the full employment national output. The collectively-bargained increase in W shifts Y_1 up to Y_2. This raises the supply-P of

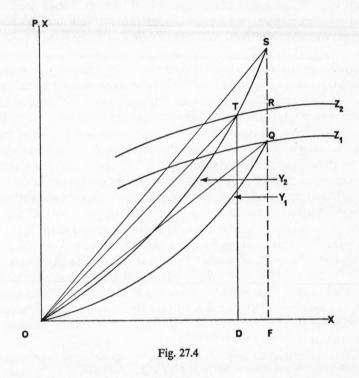

Fig. 27.4

the output OF, from the slope of OQ to the slope of OS (where point S is on Y_2, at the national output OF). The increase in W also means an increase in money wage incomes at each level of national output. Hence Z_1 shifts upwards, e.g. to Z_2.

The sequence of events under demand inflation is thus: increase in aggregate demand → excess aggregate demand → rise in P and W → upward shift in Y curve. But under a collectively-bargained increase in W it is: increase in W → upward shifts in both Y and Z curves → rise in P. Since these sequences are different, it is probable that the

[1] On p. 320 above.

timing of the changes in W and P, relative to one another, will be different as between them. This is the second respect in which the present inflationary process differs from demand inflation.

Both the Y_1 and Z_1 curves in Fig. 27.4 shift upwards when W increases. If they both shift to the *same* extent, they will still intersect at the full employment level of national output. If this happens every time there is a collectively-bargained increase in W, the inflationary process is *unstable*. Since aggregate supply and aggregate demand, at the national output OF, always increase to the same extent, a rising W will drive up the price level endlessly.

But the analysis of the preceding section of this chapter gave reasons why the Z curve may not shift upwards by as much as the Y curve, each time W increases. This will happen if the aggregate *real* demand (for consumption plus investment) *decreases* as the price level rises. The aggregate *money* demand will then increase in smaller proportion than the rise in the price level. It was seen that there are three *stabilizers* which can reduce the volumes of consumption and investment, as P rises.[1] The *expected P* may be revised upwards by less than the rise in the current P; the interest rate may rise; and real income may be redistributed between wages and profits.

If these stabilizers are effective, Z_1 shifts up by *less* than Y_1, when W increases. This is shown by Z_2 in relation to Y_2, in Fig. 27.4. The shift, from Z_1 to Z_2, is smaller than that from Y_1 to Y_2. Hence Z_2 and Y_2 intersect (at point T) *below* the full employment level of national output. The collectively-bargained increase in W has raised P from the slope of OQ to that of OT. But it has reduced the level of national output, from OF to OD. There is now some amount of unemployment.

This unemployment may not, however, be large enough to prevent W from increasing in the next round of collective bargains. It may, in terms of the Phillips Curve in Fig. 27.1,[2] be less than the rate OL. W will therefore increase again, though by less than in the initial round—as shown by the Phillips Curve. If Z_2 now shifts upwards by *less* than Y_2, because of the operation of the stabilizers, P will rise again, but national output will fall again. The unemployment rate now increases. But as long as it is below OL, in Fig. 27.1, W continues to increase from one bargaining round to the next.

However, as W increases, and national output falls, and unemployment mounts, the *rate of increase* in W diminishes. When the

[1] See pp. 323–324 above.
[2] On p. 315 above.

unemployment rate reaches *OL*, in Fig. 27.1, *W* ceases to rise.[1] The *Y* and *Z* curves in Fig. 27.4 no longer shift upwards. The price level has converged to a new (higher) equilibrium level. The inflationary process, brought about by collectively-bargained increases in *W*, is then a *stable* one.

But the stabilizing of the process is different from that under demand inflation. In the latter case, the price level converges to a new equilibrium when the excess aggregate demand, at the *full* employment level of national output, has been eliminated. The equilibrium national output is still, as it was initially, the full employment national output. But in the present analysis, when the price level has converged to its new equilibrium level, the equilibrium national output is *below* the full employment level. Some rate of *unemployment* is required to prevent *W*, and therefore the price level, from rising. Unemployment is necessary as a stabilizer in this analysis. This is the third respect in which the present inflationary process differs from demand inflation.

The inflationary process which has just been analysed is the result of collectively-bargained increases in *W* which raise costs of production. It is therefore given the name *cost inflation*. The terms 'demand inflation' and 'cost inflation' are no more than names used to distinguish different inflationary processes. There is no implication that the changes in the price level are dependent only on demand, in the one, and on costs in the other. All prices depend on both demand and costs. But as has been emphasized repeatedly, it is necessary to enquire whether a change in a price originates in a *shift* in the condition of demand, or in that of supply (costs). Only then can the consequences be correctly analysed.

Suppose that firms fix their prices by adding a percentage mark-up to average direct costs in the manner discussed earlier.[2] If they all increase the percentages in question, the price level will rise. This is called *mark-up inflation*; and it can be analysed along lines similar to that in the case of increases in *W*. Moreover, when a country has foreign trade, a rise in the prices of its imports will increase costs of production and raise the price level. The resultant fall in *real* wage rates may well stimulate trade unions to demand an increase in money wage rates, which, if they are successful, will raise the price level further. Cost inflation may thus take a variety of forms.

[1] In fact, the unemployment rate will not have to rise quite as high as *OL*. The Phillips Curve will *shift* downwards to the left as the rate of increase in *W*, and therefore in *P*, diminishes (see p. 316 above). This means that the unemployment rate, at which $\frac{\Delta W}{W} = O$, will be below *OL* in Fig. 27.1.

[2] On pp. 190–195 above.

There is also a further consideration which has not so far been taken into account. Capital accumulation and improvements in technology will, by themselves, shift the Y curve downwards to the right over time.[1] This will offset to some extent the effect on the price level of any increases in W which occur—and which would by themselves shift the Y curve upwards. Since collective bargaining only takes place periodically, the increase in W per period of time will only shift the Y curve upwards, if it exceeds the average increase in the productivity of labour, i.e. in the MPP_L. If W and MPP_L increase at the *same* rate over time, their effects on the price level exactly offset each other.

The above analyses have shown the circumstances in which inflationary processes will and will not be stable. But whichever is the case, governments usually want to prevent the price level from rising. To do so, they must eliminate or counteract the cause (or causes) of an inflationary process. A variety of possible causes have been diagnosed above. A variety of possible remedies, and their consequences, will be considered in Chapter 32 below.

DEMAND DEFLATION

It is now possible to analyse the problem referred to earlier in this chapter, namely, what will happen if there is unemployment, and all labour markets are perfectly competitive.

The Z_1 and Y_1 curves, in Fig. 27.5, are drawn on the assumption of a given W. Their intersection at point Q gives an equilibrium national output OD, which is below the full employment level OF. The latter is not achieved because, with the given W, there is an excess aggregate money supply of ST ($= FT - FS$) at the national output OF.

If all labour markets are perfectly competitive, the unemployment in the present situation will cause a fall in W. The unemployed workers will bid down money wage rates in an attempt to get jobs. This situation is the reverse of demand inflation, in which excess aggregate money demand at full employment leads firms to bid up money wage rates. It is therefore called *demand deflation*, and its analysis involves the reversal of that given above for demand inflation.

The fall in W, caused by the unemployment which exists when national output is OD, shifts *both* the Y_1 and Z_1 curves downwards. If they shift to the *same* extent, they will intersect again at the same level of national output. The price level will have fallen, but national output and the unemployment rate will be unchanged. W will therefore

[1] See pp. 272–273 above.

fall again. If the Y and Z curves *always* shift downwards to the same extent,[1] as W falls, unemployment will never be reduced. Hence W and the price level will fall endlessly, and the deflationary process will be an *unstable* one.

For this to be avoided, the Z curve must shift downwards to a *smaller*

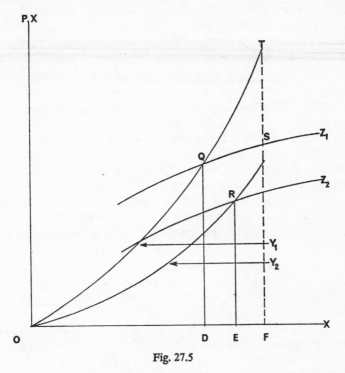

Fig. 27.5

extent than the Y curve, as W falls. Aggregate *real* demand (for consumption plus investment) will therefore have to *increase*, as W and P fall. In that case, aggregate money demand will decrease in smaller proportion than the fall in the price level. This is shown in Fig. 27.5, where the shift of Z_1 to Z_2 is smaller than that of Y_1 to Y_2, when W falls. Z_2 and Y_2 intersect (point R) at the national output OE. National output has expanded, and unemployment has been reduced. If the Z curve continues to shift downwards to a smaller extent than the Y curve, as W falls, they will ultimately intersect at the full employment national output OF. With unemployment eliminated, W will cease to fall. The deflationary process will be a *stable* one.

[1] Or if Z shifts downwards by more than Y.

Whether the process will be stable or unstable depends on the operation, or lack of it, of the stabilizers which were analysed in the case of demand inflation. As prices fall, *expected* prices may be revised downwards, the interest rate may fall, and the distribution of real income may change. These changes will alter the *volumes* of consumption and investment, and their *net* effect will determine whether the deflationary process is stable or unstable. Thus, a fall in the interest rate will increase the volume of investment (and maybe consumption); so will a downward revision of expected prices by *less* than the fall in current prices. But a downward revision of expected prices, by *more* than the fall in current prices, will decrease the volumes of consumption and investment. This would happen if the experience of falling money prices leads people to expect a continuing fall.

The whole issue here is the one which was outlined in Chapter 23 above. Will a price mechanism always converge to a general equilibrium? If it does so, it necessarily ensures the full employment of resources. For, by definition, if resources are not fully employed, they are in excess supply and their money prices will fall. But although a general equilibrium is by definition at full employment, the substantive issue is whether a price mechanism, with flexible money prices for both goods and factors, will *in fact* converge to full employment. There is the alternative that it may be unstable.

The *possible* instability of the price mechanism is basic to Keynes' macroeconomic analysis. He did not think it could be proven that reductions in W and P would always necessarily eliminate unemployment. He argued that the experience of falling W and P might well lead people to expect further falls in them. Hence they would reduce the *volumes* of consumption and investment, and this would exacerbate the deflationary process. He therefore opposed reductions in money wage rates as a means of curing unemployment[1]; and instead advocated measures which would increase aggregate money demand.[2] That is, in terms of Fig. 27.5, he proposed measures which would shift the Z_1 curve upwards, until it intersected the Y_1 curve at the full employment national output, i.e. at point T. And he opposed reductions in W, which would shift both Y_1 and Z_1 downwards, because in his view there is no assurance that they will so shift as to achieve an intersection at the full employment national output.

This was the ground on which Keynes parted from 'classical' economics. The latter maintained that flexible money prices for goods and

---

[1] As was advocated by many people in the Great Depression of the 1930s.
[2] These will be considered in Chapter 32 below.

factors would ensure full employment. It can now be seen that the classical analysis was deficient. But in recent years, a 'neo-classical' analysis has suggested a further stabilizer of the price mechanism in the form of a *real balance* effect. This effect arises because the *real* value of the money balances held by the community change as money prices change, i.e. $\dfrac{M}{P}$ changes as P changes. The operation of the real balance effect depends, however, on the manner in which money is created. The matter is too complex to be pursued in an introductory text. It is sufficient to say here that the new analysis has persuaded few economists—not even those who developed the neo-classical analysis—that reductions in W are a good *policy* for curing unemployment.

CHAPTER 28

THE DEMAND FOR MONEY

When anything is purchased, the buyer incurs a debt to the seller. This debt could be settled (or 'cleared') in a variety of ways. For example, the debt arising from the purchase of a good would be cleared if the seller accepts another good in exchange. The transaction is then a barter exchange. In developed economies, most transactions take the form of exchanges of things for 'money'. It is the payment of 'money' which clears the debts arising out of the purchase of goods, factors, resources, and financial instruments like bonds and shares. The term 'money' covers all those things which are generally used to clear debts.

There are usually three forms of money in developed economies, namely token coins, bank notes, and bank book debts. All these forms of money are themselves debts. Modern monetary systems use debts to clear debts. An understanding of this seeming paradox is needed to avoid the confusions about money which are rife.

In the UK, token coins are minted by the government. They are tokens because the market prices of the metals in them are less than the values stamped on them. These coins are, by law, valid means of clearing debts[1]: they are *legal tender*. But, although payments to the government (e.g. of taxes) can be made with them, the government is not obliged to *redeem* them with something else. They are irredeemable debts acknowledged on metal.

In England and Wales, the issue of bank notes is the monopoly of the Bank of England.[2] These notes are, by law, valid means of clearing debts. Like coin, they are legal tender; and the two together are referred to as the *cash* or *currency* part of the stock of money. The Bank of England is not obliged to redeem its notes with something else. They are irredeemable debts acknowledged on pieces of paper.

People and firms keep accounts with the *commercial banks*,[3] and use

---

[1] Except that, purely for convenience, there are limits to the amounts of different coins that may be included in the settlement of any one debt.

[2] Scottish and N. Irish banks have limited rights of note issue. For brevity, this will be ignored henceforward.

[3] E.g., Barclays, Westminster, Midland, etc.

them to clear debts. These accounts are the debts of the banks to their clients; and they are acknowledged by being entered in the books of the banks. They are therefore called bank book debts to distinguish them from bank note debts. Bank book debts are not legal tender: creditors are not obliged by law to accept them in the settlement of other debts. But they are, of course, widely accepted for this purpose. They are therefore money by convention though not by law. The banks must, on request, repay their book debts in legal tender, namely in notes and coin. The part of the stock of money made up of bank book debts is called *bank money*.

The stock of money in the UK thus consists of two parts, namely (i) *cash*, which is irredeemable debt of the government,[1] and (ii) *bank money*, which is the debt, redeemable in cash, of the commercial banks.

The debts which are money are used to clear debts which are not money. Suppose Mr *J* buys a packet of cigarettes. He now has a debt of (say) 5s to the shopkeeper. The latter gets from Mr *J* a debt of the government in the form of coins worth 5s. This transfer of ownership of the government debt clears Mr *J*'s debt to the shopkeeper.

Again, suppose that Mr *K* buys a car from Mr *L*. The former now has a debt of (say) £500 to the latter. Suppose that *K* has a credit balance of £500 in his account with a commercial bank, i.e. the latter has a debt of £500 to him. *K* instructs the bank (by writing a cheque) to transfer that debt to *L*. *K*'s account goes down by £500, and *L*'s account goes up by the same amount. The transfer of ownership of the bank debt clears the original debt of *K* to *L*.

Pounds must not be confused with debts expressed in £s. A £ is an abstract *unit of account*, in terms of which the values of things are measured. A redeemable debt is a legal obligation to make a payment, usually in the form of money, by some date. The amount of the payment, like the values of things, is expressed in terms of the unit of account. The UK monetary system uses government and bank debts (expressed in £s) to clear other debts (also expressed in £s). It is the government and bank debts which constitute the stock of money. The £ is the symbol in terms of which the stock is measured.

Units of money, namely of coins, bank notes, and bank book debts, are required to clear the debts arising out of transactions. The number of units which a community will want to have at any time depends on a variety of circumstances. The latter determine the *quantity demanded* of money.

The size of the stock of money at any time is determined by the

[1] Since the Bank of England was nationalized in 1946.

operation of the banking system. That is controlled in an overall fashion by the *central bank* of the system, which in the UK is the Bank of England. The central bank controls the quantity of money as an act of *monetary policy*. That policy can have a variety of objectives, e.g. steady economic growth, full employment, stability of the price level. It is in relation to these objectives, including the attempt to resolve any conflicts between them, that the central bank determines the *quantity supplied* of money.

The effects of the monetary system on the working of the price mechanism depend on the relationship between the demand for and the supply of money. It will be shown in Chapter 30 below that, if the quantities demanded and supplied of money are not equal, the interest rate will change. This is a link between money and the overall working of the price mechanism, since, as the preceding macroeconomic analysis has already shown, the interest rate helps to determine the aggregate demand for goods.

The theory of money will therefore be incorporated into macroeconomic analysis in Chapter 30. But it is first necessary to study in detail the determinants of the quantity demanded of money (in the present chapter) and of the quantity supplied (in the next chapter).

MONEY AND SPENDING

Money and spending must not be confused. Money is a *stock* of coins, bank notes, and bank book debts. The size of the stock of money is measured at a *moment* of time. Thus, if Mr *J* is asked how much money he has got, he must count up the coins, bank notes, and bank account balance in his possession at the time in question. Similarly, for the community as a whole, the stock of money at any time is the aggregate of the coins, bank notes, and bank account balances which people, firms, and the government jointly possess.

Spending, by contrast, is a *flow* of purchases of goods, factors, resources, and financial assets (like bonds and shares) per *period* of time. The size of the flow depends on the period of time over which it is measured. Suppose that Mr *J* earns a weekly wage of £28 and spends it all on consumption. His flow of spending is £28 per week, £112 per (four week) month, and so on. The size of his spending must always be stated in relation to some period of time.

The debts arising out of *J*'s spending have to be cleared by payments of money. The number of units of money he will require for this purpose depends on how frequently he receives his income, and on how frequently he clears the debts arising out of the purchase of consumer goods. Suppose that he spends all of his income uniformly, at the rate of £4 per day over the week, and pays for his purchases immediately in cash. The stock of money in his possession will therefore start at £28, fall to £24 at the end of the first day of the week, and so on down to zero just before he gets his next pay packet. His money-holding fluctuates over the week. How much money he has got at any time depends on the day of the week on which it is counted.

Since his money balance fluctuates, it is necessary to think of his *average* holding over time. In the above circumstances it will be £14, i.e. the average of £28 at the beginning, £14 half way through the week, and nothing at the end.

But now suppose that *J* goes over to a *monthly* (four week) salary of £112. His rate of income (and spending) is unchanged, since £28 per week is the same as £112 per month. His money-holding, however, will now be different. If he still spends uniformly over time, he will start the month with a money stock of £112, will have £56 half way through the month, and will be left with nothing at the end. His average holding is £56—four times that when he was paid weekly.

The average number of units of money required by *J* to clear his debts thus depends on how frequently he receives his income. The longer the intervals between the receipts of income, the larger will be the (average) quantity of money he holds.

But his money-holding will also depend on the frequency with which he clears the debts arising out of his spending. Suppose that his monthly salary of £112 is paid directly into his bank account, and that he makes all his purchases on credit which has to be settled at monthly intervals. He can then clear his debts at the same moment as he receives his income. The receipt of his salary, into his bank account, can be matched immediately by the total of the payments out of it, to clear the debts which arose from his purchases of consumer goods during the month. His holding of money will then be zero at all times.

The significant point about this situation is that there is perfect *synchronization* between *J*'s receipts and payments. Debts are being cleared simultaneously. Thus, at the end of each month, *J*'s employer owes him for a month's work; and *J* owes various firms for the month's purchases of consumer goods. With *J*'s income exactly equal to his expenditure, his employer's debt to him exactly offsets the sum of *J*'s own debts. His bank account, i.e. the debt of the bank to him, is the mechanism by which those various debts are cleared against one another. *J* receives a bank debt from his employer, and then transfers that debt to others in settlement of his own debts. If all the transfers of debt are done simultaneously, the bank will never be in debt to J. That is, he will never hold any money.

A monetary system is a debt-clearing mechanism. That is why bank money is overwhelmingly the most important form of money in developed economies. The transfer of ownership over bank debts is the most convenient, as well as the safest, way in which people, firms, and governments can clear the majority of the debts which arise between them. Cash is only the 'small change' of the system. It is only in relation to transactions of small value that it is sometimes more convenient to use cash than bank money.

The basic reason for holding money emerges from the above discussion. It lies in the *lack* of *synchronization* between receipts and payments. Thus, insofar as J does not settle his own debts at the same moment of time as others settle their debts to him, he holds money in the intervals of time between the settlements. The explanation of the demand for money[1] must, therefore, be sought in the reasons why receipts and payments are not perfectly synchronized.

DETERMINANTS OF THE DEMAND FOR MONEY

The operation of a price mechanism requires the observance of rules governing the settlement of debts. Firms have to establish conventions about the times at which wages, salaries, and dividends are paid, and by which trade credits granted on goods bought from other firms are settled. And they have to depend on other firms to observe similar conventions. Otherwise, the individual firm could never have any idea whether its receipts during a period of time will be adequate to cover its payments. The orderly conduct of business thus causes the acceptance of a set of conventions about the timing of various kinds of payments. Wages are paid weekly, salaries monthly, and so on.

But the times at which firms buy raw materials and components from one another, and at which households buy consumer goods, do not have entirely regular patterns. Therefore, it is unlikely that, within the established conventions about the timing of payments, any firm or household will be able to achieve a perfect synchronizing of receipts and payments. The *payments conventions* of a community are thus a determinant of the quantity of money which will be demanded.

These conventions do change through time, though not very quickly. Facilities for buying goods on credit usually develop as the standard of living of a country rises, and these permit a better synchronizing of

---

[1] Keynes called it *liquidity preference*.

receipts and payments. Thus, the growth of buying on 'credit cards'—as seen especially in the US—allows people to manage with smaller money balances.

Given the payments conventions of a community, firms and households have to plan the money balances which they will hold through time. The amounts of money required at different times will depend on the *expected* sizes of future receipts and payments, and on the dates at which they are expected to occur. The larger are the expected receipts and payments, the greater will be the amounts of money needed to cover the lack of synchronization between them. Thus, if J's monthly salary doubles from £112 to £224, he will, with payments made uniformly over the month, double his average money-holding from £56 to £112.

The demand for money by a whole community to carry out its transactions will therefore rise as its total money expenditure increases. The latter includes spending on currently-produced consumer and capital goods, on secondhand goods, on intermediate products traded between firms, and on financial assets. If all these categories of expenditure increase in the *same* proportion, the expected money value of the national output can be taken as a determinant of the quantity demanded of money. The money expenditure on national output equals $P . X$. The quantity demanded of money therefore depends both on the volume of national output, and on the price level.

Expected receipts and payments cannot be known with certainty. Receipts at any time may be less, and payments more, than expected. Some money will be held as a precaution against these contingencies. Uncertainty is a determinant of the quantity demanded of money. The greater it is, the larger the money balances which people and firms will want to hold.

Money can be lent out at interest. But the holding of money itself— coins, bank notes, and those bank book debts which are money—does not earn interest. The holding of money therefore incurs a cost, namely the interest that could be earned by lending it. The holder of a money balance has to consider whether it would be worthwhile to lend it out for the period of time during which it is not expected to be needed for the settlement of his debts.

Thus, consider the money balance of £112 which J receives each month in payment of his salary. With uniform payments over the month, he will not need £56 of the money until the second half of the month. He could therefore lend it out for two weeks and earn some interest. This would, however, involve time and trouble in seeking out a suitable borrower; and where the purchase of a financial asset (like a bond) is involved, there will be money costs attaching to the transaction (e.g. stockbroker's commission). The *transactions costs*—in terms of both effort and money—of lending out money are an offset to the interest which can be earned. A loan will not be worthwhile if the transactions costs of making it exceed the interest on it. That is why wage or salary earners do not reduce their money-holdings by lending them out in the days or weeks before they are needed for payments. The interest that could be earned is so small, that it would not cover the transactions costs.

But the position is different for large firms. The transactions costs of lending do not rise in proportion to the sum lent. The costs involved in lending out £100,000 are far from being 1000 times as great as those of lending out £100. Hence a firm which has a large money balance, that is not immediately needed for payments, may well find it profitable to lend it out for a few weeks or even days.[1] Its average money-holding is thereby reduced. As the interest rate rises, relative to transactions costs, further reductions in average money-holdings, by means of short-term lending, become profitable. The quantity demanded of money therefore falls as the interest rate rises.

This relation between the interest rate and the demand for money also involves expectations about the future levels of the interest rate. A rise in the interest rate means a fall in the prices of existing bonds. The arithmetical connection between the two is simplest in the case of an irredeemable bond, e.g. a 'perpetuity' like UK government Consols. Consider an irredeemable bond, earning $2\frac{1}{2}$ per cent p.a. interest, which was issued in the past at a price of £100. The bond therefore earns interest of £2 10s 0d p.a. Suppose that the ruling interest rate level rises to 5 per cent. The bond will now sell for only £50 on the stock exchange, since £2 10s 0d interest on an outlay of £50 means a return of 5 per cent. Nobody would pay more than £50 for this bond, since he can get 5 per cent by lending elsewhere. The higher the ruling interest rate, the lower will be the price of the bond. In general, the prices of bonds and the interest rate level are inversely related.

Hence, if people expect that the interest rate is going to rise, this means that they expect bond prices are going to fall. This is a deterrent to buying bonds, since a capital loss is expected to be made if they have to be sold before their redemption dates. The willingness to reduce money-holdings, by means of short-term lending, will therefore depend on people's expectations about future interest rates. It will, moreover,

---

[1] The term *cash budgeting* is given to the process through which firms attempt to keep their money balances to a minimum.

depend on the uncertainty surrounding those expectations. A person may not expect the interest rate to rise, i.e. bond prices to fall. But since he cannot be certain, he may prefer to avoid the risk by holding money.

At any time there will be a variety of expectations about the future levels of the interest rate. Some people will be expecting it to rise, others will be expecting it to fall, and yet others will be expecting it to remain more or less unchanged. These expectations will be formed in part on the basis of recent changes in the interest rate. They will therefore be revised from time to time in the light of recent experience. But with given expectations, an *actual* rise in the interest rate will mean that a larger section of the community now *expects* it to fall in the future. The additional people, who now expect it to fall (i.e. expect bond prices to rise), will reduce their money holdings, since they now expect to gain from a rise in the prices of bonds. This point reinforces the above conclusion that the quantity demanded of money will fall as the interest rate rises.

The demand for money arises from its use in clearing debts. The money held by a person (or a firm) is part of his wealth: it is one form in which he can hold his wealth. The other forms are durable goods and financial assets like bonds and shares. People and firms can choose how to distribute their wealth between holdings of goods, financial assets, and money. These three kinds of assets are therefore *substitutes* for one another. That is why the interest rate, i.e. the return on holding bonds, helps to determine the portions of their wealth which persons and firms decide to hold in money. In choosing to hold some amount of money, people have to consider the interest they forego in not holding bonds instead. For the same reason, the expected rates of return on shares, and the expected internal rates of return on goods, help to determine the demand for money. But money, and certain kinds of bonds (especially short-dated ones), are particularly close substitutes for each other. This is why the interest rate is especially important for the demand for money.

However, suppose that people come to expect that the prices of *goods* are going to rise. The expected rise in the price level (P) means an increase in the expected internal rates of return on goods. Or, put another way, it means an expected fall in the value of money in terms of goods $\left(\text{i.e. in } \dfrac{M}{P} \right)$. People will therefore wish to hold less money and more goods. The quantity demanded of money thus depends on expected future prices, as well as on the other influences already considered.

THE DEMAND CURVE FOR MONEY

The above analysis has shown that the quantity demanded of money depends on a variety of influences. They are: the payments conventions of the community, the expected money expenditure on national output ($\equiv P \cdot X$), the expected level of future prices, the actual and the expected levels of the interest rate, the transactions costs involved in acquiring

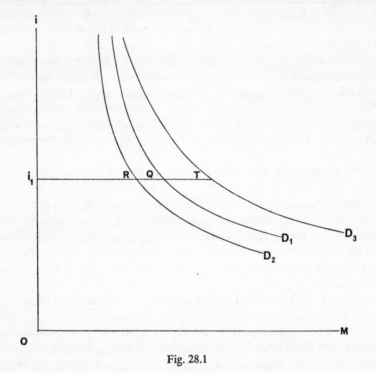

Fig. 28.1

financial assets, and the degrees of uncertainty attaching to expected receipts and payments and to expected interest rates.

The dependence of the quantity demanded of money on these influences can be expressed by means of demand curves. The present analysis is especially concerned with the connection between money and the interest rate. It is therefore convenient to work with demand curves which express the dependence of the quantity demanded of money on the interest rate. This is shown in Fig. 28.1.

The interest rate (i) is measured on the vertical axis, and the stock of money (M), comprising coins, bank notes, and bank book debts, on the horizontal. A curve on the diagram can be used to show the stock of M which the community will want to hold (on average over time) at each level of the interest rate. The three demand for money curves in the diagram are downward sloping to the right, because, as has been seen, the quantity demanded of money *expands* as the interest rate falls.

This relationship can be isolated only by taking all the other influences on the quantity demanded of money as given. The other influences listed above are therefore *parameters* of a demand curve for money. Thus, with the other influences given, the demand curve might be D_1. If any of the parameters change, D_1 will, for example, *increase* to D_3, or *decrease* to D_2; e.g. at the interest rate i_1, the quantity demanded of M increases from point Q (on D_1) to T (on D_3), or decreases from Q to R (on D_2).

The analysis above has shown the ways in which changes in the parameters will affect the quantity demanded of M. It will *increase* if the payments conventions so change as to enlarge the lack of synchronization between receipts and payments, e.g. if more people are paid on a monthly, and fewer on a weekly basis; or if the expected money expenditure on national output rises; or if people come to expect that prices are going to fall; or if more people come to *expect* that the interest rate is going to rise (i.e. that bond prices are going to fall); or if the transactions costs of acquiring financial assets rise; or if the degrees of uncertainty attaching to future receipts, payments, and interest rates increase.

When the determination of the quantity supplied of M has been studied (in the next chapter), demand curves for M—along with supply curves—will be used to explain how the level of the interest rate is determined (in Chapter 30).

THE VELOCITY OF CIRCULATION OF MONEY

It was seen above that, when Mr J spends a weekly wage of £28 uniformly over the week, his average holding of money is £14; and that, if he is paid the *same rate* of income monthly (viz. £112), his average holding of money will be £56. In both cases his rate of spending is £112 per month. But he requires, on average over time, only 14 units of money to carry out this spending when he is paid weekly, and 56 units when he is paid monthly. The ratios of his spending per month to the average number of money units used—viz. $\frac{112}{14} = 8$, and $\frac{112}{56} = 2$—are different in the two cases.

The ratio in question is called a *velocity of circulation of money* (symbolized by V). It measures the average rate, per period of time, at which units of money move around in clearing the debts arising from spending. The size of V has to be measured (like a flow quantity) in relation to some period of time. For a given rate of spending, and a given number of money units used, V is larger, the longer the period of time over which it is measured. Thus when J is paid monthly, his V as measured *per month* is $\dfrac{112}{56} = 2$; but as measured *per quarter*, it is $\dfrac{336}{56} = 6$. V, and the period of time over which it is measured, are directly proportional to each other.

V, and the quantity demanded of money, are inversely related. The larger the number of money units that J requires to carry out a particular rate of spending, the more slowly those units move around. When he is paid weekly, his average money holding is £14, and his V as measured *per month* is $8 \left(= \dfrac{112}{14} \right)$. When he is paid monthly, his average money holding is £56, and his V as measured *per month* is $2 \left(= \dfrac{112}{56} \right)$. $\dfrac{£14}{£56}$ is the inverse of $\dfrac{8}{2} \left(= \dfrac{56}{14} \right)$. The greater is the demand for money in relation to a given rate of spending, the lower necessarily is V. Hence the size of V is determined by the same influences as the quantity demanded of money. V is only another way of expressing the demand for money.

A velocity of circulation can be obtained for the whole community by aggregating from the individual level. A variety of aggregate Vs can, however, be distinguished. Thus, the money expenditure on national output, say per year, can be divided by the average stock of M in existence during that year. This ratio is called the *income velocity* of circulation (V_Y). The actual V_Y per year $\equiv \dfrac{Y}{M} \equiv \dfrac{P \cdot X}{M}$. Alternatively, the total money expenditure (T) on all things (viz. national output, secondhand goods, intermediate products, and real and financial assets) can be divided by M. This ratio is called the *transactions velocity* of circulation (V_T). Since $T > Y$, $V_T \left(\equiv \dfrac{T}{M} \right)$ is greater than V_Y.

The formula for V_Y can be re-arranged in the form $M \cdot V_Y \equiv P \cdot X$. This is called a Quantity Equation of Money. It was extensively used in monetary analysis before the development of Keynesian macroeconomics. But, as it stands, it is true by the definitions of the terms in it.[1] In itself, it does nothing to *explain* the interrelations between M, V_Y, P, and X.

The determination of P and X was analysed in earlier chapters. The determination of the demand for M—and therefore of V_Y—has now been explained. The determination of the remaining term, M, in the quantity equation, will be analysed in the next chapter. Once the determinants of M, V_Y, P, and X, and their interrelationships, are understood, a Quantity Equation can be used as a summary way of talking about them. But nothing is thereby added to the understanding of these complex matters. That is why many economists no longer find it helpful to use a quantity equation. It conceals, rather than illuminates, the functional relations between the variables in question.

[1] I.e. it is a definitional identity rather than a genuine equation.

CHAPTER 29

THE SUPPLY OF MONEY

The determination of the quantity supplied of money is very similar in all developed monetary systems. The following explanation is couched in terms of UK monetary institutions, but its principles are generally applicable elsewhere.

Bank notes are the irredeemable debts of the Bank of England. The quantity supplied of them depends on the policy of that institution. Since it is state-owned, the supply of bank notes is ultimately dependent on the monetary policy of the government.[1] The same is true of coins.

Bank money is the debt, redeemable in cash, of the commercial banks, which are privately-owned, profit-seeking institutions. They are one kind of *financial intermediary*,[2] whose business centres on borrowing and lending. Financial intermediaries earn revenue from the interest received on their loans, i.e. on the debts of others to them. They incur costs in the form of the interest paid on their borrowing, i.e. on their debts to others; and also in the form of wages, etc., paid out to the factors they use to conduct their dealings in debts. A financial intermediary, which seeks to maximize profit, will aim to borrow and lend on a *scale*, and in those *forms*, which maximize the excess of its total revenue over its total costs.

The behaviour of a privately-owned, profit-seeking commercial bank has to be explained in these terms. It borrows and pays interest. It lends and receives interest. It employs factors and pays out wages, etc. The sizes, and the forms, of its debts and its loans are governed by its attempt to maximize profit. That its debts are one form of money is an important feature of its operation. But this must not be allowed to cloak the fact that the bank is in the borrowing and lending business to make profits.

When a bank borrows, it gets receipts. When it lends, it makes payments. Any difference between its total receipts and total payments per period of time has to be settled in money. The position of the bank

---

[1] Subject to the overriding authority of Parliament.

[2] Examples of other kinds are building societies, hire purchase finance companies, and insurance companies.

in this respect is no different from that of a household or a non-banking firm. But it is different in another respect. Money to a household or a non-banking firm can be *either* cash or bank money. Both of them are equally good for clearing the debts of households and non-banking firms.[1] But the *only* money a bank can use to settle its own debts is *cash*.

It is essential, therefore, always to distinguish between cash and bank money. The word 'money' should not be used indiscriminately. That can only cause confusion about the working of modern monetary systems.

The explanation of the quantity supplied of money thus has necessarily two parts. The supply of *cash* has to be explained in terms of the monetary policy of the government. The supply of *bank money*, namely of bank book debts, has to be explained in terms of the commercial banks' attempt to maximize profits. But the two are interrelated because the banks themselves have a demand for cash. That demand will be larger, the more borrowing and lending the banks undertake. Hence, control over the quantity of cash available to the banks provides the monetary authority with a means of controlling the scale of the banks' borrowing and lending. That is, it is a means of controlling the quantity supplied of bank money.

Control over the quantity of *all* money is the prime function of a *central bank*, i.e. the Bank of England in the case of the UK. It controls the supply of cash, and thereby controls the willingness and ability of the commercial banks to supply bank money. It is best to begin the explanation of how this is done by analysing the profit-seeking behaviour of commercial banks.

COMMERCIAL BANKING

The business of a commercial bank centres on its loans and debts. These are recorded in its *balance sheet*, which has the following general form for a British commercial bank[2]:

Liabilities	Assets
Accounts:	Cash:
(i) Current accounts	(i) Coin and Notes
(ii) Deposit accounts	(ii) Account at Bank of England
	Loans

[1] Including non-bank financial intermediaries like building societies, etc. These of course keep accounts with the commercial banks, i.e. they hold bank money.

[2] Some items in the balance sheet, which are not relevant to the present analysis, have been ignored, e.g. the bank's issued capital and reserves on the liabilities side, and the value of premises, etc., on the assets side. These are quite small relative to total liabilities and assets.

The bank's liabilities are its debts to others; its assets are the debts of others to it.

The accounts which people and firms keep with the bank are the latter's debts to them. These debts are repayable in cash, i.e. in coin and notes. But they are separated into current accounts and deposit accounts. The former are repayable in cash on *demand*. The right of immediate repayment leads them to be called demand deposits. The deposit accounts are repayable in cash after seven days' notice. They are therefore also called time deposits. The requirement of seven days' notice is often waived, but the bank has the right to insist on it.

A deposit account can be repaid, not only in cash, but also by the transfer of its balance to a current account. This, in fact, is what usually happens. Thus a person, who has an insufficient balance on his current account to settle some outstanding debt, can instruct the bank to transfer some of his deposit account balance to his current account. This will put him in a position to instruct the bank (by writing a cheque) to transfer some of his current account balance to his creditor.

It is transfers between the current accounts of people (and firms) that clear the debts between them. This debt clearing is achieved by changes in the entries in the accounts with the banks, i.e by changes in the ownership of bank book debts As far as the people (and firms) are concerned, cash in no way enters into the settlement of these debts. They could, of course, use cash if they wish—but for most transactions, it is more convenient to use bank debt.

It is thus current accounts, and not deposit accounts, which are money. The balances on the latter have to be transferred to current accounts before they can be used to settle debts. The stock of money is the total of coins, notes, and current account balances in the possession of the community.

The book debts of the commercial banks will from now on be called the *accounts* of their customers. The use of the word 'deposit' for a bank account balance will be avoided because it has a misleading association. It suggests a literal depositing of cash. Interpretation in this sense produces great confusion about the ways in which a bank account balance can come into existence. It can, of course, result from the literal depositing of cash: this occurs when a person hands over bank notes to the cashier in a bank and tells him to credit the amount to the customer's account. But it is well to be clear what precisely is happening here: the person is giving up a bank *note* debt in return for a bank *book* debt.

But that is only one of the ways in which a bank book debt can be acquired. It can also be acquired by a transfer from another person's bank account. This is what happens when a person lodges a payment by cheque to his account. His bank account balance rises, and that of another person falls, without any 'deposit' of cash being involved.

Moreover, a bank book debt can be acquired without either a 'deposit' of cash or a transfer from another bank account. Bank book debts can be newly 'created' by the bank. There is nothing mysterious or difficult about the 'creation' of debt. As ordinary experience shows, it is quite obvious how to get into debt, i.e. to create debt: it is done by borrowing.

When a person borrows from a bank, he gets into debt to the bank. What he borrows is a bank book debt. The borrowing involves an exchange of debts. Thus, suppose that Mr *J* borrows £100 from a bank. He gives a written undertaking to repay £100 at the end of some period of time. That undertaking is his debt—which is an *asset* to the bank. The bank now credits *J*'s current account with a balance of £100. That is, it gives him a bank book debt in return for his personal debt. He can now use the bank book debt to settle his own debts to other people.

That, of course, is the heart of the matter. *J* has to settle his debts to other people because they refuse to hold them any longer. But they are quite willing to hold bank debts instead—because they, in their turn, can clear their debts to others with bank debts. That is why *J* is quite satisfied to accept a bank book debt in exchange for his own debt to the bank. And as long as *J* can be counted on to repay his debt, the bank is quite satisfied with the exchange of debts, because it is going to earn interest from *J*.

The 'creation' of bank money is simply an increase in bank debt to the community. That increase occurs when the community borrows more from the banks; what the latter lend is their own debt. And the community is willing to accept that debt because it is money.

The process by which modern money is created undoubtedly puzzles many people. This is probably because they expect money—i.e. what is used to settle debts—to be something *other* than debts. That was once so, when the market values of the metals in coins equalled the values stamped on the coins. But it is no longer so in developed monetary systems. Money in the form of debts has replaced money in the form of commodities like gold and silver. The explanation of a modern monetary system must therefore run entirely in terms of the creation, transfer, and cancellation of debts.

Current accounts do not earn any interest. Indeed, banks usually make a charge for managing them, according to the number of payments into and out of them per period of time. No form of money in the UK consequently earns a rate of interest. But interest is paid on deposit accounts.

The assets of a commercial bank consist of loans and cash. The loans take a variety of forms, and can be used for a variety of purposes. Households borrow from the banks in order to finance expenditure on durable consumer goods (e.g. cars). Firms borrow in order to finance expenditures on raw materials and on the holding of stocks of goods; and also sometimes on the early stages of investment in plant and buildings. Other financial institutions, like the Discount Houses of the London Money Market, and hire purchase finance companies, also borrow from the commercial banks; they use the borrowed funds to re-lend to firms and households[1] to enable them to finance investment and consumption expenditures. Thus, all the forms of bank lending detailed in this paragraph are connected with aggregate money expenditure on the national output.

The commercial banks also lend to the government by purchasing government securities.[2] The latter may be newly issued to finance government expenditures on goods and services. Hence this bank lending, like that of the previous paragraph, is connected with aggregate money expenditure on the national output. But some of the government securities bought by the banks may have been issued some time ago. In this case, the banks buy them on the stock exchange from the persons, firms, or other financial institutions which are currently holding them. This bank lending does not, therefore, finance government expenditure on goods in the *present*. Whether it has any connection with current aggregate money expenditure on the national output depends on what the households, firms, and financial institutions, which sell the securities to the banks, do with the proceeds. They may use the proceeds to finance investment and consumption expenditures; or to buy, on the stock exchange, other existing securities; or to add to their bank accounts. In the latter case, the sellers of the securities are giving up government debts in return for bank debts.

It does not necessarily follow, therefore, that all the bank lending during a given period of time is connected with current aggregate money expenditure on the national output. Some of it may be used to finance investment and consumption expenditures. But some of it may only have the function of allowing firms and persons to change the *forms* in which they hold their wealth. This is the case when the latter

[1] And to the government, e.g. when the Discount Houses buy Treasury Bills.
[2] Namely Treasury Bills and short-dated bonds.

sell government securities to the banks in order to buy other existing securities, or to hold more bank money.

Cash has been defined as coin and notes. But for a commercial bank it can also take another form, namely a balance in its account with the central bank. Commercial banks keep accounts at the Bank of England, in the same way as the community keeps accounts with them. The central bank is the 'bankers' bank'. The banks' accounts with the Bank of England are the latter's debts to them. These debts are repayable in notes and coin. Bank of England *book* debts can be exchanged for its *note* debts, and for coin. Hence the cash on the assets side of a commercial bank's balance sheet takes two forms, viz. (i) coin and notes, and (ii) the balance on its account with the Bank of England.

The former must be held to meet demands for the repayment in cash of bank accounts. The latter is convenient for the clearing of debts between the banks themselves. These arise whenever a customer of one bank makes a payment (by cheque) into the account of a customer of another bank. Such inter-bank transfers between accounts are happening continually. For example, cheques drawn against accounts in the Midland Bank are paid each day into accounts in the Westminster Bank, and vice versa. If the total value of Midland Bank cheques received by the Westminster exceeds that of the cheques going in the opposite direction, the Midland is on balance in debt to the Westminster. This inter-bank indebtedness is cleared by the former transferring some of its balance at the Bank of England to the latter. The central bank's debt to one commercial bank goes up, and that to the other goes down. This is another example of how a modern monetary system works by means of transfers of debt.

THE SUPPLY OF BANK MONEY

When a commercial bank lends, it gives the borrowers its own book debts. Thus when people or firms borrow from a bank, the balances on their accounts are automatically increased. In terms of a bank's balance sheet,[1] the loans on the assets side and the current accounts on the liabilities side both increase by the same amount.[2]

The new current account balances can now be transferred (by cheque)

---

[1] As on p. 345 above.

[2] The situation is slightly different with the British system of bank *overdrafts*. If a person is granted overdraft facilities, it is only when he uses them that he gets into debt to the bank; and it is only then that bank debts to others are created. The analysis of this system of bank lending does not, however, differ in principle from that in the text.

to others, in settlement of the debts arising out of transactions in goods, factors, resources, and financial assets. But the community is not obliged to go on holding the additional debts, namely bank money, 'created' by the banks. It can always demand cash (coin and notes) from the banks in repayment of their debts. In this case, current account balances will fall as they are repaid with cash. In the banks' balance sheets, coin and notes on the assets side, and current accounts on the liabilities side, both fall by the same amount.

When a bank lends more to the community, it must, therefore, consider whether the community will be content, at the same time, to lend more to it. In the first instance, an increase in bank lending automatically increases the community's lending to the bank. The bank simply writes up the current account balances of the borrowers by the amount of the loans. But when those balances are transferred to other people, in the settlement of debts, they may not want to hold all of them. They may prefer to hold more cash and less bank money. In that case, the additional lending *by* the bank does not lead to the same amount of additional lending *to* the bank. Current accounts will not have increased by as much as bank loans, since some of the newly created balances on current accounts have been repaid in cash.

A bank must therefore hold some cash in case its lending to the community leads the latter to demand more cash. But more generally, the many and various daily transactions of a bank may result in it having, on balance, to pay out cash. Each day it gets a variety of receipts, e.g. from repayments of loans, sales of securities, transfers from accounts in other banks, and payments in of cash by its customers; and it makes a variety of payments, e.g. by granting new loans, purchasing securities, making transfers to accounts in other banks, and making cash payments to its customers. Given the payments conventions of the community, a bank's daily total receipts and payments are unlikely to balance each other exactly. It may either gain or lose cash.

The amount of cash a bank may gain or lose on any day depends both on the lack of synchronization between its receipts and payments, and on their sizes. The amounts of the receipts and payments will be closely related to the totals of the bank's assets and liabilities. The larger its balance sheet totals, the greater will be the number of its daily transactions. Hence as a bank lends and borrows more, it will have to hold a larger amount of cash to cover the possibility of total payments exceeding total receipts on any day. That is, a bank's demand for cash, like the demand for bank money plus cash by a household or a firm, depends on the sizes of its expected receipts and payments.

But a bank, again like a household or a firm, can reduce its cash holding by making short-term loans. The worthwhileness of this depends, as has been seen,[1] on the interest rate and the transactions costs involved in lending. The higher the interest rate is, the more profitable it becomes to reduce the cash holding by means of short-term lending.[2] Thus a bank's demand for cash, like the demand for bank money plus cash by a household or a firm, depends on the interest rate.

It can now be seen that the demand for cash by a bank is explained in precisely the same way as was the demand for money in general. The analysis of the previous chapter is fully applicable to a commercial bank. It must be borne in mind, however, that the only form of money with which a bank can settle its debts is *cash*. But the quantity of cash it demands is determined by all the influences analysed in the last chapter.[3]

A commercial bank seeks to borrow and lend on a *scale*, and in those *forms*, which will maximize its profits. Its behaviour therefore depends on the interest rates on different types of loans,[4] on the transactions costs they involve, and on the other costs incurred in running a banking business. But the *scale* of a bank's borrowing and lending also depends on the cash it can acquire. The larger the bank's borrowing (i.e. liabilities) and lending (i.e. assets), the more cash it needs to hold. For, as the scale of a bank's operations increase, the probable excesses of daily total payments over total receipts will be greater.

The amount of cash available to the commercial banks depends on the policy of the central bank. The way in which this is carried out will be explained in the next section of this chapter. For the moment, assume that a given amount of cash is made available to the commercial banks. Also assume that they are free to decide the *ratio* of their cash holding to their other assets (viz. loans). The fact that they are normally obliged to observe some rule in respect of this ratio will be taken into account presently.

The quantity *demanded* of cash by all the banks depends on the scale of their borrowing and lending. The quantity available (i.e. *supplied*) of cash to them depends on the central bank. The commercial banks will

[1] On pp. 337–338 above.
[2] The opportunities open to banks in this respect are considerable, because of their close connections with financial markets. Thus, the British banks can make loans for *one* day to the London Discount Houses.
[3] As listed on p. 340 above.
[4] Interest rates, of course, differ from one kind of loan to another. There is consequently a problem of what determines the *structure* of interest rates. This is too complex to be pursued at an introductory level. Hence, 'the' interest rate of the analysis in this book is to be interpreted as an average of the various rates on different kinds of loans.

want to increase their borrowing and lending to that scale at which the quantity of cash they demand—i.e. the amount thought to be necessary for that scale of operation—equals the quantity available to them. They will not want to expand further, because they judge that their requirements for cash might then exceed their holdings of it. The latter therefore act as a constraint on bank borrowing and lending. That is, the cash available to the commercial banks acts as a constraint on the quantity *supplied* of bank money, namely of current account balances.

The nature of the supply function for bank money can now be specified. It is essential to understand that this concerns the *willingness* of commercial banks to get into debt. This willingness to supply bank money must not be confused—as it often is—with the further question of what the *actual* quantity of bank money will be. The quantity of bank money in existence depends on the community's willingness to hold it, as well as on the bank's willingness to create it. As in all markets, the condition of demand as well as the condition of supply has to be taken into account. The community's demand function for money was specified in the previous chapter. The supply function for money will now be explained. It will then be possible to analyse, in the next chapter, how the quantity of money in existence is determined.

The connection between money and the interest rate is the main problem at the present point in macroeconomic analysis. It is therefore convenient to work with supply curves which express the dependence of the quantity supplied of *bank* money on the interest rate. This is shown in Fig. 29.1.

The interest rate (i) is measured on the vertical axis, and the stock of bank money, viz. current account balances, on the horizontal. A curve on the diagram can be used to show the stock of bank money which the commercial banks will want to supply at each level of the interest rate. But the willingness of the banks to lend, and thereby create current account balances, depends on the amount of cash available to them. This has to be taken as given in order to isolate the effect of the interest rate on the quantity supplied of bank money.

Given the cash holdings of the banks, the quantity of loans, and therefore of bank money, which they are willing to supply will expand as the interest rate rises. It has already been seen that the banks' demand for cash, at a given level of assets and liabilities, will decrease as the interest rate rises. This means that, with a *given* cash holding, they will want to have a *larger* amount of assets and liabilities as the interest rate rises. This is shown by the three supply curves in Fig. 29.1 sloping upwards to the right. Each curve relates to a *different* amount of cash holding by the banks, i.e. the cash holding is a parameter of the supply curve. Thus, the shape of S_1 indicates that, given the cash holding in question, the banks will want to lend more, and thereby supply more bank money, as the interest rate rises.

If the amount of cash available to the banks rises, S_1 will shift downwards (viz. *increase*) to, e.g. S_3. If the amount of cash available is

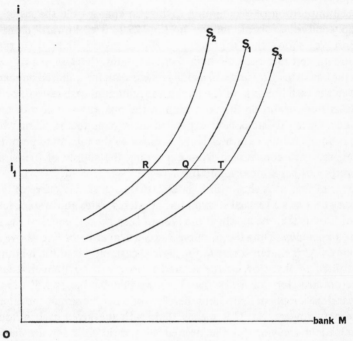

Fig. 29.1

reduced, S_1 will shift upwards (viz. *decrease*) to, e.g. S_2. Thus, at the interest rate i_1, a rise in the cash holdings of the banks will increase the supply of bank money from point Q (on S_1) to T (on S_3); and a fall in their cash holdings will decrease the supply of bank money from Q to R (on S_2).

Each supply curve assumes a given cash holding, and shows that the banks want to lend more as the interest rate rises. Total bank assets equal cash plus loans. The supply of loans expands, with cash constant, as the interest rate rises. Hence, the *ratio*, between cash and the total assets which the banks aim to have, is smaller, the higher is the interest rate. The *desired cash ratio* of the banks thus depends on the interest rate.

CONTROL OF THE SUPPLY OF MONEY

There are two elements in the control exercised by a central bank over the quantity supplied of bank money. First, the commercial banks are obliged to observe a *minimum* cash ratio. Second, the central bank can alter the amount of cash available to the commercial banks by means of *open market operations.*

The imposition of a minimum cash ratio changes the shapes of the supply curves of bank money in Fig. 29.1. The upward slope of the curves shows that the banks' *desire* to reduce their cash ratios as the interest rate rises. At higher interest rates, the *desired* cash ratio for the banks in aggregate will usually be *less* than the imposed *minimum.* Given the cash holdings of the banks, the minimum cash ratio therefore acts as a constraint on the expansion in the quantity supplied of bank money. Once the banks have expanded their loans to the point where the ratio of cash to cash plus loans is down to the minimum permitted level, they are constrained from expanding the supply of loans, and therefore of bank money, any further.

This means, as is shown in Fig. 29.2, that each supply curve of bank money becomes a vertical straight line at interest rates above some level. That level is the one at which the *desired* cash ratio is equal to the imposed *minimum.* Thus the S_1 curve is a vertical straight line above the point Q. At the interest rate i_1, the desired cash ratio is at the minimum permitted level. Below i_1, the desired ratio is *greater* than that level. The upward slope of S_1, below Q, shows that the banks will want to expand the supply of loans, and therefore of bank money, as the interest rate rises towards i_1. This means that, with the given cash holdings assumed in drawing S_1, the desired cash ratio *falls* for an upward movement along the curve towards Q.

The banks would wish to reduce their cash ratio still further as the interest rate rises above i_1. But they are not permitted to do so. Hence, the supply of loans, and therefore of bank money, will not expand any more as the interest rate rises. This is shown by the vertical range of S_1 above Q. The minimum cash ratio is thus in itself an effective constraint on the quantity supplied of bank money.

The rules governing the cash ratios of commercial banks vary from one country to another. In many countries (e.g. the US), there are legally enacted *minima* for the ratios. This still permits the banks to operate, if they so wish, with cash ratios *above* the minima—as has been allowed for in drawing the supply curves in Fig. 29.2. The banks are then said to have excess cash reserves. There is no legal provision governing the cash ratio in the UK. However, the English commercial banks are officially required to keep a *fixed* cash ratio of 8 per cent against the total of their current and deposit accounts. In this situation, the supply curve of bank money is vertical throughout its whole length.

The quantity supplied of bank money depends on the magnitude of the cash holdings of the banks. The amount of cash available to the

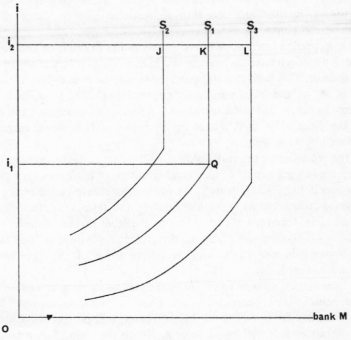

Fig. 29.2

banks is controlled by means of *open market operations*. These are purchases or sales of government securities by the central bank on the financial markets. The acquisition or sale of government debt by the Bank of England alters the balances on the accounts which the commercial banks keep with the Bank of England. These balances, together with the coin and notes they hold, constitute the cash holdings of the commercial banks.[1]

Suppose that the Bank of England sells £1 million of government securities through the financial markets to households and firms. The latter give the Bank cheques for £1 million drawn against their accounts

[1] As shown in the balance sheet on p. 345 above.

with the commercial banks. That is, they instruct the commercial banks to transfer bank account balances, amounting to £1 million, from themselves to the Bank of England. Hence the commercial banks are now £1 million in debt to the Bank and that amount *less* in debt to households and firms. The debt of the commercial banks to the Bank of England is settled by a reduction of £1 million in their accounts with the Bank, i.e. by a reduction in the Bank's debts to them. The open market *sale* of securities by the Bank has thus reduced the cash holdings of the commercial banks.

Open market operations provide yet another example of the way in which a modern monetary system works through transfers of ownership over debts. This is all that has occurred in the above example. Thus the Bank of England sells £1 million of government debt to households and firms. In return, the latter transfer £1 million of commercial bank debt to the Bank. The Bank's debt to the commercial banks is therefore reduced by £1 million.

The reduction in the cash holdings of the commercial banks causes a *decrease* in their supply of loans and therefore of bank money, e.g. the S_1 curve in Fig. 29.2 shifts to S_2. At any interest rate level, the banks will have to reduce the scale of their lending and borrowing, in order to bring their demand for cash down to the level of their smaller cash holdings. This they will do by requiring some repayment of their loans to households and firms, and by selling some of the government securities they hold.

Open market *sales* of securities by the central bank reduce the *actual* cash ratio of the commercial banks. Thus, in the above example, both cash, on the assets side of the balance sheet, and current accounts on the liabilities side, fall by £1 million. Hence the ratio of cash to cash plus loans is reduced. The consequential decrease in the supply of loans, and therefore of bank money, is directed to restoring the cash ratio to the required level.

Suppose that the commercial banks are operating at the minimum cash rate of 8 per cent: this is so when the interest rate is i_2 in Fig. 29.2. Now suppose that the fall in the cash holdings of the banks by £1 million shifts the supply curve from S_1 to S_2. The quantity supplied of bank money decreases from point K to point J. The amount KJ is $\dfrac{100}{8}$ times the £1 million fall in cash holdings. Total bank assets (cash plus loans) equal total liabilities (current plus deposit accounts). The required cash holding is $\dfrac{8}{100}$ of total assets. Hence, when the cash holding falls by

£1 million, total bank assets and liabilities must be reduced by $\dfrac{100}{8}$ times

£1 million, in order to maintain the required 8 per cent cash ratio.[1] The decrease in the quantity supplied of bank money is thus a *multiple* (viz. $12\frac{1}{2}$ in the present case) of the fall in the banks' cash holdings.

Open market *purchases* of government securities by the Bank of England increase the cash holdings of the commercial banks. The Bank gives the sellers of the securities cheques drawn against itself. The cheques are paid into accounts with the commercial banks. The latter now pass the cheques back to the Bank and have their accounts with it correspondingly increased. Once again, open market operations involve a series of transfers of ownership over debts. The Bank of England acquires government debts. The sellers of those debts acquire commercial bank debts in return. And the commercial banks acquire more Bank of England debt—which to them is cash.

The supply curve of bank money now increases, e.g. from S_1 to S_3 in Fig. 29.2. At any interest rate level, the banks will now increase the scale of their lending and borrowing, in order to bring their demand for cash up to the level of their larger cash holdings. This they will do by granting more loans to households and firms, and by purchasing more government securities. If the banks operate at the minimum cash ratio of 8 per cent, a rise in their cash holdings will lead to an increase in their total assets which is $\dfrac{100}{8}$ times the rise in cash. Thus, at the interest rate i_2, in Fig. 29.2, the increase, from S_1 to S_3 of KL in the quantity supplied of bank money, will be $12\frac{1}{2}$ times the rise in the banks' cash holdings.

The imposed minimum cash ratio, and the amount of cash available to the commercial banks, are two constraints through which a central bank can control the quantity supplied of bank money.[2] The latter constraint would be sufficient on its own insofar as the commercial banks always want to hold *some* cash. But if they can be expected—as is the case for the UK—always to operate at a fixed cash ratio, this adds more

---

[1] E.g. suppose that, initially, bank assets of £100 million are divided between cash of £8 million and loans of £92 million. If cash falls to £7 million, loans must be reduced to £80½ million, to restore the cash-to-total-assets ratio (viz. 7 to 87½) to 8 per cent. The fall in total assets, from £100 million to £87½ million, is $\dfrac{100}{8}$ times the £1 million fall in cash.

[2] A government may, of course, place constraints on the forms and the amounts of bank lending, and these may affect the total of that lending, and therefore the supply of bank money.

precision to the central bank's power of control. Because, as has been seen, changes in the quantity supplied of bank money are then related to changes in bank cash holdings by a multiple which is the inverse of the cash ratio, viz. $\dfrac{100}{8}$, when the cash ratio is $\dfrac{8}{100}$.

There is, however, an additional constraint acting on the commercial banks. Accounts with them are repayable in cash. If the 'public'—i.e. *non*-bank firms and persons—wants to hold more cash, it obtains this by reducing its accounts with the banks. The consequential fall in the banks' cash holdings forces them to decrease their supply of loans, and therefore the supply of bank money. The effect on the supply of bank money is the same as that of an open market *sale* of securities by the central bank. Thus a repayment of current accounts with cash will shift the supply curve of bank money from, e.g. S_1 to S_2 in Fig. 29.2. If the central bank wishes to keep the quantity supplied of bank money unchanged in these circumstances, it has to *purchase* securities to an amount equal to the public's additional demand for cash. The banks' loss of cash to the public is then offset by its gain of cash from the open market operations.

The amount of *cash* made available by the central bank is divided between (i) that held by the public, and (ii) that held by the commercial banks. The latter holding helps to determine, as has been seen, the quantity supplied of *bank* money. The quantity supplied of cash to the public *plus* the quantity supplied of bank money gives the *total* quantity supplied of money. The relation between the latter and the interest rate is shown in Fig. 29.3.

In this diagram, the *total* quantity supplied of money (M) to the *public* is measured on the horizontal axis. This total is the sum of (1) the quantity supplied of bank money, and (2) the public's holding of cash. A supply curve for total M is obtained by adding (2) to the appropriate supply curve for bank money (as shown in Fig. 29.2[1]). A supply curve in Fig. 29.3 has the same shape as the corresponding supply curve in Fig. 29.2, because the former is obtained by moving the latter to the right by the amount of cash held by the public.

A change in the amount of cash created by the central bank shifts the supply curve of bank money,[2] and therefore shifts the supply curve for total M in the same direction. Thus, a *purchase* of securities by the central bank will increase the cash holdings of the commercial banks, and as a result, the S_1 curve in Fig. 29.3 will shift to S_3.

[1] On p. 355 above.
[2] See pp. 355–357 above.

But the position of the supply curve for total M also depends on the *public's* demand for cash. An increase in that demand—given the amount of cash created by the central bank—reduces the cash holdings of the banks, as the public draws upon its bank accounts. The banks therefore have to contract their lending, and the quantity supplied of bank money, by a *multiple* of their loss of cash.[1] Consequently, the

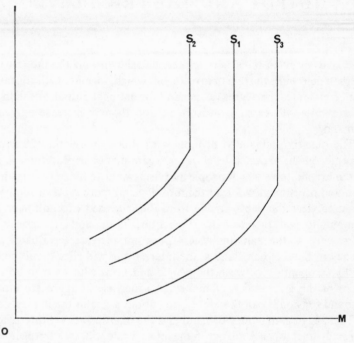

Fig. 29.3

decrease in the quantity of bank money supplied to the public outweighs the increase in the public's holding of cash. The *total* quantity of money supplied at any interest rate decreases, which means that the S_1 curve in Fig. 29.3 shifts to S_2. Thus, both the amount of cash created by the central bank, and the public's demand for cash, are parameters of the supply curve for total M.

The total supply of M is, however, ultimately under the control of the central bank through its control over the supply of cash. The effects of that control can now be understood by analysing the relation between the demand for and the supply of money.

[1] See pp. 356–357 above.

CHAPTER 30

THE INTEREST RATE, NATIONAL OUTPUT AND THE PRICE LEVEL

The analysis given in earlier chapters has shown how the interest rate helps to determine the rate of investment, which, together with consumption, constitutes the aggregate demand for national output. A fall in the interest rate will expand investment, and thereby increase aggregate demand.

The quantity demanded of money, as shown in Chapter 28 above, depends on the expected level of aggregate money expenditure. A rise in the expenditures which people and firms want to make on consumption and investment will lead them to demand more units of money in order to clear the debts arising from the increased expenditures. The community will therefore try to acquire more units of money by borrowing. If the banking system does not increase the quantity of money in these circumstances, the interest rate will rise. It will be bid up by competition between the people and firms who want to borrow more of the given stock of money. An increase in aggregate money demand for goods can therefore bring about a rise in the interest rate.

Thus, aggregate money demand and the interest rate are interrelated in *two* distinct ways. A change in the interest rate will, by altering investment, change the level of aggregate money demand. But a change in the latter will also, by altering the demand for money, change the interest rate. The two act and re-act on each other. It is not possible to explain the level of aggregate money demand, without taking the level of the interest rate into account; nor is it possible to explain the level of the interest rate without taking the level of aggregate money demand into account. It is therefore necessary to incorporate any explanation of the interest rate into the macroeconomic analysis of earlier chapters.

THE DETERMINATION OF THE INTEREST RATE

The interaction between the interest rate and aggregate demand requires the use of two *interconnected* diagrams—namely Figs. 30.1a and 30.1b—

to help with the explanation of how the interest rate is determined. First consider the natures of these diagrams separately.

Fig. 30.1a is the diagram already used[1] to explain—by means of the aggregate supply function (Y) and the aggregate demand function (Z) —the determination of national output and the price level. Only less-than-full employment levels of national output (i.e. less than OF) will be considered at the moment. Hence, since the Y curve is based on a given level of money wage rates (W), it will be assumed that trade

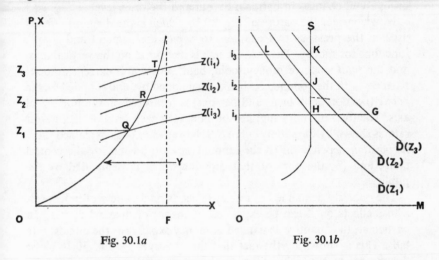

Fig. 30.1a Fig. 30.1b

unions successfully resist any attempts to reduce W, because of the excess supply of labour.

Three Z curves have been drawn for different levels of the interest rate (i). Each Z curve shows what the sum of money expenditures on consumption and investment will be at each level of national output. But the volume of investment depends on the interest rate: it will be larger, the lower is i. The level of i is taken as given in drawing any Z curve, i.e. it is a parameter of the curve. As i falls (e.g. from i_3 to i_2 to i_1), investment increases, and the Z curve shifts upwards. Thus, the curve labelled $Z(i_3)$ is the one which includes the expenditure on investment that firms will want to undertake when the interest rate is i_3. It lies below $Z(i_2)$, which includes the larger investment expenditure which will be undertaken at the lower i_2. Similarly, $Z(i_2)$ lies below $Z(i_1)$.

When the interest rate is i_3, the equilibrium level of national output is at the point of intersection (Q) of $Z(i_3)$ and the Y curve. The level of

[1] In Chapters 26 and 27 above.

aggregate money expenditure on national output is then Z_1, as shown on the vertical axis. If the interest rate falls to i_2, aggregate demand increases to $Z(i_2)$. The equilibrium level of national output now rises to the point of intersection (R) between $Z(i_2)$ and Y, at which aggregate money expenditure is Z_2. Similarly, at the interest rate i_1, the equilibrium national output is at point T, and aggregate money expenditure is then at the level Z_3. Thus, Fig. 30.1a can be used to show how changes in the interest rate alter the condition of aggregate demand, and thereby bring about changes in national output and the price level.

Now consider the nature of Fig. 30.1b, which is the diagram already used in the previous two chapters to depict the demand and supply functions for money. The interest rate is measured on the vertical axis, and the *total* stock of money (coin, bank notes, and current account balances with the commercial banks) demanded by, and supplied to, the *public* (i.e. non-bank firms and persons) is measured on the horizontal axis. The total quantity supplied of money, at each level of the interest rate, is shown by the supply curve S. It has already been explained[1] how its *position* depends on (i) the amount of cash created by the central bank, and (ii) the part of that amount which is demanded by the public.

The quantity demanded of money depends on a variety of influences, whose effects on it can be expressed by means of demand curves.[2] In particular, the quantity demanded of money expands as the interest rate falls. This is shown by the fact that the D curves in Fig. 30.1b slope downwards to the right. All the other influences on the quantity demanded of money are the parameters of these curves. Each D curve shows how the quantity demanded will vary with the interest rate, assuming that the other influences are given and constant. That is, a movement *along* a D curve shows how a change in the interest rate affects the quantity demanded of money.

But the quantity demanded of money also depends on the expected level of aggregate money expenditure (Z) on national output. If Z increases, the public will require—whatever is the level of the interest rate—a larger number of units of money to clear the debts arising from the increased expenditure. Hence, as Z rises, the quantity demanded of money increases at *each* level of the interest rate, i.e. the D curve for money shifts upwards to the right. Three D curves have been drawn in Fig. 30.1b for different levels of Z. As it increases from Z_1 to Z_2 to Z_3,

[1] By means of Fig. 29.3 on p. 359 above.
[2] See pp. 336–339 and Fig. 28.1, p. 340, above.

the demand curve shifts up from $D(Z_1)$ to $D(Z_2)$ to $D(Z_3)$.[1] That is, a *shift* in the demand curve shows how a change in Z affects the quantity demanded of money.

It will be shown presently that the interest rate will be in equilibrium only if the quantity demanded of money equals the quantity supplied, i.e. at a point of intersection between a demand curve and a supply curve for money. But the position of the demand curve depends on the level of Z. Hence, Fig. 30.1*b* can be used to explain how changes in Z alter the demand for money and thereby bring about changes in the interest rate.

The nature of the interconnections between Figs. 30.1*a* and 30.1*b* can now be seen. The position of the Z curve in Fig. 30.1*a* depends on the level of the interest rate, which is explained by Fig. 30.1*b*. And the position of the D curve in Fig. 30.1*b* depends on the level of aggregate money expenditure, which is explained by Fig. 30.1*a*. These are the diagrammatic representations of the fact that Z and i are mutually interdependent. Neither can be explained without taking the other into account. It is now possible to show how the interest rate is determined.

Suppose that the ruling interest rate happens to be at the level i_1. The amount of investment which firms will then want to undertake leads to the condition of aggregate demand given by the curve $Z(i_1)$ in Fig. 30.1*a*. The equilibrium level of national output is then at point T, where the level of aggregate money expenditure is Z_3. With that expenditure, the demand for money is given by the curve $D(Z_3)$ in Fig. 30.1*b*. It shows that, at the ruling interest rate i_1, the quantity demanded of money is given by the point G.

But the quantity of money which the banking system is willing to supply, at the interest rate i_1, is given by the point H on the S curve. Hence, when aggregate money expenditure is Z_3 and the interest rate is i_1, there is an excess demand for money equal to HG. That is, the public wishes to hold a number of units of money which is in excess of that which the banking system is willing to create. No more units of money can be obtained by further borrowing from the banks: given the banks' cash holdings, and the minimum cash ratio, they are unwilling to lend more, and thereby create more bank money.

In these circumstances, people and firms will attempt to borrow more from one another in order to satisfy their excess demand for money.

---

[1] All the D curves are shown as intersecting the S curve in its vertical range, since the UK banking system normally operates at the minimum cash ratio. But the analysis can easily be extended to allow for a variable cash ratio.

The competition between borrowers, for the *additional* units of money they require in order to spend at the rate Z_3, will bid up the interest rate. It will rise from i_1 towards i_2. *Two* effects then follow. First, the quantity demanded of money will *contract* along the $D(Z_3)$ curve. As i rises, people and firms will find it worthwhile to reduce their money holdings by means of additional short-term lending.[1] This contraction in the quantity demanded of money will reduce the excess demand for it. Thus, the movement up $D(Z_3)$ from point G towards K narrows the gap between the $D(Z_3)$ curve and the S curve.

But secondly, as the interest rate rises from i_1 towards i_2, the amount of investment which firms want to undertake will fall. The $Z(i_1)$ curve in Fig. 30.1a will shift downwards toward $Z(i_2)$. The aggregate money expenditure which the public wants to undertake therefore falls from Z_3 towards Z_2. Consequently, the $D(Z_3)$ curve in Fig. 30.1b shifts downwards towards $D(Z_2)$.

The fall in aggregate money expenditure, as a result of the rise in the interest rate, *decreases* the quantity demanded of money. This further reduces the excess demand for money. The latter is thus gradually eliminated in *two* ways. The quantity demanded of money *contracts* as i rises, and *decreases* as Z falls. Thus, starting from the excess demand HG at i_1, the rise in i causes a movement upwards *along* the D curve for money, and the fall in Z causes the D curve to *shift* downwards.

The excess demand is eliminated when the interest rate has risen to i_2. The demand for money is now given by $D(Z_2)$, since Z_2 is the level of aggregate money expenditure at the equilibrium national output which obtains when the interest rate is i_2 (i.e. at point R in Fig. 30.1a, where $Z(i_2)$ and Y intersect). The $D(Z_2)$ and S curves in Fig. 30.1b intersect at point J, thus indicating that the quantity demanded of money equals the quantity supplied at the interest rate i_2. People and firms are now holding, at this interest rate, the number of units of money they want in order to spend at the rate Z_2. Since no further borrowing need be undertaken by them, the interest rate will not change any more. Consequently, i_2 is the *equilibrium* rate of interest.

It is essential to undestand that i_2 is the equilibrium rate, not only because the quantities demanded and supplied of money are equal at i_2, but also because the aggregate supply of and demand for national output are in equilibrium when the interest rate is i_2. That is, i_2 is the equilibrium rate because *two* conditions are simultaneously satisfied, namely (i) the $D(Z_2)$ and S curves in Fig. 30.1b intersect at i_2, and (ii) the $Z(i_2)$ and Y curves in Fig. 30.1a intersect at the level Z_2. Suppose

[1] As explained on pp. 337–338 above.

that the latter condition did not hold. Then, the equilibrium national output would be at a different level of Z, and this would lead to a different demand curve for money than $D(Z_2)$. The equilibrium interest rate would not then be i_2.

It has now been seen how the levels of the interest rate and aggregate money expenditure are mutually interdependent. The spending which the public wants to carry out helps to determine the demand for money, which, in relation to the supply of money, determines the interest rate. But the latter itself helps to determine the rate of spending. Aggregate money expenditure and the interest rate act and react on each other. The one cannot be in equilibrium unless the other is simultaneously in equilibrium.

This can also be seen by supposing that the ruling interest rate is initially *above* the equilibrium level, e.g. at i_3. Aggregate demand is then shown by the curve $Z(i_3)$ in Fig. 30.1a. The equilibrium national output is at point Q, where aggregate money expenditure is Z_1. The demand for money is now given by the curve $D(Z_1)$ in Fig. 30.1b. It shows that, at the ruling interest rate i_3, there is an excess supply of money equal to LK.

The public thus wants to hold a number of units of money which is *less* than that which the banking system is willing to create at the interest rate i_3. Bank money is created by bank lending. An excess supply of bank money means an excess supply of bank loans. It means that, at the ruling levels of spending (Z_1) and the interest rate (i_3), the public does not want to borrow as much from the banks as the latter want to lend. Hence, there will be competition between the banks to lend the amount of bank money—viz. LK in Fig. 30.1b—which the public is unwilling to borrow at the interest rate i_3. The rate will be competed down towards i_2.

Two effects then follow. The quantity demanded of money *expands* as i falls, and at the same time *increases* as Z rises, because the fall in i shifts $Z(i_3)$ upwards towards $Z(i_2)$ in Fig. 30.1a. The excess supply of money is eliminated when the interest rate has fallen to i_2. The demand curve for money has shifted up to $D(Z_2)$, because aggregate money expenditure has risen to Z_2 as a result of the fall in the interest rate to i_2. At the higher Z and the lower i, the public is now willing to borrow the same amount of bank money as the banks are willing to lend.

The above analyses have shown how the interest rate will *converge*, either up or down, to its equilibrium level. It has already been seen, in various respects earlier in this book, that it is the process of convergence which enables predictions to be made about changes in economic quantities. The basis has therefore been provided for analysing the effects on economic activity of changes in the supply of money.

CHANGES IN THE SUPPLY OF MONEY

Suppose that national output and the interest rate are initially both in equilibrium at points R and J respectively in Figs. 30.2a and 30.2b. The equilibrium interest rate is i_2. This leads to the condition of aggregate demand shown by the curve $Z(i_2)$ in Fig. 30.2a. It intersects the Y

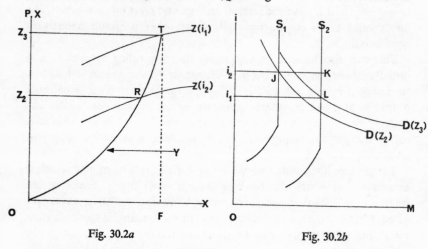

Fig. 30.2a   Fig. 30.2b

curve (point R) at the level of aggregate money expenditure Z_2. This level gives the demand for money shown by the curve $D(Z_2)$ in Fig. 30.2b. It intersects the S curve of money (point J) at the interest rate level i_2. Hence the *two* conditions for i_2 to be the equilibrium rate are simultaneously satisfied, namely (i) the quantity demanded of money equals the quantity supplied at i_2 (point J), and (ii) the aggregate demand for goods at i_2 equals the aggregate supply (point R).

Now suppose that there is an *increase* in the supply of money. This is shown by the shift from S_1 to S_2 in the supply curve of money in Fig. 30.2b. The banking system is now willing to supply a larger number of units of money at each level of the interest rate. Thus, at i_2, it is now willing to supply the quantity at point K (on S_2) as compared with that at J (on S_1). The increase in the supply of money is the result of a change in *monetary policy*: it is a deliberate act carried out by the central bank. It can be undertaken for a variety of reasons, the nature of which will become clear presently.

An increase in the willingness of the banking system to supply money—by lending more of its own debts—is initiated by the central bank. It *purchases* government securities on the open market. This increases the balances on the accounts which the commercial banks keep with the central bank.[1] The cash holdings of the commercial banks have thus been raised, and the ruling *ratio* between cash and total assets (cash plus loans) has been increased. It is therefore above the *desired* cash ratio. The banks, in seeking to maximize profits, are now willing to increase their lending to the public. This means that they are willing to supply a larger quantity of their book debts (bank money) at the ruling interest rate i_2. This is shown by the shift from S_1 to S_2 in Fig. 30.2b.

The *actual* quantity of bank money will, however, increase only insofar as the public is induced to borrow more from the banks. A fall in the interest rate is necessary for this to happen. Initially, at the interest rate i_2, the quantity demanded of money, on $D(Z_2)$, is equal to the quantity supplied, on S_1, viz. at point J. This means that at i_2, the public is willing to borrow from the banks exactly the same amount as they are willing to lend.[2] Now, however, the banks are willing— because of the increase in their cash holdings—to lend more bank money at the interest rate i_2: they are ready to move to point K on S_2. There is consequently an excess supply of money equal to JK.

The convergence analysis given in the previous section of this chapter has shown how an excess supply of money causes a fall in the interest rate. The banks, in seeking to induce the public to borrow the additional JK of bank money, will compete the interest rate down from i_2 towards i_1. Two effects then follow. First, the quantity demanded of money *expands* as i falls, i.e. there is a *movement* down along the D curve for money. Second, aggregate demand increases from $Z(i_2)$ towards $Z(i_1)$ in Fig. 30.2a, as i falls. Hence, aggregate money expenditure rises from Z_2 towards Z_3, and the quantity demanded of money *increases*: there is a *shift* in the demand curve from $D(Z_2)$ upwards towards $D(Z_3)$.

The commercial banks increase their lending in two ways. They buy existing government securities which are already in the possession of the public; and they induce the public, by lowering the interest rate, to

---

[1] As explained on p. 357 above.

[2] This has to be qualified. Banks do not always raise their interest rates to the level necessary to equate the demand for bank loans to the available supply. Sometimes there is excess demand for loans at the ruling interest rate, and the banks consequently *ration* them on some basis or other. More bank lending can therefore take place without any fall in the interest rate. No substantial modification to the analysis in the text is required to take this into account.

borrow more bank money in order to increase their rate of spending on investment (and maybe consumption).

In the first case, the banks have to bid up the prices of government securities in order to induce the public to sell some of them. The interest rate that can be earned on holding the securities falls. This makes the public willing to hold more money, i.e. it *expands* the quantity demanded of money. What has happened is that the public is now holding fewer government securities (since they have sold some to the banks), and is holding more bank money (since they now have the amount received in return for the securities).

In purchasing securities, the banks drive down the interest rate that can be earned on them. They will therefore, at the same time, lower the interest rate at which they are willing to lend to firms and persons who want finance for spending on investment (and consumption). This leads to the second effect of the increased willingness of the banks to lend. The fall in the interest rate increases the amount of investment (and maybe consumption) which the public wants to undertake. Hence the $Z(i_2)$ curve in Fig. 30.2a shifts up towards $Z(i_1)$; and at the same time, the $D(Z_2)$ curve in Fig. 30.2b shifts up towards $D(Z_3)$. The fall in i increases the spending, from Z_2 towards Z_3, which the public wants to undertake, and therefore increases the number of units of money they demand in order to carry out the higher spending. Thus, some of the increase in bank lending is used to help finance the rise in spending on investment (and maybe consumption).[1]

The interest rate converges to the lower level i_1, at which *both* conditions for its equilibrium are again satisfied. Aggregate demand, on $Z(i_1)$, is equal to aggregate supply at point T in Fig. 30.2a, with aggregate money expenditure at the level Z_3. Simultaneously, the quantity demanded of money at i_1, on the $D(Z_3)$ curve, is the equal to the quantity supplied, on the S_2 curve, at point L in Fig. 30.2b. The increase in the supply of money, from S_1 to S_2, has lowered the interest rate,[2] and has raised the level of the national output.

The quantity of money in the possession of the public has increased from point J to L. This increase will be partly in the form of bank

[1] It must be remembered that 'the' interest rate, of the present analysis, is an average of the rates on different kinds of loans. A fall in the rate on bank loans will cause a fall in the rates on other forms of lending. The latter will increase as well as bank lending, and will help in financing the rise in spending on investment (and maybe consumption).

[2] The central bank may also, but not necessarily, lower its *re-discount rate*, namely the Bank Rate of the Bank of England. The significance of this rate is explained in textbooks on banking.

money, and partly in cash. The rate of spending has risen from Z_2 to Z_3. The payments conventions of the public will require a larger cash holding, as well as a larger bank money holding, when spending increases. Hence, some of the cash gained by the commercial banks, as a result of the central bank's open market operations, will be paid out in coin and notes to the public. It will draw more cash out of the banks as the quantity of bank money increases.

The increase in the quantity of bank money will therefore not be (in the case of the UK) $\dfrac{100}{8}$ times[1] the extra cash created by the open market operations. It will be $\dfrac{100}{8}$ times the *excess* of that cash over the amount of additional cash demanded by the public, as its rate of spending rises, i.e. $\dfrac{100}{8}$ times the *net* acquisition of cash by the banks.

MONETARY POLICY

That part of a government's economic policy which is concerned with control over the supply of money is called *monetary policy*. It is put into effect by the central bank. It has now been seen that changes in the supply of money affect the interest rate. Monetary policy, therefore, necessarily implies a policy with respect to the level of the interest rate.

The level of aggregate demand depends on the interest rate. Aggregate money expenditure can be increased or decreased by lowering or raising the interest rate. The level of national output, and the associated level of employment, depend on the condition of aggregate demand in relation to that of aggregate supply. Hence a change in the supply of money can, by altering the interest rate, and therefore the level of aggregate money expenditure, affect the levels of national output and employment.

This provides one criterion by which the central bank can judge what is the appropriate quantity of money to supply to the public. It can attempt—by changing the quantity of money and therefore the interest rate—to bring aggregate money expenditure to the level which ensures the full employment of resources. Full employment is one possible objective of monetary policy.

The *possibility* of achieving full employment by means of monetary policy can be illustrated in terms of Figs. 30.2a and 30.2b.[2] When the

[1] I.e. the inverse of the cash ratio; see pp. 356–357 above.
[2] On p. 366 above.

supply of money is that given by the curve S_1, the equilibrium interest rate is i_2. Aggregate demand is then given by the curve $Z(i_2)$. The equilibrium national output (at point R) is *below* the full employment level OF. An increase in the supply of money to S_2 lowers the interest rate to i_1. Aggregate demand increases to $Z(i_1)$, and the equilibrium national output rises to the full employment level (at point T). Thus, the elimination of unemployment by means of monetary policy depends on (i) the ability and willingness of the monetary authority to lower the interest

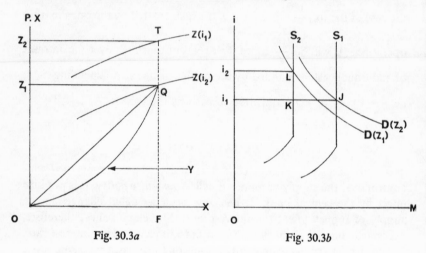

Fig. 30.3a   Fig. 30.3b

rate, and (ii) the extent to which aggregate demand will increase as the interest rate falls. These points will be considered in the next section of this chapter.

But the price level, as well as the level of national output, depends on the conditions of aggregate demand and supply. If the level of aggregate demand exceeds that of aggregate supply at the full employment national output, a *demand inflation* results. The consequential rise in the price level was analysed in Chapter 27.[1] This provides a second criterion by which the central bank can judge what is the appropriate quantity of money to supply. It can attempt to provide that quantity which leads to a level of the interest rate that avoids a demand inflation which would raise the price level. Price level stability is a second possible objective of monetary policy.

This can be explained by means of Figs. 30.3a and 30.3b. Suppose that initially the supply of money is given by the curve S_1 in Fig. 30.3b.

[1] See pp. 320–324 above.

Also suppose that the ruling interest rate is at the level i_1. Aggregate demand, at that interest rate, is given by the curve $Z(i_1)$ in Fig. 30.3a; aggregate supply is shown by the curve Y. There is excess aggregate demand of QT at the full employment national output OF. The aggregate money expenditure which the public wants to undertake is Z_2. The demand for money is then given by the $D(Z_2)$ curve in Fig. 30.3b, which intersects S_1 (point J) at the ruling interest rate i_1.

This is *not* an equilibrium situation. Only one of the two conditions necessary for the interest rate to be in equilibrium is satisfied. The quantity demanded of money, at the rate of spending Z_2, equals the quantity supplied at the interest rate i_1. That is, $D(Z_2)$ intersects S_1 at i_1. But there is excess aggregate demand of QT for national output. This means that the price level is not in equilibrium. The Y curve shows that firms in aggregate are willing to supply the national output OF (at the ruling money wage rate) at the price level given by the slope of OQ. But at that supply-P, and the interest rate i_1, aggregate money demand is given at point T on $Z(i_1)$, and T lies above Q.

The earlier analysis of demand inflation explained what will happen in this situation.[1] The excess demand for goods raises the price level above that given by the slope of OQ; and at the same time, the excess demand for labour raises the money wage rate. Both the Y and $Z(i_1)$ curves therefore shift upwards. The increase in the $Z(i_1)$ curve means that, at the ruling interest rate i_1, the public now wants to raise its aggregate money expenditure above the level Z_2, given at point T on $Z(i_1)$. To do this, it will increase its demand for money. That is, the $D(Z_2)$ curve, in Fig. 30.3b, will shift upwards to the right. In relation to S_1, there will now be excess demand for money at the interest rate i_1. It will therefore rise above that level. Thus, i_1 is not the equilibrium interest rate, inasmuch as the price level is not simultaneously in equilibrium.

The central bank can prevent the rise in the price level by decreasing the supply of money below S_1. It *sells* government securities on the open market and thereby reduces the balances on the accounts which the commercial banks keep with it. The cash holdings of the banks have thus been lowered, and the ruling ratio between cash and total assets (cash plus loans) is now *below* the desired ratio. The banks have therefore to decrease their lending, i.e. the supply of bank money. The S_1 curve shifts to S_2 in Fig. 30.3b.

With the $D(Z_2)$ and S_2 curves, there is now an excess demand for money, of KJ, at the ruling interest rate i_1. That is, in order to spend at the rate Z_2, the public is demanding more units of money than the

[1] On pp. 321–322 above.

banking system is willing to create. People and firms will therefore attempt to borrow more from one another, and the interest rate will rise above i_1 towards i_2. As already seen, two effects follow. First, the quantity demanded of money *contracts* as i rises. Second, aggregate demand decreases as i rises. The $Z(i_1)$ curve in Fig. 30.3a shifts downwards towards $Z(i_2)$, and the aggregate money expenditure which the public wants to undertake falls from Z_2 towards Z_1. The demand for money therefore *decreases* from $D(Z_2)$ towards $D(Z_1)$ in Fig. 30.3b.

The interest rate will be in equilibrium at i_2, with the S_2 supply of money. The rise from i_1 to i_2 has eliminated the excess demand for national output: the $Z(i_2)$ and Y curves intersect at the full employment level of output. The price level is therefore in equilibrium at the level given by the slope of OQ. With aggregate money expenditure at the level Z_1, the demand for money is given by $D(Z_1)$, and it intersects S_2 at point L, i.e. at i_2. This is the equilibrium intersect rate, since (i) the quantity demanded of money now equals that supplied, and (ii) the price level and national output are simultaneously in equilibrium.

The central bank, by decreasing the supply of money from S_1 to S_2, can thus eliminate the excess demand which would raise the price level. But the analysis given above showed what would happen if the supply is kept unchanged at S_1. The excess demand QT in Fig. 30.3a, which exists at the interest rate i_1, raises the price level and the money wage rate. The $Z(i_1)$ and Y curves shift upwards. The aggregate money expenditure which the public wants to undertake therefore rises above Z_2. Hence, the $D(Z_2)$ curve in Fig. 30.3b, shifts upwards to the right. In relation to S_1, there is now an excess demand for money at i_1. The interest rate thus rises when the supply of money is held constant.

This consequence of a demand inflation was allowed for in the analysis given in Chapter 27.[1] It was there shown how a rise in the interest rate would, by reducing the *volume* of investment, act as a stabilizer on a demand inflationary process. If the central bank holds the supply of money at S_1—rather than decreasing it to S_2—the price level will rise. But it will eventually converge to equilibrium at a higher level. It can now be seen, by means of Figs. 30.3a and 30.3b, how the rise in the interest rate comes about in this situation when the supply of money is kept unchanged.

The maintenance of full employment, and the avoidance of demand inflation, are two objectives in relation to which the central bank can exercise its control over the supply of money. The principle governing monetary policy in these respects can be summarized as follows:

[1] See especially pp. 323–324 above.

increase the supply of M, and lower i, to avoid unemployment; decrease the supply of M, and raise i, to avoid demand inflation. There is no conflict between these principles. They both require the creation of a supply of M, and the fixing of the corresponding i, which equates aggregate demand and supply at the full employment level of national output. This equality avoids both unemployment and *demand* inflationary rises in the price level.

THE LIMITATIONS OF MONETARY POLICY

It must now be considered whether monetary policy is capable, in all circumstances, of eliminating unemployment on the one hand, and inflation on the other. This depends, in the case of unemployment, both on the ability and willingness of the monetary authority to lower the interest rate, and on the extent to which aggregate demand will increase as the interest rate falls.

A fall in the interest rate means a rise in the prices of existing bonds.[1] The willingness of people to continue holding bonds when this happens depends in part on their *expectations* about future bond prices. If the rise in the current prices of bonds leads some holders of them to expect a reversal of this movement, they may sell their bonds *now*, in order to avoid an expected capital loss on a sale at a future time. Hence, if the interest rate *is* to fall (i.e. bond prices to rise), the banking system has to purchase any bonds which the public is unwilling to hold at higher prices. The more unwilling the public is in this respect, the larger is the quantity of bonds which the banking system has to buy in order to get the interest rate down (bond prices up) by a given amount.

The public gets bank money in return for the bonds which it sells to the banking system. Hence the extent to which the public is unwilling to hold bonds, as their prices rise, is shown by the extent to which the quantity demanded of money expands as the interest rate falls, i.e. by the *interest elasticity of the demand for money*.[2] The more unwilling the public is to hold bonds, as their prices rise, the greater is the interest elasticity of the demand for money. This elasticity may be very large at low interest rates, since the correspondingly high bond prices may lead a large part of the public to fear a fall in them. In these circumstances, the demand curve for money will come near to being a horizontal

---

[1] See p. 338 above.

[2] As measured, in the usual way for an elasticity, by $\dfrac{\Delta q_M}{q_M} \Big/ \dfrac{\Delta i}{i}$, where q_M stands for the quantity demanded of money.

straight line at low interest rates. This means—as can be seen from Fig. 30.2b[1]—that a large increase in the quantity of money (i.e. rightward shift of the S curve) is required to get the interest rate down by a small amount.

However, with its power to create money, the monetary authority could buy any amount of bonds it wishes—including, ultimately, all the existing stock of them. Thus the monetary authority does in principle have the ability to fix the interest rate at any level. But it is unlikely to be willing to do so for the following reason.

A change of a few percentage points in the interest rate implies large capital gains or losses for the holders of existing bonds. For example, consider a bond bearing interest at 5 per cent, which was issued at a price of £100, and which (for simplicity of calculation) has no redemption date. The market price of the bond will rise to £200, if the interest rate falls to $2\frac{1}{2}$ per cent; and it will fall to £66$\frac{2}{3}$, if the interest rate rises to $7\frac{1}{2}$ per cent. The profitability of financial intermediaries, which are the most important dealers in bonds, depends in part on changes in bond prices. Rapid and/or considerable changes in the interest rate would make financial intermediation a very uncertain business, and would be likely to disturb the smooth flow of finance for investment. The monetary authority will probably wish to avoid policies which run the risk of disrupting the operation of the financial markets. This consideration constrains both the extent to which the interest rate may be changed, and the speed with which changes in it may be made. This constraint may in itself prevent monetary policy from having a sufficient effect on aggregate demand to eliminate either unemployment or inflation.

But even if the constraint did not operate, the reduction of the interest rate to a very low level will not necessarily increase aggregate demand sufficiently to eliminate an existing amount of unemployment.[2] The volume of investment (and consumption) may respond little to the fall in the interest rate, i.e. the *interest elasticity of investment*[3] may be very small. Investment depends not only on the cost of the finance for it, but also on the expectation that the outputs of additional capital goods can be sold at profitable prices in the future. During depressed business conditions, expectations about future sales can be so pessimistic that even a large reduction in the interest rate will not make

---

[1] On p. 366 above.

[2] I.e. in terms of Fig. 30.2a (on p. 366 above), the $Z(i_2)$ curve might not shift all the way up to $Z(i_1)$, when i is reduced to a very low level.

[3] As measured, in the usual way for an elasticity, by $\dfrac{\Delta I}{I} \bigg/ \dfrac{\Delta i}{i}$.

many firms think it worthwhile to expand their productive capacities. In these circumstances, monetary policy on its own may be incapable of increasing aggregate demand sufficiently to eliminate unemployment.

It was seen above that the risk of upsetting the smooth operation of the financial markets may restrain the monetary authority from raising the interest rate (i.e. lowering the prices of existing bonds) to an extent sufficient to prevent a *demand* inflation. But even if the interest rate is raised sufficiently, for this purpose, the stability of the price level may not be ensured. As has been seen,[1] *cost* inflation may cause the price level to rise. This will happen if the rate at which W rises, per period of time, is greater than that at which the MPP_L increases. The rate of rise in W will be the greater, the lower is the level of unemployment. But at some amount of unemployment, W will not rise more rapidly than the MPP_L.

Cost inflation can thus be avoided, and the stability of the price level ensured, at the price of leaving some resources unemployed. That unemployment can be brought about by restricting the supply of money in order to keep the interest rate *higher* than the level which would ensure full employment. Monetary policy can be used to combat cost inflation; but this involves a conflict between the objectives of full employment and price-level stability. Both cannot be attained at the same time by monetary policy. It can, however, be used in conjunction with other policy weapons. Its role in this context will therefore be pursued further when government economic activity has been taken into account.[2] But the analysis so far is sufficient to show that the connection between the supply of money and the behaviour of the price level is a complex one.

A rise in the interest rate reduces the volume of investment, and thereby retards the rate at which national output can grow, since the stock of capital will now increase less rapidly. This provides a third criterion by which the central bank can judge what is the appropriate quantity of money to supply to the public. Monetary policy can be used to influence the rate of economic growth.[3] But in this case, the question is the *rate* at which the supply of money should be *increased* over time. The role of monetary policy in this respect cannot be pursued, however, until the problems of economic growth are analysed in the next chapter.

---

[1] On pp. 324–328 above.
[2] In Chapter 32 below.
[3] It will be seen, in Part IV below, that the state of a country's balance of payments with the rest of the world provides a fourth possible criterion for monetary policy.

CHAPTER 31

INVESTMENT AND ECONOMIC GROWTH

A microeconomic analysis of investment decisions was given in Chapter 21 above. This considered the influences which determine whether or not a firm will *expect* it to be profitable to make a net addition to its stock of capital, e.g. to acquire another machine. The relevant influences are the *expected* internal rate of return on the machine (r), the interest rate (i), and an allowance for uncertainty in the form of a risk premium (p). An investment project is expected to be profitable if $r > i + p$, for example, when r is predicted at 12 per cent p.a., i is 7 per cent, and p is assessed at the level of 3 per cent.

The expected r is obtained by discounting the capital rentals, expected to be earned by using the machine over its estimated life, to a present value equal to the supply price of the machine. This is shown by the formula[1]:

$$S = P = \frac{a_1}{(1 + r)} + \frac{a_2}{(1 + r)^2} + \cdots + \frac{a_n}{(1 + r)^n}$$

where S is the price which has to be paid to acquire the machine, a_1 to a_n are the capital rentals expected to be earned in each year of the machine's life, and n is the estimated number of years for which it will be used. r is then the rate of discount which makes the present value (P), of a_1, a_2 to a_n, equal to the machine's supply price (S).

It was explained earlier[2] that discounting and accumulating at interest are two ways of looking at the same process. Thus, suppose that r, in the above discounting formula, comes out at 12 per cent p.a. for a particular machine. This means that the investor in the machine expects an outlay of S to yield (i.e. accumulate to) a series of revenues (a_1 to a_n) which represent a 12 per cent rate of return on his outlay. That is, he expects to obtain a total of revenues in *excess* of his outlay, i.e. he expects the *sum* of a_1 to a_n to exceed S. The 12 per cent means an expected rate of return *over and above* the outlay.

[1] See especially pp. 234–235 above.
[2] On p. 232 above.

Obviously an explanation is needed of why this can be so. The analysis of Chapter 21 simply assumed that there are investment projects each of which promises a series of capital rentals whose sum exceeds the outlay on the project. It was taken for granted, without proof, that there will be projects for which the internal rate of return is greater than zero. It is now necessary to explain why the accumulation of capital can yield a return over and above its cost. This will also help to explain how economic growth is possible.

THE NET PRODUCTIVITY OF CAPITAL

Consider the matter first of all in *physical* terms. Capital goods are used to produce other goods—both consumer goods and more capital goods. Existing resources have to be employed to produce the capital goods. But those resources could alternatively be used to produce consumer goods.

At any time, therefore, a community is faced with a choice. It can use *all* of its existing resources to produce consumer goods. Let this be called the *direct* use of the resources. Alternatively, some of them can be used to produce more capital goods, which in due course will help to produce consumer goods.[1] Let this be called the *indirect* use of the resources. That is, existing resources can be used directly to produce consumer goods, or they can be used to that end indirectly by means of the accumulation of capital.

The community's choice between the direct and the indirect methods of producing consumer goods will depend, in part, on which is *physically* the more efficient method. Consider a simple example. It is possible to catch fish by using only the productive services of labour. A man can wade into a river and try to catch them with his hands. Suppose that, by this *direct* method, he can catch 2 fish per day. Alternatively, he can construct and use a fishing rod. Suppose that it takes 1 day to make a rod which will last 9 days, i.e. will wear out after 9 days' fishing. Also suppose that, by this *indirect* (capital-using) method, he can catch 10 fish per day. Hence, 10 days' fishing with the hands produces 20 fish. But 9 days' fishing with the rod, plus 1 day to make it, produces 90 fish. Over 10 days, there is a *gain* of 70 fish from constructing and using the rod. The indirect method of using some of the existing resources (namely 1 day's labour on making the rod) is *physically* much more efficient than the direct method: 1 day's fishing with the hands produces

[1] Capital goods may, of course, produce other capital goods, which produce others, which at last help to produce consumer goods.

2 fish, while 1 day's labour making a rod *adds* 70 fish to output over the life of the rod.

The gain of 70 fish is a measure of the *net* physical productivity of the rod over its life. This contribution of the rod, to the output of fish, is *net* in the sense that it is computed after an allowance has been made for the cost of making the rod, i.e. the 2 fish which the man would have caught, if he had not taken a day off from fishing in order to make the rod. It is the rod's *net* physical productivity that indicates the technical superiority of this indirect—or capital-using—method of production over a direct one.

It is clear from the experience of the modern world that, with a given state of technology, there are very many capital-using methods of production which are physically more efficient than non-capital-using ones. That is, the net physical productivities of many capital goods over their lives are positive.

This is why the accumulation of capital increases the amount of national output which a community can produce. Consider the matter in terms of the macroeconomic production function, $X = F(N, K)$, where K, as before, includes the stock of land. In order to increase K, some N and some of the existing K have to be used to produce more capital goods. Those quantities of N and existing K could alternatively have been used directly to produce consumer goods. Suppose that the new capital goods will produce,[1] over their lives, a total of consumer goods which is *greater* than that which could have been produced directly by the quantities of N and existing K needed to create the capital goods. Then, over the period in question, X will be larger than it would have been if no more capital had been accumulated. The contribution to X (in the form of consumer goods) of the new capital goods outweighs the contribution to X (again in the form of consumer goods) which would have been made by the resources which were used to produce the new capital goods. X is thus higher, over the period in question, because the *net* physical productivity of the new capital is positive.

The higher level of X, resulting from the use of more K, will of course only be maintained if capital is replaced as it wears out. Not to replace capital means reverting from indirect to direct methods of production. Thus, the fisherman who does not replace his rod when it wears out, will revert from an output of 90 fish in 10 days to one of 20 in that period. To prevent this, he must always set aside time, equivalent to 1 day in 10, for the replacement of capital. The replacement costs him the 2 fish which he could have caught with his hands during that day,

[1] After allowing for the contribution of the labour working with them.

but it ensures that his output continues to be 70 fish per 10 days *higher* than it would be without the rod. The gain of 70 has been computed after allowing for the cost of 2 fish involved in replacing capital. The gain is the *net* physical productivity of the capital. It will be lost unless the stock of capital is maintained at the level in question. *Replacement* investment is required to prevent X from *falling*.

Consider now what will happen if the stock of capital is increased by *net* investment. Suppose, initially, that this happens with an unchanging state of technology, and a constant size of the labour force. There is no improvement in technical knowledge which would make it possible for previously unknown *kinds* of capital to be produced; and there is no increase in the amount of labour services available to work with the additional capital. An increase in the stock of capital then means an increase in the capital-to-labour $\left(\dfrac{K}{L}\right)$ ratio. Whatever the level of employment of the existing labour force, *each* man will now have a larger amount of capital to work with. The capital per head of the employed labour force has risen.

As the $\dfrac{K}{L}$ ratio rises, there are likely to be *diminishing returns* to K. The marginal physical product of capital (MPP_K) falls[1]; and at the same time, that of labour (MPP_L) rises. The fall in MPP_K has to be interpreted, in accordance with the above analysis, in terms of the *net* physical productivity of capital. The increase in the stock of K lowers its *marginal net* physical productivity.

The meaning of this can be seen in terms of the fishing example. The construction of one rod, and its continual replacement as it wears out, enables the fisherman to maintain his output at 90 fish per 10 days, as compared with 20 per 10 days without the rod. He can now consider adding to his stock of capital by, for example, constructing a boat to fish from, a second rod to use at the same time as the first, and so forth. These additions to his stock of capital, and their continual replacement as they wear out, will increase the output of fish above the level of 90 per 10 days which can be achieved with one rod. The boat and the second rod will have positive *net* physical productivities over their lives.

But as the fisherman accumulates more and more items of capital, he will find it increasingly difficult to operate them all at the same time. A second rod will make some *addition* to his catch after allowing for the cost of constructing it. But a third rod will make a smaller addition, and

---

[1] For the reasons explained on pp. 100–102 above.

a fourth one a still smaller addition. The *net* physical productivities of the *additional* items of capital get smaller and smaller as the fisherman's stock of capital increases. That is, the *marginal net* physical productivity of capital falls as the stock of it increases.

Ultimately, the fisherman can increase his stock of capital to the level at which its *marginal net* physical productivity has fallen to zero. Any further increase in the stock will not now raise his catch of fish.[1] He has exhausted all the worthwhile possibilities of switching from the direct, to the indirect, use of existing resources. The output of this one man is now at the maximum possible with his given technical knowledge.

THE SOURCES OF ECONOMIC GROWTH

The implications of the above analysis for the *possibility* of economic growth can now be seen. Suppose that initially a community has a constant labour force which is kept fully employed, and also that it has unchanging technical knowledge. The accumulation of capital raises the national output if the marginal *net* physical productivity of capital ($MNPP_K$) is positive. The $\dfrac{K}{L}$ ratio is rising: each man has more capital to work with. The $\dfrac{X}{L}$ ratio is also rising: the constant labour force is producing, with the help of the additional capital, a rising X.[2] Output per man is going up, and hence the standard of living of the community is improving.[3]

The term 'economic growth' is (unfortunately) used in two senses. It can mean *either* an increase in X *or* an increase in $\dfrac{X}{L}$. That is, it can mean either an increase in the total output of a community, or an increase in output *per head* of the labour force. An explicit distinction between the two meanings must always be made.

With a constant labour force, both X and $\dfrac{X}{L}$ will rise, as capital is accumulated, if the $MNPP_K$ is positive. But the $MNPP_K$ diminishes as

---

[1] Indeed, it will *reduce* his catch. He will then have so much capital equipment that it impedes his efforts to use it, thus making its marginal net physical productivity negative; see pp. 204–205 above.

[2] But the $\dfrac{X}{K}$ ratio is falling. Because of diminishing returns to capital, X is increasing less rapidly than K, and the $MNPP_K$ is falling.

[3] In average terms. This and the ensuing analysis ignores the problems connected with changes in the *distribution* of income.

the stock of capital increases, and at some size of the stock it will be zero. Both X and $\dfrac{X}{L}$ are then at the highest levels possible with the given technical knowledge of the community.

Thus, with a given labour force, and a given state of technical knowledge, there is a *limit* to the economic growth—in both senses of the term—which can be achieved by capital accumulation.

Now suppose that the population rises, and that the employed labour force increases at the *same* rate as the stock of capital. The $\dfrac{K}{L}$ ratio then remains unchanged over time. The increase in the stock of capital simply equips each additional man with the *same* amount of capital as each existing man already has. For example, the number of fishermen increases, but each one always works with a single rod.

With constant returns to scale[1] in this situation, X, K, and L all increase at the same rate. There is economic growth in the sense that total national output is rising. But $\dfrac{X}{L}$ remains constant: there is *no* economic growth in the sense of a rise in output per man. As the above analysis has shown, that requires[2] an increase in the amount of capital *per man*. Only then will output per man be raised by the positive *net* physical productivity of the additional capital per man.

Thus, if the employed labour force increases, the stock of capital must increase in the same proportion merely to prevent output per man from falling.[3] A continual increase in the employed labour force makes a continual increase in the stock of capital worthwhile. X will continue to grow in these circumstances. But $\dfrac{X}{L}$ will grow only if $\dfrac{K}{L}$ rises, i.e. if the accumulation of capital outstrips the increase in population.

Now take changes in technology into account. An improvement in technical knowledge increases the output which can be obtained from given quantities of productive services. Thus, it increases the X which can be produced with given quantities of N and K. Technical progress can lead to economic growth in *both* senses of the term: that is, it can increase both X and $\dfrac{X}{L}$.

---

[1] See p. 97 above.

[2] With given technical knowledge.

[3] This is the pressing problem which confronts underdeveloped countries (e.g. India, China) which have rapidly growing populations.

But it can take two contrasting forms. On the one hand, an increase in knowledge may allow the existing *kinds* of N and K to produce a larger X. It leads to the existing kinds and quantities of N and K being used, or combined, in new ways, so that their physical productivities are increased. On the other hand, an improvement in technical knowledge may require investments in both material and human capital in order to increase X. It may be necessary for new *kinds* of capital goods to be introduced, or for labour skills to be improved by education and training, before X can be increased.

The second form of improvement is called *embodied* technical progress. It has to be embodied, through investment, in new kinds of capital goods and labour skills, whereas the first firm—*disembodied* technical progress—does not require any investment in order for its benefits to be reaped. It involves only a re-arrangement of the ways in which existing resources are used.

Embodied technical progress changes the *nature* of the stock of capital goods which a community will want to use. It will want to substitute the technically more advanced kinds of capital for the existing kinds. This it can do through *replacement* investment. As existing capital goods wear out, they are replaced by technically more advanced ones. This will raise both X and $\dfrac{X}{L}$.

But the change in technology will also probably alter the *size* of the capital stock that it is worthwhile to accumulate. It was seen above that, with a given labour force, and a given state of technical knowledge, there is a quantity of capital at which the $MNPP_K$ will be zero. The community will not want to accumulate more than that quantity, since X and $\dfrac{X}{L}$ cannot thereby be raised any further. An improvement in technology will probably change the size of the capital stock at which the $MNPP_K$ is zero, i.e. at which X is at a maximum. It will now be worthwhile to accumulate a *different* quantity of capital than before.

The new quantity of capital, which it is now worthwhile to accumulate, may be larger, or smaller, than the old one. Technical progress may be of a character which increases the stock of capital needed to make X as great as possible: it is then said to be *capital-using*. But it is just as conceivable that technical progress reduces the stock of capital needed to maximize X: it is then said to be *capital-saving*. Little is yet known about the nature, in this respect, of contemporary technical improvements.

This means that it is not possible to say how technical progress will affect *net* investment. If a community has not yet accumulated the stock of capital which maximizes X (i.e. at which $MNPP_K$ is zero), net investment is still required to reach that objective. If technical progress occurs in this situation, it can either increase or decrease the size of the stock of capital which will maximize X. It can therefore either increase or decrease the amount of net investment still required to reach that objective.

PRODUCTIVITY AND INVESTMENT

The connection between the $MNPP_K$ and the expected internal rates of return on investment projects can now be explained. Consider this in terms of the formula:

$$S = P = \frac{a_1}{(1 + r)} + \frac{a_2}{(1 + r)^2} + \cdots + \frac{a_n}{(1 + r)^n}$$

from which the internal rate (r) on individual capital goods is calculated.

The factors needed to produce a capital good could alternatively be used to produce a quantity of consumer goods—say a quantity d. The capital good will itself be able, over its life, to produce a certain quantity of consumer goods[1]—say a quantity e. The quantity e will be greater than the quantity d, if the *net* physical productivity of the capital good is positive.

The supply price (S) of the capital good is the sum of the payments which have to be made to the factors to induce them to produce *either* the capital good *or* alternatively the quantity d of consumer goods. Let P_C be the money price level of consumer goods. Then $P_C = \frac{S}{d}$; that is, consumer goods will sell at a price level which equals the total of the payments, which have to be made to factors, *divided by* the number of units of consumer goods which they can produce.

Now suppose that P_C is *expected* to remain *unchanged* in the future. Then the revenues expected to be earned by selling the quantity e of consumer goods, which will be made by the capital good, equal $P_C \cdot e$. That is, $a_1 + a_2 + \ldots + a_n = P_C \cdot e$. It has just been seen that $P_C = \frac{S}{d}$, i.e. that $S = P_C \cdot d$. Hence, since $e > d$, $P_C \cdot e > P_C \cdot d$; which means that $a_1 + a_2 + \ldots + a_n > S$. Thus, the capital good is expected to earn a positive internal rate of return, i.e. $r > 0$.

[1] After allowing for the contributions of the other factors working with it.

An answer has now been provided to the question asked at the beginning of the chapter,[1] namely, how is it possible for the internal rate of return on an investment project to be greater than zero? It is possible, if the *net* physical productivity of the capital good is greater than zero.

But this will *not ensure* that the internal rate is greater than zero, since the expected revenues from the investment depend on the *expected* P_C, as well as on the physical productivity of the capital good. *If*—as assumed above—the expected P_C equals the current P_C, then a positive net physical productivity for the capital good implies that the internal rate of return is greater than zero. But if the P_C is expected to be *lower* in the future, this reduces the expected revenues from the investment. In this case, the internal rate may *not* be greater than zero, despite the fact that the capital good has a positive net physical productivity.

Thus, in general terms, *both* the expected P_C, and the $MNPP_K$, play a part in determining the expected internal rates of return on investment projects. Investors have to attempt to predict P_C before they can compute the expected internal rates. This means attempting to predict the future levels of aggregate demand for goods, upon which the future prices of consumer goods will depend. Pessimistic expectations about aggregate demand will depress the expected internal rates of return, and —given the interest rate—will therefore reduce the number of investment projects which firms expect to be profitable. Hence, a positive $MNPP_K$ is not a sufficient condition for investment to be undertaken; it is also necessary for investors to expect that the outputs of the additional capital goods will be sold at profitable prices.[2]

A positive $MNPP_K$ means that capital accumulation will, if it is undertaken, raise the level of national output. It has now been seen that the *possibility* of economic growth, in this sense, will not of itself ensure that it actually takes place. For growth to occur, investors must expect an adequate level of aggregate *demand* in relation to the larger aggregate *supply*, that capital accumulation makes possible. If they do not expect this, the *potential* economic growth will not be realized.

The interconnections between investment and economic growth therefore depend on the conditions of aggregate demand and aggregate supply. But before this can be analysed, one further matter has to be dealt with. It has to be explained what determines the *rate* of net investment per period of time.

[1] On p. 377 above.
[2] As was not the case, for example, in the early 1930s. The $MNPP_K$ was certainly positive during the Great Depression. But little net investment was undertaken because firms did not expect that they could sell profitably the output of additional capital goods.

THE RATE OF NET INVESTMENT

With modern technology, there are very many capital-using methods of production which are physically more efficient than non-capital-using ones. The production of capital goods requires the use of existing resources which could, alternatively, be used to produce consumer goods. The maximum rate, per period of time, at which net investment can proceed therefore depends on the willingness of the community *not* to use all its existing resources in the production of consumer goods. The larger is the volume of consumption—i.e. the smaller is the volume of saving—which the community wants to undertake, the fewer will be the existing resources which can be devoted to producing capital goods.

It is likely that the quantity of existing resources, which will be available in any year for investment, will be quite small compared with the total quantity required to produce all the capital goods which have positive net physical productivities.[1] Net investment cannot, therefore, proceed at the rate which would quickly accumulate the stock of capital at which $MNPP_K = 0$. It would take many years, even at much higher rates of net investment than are usually found, for a community to raise the stock of capital to the level which maximizes national output. Suppose that the price mechanism works so as to move the economy towards that situation. The question then arises: how will the rate of net investment per period of time be determined? What will determine the speed at which capital is accumulated?

Both the rate of interest, and the prices of capital goods (P_K) *relative* to the prices of consumer goods (P_C), help to determine the rate of net investment. The latter influence will be considered first of all.

If existing resources are fully employed, the level of investment can be increased only if the level of consumption is reduced. Some factors have to be shifted out of the consumer goods industries into the capital goods industries. In order to increase the rate of investment, the latter industries have, therefore, to draw factors away from the former. The marginal cost of capital goods will rise *relatively* to the marginal cost of consumer goods as the output of the former expands and that of the latter contracts.[2] P_K will rise relatively to P_C.

The supply price (S) of a new capital good is given by P_K. The expected capital rentals from it (a_1 to a_n) depend on the *expected* P_C. Suppose that the expected P_C is the *same* as the current P_C. The effect,

[1] Given the size of the labour force, and the state of technology.
[2] A rigorous proof of this proposition is not easy; it depends on the (plausible) assumption that the production functions for capital goods and consumer goods are different. But at least it seems intuitively reasonable.

on the expected internal rates of return on investment projects, of a rise in P_K *relative* to P_C, can now be seen from the discounting formula.[1] As P_K rises relatively to P_C, S rises relatively to a_1 to a_n. Hence, the expected r falls. Thus, as capital goods become more expensive relative to the consumer goods which they are going to produce, it becomes less worthwhile to invest in capital goods. In general, the expected internal rates of return on investment projects *fall* as P_K rises relatively to P_C.

The expected internal rates of return therefore depend on the *rate* of investment per period of time which the community attempts to undertake. To increase the rate of investment, more of the community's factors must be drawn into the capital goods industries. As this takes place, P_K rises relatively to P_C, and the internal rates of return on all investment projects consequently fall. This is one aspect of the way in which the price mechanism controls the *rate* of investment over time.

The relationship between this aspect and the rate of interest can now be seen by means of Fig. 31.1. The rate of investment per period of time is measured on the horizontal axis. An investing firm will always undertake a project with a higher internal rate of return before one with a lower internal rate. Hence, whatever the rate of investment per period happens to be, it will include only the investment projects with the highest internal rates of return at the time.

Consider the rate of investment OE. A particular $\dfrac{P_K}{P_C}$ ratio must exist for this rate of investment to take place, namely, the one at which the capital goods industries will supply the investment goods included in OE. This $\dfrac{P_K}{P_C}$ ratio helps to determine the expected internal rates of return on different projects. The *lowest* internal rate, which is expected from any of the projects included in the OE rate of investment, is measured on the vertical axis of Fig. 31.1. It is usually called the *Marginal Efficiency of Investment* (*MEI*). The *MEI* is the internal rate of return on the *marginal*, or least worthwhile, project included in any rate of investment per period of time.

Suppose that the rate of investment increases from OE to OF. The $\dfrac{P_K}{P_C}$ ratio will therefore rise as the output of the capital goods industries expands. Hence, the internal rates of return on all investment projects fall. In particular, the internal rate on the marginal project included in

[1] On p. 383 above.

OF will be lower than that on the marginal project included in OE. Thus the MEI falls as the rate of investment per period increases.

This is shown by the points Q and R in the diagram. EQ is the MEI of the OE rate of investment: it is the internal rate of return on the marginal project included in OE. Similarly, FR is the MEI of the OF

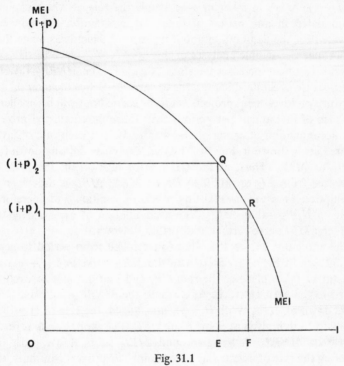

Fig. 31.1

rate of investment. $EQ > FR$ because, as the rate of investment per period increases, $\dfrac{P_K}{P_C}$ rises and the internal rates of return on all projects fall. The MEI curve, showing how the MEI varies with the rate of investment per period of time, is therefore downward sloping to the right.

An investment project is expected to be profitable if $r > i + p$. With $(i + p)$, as well as MEI, measured on the vertical axis of Fig. 31.1, the determination of the rate of investment per period can now be explained. It will be OE per period when $(i + p)$ is at the level $(i + p)_2$. At the point Q on the MEI curve, $(i + p)_2$ equals the r of the *marginal* project (as measured by EQ) in the OE rate of investment. It is therefore just worthwhile to undertake investment at the rate OE. At a greater rate,

MEI will be lower, and therefore some projects will have internal rates of return which are less than $(i + p)_2$.

But if $(i + p)$ falls to $(i + p)_1$, the rate of investment will expand to OF. It is now worthwhile to raise the rate of investment until the r on the marginal project in that rate (as measured by FR) is once again equal to $(i + p)$. A fall in i—or in p—expands the *rate* at which capital is accumulated in any period of time. An explanation has now been provided for the assumption about investment which was made in the earlier macroeconomic analyses of this book.

Net investment increases the stock of capital. The $MNPP_K$ therefore falls because of diminishing returns to capital.[1] Hence the internal rates of return on investment projects yet to be carried out will be smaller (at any rate of investment per period) than those on completed projects. The accumulation of capital *decreases* the *MEI* at each rate of investment. This is shown in Fig. 31.2 by the *MEI* curve shifting down from MEI_1 to MEI_2. Thus, at the OE rate of investment, the *MEI* has decreased from EQ on MEI_1 to ET on MEI_2. MEI_1 is drawn on the assumption of a *smaller* existing stock of capital—and therefore a higher $MNPP_K$—than MEI_2. The accumulation of capital over time shifts the *MEI* curve further and further downwards.

The effect this has on the rate of investment from period to period can be seen in Fig. 31.2. Start with the MEI_1 curve and $(i + p)_2$. Net investment takes place at the rate OE, and that amount of capital is added to the existing stock. As a result, the $MNPP_K$ falls, and MEI_1 shifts down to MEI_2. With $(i + p)_2$ unchanged, the rate of investment now falls to that given at point R on MEI_2. The capital stock is further increased. $MNPP_K$ falls again, and MEI_2 shifts downwards, thus lowering the rate of investment once again. The process continues, with the rate of investment falling over time, as long as $(i + p)_2$ remains unchanged. Finally, the stock of capital reaches the size which gives the MEI_3 curve. Net investment per period is now zero, since there is no project, in the MEI_3 curve, which promises an r greater than $(i + p)_2$.

The fall in the rate of investment, as capital is accumulated,[1] can be postponed by a reduction in i (or p). Thus, if $(i + p)_2$ is reduced to $(i + p)_1$, when MEI_1 shifts down to MEI_2, the rate of investment (at point T) remains unchanged at OE. But as capital continues to accumulate, the rate of investment must ultimately fall. Even if $(i + p)$ falls to zero,[2] net investment will become zero when enough capital has been

---

[1] Given the size of the labour force and the state of technology.

[2] $(i + p)$ cannot be less than zero, since no one will lend at a negative interest rate when he can hold money at a zero interest rate.

accumulated to make $MNPP_K = 0$. There will then remain *no* investment project for which the internal rate of return is greater than zero.

This analysis of the *path*, which the rate of investment follows over time, can now be extended to allow for population growth and for technical progress. If the employed labour force grows at the same rate as the stock of capital, $MNPP_K$ does not change.[1] Suppose, as before,

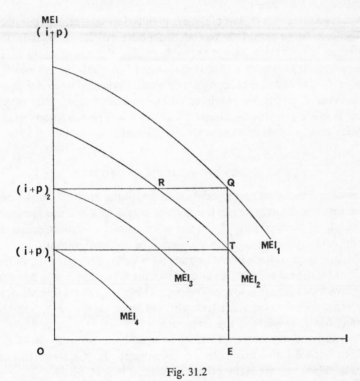

Fig. 31.2

that the expected P_C equals the current P_C. The *MEI* curve therefore does not shift downwards as capital is accumulated. The rate of investment, at a given $(i + p)$, will remain unchanged through time. More and more capital is produced to equip a continually growing labour force.

Technical progress may either increase, or decrease, the size of the capital stock at which $MNPP_K = 0$.[2] It cannot be said, therefore, whether it raises or lowers the $MNPP_K$ of the *existing* capital stock. That is, the effect of technical progress on the *MEI* curve cannot be

[1] See p. 381 above.
[2] See p. 382 above.

predicted. A continual stream of *capital-using* innovations could prevent the $MNPP_K$ from falling as capital is accumulated, and thus stop the *MEI* curve from shifting downwards over time. Or it could even shift the *MEI* curve steadily *upwards* over time, and thus increase the rate of net investment, at a given $(i + p)$, from period to period. We live in a world of rapid technical progress. But we do not yet know if it has this effect on net investment.

Net investment per period of time may thus decrease, remain constant or increase from period to period depending on the changes in the employed labour force and in technology. But the above analyses, in these respects, all assumed that the *expected* P_C equals the *current* P_C. That is, they assumed that aggregate demand is expected to be sufficient, at unchanged prices, to purchase all the increased aggregate supply which is made possible by capital accumulation. The conditions necessary for this to be so must now be investigated.

THE THEORY OF ECONOMIC GROWTH

Investment has a *dual* role in relation to economic growth. On the one hand, net investment increases the stock of capital (K), and this increases the *supply* of national output. On the other hand, investment plus consumption comprise the aggregate *demand* for national output.

The two roles of investment interact with each other. Growth in the supply of national output (X) is only worthwhile if aggregate demand (Z) grows by the same amount. The path which investment follows over time must therefore be consistent with both the supply of X, and the demand for it, growing at the *same* rate.

The study of economic growth must start from an analysis of the relation between the two roles of investment (I). Consider this in physical terms, on the assumption of constant money prices.

The increase in the *supply* of X, which results from an increase in K, depends on the size of the $MNPP_K$. But, as has been seen, the $MNPP_K$ depends on what is happening to the employed labour force, and to the state of technology. Assume, initially, that these remain unchanged. The $MNPP_K$ will then fall as capital is accumulated (because of diminishing returns to capital).

This is illustrated by Table 31.1. The columns 1, 2, and 3 are successive time periods (e.g. years). Net I in period 1 adds to the stock of K which can be used in period 2, and therefore increases the supply of X in period 2 above that in period 1. Similarly, the net I of period 2 increases the K, and the supply of X, of period 3.

TABLE 31.1

	Time periods		
	1	2	3
Net I per period	10	10	10
Stock of K	400	410	420
Supply of X per period	100	102	103

Ten units of the 100 units of X in period 1 go into net I (and therefore 90 units go into C). The stock of K rises from 400 units in period 1 to 410 in period 2. The supply of X is thereby raised from 100 to 102. This means that the $MNPP_K$ per period, of the additional 10 units of K, is 2 units of X. Similarly, the net I of 10 units, in period 2, raises K to 420 units in period 3, and increases the supply of X from 102 to 103 units. The $MNPP_K$ per period, of these 10 additional units of K, is 1 unit of X. The $MNPP_K$ thus *falls* (namely from 2 to 1) as K increases from 400 to 410 to 420 units. This is reflected in the $\dfrac{K}{X}$ ratio *rising* from $\dfrac{400}{100}$ to $\dfrac{410}{102}$ to $\dfrac{420}{103}$. It is taking more K to produce each unit of X.

Net I is constant at 10 units from period to period. Since $MNPP_K$ is falling, the interest rate must also be falling in order to keep net I constant. As was seen above,[1] a falling $MNPP_K$, with given money prices, decreases the MEI for any rate of I, i.e. the MEI curve shifts downwards. The interest rate must therefore fall in order to maintain net I at a constant rate.

Now consider changes in the employed labour force and in the state of technology. A rise in the former increases the $MNPP_K$. Technical progress, if it is capital-using, will also increase the $MNPP_K$. These increases in the $MNPP_K$ offset the fall in it which would result (because of diminishing returns) as the stock of K increases. On balance, the $MNPP_K$ may not change as K increases. This is illustrated by Table 31.2.

The constant net I of 10 units per period increases the stock of K from 400 to 410 to 420 units between the three time periods. The supply of X rises from 100 to 102·5 to 105 units. The $MNPP_K$ per period, of each additional 10 units of K, is constant at 2·5 units of X. This is reflected in the $\dfrac{K}{X}$ ratio remaining constant $\left(\text{i.e. } \dfrac{400}{100} = \dfrac{410}{102\cdot5} = \dfrac{420}{105}\right)$. It is taking the same amount of K to produce each unit of X.

[1] On pp. 388–389.

TABLE 31.2

	Time periods		
	1	2	3
Net I per period	10	10	10
Stock of K	400	410	420
Supply of X per period	100	102·5	105

Net I is constant at 10 units from period to period. The $MNPP_K$ is constant as K increases, because the employed labour force is rising, and/or capital-using technical progress is taking place. Hence, the MEI curve, with given money prices, remains unchanged through time. The interest rate must therefore remain unchanged to keep net I constant from period to period.

Tables 31.1. and 31.2 illustrate the role of I in relation to the *supply* of X. Now consider its role in relation to the *demand* for X. This is illustrated by Table 31.3.

TABLE 31.3

	Time periods		
	1	2	3
Supply of X per period	100	102·5	105
C per period	90	92·5	95
Net I per period	10	10	10

The figures for the supply of X and net I per period are the same as those in Table 31.2, and are based on the same assumptions used in relation to that table. The supply of X rises from 100 to 102·5 to 105 units between the three time periods. The aggregate demand (Z), for the supply of X, is the sum of I and C. I is constant at 10 units per period. Hence, if *all* the X supplied in each period is to be demanded, C must increase from 90 to 92·5 to 95 (as shown in the table). These increases mean a rise in the $\dfrac{C}{Y}$ ratio (the average propensity to consume) from $\dfrac{90}{100}$ to $\dfrac{92·5}{102·5}$ to $\dfrac{95}{105}$. That is, the APC of the community has to rise if Z is to increase at the same rate as the supply of X.

If the *APC* does *not* rise in these circumstances, there will be *insufficient Z* to buy the increasing supply of *X*. Thus, if the *APC* remains constant $\left(\text{namely at } \dfrac{9}{10}\right)$, *C* will expand from 90 to 92·25 to 94·5 as *X* increases from 100 to 102·5 to 105. Adding in the constant net *I* of 10 per period, *Z* will then increase from 100 to 102·25 to 104·5. *Z* is therefore growing more *slowly* than the supply of *X*.

Thus some of the growing *X* will not be sold. This means that the revenues of the firms, which invested in additional capital in order to increase the supply of *X*, are less than was expected. The *actual* capital rentals on the new capital are less than the *expected* capital rentals. The disappointment of the expectations, on which recent investment was based, will probably lead to a downward revision of expected capital rentals from *new* investment projects. That is, investors will now expect *Z* to increase more slowly in the future, than they had previously expected. The resultant downward shift in the *MEI* curve leads, with a given interest rate, to a fall in net *I* per period. The supply of *X* therefore increases more slowly from period to period.

This outcome could, however, be avoided if, with the *APC* constant, net *I* increases from period to period. *Z* would then increase more rapidly than when net *I* is constant. But if net *I* increases from period to period, the stock of *K* and the supply of *X* will also increase more rapidly than when net *I* is constant. The increase in net *I* from period to period has therefore to be such that *both Z* and the supply of *X* increase at the *same* rate. This is illustrated by Table 31.4.[1]

TABLE 31.4

	Time periods		
	1	2	3
Supply of *X* per period	100	102·5	105·06
C per period	90	92·25	94·55
Net *I* per period	10	10·25	10·51
Stock of *K*	400	410	420·25

Net *I* increases from period to period, and does so at a constant rate of $2\frac{1}{2}$ per cent per period. Thus, 10·25 exceeds 10 by $2\frac{1}{2}$ per cent; similarly, 10·51 is $2\frac{1}{2}$ per cent greater than 10·25. The stock of *K* increases at the same rate, from period to period, as does net *I*, i.e. $2\frac{1}{2}$ per cent per period.

[1] In which the figures are rounded to the second decimal place.

The $MNPP_K$ is assumed to be constant, as K increases, because the employed labour force is rising and/or technical progress is taking place. The stock of capital is increasing more rapidly, in Table 31.4, than it was in Table 31.2 above. Table 31.4 therefore requires more rapid growth in the employed labour force and/or in technical progress, than did Table 31.2, in order to keep $MNPP_K$ constant. With the latter assumption, the supply of X increases at the same rate as the stock of K, i.e. $2\frac{1}{2}$ per cent per period, and the $\frac{K}{X}$ ratio remains constant.

The APC is assumed constant $\left(\text{namely at } \frac{9}{10}\right)$. C therefore increases at the same rate as X, i.e. $2\frac{1}{2}$ per cent per period.

X, C, I, and K in Table 31.4 are *all* growing at the same rate of $2\frac{1}{2}$ per cent per period. Hence $Z \,(\equiv C + I)$ grows at the same rate as the supply of X. As the figures show, there is sufficient aggregate demand to buy all that is produced in each period.

The significant point, about the situation portrayed in Table 31.4, is the consistency between the *two* roles of investment. The increasing net I raises the level of Z. It also, by increasing the stock of K, raises the supply of X. Given the assumptions on which Table 31.4 is based, an increase in net I, by $2\frac{1}{2}$ per cent per period, will make Z, and the supply of X, both increase at the same rate. This growth rate will be sustained, since firms are able to sell all of their increasing outputs. But if net I increases by *less* than $2\frac{1}{2}$ per cent per period, Z will grow more *slowly* than the supply of X. Firms will not sell all of their increasing outputs. Growth will not then be sustained.

The analysis illustrated by Table 31.4 is the starting point of the theory of economic growth. It is generally known as the 'Harrod-Domar model'.[1] Its properties can now be put in a general form.

The $MNPP_K$ is taken as constant: each additional unit of K (ΔK) is assumed to increase X by the same amount (ΔX). Hence, the ratio $\frac{\Delta K}{\Delta X}$ is a constant, which is usually symbolized by v. Thus, in Tables 31.2 to 31.4, each additional 10 units of K increase X by 2·5 units, so that $\frac{\Delta K}{\Delta X} = 4$. $\frac{\Delta K}{\Delta X} = v$ can be rewritten as $\Delta K = v \, . \, \Delta X$, or again as $I = v \, . \, \Delta X$, since net I means the same thing as ΔK. Thus the requirement that net I equal a constant multiple (v) of the *increase* in X

---

[1] After Sir Roy Harrod and Professor E. D. Domar who developed it, independently and in somewhat different forms, just after the Second World War.

is another way[1] of expressing the assumption that the $MNPP_K$ is constant.

The average propensity to consume (c) is also taken as constant. Hence, $\dfrac{C}{X} = c$, and $C = c \cdot X$. Thus, in Table 31.4, the APC is constant at $\dfrac{9}{10}$, so that C is always nine-tenths of the corresponding X.

The two basic assumptions of the analysis—that $\dfrac{\Delta K}{\Delta X}$, and the APC, are both constant—are now combined with the equilibrium condition for X. In equilibrium, the aggregate supply of goods (X) equals the aggregate demand for them (Z), which is made up of C and I. On the above assumptions, $C = c \cdot X$, and $I = v \cdot \Delta X$. Hence, for X to be in equilibrium, $X = c \cdot X + v \cdot \Delta X$. This can be re-written as $X(1 - c) = v \cdot \Delta X$, which gives the solution[2] $\dfrac{\Delta X}{X} = \dfrac{1 - c}{v}$. The term $\dfrac{1 - c}{v}$ is a constant, since both c and v are constants. Hence, $\dfrac{\Delta X}{X} = \dfrac{1 - c}{v}$ states that, for X to be in equilibrium in every period of time, is has to increase at the constant rate $\dfrac{1 - c}{v}$ from period to period. If this *rate of increase* in X is sustained, $X = C + I$ at all times.

This conclusion was illustrated by the earlier arithmetic. Thus, in Table 31.4, v has a constant value of 4 (e.g. 10 units of I, in period 1, increase X by 2·5 units in period 2); and c has a constant value of $\dfrac{9}{10}$ $\left(\text{e.g. } \dfrac{C}{Y} = \dfrac{90}{100} \text{ in period 1}\right)$. Hence, $\dfrac{1 - c}{v} = \dfrac{1}{10} \Big/ 4 = \dfrac{1}{40}$, which is converted into percentage terms by multiplying by 100. Thus, $\dfrac{1}{40} \cdot 100 = 2\frac{1}{2}$ per cent. As was seen above, X must increase by $2\frac{1}{2}$ per cent per period in order to keep $X = C + I$ at all times.

The Harrod-Domar model brought to light the central problem of economic growth, namely, under what conditions will Z, and the supply of X, grow at the *same* rate? It gives *one* set of conditions in which the growth of X can be sustained. The model is, of course, a highly simplified

---

[1] This relationship between I and ΔX is called the *Acceleration Principle*, because it makes I dependent on the *rate of change* of X.

[2] Which can also be written $\dfrac{\Delta X}{X} = \dfrac{s}{v}$, where s ($\equiv 1 - c$) is the average propensity to save.

picture of economic growth. Moreover, the constant $MNPP_K$ and the constant APC, assumed by it, seem unlikely to hold true over time. Nevertheless, like all advances in any subject, the model clarifies the nature of a *problem*, as well as providing one possible solution to it. The model has therefore been the starting point for enquiries into such questions as (1) whether there are other conditions in which the growth of national output can be sustained, and (2) what will happen if the growth of national output is disturbed by changes in the economy.[1] These important problems must, however, be left to more advanced study.

[1] This question leads into the problem of the Trade (or Business) Cycle, namely the fluctuations in national output which have been a prominent feature of industrialized economies.

CHAPTER 32

GOVERNMENT

The effects of government[1] economic activity on the overall working of the price mechanism were described by means of Fig. 5.4 in Chapter 5.[2] Those effects will now be analysed in terms of the conditions of aggregate demand and aggregate supply. It will then be seen how the actions of government can affect the levels of the national output (X) and prices (P).

Government expenditure has to be classified under two heads, namely (i) expenditure on *goods and services* (e.g. defence, education, hospitals), and (ii) expenditure in creating *transfer incomes* (e.g. social security benefits, like unemployment benefit and retirement pensions). The former is a demand for the productive services of some of the community's resources. In employing, for example, civil servants, teachers, and doctors, and in buying, for example, school and medical supplies from the private sector, government expenditure directly calls forth some national output, and at the same time creates *factor* incomes for the people who produce that output. This form of government expenditure may be either on 'collective consumption' goods and services, or on capital goods (e.g. investment in roads).

On the other hand, government expenditure on *transfer incomes* is not, in itself, a demand for productive services: it does not directly call forth any national output. What it does is to provide *personal* income to the unemployed, the retired, etc., who are not supplying any productive services at the time. It is only when the recipients of transfer incomes spend them on goods, that some national output will be called forth. Not all of the transfer incomes may be spent on goods; some may be saved. Hence, not even indirectly will the whole of government expenditure on transfer incomes necessarily lead to a demand for national output.

Government revenue from taxation has to be classified according to its effects on the private sector. The taxes on personal incomes reduce

[1] The term 'government' covers *all* the public authorities; in the case of the UK it includes the central government, the local authorities, and the National Insurance Scheme.
[2] On pp. 47–49 above. It is strongly recommended that the reader refresh his memory of the details, and of Fig. 5.4, before proceeding.

the amounts of them which are at the disposal of households for consumption and saving. The taxes (e.g. corporation tax) on company incomes reduce the amounts of profits which are at the disposal of companies for the payment of dividends to their shareholders and for business saving.

The decisions of households, as to how much to spend on consumption, will depend on the sizes—both current and expected—of their personal incomes *after* the payment of income taxes, i.e. on personal *disposable* incomes. The total of personal incomes (before tax) is made up of wages, salaries, and the interest, rents, and dividends which go to households, and of transfer incomes. This total thus depends on *both* the amount of corporation tax paid by companies, and the amount of business saving (viz. undistributed profits). The higher the rate of corporation tax, and the greater the rate at which businesses want to retain profits as a source of finance to themselves, the smaller will be the proportion of total profits which is distributed to households in dividends. Thus the government can influence the total of personal *disposable* incomes in two ways by means of income taxes. By changing the rate of corporation tax, it will probably alter the proportion of profits which is paid out in dividends; and by changing the rates of personal income taxes, it will alter the total of personal incomes which is at the disposal of households.

But personal income comprises not only *factor* incomes in the form of wages, salaries, interest, rents, and dividends. It also includes *transfer* incomes. Hence the government can alter the total of personal disposable income, not only by changing income tax rates, but also by changing the rates at which it pays out transfer incomes (e.g. the rate of unemployment benefit).

Outlay taxes on goods have already been analysed at the microeconomic level in Chapter 15.[1] It was there seen that they raise the *supply* prices, of the taxed goods, above what they would otherwise have been. Outlay subsidies—which can be regarded as negative outlay taxes—have the reverse effect.

Taxes on capital (e.g. death duties) reduce personal wealth, which is one of the influences determining the level of consumption.

TAXES AND TRANSFER INCOMES

The conditions of aggregate demand and aggregate supply, as used in the analyses of earlier chapters, relate only to the *private* sector of the

[1] On pp. 169–172 above.

economy. They must now be extended to allow for government economic activity. In order to do this, it will be well to recall, by means of Fig. 32.1, the meanings of the aggregate supply (Y), and the aggregate demand (Z), curves *as used so far*.

Consider the information given by any point on each curve, e.g. by point Q (on Y), and point R (on Z). Firms in aggregate are willing to

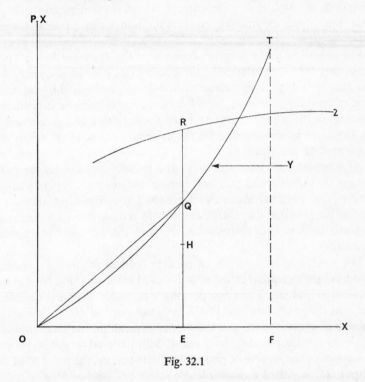

Fig. 32.1

supply, at a given money wage rate, the national output OE if they expect to get a total revenue of EQ from the sale of it. The price level at which the output OE will be offered for sale (i.e. its *supply-P*) is given by the slope of OQ. The total of wage (and salary) incomes earned at this level of national output equals the level of employment (N) multiplied by the average money wage rate (W). The wage bill ($W . N$), at the national output OE, is shown by EH. Expected profits[1] therefore equal HQ.

Total personal income is made up of the actual money wage income

---

[1] Which, as earlier, are defined here to include interest and rents.

EH, and the expected money profit income HQ. This assumes that all profits will be distributed in dividends. That personal income, in relation to the *supply-P* of the output OE (viz. the slope of OQ), gives the *real* income of the community. The volume of consumption, at this real income, depends on the personal attributes and the real wealth of households, and on the distribution of income. This volume of consumption, multiplied by the price level of consumer goods (P_C), gives the *money expenditure* on consumption when national output is OE.

The *volume* of net investment depends on the *Marginal Efficiency of Investment* (MEI) in relation to the interest rate plus an allowance for uncertainty ($i + p$). This volume of investment, multiplied by the price level of capital goods (P_K), gives the *money expenditure* on investment. The sum of the money expenditures on consumption and investment is the aggregate money demand for the national output OE. It equals ER at point R on the Z curve.

Now consider the effects of taxes and transfer incomes on the positions of the points R and Q. The volume of consumption depends on the total of real personal *disposable* incomes. The government affects the amount of personal disposable incomes in money terms by means of personal income tax, corporation tax, and the payment of transfer incomes.

The levying of income tax on persons reduces the *money* personal income at their disposal below what it would otherwise have been at the national output OE. Their *real* personal disposable income is therefore lower at the given supply-P of OE (viz. the slope of OQ). Hence, the volume of consumption, and the money expenditure on consumption, will be lower.[1] Aggregate money demand for national output is reduced as a result of the levying of personal income tax, i.e. the point R, at the output OE, is shifted downwards.

The levying of corporation tax has a similar effect. It reduces the amount of profits available for the payment of dividends to persons. Their real personal disposable income may therefore be less than it would otherwise have been. It can also be seen that business saving has the same effect. Because some amount of profits (after corporation tax is paid) is not distributed in dividends, the incomes at the disposal of persons are not as high as they would otherwise have been.

---

[1] The *structure* of income tax rates is important in this respect. The proportions of disposable incomes spent on consumption are different as between income levels. The extent to which consumption is reduced by a given total of income tax will therefore depend on how the payment of it is distributed between the different income gro ups.

Taxes on capital (e.g. death duties) reduce the real wealth of households, and therefore decrease the *volume* of consumption. This shifts the point *R* downwards.

The payment of transfer incomes has the reverse effect to that of income taxes, since the former increase personal disposable incomes in money terms. The volume of, and the money expenditure on, consumption are higher on this account. The point *R*, at the national output *OE*, is shifted upwards as a result of the receipt of transfer incomes.

Corporation tax is levied on the capital rentals (viz. profits) earned from the use of capital goods. The worthwhileness of investment projects will therefore depend on the sizes of the expected capital rentals *after* the payment of this tax: investors will compare the expected internal rates of return, *net* of corporation tax, with $i + p$. Corporation tax therefore decreases the *MEI* at each rate of investment.[1] With a given $i + p$, the volume of, and the money expenditure on, investment will be reduced. The point *R*, at the national output *OE*, is therefore shifted downwards. Corporation tax thus reduces aggregate money demand by decreasing both consumption and investment.

Income taxes, capital taxes, and transfer incomes mainly affect the condition of aggregate demand in the short period. The condition of aggregate supply will, however, be altered insofar as the payment of income taxes, and the receipt of social security benefits, affect the quantity supplied of labour, and the money wage rate. The willingness to work, as against the taking of leisure, may be altered by income taxes and social security benefits. The periodic claims by trade unions, for higher money wage rates, may be influenced by changes in income tax rates. In the longer run, the growth of aggregate supply will depend on the effect that a corporation tax has on the rate of net investment.

Outlay taxes alter the condition of aggregate supply.[2] Suppose that the government levies a 'sales tax' on all finished goods in the form of a uniform percentage of their selling prices. The *supply-P* of the national output *OE*, in Fig. 32.1 (viz. the slope of *OQ*), will then be increased by that percentage. Firms will require the prices of their goods to cover not only their costs (including profit), but also the sales tax. The expected total revenue, which is now necessary to induce the firms to produce the national output *OE*, will exceed *EQ* by the percentage level of the sales tax. The point *Q* shifts upwards.

The rise in the supply-*P* of the output *OE* reduces the *real* personal

---

[1] I.e. it shifts the whole *MEI* curve downwards.

[2] Just as at the microeconomic level (as shown by Fig. 15.4 on p. 170 above) they alter the supply conditions of individual goods.

disposable incomes of the community. The total of personal disposable incomes in *money* terms (Y^d), which is earned when national output is *OE*, will now only buy a smaller quantity of goods. This fall in *real* incomes reduces the *volume* of consumption. Outlay taxes thus affect the condition of aggregate demand, as well as that of aggregate supply.

The effect of the sales tax on the total of *money* expenditure on consumption, at the national output *OE*, depends on the extent to which the volume of consumption is reduced. The supply-P_C has risen by the percentage amount of the sales tax. If the volume of consumption falls by the same percentage, the total money expenditure on consumption is unchanged. This will happen only if the *Average Propensity to Consume* $\left(\text{i.e. the } APC, \text{ which equals } \dfrac{C}{Y^d}\right)$ is constant over the range of *real* income in question. With $\dfrac{C}{Y^d}$ constant, the level of *money* expenditure on consumption, at a *given* Y^d, remains constant as real income falls. But if the *APC* is larger at *lower* levels of real income, the money expenditure on consumption, at the national output *OE*, will increase when the supply-P_C is raised by the sales tax. This is so, because $\dfrac{C}{Y^d}$ will increase when the real value of the given Y^d is reduced by the rise in the supply-P_C. Point *R*, in Fig. 32.1, then shifts upwards—but by *less* than point *Q*. It has been seen that the latter shifts up by the percentage amount of the sales tax. Point *R* shifts up by the amount of the increase in the money expenditure on consumption. This is less than the percentage rise in the supply-P_C (as a result of the sales tax), since the volume of consumption has decreased.

The sales tax on capital goods raises the supply-P_K. If the *expected* P_C rises in the same proportion, expected internal rates of return on investment projects are not affected.[1] The *volume* of investment, at a given $i + p$, will be unchanged. But, as was seen at the microeconomic level,[2] the market prices of goods are unlikely to rise by the full amounts of the outlay taxes imposed on them. Hence, investors may well not revise the *expected* P_C upwards to the full extent of the sales tax. In that case, the *MEI* will decrease, and the *volume* of investment will fall. But the level of *money* expenditure on investment can increase, remain constant, or decrease—according to the extent of the decrease in the volume of investment relative to the rise in the supply-P_K. It cannot,

[1] As was explained on pp. 306–307 above.
[2] On pp. 170–171 above.

therefore, be said in general how the effect of the sales tax on investment will affect point R in Fig. 32.1.

Thus, outlay taxes affect both the conditions of aggregate supply and aggregate demand. The point Q (on the Y curve) is shifted up by the percentage amount of the outlay taxes. The point R (on Z) may be shifted up or down, or remain unchanged, depending on the extents of the decreases in the *volumes* of consumption and investment. However, R will not shift upwards, if it does so, by as much as Q does—because the volumes of consumption and investment have fallen.

The effects of income taxes, capital taxes, transfer incomes, and outlay taxes, on aggregate demand and aggregate supply, have been explained in relation to one point (R) on the Z curve, and one point (Q) on the Y curve. The same analysis applies to all the other points on both the curves. The main conclusions of the above analyses can therefore be summarized in the following way.

The *rates* at which the taxes on incomes, capital, and outlay are levied, and the *rates* at which transfer incomes are paid, are *parameters* of the Z and Y curves. If these rates are changed by the government, the Z, and/or Y, curves will shift their positions.

Thus, if the rates of personal income tax are increased, the total of personal disposable incomes in money terms will be lower at *any* level of national output. Expenditure on consumption will therefore be lower at *any* level of national output. The Z curve shifts downwards (i.e. decreases). An increase in capital taxes, by causing a greater decrease in the wealth of households, has the same effect.

If the rates of company income tax (corporation tax) are increased, the *MEI net* of tax is decreased. Expenditure on investment will therefore be lower at *any* level of national output. The Z curve shifts downwards.

If the government increases the rates at which social security benefits are paid, transfer incomes, and therefore the total of personal disposable incomes, will be higher at *any* level of national output. Expenditure on consumption will, therefore, be higher at *any* level of national output. The Z curve shifts upwards (i.e. increases).

If the rates of outlay taxes are increased, the supply-P of national output will be higher at *any* level of national output. The Y curve shifts upwards (i.e. decreases). The rise in the supply-P decreases the volumes of consumption and investment at *any* level of national putput. But the *money* expenditures on consumption and investment may decrease, increase, or remain constant at *each* level of national output—depending on the extents of the decreases in the volumes of consumption and investment relative to the rises in P_C and P_K. The Z curve can, therefore, shift downwards or upwards, or remain unchanged.

EXPENDITURE ON GOODS

The remaining element to be taken into account in government economic activity is its expenditure on goods and services. The government provides collective consumption goods and services (e.g. defence), and capital goods (e.g. new roads) to the community. But it does not charge any prices for their use.[1]

Some of these goods and services (e.g. school and medical supplies) are bought by the government from firms in the private sector. The condition of *supply* for them is, therefore, already allowed for in the Y curve. The supply-P at any point on that curve shows the price at which firms will sell units of national output to the government as well as to the private sector.

But the government itself produces most of the services which it provides to the community. This is what it employs civil servants, teachers, doctors, etc., to do. Thus, it is supplying its own demand for these services—which it then provides free of charge to the community. Consequently, there is no market *supply price* for the government's output. Nevertheless, it has a marginal cost in exactly the same sense as the output of the private sector. That MC is given by the marginal physical product of government employees in relation to their average money wage rate. The implied supply price of government output is its MC.

The Y curve must now be interpreted to relate to the *sum* of the outputs of the government and the private sector. National output is produced jointly by the public and the private sectors. The MC of government output in the short period is likely, like that of the private sector, to rise as national output increases. Hence the Y curve, now interpreted to include government output, will have the same shape as heretofore.

Government expenditure on goods and services (symbolized by G) is a demand for some of the productive services of the community's resources. Like C and I, G is an element in the aggregate *demand* for national output. That is, $Z \equiv C + I + G$. Hence, each point on the Z curve must now be interpreted to include the money expenditure on G, as well as on C and I, at the national output in question.

The *volume* of G depends on the government's social and military policies. In the long run, most governments increase the volume of G

[1] With quite minor exceptions.

as national output rises.[1] But in the short period, the relation between the volume of G and national output is less certain. On that account, the volume of G will be taken as a *constant* (given by public policy) in drawing any particular Z curve. It will not vary as national output changes,[2] as for example, the volume of consumption does when national output changes. That is, it will be treated as a parameter of the Z curve. Hence, if government policy changes, and the volume of G is increased, the Z curve shifts upwards. If the volume of G is decreased, the Z curve shifts downwards.

BUDGETARY CHANGES

The Z and Y curves can be used to analyse the effects which the different elements in government economic activity have on the levels of national output and prices. However, many governments throughout the world now manipulate these elements *in relation to one another* so as to achieve certain objectives. The most important objectives, at the macroeconomic level, are usually the maintenance of the *full employment* of resources, the *stability* of the price level, and *steady growth* in national output.[3]

The manipulation of the various elements in government expenditure and revenue from taxation constitutes its *budgetary* (or fiscal) policy. It will be most convenient to consider the effects of those elements within the context of *overall* budgetary policy. The ways in which they influence national output and the price level can then be understood, not only in isolation, but also in relation to the government's pursuit of full employment, price stability, and economic growth.

These objectives may conflict with one another to some extent. This possibility must be taken into account in any analysis of *budgetary policy*. But the latter is not the only economic policy weapon at the disposal of governments: they can also use *monetary policy*. Moreover, some governments now attempt to control the rate at which money wage rates change over time. This is known (in the UK) as a *national incomes policy*. These three forms of macroeconomic policy have to be analysed as *complementary* measures to promote full employment, price stability, and economic growth.

First consider the use of budgetary policy in relation to the promotion

[1] Often in proportionate, as well as in absolute terms.

[2] This means, however, that the *money* expenditure on G rises as national output increases, since the supply-P of X rises as X increases. This has to be allowed for in the *shape* of the Z curve.

[3] The state of the country's balance of payments may also be taken into account, as will be seen in Part IV below.

of full employment and the avoidance of *demand* inflation. In Fig. 32.2*a*, the Z_1 curve intersects (point T) the Y curve at the full employment (OF) level of national output. There is neither excess aggregate supply which would lead to unemployment, nor excess aggregate demand which would lead to demand inflation. Z_1 is therefore the condition of aggregate demand which, in relation to the Y curve, budgetary policy should aim to bring about.

But suppose that at the ruling rates of taxation, transfer incomes,

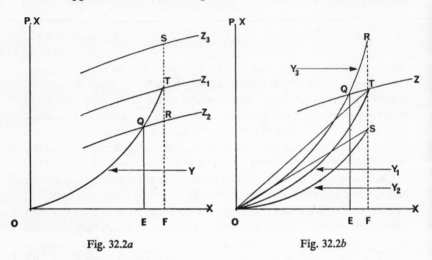

Fig. 32.2*a*   Fig. 32.2*b*

and government expenditure on goods, aggregate demand is given by the Z_2 curve. There is excess aggregate supply (RT) at the output OF. The equilibrium output (point Q) is OE, at which some resources are unemployed. The government can change one or more of the elements in its budgetary policy in order to shift Z_2 up to Z_1, and so promote full employment. The earlier analyses of this chapter have shown what budgetary changes will do this.

If the *rates* of personal income tax are reduced, or the *rates* of social security benefits (viz. transfer incomes) are increased, the total of personal disposable incomes in money terms, at the national output OE (and at any other output), is increased. The volume of consumption, and the money expenditure on it, increase at the output OE (and at any other output). Z_2 shifts upwards.[1] The same effect will result from a

[1] The same kind of effect can be achieved by a reduction in the rates of capital taxes. But these are relatively so unimportant in magnitude, that even their complete abolition would have little effect on Z_2.

reduction in the rate of company income tax (corporation tax). Companies will probably now distribute more profits in dividends, which means an increase in personal disposable incomes. Moreover, the reduction in corporation tax will increase the *MEI after* tax.[1] This will increase the rate of investment, and so help to shift Z_2 upwards. Finally, an increase in the government's own expenditure (G) on goods and services will shift Z_2 upwards.

The increase in aggregate demand, at the national output OE in Fig. 32.2a, resulting from *any* of the above budgetary changes, will lead to a multiplier process. The initial rise in aggregate demand following upon the budgetary change—irrespective of whether it is in C or I or G—raises the level of national output. The total of personal disposable incomes increases as national output rises. Expenditure on consumption therefore *expands*. This expands aggregate demand, and therefore national output, once again; and so on, in the multiplier process as already explained.[2] It follows that, in aiming to raise national output from OE to OF, the government must take into account the multiplier effects of its budgetary change. That is, it has to predict the magnitude of the budgetary change, which *together with* its multiplier effects, will just eliminate the excess aggregate supply of RT at the national output OF. Although any of the changes discussed above will bring the multiplier into operation, its size, however, is likely to differ from one kind of budgetary change to another.[3]

Now suppose that at the ruling rates of taxation, transfer incomes, and government expenditure on goods, aggregate demand is given by the Z_3 curve in Fig. 32.2a. There is excess aggregate demand (TS) at the national output OF. The price level will therefore rise above the supply-P (given by the slope of OT), unless budgetary policy is changed so as to shift Z_3 down to Z_1. Budgetary changes, which are the reverse of those needed to eliminate unemployment, will do this. Increases in the *rates* of personal and company income tax, decreases in the *rates* of social security benefits, and a reduction in government expenditure (G) on goods can be used singly, or in combination, to eliminate the excess aggregate demand.

An appropriate combination of the above elements in budgetary policy can thus bring about the Z_1 condition of aggregate demand, with which there will be neither unemployment nor demand inflation.

---

[1] This could also be brought about by the payment of subsidies on the purchase of new capital goods (as has been the case—in a selective fashion—in the UK in recent years). The consequential reduction in the supply prices of capital goods increases *MEI*.

[2] On pp. 293–298 above.

[3] For reasons which are analysed in more advanced texts.

Changes in the *rates* of outlay taxes can be used to the same end. They operate in a different way, however, from changes in income tax rates. Thus, an increase in outlay tax rates raises the supply-P at any level of national output: the Y curve is shifted upwards. The total of personal disposable incomes in *money* terms is not affected by the increase in outlay tax rates. But *real* disposable incomes are reduced. Hence, the Z curve may also shift—depending on the magnitudes of the decreases in the *volumes* of consumption and investment. For brevity—and simplicity in drawing a diagram—it will be assumed that the Z curve does not shift.[1] This will be sufficient to establish the qualitative principles of the analysis.

Consider the matter with the help of Fig. 32.2b. With the Y_2 and Z curves, there is excess aggregate demand (ST) at the full employment (OF) level of national output. The price level will therefore be competed above the supply-P (given by the slope of OS), unless budgetary policy is changed.

An appropriate increase in the rates of outlay taxes will shift Y_2 up to Y_1. This raises the price level from the supply-P at point S (viz. the slope of OS) to the supply-P at point T (viz. the slope of OT). But it eliminates the excess aggregate demand. That is, it prevents the price level from being competed up *any further*. It is this that explains the seeming paradox of eliminating demand inflation by budgetary action which raises the price level. The excess aggregate demand of ST (with the Y_2 curve) means that the community wants to buy a larger *quantity* of goods than the output OF. The increase in outlay tax rates raises the price level, but leaves the total of personal disposable incomes in *money* terms unchanged. *Real* incomes fall and the quantity demanded of goods is reduced. Hence, the *excess quantity* demanded is eliminated.[2]

The contrast between the use of increases in the rates of income taxes, and in the rates of outlay taxes, to eliminate demand inflation, can now be seen. The former decrease aggregate *real* demand by reducing *money* disposable incomes in relation to the price level. The latter do so by raising the price level in relation to money disposable incomes. *Real* incomes are reduced in both cases—but by different methods.

Now suppose that aggregate supply is initially given by Y_3 in Fig. 32.2b. There is excess aggregate supply (RT) at the national output OF. The equilibrium output (point Q) is OE, at which some resources are

---

[1] Which means that the *volume* of consumption plus investment decreases in the same proportion as the supply-P rises: see pp. 402–403 above.

[2] If Z shifts (either up or down), when Y_2 shifts up to Y_1, the magnitude of the rise in the price level will be different from that in Fig. 32.2b. But the analysis still follows the same lines as that in the text.

unemployed. An appropriate reduction in the *rates* of outlay taxes will shift Y_3 down to Y_1: the supply-P falls at each level of national output. Personal disposable incomes in *money* terms are unchanged at the output *OE*. *Real* incomes are therefore increased, and the *volume* of consumption increases.[1] This brings the multiplier into operation, and national output rises from *OE* to *OF* (point *T*, where Y_1 and *Z* intersect).

Thus, an appropriate level of outlay tax rates can bring about the conditions of aggregate supply (Y_1) and aggregate demand (*Z*), with which there be neither unemployment nor demand inflation.

MACROECONOMIC POLICIES

Budgetary changes alter the level of aggregate money expenditure which the community wants to undertake. This alters the quantity demanded of money. If *monetary policy* is kept unchanged in these circumstances— i.e. if the quantity supplied of money is kept constant—the rate of interest will alter. Thus, if tax rates are reduced or government expenditure increased, so as to raise national output and the level of employment, the rising money expenditure increases the quantity demanded of money. With the quantity supplied of money constant, there will now be excess demand for it, and the interest rate will rise.[2]

In the first instance, this will be caused by the change in the balance between total government expenditure and total revenue from taxation. Suppose that initially the former exactly equals the latter, i.e. the government's budget is 'balanced'. A decrease in tax rates, and/or increase in government expenditure, puts the budget into 'deficit', i.e. total expenditure now exceeds total tax revenue. The government has to borrow—by selling newly created bonds—to finance the deficit. It must therefore compete with other borrowers in the financial markets. It is the increased demand for finance by the government which initiates the rise in the interest rate.

That rise will decrease the volume of investment (and maybe consumption as well). This decrease in money expenditure by the private sector will *partly* offset the expansionary effects on national output of the budgetary changes.[3] The attempt to promote a higher level of employment by means of *budgetary policy* is thus thwarted to some extent by the unchanged *monetary policy*. This can be avoided, of course, if the

---

[1] The volume of investment may also increase; see pp. 402–403 above.

[2] As explained on pp. 363–364 above.

[3] The offset is only partial, since investment (and consumption) will only be reduced if the interest rate rises, and it will rise only if there is *some* increase in aggregate money expenditure.

quantity supplied of money is increased at the same time as the budgetary changes.

It is essential, therefore, not to confuse changes in *budgetary* policy with those in *monetary* policy. This can be seen in terms of the following three situations: (i) an increase in the supply of money—brought about by central bank open market operations[1]—which is *not* accompanied by any budgetary changes; (ii) tax rate decreases, and/or government expenditure increases, which are *not* accompanied by any change in the supply of money; and (iii) the same budgetary changes as in (ii) which *are* this time accompanied by an increase in the supply of money. The effects on the levels of national output and employment will be *different* as between these three situations.

In (i), the interest rate falls and this increases investment (and maybe consumption). The extent of the consequent increase in national output, through a multiplier process, depends on the responsiveness of investment (and consumption) to the fall in the interest rate. In (ii), the budgetary changes increase consumption, and/or investment, and/or government expenditure on goods and services. National output increases through a multiplier process. But the interest rate rises (because the supply of money is constant), and the consequent fall in investment (and maybe consumption) prevents national output from increasing as much as it would otherwise have done. In (iii), the supply of money can be increased so as to prevent the interest rate from rising and thereby reducing investment (and consumption). The increase in national output will, therefore, be greater than in (ii).

Budgetary and monetary policies can therefore be treated either as alternative or as complementary measures for raising national output and the level of employment—or of eliminating demand inflation. The level of aggregate money expenditure, in conditions of excess aggregate supply, can be raised by tax rate decreases and/or government expenditure increases, or by an increase in the supply of money which lowers the interest rate, or by some combination of both sets of measures. And the reverse changes, or combination of changes, can be used to reduce the level of aggregate money expenditure in conditions of excess aggregate demand.

A variety of considerations are relevant to the choice of the combination of changes in budgetary and monetary policies to be used in any particular situation. A change in the interest rate, brought about by a change in the supply of money, probably has a relatively greater effect on investment than on consumption. Budgetary changes can also affect

[1] As explained on p. 357 above.

investment, e.g. by changes in the rate of corporation tax, and in subsidies granted on new capital goods, and in the government's own expenditure on investment (e.g. roads, schools). But budgetary changes can be used especially to alter consumption, e.g. by changes in income and outlay tax rates, in transfer incomes, and in the government's own expenditure on collective consumption goods and services. Investment helps to determine the rate of growth of national output by increasing the stock of capital. Hence the combination of budgetary and monetary changes chosen will depend, because of their effects on the ratio between consumption and investment, on government policy with respect to economic growth.

However, investment usually responds rather slowly to monetary and budgetary changes. Investment projects already under construction, or even in a late stage of planning, are seldom abandoned. A reduction in the rate of investment therefore depends on how quickly existing projects are completed, as well as on a decrease in new projects. Similarly, an increase in the rate of investment will be delayed by the need to plan and execute new investment decisions. On the other hand, a change in consumption can probably be brought about more quickly by means of a change in real disposable incomes. Hence, if a change in aggregate money expenditure is thought to be urgently needed, budgetary policy —through its effects on consumption—would be a more effective weapon than monetary policy.

But this depends, of course, on the relative speeds with which monetary and budgetary changes can be made. The central bank can change the quantity of money from day to day: monetary policy is a flexible weapon in this respect. It is, however, subject to the limitations which have already been discussed.[1] Changes in budgetary policy depend on the machinery of government. Delays in legislating on taxes and government expenditure make budgetary policy an inflexible weapon. That is why, in recent years, budgetary changes in the UK have ceased to be restricted to the traditional annual Budget day.

However, the maintenance of full employment and the avoidance of *demand* inflation, by means of monetary and budgetary policies, will not necessarily ensure the stability of the general price level. *Cost* inflation will still occur if the trade unions are successful in raising money wage rates from period to period more rapidly than the average rate at which labour productivity is rising. It has already been seen[2] that a restrictive monetary policy can, by raising the level of unemployment, eliminate the

[1] On pp. 373–375 above.
[2] On p. 375 above.

cost inflation. Budgetary policy can be used to the same end. But this involves a conflict between the objectives of full employment and price stability.

Modern industrial economies do seem to be prone to cost inflation at (and near) the full employment level of national output. Some govern-

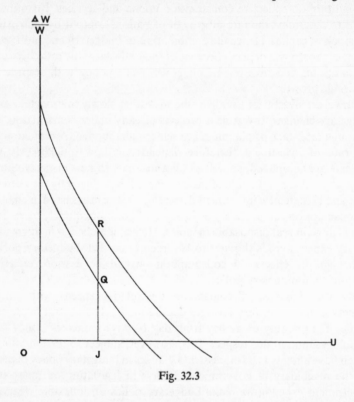

Fig. 32.3

ments—especially post-war ones in the UK—have therefore attempted to develop *national incomes policies*, through which the rate of increase in money wage rates can be constrained. In that way, they hope to resolve in time the conflict between the objectives of full employment and price stability.

An incomes policy can be regarded as an attempt to shift the Phillips Curve[1] for the economy downwards to the left. This is shown by means of the two Phillips Curves in Fig. 32.3. Suppose that the higher curve is shifted downwards to the left to the position of the lower one. The rate

[1] See pp. 314–316 above.

of increase in money wage rates, per period of time, is now smaller at each level of unemployment, e.g. it is JQ, rather than JR, at the unemployment rate OJ. There will always be some amount of 'frictional' unemployment, namely people moving between jobs. Hence, the problem for a national incomes policy is to shift the Phillips Curve so that, at full employment (after allowing for frictional unemployment[1]), the rate of increase in money wage rates per period does not exceed the average rate of growth of labour productivity.

Shifting the Phillips Curve means that the government must intervene in the collective bargains between trade unions and employers' associations. It can attempt to influence them by persuasion and/or legislation. In either case, the government gets involved in the rival strategies of the two parties.[2] Ultimately, the success of its intervention will depend on (i) its willingness to accept some industrial strife (and maybe electoral unpopularity) as the cost—though not necessarily a continuing one—of moderating the rate of increase in money wage rates per period, and (ii) its ability to educate people to see that there is no *real* advantage to the community in an increase in money wage rates which is followed by an equal increase in the price level. A difficulty, in the latter respect, is the hope of some that *their* money wage rates will rise by more than the price level—or the fear that others will gain at their expense in this way. The problem of education is the greater, moreover, since some changes in wage rates, *relative* to one another, are required over time in order to shift labour between industries. The opponents of national incomes policies doubt if they can be consistent with the appropriate changes in relative wage rates. The proponents of the policies rest their hopes on the power of education—and point to the alternatives of continuing cost inflation, or higher unemployment to prevent it.

Modern governments seek steady economic growth, as well as full employment and price stability. It was seen in the previous chapter that steady growth requires that aggregate demand increases over time at the same rate as aggregate supply. This is the context in which budgetary and monetary policies have to be framed. They have to be consistent with a steadily increasing level of aggregate money expenditure.[3] What the rate of increase should be depends on the potential growth in

---

[1] The government has, therefore, to make a judgment as to what is the amount of frictional unemployment which is necessary to allow resources to be switched between industries—as will be required, especially in conditions of economic growth. A balancing of the totals of job vacancies and unemployment provides a rough criterion in this respect.

[2] See pp. 221–222 above.

[3] Assuming that the price level does not fall over time.

aggregate supply. Hence, the choice of particular policies, and changes in them from time to time, have to be based on predictions about the future course of the whole economy. Keynesian macroeconomics provides the framework for those predictions; and their content is increasingly supplied by econometric studies.

FURTHER READING

More advanced analysis of the problems of macroeconomics is given in F. S. Brooman, *Macroeconomics* (third edition, 1967), in G. Ackley, *Macroeconomic Theory* (1961), and in P. Davidson and E. Smolensky, *Aggregate Supply and Demand Analysis* (1964). J. M. Keynes, *The General Theory of Employment, Interest and Money* (1936), is the source of modern macroeconomics. Its antecedents and content are analysed in L. R. Klein, *The Keynesian Revolution* (second edition, 1966). Chapter VIII of this book surveys the developments in macroeconomics which have followed upon that revolution. A variety of views on the content and significance of Keynesian macroeconomics can be found in R. Lekachman (ed.), *Keynes' General Theory* (1964).

A full account of the meaning and measurement of national income and the other concepts which are used in macroeconomics is given in W. Beckerman, *An Introduction to National Income Analysis* (1968).

Chapters I and II of H. G. Johnson, *Essays in Monetary Economics* (1967), are recent surveys of work on monetary theory and policy; the first chapter contains a bibliography. This book also has a chapter on the theory of inflation. A description and analysis of the working of the British financial system is given in R. S. Sayers, *Modern Banking* (seventh edition, 1967). A. B. Cramp, 'The Control of Bank Deposits', *Lloyd's Bank Review*, October 1967, surveys recent controversy about how the quantity of money in the UK is determined.

The study of growth theory can be pursued by means of F. H. Hahn and R. C. O. Matthews, 'The Theory of Economic Growth: A Survey', *Economic Journal*, December 1964, to which a bibliography is attached. Fluctuations in economic activity are analysed in R. C. O. Matthews, *The Trade Cycle* (1959). A mathematical approach to macroeconomics, including the theory of economic growth, can be found in R. G. D. Allen, *Macro-Economic Theory* (1967).

Both the microeconomic and macroeconomic aspects of government economic activity are analysed in A. R. Prest, *Public Finance in Theory and Practice* (third edition, 1967), and in R. A. Musgrave, *The Theory of Public Finance* (1959).

PART IV
INTERNATIONAL ECONOMICS

CHAPTER 33

THE COMPOSITION OF
INTERNATIONAL TRADE

The analysis in this book has so far been restricted to a *closed* economy —one which has no trading or financial relations with other countries. The methods of analysis developed have centred on how the prices and quantities of goods and of factors, taken both individually and in aggregates, are determined.

In an *open* economy, trade takes place not only between the households and firms resident there, but also between them and foreign households and firms. The prices and quantities of goods—and of factors— are therefore determined by both domestic and foreign trade. The influence of foreign trade obviously depends on the kinds and quantities of goods which enter into it. What determines the composition of international trade is consequently the first problem in an extension of the analysis to an open economy.

Goods and services are classified, for present purposes, as:

(1) Export goods: those produced for sale in foreign markets as well as in the domestic market.
(2) Import goods: those purchased from abroad but which may at the same time be produced at home.
(3) Domestic goods: those that are neither exported nor imported.

The category into which any good will fall at a particular time depends on the demand and supply conditions for foreign trade. These conditions specify the circumstances in which various quantities of each good will be demanded and supplied internationally.

Consider first the willingness to supply exports. Under perfect competition, a firm will not export at less than the domestic market price, since it can sell as much as it wishes on the home market at that price. But because of the costs of transport between countries, its supply price to foreign markets will exceed its domestic price. Moreover, the excess will be increased by any tariff (import duty or tax) imposed on the good by the government of the importing country. The export supply price, which is obtained by adding the transport cost and the tariff (if any) to the domestic price, can be expressed either in terms of the money of the exporting country, or in that of the importing country. The relation between the home currency and foreign currency values of the export supply price is given by the rate of exchange between the two currencies. The price in terms of foreign currency is, of course, the relevant one for the export market. Hence the quantity of a good offered for export depends on its domestic price, the costs of transport, tariff levels, and the rates of exchange between currencies.

Whether the quantity offered at any export supply price will actually be sold depends on the condition of *import* demand in foreign markets. The import demand itself depends not only on the willingness of foreigners to buy the good in question (as indicated by their demand curve for it) but also on the competition from local producers to supply it. An exporter attempting to sell in a foreign market must at least be able to match the price charged by that market's own producers. Hence the quantity demanded of a good for import depends on the relation between prices at home and abroad, as well as on the incomes and preferences of the purchasers; and the relation between home and foreign prices depends, in part, on the rates of exchange between currencies.

It can thus be seen that the demand and supply conditions for foreign trade are fairly complex. An analysis of how their interaction determines the composition of international trade must therefore be taken one step at a time. As always in economics, it is essential to be quite explicit about the assumptions made at each stage of the analysis. In the following analysis, there will be only two countries, the UK and the US. With two currencies, the pound and the dollar, there is only one rate of exchange. This can be expressed either as the price of the pound in terms of the dollar (e.g. $3), or as its reciprocal, the price of the dollar in terms of the pound (e.g. £⅓). Three goods (A, B, and C) will be sufficient to demonstrate the analytical principles involved.

The above simplifications will hold throughout the analysis. In addition, the following assumptions will be made initially, and will then be relaxed one at a time, in order to show how the different influences in the demand and supply conditions help to determine the composition of trade. The rate of exchange will at first be taken as given. Transport costs, tariffs, and financial transactions between countries will be ignored. Perfect competition will be assumed for all markets. It will be supposed that goods are produced under conditions of constant marginal cost. This means that the supply curve for each good is a horizontal straight line.[1]

MONEY PRICES AND THE EXCHANGE RATE

The last assumption makes it easy to illustrate the analysis arithmetically. In Table 33.1, the figures in column (i) represent the prices, in pounds, at which British firms are selling the goods A, B, and C on the domestic market.

TABLE 33.1

	Prices of U.K. goods		Prices of U.S. goods	
	in £s (i)	in $s (ii)	in $s (iii)	in £s (iv)
A	3	9	12	4
B	1	3	3	1
C	9	27	18	6

Exchange rate: £1 = $3.

Since supply price is assumed not to vary with output, the whole supply condition for each good can be specified in this way (e.g. industry A is willing to supply any amount of its good at £3 per unit). Column (iii) gives the same kind of information about prices, in dollars, in the US (e.g. the American industry producing C is willing to supply any amount of its good at $18 per unit).

In the absence of transport costs and tariffs, a knowledge of the exchange rate is sufficient to enable export supply prices to be derived from these domestic prices. With the pound worth $3 (and therefore the dollar worth £⅓) in the foreign exchange market, the export supply prices for the UK and the US respectively are those given in columns (ii) and (iv). Thus, British firms will be ready to sell A in the US for $9 (which can be exchanged for £3), since that price will earn the same profit as sales on the home market. Similarly, the American industry C will be ready to sell in the UK at £6 (= $18).

Even without any information about import demand conditions in the two countries, it is now possible to see how trade will flow between them. From the UK viewpoint, A will be an export good, C an import

[1] See pp. 136–137 above.

good, and B a domestic good. This can easily be seen by comparing the corresponding prices in columns (ii) and (iii), or those in columns (i) and (iv). For A, the British export supply price of \$9 undercuts the American domestic price of \$12. American consumers (as well as those in the UK) will buy A from British firms. The UK industry A will expand in order to supply the foreign as well as the domestic market, and the US industry A will go out of business. Similarly, the American industry C, by supplying its product at £6 against the British domestic price of £9, will expand and eliminate its UK rival. Industry B has a competitive advantage in neither country, and so B will be produced in both countries for domestic consumption only.

The composition of international trade in the present situation is determined by two sets of influences, namely (i) the supply prices of goods in the two countries, and (ii) the rate of exchange between their currencies. The role of each set must now be investigated—and this can be done by considering the effects of changes in them.

Suppose that the exchange rate varies from the £1 = \$3 which was assumed in Table 33.1. When the rate changes, the figures in column (ii) have to be recalculated by multiplying the corresponding figures in column (i) by the *new* dollar price of the pound. Similarly, revised figures for column (iv) are got by multiplying the corresponding ones in column (iii) by the *new* pound price of the dollar. A few examples, of the effects of a change in the exchange rate upon the prices in columns (ii) and (iv), quickly show the relevance of that rate for the composition of trade. If the pound *depreciates* to £1 = \$2 (which is the same as saying the dollar *appreciates* to \$1 = £$\frac{1}{2}$), then the *dollar* supply prices (in column (ii)) of British goods fall, and the *sterling* supply prices (in column (iv)) of American goods rise. The prices (in columns (i) and (iii)) of both countries' goods in terms of their *own* currencies are not directly affected by the exchange rate alteration.[1] At the £1 = \$2 rate, both A and B are British exports (with an export supply price of \$2, the British B now undersells the American one), and C becomes a domestic good. On the other hand, if the pound *appreciates* to \$4 (i.e. the dollar depreciates to £$\frac{1}{4}$), B and C are now American exports, and A is a domestic good.

The generalization from these examples is clear: the lower the foreign exchange value of a country's currency, the *greater* the range of goods it will export, and the *smaller* the range it will import. Trade occurs because of price differences between countries. But, for comparisons to

---

[1] To avoid confusion, it is therefore essential to state the currency in which any price is measured.

be made between the prices, all of them have to be stated in the same currency (it does not matter which), and for this to be done an exchange rate is necessary. The level of the exchange rate therefore enters into the price comparisons. Change the exchange rate, and the prices of one country's goods necessarily alter relatively to those of the other country. In this way, the exchange rate helps to determine the composition of trade.

Now consider the role played by the money prices of goods in determining the composition of international trade. It is the *ratios* between the money prices in the two countries that determine which particular goods will be exported and imported at any level of the exchange rate. The ratios between the UK (sterling) and US (dollar) prices of each good in Table 33.1 are: for A, $\frac{3}{12} = \frac{1}{4}$; for B, $\frac{1}{3}$; and for C, $\frac{9}{18} = \frac{1}{2}$. These ratios can be compared with one another, because their numerators are all measured in pounds and their denominators all in dollars.

The principle governing the composition of trade can now be seen. If the UK–US price ratio for a good is *less* than the pound-dollar exchange rate, that good will be a British export; if the UK–US price ratio is *greater* than the pound-dollar exchange rate, the good will be a British import. Thus, with £1 = \$3 (i.e. a pound-dollar exchange ratio of $\frac{1}{3}$), good A, with a UK–US price ratio of $\frac{1}{4}$, is a British export, and C, with a price ratio of $\frac{1}{2}$, is a British import. This follows because, if the UK–US price ratio for a good is less than the pound-dollar exchange ratio, the export price of the UK good (got by multiplying its domestic price by the dollar price of the pound) will be less than the US domestic price of the same good. Thus, with £1 = \$3, the UK export price in dollars of A is 3 times its sterling price of 3; whereas, since the UK–US price ratio for A is $\frac{1}{4}$, the good has a dollar price of 4 times 3 in the US. By the same reasoning, a domestic good is one whose price ratio is the *same* as the exchange ratio.[1]

The respective roles of money prices and the exchange rate in determining the composition of trade can now be put more generally. Imagine a table with all goods and services placed in an order of *increasing* UK–US price ratios as one reads downwards (as in Table 33.1). The exchange rate will divide the table into three sections. In the top section will be the UK export goods with price ratios less than the exchange rate; in the bottom section, UK import goods with price ratios greater than the exchange rate: and in between, the domestic goods with

---

[1] The principles outlined in this paragraph are exactly the same when the details are presented from a US viewpoint, with all the ratios reversed (i.e. dollar quantities in the numerators).

price ratios equal to the exchange rate. A change in that rate will shift the dividing lines between the sections—upwards for an appreciation of the pound, and downwards for a depreciation.

Hence, at some high rate for the pound, there will be no UK exports at all (as with £1 $\geq$ \$4 in Table 33.1); while at some low rate for the pound (i.e. high for the dollar), there will be no US exports (as with £1 $\leq$ \$2 in Table 33.1). Neither of these situations could, however, continue for long. In the former, the lack of UK exports would mean that no dollars were forthcoming to pay for imports from the US. The exchange value of the pound would have to fall, in order to induce some dollar-earning exports. In the latter situation, the lack of pounds to pay for US imports would drive up the sterling exchange rate. The rate, therefore, must be at a level which, given the price ratios of goods, allows trade to flow in *both* directions. The explanation of the level at which the rate will settle cannot be undertaken until import demand conditions are brought into the analysis in the next chapter.

RELATIVE COSTS AND PRICES

It is differences in the *ratios* between the money prices of goods that are fundamental to the explanation of international trade. That is, it is *relative*, and not *absolute*, prices which provide the basis for trade.[1] A country will export those goods which it can produce *relatively* more cheaply, and import those goods which it could only produce *relatively* more dearly, in comparison with other countries.

This theory, known as the Principle of Comparative Costs, was stated by David Ricardo more than a century and a half ago.[2] It is usually put in the form: the basis of trade lies in differences in *relative* costs (cost ratios), and not in differences in the *absolute* levels of costs. But ambiguities in the term 'costs' can cause misunderstanding. The matter requires further explanation.

It can easily be shown that continuing trade would not be possible if the price ratios for *all* goods were the same. Suppose that the domestic prices of US goods *A*, *B*, and *C*, in column (iii) of Table 33.1, are re-written as 9, 3, and 27, thus making all the UK–US price ratios the same (at $\frac{1}{3}$). With the exchange rate £1 = \$3, all the goods are domestic ones. Higher or lower exchange rates lead to trade in *one* direction only.

---

[1] Thus, once again it is seen how important it is to distinguish between relative and absolute prices; cf. pp. 264–265 above.

[2] The exposition of the Principle, given above in terms of the ratios of money prices, differs in form from that of Ricardo; see p. 427 below.

As was explained above, this will force the rate back to £1 = $3. Hence, whatever the *absolute* sizes of the domestic prices inserted in Table 33.1, it is only possible to get continuing trade if the *ratios* of prices are different.

That statement is true whatever may be the differences between the absolute levels of physical productive efficiency in the two countries. Even if the US were absolutely more efficient (in the sense of using smaller quantities of all factors per unit of output) than the UK in the production of all goods, continuing trade would not be possible without differences in price ratios. An extreme example will make this clear.

Suppose that the US suddenly experiences a miraculous hundredfold increase in the physical productivity of all its factors of production. This would certainly give it a productivity advantage over the UK in all goods. With given money prices for factors, the money prices of US goods will all fall to one-hundredth of their previous levels. Column (iii) in Table 33.1 can, therefore, be re-headed 'cents' rather than 'dollars'. With the exchange rate still at £1 = $3, all goods become US exports. The pound must therefore depreciate. At a new rate of £1 = 3¢, the original pattern of trade is restored, despite the absolute productivity gulf between the countries.

Moreover, suppose that the figures in column (iii) are again re-written as 9, 3, and 27. Continuing trade is then impossible both *before*, and *after*, the miracle. Thus, *absolute* differences in physical productive efficiency between countries are neither a sufficient obstacle to, nor a sufficient condition for, the existence of trade.

It is the significance of physical productivity differences for international trade that causes most misunderstanding of the Principle of Comparative Costs. The lament is often heard, 'How can the UK compete with the US where productivity is so much higher?' Whatever superficial plausibility that may have, it is spoilt when it is coupled with 'How can the UK compete with Japan where wages are lower?' Because, of course, *real* wages in a country are high, or low, according as physical productivity is high or low. So, 'How can Japan compete with the UK where productivity is higher?' The lament in relation to Japan is ambiguous, because it does not distinguish between real and money wages. Even so, both laments are *non sequiturs*, because they only allow for one or other, but not both, of the two elements which determine costs, viz. the prices and the physical productivities of the factors.

Here again is an opportunity to stress the unity of analytical methods in economics. The false reasoning in the previous paragraph can be avoided by using the analysis of costs and prices set out in Part II above. The cost condition for a good depends on the prices of factors and on their physical productivities as given by the production function. Under perfect competition, the supply price for each output of a good is equal to the corresponding marginal cost. This is the way in which the prices in columns (i) and (iii) of Table 33.1 have to be explained.

Consider the relation of those prices to factor productivities in the two countries. This can be simplified for the moment by assuming that labour is the only factor needed to produce goods. Moreover, suppose that money wage rates (at 10s per hour) are the same in all UK industries; and similarly for the US (at $3 per hour). The figures in Table 33.2 represent the man-hours needed to produce a unit of each good in the two countries. They do not vary with the level of output, since the marginal cost of each good is assumed to be constant. The reciprocals of these figures are the (constant) marginal physical productivities per hour of labour in each industry, e.g. the *MPP* of labour in the UK industry A is $\frac{1}{6}$ unit of A per hour.

The prices in columns (i) and (iii) of Table 33.1 above follow from Table 33.2 and the given money wage rates. Thus, the price of A in the

TABLE 33.2

	Man-hours per unit of output	
	UK	US
A	6	4
B	2	1
C	18	6

UK is £3, because one unit requires 6 hours of work at 10s an hour. The roles of factor prices and productivities, in determining the composition of trade, can now be explained.

American labour is $1\frac{1}{2}$ times as productive as British labour in producing A (4 hours per unit requred as against 6 hours); but it is twice as productive in relation to B, and three times as productive in relation to C. Since money wage rates are uniform between industries in both countries, the differences in the price ratios of goods are due to the differences in the factor productivity ratios. Thus, it is the *higher* US to UK productivity ratio (of $3:1$) in C, as compared with that (of $1\frac{1}{2}:1$) in A, which makes the price ratio of C to A in the US (at $18:12$) *lower* than that ratio in the UK (at $9:3$).

American labour is *absolutely* more productive than British labour in *all* three goods. But it is *relatively* more productive in industry *C* than it is in industry *A*. It is the relative productivity differences, as between goods, that bring about the differences in the price ratios of goods—which are the immediate reason why international trade takes place.

But if the American productivity advantage is the *same* for all goods, there is, with uniform money wage rates, no basis for trade. Re-write the figures in the US column of Table 33.2, as 3, 1, and 9. American labour is now twice as productive as British labour in *all* three goods. At the given money wage rate of $3, the American supply prices of *A*, *B*, and *C* are now 9, 3, and 27 respectively (which are those used on pp. 424–425 above, in the analysis of the re-written version of column (iii) of Table 33.1). The UK–US price ratios are all the same (at $\frac{1}{3}$). The three goods are domestic ones and no trade takes place.

Ricardo used an example similar to that in Table 33.2 in order to demonstrate the Principle of Comparative Costs. The meaning of the Principle, in its Ricardo presentation, is clarified by the above analysis of the significance of money wage rates and labour productivity for the price ratios of goods. In the Ricardian principle—namely, that the basis of trade lies in differences in *relative* costs, and *not* in differences in the *absolute* levels of costs—the term 'costs' means the physical quantities of labour required to produce goods. 'Costs,' in that sense, are determined entirely by the physical productivities of labour, as given in the production functions of goods. The money wage rates of labour do not enter into this conception of 'costs'. It is this ambiguity in the use of the term 'costs' which causes a lot of confusion about the Principle of Comparative Costs.

Ricardo's perfectly valid point is this: trade in goods can be explained by differences in factor physical productivities between countries. But it is *relative* and not *absolute* differences that count. Neither the high productivity level of the rich, developed, country, nor the low real wage rates (i.e. low productivity per head) of the poor, underdeveloped country, is the relevant consideration. Rather, as long as the developed country's productivity advantages differ from good to good, there will be the differences in price ratios which make trade possible. The analysis based on Table 33.2 was directed to proving that point.

FACTOR PRICES AND TRADE

But the analysis above also implies that relative productivity differences are not the only basis for trade. Differences in the industrial patterns of money wage rates in the two countries provide another basis.

Consider the re-written version (used on p. 427 above) of the US column in Table 33.2, with the man-hours required to produce A, B, and C set at 3, 1, and 9 respectively. American labour is then twice as productive as British labour in all goods, and there are no relative productivity differences to cause trade. Continue the assumption that money wage rates (at 10s per hour) are the same in all UK industries. This gives the prices in column (i) of Table 33.1. But now suppose that, because of the Americans' preferences as between different kinds of work, a \$4 wage rate is required to attract labour into industry A, while \$3 and \$2 rates need only be paid by industries B and C respectively. The US prices of A, B, and C will therefore be 12, 3, and 18 respectively, namely those in column (iii) of Table 33.1. Therefore trade will occur, as shown earlier.

Thus *relative* differences, as between countries, in money wage rates, as well as in labour productivities, will bring about the differences in price ratios which cause trade to take place.

This conclusion can now be generalized to cover realistic situations, in which goods are produced by many different kinds of labour, capital, and natural resources. In any country, the marginal cost of a good will depend on the kinds and the prices of the factors used to make it. The proportions in which the factors are combined will vary with their prices.[1] The *kinds* of factors available are the outcome of the country's population and investment histories, and of its geology. Countries differ a lot in these respects. Certain kinds of resources (e.g. minerals, machinery, specialized labour) are available in some countries, but not in others. As a consequence, the technology used in the production of any good can vary a lot from one country to another, i.e. the same good will have different production functions in the various countries. The variety of technologies is likely to lead to relative productivity differences, which cause the cost ratios of goods to differ between countries.

The prices of the factors available in a country depend on their relative scarcities, as determined by the demands to use them in relation to their supplies. The relative scarcities of the *same* kinds of factors differ a lot from country to country. Some, for example, are well endowed with land relatively to population as compared with others (e.g. the US as compared with the UK). The ratios between the supplies of the different factors, with which a country is endowed, help to determine factor prices. When these factor endowment ratios differ between two countries it is likely[2] that the factor price ratios in them will also be different. A

---

[1] As explained on pp. 205–206 above.
[2] I.e. unless factor demand conditions act in the contrary direction.

country well endowed with land relative to population will have a lower rent-to-wage-rate ratio than a country poorly endowed in this respect. Consequently, even if two countries use the same technology, they will combine the factors in different ratios in producing any particular good —because their factor price ratios are different.[1] The cost ratios of goods will therefore differ between countries.[2]

The effects on the composition of trade of two sets of influences—the supply prices of goods and the rate of exchange—have now been explored. It is differences between countries in the *ratios* of the prices of goods that make trade possible. Those differences depend, in turn, upon differences in technologies, and/or in factor price ratios. The latter result from differences in factor endowment ratios. Given the different price ratios between goods, the level of the exchange rate determines which goods are exports, imports, and domestic ones. The next step is to enquire how the exchange rate itself is determined as an integral part of the system of international transactions.

[1] Once again see pp. 205–206 above.
[2] There is a subtle exception to this that cannot be dealt with here.

CHAPTER 34

THE EXCHANGE RATE

The analysis of the previous chapter was based entirely on the conditions of *supply* for the export of goods A, B, and C by the UK and the US. Those supply conditions were illustrated by means of Table 33.1. But there was no information in the table about the quantities of the goods which the two countries will want to buy from each other. The conditions of *demand* for the *import* of goods by the UK and the US have now to be added to the analysis in order to explain how the exchange rate between the pound and the dollar is determined.

Table 34.1 extends Table 33.1[1] to include the demand conditions for imports by the UK and the US. Column (i) of Table 34.1 gives the domestic prices, in pounds, of A, B, and C in the UK; column (ii) gives their export supply prices in dollars on the assumption of an exchange rate of £1 = $3.[2] Similarly, column (iv) gives the domestic prices in dollars of the goods in the US, and column (v) gives their export supply prices, in pounds, again on the assumption of an exchange rate of £1 = $3. Thus, columns (i), (ii), (iv), and (v) of Table 34.1 are the same respectively, and have the same figures in them, as columns (i), (ii), (iii), and (iv) of Table 33.1. The additional columns (iii) and (vi), in Table 34.1, provide information about import demand conditions in the US and the UK respectively.

The heading to column (iii), in Table 34.1, means the quantity demanded per period of time (q_D) for import, by the US, of goods from the UK—that is, the quantity demanded of UK exports. If the exchange rate is £1 = $3, the UK will export only A[3]—and will do so at a price of $9 (as in column (ii)). The figure 100, in column (iii), then shows that people in the US will buy (i.e. import) 100 units of A from the UK at that price. It is essential to understand how the quantity 100 is determined.

The quantity demanded of A in the US depends on its dollar price. How much will be demanded, at any dollar price, is indicated by the US *demand curve* for A. The quantity of 100 in column (iii) is that given by

[1] On p. 421 above.
[2] Transport costs and tariffs are still ignored.
[3] B being a domestic good, and C a US export, at that exchange rate.

TABLE 34.1

	Prices of UK goods		US q_D of UK goods	Prices of US goods		UK q_D of US goods
	in £s (i)	in $s (ii)	(iii)	in $s (iv)	in £s (v)	(vi)
A	3	9	100	12	4	
B	1	3		3	1	
C	9	27		18	6	50

Exchange rate: £1 = $3.

one point on the US demand curve, namely the point corresponding to the $9 price of *A*. If the price of *A* is different from $9, the US quantity demanded of *A* will be different from 100. Thus, if the UK export supply price of *A* happens to be *less* than $9, the US quantity demanded of *A* will be *larger* than 100 units, and vice versa. In general, the sizes of any figures in column (iii) *depend* on the sizes of the corresponding prices in column (ii). A change in the export supply price in dollars[1] of a UK export good will alter the quantity imported into the US.

Moreover, it must be remembered that the *position* of the US demand curve for *A* depends on the incomes, and the preferences between goods, of US households, and on the prices of other goods. If any of these parameters of the demand curve change, it will *shift* (increase or decrease) to a new position. The US quantity demanded of *A* will then be different at *any* dollar price for it.

The heading of column (vi), in Table 34.1, means the quantity demanded per period of time (q_D) for import, by the UK, of goods from the the US—that is, the quantity demanded of US exports. Any figures in this column have to be interpreted in the same manner as those in column (iii). If the exchange rate is £1 = $3, the US will export only *C*— and will do so at a price of £6 (as in column (v)). The figure of 50 in column (vi) is given by the point on the UK *demand curve* for *C* corresponding to a £6 price for it. This UK quantity demanded of *C* would be different if the US export supply price in pounds of *C* were to change from £6. In general, the sizes of any figures in column (vi) *depend* on the sizes of the corresponding prices in column (v). Moreover, the quantities demanded, by the UK, of US goods depend on the *positions*

[1] It must be emphasized again that, in analysing international trade, the *currency* in which any price is measured must always be stated.

of the UK demand curves for the goods. These positions are dependent on the incomes, and the preferences between goods, of UK households, and on the prices of other goods.

Table 34.1 thus illustrates both the export *supply* conditions and the import *demand* conditions for goods, which prevail in the UK and the US. Consider the figures in the table. With the exchange rate assumed to be £1 = $3, the UK exports A at a price of $9 and the US buys 100 units of it. The *total* expenditure on A by US households is $900. This is what they have to pay to the UK industry A. But that industry will want payment in pounds, rather than in dollars, since its costs are incurred in pounds and its shareholders will want their dividends in pounds. Therefore, either the US importers of A will have to exchange $900 for pounds on the foreign exchange market, or the UK exporters, having received $900, will have to exchange them for pounds. This means that, at the assumed exchange rate of £1 = $3, $900 are sold to the foreign exchange dealers[1] in return for £300.

The supply of dollars and the demand for pounds are the two sides of one and the same transaction. The one currency is bought with the other. The quantity demanded of pounds necessarily equals the quantity supplied of dollars multiplied by the exchange rate for the dollar, e.g. as above, £300 = 900 × £$\frac{1}{3}$. The quantity of dollars *supplied* to the foreign exchange market—and the corresponding quantity of pounds demanded from it at the ruling exchange rate—is determined by the total value in dollars of US imports (i.e. UK exports).

Similarly, the quantity of dollars *demanded* from the foreign exchange market—and the corresponding quantity of pounds supplied to it at the ruling foreign exchange rate—is determined by the total value in dollars of US exports (i.e. UK imports). With the exchange rate assumed at £1 = $3 in Table 34.1, the US exports C at a price of £6 and the UK buys 50 units of it. The *total* expenditure on C by UK households is £300. The UK importers of C will therefore supply £300 to the foreign exchange dealers and demand $900, in order to pay the US industry C.

The figures in the table have been deliberately chosen so that the total values—measured in either currency—of UK exports (US imports) and UK imports (US exports) are the same per period of time (at £300 = $900). Hence, the quantity demanded of pounds, to pay for UK exports, is equal to the quantity supplied of pounds, to pay for UK imports. Or—what amounts to the same thing—the quantity supplied of dollars to pay for US imports is equal to the quantity demanded of

---

[1] The most important of whom are the foreign exchange departments of the commercial banks in both countries.

dollars to pay for US exports. The significance of this situation for the foreign exchange market must now be analysed.

Foreign exchange dealers buy and sell currencies for one another. They therefore have to hold working balances of the various currencies. Despite the customary use of the term 'currency' in this context, these balances of different monies are mainly bank money,[1] i.e. they are accounts with commercial banks. The commercial banks are themselves the main foreign exchange dealers. Hence, the banks in one country keep accounts with banks in the other countries in whose currencies they want to deal. A UK bank will keep a dollar account with a 'correspondent' US bank. When the former sells dollars to a customer (in return for pounds from him), it gives him a cheque drawn against its account with its US correspondent bank. When it buys dollars, they are paid into that account. US banks similarly operate sterling accounts with their UK correspondent banks.

These accounts of internationally correspondent banks with one another are their working balances of foreign currencies.[2] The balances are reduced when they sell foreign currencies, and are increased when they buy them.

In the situation portrayed in Table 34.1, the foreign exchange dealers in aggregate (in both countries) are selling the same amount of dollars per period of time as they are buying, at the ruling exchange rate of £1 = $3. This also means that they are buying the same amount of pounds as they are selling. Hence their working balances of foreign currencies remain unchanged. There is no reason, therefore, for them to change the rate at which they exchange pounds for dollars. £1 = $3 is an *equilibrium* exchange rate.

Thus, under present assumptions, an equilibrium exchange rate is one at which the total values of trade in each direction between the UK and the US are equal. Symbolize the total value of exports by E, and the total value of imports by M, with subscripts to indicate the country in question. Let D and S, with subscripts to indicate the currency, stand for the quantities demanded and supplied of currencies. Then

$$D_£ \equiv E_{UK} \text{ measured in pounds}$$
$$S_£ \equiv M_{UK} \text{ measured in pounds}$$

[1] Because most international transactions—except e.g. minor travel expenses—are settled by transfers of bank money.

[2] They do not hold balances of domestic monies, since their own debts—which they create by lending them—are domestic (bank) money, as was explained in Chapter 29 above.

$$D_{\$} \equiv E_{US} \,(\equiv M_{UK}) \text{ measured in dollars}$$
$$S_{\$} = M_{US} \,(\equiv E_{UK}) \text{ measured in dollars}$$

Hence, if $E_{UK} = M_{UK}$—i.e. if $M_{US} = E_{US}$—then $D_{\pounds} = S_{\pounds}$, i.e. $S_{\$} = D_{\$}$.

The analysis based on Table 34.1 thus shows that if $E = M$ at the ruling exchange rate, the rate is an equilibrium one. The next question clearly is: what will happen to the exchange rate if E is not equal to M at the ruling rate?

EXCHANGE RATE CHANGES

Suppose that the exchange rate is a *freely fluctuating* one.[1] This means that monetary authorities (i.e. central banks or government treasuries) do not attempt to influence the rate in any way. Its level is determined entirely by the free working of the foreign exchange market. This, in fact, is seldom the case. But an understanding of freely fluctuating rates will make it easier to explain—in the next chapter—how monetary authorities can control the rates.

Now suppose that, in terms of Table 34.1, the quantity demanded of A per period of time for import by the US, is 90 units rather than 100 (in column (iii)) at the UK export supply price of $9. This means that the US demand curve for A has a lower (i.e. decreased) position than was previously assumed. The total value of UK exports (of good A), measured in dollars, now equals $810 ($= 9 \times 90$); and measured in pounds, it now equals £270 ($= 3 \times 90$). The total value of UK imports (of good C) is unchanged at $900 (£300). Hence the $D_{\$}$ at 900 now exceeds the $S_{\$}$ at 810; or put the other way, the $S_{\pounds}$ at 300 exceeds the $D_{\pounds}$ at 270.

Foreign exchange dealers are therefore selling more dollars than they are buying, at the ruling rate of £1 = $3; and are buying more pounds than they are selling. UK banks' dollar accounts with US banks *fall*; and US banks' sterling accounts with UK banks *rise*. In an attempt to prevent this from continuing, the banks will reduce the $ price of the £, i.e. increase the £ price of the $. The pound depreciates (the dollar appreciates) as a result of the excess supply of pounds (excess demand for dollars).

When the pound depreciates below $3 (i.e. when the dollar appreciates above £⅓), the export supply prices in dollars of UK goods *fall* below those in column (ii). If the pound falls to $2.80, the dollar prices of UK goods A, B, and C become 8.40, 2.80, and 25.20 respectively. On the

[1] Sometimes also called a *floating* rate.

other hand, the export supply prices in pounds of US goods A, B, and C, in column (v), *rise* to (approximately) £4·3, £1·1, and £6·4. B ceases to be a domestic good and joins A as a UK export; C remains a US export.

The US quantity demanded of A will *expand*,[1] as its dollar price falls as a result of the depreciation of the pound: say from 90 units at $9, to 98 at $8.40. The US also now buys B from the UK: say 8 units at $2.80 each. On the other hand, the UK quantity demanded of C will *contract*,[2] as its price in pounds rises as a result of the depreciation of the pound: say from 50 units at £6, to 47 at £6·4. The US supply price of C is, however, unchanged in terms of dollars.[3] The UK therefore now buys 47 units of it at $18 each.

E_{UK} measured in dollars now equals 845.6 (823.2 for A, and 22.4 for B); and M_{UK} measured in dollars equals 846 (for C). The depreciation of the pound has increased the dollar value of E_{UK} (from 810), and has decreased the dollar value of M_{UK} (from 900). The initial excess $D_\$$, of 90 at £1 = $3, has practically been eliminated at the exchange rate of £1 = $2.80.[4] The exchange rate has converged to a new equilibrium level.

The £1 = $3 exchange rate was a disequilibrium one, because the $D_\$$ exceeded the $S_\$$ (i.e. $S_£$ exceeded $D_£$) at it. The excess $D_\$$ (excess $S_£$) existed because M_{UK} was greater than E_{UK}, i.e. because the UK had an *import surplus*. The exchange rate *converges* to a new equilibrium insofar as the depreciation of the pound eliminates the import surplus. It was shown above to do this as a result of (i) the expansion in the quantity sold of the UK's existing export good A, (ii) the widening of the range of UK exports to include good B, and (iii) the contraction in the quantity bought of the UK's existing import good C. (i) and (ii) occur because the depreciation of the pound lowers the *dollar* prices of UK exports (their *sterling* prices remaining unchanged on present assumptions[5]). (iii) occurs because the depreciation of the pound raises the *sterling* prices of the UK import (its *dollar* price remaining unchanged on present assumptions[5]).

However, the expansion in the quantities of goods exported, and the contraction in the quantities imported, which occur as the pound depreciates, may not be *large enough* to eliminate an import surplus. In that case, the exchange rate will *not* converge to a new equilibrium. This possibility can be illustrated by inserting new figures, for the changes

---

[1] I.e. there will be a *movement down* the US demand curve for A.
[2] I.e. there will be a *movement up* the UK demand curve for C.
[3] Under the assumption that *domestic* supply prices do not vary with output.
[4] All of this can, of course, be expressed in terms of pounds rather than of dollars.
[5] Note again how it is necessary to state the currencies in which prices are measured.

in trade, in the above example of disequilibrium. Take the same starting point, with M_{UK} greater than E_{UK} at £1 = \$3,[1] and suppose that the rate again falls to £1 = \$2.80.

Now suppose that, when the export price in dollars of A falls to 8.40, the US quantity demanded expands to 92 (rather than 98 as above); and that, when the export price in dollars of B falls to 2.80, the US buys 4 units (rather than 8 as above). Moreover, suppose that when the import price in pounds of C rises to 6·4, the UK quantity demanded contracts to 49 (rather than 47 as above). The UK therefore buys 49 units of C at its unchanged dollar price of 18.

E_{UK} measured in dollars now equals 784 (772.8 for A, and 11.2 for B). It has *decreased* from the initial level of 810. M_{UK} measured in dollars now equals 882 (on C). It also has decreased from the initial level of 900. But the decrease in the dollar value of E_{UK} is *greater* than that in the dollar value of M_{UK}. The import surplus has been *increased* by the depreciation of the pound. Hence, the excess $D_\$$ (and excess $S_£$) has been increased—it is now 98 as against the initial 90. The pound will continue to depreciate as long as there is any excess $D_\$$. And this will not be eliminated if the dollar value of E_{UK} decreases by as much as, or more than, the decrease in the dollar value of M_{UK} as the pound falls. The exchange rate may therefore not converge to a new equilibrium level.

Whether or not the exchange rate will converge to equilibrium depends on the behaviour of the *quantities demanded* of exports and of imports when their prices change as a result of the exchange rate alteration. This can be seen from the two sets of figures used above to exemplify convergence, and lack of convergence, respectively.

In the first example, where the rate converges to equilibrium at £1 = \$2.80, the US quantity demanded of A expands from 90 to 98, and that of B from 0 to 8; and the UK quantity demanded of C contracts from 50 to 47. In the second example, where the rate does not converge to equilibrium at £1 = \$2.80, the US quantity demanded of A expands from 90 to 92, and that of B from 0 to 4; and the UK quantity demanded of C contracts from 50 to 49. As between the two examples, the quantities demanded of all the goods change to a *smaller* extent in the second than in the first. That is, the *price elasticities of demand* for the goods are *smaller* in the second example than in the first.

It is *small* price elasticities of demand, for *both* export and import goods, that prevent the depreciation of a currency from eliminating an import surplus. It will be recalled[2] that the change in the *total*

---

[1] I.e. with the US buying 90 units of A (rather than 100, as in Table 34.1).
[2] See pp. 86–87 above.

expenditure (i.e. $p \cdot q$) on a good, when its price alters, depends on its price elasticity of demand (ε_D). If $\varepsilon_D > 1$, then as *p falls* and *q* expands, $p \cdot q$ *increases*. This is the case for good *A* in the first of the two examples above: when p_A falls from \$9 to \$8.40, q_A expands from 90 to 98, and $p_A \cdot q_A$ increases from \$810 to \$823.2. But if $\varepsilon_D < 1$, then as *p falls* and *q* expands, $p \cdot q$ *decreases*. This is the case for good *A* in the second example above: when p_A falls from \$9 to \$8.40, q_A expands from 90 to 92, and $p_A \cdot q_A$ decreases from \$810 to \$772.8. And despite *B* becoming a UK export, as the pound depreciates, the total dollar value of E_{UK} drops from \$810 to \$784.

This fall in the total dollar value of E_{UK} in itself increases the UK import surplus. But if the total dollar value of M_{UK} falls to a *greater* extent, the import surplus will, on balance, be reduced. That will happen if the ε_D for imports is large enough. But it is not large enough in the second example above. When the depreciation of the pound causes the price of *C* to rise from £6 to £6·4, the quantity demanded contracts only from 50 to 49. Hence, at the unchanged dollar price of 18 for *C*, the total value in dollars of M_{UK} falls only from 900 to 882. This reduction is *less* than that in the total dollar value of E_{UK}. The UK import surplus—and the excess $D_{\$}$—increases. The pound therefore continues to depreciate.

Thus the price elasticities of demand, for *both* export goods and import goods, determine whether or not the exchange rate will converge to an equilibrium level. It can be shown that, under simplified conditions, the *sum* of the average ε_D for exports and the average ε_D for imports must be *greater* than 1 for convergence to take place.[1] In that case, the depreciation of a currency will eliminate an import surplus, and an appreciation will eliminate an export surplus (i.e. $E > M$). But if the *sum* of the elasticities is *less* than 1, a depreciation will *increase* an import surplus, and an appreciation will *increase* an export surplus. A freely fluctuating exchange rate will depreciate if there is an import surplus, since the quantity supplied of the currency in question then exceeds the quantity demanded; and vice versa if there is an export surplus. Hence a freely fluctuating rate will be *unstable* if the sum of the elasticities is *less* than 1.[2]

[1] This is proven in general terms in more advanced texts on international economics. The reader can, however, test the principle, in terms of Table 34.1 above, by using different arithmetic values for the elasticities.

[2] It follows that, in these circumstances, an *appreciation* would eliminate an *import* surplus, and that a *depreciation* would eliminate an *export* surplus. But a freely fluctuating exchange rate will not change in the appropriate direction—rather, market forces will move it in the opposite one.

However, as the formula shows, the elasticities do not need to be large, in order to ensure the stability of the exchange rate: for example, elasticities greater than 0·5 for *both* exports and imports will be sufficient. The exports of most countries compete in a world market with those of quite a number of other countries. There is consequently considerable scope for *substitution effects* between the goods of different countries as their prices change relatively to one another. The presumption is, therefore, that the price elasticities of demand for the exports of a *single* country will be large rather than small. There is some empirical evidence to this effect, though it is by no means conclusive.

It has now been shown how a freely fluctuating exchange rate is determined as an integral part of the system of international trade. Given the domestic prices of goods in the different countries, the exchange rates between currencies determine the export supply prices of the goods. The quantities demanded in each country of the goods of the other, at those export prices, determine the total values of exports and imports. The quantities demanded and supplied of currencies, at the ruling exchange rates, are given by the total values of exports and imports. If E does not equal M for each country, exchange rates will alter. Export supply prices, in terms of foreign currencies, will therefore alter and bring about changes in the flows of trade. This process will continue until $E = M$ for each country—assuming that the price elasticities of demand for goods are large enough to bring this about. Exchange rates are then in equilibrium.

It is now possible to relax some of the assumptions on which the explanation of the interconnections between trade and exchange rates has so far been conducted.

TRANSPORT COSTS AND TARIFFS

Because of the costs of transporting goods between countries, their supply prices to foreign markets will exceed their domestic prices. This can be seen in terms of good A in Table 34.1.[1] The UK export price in dollars is there given as 9. Now suppose that the cost of transporting it to the US is $1 per unit. It will then be offered for sale in the US at $10, which is still below the $12 supply price of domestic producers. But the US quantity demanded of this UK export will be less at $10 per unit than at $9, i.e. it will be less than the 100 units in column (iii) of the table.

But if the transport cost for A is equal to, or greater than, $3 per

[1] On p. 431 above.

unit, its dollar price as a UK export will equal, or exceed, the $12 supply price of US producers. *A* then ceases to be a UK export, and becomes a domestic good. The transport cost is prohibitive of trade. This is, in fact, the reason why a large number of goods do not enter into international trade.

Tariffs have the same effect on trade as transport costs. Suppose that the US government levies a tariff (i.e. an import duty or tax) of $1 per unit on the import of *A*. If the transport cost is $1 per unit, the UK will now offer *A* for sale in the US at $11.[1] This is still below the domestic supply price. But the quantity demanded of *A* in the US will contract when its price is raised by the tariff.

If the tariff on *A* is equal to, or greater than, $2 per unit, its dollar price as a UK export will equal, or exceed, the $12 supply price of US producers. The tariff is then prohibitive of trade and *A* becomes a domestic good. The tariff has a *protective effect*. It shields the US industry *A* from UK competition and allows it to continue in business. But as a result the US consumer has to pay a higher price for *A*.

Both transport costs and tariffs reduce the volume of international trade in two respects. By raising the prices of *traded* goods, they reduce the quantities demanded of them. And when they are high enough to be prohibitive of trade in particular goods, they narrow the *range* of goods traded.

CHANGING COSTS AND IMPERFECT COMPETITION

All the analysis so far has assumed that the domestic supply prices of goods do not change as their outputs alter. It is more probable, under perfect competition, that marginal cost, and therefore supply price, will rise as output increases.[2] The significance of this for international trade can be analysed with the help once more of Table 34.1.[3]

Suppose that the domestic supply prices in columns (i) and (iv) are those which would rule in the *absence* of trade between the UK and the US. When trade takes place, the UK exports *A* and imports *C*. UK industry *A* must therefore expand to supply the foreign as well as the domestic market. To do this, it uses the factors which are no longer required by industry *C*, because the competition from its US counterpart has forced it to contract. The reverse occurs between industries *A* and *C* in the US.

As UK industry *A* *expands*, its supply price rises above the £3 shown

---

[1] Since the supply curve of *A* is here assumed to be perfectly elastic, the whole of the tariff (tax) is passed on to the consumer; cf. pp. 171–172 above.

[2] See pp. 136–137 above.

[3] On p. 431 above.

in column (i). As US industry *A contracts*, its supply price falls below the $12 shown in column (iii). It may happen, therefore, that the two supply prices reach equality, at the exchange rate £1 = $3, *before* all the firms in US industry *A* are driven out of business. Thus, when the supply price of the enlarged UK industry *A* has risen to £3⅔ (= $11), there may still be some US firms which can supply *A* at $11. In that case, the US will *both* import *A* and produce some *A* at home.

The earlier analysis, with constant supply prices, showed the UK and the US *specializing completely* in the production of *A* and *C* respectively. It is now seen that, with rising supply prices, international trade may lead only to *partial* specialization as between countries in the production of different goods. This in fact frequently occurs, e.g. the UK imports many of its foodstuffs, but also produces quantities of certain of them at home.

Under imperfect competition, the supply price of a good may actually *fall* as its output increases.[1] The enlargement of an industry, to supply the foreign as well as the domestic market, can therefore increase its competitive advantage in relation to other countries. But imperfect competition is usually characterized by differences between the products of competing firms. Thus, suppose that industry *A* operates under monopolistic competition or imperfect oligopoly. The products of the different firms in UK industry *A* are not then identical in the eyes of consumers; and they also differ from the products of the different firms in US industry *A*. The products of both industries could therefore sell simultaneously at the same or different prices, in *both* countries. This is possible because UK and US consumers choose between the products on the basis of their various characteristics, as well as their prices. Thus, product differentiation, as well as price differences, plays a part in determining the composition of international trade (e.g. as in cars, clothes).

CAPITAL TRANSACTIONS

The households, firms, and government of one country can purchase real assets (e.g. land, factories) which are located in other countries. They can also make loans to foreign households, firms, and governments. These international *capital transactions*[2] help, along with trade, to determine exchange rates.

[1] See p. 188 above.
[2] The word 'capital', in this context, is used in a wider sense than it was earlier, since it here includes loans as well as capital goods.

The volume and composition of international capital transactions depend on the differences, as between countries, in expected internal rates of return on capital goods, in interest rates, and in expected future interest rates. They also depend on people's expectations about future exchange rates. Moreover, the degrees of uncertainty which attach to all these expectations also influence the capital transactions.

In making its domestic investment decisions, a firm will undertake projects which promise high internal rates of return before it considers those which promise lower ones. It will choose projects abroad, rather than at home, on the same basis. Investment in capital goods (and land) located in foreign countries thus depends on the *expectations* of higher rates of return on them than on domestic capital goods.

It was seen in Chapter 31[1] that the expected internal rates of return on investment depend on the size of the existing capital stock in relation to population. The more capital per head of its labour force a country has, the lower will be the marginal net physical productivity of capital, and therefore the Marginal Efficiency of Investment (*MEI*). This suggests that foreign investment will usually be undertaken by developed, capital-rich countries in underdeveloped, capital-poor countries.

But it was also seen in Chapter 31,[2] that the *MEI* depends on the expected increase in aggregate demand for the goods made by capital. That demand may come, not only from within the country in question, but also from other countries. That is, the expected increase in the *export* demand for the goods made by capital helps to determine the *MEI*. Thus, many investments in the production of foodstuffs and raw materials in underdeveloped countries have in the past been directed mainly to meeting the demands for them from industrial countries. Insofar as an underdeveloped country has resources which can be used to this end, it will attract investment from capital-rich countries. But if it does not have such resources, and if its domestic economy shows little promise of expansion, then its capital-poverty will not be sufficient to attract foreign investment.

On the other hand, sustained economic growth in industrial countries will probably cause them to invest in one another. In these circumstances, some firms in each country will continually weigh the profitability of expanding abroad as against that of expansion at home. With variations in the growth rates of countries, and of the industries within them, differences in profit prospects are bound to appear. These will attract foreign investment.

[1] See especially pp. 388–389 **above.**
[2] See especially p. 384 above.

Moreover, the existence of transport costs and tariffs are of importance in this respect. In order to avoid them, firms will set up factories in other countries. Economic growth in these other countries then leads to more foreign investment in them, in order to expand the foreign-owned factories. There has been, in fact, a high level of foreign investment by some industrial countries in one another since the last war.

Differences in interest rates make it worthwhile to lend, for short or long periods, in one country rather than another. But expected changes in interest rates are also of importance in this respect. An expected fall in interest rates means an expected rise in the prices of bonds.[1] Hence a person may lend at a lower rate abroad, rather than at a higher rate at home, if he expects that foreign interest rates are going to fall. He then expects to make a capital gain on the foreign bonds.

The willingness to lend abroad also depends on expectations about exchange rates. Suppose that the pound is expected to depreciate, i.e. the dollar is expected to appreciate. This means that loans made in pounds are expected to *fall* in value in terms of dollars; and that loans made in dollars are expected to *rise* in value in terms of pounds. Hence, an expected depreciation of the pound is an incentive for UK residents to lend to the US, and for US residents to reduce their lending to the UK. In this situation, people will speculate against the pound, by shifting out of assets (both real and financial) in the UK into assets in the US.

Speculation against a currency, because of an expected depreciation in it, may lead people to hold foreign currencies, e.g. accounts with commercial banks in other countries. They are then lending to the foreign commercial banks, i.e. they are holding the latters' debts. The foreign bank money is held because, though it may not earn any interest, it is expected to appreciate in terms of the currency of the holders' country.

Foreign investment, and foreign lending, by a country involve a supply of its domestic currency to the foreign exchange market, and a corresponding demand for foreign currency from it. When the UK invests in, and lends to, the US, pounds are sold to the foreign exchange dealers in return for dollars with which to make the investments and loans in the US. Similarly, US investment in, and loans to, the UK means that dollars are sold to the dealers in return for pounds.

Let L, with a subscript to indicate the country, stand for the sum of its foreign investment and lending; and let B, with a subscript to indicate the country, stand for the sum of its foreign borrowing and the other

[1] See p. 338 above.

country's investment in it. Taking these capital transactions per period of time along with the trade in goods, it follows that:

$D_£ \equiv E_{UK} + B_{UK}$ measured in pounds

$S_£ \equiv M_{UK} + L_{UK}$ measured in pounds

$D_\$ \equiv E_{US} (\equiv M_{UK}) + B_{US} (\equiv L_{UK})$ measured in dollars

$S_\$ \equiv M_{US} (\equiv E_{UK}) + L_{US} (\equiv B_{UK})$ measured in dollars

Hence, if $E_{UK} + B_{UK} = M_{UK} + L_{UK}$—i.e. if $M_{US} + L_{US} = E_{US} + B_{US}$—then $D_£ = S_£$, i.e. $S_\$ = D_\$$. This is the condition for the equilibrium of the exchange rate.

A freely fluctuating exchange rate will therefore move to the level at which the *sum* of a country's exports, its borrowing from abroad, and other countries' investment in it, equals the *sum* of its imports, its foreign lending, and its foreign investment. The significance of this statement becomes clearer if it is rephrased. Thus,

$$\text{if} \qquad E + B = M + L$$
$$\text{then} \quad E - M = L - B$$

The left-hand side of the latter equation is the country's *export surplus*; if it is negative, it is the import surplus. The right-hand side is the country's *net* addition per period of time, by lending and investment, to its *foreign wealth*; if it is negative, it is the net reduction in its foreign wealth.

Hence, if a country wants to undertake *net* lending and investment abroad, a freely fluctuating exchange rate has to be at a level which makes the total value of exports exceed that of imports. Thus, suppose that initially $E = M$. If net foreign lending and investment is now undertaken, this creates an extra supply of domestic currency (i.e. demand for foreign currency) on the exchange market. The country's currency depreciates in terms of others. The range and quantities of its exports increase, and the range and quantities of its imports decrease. The exchange rate continues to fall until a sufficient export surplus has been created to offset the net foreign lending and investment. The reverse occurs when there is net foreign borrowing and investment in the country by others.

The analysis of the relations between exchange rates and international trade and capital transactions can now be carried further by showing how all these transactions are recorded in balances of payments.

CHAPTER 35

THE BALANCE OF PAYMENTS

The *balance of payments* of a country is the classified record of its foreign trade in goods and services and its foreign capital transactions per period of time. The trade and capital transactions are grouped separately. The former comprise the *current account* of the balance of payments and the latter its *capital account*.

The nature of these accounts will be explained first of all on the assumption that the country's exchange rate is a freely fluctuating one. It will then be shown how monetary authorities can intervene in the foreign exchange markets in order to control (or *peg*) the levels of exchange rates. They do this by buying and selling currencies for one another. These *official monetary transactions* will be grouped in a third account of the balance of payments, namely the *official monetary account*. They are a sub-category of capital transactions, but they are classified separately in order to bring out their function of pegging exchange rates.

The current and capital accounts of the balance of payments, when the exchange rate is freely fluctuating, are shown in Table 35.1. All the transactions which give rise to *payments* by the country in question to the rest of the world are on the right-hand sides of the accounts; and all those which give rise to *receipts* from the rest of the world are on

TABLE 35.1

The Balance of Payments

RECEIPTS	PAYMENTS
Current Account	
Exports:	Imports:
(i) goods	(i) goods
(ii) services	(ii) services
Capital Account	
Borrowing from foreign countries	Lending to foreign countries
Direct investment by foreign countries	Direct investment in foreign countries

the left-hand sides. The payments involve a supply of the domestic currency of the country in question and a demand for foreign currencies; the receipts involve a demand for domestic currency and a supply of foreign currencies. The balance of payments is usually set out in terms of domestic currency; but it can of course be expressed in any foreign currency at the ruling exchange rate.

The payments on current account are for the imports of goods and services. The latter include the expenditures by the country on foreign transport services and on foreign financial and insurance services, the expenditures of its tourists and businessmen when they are travelling abroad, and the remittances out of income made to foreigners. Government foreign expenditures (e.g. on maintaining armed forces abroad, on embassies, and on grants made to foreign countries) are included under the head of imported services. Lastly, these also include any rents, interest, and profits which are paid to foreigners in respect of land, securities, and capital they own in the country in question. These are payments to foreigners for the services yielded by the wealth they own in the country.

The values of imported goods entered in the current account do not include any tariffs levied on them, nor the freight and insurance charges incurred in bringing them to the country. The tariffs are paid to the government of the country and not to foreigners. The freight and insurance services may be provided by the country's own firms. If not, they are entered under imported services.

The receipts on current account come from the exports of goods and services. The latter can include the same kinds of items as already listed for imported services, viz. expenditures by foreigners on the country's transport, financial and insurance services, and by them during visits to the country; remittances to residents made by foreigners out of income; foreign goverments' expenditures in the country; and any rents, interest, and profits received on the country's ownership of wealth in foreign countries. The values of exported goods include any taxes levied on them by the exporting country, since these are paid by foreigners. But they do not include the freight and insurance charges incurred in taking the exports abroad. If any of these are received by domestic firms, they are entered under exported services.

The *balance* on the current account[1] of the balance of payments may be *positive*, i.e. an excess of receipts over payments resulting from an export surplus; or it may be *negative*, i.e. an excess of payments over receipts resulting from an import surplus. The positive or negative

---

[1] I.e. the difference between the totals of the two sides of the account.

balance of trade is the sum of the balance of trade in goods and the balance of trade in services.[1] Some developed countries (e.g. the UK) often have a negative balance of trade in goods, but a positive balance of trade in services.

Lending to foreign countries involves the *payment* of the loans to foreigners. It is therefore entered on the *right-hand* side of the capital account. So is investment in real assets (e.g. land, factories) abroad, since it also involves payments to foreigners. This is usually called *direct* investment in foreign countries. The prefix 'direct' is used to distinguish it from the *total* foreign investment by the country. The latter term is used for the addition, per period of time, to the country's foreign wealth. A country adds to its foreign wealth both by lending abroad and by acquiring foreign real assets. Hence foreign investment by a country, in the broader sense, equals the *sum* of its lending to, and *direct* investment in, other countries. The amount of foreign investment in total has, of course, to be measured after taking into account any repayment by foreigners of past loans, and any sale of foreign real assets in the period in question.

The receipts on capital account arise out of borrowing from foreign countries, and direct investment in the country by foreigners. Borrowing from foreign countries involves the *receipt* of loans from foreigners. It is therefore entered on the *left-hand* side of the capital account. So are the sales of real assets to foreigners, since these involve receipts from them. *Total* foreign investment in the country per period of time is the *sum* of the borrowing from foreign countries and the *direct* investment in the country by foreigners. Its amount has, of course, to be measured after taking into account any repayment to foreigners of past borrowing, and any purchase of domestic real assets from foreigners in the period in question.

Total foreign investment by the country *less* total investment in it by foreigners measures the *net* addition, per period of time, to the country's foreign wealth. It is therefore called *net* foreign investment. It may be positive or negative: a country can add to its foreign wealth by lending more to foreigners than it borrows from them, and by acquiring more foreign real assets than the domestic real assets which are acquired by foreigners; or the reverse.

The *balance* on the capital account[2] of the balance of payments may be *positive*, i.e. an excess of receipts over payments; or it may be

---

[1] Trade in goods is sometimes referred to as visible trade, and trade in services as invisible trade.

[2] I.e. the difference between the totals of the two sides of the account.

negative, i.e. an excess of payments over receipts. A *negative* balance on capital account therefore means that the country's net foreign investment is *positive*. The latter is a net addition to its foreign wealth. It has to be paid for; and that is why the capital account shows an excess of payments over receipts, viz. a negative balance. Similarly, a *positive* balance on capital account means that the country's net foreign investment is *negative*, i.e. it is disinvesting. The foreign disinvestment provides an excess of capital account receipts over payments.

It was shown in the previous chapter how a freely fluctuating exchange rate will move to the level which equates the quantity demanded of a currency with the quantity supplied. The quantity demanded is given by the total of the receipts on the left-hand side of the balance of payments; and the quantity supplied is given by the total of the payments on the right-hand side. A freely fluctuating exchange rate will therefore bring the two totals into equality. The balance of payments is then said to be in *equilibrium*. That is, equilibrium in the exchange rate, and equilibrium in the balance of payments, are two aspects of the same situation.

Equilibrium in the balance of payments means that any positive balance on its current account is exactly offset by a negative balance on its capital account; and vice versa. This situation is, as was seen in the previous chapter,[1] the one required for equilibrium in the exchange rate, namely, $E - M = L - B$, or $(E - M) - (L - B) = 0$.

THE PEGGING OF EXCHANGE RATES

Most governments, most of the time, prefer to have stable exchange rates for their currencies. These are thought to increase the volumes of foreign trade and investment as compared with fluctuating rates. With stability in exchange rates, exporters know the amounts of domestic currency which they can obtain from their earnings of foreign currencies, and lenders know the amounts of domestic currency which they will get when their loans to foreign countries are repaid. If the rates are free to fluctuate, international trade and investment are subject to an additional uncertainty, i.e. additional to those which obtain for domestic trade and investment. A depreciation in *foreign* currencies, in the interval between the planning and the selling of exports, will reduce exporters' earnings of *domestic* currency below what they had expected; and it will also reduce the domestic currency value of loans to foreign countries. Because of this risk, less foreign trade and investment may be undertaken.

[1] See pp. 442–443 above.

Moreover, when exchange rates are free to fluctuate, speculation against currencies may *amplify* any changes in them. Thus, when a currency depreciates, some people may fear that it will depreciate further. They will then, as far as possible, sell domestic assets and buy foreign ones. This makes the currency depreciate further. If speculation produces this de-stabilizing effect on exchange rates, the exchange risks to foreign trade and investment are increased.

For the above reasons, governments peg exchange rates at particular levels for shorter or longer periods of time. They, or their central banks, do this today by buying and selling currencies on the foreign exchange market. This will be exemplified in terms of the pound and the dollar, to the exclusion of all other currencies.

Suppose that the UK and the US governments agree to stabilize the exchange rate at £1 = $2.40.[1] They will not, of course, need to take action if the total of payments, on both current and capital accounts of the UK balance of payments, happens to equal the total of receipts on both accounts, when the rate is £1 = $2.40.[2] The rate will then be in equilibrium at that level. But action will be required if total payments do not equal total receipts, since a freely fluctuating exchange rate would then, in the absence of official action, move away from £1 = $2.40.

This can be prevented by intervention in the foreign exchange market by one, or other, or both, of the countries' central banks, namely the Bank of England and the US Federal Reserve System. Strictly speaking, the banks are acting in this respect as agents of their governments' Treasuries; and they use the latters' *Exchange Stabilization Accounts*.[3] These accounts are the devices employed to stabilize (i.e. peg) exchange rates in the following way.

Suppose that the UK total foreign payments per day exceed its total foreign receipts by £1 million, when the rate is £1 = $2.40. There is a 1 million *excess supply* of pounds. To prevent the pound from depreciating, the Bank of England (B/E for short) will buy £1 million in the foreign exchange market. It pays for these pounds by drawing upon its dollar account[4] with the Federal Reserve Bank of New York (FRB for short). The B/E banks with the FRB in the same way as a UK commercial bank keeps an account with its 'correspondent' US commercial bank.

---

[1] Which is the present (1968) stabilized rate, with the minor qualification that the rate is allowed to vary within the narrow range of £1 = $2.38 to £1 = $2.42.

[2] This means, of course, that total receipts also equal total payments on the US balance of payments, when only the two countries are considered.

[3] This is the general term used throughout the world, but in the UK the account is called the Exchange Equalization Account.

[4] Strictly speaking, that of the UK Exchange Equalization Account.

By selling dollars from its account with the FRB, the B/E buys up the excess supply of pounds on the foreign exchange market. This prevents the pound from depreciating. Or put the other way round: by selling dollars, the B/E offsets the *excess demand* for dollars on the market and prevents the dollar from appreciating.

The FRB can act to the same end. It[1] keeps a sterling account with the B/E. By purchasing pounds—which are added to that account—and selling dollars, the FRB can offset the excess supply of pounds (the excess demand for dollars), and prevent the pound from depreciating (the dollar from appreciating).

These central bank actions to prevent the pound depreciating are called *support* for the pound. Hence the B/E can support the pound by reducing its dollar account with the FRB; and the latter can do likewise by increasing its sterling account with the B/E. Contrariwise, if the US total foreign payments exceed its total foreign receipts, the FRB can support the dollar by selling pounds from its account with the B/E; and the latter can do likewise by purchasing dollars and adding them to its account with the FRB.

A central bank has unlimited power to support *foreign* currencies. That is, it has unlimited power to prevent its own currency from *appreciating*. A freely fluctuating pound will appreciate if there is an excess demand for it. The B/E can prevent the appreciation by supplying additional pounds to the exchange market. The B/E controls the creation of pounds, i.e. of UK bank debts,[2] and can therefore provide any amount necessary to prevent the pound appreciating (the dollar depreciating). But in doing this, the B/E adds to its dollar account with the FRB. Thus support of a foreign currency by a central bank implies a willingness by it to hold more of that currency.

On the other hand, a central bank has only limited power to support its *own* currency. A freely fluctuating pound will depreciate if there is an excess supply of it. The B/E can prevent the depreciation only insofar as it has a dollar balance with the FRB, which can be used to buy up the excess supply of pounds. The B/E cannot create dollars—as it can create pounds. Its power to prevent the pound from depreciating therefore depends on the size of its dollar holding, and on its ability to acquire more dollars.

There are a number of ways in which the UK government may be able to acquire more dollars for the Exchange Equalization Account. It can sell any assets (e.g. securities) that it may own in the US, and it can

---

[1] Strictly speaking, the US Exchange Stabilization Account.
[2] As explained in Chapter 29 above.

purchase with pounds (by agreement or compulsion) US assets owned by its citizens and sell them for dollars. It may be able to borrow dollars from other central banks and from the International Monetary Fund.[1] The B/E can also sell gold held by the Exchange Equalization Account. This is the immediate way in which additional dollars will be acquired for the B/E account with the FRB, when it falls to a low level.

Gold has ceased for some time to be used as a *domestic* money in most developed countries. Nor is it now used to settle international transactions between people and firms. That is done, as has been seen, by bank money transfers between internationally correspondent commercial banks. But gold is still used as one means—though not the only one—of settling debts between central banks. It is one form of world money at the *central bank level*. Its value for this purpose is $35 per oz, which is the price at which the US Treasury is willing to buy it—and sell it, but *only* to monetary authorities.

If the US Treasury ceased to be willing to buy gold at $35 per oz, it seems likely that its price would fall below that level. Gold has commercial and industrial uses, and some people, especially in the Middle and Far East, hold it as a form of wealth. But if the central banks' monetary demand for gold disappeared, the other demands for it would probably be insufficient to sustain its price at $35.[2]

The gold and dollars (and a few other currencies) held by the Exchange Equalization Account are the *official foreign exchange reserves*. Their function is to be used, as required, to peg the exchange value of the pound. The pegging operation is carried out, as explained above, by purchases or sales of dollars through the B/E account with the FRB. That account rises (falls) according as UK total foreign receipts are greater than (less than) its total foreign payments.[3] Any large addition to the account is used to buy gold; any large fall in it is replenished by a sale of gold. A continuing *rise* in the official foreign exchange reserves may require, and a continuing *fall* in them certainly will require, some form of action to change the foreign receipts and payments situation that is causing the alteration in the reserves. This matter will be analysed in Chapters 36 and 37 below.

---

[1] Whose working will be explained in Chapter 37 below.
[2] The fact that gold now (1968) sells for more than $35 per oz., on some markets in the world, depends on the belief that the US Treasury will raise its buying price.
[3] This statement has to be qualified, because of the operation of the Sterling Area, which is explained in texts on the UK banking system.

EQUILIBRIUM AND DISEQUILIBRIUM

The purchases and sales of currencies by monetary authorities, for the purpose of pegging exchange rates, will be called official monetary transactions. They are entered in a separate *official monetary account*

TABLE 35.2
The UK Balance of Payments

RECEIPTS	PAYMENTS
Current Account	
Exports:	Imports:
(i) goods	(i) goods
(ii) services	(ii) services
Capital Account	
Borrowing from foreign countries	Lending to foreign countries
Direct investment by foreign countries	Direct investment in foreign countries
Official Monetary Account	
Increase in:	Increase in:
foreign official holdings of pounds	UK official reserves of gold and foreign currencies

in the balance of payments. This is done, in Table 35.2, in a form appropriate for the UK. The current and capital accounts have the same form as in Table 35.1. above.

When the B/E sells, i.e. makes *payments* of, pounds to prevent the pound appreciating, it acquires gold and/or foreign currencies in return. *Increases* in the UK official reserves of gold and foreign currencies therefore go on the right-hand (payments) side of the official monetary account. When the B/E buys pounds to prevent the pound depreciating, its reserves of gold and/or foreign currencies *decrease*. The item on the right-hand side of the monetary account then has a *negative sign*.

Foreign monetary authorities can buy pounds to prevent their own currencies appreciating (the pound depreciating). Increases in foreign official holdings of pounds are *receipts* to the UK, and go on the left-hand side of the monetary account. This item has a *negative sign* when foreign monetary authorities sell pounds in order to support their own currencies.

The *balance* on the official monetary account[1] is necessarily the *same* size as, but of *opposite* sign to, the *sum* of the balances on the current

[1] I.e. the difference between the totals of the two sides of the account.

and capital accounts. Suppose that the current account balance is positive at £300 million, i.e. exports exceed imports by that amount; and that the capital account balance is negative at −£200 million, i.e. lending to foreign countries, etc., exceeds borrowing from foreign countries, etc., by that amount. The sum of the balances is positive at £100 million, i.e. UK total foreign receipts from trade and capital transactions exceed its total foreign payments by that amount. There is therefore an excess *demand* for pounds of 100 million.

To prevent the pound appreciating, the B/E can sell 100 million of pounds and add a corresponding amount to its reserves of gold and foreign currencies. This item is on the right-hand (payments) side of the monetary account, which therefore has a *negative* balance, viz. of −£100. That balance is equal to, but of opposite sign to, the sum of the current and capital account balances, because the monetary account transaction is exactly *offsetting* the excess of receipts over payments on the other two accounts.

Alternatively in this situation, foreign monetary authorities can sell 100 million of their holdings of pounds to prevent their currencies depreciating (the pound appreciating). This *decrease* in foreign official holdings of pounds means that the entry of £100 million on the left-hand side of the monetary account has a *negative sign*. Once again the balance on the monetary account is −£100 million. This time it is the foreign monetary authorities which are offsetting the excess of UK receipts over payments on current and capital accounts. The offset can, of course, be brought about in part by an increase in UK official reserves, and in part by a decrease in foreign official holdings of pounds.

Thus, when monetary authorities peg exchange rates, the balance on the official monetary account of the balance of payments is *necessarily* equal to, but of opposite sign to, the sum of the balances on the current and the capital accounts. Hence, the sum of the balances on all *three* accounts is necessarily zero. This means that the sum of the receipts on all three accounts necessarily equals the sum of the payments on all three accounts. That is, when the balance of payments is presented in the form of Table 35.2, the totals of its two sides are necessarily the same.

Since the balance of payments necessarily *balances* in this way, what meaning can now be given—under a régime of pegged exchange rates —to the distinction between *equilibrium* and *disequilibrium* in the balance of payments?

One possibility is to argue by analogy from the case of freely fluctuating exchange rates. As was seen above,[1] such rates are in

[1] On p. 447.

equilibrium—in the usual *market* sense of the term—when the quantities demanded of currencies are equal to the corresponding quantities supplied. This obtains when the total of receipts, on both the *current* and the *capital* accounts of each country's balance of payments, is equal to the total of payments on these accounts. The balance of payments is then said to be equilibrium. The equilibrium of freely fluctuating exchange rates, and of balances of payments, are thus two aspects of the same situation.

This *market* concept of equilibrium can be carried over to the case of pegged exchange rates. The criterion for equilibrium in the balance of payments would then be that sum of the balances on the *current* and *capital* accounts is zero. This necessarily means that the balance on the official monetary account is zero. Disequilibrium would obtain if the sum of the balances on current and capital accounts is positive or negative, i.e. if the balance on the monetary account is negative or positive.

On this basis, the balance of payments is said to be in *surplus* if the sum of the balances on current and capital accounts is *positive*; and in *deficit*, if the sum of the two balances is *negative*. That is, a deficit on the balance of payments means that a country is losing foreign exchange reserves, and/or other countries are increasing their official holdings of its currency; and the reverse for a surplus.

These concepts of surplus and deficit on the balance of payments need to be given further consideration. That will be done during the following analyses of the ways in which disequilibrium in balances of payments can be corrected.

CHAPTER 36

ADJUSTMENTS IN BALANCES
OF PAYMENTS

Equilibrium in balances of payments can be disturbed in a number of ways. The disturbance may occur in the current account: the values of imports or exports may change. Or it may occur in the capital account: the total of lending and direct investment abroad by the country, or that of borrowing from abroad and direct investment in it by other countries, may change. Each kind of disturbance has a number of possible causes. This can be seen from the analyses, in terms of the UK and the US, of Chapters 33 and 34 above.

At any exchange rate for the pound, the range and volumes of UK exports depend on the US conditions of demand for these goods, and on the UK conditions of supply for them; and also on transport costs and US tariffs. The US conditions of demand—as indicated by the demand curves for the goods—show the quantities of UK exports which will be bought at different dollar prices for them. But those quantities also depend on US real incomes and preferences between goods (which are parameters of the US demand curves). If the incomes or preferences change, the demand curves will shift their positions. In that case, the US will buy *different* quantities of UK exports at *any* set of dollar prices for them.

If the US real national income increases, or if US preferences change in favour of UK goods, the volume and value in pounds of UK exports will increase. Starting from a position of equilibrium, the UK balance of payments will then move into surplus. It will, on the other hand, move into deficit if the US real national income decreases, or if US preferences change away from UK goods in favour of US ones.

The conditions of supply for UK export goods—as indicated by the supply curves for them—show the sterling prices at which different quantities of them will be offered for export. Their dollar export prices will then depend on the exchange rate, transport costs, and US tariffs. The supply prices in pounds depend on cost conditions in the UK which, in their turn, depend on factor prices in pounds and on physical productivities. If the factor prices rise, or if physical productivities decrease, the sterling supply prices of UK export goods will rise. Hence their dollar export prices, at *any* exchange rate, will be higher.

The increase in the dollar supply prices of UK exports will, with given US demand conditions, cause a contraction in the range and volumes of those exports. What will happen to their *total value* in pounds (or dollars) depends on the average US price elasticity of demand (US ε_D) for them. If that is greater than 1, the total value in pounds of UK exports will *decrease*. Starting from equilibrium, the UK balance of payments will then move into deficit as a result of the rise in prices in the UK. But if the US ε_D happens to be less than 1, the total value in pounds of UK exports will increase as UK prices rise. The UK balance of payments will then move into surplus. These principles apply in reverse to the case where prices fall in the UK as a result of improvements in technology or reductions in factor prices.

The levels of transport costs, and of US tariffs, also influence the range and volumes of UK exports. If the US raises its tariff rates, the dollar export prices of UK goods rise and their range and volume contract. The total value in pounds of UK exports—*excluding* the tariffs, which are paid to the US government—will therefore decrease at any exchange rate. Starting from equilibrium, the UK balance of payments will then move into deficit. It will, on the other hand, move into surplus if the US lowers its tariff rates.

A similar analysis explains disturbances in the sterling value of UK imports. The range and volumes of these depend on the UK conditions of demand for them, and on the US conditions of supply; and also on transport costs and UK tariffs. If the UK real national income increases, or if UK preferences change in favour of US goods, the volume and value in pounds of UK imports will increase. Starting from equilibrium, the UK balance of payments will then move into deficit. It will, on the other hand, move into surplus if the UK real national income decreases, or if UK preferences change away from US goods in favour of UK ones.

An improvement in US technology, or a fall in US factor prices, will lower the dollar (and pound) supply prices of US export goods. What will happen to the total value in pounds (or dollars) of UK imports depends on the average UK price elasticity of demand (UK ε_D) for them. If it is greater than 1, the total value in pounds of UK imports will increase, and the UK balance of payments will move into deficit. But if the UK ε_D happens to be less than 1, the UK balance of payments will move into surplus as the prices of US exports fall. These principles apply in reverse when US export prices rise.

However, it must now be remembered that a fall in the domestic prices of a country's goods will affect the volumes of *both* its exports and imports. Suppose that technology improves, or factor prices fall, in the UK, so that the sterling prices of *all* goods produced in the UK fall. The range and volume of UK exports will expand. At the same time, the range and volume of UK imports will contract, since the now cheaper UK goods will be substituted, to some extent, for goods imported from the US. Hence, the *direction* (i.e. into surplus or deficit) in which the UK balance of payments is disturbed—when UK prices fall—depends on what happens to the total values in pounds of *both* exports and imports.

As the sterling prices of UK exports fall, their total value in pounds will increase or decrease according as the US ε_D for them is greater or less than 1. As the sterling prices of UK goods fall, this means a *rise* in the prices of imported US goods *relatively* to them. There is, however, no change in the *absolute* levels of the prices in pounds of US goods. The volume of UK imports, and their total value in pounds, at the ruling sterling prices of US goods, will therefore contract as long as the UK ε_D for US goods is greater than 0.

If the US ε_D is greater than 1, and the UK ε_D is greater than 0, the UK balance of payments will (starting from equilibrium) move into surplus, when UK prices fall. The total value in pounds of UK exports *increases* when the US ε_D is greater than 1, and the total value in pounds of UK imports *decreases* when the UK ε_D is greater than 0. But if the US ε_D is less than 1, the total value in pounds of UK exports will *decrease*. If this decrease is *less* than that in the total value in pounds of UK imports, the UK balance of payments will still move into surplus. But if it is *greater*, a deficit will result.

It is thus the sizes of *both* the US ε_D and the UK ε_D which determine the *direction* of change in the UK balance of payments, when UK prices fall. The general principle is: the balance of payments will move into surplus if US ε_D *plus* UK ε_D is *greater* than 1; and into deficit, if US ε_D *plus* UK ε_D is *less* than 1. This is most easily illustrated by supposing that the UK ε_D equals 0. The volume of UK imports is then unchanged when UK prices fall; and their total value in pounds remains *constant* (the sterling prices of US goods being unchanged). If the US ε_D is greater than 1— so that the *sum* of the two elasticities is greater than 1—the total value in pounds of UK exports *increases*, and the balance of payments moves into surplus. But if the US ε_D is less than 1—so that the *sum* of the two elasticities is less than 1—the total value in pounds of UK exports *decreases*, and the balance of payments moves into deficit.

These relationships, between the price elasticities of demand for exports and imports and the overall change in the balance of payments, have been met before. It has been shown[1] how a depreciation of the pound will eliminate a deficit on the UK balance of payments, if US ε_D plus UK ε_D is greater than 1; but that it will enlarge the deficit, if US ε_D plus UK ε_D is less than 1. The above analysis reaches the same conclusions in respect of a fall in the sterling prices of all UK goods. This is to be expected, since a change in the exchange rate for the pound, and a change in the UK price level, are alternative ways of altering the prices of UK goods *relatively* to those of other countries' goods. UK goods prices can be lowered, relatively to US goods prices, either by depreciating the pound, or by lowering the UK price level.[2] The overall effect on the balance of payments then depends, in both cases, on the price elasticities of demand for exports and imports.

Thus, when the price level of a country changes, equilibrium in its balance of payments will be disturbed by alterations in both its exports and imports. The *sum* of the price elasticities of demand for the exports and imports of a single country is likely to be greater than 1.[3] Hence, a rise in its price level will probably move its balance of payments into deficit; and vice versa.

Finally, a disturbance in the balance of payments can occur in the capital account. Lending and direct investment between countries will change if interest rates and expected internal rates of return on investment projects alter, and if people come to expect a change in exchange rates. Thus, a rise in UK interest rates will reduce its lending abroad, and will attract more lending to it by foreigners. Starting from a position of equilibrium, the UK balance of payments will then move into surplus.

THE EFFECTS OF DISTURBANCES

The different kinds of disturbance in balances of payments have different effects on the economies of the countries involved. These have to be distinguished in analysing the adjustment processes through which disequilibrium is corrected. In particular, it is essential to distinguish disturbances which arise in the current account from those which arise in the capital account.

Contrast, for example, the following two ways in which the UK balance of payments can move into deficit: (i) through a change in US preferences away from UK goods, and in favour of US goods, which decreases UK exports, and (ii) through a rise in US interest rates, resulting

[1] On pp. 434–437 above.
[2] As can easily be seen by means of Table 33.1 on p. 421 above.
[3] See p. 438 above.

from a change in US monetary policy, which decreases US lending to the UK. Suppose, in both cases, that the exchange rate is kept pegged at a particular level.

In the former case, the decreased demand for UK goods will lower the national output and/or the price level in that country. The fall in real income, and/or in prices, in the UK will reduce its demand for US goods. This decrease in UK imports will offset, at least to some extent, the initial fall in UK exports. At the same time, the change in US preferences towards its own goods increases the demand for them and raises the national output and/or the price level in that country. The rise in real income, and/or in prices, in the US will increase its demand for UK goods. This increase in US imports will offset, at least to some extent, the initial decrease in them because of the change in preferences.

Now consider the case where a rise in US interest rates reduces its lending to the UK. The reduced flow of lending on the UK financial markets will raise interest rates in that country as well. The higher interest rates will reduce expenditure on investment in both countries, and therefore lower their national outputs and/or their price levels. If real incomes are reduced in both countries, their imports from each other will fall. If their price levels change, exports will increase and imports decrease for the country whose price level falls to the *greater* extent.

Thus the changes in US preferences and US interest rates both move the UK balance of payments into deficit. But beyond that, their effects are different. The former change lowers the national output, and/or the price level, in the UK, and does the reverse in the US. The latter change lowers the national output, and/or the price level, in both countries.

The general point which this illustrates is that changes in balances of payments disturb the equilibrium of national outputs and price levels, and that different changes do so in different ways. Moreover, the changes in national outputs and price levels themselves have effects on balances of payments, since they help to determine the quantities of goods traded between countries. The 'internal' and 'external' sides of economic systems act and react on each other. Adjustment in balances of payments therefore involve the interconnections between *internal equilibrium* (in national output and the price level) and *external equilibrium* (viz. in the balance of payments).

This complex matter will be analysed one step at a time, by considering separately the *five* different ways in which disequilibrium in balances of payments can be corrected, namely by (i) changes in *exchange rates*, (ii) changes in the *national outputs* of countries, (iii) changes in the *price levels* of countries, (iv) changes in *capital transactions* between countries, and (v) changes in *direct controls* like tariffs, subsidies, quantitative restrictions, and exchange control.

The way in which changes in exchange rates correct disequilibrium has already been explained in Chapter 34 above. For the rest of this chapter, the exchange rate will be assumed to be pegged at a constant level, in order to separate out the effects of the other four methods of adjusting balances of payments.

CHANGES IN NATIONAL OUTPUTS

It is now necessary to extend the macroeconomic analysis of Part III above to an *open* economy. In a closed economy, the aggregate supply of goods comes entirely from domestic production (Y). The aggregate demand for goods comprises consumption (C), domestic investment (I), and government expenditure on goods and services (G). A closed economy is in equilibrium when $Y = C + I + G$. The money value of Y is the product of the volume of national output (X) and the price level (P).

In an open economy, imports (M) are a source of supply of goods in addition to domestic production. Aggregate supply now equals $Y + M$. Exports (E) are an additional element in the demand for the goods available in an open economy. Aggregate demand now equals $C + I + G + E$. The economy will therefore be in *internal* equilibrium when

$$Y + M = C + I + G + E$$

Since internal equilibrium is the equilibrium of Y, it is convenient to re-arrange this equation by taking M over to the right-hand side. It can then be seen that Y is in equilibrium when

$$Y = C + I + G + (E - M)$$

Brackets have been put around $E - M$ to draw attention to the fact that the difference between them—which can be positive or negative— is the balance on the *current* account of the balance of payments. The *sum* of it, and the balance on the *capital* account, indicates whether or not the economy is in *external* equilibrium, i.e. whether or not the balance of payments is in equilibrium. This is so if the sum of the balances on both accounts is zero.

With a pegged exchange rate, an economy can be in internal equilibrium without necessarily being in external equilibrium at the same time. Y will be in equilibrium if it equals $C + I + G + (E - M)$. But the value of $(E - M)$ in this situation may not be equal to, and of opposite sign to, the balance on the capital account of the balance of payments. Thus, suppose that E exceeds M, when Y is in equilibrium. This export surplus must be offset by a *negative* balance, of equivalent size, on the capital account, if the balance of payments is to be in equilibrium. That is, the *net* amount of lending and direct investment abroad must equal the export surplus. If it does not, there will either be excess demand for, or excess supply of, the country's currency on the foreign exchange market. Monetary authorities will therefore have to undertake official transactions in currencies in order to keep the exchange rate pegged at the chosen level.[1]

The net amount of lending and direct investment abroad depends on interest rates and on expected internal rates of return on investment projects, both at home and abroad. These various influences may not be such as to produce, at the pegged exchange rate, a *negative* balance on capital account which just offsets the export surplus. Hence, there is no necessity for external equilibrium to exist simultaneously with internal equilibrium.

If it does not, and if governments wish to maintain stable exchange rates, they must use some other methods (i.e. than changes in exchange rates) to correct the balance of payments disequilibrium. They have a choice between changes in national output levels, in price levels, in capital transactions, and in direct controls. The macroeconomic analysis of an open economy can now be used to explain how these various changes can correct external disequilibrium. First, consider changes in national outputs; and, in order to isolate their effects, assume that price levels remain constant.

It has already been explained how the volume of a country's imports depends on the level of its real national income. As its national output (X), and therefore its real income, rises, the demand curves for imported goods will shift upwards (i.e. *increase*). At given prices and exchange rates, the volume and value of imports will therefore expand. Similarly, the volume and value of a country's exports depend on the level of *other* countries' national outputs. As real incomes rise in the rest of the world, it will buy more of the exports of the country in question.

The way in which a country's imports depend on its national output is called its *import function*.[2] Like any functional relation between economic quantities, it can be expressed in a total, an average, or a

[1] See pp. 451–452 above.
[2] Or its propensity to import.

marginal form. Total M expands as X rises. The *average propensity to import*, at any level of X, is measured by $\dfrac{M}{X}$: it shows the average amount of M per unit of X. The *marginal propensity to import*, at any level of X, is measured by $\dfrac{\Delta M}{\Delta X}$: it shows by how much M will *change* when X changes.

Suppose that the UK balance of payments moves into deficit; and that the US is taken to stand for the rest of the world. The UK deficit could be eliminated by a *fall* in the UK national output (X_{UK})—because this will reduce UK imports (M_{UK}); or it could be eliminated by a rise in the US national output (X_{US})—because this will increase US imports (M_{US}), which are the same thing as UK exports (E_{UK}). Thus, suppose that the UK balance of payments deficit is £100 million; that the UK marginal propensity to import is $\frac{1}{5}$ over the relevant range of X_{UK}; and that the US marginal propensity to import is $\frac{1}{20}$ over the relevant range of X_{US}. The deficit could be eliminated by a fall of £500 million in X_{UK}, since M_{UK} will then be reduced by $\frac{1}{5}$ of that amount; or it could be eliminated by a rise of £2,000 million in X_{US}, since M_{US} ($\equiv E_{UK}$) will then be expanded by $\frac{1}{20}$ of that amount. Some combination of a fall in X_{UK}, and a rise in X_{US}, will, of course, also eliminate the deficit.

The changes in X_{UK}, and/or X_{US}, required to restore equilibrium to the UK balance of payments, can be brought about by deliberate acts of economic policy. The UK and/or US governments could, by changes in their monetary and fiscal policies, lower X_{UK} and/or raise X_{US} (insofar as there unemployed resources available to do this). However, the required changes in X_{UK} and X_{US} may come about *in part* through the ordinary working of the two economies. *Some* amounts of change in X_{UK} and X_{US}, in the required directions, may follow automatically when the UK balance of payments moves into deficit.

It was shown above[1] how disturbances in balances of payments will probably also disturb the equilibrium of national outputs. For example, if US preferences change in favour of US goods, and against UK goods, M_{US} ($\equiv E_{UK}$) decreases and the UK balance of payments moves into deficit. At the same time, the decreased demand for E_{UK} lowers output, employment, and real income in the UK export industries. This starts a downward *multiplier* process, in exactly the same way as a decrease in C, or I, or G would. The initial fall in UK real income—because of the

[1] On pp. 457–458.

decrease in E_{UK}—causes a contraction in C, which reduces output, employment, and real income in the consumer goods industries. This secondary fall in UK real income causes a further contraction in C— leading to still further contractions in the way already analysed.[1]

However, the multiplier process in an *open* economy differs in one respect from that in a closed economy. When aggregate expenditure falls, the demand for imports decreases, as well as the demand for domestically produced goods. *Not all* of the decrease in aggregate expenditure causes a corresponding reduction in domestic output, employment, and real income. The part of it which falls on imports reduces output, employment, and real income in the other countries which were supplying the imports. The *domestic* effect of the downward multiplier process is *smaller*, to the extent that part of its total effect operates abroad through the contraction in imports. The size of the multiplier within an open economy is thus *smaller* than it would be if the economy were closed.

The extent to which the size of the multiplier for an open economy is reduced in this way depends on the magnitude of the country's marginal propensity to import. The larger it is, the greater is the part of any decrease in aggregate expenditure which falls on imports, and the smaller is the part which falls on domestic production. The multiplier for an open economy will be the smaller, the larger is its marginal propensity to import.

Thus the decrease in E_{UK}, caused by the change in US preferences, automatically causes a fall in X_{UK} and, consequentially, in M_{UK}. At the same time, aggregate expenditure in the US rises because of the increased preference for US goods. This starts an upward multiplier process, whose size will depend on the magnitude of the US marginal propensity to import. The smaller it is, the greater is the part of the increase in aggregate expenditure which raises X_{US}, and the smaller is the part which raises M_{US}.

It has now been seen how the disturbance, in the UK balance of payments, has upset the equilibria of X_{UK} and X_{US}; and how the changes in them have had consequential effects on the balance of payments. The fall in X_{UK} reduces M_{UK}; and the rise in X_{US} expands E_{UK}. The contraction of M_{UK} and the expansion of E_{UK} will at least partially offset the initial *decrease* in E_{UK}. Thus, *this* disturbance in the balance of payments has automatically caused changes in national outputs, which, through their effects on imports and exports, have (at least in part) helped to correct the disequilibrium in the balance of payments.

[1] On pp. 293–298 above.

It was emphasized earlier,[1] however, that different kinds of disturbance in balances of payments have different effects on the economies of the countries involved. It cannot, therefore, be said in general whether the changes in national outputs, which result from such disturbances, will or will not in themselves help to correct the disequilibrium which has arisen in balances of payments. Moreover, even if they do so help, the extent of their contribution to the correction of disequilibrium will vary from case to case. It will, for example, depend on the magnitudes of the marginal propensities to import of both the UK and the US in the above analysis. The larger these are, the greater will be the contraction in M_{UK} and the expansion in E_{UK}; and thus the greater will be the offset to the initial decrease in E_{UK}.

National output changes can thus correct balance of payments disequilibrium. The required changes may come about, *in part*, through the automatic responses of price mechanisms to disturbances in balances of payments. But they may have to be induced, in part, by deliberate changes in the monetary and fiscal policies of governments.

CHANGES IN PRICE LEVELS

Disturbances in balance of payments can cause changes in price levels, as well as in national outputs. The simultaneous determination of the price level and national output, by means of the conditions of aggregate demand and aggregate supply, was analysed in Chapter 27 above. The principles of that analysis are not altered by extending it to an open economy.

An increase in aggregate demand (i.e. an upward *shift* in the Z curve) in an open economy can come from an increase in C, or I, or G, or E—or from a switch in expenditure away from M and towards domestically produced goods. The effect on the price level then depends on the condition of aggregate supply (i.e. the *shape* of the Y curve), and on any changes in it (i.e. *shifts* in the Y curve) that may result from the increase in aggregate demand. Suppose that—starting from equilibrium in the balance of payments—there is an increase in E_{UK}. If there are unemployed resources in the UK, and if the money wage rate (W) remains unchanged, the increase in aggregate demand will raise the price level insofar as marginal cost rises as X_{UK} expands. If there are no unemployed resources, a demand inflation will be caused by the increase in

---

[1] On pp. 457–458.

E_{UK}. In this case, W increases (because of the excess demand for labour), the Y curve shifts upwards, and the UK price level rises.

The rise in the prices of UK goods, *relative* to those of foreign goods at the pegged exchange rate, will contract the volume of E_{UK}, and expand the volume of M_{UK}. If the *sum* of the average price elasticities of demand for UK exports and imports is greater than 1, the balance on the current account of the balance of payments moves in a *negative* direction.[1] The surplus on the balance of payments—caused by the increase in E_{UK}—is therefore at least reduced, if not eliminated, by the rise in UK prices.

The effect of a decrease in E_{UK} on the UK price level depends on whether or not W is flexible in a downwards direction. If trade unions successfully resist a reduction in W in conditions of unemployment, a decrease in E_{UK} will lower X_{UK} through a multiplier process. The price level will fall to some extent, even with W constant, insofar as marginal cost falls as X_{UK} decreases. The fall in UK goods prices, *relative* to those of foreign goods at the pegged exchange rate, will move the balance on the current account in a *positive* direction, if the *sum* of the price elasticities of demand for UK exports and imports is greater than 1. Together with the contraction in M_{UK}, resulting from the fall in X_{UK}, this will at least reduce, if not eliminate, the deficit on the balance of payments caused by the decrease in E_{UK}.

Thus, the changes in price levels, which follow from disturbances in balances of payments, may cause at least a *partial* correction of the payments disequilibrium. The degree of that correction will depend on the extent to which the price level falls or rises as a result of a disturbance. If the price level change is not sufficient to bring about a complete correction of the payments disequilibrium, the government might attempt to induce a further change by means of monetary and fiscal policies. This would involve decreasing or increasing aggregate money expenditure in order to lower or raise the price level.

However, unless W is flexible downwards, the decrease in aggregate money expenditure will have its main effect in lowering national output, employment, and real income. It will then be mainly the fall in national output, rather than in the price level, which completes the correction of a deficit on the balance of payments. A policy of price level reductions, to cure balance of payments deficits, is feasible only if workers will agree to cuts in money wage rates.

Price level increases to correct surpluses on balances of payments are not subject to the same constraint: W is certainly flexible upwards. But

[1] As explained on pp. 456–457 above.

there is another constraint: the unwillingness of governments to bring about inflation as a deliberate act of policy.

CHANGES IN CAPITAL TRANSACTIONS

An increase in interest rates in one country, relative to those in the rest of the world, will reduce the incentive to lend abroad, and increase that to borrow from abroad. Monetary policy can therefore be used to alter the balance on the capital account of the balance of payments as a means of correcting external disequilibrium. A reduction in the quantity of money, which will raise interest rates,[1] is required in the case of a payments deficit.

The use of monetary policy to influence the balance of payments is, however, subject to two complications when exchange rates are pegged. First, international capital transactions depend partly on people's expectations about the future levels of exchange rates.[2] These expectations will be conditioned to some extent by the current situation on balances of payments. Thus, if a country is in payments deficit, people may come to expect that the pegged exchange rate for its currency will have to be lowered. The expected depreciation (or devaluation[3]) increases the incentive to lend abroad, and reduces that to borrow from abroad. It will therefore work against the effects on the balance of payments of higher interest rates.

Second, the higher interest rates will decrease the level of domestic investment, and thereby reduce either the level, or the rate of growth, of national output. In these circumstances, the expected internal rates of return on investment projects are likely to fall. Direct investment in the country by foreigners will therefore be discouraged, and this will counter the effects of the higher interest rates on the capital account of the balance of payments.

That outcome could, however, be avoided by using fiscal policy to offset the *domestic* effects of the higher interest rates. A reduction in tax rates, and/or an increase in government expenditure—simultaneous with the increase in interest rates—would prevent the level, or the rate of growth, of national output from falling. This is one example of how a

---

[1] See pp. 366–368 above.
[2] See p. 442 above.
[3] The term 'devaluation' is often used for the deliberate lowering of a *pegged* exchange rate by the monetary authority, in distinction from the 'depreciation' of a *freely fluctuating* exchange rate. The raising of a pegged exchange rate is called a revaluation (or up-valuation).

combination of monetary and fiscal policies can be used to influence the external and the internal working of the economy at the same time.

CHANGES IN DIRECT CONTROLS

The term 'direct controls' covers all those policy measures which can be used, in a selective manner, to influence *particular* items in the balance of payments. Their selective operation is in contrast to the *general* effects on the balance of payments of changes in exchange rates, national outputs, and price levels.

Tariffs can be levied at different rates on the various goods which are imported and exported.[1] Similarly, *subsidies* can be granted at different rates on the various goods which are imported and exported.[2] The quantities (or values) of particular goods, which may be exported and imported, can be limited by 'quotas'. The degrees of these *quantitative restrictions*[3] can differ as between the various traded goods. *Exchange control* limits the amount of foreign currency which may be used for particular forms of expenditure abroad, and can be applied in a selective fashion. It is usually employed to restrict expenditures on foreign services (e.g. travel abroad), and to reduce the amounts of foreign lending and direct investment abroad.

Direct controls can be used for a variety of reasons.[4] The present concern is with the changes in them, by a single country, which will eliminate a deficit or a surplus in its balance of payments. An increase in the rates of tariffs on imports can eliminate a deficit. This will raise the *domestic* currency prices of imports, and contract the quantities purchased of them. The *total* value of imports—*excluding* the tariffs, which are paid to the home government—will therefore fall.

An increase in the rates of subsidy on exports can eliminate a deficit only if the average foreign price elasticity of demand for exports is greater than 1. The subsidies will lower the *foreign* currency prices of exports, and expand the quantities purchased of them. The foreign price elasticity of demand has then to be greater than 1 for the *total* value of exports to increase.

The severity of quantitative restrictions on imports, and of exchange control on foreign expenditure, can be increased to the extent necessary to eliminate a deficit. But in this respect, and also for the other direct

---

[1] They are more often levied on imports than on exports.
[2] They are more often granted to exports than to imports.
[3] Which are more often applied to imports than to exports.
[4] Which will be discussed in Chapter 38 below.

control measures, it must be remembered that other countries may retaliate by increasing the severity of their own direct controls. That would increase the amounts of the changes in them required by the first country to eliminate its deficit.

The five different ways in which disequilibrium in balances of payments can be corrected have now been analysed. The choice between them involves agreement among countries on the nature of the international monetary system and of their international commercial policies.

CHAPTER 37

THE INTERNATIONAL MONETARY SYSTEM

A *domestic* monetary system has two aspects. On the one hand, it is a debt clearing mechanism; on the other, it is a means by which the government can influence the *internal* equilibrium of the economy. Units of domestic money are required to clear the debts arising from transactions between households, firms, and the government. These units are provided by the banking system, their total quantity being under the control of the central bank.[1] The level of interest rates can be changed by means of alterations in the quantity of money. A change in interest rates will, by its effect on investment expenditure (and maybe consumption as well), influence the internal equilibrium of national output and the price level.[2]

An *international* monetary system has, similarly, two aspects. It is a clearing mechanism for the debts which arise from the transactions between countries. And it is a means by which the *external* equilibrium of countries (i.e. in their balances of payments) can be influenced. Both aspects are essential to the working of an international monetary system; and their *interrelationship* is the central problem of the system.

A system of *freely fluctuating* exchange rates is one possible kind of international monetary system. The different national currencies would then be exchanged for one another at rates determined by the conditions of demand and supply for them in the foreign exchange markets. Those conditions, as has been seen, derive from the trade and capital transactions which people and firms find it worthwhile to undertake. The exchange of national currencies is the way in which people and firms, in one country, are enabled to clear their debts to people in other countries.

With such a system, there is no need for an *international currency*, distinct from the different national currencies. The foreign exchange dealers can, through the buying and selling of national currencies, provide an adequate means for the settlement of debts between countries.

[1] As explained in Chapter 29 above.
[2] As explained in Chapter 30 above.

The dealers will, of course, have to hold *working balances* of the various national currencies, in order to be able to sell them on demand to their customers. Where the dealers are commercial banks, this will be done by each bank having accounts with foreign 'correspondent' banks in the countries in whose currencies it wishes to deal.[1]

It is likely, however, that a few national currencies will come to be widely used for the clearing of debts between *most* countries. That is, the prices of all traded goods—irrespective of the countries involved—will be quoted in terms of one, or other, of these few currencies, and the debts arising from the trade will be settled with these currencies. And similarly for capital transactions. The commercial and financial dominance, internationally, of a few countries will bring this about, as it has done, in fact, for the pound sterling and the American dollar. The international scope of British and American banks has made it convenient for the traders of most countries to use pounds or dollars to settle their debts. These national currencies therefore act as international *trading currencies*.

In addition to its debt clearing function, a system of freely fluctuating exchange rates would maintain equilibrium in balances of payments. It would do this, as has been seen,[2] through the effects of exchange rate changes on the ranges and volumes of goods exported and imported.

But such a system is not advocated by many people. For a number of reasons,[3] most governments prefer to have stable exchange rates most of the time. This does not, in itself, affect the way in which people and firms in one country will clear their debts to those in other countries. The system of correspondent commercial banking between countries, working mainly in terms of a few national currencies (as with the dollar and the pound today), will still operate for the day-to-day settlement of most international debts.

However, the pegging of exchange rates requires an additional element in the international monetary system: one that operates at the *central bank* level. It has already been seen[4] how central banks can peg exchange rates by means of official transactions in currencies. To do this, they must have *foreign exchange reserves* with which to offset any *excess supply* of their currencies on the exchange markets, so as to prevent them from depreciating.

While exchange rates are pegged at particular levels, these rates do

[1] As explained on p. 433 above.
[2] On pp. 434–438 above.
[3] As explained on pp. 447–448 above.
[4] On pp. 448–450 above.

not, of course, perform the function of maintaining equilibrium in balances of payments. They could, however, be changed from time to time for this purpose. The system of altering the exchange rate for a currency, only when it is thought necessary to correct external disequilibrium, is known as that of the *adjustable peg*. Alternatively, if it is desired to keep the exchange rate fixed indefinitely at a particular level, the government can attempt to bring about such changes in the national output, the price level, capital transactions, or direct controls, as will correct the payments disequilibrium.[1]

As compared with freely fluctuating exchange rates, an international monetary system based on pegged exchange rates thus has two distinctive and interrelated features: (i) the *official* monetary operations by means of which rates are pegged, and (ii) the choice confronting governments as to the *method*[2] by which external disequilibrium is to be corrected when it occurs from time to time. That it will so occur is certain for any economy. In a changing world, there is a great variety of disturbances[3] which are bound to upset the equilibrium of even the best regulated economy from time to time.

Official monetary operations to peg exchange rates can, in principle, be based on foreign exchange reserves which are held in the form of *gold*, and/or of *national* currencies, and/or of an *international* currency. The international monetary system has been in a process of transition in this respect for the past half-century or so—and it is still changing. In the latter part of the nineteenth century, gold came to be widely accepted as the appropriate form in which to hold official foreign exchange reserves. The *international gold standard system* then achieved its widest acceptance by the countries of the world. But it was abandoned during the 1930s, and this accelerated the developing custom among many countries of holding foreign exchange reserves in pounds and dollars.[4] This custom derived from the already widespread use of these national currencies as international *trading* currencies for the day-to-day settlement of debts between countries. That is, the acceptance of pounds and dollars as trading currencies at the *commercial* bank level led to their acceptance as *reserve* currencies at the *central* bank level. It is essential to distinguish between the international *trading* and *reserve* functions which national currencies may take on.

[1] In the ways explained in the previous chapter.
[2] I.e. the adjustable peg, or changes in national output, the price level, capital transactions or direct controls.
[3] See pp. 454–457 above.
[4] I.e. in the form of accounts with the British and the American banking systems, and in easily marketable British and American securities.

During the last war, the allied countries decided to reconstruct the international monetary system, and reached agreement on this at a conference in Bretton Woods, New Hampshire, in 1944. The central institution of the new system is the *International Monetary Fund*, and the central idea of the system is the *adjustable pegging* of exchange rates by international agreement. The Fund is the meeting ground for agreement, between its member countries, on changes in exchange rates, and at the same time it provides, according to certain rules, additional foreign exchange reserves to its members, to enable them to peg their exchange rates when they are in balance of payments deficit. The Fund has not brought to an end the holding of gold, pounds, and dollars, as official foreign exchange reserves by member countries. Nor has it, as yet, led to the creation of an international currency quite distinct from national currencies. But, for some time, there has been pressure for its reform in that direction. However, to understand all this, it is necessary to consider further the antecedents of the Fund.

THE INTERNATIONAL GOLD STANDARD

The international gold standard system was supposed to perform two functions simultaneously: (i) to peg exchange rates indefinitely at particular levels, and (ii) to provide a mechanism for correcting balance of payments disequilibrium as it arose. The first function required the fixing of the prices of gold in terms of national currencies, and the free private buying and selling of it between countries. The second function required that the quantities of money in each country were determined by the gold holdings of their monetary authorities, and that price levels were flexible both downwards and upwards.

Consider an illustration of this in terms of the UK and the US. Suppose that the Bank of England is obliged to buy *and* sell gold, in any quantity, at a fixed price of £4 per oz; and that the US Treasury is similarly obliged to deal at $20 per oz. The pound and dollar market prices of gold will not then diverge from these figures, since no one will buy at higher prices, or sell at lower ones. That being so, the foreign exchange rate between the currencies will only be able to diverge from the *mint parity* of £4 = $20, or £1 = $5, by a very small amount.[1]

Suppose that it costs 4¢ to insure and transport an oz of gold across the Atlantic. An Englishman can then buy a $\frac{1}{4}$ oz of gold from the Bank of England for £1, ship and sell it to the US Treasury for $5, and end up with $4.99 after paying 1¢ for insurance and transport. Similarly,

[1] Before 1914, and from 1925–31, the mint parity was £1 = $4.86.

an American could buy $\frac{1}{4}$ oz gold for $5 from the US Treasury, and sell it for £1 to the Bank of England, which means that the £1 costs him $5.01 after the payment of insurance and transport of 1¢. In these circumstances, the exchange rate will not move outside the range £1 = $4.99–5.01. No one will sell a pound on the exchange market for less than the $4.99 which he could get through the gold market; or pay more than the $5.01 which it would cost him through the gold market. The fixing of gold prices by the monetary authorities, and the free export and import of gold, is thus a device for pegging exchange rates.

This device means that a country, whose balance of payments is in deficit, will lose gold; and that one in payments surplus will gain gold. If the UK is in deficit, the excess supply of pounds on the exchange market will drive the rate down to £1 = $4.99. At this point (called the 'gold export point' for the pound), gold will be sold to the US to the same amount, per period of time, as the UK payments deficit; otherwise, the excess supply of pounds would push the exchange rate below £1 = $4.99. The outflow of gold, in offsetting the UK deficit, corresponds to the sales of dollars by the Bank of England, which are the present-day means of pegging the pound in face of a UK deficit.[1] Similarly, a UK payments surplus, which causes an excess demand for pounds, will drive the exchange rate up to £1 = $5.01 (the 'gold import point' for the pound). The UK will now gain gold to an amount, per period of time, equal to its payments surplus (the US deficit).

The increase in the gold holding of the Bank of England will automatically expand the supply of bank money in the UK. The Bank purchases the additional gold with cheques drawn against itself. These are paid into commercial bank accounts, and thereby increase the cash reserves of the commercial banks in exactly the same way as an 'open market' *purchase* of securities by the Bank of England will.[2] The commercial banks are now able to expand their lending and the supply of bank money. At the same time, the reverse is happening in the US: its loss of gold causes a contraction in the supply of bank money in the same way as would an 'open market' *sale* of securities by its monetary authority.

These were the monetary mechanics of the international gold standard system. In the 'classical' theory of the system, it was supposed to provide a mechanism for correcting balance of payments disequilibrium in the following way. The price levels of countries were supposed to be flexible, both downwards and upwards, so that the full employment of

[1] As explained on pp. 448–449 above.
[2] See p. 357 above.

resources was automatically brought about.[1] If, in these circumstances, the UK moves into payments surplus and gains gold, the supply of money expands and the interest rate falls. This increases expenditure in the UK, and raises its price level. At the same time, the reverse is occurring in the US: it loses gold, the money supply contracts, the interest rate rises, expenditure decreases, and the price level falls. The rise in the UK price level, relative to that of the US, decreases the range and volumes of UK exports, and increases those of UK imports,[2] and thereby corrects the external disequilibrium.

It is now doubted whether price levels were ever sufficiently flexible for the gold standard to have worked entirely in the 'classical' manner. However, as the twentieth century progressed, they certainly became less flexible in a downwards direction, because of the rise of trade unions, and the spread of imperfect competition in the markets for goods. As a consequence, the deflationary effects of gold outflows reduced national output levels, rather than price levels. The resulting unemployment was, of course, unwelcome to governments. Moreover, some governments became less willing to countenance the inflationary effects of gold inflows. They therefore 'neutralized' the effects on the money supply of the inflows, by means of 'open market' *sales* of securities.

The immediate historical reasons for the abandonment of the international gold standard system by successive countries from 1931 onwards[3] are too complex to be discussed here. However, it is clear for the reasons just given, that the correction of external disequilibrium by means of *price level changes* would sooner or later have been recognized as unworkable. For that reason, the 'classical' form of the gold standard system was bound to have been abandoned sometime, and is unlikely to be put into practice again.

The pound became freely fluctuating after the UK left the gold standard in September 1931. But in 1932, the UK set up the world's first *exchange stabilization account*[4] with the objective of limiting the day-to-day changes in the exchange rate, by means of official monetary transactions in the ways already explained.[5] Certain other countries established similar accounts in the following years. This gave rise to the possibility of competition between the different national exchange stabilization accounts in the fixing of the rates favoured by their governments, e.g.

[1] This 'classical' theory has already been discussed on pp. 328–331 above.
[2] As explained on pp. 456–457 above.
[3] The Bank of England was relieved of its obligation to buy and sell gold at a fixed price in September 1931.
[4] Viz. the Exchange Equalization Account.
[5] On pp. 448–450 above.

the UK and US accounts might differ on what should be the £–$ exchange rate. A struggle between the accounts was avoided by the Tripartite Monetary Agreement of 1936, between the UK, US, and France, under which these countries' stabilization accounts concerted their policies of intervention in the foreign exchange markets. As a result, exchange rates were much more stable in the three years before the last war than they had been in 1931–36. This form of international monetary co-operation was of great importance for the framing of the new system which was agreed at Bretton Woods in 1944.

THE INTERNATIONAL MONETARY FUND

The International Monetary Fund (IMF) is an *international* exchange stabilization account. Its basic conception clearly derives from the 1936–39 experience of co-operation between national exchange stabilization accounts. The new system centring on the IMF is thus one of *international agreement* on the *pegging* of exchange rates. A system of pegged exchange rates involves, as has been seen, two *interrelated* problems: (i) the nature of the official monetary operations by means of which the rates are to be pegged, and (ii) the nature of the method by which balance of payments disequilibrium is to be corrected, namely by the adjustable peg, or by changes in national outputs, price levels, capital transactions, or direct controls. Consider in turn the ways in which the IMF system tackles these two problems, before going on to an analysis of their interrelationship.

National stabilization accounts still continue in existence under the IMF system. Each country's account has the direct responsibility of keeping its exchange rate pegged within 1 per cent of its agreed *par value*. Thus the present par value of the pound is $2.40, and the Bank of England will intervene, if necessary, in the exchange market to prevent the pound rising above $2.42, or falling below $2.38. In the latter case, the Bank has to purchase pounds by selling some of the UK official foreign exchange reserves held in the Exchange Equalization Account. The IMF is therefore not involved in the day-to-day process of pegging exchange rates. It only enters the picture when a *national* stabilization account's holding of foreign exchange is likely to be insufficient to prevent the currency of the country in question from depreciating below the agreed level.

When this happens, the IMF can lend the country additional reserves, in the form of other national currencies, for a period of time (usually 3–5 years). The IMF has a fund of national currencies and gold, subscribed by the member countries. The subscription of each member is based on its *quota*, which depends on the country's relative economic importance in the world. The normal rule is for each country to put into the fund an amount of its own national currency equal to 75 per cent of its quota, and to put in gold equal to the remaining 25 per cent. In this way, an international stabilization account is provided to help in the pegging of exchange rates.

. Each member country is allowed, according to certain rules, to 'draw' foreign currencies from the IMF, and add them to its national reserves. It does this by 'purchasing' those currencies with its own, i.e. by giving the IMF an equivalent amount of its own currency at ruling exchange rates. This means that the IMF's holding of the currency in question now rises above the initial 75 per cent of the country's quota; and that its holdings of the other currencies 'sold' by it fall below the initial 75 per cent of their respective quotas. The country which obtains more exchange reserves in this way is obliged to 're-purchase' (within 3–5 years) the amount of its own currency which the IMF then holds in *excess* of 75 per cent of its quota. It does this by paying the equivalent amount of foreign currencies into the IMF. Thus, the terms 'purchase' and 're-purchase' are just another way of saying that the IMF will *lend* other currencies to a country for a period of time. The intention is that the IMF should be a *revolving fund*, which lends only on a *short term* basis to member countries.

The main principles which now govern IMF lending are as follows. A country may draw foreign currencies (and put in more of its own in return) up to the equivalent of 25 per cent of its quota within any period of one year, up to a limit which obtains when the IMF holds an amount of its currency equal to 200 per cent of its quota. Thus, suppose that a country's quota is 100 units of its currency. It will, initially, subscribe 75 units of its currency, and the equivalent of 25 units in gold, to the IMF. If it now draws the equivalent of 25 in foreign currency, the IMF's holding of its currency goes up to 100. If it then draws another 25 in *each* of the following four years, the IMF holding goes up to the limit of 200, i.e. 200 per cent of its quota. This limit is a firm one, but the IMF has discretion to allow a country to draw more than 25 per cent of its quota within any single year. This discretion has been exercised in a number of cases (e.g. more than once for the UK).

A country is free to draw foreign currency from the IMF as long as the latter's holding of its currency does not exceed 100 per cent of its quota. But beyond that, further drawings are at the discretion of the IMF, which has to be satisfied that the country will pursue a policy designed to correct the balance of payments deficit, to offset which the drawings are required. The provision by the IMF of additional foreign exchange, to help in the pegging of exchange rates, is thus 'automatic' only to a limited extent. This leads into the question of how disequilibrium in balances of payments is to be corrected under the IMF system.

The Articles of Agreement governing the IMF make provision for a change in the exchange rate of a country which is in '*fundamental disequilibrium*'. Moreover, they can be interpreted, at least by inference, as regarding this system of the *adjustable peg* as the appropriate one for correcting external disequilibrium. Among the objectives of the IMF, as set out in its Articles, are the promotion of high levels of employment in member countries, and the expansion of international trade. These objectives rule out—as *appropriate* means for the correction of disequilibrium—deliberate changes in national output levels (by means of monetary and fiscal policies), and in direct controls. Exchange control over capital transactions is allowed under the Articles, but only as an interim measure while a payments deficit is being eliminated by other action. There is no indication in the Articles that alterations in capital transactions, by means of changes in domestic monetary policies, could be depended on to correct all cases of external disequilibrium. Moreover, it is unlikely that the founders of the IMF envisaged changes in price levels as the main means of correcting disequilibrium, in view of their downward inflexibility, and the widespread antipathy to inflation.

Hence, both the provisions in the Articles for exchange rate changes, and the negative inferences from them with respect to all the alternative ways of correcting 'fundamental disequilibrium', would seem to indicate the *adjustable peg* as the appropriate way. There is dispute, however, as to whether the founders of the IMF in fact envisaged frequent changes in the exchange rates of, at least, the major currencies of the world. Moreover, the term 'fundamental disequilibrium' is nowhere defined in the Articles. However, if the objectives of high employment levels and expansion in world trade are to be pursued, it must mean *more* than the provisional definition, given earlier,[1] of balance of payments disequilibrium when exchange rates are pegged.

The earlier definition was derived by analogy from the case of freely fluctuating exchange rates. Under the latter, an exchange rate is in equilibrium (in the *market* sense of that term) when the *sum* of the balances, on the current and the capital accounts of the balance of payments, is zero. This definition has so far been used also for the case of a pegged exchange rate; which has meant that it is in equilibrium as long

[1] On pp. 452–453 above.

as the country is neither losing nor gaining official foreign exchange reserves. But this might be so only because the country is holding down the amount of its imports, either by keeping national output below the full employment level, or by having more severe direct controls than it would otherwise wish to have. In this event, a rise in national output, or a relaxation of direct controls, would increase imports and push the balance of payments into deficit. While the country is not, in fact, losing foreign exchange reserves, it *would* lose them if it pursued the desired policies on employment and direct controls.

The concept of 'fundamental disequilibrium' has thus—for consistency with the objectives of the IMF—to be interpreted in relation to what the positions on balances of payments *would be*, if policies directed towards the maintenance of high employment levels, and the expansion of international trade, are pursued. The concept is then no longer defined in objective market terms: its meaning depends on the policy judgments of the persons who use it. The variety of views which exist on the need for a reform of the IMF reflect, in part, the differences in the policy judgments which underlie the meaning of 'fundamental disequilibrium'.

REFORM OF THE IMF

Under a system of pegged exchange rates, official foreign exchange reserves are used to offset deficits in balance of payments. The amount of reserves, which will be required for this purpose by *all* countries in total, depends on the *extent* and the *duration* of external disequilibrium. The more frequently balances of payments are disturbed, and the longer it takes to correct the resulting disequilibrium, the larger is the amount of reserves required to prevent some currencies from depreciating, and others from appreciating. The world's 'need for reserves' is therefore *relative* to the nature and speed of operation of the method (or methods) which governments choose to use for the correction of balance of payments disequilibrium. Any assessment of the *amount* of international money required, at the *central bank level*,[1] can be made only in the context of a judgment on the appropriate way (or ways) of correcting disequilibrium.

Moreover, it seems likely that, given the methods of correcting disequilibrium, the required amount of international reserve money will increase as the volume and value of world trade, and of capital

[1] I.e. of international *reserve* money, as distinct from international *trading* money at the commercial bank level.

transactions, expand. Increases in the absolute sizes of the payments and receipts on balances of payments are likely to bring about increases in the absolute sizes of the deficits and surpluses on them which appear from time to time. Hence, there is not only a problem of assessing the appropriate quantity of international reserve money at any one time; there is also the problem of deciding the *rate* at which that quantity should be *increased* over time.[1]

At the present time (1968), foreign exchange reserves are held in the form of gold, dollars, and pounds. The *increases*, from year to year, in the supplies of these international reserve monies, depend on a number of influences. The increase in the supply of gold for monetary use by central banks depends on the annual production of gold *less* the demands for it for industrial and commercial purposes, and for private hoarding. The rate of annual production is determined by the cost condition of the gold-mining industry in relation to the price of gold. The latter is effectively set by the US Treasury,[2] although, in principle, it rests with the IMF. Increases in the supply of monetary gold thus depend on a policy decision with respect to its price.

Increases, from year to year, in the supplies of dollars and pounds for international monetary use, flow from *deficits* in the US and UK balances of payments. If these countries' foreign payments exceed their foreign receipts, the excesses may result in additions to the dollar and the pound holdings of foreign monetary authorities. But beyond this, the sizes of countries' foreign exchange reserves depend on the lending operations of the IMF. These can have complex effects on reserves, since they are conducted in the various national currencies held by the IMF. In general, however, the drawing of currencies from the IMF expands the reserves available to member countries. Hence the increase, from year to year, in international reserve money, depends on whether or not the quotas, and therefore the subscriptions, of IMF member countries are enlarged. An increase in the international fund of *national* currencies is one means by which the supply of *international* reserve money can be expanded.

The total supply of world reserve money (and changes in it) is thus not determined in a unified way. This is the basis of most criticism of the present international monetary system. The *appropriate* year-to-year increases in the supply of world reserve money—as required by the growth of trade and capital transactions—are unlikely to result from

[1] Just as there is the question of deciding the rate at which the supply of *domestic* money should increase in conditions of economic growth; see p. 375 above.

[2] The free market price of gold depends on expectations about the *future* US Treasury price.

such multifarious influences as US policy on the price of gold, the cost condition of the gold industry, US and UK policies towards their balances of payments, and the political process of getting agreement to increases in countries' IMF quotas. Moreover, such a monetary system is liable to contract in an *unstable* fashion. Deficits in the US and UK balances of payments may give rise to expectations that the dollar and the pound will have to be devalued.[1] This will cause a movement out of these reserve currencies, and into gold,[2] since its prices in terms of them would be raised by devaluation. A reduction in the exchange reserve holdings of dollars and pounds would decrease the *total* amount of world reserve money.

Dissatisfaction with the present system has produced many schemes for reform—from individuals, governments, and international institutions (like the IMF itself). These include raising the price of gold in terms of *all* currencies,[3] changing or eliminating the *reserve* (as distinct from the trading) currency function of the dollar and the pound, and reform of the IMF. If *unified* control over the supply of world reserve money is to be achieved, it is likely to come through a change in the structure of the IMF, analogous to that which has already taken place in all developed domestic monetary systems.

It was seen earlier[4] how the commercial banks of a country all keep accounts with the central bank. They use these central bank debts to them to clear the debts *between* themselves, which arise from the transactions of their customers. Moreover, the central bank can—through the effects of open market operations on the commercial bank accounts with it—alter the supply of domestic money.

The IMF could be transformed into a *world* central bank for *national* central banks.[5] The latter would keep accounts with the reformed IMF, just as the commercial banks keep accounts with them. These debts of the reformed IMF to national central banks[6] would then be their foreign exchange reserves. Consider this in terms of the UK and the US. It has been seen[7] how the Bank of England (B/E), and the Federal Reserve

---

[1] Especially since the pound has been devalued in the past (in 1949 and 1967).

[2] As happened on a considerable scale both in 1961 and 1968.

[3] Which would not, in itself, alter the exchange rates *between* currencies.

[4] On p. 349 above.

[5] This was the essence of the original proposal, during the last war, by the UK Government, for the setting up of an International Clearing Union to operate the post-war international monetary system. The proposal was largely the work of John Maynard Keynes (Lord Keynes).

[6] At present, the reverse occurs: the IMF keeps accounts with the central banks, i.e. it holds *their* debts (currencies).

[7] On pp. 448–449 above.

Bank of New York (FRB), have to buy or sell pounds and dollars to peg
the exchange rate in conditions of external disequilibrium. If the UK
balance of payments is in deficit, the B/E has to sell dollars (from its
account with the FRB), and/or the FRB has to buy pounds (and add
them to its account with the B/E), to prevent the pound from depreciating. The sum of the changes (say over a month) in the B/E's
holding of dollars, and in the FRB's holding of pounds, equals the UK
deficit.

Now suppose that the two banks have accounts with a reformed IMF.[1]
The B/E could then transfer, from its account to that of the FRB (say at
the end of each month), an amount equivalent to the UK payments
deficit. This transfer would reduce the FRB's holding of pounds, and
raise the B/E's holding of dollars, to what they had been at the beginning
of the month. That is, the transfer of IMF debt, from one central bank
to the other, clears the debts (in pounds and dollars) between the banks,
which have arisen from the month's international transactions. This is
analogous to the way in which the commercial banks within a country
clear the debts between themselves, which arise from the transactions
of their customers, by means of transfers of the central bank's debts
to them.

The fall in the B/E's account with the reformed IMF means a fall in the
UK's foreign exchange reserves. The size of that account, in relation to
the rate of the UK deficit, determines the length of time within which the
external disequilibrium has to be corrected. Thus, if gold, dollars, and
pounds ceased to be world reserve monies, international monetary
control over balance of payments disequilibrium could be *unified* in a
reformed IMF. The degree of this control would depend on the initial
sizes of the IMF accounts to be created[2] for member countries, and on the
rate at which they were increased from time to time as world trade and
capital transactions expand.

The mechanics of such a system are well understood from the domestic
analogy; and, indeed, were put into practice on a regional basis from
1950–58 by the European Payments Union. The IMF is at present (1968)
discussing a limited step in this direction through the institution of
Special Drawing Rights. However, the basic problem of establishing a
unified international monetary system is that of getting agreement on
the kind and the degree of *control* which it should exercise over *national*

---

[1] It does not matter, given exchange rates, in what currency unit these accounts
are kept; a new international currency unit might even be devised for the purpose.
[2] In the same way as commercial banks create domestic money (see p. 347 above),
i.e. the reformed IMF would lend its own debts.

economic policies. In this respect, the analogies between domestic and international monetary systems can be misleading.

A domestic monetary system influences internal equilibrium through the effects of interest rate changes on the spending of investors and consumers. An international monetary system of pegged exchange rates influences external equilibrium through the effects of changes in foreign exchange reserve on the *economic policies* of governments. When falling exchange reserves require the correction of balance of payments deficits,[1] governments have to choose some method (or methods) to bring this about. International monetary control operates by forcing governments to change their economic policies. It was argued above that the Articles of the IMF imply that the *adjustable peg* is the appropriate method of correcting external disequilibrium. But, in the event, changes in the exchange rates of major currencies have been few in number since the IMF started to operate in 1947. Concern about speculation against the reserve currencies (the dollar and the pound), which would be likely to result from frequent changes, has helped to bring this about.

The relative inflexibility of exchange rates, together with the dislike which most governments have for *all* the alternative methods of correcting external disequilibrium—namely, changes in national outputs, price levels, capital transactions, and direct controls—makes it exceedingly difficult for countries to agree on the nature and the degree of international monetary control. This means that they can have widely different views with respect to the appropriate quantity, and rate of increase, of international reserve money. As emphasized above, the 'need for reserves' is *relative* to the nature, and speed of operation, of the method (or methods) used to correct external disequilibrium. The less agreement there is on such methods, the more difficulty there will be in reaching agreement on the reform of the international monetary system. This consideration is basic to any judgment between alternative plans for reform.

---

[1] The elimination of a payments surplus is usually regarded as a less pressing problem.

CHAPTER 38

INTERNATIONAL COMMERCIAL POLICY

It has been seen[1] how changes in direct controls can be used to eliminate a deficit or a surplus on the balance of payments. Thus, in the case of a deficit, the volume and value of imports can be reduced by raising the level of tariffs on them, and by increasing the severity of quantitative restrictions and of exchange control. The volume of exports can be expanded by the granting of subsidies on them, and if the average price elasticity of demand for them is greater than 1, this will increase their total value, and so help to eliminate the payments deficit. However, the elimination of external disequilibrium is not the only reason why direct controls on international trade may be used.

They may also be used with the intention of *protecting* domestic industries from foreign competition. This was explained earlier[2] in the analysis of how the composition of international trade is determined. Thus, if the domestic supply prices of goods do not vary with output, a tariff which exceeds the difference between the respective prices[3] of good A in two countries will be prohibitive of trade in it. Industry A in the country imposing the tariff will be protected—it will not now be competed out of existence by the export of A from the other country. In the case where domestic supply prices rise as outputs increase, a country may itself produce some quantity of a good, as well as importing an additional quantity.[4] The imposition of a tariff in this situation will contract the quantity imported and will expand the domestic production of the good. A degree of protection is thereby given to the domestic industry, to the extent that it will be larger than it would have been without the tariff.

A government may give tariff protection to an industry with the intention of continuing it indefinitely. This is frequently done on the argument that some domestic production of the good in question (e.g. aircraft) must be ensured as a precaution against the event of war.

[1] On pp. 466–467 above.
[2] On p. 439 above.
[3] At the ruling exchange rate, and after allowing for transport costs.
[4] See pp. 439–440 above.

Alternatively, the intention may be to give protection only for such time as is necessary for a newly-established industry to become competitive with the corresponding, already-established industries in other countries. This is the *infant industry* argument for protection. It is based on the assumption that the marginal cost of production will fall as output increases. If this is so, then the growth of a newly-established industry *might*, in time, so reduce its *MC* as to enable it to supply at a price which is not undercut by foreign competitors. Protection is thus needed for a time to allow the industry to grow and thereby lower its supply price. The case for the protection of infant manufacturing industries in developing countries is often advanced on this ground. In this respect, however, their governments have the difficult problem of predicting *which* industries will be able to survive without indefinite protection.

A change in direct controls, which contracts the volume of imports of a country, and/or expands its volume of exports, will increase the aggregate demand for that country's goods. The contraction of imports means that some expenditure is switched to domestically-produced goods. Direct controls on international trade can thus be used with the intention of influencing *internal* equilibrium, and in particular, of raising the level of national output and employment. This is a 'beggar-my-neighbour' policy of bringing about internal expansion, since it simultaneously lowers aggregate demand in the countries which provide the imported goods.

Just as there is a variety of reasons why countries may increase their direct controls on trade, so there is a similar variety of grounds on which they may attempt to reach an agreed *international commercial policy* for the reduction of barriers to trade. In the main, two methods have been used in this respect since the end of the last war, namely the *General Agreement on Tariffs and Trade* (GATT) and the setting up of *Customs Unions* and *Free Trade Areas*.

The GATT performs two functions with regard to international commercial policy. First, it embodies an agreed set of rules governing the use of direct controls by member countries. Broadly speaking,[1] these rules do not permit increases in existing tariff rates, do not allow the use of subsidies specifically directed to the promotion of exports, and forbid the use of quantitative restrictions on trade, except by countries in an early stage of economic development, and by those with serious deficits in their balances of payments. Secondly, the GATT is the means by which the large number of member countries can negotiate,

---

[1] There are complex exceptions to all the rules in the GATT.

periodically, for a general reduction in the levels of tariffs. Since 1948, a series of very long, tariff-bargaining rounds has lowered the overall level of tariffs considerably.

The formation of a Customs Union, between a number of countries, involves agreement on (i) the elimination of all tariffs on trade *between* them, and (ii) the imposition by *each* of them of the *same* tariff rates on trade with the rest of the world. A Customs Union has a common set of external tariffs, and differs in this respect from a Free Trade Area. The latter also involves agreement on the elimination of all tariffs on trade between its member countries, but does not oblige them to have the same tariffs on trade with the rest of the world. The European Economic Community (the 'Common Market') is, *inter alia*, a Customs Union; the European Free Trade Area (EFTA) is what its name indicates. Both have secured reductions in tariffs on a regional basis in addition to those achieved by the more comprehensive operation of the GATT.

Any agreement between countries to reduce the barriers to international trade will undoubtedly be based on a variety of economic and political considerations. However, the Principle of Comparative Costs provides a strong argument in favour of freeing trade from all restrictions.

THE GAINS FROM TRADE

It was shown, by means of Table 33.2,[1] that international trade can result from *relative* (comparative) differences in the physical productivities of factors in two countries. The same illustration will now be used to demonstrate, in *real terms*, the gains from trade which both countries can get.

Only two goods are required for the present analysis; Table 38.1a repeats the information given for goods *A* and *B* in Table 33.2. It shows the man-hours needed to produce a unit of each good in the two countries, on the simplifying assumption that labour is the only factor required. The US has an *absolute* productivity advantage in both goods, since it can produce each of them with fewer man-hours than can the UK. But the US has a *comparative* productivity advantage in respect of *B*, since it is 2 times as efficient as the UK (i.e. 1 man-hour against 2) in producing it, while it is only $1\frac{1}{2}$ times as efficient (i.e. 4 man-hours against 6) in respect of *A*. The US has deliberately been given an *absolute* advantage in both goods, in order to show that, despite this, it can still get a *real* gain from trade.

[1] On p. 426 above.

The information in Table 38.1a can be put in a different form, which is more convenient for the present purpose. If the UK reduces the output of A by 1 unit, 6 man-hours of work can then be transferred to produce an additional 3 units of B (at 2 man-hours per unit). The cost, in *real* terms, of the 3 units of B is the 1 unit of A which has to be foregone in order to produce the additional amount of B. This *alternative* real cost of B, in terms of A, for the UK—and, of course, of A in terms of B—is shown in Table 38.1b: either 1 unit of A or 3 units of B can be produced with the same number of man-hours. The real cost of $1A$ is $3B$—or, what is the same thing, the real cost of $1B$ is $\frac{1}{3}A$.

TABLE 38.1a		
	Man-hours per unit of output	
	UK	US
A	6	4
B	2	1

TABLE 38.1b		
	Alternative costs in units of output	
	UK	US
A	1	1
B	3	4

Similarly, Table 38.1b shows that either 1 unit of A or 4 units of B can be produced in the US with the same number (4) of man-hours. The real cost in the US of $1A$ is $4B$, i.e. the real cost of $1B$ is $\frac{1}{4}A$. The cost of A in terms of B (or vice versa) is different in the two countries, and this is the reason why *both* countries can gain in real terms by trading with each other. Consider a number of illustrative possibilities.

Suppose that the UK increases its output of A by 1 unit, and that the US decreases its output of A by 1 unit, so that their joint output of A is unchanged. As a result of these changes, the UK has to decrease its output of B by 3 units, and the US can increase its output of B by 4 units. There is a *net gain* of 1 unit in their joint output of B. If this is shared by means of trade, both countries will be better off in real terms.

The possibility of a mutual real gain from trade can also be illustrated in terms of good A. Suppose that the UK increases its output of A by $1\frac{1}{3}$ units, and therefore has to decrease its output of B by 4 units; and that the US increases its output of B by 4 units, and therefore has to decrease its output of A by 1 unit. Their joint output of B is unchanged, but there is a *net gain* of $\frac{1}{3}$ unit in their joint output of A, which can be shared by means of trade.

Yet again, the possibility of gain can be illustrated in terms of both goods. The UK can increase the output of A by $1\frac{1}{8}$ units, as a result of decreasing the output of B by $3\frac{1}{2}$ units; and the US can increase the output of B by 4 units as a result of decreasing the output of A by 1 unit. In this case, there is a *net gain* of $\frac{1}{8}$ unit in the joint output of A, and of $\frac{1}{2}$ unit in the joint output of B, which can be shared by means of trade.

In all the above illustrations, the UK increases its output of A, and the US increases its output of B, since the US has a *comparative* productivity advantage in respect of B.[1] The UK will export A and import B. The terms on which trade takes place—i.e. the price of A in terms of B—determines the division between the two countries of the real gain from trade.

The UK can obtain $3B$ at a cost of $1A$ by shifting labour out of industry A into industry B. It will therefore not export A to the US unless it gets at least $3B$ for every $1A$. If it gets *more* than $3B$ for every $1A$—i.e. if the price of A exceeds $3B$—it will get a *real* gain from trade, i.e. the total quantity of A plus B which it can obtain will be increased.

The US can obtain $1A$ at a cost of $4B$ by shifting labour out of industry B into industry A. It will therefore not export B to the UK unless it gets at least $1A$ for every $4B$. But if it has to give *less* than $4B$ for every $1A$—i.e. if the price of A falls short of $4B$—it will get a *real* gain from trade, i.e. the total quantity of A plus B, which it can obtain, will be increased.

Thus, the UK will gain from trade if the price of A exceeds $3B$, and the US will gain if the price of A is less than $4B$. Therefore, *both* can gain if the price of A lies between $3B$ and $4B$. The price of A in terms of B is called the *barter terms of trade*.

The *range* over which the barter terms of trade for two goods can lie is determined by their cost ratios in the two countries. In the above example, the UK cost ratio is $1A$ to $3B$, and the US cost ratio is $1A$ to $4B$. The barter terms of trade cannot lie outside the range $1A$ for $3B$ and $1A$ for $4B$, since the UK will not sell $1A$ for less than $3B$, and the US will not buy $1A$ for more than $4B$.

The point at which the barter terms of trade will settle depends on the respective strengths of the US demand for A, and the UK demand for B. The greater the US demand for A, relative to the UK demand for B, the higher will be the price of A in terms of B, i.e. the closer it will lie to $4B$ rather than to $3B$. That is, the greater the relative strength of US demand,[2] the closer will the barter terms of trade lie to the US cost ratio

---

[1] Which means, of course, that the UK has a *comparative* productivity advantage in respect of A.

[2] Which depends on the size of the US national income relative to that of the UK, and on the preferences between A and B of US and UK consumers.

(of 1*A* to 4*B*). This means that the real gain from trade will be the smaller to the US, and the larger to the UK. The US gains from trade, to the extent that it can *import A* on better terms than it could obtain it by *production*. It can produce 1*A* at a real cost of 4*B*. It gains if it can buy 1*A* for less than 4*B*. The gain to the US will be the smaller—and that to the UK will be the larger—the closer the barter terms of trade lie to 1*A* for 4*B*.

International trade does not, of course, take place in barter terms. Nevertheless, changes in a country's terms of trade can be measured by changes in the *ratio* between the average prices of its export goods and the average prices of its import goods.[1] If export prices rise *relatively* to import prices, there is an improvement in the country's terms of trade, since a given volume of exports will now buy a larger volume of imports. The terms of trade deteriorate if export prices fall *relatively* to import prices. Changes in the terms of trade alter the *real* national income of a country by altering the amount of the national output which has to be given up in exchange for a given volume of imports. This is the way in which changes in the gain from trade are measured at the macroeconomic level.

It is essential, however, to be clear about what the Principle of Comparative Costs does—and does not—prove in relation to the gains from trade. In terms of the example above, it shows that the *joint* outputs of *A* and *B*, produced by given resources in the UK and the US, will not be at a maximum unless each country specializes in producing the good in which it has the *comparative* productivity advantage. Freedom of trade from all restrictions will be required for such specialization to occur. In general, therefore, the level of *world* output from given resources will be maximized if, through trade which is free of all restrictions, each country is able to specialize in production according to its comparative advantages.

But this does *not* prove that the real national income of an *individual* country is maximized by complete freedom of trade. A single large country can attempt to improve its terms of trade by restricting the volume of its imports. Thus, if it imposes tariffs on them, this will cause their foreign supply prices to fall. The benefit to the country from improved terms of trade will, however, be offset to some extent by a loss from the reduction in the volume of trade. Nevertheless, there will be a tariff level[2] which will give it a maximum net gain from restricting its imports. Its real national income (assuming no retaliatory imposition

---

[1] Both sets of prices being expressed in terms of the same currency.
[2] Known as the *optimum tariff*.

of tariffs by other countries) will therefore be increased—but at the expense of other countries, since the restriction on trade has reduced world output. Of course, if the other countries *do* retaliate by imposing tariffs on their imports, the level of world output may be so reduced that the real incomes of *all* countries are lowered.

It might appear that the Principle of Comparative Costs provides an argument for the formation of Customs Unions, as a step towards the maximization of world output through a partial removal of restrictions on trade. This, however, is not necessarily so. The elimination of tariffs, within a Customs Union, *creates* additional trade between the member countries; but it also *diverts* some trade away from the rest of the world. The supply prices, at which member countries can export to one another, are reduced when tariffs are eliminated within the Union. But the supply prices of goods from the rest of the world are still subject to the Union's common external tariffs. As a consequence, it may now be cheaper, in money terms, for an individual member country to buy some goods from another member country, rather than, as before the formation of the Union, to buy them from the rest of the world. Trade is thereby diverted into the Union, and away from the rest of the world. When the effects of trade creation and trade diversion are both taken into account, it is not possible to say, in general, whether or not the real incomes of the Customs Union, and/or the rest of the world, will be increased. The Principle of Comparative Costs is, in some respects, a simple and powerful weapon for analysing the problems of international trade; but its implications are now always easy to derive.

It is more important to learn how to *do* economic analysis than to learn particular pieces of economic analysis. Economic systems are complex, and their details change over time. They cannot be understood in terms of stereotyped explanations: each new situation must be analysed afresh.

The intention in this book has been to emphasize the similarities between the *methods* of analysing different economic problems, as a means of showing the general way in which economic analysis is done. Thus, it has been seen how each economic quantity depends on a number of influences, and how different economic quantities are interrelated. To predict the behaviour of any one quantity, it is necessary to trace out its interactions with other quantities. Progress in learning to do economic analysis means acquiring the ability to cope with a larger and larger number of interconnections between economic quantities.

This is the sense in which the process of learning the subject—like that of adding new knowledge to it—must progress from the simple to the complex. In both cases, broad generalization is the starting point. This provides an initial insight into the relations between things; but it also suggests new lines of enquiry. In that way, both the student and the researcher are led to probe more deeply into the nature of things.

FURTHER READING

INTERNATIONAL ECONOMICS

More advanced analysis of the problems of international economics is given in C. P. Kindleberger, *International Economics* (fourth edition, 1968), and in R. A. Mundell, *Theory of International Trade* (1968). The problems are covered more briefly in G. Haberler, *A Survey of International Trade Theory* (revised edition, 1961), and in W. M. Corden, *Recent Developments in the Theory of International Trade* (1965), both of which are published by the International Finance Section of Princeton University. Many of the main problems are analysed in articles contained in W. R. Allen and C. L. Allen (eds.), *Foreign Trade and Finance* (1959), and in H. G. Johnson, *International Trade and Economic Growth* (1958).

The issues involved in reforming the international monetary system are investigated in F. Machlup, *Plans for Reform of the International Monetary System* (revised edition, 1964), and in the report of an International Study Group of thirty-two Economists entitled *International Monetary Arrangements: The Problem of Choice* (1964). Both of these are published by the International Finance Section of Princeton University.

OTHER FIELDS

The general characteristics of different kinds of economic system, together with present-day examples of them, are analysed in M. Bornstein (ed.), *Comparative Economic Systems* (1965).

A variety of views on the nature and methods of economics can be found in S. R. Krupp (ed.), *The Structure of Economic Science* (1966).

The historical development of economic analysis is set out and discussed in M. Blaug, *Economic Theory in Retrospect* (second edition, 1968).

The nature and methods of econometrics are explained and exemplified in L. R. Klein, *An Introduction to Econometrics* (1962), and in A. A. Walters, *An Introduction to Econometrics* (1968).

INDEX

GEORGE ALLEN & UNWIN LTD

Head office:
40 Museum Street, London, W.C.1
Telephone: 01-405 8577

Sales, Distribution and Accounts Departments
Park Lane, Hemel Hempstead, Herts.
Telephone: 0442 3244

Athens: 7 Stadiou Street, Athens 125
Barbados: Rockley New Road, St. Lawerence 4
Bombay: 103/5 Fort Street, Bombay 1
Calcutta: 285J Bepin Behari Ganguli Street, Calcutta 12
Dacca: Alico Building, 18 Motijheel, Dacca 2
Hornsby, N.S.W.: Cnr. Bridge Road and Jersey Street, 2077
Ibadan: P.O. Box 62
Johannesburg: P.O. Box 23134, Joubert Park
Karachi: Karachi Chambers, McLeod Road, Karachi 2
Lahore: 22 Falettis' Hotel, Egerton Road
Madras: 2/18 Mount Road, Madras 2
Manila: P.O. Box 157, Quezon City, D-502
Mexico: Serapio Rendon 125, Mexico 4, D.F.
Nairobi: P.O. Box 30583
New Delhi: 4/21-22B Asaf Ali Road, New Delhi 1
Ontario, 2330 Midland Avenue, Agincourt
Singapore: 248C-6 Orchard Road, Singapore 9
Tokyo: C.P.O. Box 1728, Tokyo 100-91
Wellington: P.O. Box 1467, Wellington